Studia Fennica
Historica 13

THE FINNISH LITERATURE SOCIETY (SKS) was founded in 1831 and has, from the very beginning, engaged in publishing operations. It nowadays publishes literature in the fields of ethnology and folkloristics, linguistics, literary research and cultural history.

The first volume of the Studia Fennica series appeared in 1933. Since 1992, the series has been divided into three thematic subseries: Ethnologica, Folkloristica and Linguistica. Two additional subseries were formed in 2002, Historica and Litteraria. The subseries Anthropologica was formed in 2007.

In addition to its publishing activities, the Finnish Literature Society maintains research activities and infrastructures, an archive containing folklore and literary collections, a research library and promotes Finnish literature abroad.

Seija-Riitta Laakso

Across the Oceans

*Development of Overseas Business
Information Transmission 1815–1875*

Finnish Literature Society • Helsinki

Studia Fennica Hisrtorica 13

The publication has undergone a peer review.

VERTAISARVIOITU
KOLLEGIALT GRANSKAD
PEER-REVIEWED
www.tsv.fi/tunnus

The open access publication of this volume has received part funding via
a Jane and Aatos Erkko Foundation grant.

A digital edition of a printed book first published in 2007 by the Finnish Literature Society.
Cover Design: Timo Numminen
EPUB: eLibris Media Oy

ISBN 978-951-746-904-3 (Print)
ISBN 978-952-222-808-6 (PDF)
ISBN 978-952-222-809-3 (EPUB)

ISSN 0085-6835 (Studia Fennica)
ISSN 1458-526X (Studia Fennica Historica)

DOI: http://dx.doi.org/10.21435/sfh.13

Contents

Preface

The origins of this work go back to *Italia '98*, an international philatelic exhibition in Milan, where a well-known French dealer happened to have a box of old letters on his desk. Two of these letters appeared to be especially interesting. They were business correspondence, sent from New York to August Martell in Cognac, France, in the late 1820s, by the ships *France* and *Charlemagne*.

At that time, all overseas mail was carried across the oceans by sailing ships. A further examination of these two letters opened up a new world to me. The *France* and the *Charlemagne* were American sailing packets on regular line service between New York and Havre. As will be noticed in this study, the idea of 'sailing on schedule' instead of general merchant shipping was one of the most important conditions for the development of business information transmission, whether conducted by sail or by steam.

A few years later, when I started this study, Professor Yrjö Kaukiainen's article on the Shrinking World gave my thesis a firm direction at the point when the idea was still more or less open. Without that article, my work on this theme would probably never have been started. I would like to thank Professor Kaukiainen for his patient guidance, which continued even after his retirement from his university post.

I would also like to thank Professors Riitta Hjerppe and Markku Kuisma for their support and many useful conversations in their research seminars, and Professor Päiviö Tommila for his earlier counsel on the history of communications. I am also indebted to Professor Laura Kolbe, who took the time to read my thesis in an early stage, thank you for your support.

My warmest thanks also go to Professor Robert Lee, School of History at the University of Liverpool, and Dr Adrian Jarvis, Centre for Port and Maritime History, for facilitating and supporting my studies in Liverpool.

The pre-examiners of my thesis, Professor Jari Ojala and Docent Mika Kallioinen gave many insightful comments on the work. Especially the detailed observations and recommendations by Jari Ojala were extremely valuable in the final phase of the study. The international group of researchers led by him and Leos Müller also shared ideas of good value during the congresses under the title 'Information Flows 1600-2000' in Jyväskylä (2005) and in Helsinki (2006), and many e-mails and articles have been sent across the oceans between the participants later on. Thank you for your contribution, all of you.

Graeme J. Milne, Sari Mäenpää and Tage Lindfors, thank you very much to you, too, for reading my texts and giving your useful comments, and thanks for all our good conversations. And without Tim Voelcker's help in London, some of my East India records would never have been finalized – thanks a lot.

I would also like to add my grateful thanks to my opponent at the defence of my doctor's dissertation in Helsinki in December 2006, Professor John J. McCusker from Trinity University, San Antonio, Texas, USA, who still keeps 'nudging' me to continue studies on this topic.

Thank you, Heikki Hongisto, Johan Snellman and Seppo Talvio for kindly providing me with copies of relevant correspondence from your philatelic collections. And thanks for the whole philatelic society – collectors, dealers, writers, and colleagues in different countries – for all the discussions, articles and useful tips over the years. It has really been fun.

After publishing the web version of my thesis, I have had the pleasure of receiving encouraging comments as well as updates and unpublished information on their own studies from the well-known maritime postal historians Colin Tabeart and Richard Winter. Thank you very much for your kind help and observations.

Many thanks to Derek Stewart and his team for the final language checking of my work and to Professor Lewis R. Fischer and Maggie Hennessey, Managing Editor of the IJMH, for their useful advice concerning academic writing.

Research work could hardly be successful without the help of skilled personnel in the libraries and archives. I would like to direct my grateful thanks to the directors and personnel of the Merseyside Maritime Museum Library & Archives; the University of Liverpool's Sydney Jones Library & Archives; the Liverpool Public Record Office Library & Archives; the India Record Office and the Philatelic Collections of the British Library in London; the Library of the Royal Philatelic Society London; and the Library of the Post Museum in Helsinki.

For financial support, I wish to express my warm thanks to the Helsingin Sanomat Centennial Foundation, which enabled my studies in the Liverpool archives, and to the University of Helsinki.

Finally, of course, my greatest gratitude goes to my family and to all my friends, whether mentioned above or not. Without you my thesis would probably have been completed much earlier, but I would definitely have lost something else of personal importance in my life. Thank you all.

I dedicate this book to my parents: to my late father, who always encouraged me to study further, and to my mother, whose warm support helped me through many difficulties during the years when I was involved in this research.

Helsinki, June 2007
Seija-Riitta Laakso

I Introduction

Earlier studies have shown that the speed of information transmission increased markedly in all parts of the world during the 19th century. Before that period, the development in duration and frequency of sailings had been very much slower.[1] The fast progress was primarily based on the change from sailing ships and horse-driven coaches to steamers and railways. The telegraph, introduced by the mid-19th century and taken into intercontinental use twenty years later, finally revolutionized the speed of information transmission over long distances. This development has generally been described as a chain of technical improvements. In the real world, things were of course more complicated.

The title of this study, *Across the Oceans – Development of Overseas Business Information Transmission 1815–1875*, has been chosen to indicate that shipping and overseas information transmission were unquestionably linked in the 19th century, before the time of aircraft or electric communications. Maritime history is usually seen as the history of shipping, while the development of the speed of information transmission is often included in the history of communications. In particular, Yrjö Kaukiainen, Ian K. Steele and Allan R. Pred have carried out important research by combining these aspects.

The starting point for this particular study was Yrjö Kaukiainen's article, in which he showed that the general duration of information transmission had continuously decreased several decades before the breakthrough of the electric telegraph. Kaukiainen based his arguments on maritime intelligence published by *Lloyd's List*, calculating how many days it took for the information on ship arrivals in different ports around the world to reach London and be published.

Interestingly, the shortest time lag e.g. between Barbados and London was 38 days in 1820, but only 20 days in 1860. Similarly, the time lag decreased on the route between Buenos Aires and London from 72 to 40 days; between Valparaiso and London from 109 to 49 days; and between New York and London from 23

---

1   See Yrjö Kaukiainen, 'Shrinking the world: Improvements in the speed of information transmission, c. 1820–1870'. *European Review of Economic History, 5* (Cambridge, 2001), 1–28; Ian K. Steele, *The English Atlantic 1675–1740. An Exploration of Communication and Community* (Oxford, 1986); and Allan R. Pred, *Urban Growth and the Circulation of Information: The United States System of Cities, 1790–1840* (Harvard, 1973).

to ten days during the same period. The most remarkable changes were seen on the East India route, where the time lag between Bombay and London decreased from 121 to 25 days; and between Calcutta and London, where it decreased from 128 to 35 days between 1820 and 1860.[2] All this happened before the long distance telegraph was brought into use. The Atlantic cable was laid successfully in 1866, and a direct connection from London to India was opened in 1870. A direct telegraph line to Buenos Aires was available in 1875.

A great part of the development can naturally be explained by the overall change from sail to steam and the opening of railways over the isthmuses of Suez and Panama. But it is also evident that such changes took time. The networks – shipping routes and regular sailings, railways, canals, and telegraph lines – had to be established, financed and built, as well as coordinated to serve the mail system. Everything could not be done immediately when a new innovation was made. Sometimes a new innovation had to be technologically improved for years before becoming commercially successful, as with the different steam engine solutions for ocean transport.

Earlier research has already shown that the shift from sailing ships to steamers in bulk transport was mainly based on reducing fuel costs, extending from short trade voyages to longer distances over several decades, instead of just being one technological event.[3] Also the cost development of shipping during the shift period, particularly the freight rates as well as capital, fuel and labour costs, have been thoroughly examined by maritime historians.[4] However, most of these studies cover primarily cargo shipping. Mail and passenger services were a rather different business, where speed and regularity were highly valued and the (bulk) freight rates only played a minor role.[5]

New technology was always more expensive to build and use than the old, and included more risks. Financing depended on the expected benefits of

---

2   Kaukiainen (2001), 1–28. – Westbound, the difference on the New York route would obviously have been much greater due to the prevailing winds and currents.

3   Charles K. Harley, 'The shift from sailing ships to steamships, 1850–1890: a study in technological change and its diffusion' in Donald N. McCloskey (ed.), *Essays on a Mature Economy: Britain after 1840* (London, 1971), 215–237. Harley's study does not cover the mail and passenger steamship services, which competed in a very different market. In accordance with Harley's paper, it has also been argued that the huge increase in cargo carrying capacity was the end result of a century of evolution, starting from the 1860s and ending in the 1960s. The process was basically a matter of successive relatively small increments in size and speed, in carrying capacity and fuel efficiency. The two major 'revolutions' in technology were the interaction of metal construction and steam propulsion to produce ships capable of operating economically over long distances on regular schedules, and the introduction of containerization. See Malcolm Cooper, 'From *Agamemnon* to *Priam*: British liner shipping in the China Seas, 1865–1965' in Richard Harding, Adrian Jarvis & Alston Kennerley, *British Ships in China Seas: 1700 to the Present Day* (Liverpool, 2004), 225.

4   In addition to the above, see for example Yrjö Kaukiainen, 'Coal and Canvas: Aspects of the Competition between Steam and Sail, c. 1870–1914' in Lars U. Scholl and Merja-Liisa Hinkkanen (eds), *Sail and Steam. Selected Maritime Writings of Yrjö Kaukiainen. Research in Maritime History No. 27* (St. John's, 2004), 113–128. For the investment cycles and development of capital and labour costs, see also Yrjö Kaukiainen, *Sailing into Twilight. Finnish Shipping in an Age of Transport Revolution, 1860–1914.* (Helsinki, 1991), 73–128.

5   A good overview to the financial management of a government-sponsored joint-stock company can be found in Francis E. Hyde, *Cunard and the North Atlantic, 1840–1973. A history of shipping and financial management* (London, 1975).

the business. To find entrepreneurs or investors for such experiments, there had to be a clear demand for the service. Distant places far from the world's business centres, such as California or Australia, had to wait for a gold rush to become interesting enough for regular communications services.

To date, no attention has been paid in discussion on the speed of information transmission to the somewhat varying needs of the heavy users of long distance mail services, especially newspapers and business enterprises. For newspapers, it was extremely important to receive urgent news as quickly as possible, and special arrangements were frequently made to beat the competitors. While fast one-way information transmission was clearly also important from the merchants' point of view, they needed a system which would work efficiently in both directions. This is the reason why the name of this study includes the term 'business information transmission' instead of just 'information transmission' or 'market information transmission'. Although the business enterprises certainly took all the advantage they could of, for example, the telegraph, there was always the need of physical mail transmission as well. This study is about the business information transmission: how new systems were introduced and developed during the period, and how the merchant houses and their trade partners used the growing network of world communications for their different needs.

TABLE 1. *Differences between the nature of information transmission for newspapers and for business enterprises.*

	General information transmission	Market information transmission	Business information transmission
Main target groups	Newspapers	Newspapers & business enterprises	Business enterprises
Special needs	Asap. The first one receiving the news was the winner.	Asap. The first one receiving the news was the winner.	Asap. Also the possibility to react rapidly was important.
Contents	Any news of general interest.	News of market situation, changes in prices, etc.	Market information, business documents, personal letters between business partners, agents, etc.
Means of communications	The fastest possible means of communications, including pigeons, telegraph, etc.	The fastest possible means of communications, including pigeons, telegraph, etc.	The fastest possible means of communications suitable for carrying physical documents.

In addition to newspapers and business enterprises, there was also a third major group of interests, i.e. the governmental and military needs for rapid information transmission. As administrative letters could also be carried by naval ships, it has not been possible to include them in this study, except in the cases where the naval vessels also carried ordinary mail, e.g. in the Mediterranean as part of the East India mail route in 1830–1857, or when they were replacing the Admiralty-governed Falmouth packets for one reason or another. Private letters were carried in the same way as the commercial ones, and they are implicitly included in this research without further remarks.

As this is a study of the logistical development of mail transmission, it will not discuss the networks of the specific merchant houses or the contents of the letters carried. These will be described only by way of example in a few cases.

In the business world, information flows often consisted of multiple transactions. Although fast one-way information could be crucial in the trade – for example the news of changes in the market situation – it was at least equally important that there was a possibility to react rapidly. Overseas business consisted of numerous letters sent back and forth across the oceans. It was not only important to know the market situation and the prices before making an order, it also had to be known when and by which vessel the freight would be shipped, a bill of lading should be sent to confirm the shipping and a bill of exchange should be sent for the payment.

Regular correspondence with different companies and agents was often necessary throughout the year. The role of agents has been recently covered by e.g. Jari Ojala, according to whom the constant flow of information was needed not only for the business itself or for vital market information, but also as an important way to achieve trust between the parties undertaking transactions.[6]

Improvements in the speed of communications were crucial for many commercial, financial and shipping business activities. Speedier information made capital move faster, directly affecting world trade. Or, as it was seen in Victorian England: 'Increased postal communications... implies increased relations with that country, increased commerce, increased investment of English capital, increased settlement of energetic middle-class Englishmen; and from all these sources, the wealth and prosperity of England... are greatly increased.'[7]

To what extent economic growth was based on improving communications is difficult to show. There was clearly a connection between them and it seems that the growth in exports correlated positively with the need to create and improve systems for long distance mail transmission.

In Britain and the United States, the value of merchandise exports grew tenfold between 1820 and 1870, and many other countries followed closely.

6   Jari Ojala, 'The Principal Agent Problem Revisited: Entrepreneurial networks between Finland and 'world markets' during the eighteenth and nineteenth centuries' in Margrit Schulte Beerbühl and Jörg Vögele (eds.) *Spinning the Commercial Web. International Trade, Merchants, and Commercial Cities, c. 1640–1939* (Frankfurt-am-Main, 2004).

7   A quote from Sir Charles Wood by Michael Pearson in *The Indian Ocean* (London, 2003), 203.

As Britain in the early 19th century was so much ahead of any other country in economic performance due to the early industrial revolution, its real figures show an even more impressive increase during the period in question. In 1870, the value of British merchandise exports equalled the corresponding figures of the United States, France and Germany combined, even though colonies such as India were not included.[8]

TABLE 2. *Value of merchandise exports at constant prices 1820–1870 (million 1990 USD)*.

	1820	*1870*
Britain	1,125	12,237
France	486	3,512
USA	251	2,495
Germany	–	6,761

Source: Maddison, 236–237.

In 1820, employment between major economic sectors in Britain differed markedly from any other country. While agriculture, forestry and fisheries employed 37.6% and mining, manufacturing, construction and utilities 32.9%, services already employed 29.5%.[9] The service sector included financing activities and shipping, both of which were strongly dependent on fast information transmission. 19th century Britain was the world's main source of foreign capital, investing mainly in Europe and Latin America until 1830, but thereafter increasingly in canal and railway construction in the United States and India.[10]

In 1870, less than a quarter (22.6%) of British employment came from agricultural activities, more than 42% came from industry and 35% from the service sector. At the same time, agriculture still accounted for almost half of employment in France and Germany, and for as much as 70% of employment in the United States, where business activities were concentrated in the large cities of the north eastern coast.[11]

In the light of these figures, it is no wonder that the development of faster business information transmission was especially in British interests. The economic structure of other comparable countries did not require it to the same extent. And in terms of potential, the British had coal, iron and the

---

8   Angus Maddison, *Monitoring the World Economy 1820–1992. OECD Development Centre Studies,* (Paris, 1995), 236–237.

9   Maddison, 39. See also James Foreman-Peck, *A History of the World Economy. International Economic relations since 1850* (Sussex, 1983), 18–21.

10   See A.G. Kenwood and A.L. Lougheed, *The Growth of the International Economy 1820–1980* (London, 1985), 40–45.

11   Maddison, 39.

13

technological knowledge to develop steamship services; a manufacturing industry that created new capital to the market; and tolerable labour costs on board the ships.[12] Additionally, there was the long tradition of overseas mail services by the British Post Office sailing packets, starting on the route between Falmouth and Lisbon in 1689.

The aim of this study, methods, structure and sources in brief

This study aims to find out how efficiently the information transmission systems used on the world's most important mail routes served business during the period 1815–1875. Several concrete cases have also been examined to see how efficiently these services were used in practice.

We can of course not judge the effectiveness of the 19th century mail systems by any modern criteria. What could be extremely slow in our view, might have been acceptable and even good performance in those circumstances. Thus the development of mail services can only be measured by comparable criteria such as speed, frequency, regularity and reliability. Of these criteria, reliability is the most intangible. It is viewed here from the perspective of information transmission, observing the regularity of sailings as well as the safety of shipping measured by the number of wrecks, both of which varied greatly between the different companies.

As the study covers a period of six decades, as well as several of the world's most important trade routes and different mail-carrying systems operated by merchant ships, sailing packets and several nations' mail steamship services, a specific method has been developed to measure the duration of business information transmission in a systematic and commensurable way.

The method of calculating consecutive information circles enabled by different means of communications gives a clear picture of the best options available for business information transmission during the year. The development of communications can easily be seen from the comparative figures of different time periods. To complete the picture, the business correspondence of several merchant houses has been used for postal historical research to illustrate how the system worked in practice.[13] Much emphasis has also been put on the research of the historical context, which is essential for understanding why and how things changed.

As world trade was so much in British hands during the time period in question, and the most important long distance mail routes were mainly

---

12   E.g. in the 1860s, the average wages of able-bodied seamen were 3.1 pounds sterling per month in England, compared with 6.0 in British North America. The average in Europe was 2.8. but for example in Finland and Norway less than 2.0. See Yrjö Kaukiainen, 'Finnish sailors, 1750–1870' in Lars U. Scholl and Merja-Liisa Hinkkanen (eds), *Sail and Steam. Selected Maritime Writings of Yrjö Kaukiainen. Research in Maritime History No. 27* (St. John's, 2004), 19.

13   Postal historical research focuses on the postal markings and handstamps of the letters instead of their contents. In a few cases, some attention has also been paid to the contents to shed more light on the circumstances in which the information was transmitted. As will be explained in Chapter II, this study is not about mercantile networks but about how the systems of business information transmission developed during the chosen period.

those connecting Britain and its (former) colonies or other important trade partners, the approach of this study is unavoidably British in orientation. Yet the overseas mail services of American, French and German steamship companies have been included where the sailing data has been available. It should be noticed that these services started much later than the British and many of them were active only for a short period.

Before 1840, the British Post Office sailing packets carried mails from England to North America, the West Indies and South America, while the route to India was covered by the British East India Company until the end of its monopoly. In the 1820s and 1830s, most of the North Atlantic mails were carried by the commercial American sailing packets. At the end of the 1830s, the British Post Office made three important mail contracts: one for the route from England to Halifax (Nova Scotia) and Boston with the Cunard Line, starting in 1840, another for the service to the West Indies with the Royal Mail Line, starting in 1841, and a third for the service via the Mediterranean and Suez to India with the P&O, starting gradually in 1840. The mail steamship service to South America by the Royal Mail Line started in 1851, and the P&O also extended their Asian network markedly during the years thereafter.

American competition on the North Atlantic route was extremely hard in the 1850s but declined sharply after 1857, when the U.S. Congress made a decision to terminate the government subsidies for mail steamship companies. After the Civil War, the government's interest was mainly in developing internal structures such as canals and railways, and foreign trade did not expand to the same extent.

Excluding the short experiment on providing government subsidies for a French steamship company in 1847, the French did not organize corresponding mail services on long-distance routes before the 1860s. The German steamship companies Hamburg-Amerika Linie and Norddeutscher Lloyd were established in the 1850s but they gained greater importance only later, when the emigration to North America expanded after the Civil War and the frequency of the sailings increased. For these obvious reasons, the space given to the different mail services and companies in this study depends very much on the length of the time the services existed. The electric telegraph entered the picture rather late from this study's point of view. The importance of telegrams as business communication tools increased notably later, towards the end of the century, when the prices of the service were reduced to a more reasonable level.

John J. McCusker has compressed the overall development of business press and the 'Information Revolution' during the last five centuries in three words: 'better, faster and cheaper'.[14] However, the question of information costs could not easily be covered here. There would not only be the angle of the users of different mail services, but also the viewpoints of mail-carrying shipping companies as well as the governments that paid for the services by awarding mail contracts.

---

14 John J. McCusker, 'The Demise of Distance: The Business Press and the Origins of the Information Revolution in the Early Modern Atlantic World' In *The American Historical Review*, Vol. 110, Number 2, April 2005, 295–321.

During the period in question – the time before the Universal Postal Union, or the UPU – there was no uniformed system for overseas mail, but only bilateral postal treaties between the countries. The contents of the treaties varied and they were renegotiated several times over the decades in question. The postage rates varied in each case depending on the ship by which the letter was carried (private or official mail-carrier), on the route and the mail contract under which the letter was carried, as well as the length of the inland voyage at both ends of the journey. Even during the same period there were alternatives for sending mail with different costs.[15] And furthermore, in the first half of the 19th century it was mostly the recipient who paid for the letters when receiving them, not the sender who chose the means of communication.

From the operator's – the mail-carrying shipping company's – perspective, faster communication increased costs. The expenses of building and operating steamships were manifold compared with sailing vessels. And newer and faster steamers were needed all the time to keep up with the competitors. Also the laying of submarine cables was conducted by huge expenses. Many companies failed, and only a few succeeded. For the governments, the mail contracts were usually a fiscal burden and a subject for continuous political debate.

Due to the wide spread of the subject, the costs of information transmission are touched here only as examples of different aspects. The intention of this study is mainly to try to find an answer to the question: was there a 'revolution' in the way of organizing the global business information transmission in the 19th century. And if there was, when was it and what happened really?

Earlier research on business communications will be discussed in Chapter II and the use of different methods and sources in measuring the speed of information transmission in Chapter III. A short introduction to the overseas mail systems and the development of the speed of communications before 1815 will be presented in Chapter IV.

The study covers the time period from the end of the Napoleonic Wars in 1815 to the formation of the UPU in 1875, which finally uniformed the regulations of the world's mail systems and rates. Two important shift periods are thus included: the transition from sail to steam in overseas mail transport, and the introduction of the intercontinental telegraph.

There would have been at least two different ways of organizing the main contents (chapters V–VII) of the study. The first would have been a chronological approach:

- Sail vs. sail
- Sail vs. steam
- Steam vs. steam
- Steam vs. telegraph

---

15 There are several distinguished postal historical studies of the postage rates of the period. See George E. Hargest, *History of Letter Post Communication Between the United States and Europe 1845–1875* (Massachusetts, 1975); Jane Moubray & Michael Moubray, *British Letter Mail to Overseas Destinations 1840–1875* (London, 1992); Richard Winter, *Understanding Transatlantic Mail, Vol. 1.* (Bellefonte, PA, 2006).

These periods of different means of overseas communication, including the two shift periods, would then have been examined geographically. To make it easier for the reader to follow the long-term development of communications on each main trade route, another approach has been chosen. The development of the speed of communications is examined route by route with the North Atlantic, the West Indies, South America, Panama, East India, China, Australia and South Africa being the main areas of interest. This appeared to be the right solution, as the improvements in the mail systems did not take place simultaneously but each route had its own character, depending on historical background, economic importance, geographic location, technological challenges and other matters.

Of all the sources available, the sailing data of the mail-carrying ships give an answer to most of the general questions about how overseas business information transmission was organized during the different time periods. Therefore the sailing lists, to date rather unknown in academic research, have been chosen to form the basis of this study. Postal historians have worked for several decades collecting the sailing data of mail-carrying ships from different newspapers and organizing all the information into comprehensive lists. The objective has been to serve philatelists, who need this kind of accurate information to verify the authenticity of letters in their collection.

The published lists cover the sailings of the Falmouth packets to Halifax and New York between 1815 and 1840, and to South America until the end of 1850. They cover all the North Atlantic mail sailings of more than 30 shipping companies between 1838 and 1875; the mail steamship services to the West Indies by the Royal Mail Line from 1841 onwards; all British mail steamship contract services to South America from 1851; and the French services from the early 1860s. They also cover the P&O's various routes from the 1840s, the British Admiralty's services on the Mediterranean between 1830 and 1857; and American coastal steamship services of the early 1850s, to name but a few of the most important ones.

To get an impression of the number of sailings listed, we can look at Walter Hubbard's and Richard Winter's extremely useful *North Atlantic Mail Sailings 1840–1875,* which alone includes some 14,000 Atlantic crossings with all relevant data from the ship's departure port and sailing date to the details of the arrival. The ports of call are also included, and delays are often explained in the notes.[16] The lists do not repeat the schedules advertised before the trip by agents or shipping companies, but they are based on factual sailing data published by newspapers, thus describing what happened in reality. During the age of sail and steam, this was often a very different story.

Although much has been done, there are also gaps in the published sailing data. The writer of this study has not been able to find sailing lists of the Falmouth packet sailings to the West Indies or Central America. The departure and arrival dates of the American sailing packets have not been published either. The historian Robert Albion, who calculated the duration of each of the more than 4,000 westbound voyages of these packets for his

---

16 Walter Hubbard & Richard F. Winter, *North Atlantic Mail Sailings 1840–1875* (Ohio, 1988), passim.

book *Square-Riggers on Schedule,*[17] never published the actual sailing dates. And furthermore, sailing data has not been systematically collected from journeys made by merchant vessels, which also carried mail.

If the sailing data needed for this study has not been found from previously published postal historical sources, it has been collected from *Lloyd's List,* with a few years' double-checking from the *Liverpool Customs Bills of Entry.* In addition to the new details about the Falmouth and American sailing packet services, this work includes nearly 600 records from the merchant ship traffic between Britain and British Guiana in 1840, as well as all port calls of the whole round trip of nearly 400 British merchant vessels between around 20 ports on the way from England to India, China, Southeast Asia and Australia in January 1832 – June 1834. The number of recorded dates in the last mentioned period exceeds 2,000.

To find out the difference between the duration of the mail transport itself and the duration of the whole process between writing a letter and receiving it, postal historical studies of merchant correspondence have also been included in this research. For this, the overseas correspondence of several Liverpool and London merchant houses, as well as the honourable East India Company have been studied and compared with respective sailing data.[18]

The material includes correspondence of the following merchant houses:

- Sandbach, Tinne & Co., 1825–1870 (West Indies–Liverpool)
- Thomas and William Earle & Co., 1836–1870
  (West Indies–Liverpool)

---

17 Robert Greenhalgh Albion, *Square-Riggers on Schedule. The New York Sailing Packets to England, France, and the Cotton Ports* (Princeton, 1938).

18 Liverpool, being the European port of three American sailing packet lines with weekly transatlantic service, as well as of the most important transatlantic mail steamship companies (Cunard Line, Collins Line, Inman Line, White Star Line, etc.), was the most important information hub in the North Atlantic communications ca. 1820–1870 and the second trade port of England after London only, when it comes to business with e.g. the West Indies, South America or East India. The merchant correspondences have been chosen here mainly from the philatelic point of view: there had to be postal markings on the covers received. For example, the letter copy books of senders (which normally form a great part of the correspondence examined in network studies) are not at all useful from this point of view. In earlier times, letters were not put into covers but just folded and sealed. In these cases, the postal markings have been saved on the backside of the received documents. Later, only the contents were often saved while the merchant houses threw away the unnecessary covers or they have later been sold to philatelic markets by the descendants of the merchant families, or other persons involved in the business. Much material has been destroyed in wars, fires, mergers, etc. All this limits the possibilities to find relevant merchant correspondence especially for postal historical studies. In the case of the East India Company, their letters were carried in bundles with no Post Office markings. However, the clerks of the India House have carefully documented the date of arrival of each letter as well as by which ship the letter has arrived. By using this information, it is possible to find out from the sailing data published by *Lloyd's List,* how long time the sea journey took in each case from the entire duration of the information transmission. All the letters of these merchant correspondences have been compared with the existing sailing data from other sources to ascertain how the existing services were used in practice.

- Rathbone Bros & Co., 1841–1870 (North Atlantic)
- Daniel Williams, 1854–1870 (South America–Liverpool)
- Henry Eld Symons, of Kirkdale, 1857
  (Australia & New Zealand–Liverpool), and 1857–1858
  (South America–Liverpool).
- The East India Company, 1832–1833 (India–London)
- Frederick Huth & Co., 1836–1850 (North America–London)

The total number of letters analysed exceeds 2,000. For the published sailing lists, see the Bibliography: 'Printed sources with important postal historical sailing data'.

II Business Perspectives in the History of Communications

Where does this study stand in the history of communications? It is obvious that the history of communications can be viewed from several different perspectives. It might be understood as the history of logistics or transport, the history of journalism, or postal history, the history of postal organizations, the history of personal networks, or the history of the development of the speed of communications, just to mention a few.

Also the history of information transmission includes different angles. Roughly, it can be divided into two: personal contacts and public communications. In both cases, information is transmitted in spoken or written (or printed) form through various networks or public transport and delivery systems.

Traders – whether they were merchants, agents, brokers, bankers, shipowners, underwriters or other businessmen, sometimes even women – were individuals, who used all kinds of personal communications in their everyday life. They were also heavy users of public communications, sometimes also involved in their contents. In principle, any kind of communication could include a business aspect.

A short introduction to the research already conducted in the fields of personal as well as public information transmission may be useful for the reader. Both these 'categories' may include a local and an overseas dimension, although their respective emphasis may vary.

For example, Graeme J. Milne has studied the information order of the mercantile community of Victorian Liverpool, i.e. which members of society had access to which kinds of information, how much it cost to acquire it, and how institutions were formed to disseminate or restrict it.[19] This approach includes a question about the limits between personal and public communications. As Milne noted, although frequently marginalised in economic theory, information of all sorts was a central preoccupation of 19th-century business. For example, placing information with its costs, benefits and uncertainties, at the centre of the historical analysis of these operations can

---

19 Graeme J. Milne, 'Knowledge, Communications and the Information Order in Nineteenth-Century Liverpool', *Forum: Information and Marine History*, International Journal of Maritime History, Vol. XIV No.1 (2002), 209–224.

therefore offer a more appropriate interrogatory approach than the powerful, but sometimes ahistorical, tools of classical economics.[20]

Several other historians have lately studied the personal networks of particular merchant houses or mercantile communities. As an example, Sheryllynne Haggerty has examined the transshipment of knowledge in the business environments of Philadelphia and Liverpool in the late 18th century. She notes that various means of communications were already available for traders, allowing them to assess, manage and reduce their risks. Newspapers were crucial in providing information in an increasingly impersonal environment, but the written word in the form of personal letters was also important, not only for recording and directing business, but for introductions and transmitting gossip – very necessary in keeping up to date with the state of people's reputations. Haggerty divides the field of communications into printed, written and spoken word, with a fourth category of religion, family and friendships.[21]

Gordon Boyce continues the idea with a more economic viewpoint as follows: the commercial communities, where business, family, religious and political ties were often interwoven, provided necessary information and capital even for large enterprises. Within the closely-knit commercial communities of British ports, successful operation of the basic network mechanism generated over time the interpersonal learning, mutual interest and enhanced reputations needed to support larger operations.[22]

In a local business environment, the reliability and reputation of business partners and counterparts were continuously under the microscope in different formal and informal business activities, including correspondence, participation in events, associations, etc. When considering foreign business opportunities, the reputation of foreign partners was extremely important. All means were used to keep the most reliable connections for foreign business up to date.[23]

In Finland, Mika Kallioinen and Jari Ojala have recently studied the business communications networks of specific merchant houses with overseas trade.[24] In Britain, e.g. Graeme J. Milne's *Trade and Traders in Mid-Victorian Liverpool* covers several aspects of this topic.[25] There is also a major ongoing project by the name *Mercantile Liverpool* at the University of Liverpool, involving a mix of quantitative and qualitative studies to broadly cover the networks of Liverpool merchants in 1851–1911. Kalevi Ahonen

---

20   Milne (2002), 224.
21   Sheryllynne Haggerty, 'A Link in the Chain: Trade and the Transhipment of Knowledge in the Late Eighteenth Century', *Forum: Information and Marine History*, International Journal of Maritime History, Vol. XIV No.1 (2002), 157–172.
22   Gordon Boyce, *Information, mediation and institutional development. The rise of large-scale enterprise in British shipping, 1870–1919* (Manchester, 1995), 32–39.
23   Mika Kallioinen, *Verkostoitu tieto. Informaatio ja ulkomaiset markkinat Dahlströmin kauppahuoneen liiketoiminnassa 1800-luvulla* (Helsinki, 2002), 90–96, 113–115, 200.
24   For the latter, see Jari Ojala, *Tehokasta liiketoimintaa Pohjanmaan pikkukaupungeissa. Purjemerenkulun kannattavuus ja tuottavuus 1700- ja 1800-luvulla* (Helsinki, 1999), especially 311–332, 440–441.
25   Graeme J. Milne, *Trade and Traders in Mid-Victorian Liverpool. Mercantile business and the making of a world port* (Liverpool, 2000), passim.

has also examined a great number of merchant house correspondences in the United States to cover the trade between America and Baltic Russia, touching furthermore upon the difficulties in obtaining information on both sides of the Atlantic.[26]

Merchant networks can be studied from different angles. A good recent example is Mika Kallioinen's *Verkostoitu tieto,* which covers the networks of a Turku-based merchant house in the mid-19th century. It is based on the following classification: 1) technology, meaning new forms of communications, their adaptation, improvements in the speed of information transmission, 2) communications as means of social interaction, network as a channel of information, 3) cultural basis of communications; confidence, international 'entrepreneurial culture', and 4) information of business activities; contents, availability, usefulness.[27] Even if the perspective is wide, the merchant house aspect predominates in the study, and it does not therefore cover the public communications aspect.

In addition to the research on personal networks, important studies also exist covering different kinds of public communications: the general news circulation, early newspapers, carrying mails, and speed of communications.

Ian K. Steele's *The English Atlantic*[28] includes several interesting viewpoints concerning early overseas information transmission. Steele divides the English Americas of 1675–1740 into four main areas which received and forwarded information from the mother country in a very different way. The sugar route for the West Indies, the tobacco route for Chesapeake, the Western route for Philadelphia, New York and Boston, as well as the Northern routes for Canada all had their typical traffic and information streams. Steele's work covers the development of sea transport ('news-bearing ships'), mail routes and post offices, newspapers and packet boat service, as well as some good case examples of news circulation following important historical events. Additionally, Steele notes that emigrants and diseases, e.g. smallpox and yellow fever, also spread along the same routes.

Another extensive and equally interesting study about the development of the speed of information transmission is made by Allan R. Pred. Although mainly concentrating on this development between American cities, the *Urban Growth and the Circulation of Information* gives a wide view of the ways in which the information flows proceeded during the last 'pre-telegraphic' half century. Pred's study covers the spread of information through newspapers, postal services and coastal trade, as well as inter-urban travelling, and the spread of innovations and diseases. His model of large-city rank stability is of special interest.[29]

What Pred describes as an urban city system on the north eastern coast of the United States, was rather parallel with the major cities in Britain. The

---

26   See Kalevi Ahonen, *From Sugar Triangle to Cotton Triangle. Trade and Shipping between America and Baltic Russia, 1783–1860* (Jyväskylä, 2005), 163–168.
27   See Kallioinen, 20.
28   Steele (1986), passim.
29   Pred, passim.

city merchant middlemen (e.g. importers and shipping merchants), agent middlemen (e.g. auctioneers, brokers, commission merchants, and factors) and retailers were the most important capital accumulators, but even the so-called manufacturing establishments combined small scale production with retailing or wholesaling functions, or gained provisions by offering repair services. The system included coastal and interregional distribution of hinterland production, hinterland and coastal distribution of interregional and foreign imports, foreign export of hinterland commodities and re-export of trade commodities. While the wholesaling-trading system dominated the urban economy, the relative importance of its functions varied over time and from city to city.[30] The more developed the urban systems of an area were during the period, the more important was the speed of business information transmission.

The history of printed business communications goes back to ancient times, as John J. McCusker has shown in his studies on the early modern Italian business press, and the business press in England before 1775. His essays on the early financial and commercial newspapers published in the Italian and other European business centres cover a period of more than two and a half centuries prior to the 1780s.[31]

At the turn of the 18th century there were four basic types of commercial and financial newspapers published in London during a business week: the *Bills of Entry*, the *Commodity Price Current*, the *Marine List* and the *Exchange Rate Current*. Several hundred *Bills of Entries* were printed and published every day. They were subscribed to not only by individual merchants but by the London coffee houses, government agencies, etc. Merchants also subscribed to the newspapers for their overseas correspondents on a regular basis.[32]

The business newspapers – as well as the national papers – were widely spread. Large numbers of commodity price currents of Venice can be found in the archives of the Netherlands, and large numbers of Amsterdam commodity price currents in the archives of Indonesia. The British Post Office prioritized incoming *Lloyd's List* news in its London Post Office, and all newspapers carried by mail were for long periods free of postage fees and stamp duty.[33]

According to McCusker, 'quicker distribution of business news meant that businessmen could react more rapidly to changes in market conditions', while newspapers were 'filled with information gathered, published, distributed, and sent off in the post all in the same afternoon or evening; these business newspapers spread the news of prices and the rest much more quickly than in the past'.[34]

---

30 Pred, 189.

31 See John J. McCusker, 'The Italian Business Press in Early Modern Europe' and 'The Business Press in England before 1775', in McCusker, *Essays in the Economic History of the Atlantic World* (London, 1997), 117–176.

32 See McCusker, 149–172.

33 See McCusker, 138–139; Charles Wright & C. Ernest Fayle, *A History of Lloyds, from the Founding of Lloyd's Coffee House to the Present Day* (London, 1928), 73–74.

34 McCusker, 139.

In practice, however, the newspapers could not be in Indonesia faster than the following sailing ship would take them there, forwarded by the ship's captain or an individual traveller. This meant something like an approximately five months delay after the rapid 'posting' of the news. In Central Europe, the mail coaches normally managed to bring the news from one country to another within a couple of weeks or even a shorter time, depending on the distance.

Why then was the speed of information so important for a trader, whether he was a merchant, an agent, a broker or a banker? Those who knew first about the market changes – prices, exchange rates, declining or growing stocks, etc. – could naturally make money. Businesses like the cotton trade across the Atlantic were typically influenced by speculations. New York merchants, usually being the first to learn of radical price changes for cotton in Liverpool were often ruthless in their exploitation of the market in Charleston, Savannah, Mobile and New Orleans, while interests in those cities, being the first in the South to acquire New York news, could make quick back-country purchases before the word of price adjustments became public property. Similarly, hastily dispatched representatives of New York mercantile houses could frequently take advantage of early news of domestic price changes in Philadelphia, Baltimore, and other major cities, with entrepreneurs in those cities frequently repeating the process in their respective hinterlands.[35] In this kind of trade, the impact of the telegraph would be the greatest.

Despite the progress in developing electric communications, which started in the mid-19th century, most business activities still required physical movements of documents, as they did up to the age of the fax and Internet. As Yrjö Kaukiainen has pointed out, the improvements in communications widened the already existing speed gap between the transport of information and of bulk goods, giving merchants an opportunity to sell the cargo further before it had even arrived. The bill of lading, a certificate of specific goods being loaded on a specific ship, normally signed by the master, legally respected the actual cargo. This document could be sent by a fast mail steamer to the port of arrival, and the recipient of the goods could make further transactions before the actual arrival of the ship.[36] Money was changing hands quicker than ever before.

While the pace of business transactions was typically slow, merchants could gain from completing sales deliveries and purchase acquisitions as quickly as possible, being able to avoid the unnecessary tying up of capital in goods-in-transit or goods-in-stock. In places where the intervals between information receipt were shorter and transport services were more frequent and rapid, the merchant could in the course of a year complete a greater number of capital turnovers, or action cycles, than his counterpart with similar capital resources but slower communications.[37]

Shipments were usually paid by a bill of exchange, which was considered a legal promise to pay a certain sum of money on a particular date, most usually

---

35 See Pred, 221.
36 Kaukiainen (2001), 21–22.
37 Pred, 222–223.

in three month's time. A supplier issued a bill for the value of the goods he was shipping and for which he expected to be paid at some definite future date; the supplier agreed to 'draw a bill' on the buyer, who acknowledged responsibility for eventual payment by writing on the bill his 'acceptance'. The acceptance signified that the buyer was a good risk for a lender, as the acceptance house was liable to the financing house in the event of default. After acceptance the bill was sold to a financier; a lender would then 'discount' the bill (buy it for less than the sum payable in the future) and the supplier would thereby borrow. The difference was the interest charged on the loan. When the goods were sold, the supplier was able to pay the debt and withdraw the bill. The bill could change ownership (be rediscounted) during its currency should the original lender suddenly need cash. Bills of exchange therefore were a valuable means of facilitating both national and international trade at a time when transport was slow and communication difficult.[38]

The German Ernst Samhaber depicts in his book *Merchants make history* how a Hamburger merchant, John Parish, used the system for his credit. He shipped Baltic grain to Western Europe and imported West Indian merchandise – coffee, sugar, rum, tobacco and tea – via Liverpool. He paid for the grain with colonial merchandise and for the colonial merchandise with grain. While the cargo was still at sea, he made out a bill of exchange, on which they advanced money. As security he handed over the ship's papers, the bills of lading. He himself bore the major part of the risk, only partly covered by insurance, and simply added the premium to the price of the grain and the colonial merchandise.[39]

In the North Atlantic cotton trade, where prices could change sharply, importers in Liverpool tried to guard themselves against price falls by making forward sales as soon as they had made their purchases in America. Speculators and others purchased the forward-sold cotton either to safeguard their future supply or in the hope of profiting if the price of cotton did rise while in transit.[40]

Until the early 19th century, notable financial development had already taken place. There was the establishment of a de facto gold standard, the evolution of specialised merchant banks, the growth of a market in mortgages, the increasing use of bills of exchange to settle domestic and international

38 Foreman-Peck, 68–69. Kalevi Ahonen describes in his doctor's thesis different means of financing trade between America and Russia. While bills of exchange, based on sterling dominated international trade, and were especially popular in Anglo-American trade, the Americans often operated with Russia on credit accounts arranged by the 'American houses' in London, and 'as London was the centre of world trade an importer of any kind of product could manage his payments using bills drawn on his London banker'. Ahonen also describes how direct barter trade was used in the Havana sugar trade, as well as the use of Spanish silver dollars, where the right moment to buy and use specie was always a topical question for shippers interested in Cuba. See Ahonen, 257–282.

39 Ernst Samhaber, *Merchants make history* (New York, 1964) 279. Graeme J. Milne describes the use of bills of exchange by Liverpool merchants in the mid-19th century, see Milne (2000), 114, 154–155. For more about the credit systems in the international trade in 1850–1875, see Foreman-Peck, 67–70.

40 Nigel Hall, 'The Liverpool Cotton Market', *Transactions of the Historic Society of Lancashire and Cheshire, Vol 149* (1999), 105.

obligations, the rise of the stock exchange, the development of marine and fire insurance, and the appearance of a financial press. The effects of these innovations were felt on other activities. Improvements in credit and commercial services boosted the shipping industry, promoted overseas trade and assisted the balance of payments by generating invisible earnings. The expansion of overseas commerce encouraged the rise of mercantile firms whose size enabled them to mobilize the capital and credit needed for long-distance trade.[41]

International bankers like the Rothschilds and Barings, both of German origin, were very powerful in the British overseas business. While the Rothschilds established banks in Vienna, Paris, London and Naples, the Barings concentrated to a much greater extent on overseas transactions. They bought and sold merchandise and securities on commission as well as for themselves, they operated their own ships, kept the accounts of selected depositors, and acted as financial agents for merchant houses and governments all over the world, especially in Latin America and the British Empire.[42]

The business practices and the common use of financial instruments, combined with growing world trade and investment flows, caused a growing need for fast business information transmission. Although there was a continuous improvement in the speed of communications during 1820–1870, the improvements were far from even.[43] Each of the important world trade routes had its own historical background, and the development of the speed of information transmission varied markedly from one place to another. In fact, technical improvements played only a partial role in the development, while many other factors have been rather untouched in historical research.

To put this specific study on the 'map' of the history of communications, its focus is on the public long-distance mail systems, concentrating on the current *possibilities* to maintain personal networks of overseas business relations. Whether the mail carried consisted of personal letters or trade documents has no specific importance from this perspective.

The study thus concentrates on overseas business information transmission, leaving out the local merchant networks and means of communications. Spoken information, like 'news of mouth', rumours and personal travelling, is only implicitly involved – mails and passengers were usually carried by the same ships. Before the time of the telegraph, the speed of information transmission was the same as the speed by which a person could travel. While studying the development of mail transport, the other related aspects are also automatically involved. The chosen methods will be explained in the following chapter.

---

41   P.J. Cain & A.G. Hopkins, *British Imperialism, 1688–2000* (London, 2002), 68.
42   See Foreman-Peck, 67–68.
43   See Kaukiainen (2001), 1–28.

TABLE 3. *Different forms of information transmission (before telegraph).*

Means of communications		Local	Overseas
Personal	Spoken	Face-to-face	News by mouth (travelling individuals)
	Written	Letters	Letters
	Networks	Personal networks - family, religion - social - business or other professional	<u>Personal networks, maintained by travelling and writing letters</u>
Public	Spoken	Speeches for large audience	News by mouth, rumours
	Printed	Newspapers, books Circulars Advertising	Newspapers, books Circulars Advertising
	Systems	Local mail & newspaper delivery	<u>Long distance mail systems</u>

This study concentrates on public long-distance mail systems and the possibilities to maintain personal overseas networks (mainly business relations) by using these systems.

III Measurement of the Speed of Communications – Methods and Sources

Introduction to the different methods of measuring the speed and frequency of communications – Consecutive information circles as tools in measuring the speed of business information transmission

Introduction to the different methods of measuring the speed and frequency of communications

Historians often find it difficult to receive an accurate answer to the question of the duration of information transmission. Problems vary depending on the mail route (sea, overland, or mixed), the time period (war times, seasonal variations, general level of technological development) and the source material in question (correspondence, newspapers, administrative documents).

The nature of sources available, as well as their quality and quantity, gives firm limits to what can be attained by examining the information flows. If the interest is in personal contacts, for example the speed of a particular merchant's business information transmission, the main sources are the received letters in the company's correspondence. Yet they can be complemented with maritime intelligence from contemporary newspapers or postal historical studies. Sailing data from newspapers, customs bills etc. are the main sources if the interest is in the general conditions of information transmission. Letters with postal markings and handstamps give more and better information on the transmission than privately sent or very early letters with only the writer's and recipient's handwritten markings.

Generally speaking, there are three main aspects to consider when choosing the method for measuring the speed of information transmission:

- measurement of the duration of information transmission from the sender to the recipient of the message
- measurement of the duration of transport between two places
- measurement of the frequency of transport between two places

These aspects have often been used for the measurement of the speed of information transmission without clearly distinguishing the difference between what has been measured and what is talked about.

The information transmission from the writer to the recipient obviously includes the second aspect, the duration of transport between the two places in question, and is very much dependent on the third one, the frequency of the transport available.

The first aspect deals mainly with correspondence between two individuals and leads to the research of personal communications, while the two other aspects generally deal with public sources – like newspapers, customer bills, post office records and collected sailing data in postal historical studies – and focuses on public communications. The two latter aspects *explain* the duration of personal communications, while the personal correspondence with its postal markings and handstamps can *verify* the data and statistics given by public sources. Therefore, the use of different aspects together can portray an issue better than the use of one aspect only.

The most common method in measuring the speed of information transmission in history studies has been the simple calculation of days between writing and receiving letters. This method can only give limited results, however.

Firstly, only received letters are useful in the research, as the copies of letters sent do not include information about the arrival date in the other end. Copy books of sent letters can sometimes complete the picture shedding light on the information circulation or the frequency of communications. By using only the writing and arrival dates of the letters for measuring the speed of information transmission, several important aspects remain unknown.

The transmission of an overseas letter can be described as a process, which is sliced into several independent parts: how long it took for the writer to send the letter after writing it, how long it took for the local system (coffee house, forwarding agent, post office) to forward it to an ocean going vessel (if overseas mail), how long it took before the ship was ready to leave from the port, how long the sea journey was, and how efficiently the letter was forwarded and finally delivered at the other end. Naturally, the duration of the whole process also depended on the frequency of the mail transport available.

To understand how the process worked and thus be able to distinguish the fixed elements of information transmission from occasional delays, it is useful to learn to understand the postal historical elements of the material examined.

Postal handstamps and other markings on the letters made by post offices are of great help when examining the factual speed of information transmission. They give accurate dates of departures and arrivals of the letters, as well as the transit places. The handstamps were needed to inform the receiving post office, as well as the final recipient who had to pay for the transport, by which route the letter had been carried. The inland postage rates depended on the length of the route by which the letter was carried, while the ship letters had their own instructions. For fiscal purposes, it was important that the system worked promptly, and much effort was put into correcting mistakes instantly.

Handwritten instructions on the covers are also very useful for a historian, regarding the means of communications ('per Packet', 'per English Steamer', 'per Neptune', 'p. Capt. Read') or the route ('via Panama', 'via Marseilles').

Also these markings are usually reliable, as there were strict regulations about the rates depending on different mail routes, mail contracts, etc. The changes *en route* were most often corrected on the cover, or they can be noticed from differing postal handstamps.

By carefully reading the postal markings of the covers and examining the postal history, it is usually possible to discover further information regarding the letter's trip from the writer to the recipient instead of just calculating the days between writing and receiving it.

One of the rare academic studies crossing the border of philatelic postal history has been conducted by John J. McCusker, who examined the origins of one single letter in his essay *New York City and the Bristol Packet*.[44]

The letter, found by McCusker himself as a boy, appeared to be an important document in the history of the first packet service between Bristol and New York in 1710–13. As the author puts it, 'administrative, philatelic, archival and genealogical evidence united to support the validity of the conclusion' that the letter was really sent from New York early in May 1711 by one of the packets. 'The letter traveled on precisely the business and precisely the route that the organizers of the packet service had intended. It linked English and colonial merchants and secured their communications during a time of war. London merchants, like Joseph Levy [the recipient of the letter], had been the ones who had pressed for the packet. For Levy and Simson, and many more like them, the mails meant the continuation of their business but government, too, realized the need, and reaped the advantages of secure lines of communications with the Continental Colonies.'[45]

Complementary methods obviously add value to the research. In addition to the data collected from personal correspondence, and especially if the main interest of the study is in public communications, general news flows or the efficiency of mail systems, maritime intelligence from contemporary newspapers or relevant postal historical studies are of great help. As already mentioned in the Introduction, most British and French mail steamship routes as of 1838 are well covered by postal historians at least to 1875, the year when the Universal Postal Union, or UPU, was established and the international postal rates were uniformed. Earlier mail sailings are also often well documented in postal historical studies, or the data can be found from contemporary newspapers.

An example from the writer's postal historical collection may clarify the usefulness of combining the classic method of calculating the difference between the dates of writing a letter and receiving it, the postal markings on the letter and the sailing data published in the contemporary newspapers or postal historical studies:

In the late 18th century, there was a monthly British Post Office sailing packet service between Falmouth, England, and New York. A letter from Richmond, Virginia, with the note 'p. Packet', was handstamped in the

---

44   John J. McCusker, 'New York City and the Bristol Packet. A chapter in eighteenth-century postal history', in John J. McCusker, *Essays in the Economic History of the Atlantic World* (London, 1997), 177–189.
45   McCusker (1997), 189.

Richmond Post Office on 2 September, 1796 and on arrival in London 18 weeks later, 5 January, 1797.[46] (See Fig. 1) As the letter was obviously written in Richmond (it is not dated) and it was addressed to London, there should not have been any delays at either end of the journey. But how could it take 125 days to bring the letter from South Carolina to England?

According to *Lloyd's List*, two mail packets had arrived at Falmouth from New York on the same day, 2 January, 1797. This matched perfectly with the arrival handstamp of London on 5 January. One of the packets was the *Countess of Lei[ce]ster*, which had sailed 'in 7 weeks', and the other was the *Princess of Wales*, 'in 5 weeks'.[47] As the mails should have arrived once a month, at least one of the ships was at least two weeks late. There had been problems in the westbound packet service already, as the writer starts his letter by complaining that 'your last of 2d May only reachd me last week owing to the delay of the Packet'. Due to the war time (French war 1793–1802), dozens of mail packets were captured, including one in June which probably should have carried the letter if available.[48]

The unlucky combination of a late incoming packet and the need for waiting at port, primitive inland connections between Richmond and New York – only one post rider was in service, as the mail coaches would start on the Virginia route just a few years later[49] – and the five to seven weeks sailing from New York to England caused an accumulated delay to the information transmission. However, the facts known verify that the sea transport had taken only 30–40 per cent of the whole transmission time. Studying only the writer's and recipient's markings on the letter would have given an incorrect picture of the overseas communications, and studying only the sailing data would have given a mistaken picture of the whole process of information transmission.

Sometimes the historian's interest is not only in the duration of the information transmission but in learning more about the process of how the mail was carried. The letter itself may give little to start with but even those markings may open a path to an exciting story about how information was transmitted during that period.

For example, a letter (see Fig. 2) to 'Messrs Magowe & Son, Boston' was written in Calcutta on 6 December, 1851, and handstamped on the reverse by the Calcutta General Post Office on the 8th. Additionally, there are the British handstamps of London and Boston on 15 January, 1852; 'INDIA' by red letters; a few rate markings; and a handwritten remark 'America'. The recipient has finally marked the arrival date on the reverse, February 9th. All the needed information exists to find out the duration of information transmission: 65 days from the writer to the recipient. We even learn that the

---

46   A ship letter from Richmond, Virginia, 2.9.1796 to Duncan Davidson Esq., London. In Seija-Riitta Laakso, *Development of Transatlantic Mail Services from Sail to Steam (2005)*. Postal historical collection. (SRLC).

47   *Lloyd's List* 6.1.1797.

48   The *Countess of Leicester* was also captured by a French privateer in December 1797 and the *Princess of Wales* in May 1798. See Howard Robinson, *Carrying British Mails Overseas* (London, 1964), 312.

49   Pred, 91.

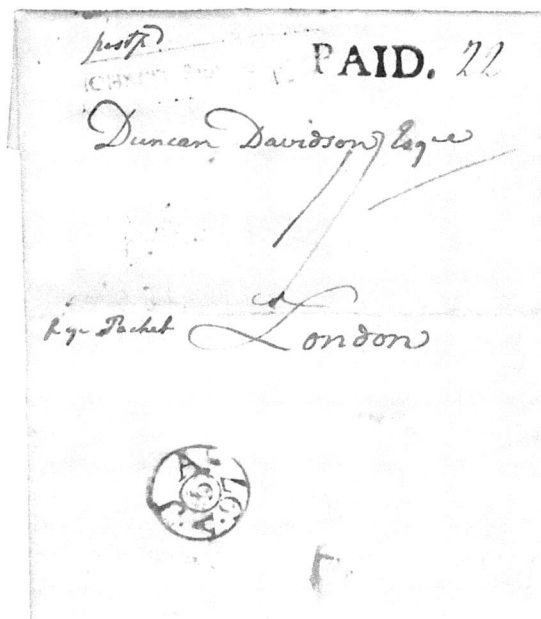

FIG. 1. *War time communications was slow and unpredictable. The letter, sent on 2.9.1796 from Richmond, Virginia, was delayed for more than two months in the United States until it was finally carried from New York to England by one of the Falmouth packets. The letter arrived in London on 5.1.1797, in 125 days. (See the text.)*

letter was handled by the Calcutta G.P.O. only two days after the writing, so there was not much delay. The British markings show that the letter has been carried via England.[50]

But how did the letter arrive in Britain and further to the United States? By combining the facts available on the cover and what can be achieved from existing postal historical studies, we learn a lot more about the information transmission process. After being written in Calcutta on December 6th and handstamped by the Post Office on the 8th, the letter was taken by the Peninsular & Oriental Steam Navigation Company's, or the P&O's, branch steamer to Galle, Ceylon, and from there on the 16th by a larger P&O vessel, the *Oriental*, via Aden to Suez, arriving there on 1 January, 1852. From Suez the letter was taken overland across the desert by donkey, dromedary and riverboat services to Alexandria, Egypt, from where the letter continued on 5 January by a third P&O vessel, the *Ripon*, to Malta. It arrived on the 9th and proceeded on the same day by the British Admiralty steam packet *Banshee*, Lieutenant Hosken as the Captain, to Marseilles, arriving on the 11th.[51]

The mails were taken by railway to Calais, across the Channel by a branch steamer, and again by train to London, from where the letter was forwarded to Boston on 15 January. However, the letter was meant to be delivered to

50   A letter to Messrs Magowe & Son, Boston, from Calcutta 6.12.1851. (SRLC)
51   Reg Kirk, *The P&O Lines to the Far East.* British Maritime Postal History, Vol. 2 (printing data missing), 30; Colin Tabeart, *Admiralty Mediterranean Steam Packets 1830 to 1857* (Limassol, Cyprus 2002), 212. For the Overland trip, see Boyd Cable, *A Hundred Year History of the P&O, Peninsular and Oriental Steam Navigation Company, 1837–1937* (London, 1937), 85–93.

FIG. 2. *The letter sent on 6.2.1851 from Calcutta, India, was carried by P&O, Admiralty and Cunard Line mail steamers, as well as railways, camels and donkeys, via Galle, Suez, Alexandria, Malta, Marseilles, London and Liverpool, before being received in Boston, United States, on 9.2.1852, in 65 days. (See the text.)*

Boston in the United States, not in Britain. The word 'America' was added to the address, and the letter was sent across the Atlantic by the Cunard Line mail steamer *Niagara*, which departed from Liverpool on 17 January and arrived in New York on 7 February, or by the same company's *Europa*, which departed on 24 January and arrived in Boston on 8 February.[52] In both cases the letter would have been dispatched in Boston on the 9th, as it happened. The trip by the *Niagara* took 21 days but that of the *Europa* only 15 days. The rough winter winds in the Atlantic were sometimes unpredictable, and the *Niagara's* trip had been lengthened so much that the ship had to put into Halifax for coal on 4 February.[53]

By slicing into pieces the letter's trip from Calcutta to Boston according to the means of transmission during the voyage, we discovered a great deal of information not available in the original letter. Instead of just finding out the duration of the information transmission, we learnt that the letter was carried by six different mail steamers and several trains, as well as donkey, dromedary and river boat. We could notice that the international mail system worked smoothly already in the mid-19th century, especially when the letters were carried by British services all the way. The waiting times were short, but there could be some variation in the duration of longer sea journeys as in the Atlantic crossing.

In addition to the use of personal correspondence, the speed of arriving news has generally been measured from the time lag of foreign news published in the newspapers. Päiviö Tommila calculated in his pioneering article in

52   Sailing lists of Hubbard & Winter, 30.
53   J.C. Arnell, *Atlantic Mails. A History of the Mail Service between Great Britain and Canada to 1889*, National Postal Museum (Ottawa, 1980), 311.

1960, how long it took for the news of *Finlands Allmänna Tidning,* an official newspaper, to arrive in Finland from different countries in 1830.[54] Ian K. Steele used the same method to calculate the age of London-based news in some American newspapers in 1705–1740, and Allan R. Pred for calculating the spread of news between the major American cities in 1790–1840.[55]

The method of comparing known facts of historical events with the dates on which the news was published in the newspapers in other countries leave several questions open. By which means was the news carried, how long was the waiting time before the transport, what was the duration of the transport, how long did it take before the next issue of the newspaper was published, and finally, how long did it take before the newspaper was delivered to the readers, probably again far from the place where the paper was printed.

To measure the duration of maritime news transmission, Yrjö Kaukiainen calculated the difference between the dates on which the sailing lists from distant ports were sent and on which they were published by *Lloyd's List* in London. This method gives comparable knowledge from different routes and different time periods, and is very useful for measuring the speed of one-way information transmission.[56] However, it does not tell the whole truth about the duration of information transmission from the recipient's point of view. As the news in the earlier times was carried by occasional merchantmen, the readers in Britain often had to wait one or two extra months to learn e.g. of a particular ship's arrival, simply because there were no vessels arriving from that port to bring the news.

For example, a sailing list from Hong Kong published in *Lloyd's List* on 25 October, 1845, included arrivals and departures from that port between 20 June and 26 August. Thus, the age of the earliest news was 127 days while the latest news was only 60 days old when published in the same day's newspaper.[57] The frequency of mail transmission definitely played an important role in the information flows. When interpreting the figures, it is important to keep in mind the difference between the measurement of duration of the mail transportation itself (which was chiefly examined by Kaukiainen) and the measurement of the duration of spreading the news contents.

Similarly, when using Allan Pred's figures of the 'relative level of interregional shipping interaction' between the coast ports of the United States, it should be remembered that the 'weighted arrivals' are not the same as the factual sailings.[58]

Ian K. Steele calculated the duration of early North Atlantic sailings using British port records of customs entrances and clearances, finding important information on the frequency and duration of sailings during the period 1675–1740. Yet, as Steele noted, by this method the duration of sea journeys is calculated only from customs to customs.[59]

---

54 Päiviö Tommila, 'Havaintoja uutisten leviämisnopeudesta ulkomailta Suomeen 1800-luvun alkupuolella', *Historiallinen Aikakauskirja, vol. 81*(1960), no. 1, 83–84.
55 Steele (1986), 158–159, 302; Pred, 35–57.
56 Kaukiainen (2001), 1–28.
57 *Lloyd's List* 25.10.1845.
58 Pred, 115–126.
59 Steele (1986), 283.

In real life, the final departure dates could vary several days from the customs records. It often took days after the clearance before the ship really departed, due to bad weather or other delays. The ship could even put back having already sailed due to damage caused by storm or other unexpected events.[60] Thus, the figures do not reflect the duration of the sea voyage only, but may include other elements.

A comparison between the customs records and the final sailing data from the port of Liverpool in 1825 give a good example of the difference. The American sailing packets, although scheduled for regular line service, did not always depart on the given date, even if they had cleared in good time to be able to do that. The clearance usually took place on the scheduled departure date or the day before, but in half of the cases in 1825 the ship was delayed, the average delay being four days and the variation from one to 12 days.[61] When measuring the duration of sailings, there can thus be a major difference in the results depending on which method has been chosen.

Naturally, the newspaper dates may have included more errors, while the customs bills were administrative records with most obviously correct data. Yet the maritime intelligence of *Lloyd's List* was at least 'semi-official', being collected by Lloyd's agents and correspondents for the use of underwriters. A general rule in using newspaper data is that the longer the distance between the event (e.g. ship arrival) and the place of publishing it, the more potential there is for errors. In those cases where postal historical studies have been based on e.g. Caribbean newspapers, some additional caution is needed when considering the precision of the dates given.

Carl C. Cutler used a combination of custom house records, log books and maritime intelligence of contemporary newspapers to collect sailing lists of the American tea clipper voyages in the 1850s.[62] Colin Tabeart based his study of the Admiralty Packets in the Mediterranean on data collected from the ships' logs and maritime intelligence from the newspapers, combining these with factual postal information from the letters carried on the route.[63] The latter one is an especially excellent combination, but seldom available.

Some historians give figures of exactly how many days, hours and minutes a transatlantic crossing took by a specific vessel.[64] These figures are usually based on newspaper reports or the ships' log books, sources which are not

---

60   An extreme example from the 1840s: 'Liverpool, put back: 14 Aug, *Thomas Bennett*, late Halsey, for Charleston, the Master having been killed by the Cook, 8th inst.' *Lloyd's List 15.8.1844.*

61   Calculated from the *Liverpool Customs Bills of Entry*, 1825; *Lloyd's List* 1825.

62   Carl C. Cutler, *Greyhounds of the Sea. The story of the American clipper ship* (Maryland, 1930), 475.

63   Tabeart (2002), x–xi.

64   See e.g. N.R.P. Bonsor, *North Atlantic Seaway* (New York, 1975), vol. 1, 203–205, 230–237; Jack C. Arnell, *Steam and the North Atlantic Mails: The impact of the Cunard Line and subsequent steamship companies on the carriage of transatlantic mails* (Toronto, 1986), 241, 248, 254.

available in all cases.[65] To be consistent, all voyages in this study have been calculated by using the same sources: sailing lists of mail-carrying ships, published by *Lloyd's List* or relevant postal historical studies.[66]

These sources can only afford sailing dates, not hours or minutes. There is naturally a difference, if the ship departs early in the morning and arrives at the destination port a few days later in the evening, or if she departs in the evening and arrives in the early morning. Even if the method of calculating the duration of journeys only by dates cannot be really accurate in a particular case, it gives a good overview of the situation. The 'grey margin' remains the same throughout the period, and the system treats all companies evenly. A comparison of sailing data published by Hubbard & Winter in *North Atlantic Mail Sailings 1840–75* and the Cunard Line records for the Admiralty 1840–1846,[67] gives the following results:

The Cunard Line's ships sailed from Liverpool on regular dates but the departing hour varied greatly. There may have been several reasons for this, one of which was the exceptionally strong tide at the River Mersey. Besides that, especially during the latter part of the period, departures often took place in the afternoon or even in the evening, perhaps waiting for the latest business correspondence. At the other end of the journey, arrivals often occurred in the early morning, but could also take place at any other time of the day.

Comparison between the duration of passages, calculated from the sailing lists of Hubbard & Winter and the Cunard statistics, show that even if there were several hours' differences in the duration of sailings on particular voyages, the differences balanced each other rather well in the long run. Between 4 July 1840 and 5 May 1846, the difference between the sailing lists of Hubbard & Winter and the company records concerning 112 westbound sailings was only three hours on average. The duration of trips calculated using the dates only was longer each year than if the duration was calculated by using the exact sailing hours. However, in specific cases the difference could be positive as well as negative.

What methods should be used to estimate the mass of information transmitted? For example, the statistics of income from postage rates to the post offices have sometimes been used to figure out the growth of the number

---

65   There are exceptions. E.g. the Cunard Papers (CP) in the Sydney Jones Library Archives (SJ) at the University of Liverpool include record books of the Cunard ship departures and arrivals. The precision of the record keeping varies but the sailing and arrival times are normally given in an accurate form. A considerable problem is, however, that the time difference between Europe and North America has been calculated in different ways on the voyages, or totally ignored, in each direction. The use of the Passage Books for the Cunard voyages would mislead the study, as there are no similar sources available from all shipping companies included. *Cunard Passage Books 1–4* cover the years 1848–1881. CP, GM2/1–4 (SJ). About problems in using these records as sources for measuring the duration of the voyages, see also N.R.P. Bonsor, *North Atlantic Seaway* (New York, 1980), vol. 5, 1868–1870.

66   The issues of *Lloyd's List* used in this study have been reprinted up to 1826 and microfilmed from 1827 onwards. They are kept e.g. in the Merseyside Maritime Museum Library and Archives (MMM) in Liverpool.

67   Sailing lists of Hubbard & Winter, 17–21; 'Tenders and Contracts for Carrying the Mails by Steam to and from North America. N:o 10. Return of the Dates of Sailing and Arrival of the Steamers Employed in Performing the Contract', 28–29. CP, PR 3/1/12. (SJ)

of letters sent during a time period.[68] Yet the rates of single letters may have changed markedly during the period, the relation between cheaper short-distance and much more expensive long-distance mail may have changed – and these figures could not be compared with other cities of different geographic location even in the same year. Finally, the newspapers were normally not included in the postage rate figures.[69] Therefore, these figures probably describe best the fiscal importance of the postal services. Numbers of letters sent during a specific period can naturally be compared with numbers of letters sent during another period of the same length.

As has been noted, there is no single method which would answer all questions regarding information transmission. Even though all methods can be used to measure something, it should be kept in mind that there is a great difference in what can be achieved by using the alternative methods. Table 4 may be of help in the consideration.

Consecutive information circles as tools in measuring the speed of business information transmission

The need for fast information transmission often varied between the different parties in mercantile societies. Newspapers wanted to get the freshest news as quickly as possible, and for them rapid one-way information flow was critical. But for traders – depending on the nature of their business – it was often at least equally important that the system enabled them to answer the business letters rapidly, and again to receive fast answers to their letters.

A practical tool which has not previously been used for measuring the speed of business information transmission in published studies is to calculate the number of consecutive information circles enabled by a particular service within a calendar year. This tool enables us to examine in a commensurable way the efficiency and development of the information circulation during different time periods and on different routes.

One information circle is equal to the time between sending a letter and getting an answer to it. While a round trip of a mail-carrying ship means the period from the ship departure from the home port to the arrival back home, an information circle could be shorter, if there were other mail-carrying vessels departing earlier from the other end, and they were able to carry the answer. Thus, the length of an information circle depended not only on the duration of two one-way trips but also on the frequency of the sailings.

The duration of the sailings can be calculated from the sailing data published in different postal historical studies, or if such a study is not obtainable for a specific route or time period, from the maritime intelligence published by *Lloyd's List* or other contemporary newspapers. By combining information on the arrivals and departures of mail-carrying ships, it is easy to find out how the system worked at both ends of the trip. A combination of these facts gives us the length of one information circle and enables the calculation of numbers of consecutive information circles per year.

---

68   Steele (1986), 124; and Pred, 80, 96–101.
69   Pred, 94.

TABLE 4. *Methods for measuring the speed of information transmission.*

What is calculated	*Focus*	*Source material*	*Comments*
Duration between dates of writing & arrival of letters		Correspondence (only received letters useful)	Includes unclear delays between the two dates. Real duration of transport will remain unknown. Sent letters are not useful for speed calculations, but they shed light on the information circulation as a whole.
Duration between dates of arrival & answer of letters		Correspondence	Not very useful, as there might have been several reasons for delays in answering. However, the method sheds some light on the frequency of business relations.
Duration between an event & the news spread by newspapers		Newspapers, their contents (maritime intelligence give added value)	Includes uncertainties in both ends, e.g. how long it took for the newspaper to receive the specific piece of news, and how long it took for the recipient to receive the newspaper after printing.
Duration of transport	From departure of mail to arrival (from post office to post office)	Correspondence (postal markings, only received letters useful)	Gives a true picture of duration of mail transmission from the post office of departure to the post office of arrival, and all transits. Can be used only if the letters were carried by official mail. Not useful when examining the frequency of mail transport.
Duration of transport	From the latest news to the date of publishing	Newspapers, the technically latest news	Gives a proper picture about the speed of news transmission (e.g. maritime intelligence for newspapers). Includes a gap between the arrival of news to the publisher and the printing. Should not be mixed with the speed of news spread.
Duration of transport	From departure of ship to its arrival	Sailing lists, published in newspapers & postal historical studies	Gives a solid picture of the duration of transport in general, and if the date of sending is known, also about the duration of transport of a specific letter. There may be gaps or faults in the newspaper based data.
Duration of transport	From departure of ship to its arrival	Log books of ships	Gives quite exact data about duration of transport (with some reservations). The log books of specific sailings are not easily available, and many have been destroyed.
Duration of transport	From customs to customs	Customs records of clearances and entrances	Includes unclear delays between the dates of customs clearances and the ship departure. The real duration of transport remains unknown.
Frequency of transport	From departure of ship to its arrival	Sailing lists, published in newspapers & postal historical studies	Gives useful data about the frequency of transport. There may be gaps in the information, as all details have not always been published.
Frequency of transport	From customs to customs	Customs records of clearances and entrances	Very useful, if all records are available, but early mail ships (e.g. Falmouth packets and Admiralty vessels) did not sail via customs.
Frequency of transport	Postage rate incomes	General Post Office records	Includes uncertainties in form of changing postage rates and different types of mail.

How this system worked in reality, and whether the trade partners really used it in an optimal way, can be examined from the correspondence of the various merchant houses. The handstamps and other postal markings of the letters also give us a clear idea of which postal service has been used in cases where there were several possibilities, for example the alternating British and French government mail services for South America in the 1860s.

It should be noticed that this tool measures the best possible information circulation (the maximum number of consecutive information circles) between two places within a time period, for example one year. There may have been many other possibilities to send mail in one direction, but this method gives us an idea about how the two-way communications worked in practice. It was surprisingly often a very different story.

IV Overseas Mail and Speed of Communications before 1815

Overseas mail systems before 1815 – Background for the development in speed

From the 17th century, merchant letters had arrived at British ports by private ships, while official correspondence was often carried by naval vessels. The arriving private ship letters were sent from the port of arrival to London, where they were marked up with three charges: the ship letter charge, the fee paid to the ship's master for each letter handed over, and the inland postage according to the number of miles the letter had been conveyed by road from the port of entry via London to the place of address. The addressee could not receive his letter before having paid the total amount due.

At first, the only means of identifying incoming ship letters was from the endorsements in the manuscript on the letter, such as the name of the incoming ship or the name of her master. From the 1760s, the Post Office issued individually named ship letter handstamps to postmasters at ports in all parts of Britain. Similar kinds of arrival handstamps on ship letters were also introduced in France at about the same time.[70] The purpose was to identify the letter as a ship letter and also name the specific port of entry, so that the inland postal charges on the mileage basis could be accurately assessed. These handstamps are often very useful for a historian who tries to reconstruct a ship letter's voyage.

Between 1770 and 1840, hundreds of different arrival handstamps succeeded each other with a wide distribution of ports, large and small. In

---

70   In Britain, the first ports to use this type of handstamps were Liverpool 1757; London 1760; Cork 1761; Londonderry 1762; Greenock 1763; Dover 1765; and Deal, Plymouth, Poole and Portsmouth 1766. See Colin Tabeart, *Robertson Revisited. A study of the Maritime Postal Markings of the British Isles based on the work of Alan W. Robertson* (Cyprus, 1997), passim. – According to Tabeart, the first ship letter handstamp of Deal is from 1767, but a letter in the writer's collection, dated 26 June and arrived in London 30 July 1766, verifies an earlier date. (SRLC). – In France, the first ship letter arrival handstamps of this type were introduced in Marseille 1757, Brest and Rouen 1760, Bayonne and Port-Louis 1761, Bordeaux and Havre 1763, Ile de Rhé 1764 and La Rochelle 1764 and Nantes 1766. See Raymond Salles, *La Poste Maritime Française. Tome 1, Les Entrées Maritimes et les Bateaux a Vapeurs* (Cyprus, 1992), 7–9, Addendum, 1–4.

the days of sail, ships put in at convenient ports for shelter from the weather, for water and stores, and also to report safe arrival and receive orders at the first opportunity. As the letters carried were required by law to be handed over at the first port of call, any port or haven was a potential landing place for ship letters carried by the early sailing ships.

The outward letters were sent similarly by ship passengers, by courier or, in most cases, by masters of ships sailing from British ports. The agents of shipowners also accepted letters in their offices, and handed them to the care of their captains. In London and other major ports, the owners of coffee houses collected outward letters in a bag, which was then forwarded to the ship's captain, who took them on board and delivered them in the port of destination to the local Post Office or coffee house, getting the nominal two pence charge per dispatched letter.

The unofficial system of private arrangement with ship masters continued to be the main channel through which letters to overseas destinations left from Britain throughout the 18th century. The Act of 1711 made it illegal to dispatch by private ships letters which could be sent by regular packets, but to places for which no Post Office packet service existed, ship masters were free to carry letters. Enforcement was difficult, and little respect was forthcoming from the letter-writing public.[71]

In 1799, a ship letter rate of four pence was imposed on single letters brought into Britain with a gratuity of two pence to the ship's master. Outwards, the rate for private ship letters was fixed at one half of the packet ship postage, while the gratuity to the ship's captain was increased from one penny to two pence. Merchants were encouraged to take their letters to the Post Office, which would undertake to find a suitable ship to carry them. Even though the Post Office repeated offers to the owners of coffee houses and taverns to become its salaried agents, the old practice continued as it had done for nearly two centuries. The coffee house proprietors were not interested, and the general public could not see any advantage in sending to the Post Office mail that was going out of Britain by private ships. Due to treasury needs after the war in 1814, the sea postage of incoming letters was raised from four to six pence, and a year later to eight pence, which was a very high rate, to be collected when the letter was delivered. The rate of outgoing private ship letters was decreased from one-half to one-third of what was charged by outgoing packets to make the government option more attractive, but to no avail.[72]

In addition to private merchant ships, British Post Office sailing packet services sailed from Falmouth at the south western coast of England to Halifax, Bermuda, the West Indies, Mexico and South America. The packet service started between Falmouth and Lisbon in 1689 and continued on that route until the Peninsula Steam Navigation Company, or the P&O, took over in 1837.

---

71   Alan W. Robertson, *A History of the Ship Letters of the British Isles.* An Encyclopaedia of Maritime Postal History (Bournemouth, 1955), A 1, A 3.
72   Frank Staff, *The Transatlantic Mail* (Massachusetts, 1956), 46, 54; Robinson (1964), 114–115.

The Falmouth packets were speedier than the non-scheduled merchant ships, for which time was of little concern, while a fully loaded ship could bring the owners a satisfactory financial return. To carry only mail, as the government packets did, was primarily regarded as expensive misuse of shipping capacity. The armed mail packets carried just a few passengers, and fine freight like bullion and specie. The service was costly to maintain, and the Post Office packet charges to meet these costs were much greater than the nominal two pence charged by the master of a private ship. The public in general preferred private ships, thus avoiding the extra costs paid for Post Office packets according to the number of sheets and weight.[73]

The first transatlantic mail service from Falmouth to the West Indies was run monthly by Edward Dummer, a former Surveyor General of the Navy, in 1702–1711. This was the first mail contract, by which the government sponsored private shipowners for transatlantic mail transmission. The service, even though originally very promising from the viewpoint of speed and regularity of mail transport, collapsed due to problems in financial management and expenses caused by losses of several packets and replacement of them.[74] Another early attempt to start a regular transatlantic packet service was made by William Warren, with sailings between Bristol and New York in 1709. This service ceased in 1711 or 1712.[75]

From 1755, a monthly mail service was usually carried out between Falmouth and the West Indies, with several unavoidable delays and interruptions during times of war. This route later included a variety of colonies – a rather difficult service, as the ports of call were so widely spread in the Caribbean. By 1810, six local West Indian mail boats supplemented the sailing packets that crossed the Atlantic. Communication from England was then bi-monthly. The packets were owned by private shipowners, usually the captains themselves, and they each had their separate contracts with the Post Office. The Postmaster organized the departures depending on the availability of vessels at port.[76]

The packet service from Falmouth to New York also started in 1755. The New York packets stopped regularly in Boston from 1773 onwards. A third leg for the service was established at Charleston, South Carolina, in the 1760s but remained occasional. After the American Revolution, the New York service was re-established in 1783. It was not conducted during the war years 1813 and 1814.[77] From 1806, it was common practice to route the New York packets via Bermuda from November to February and via Halifax during the rest of the year to serve the British naval stations. Finally, a packet service for South America was added in the Falmouth schedules

---

73 Robertson, A 3; See also Tony Pawlyn, *The Falmouth Packets, 1689–1851* (Truran, 2003), 6. Despite its name, the latter study is mainly focused on the 18th century.

74 See L.E. Britnor, *The History of the Sailing Packets to the West Indies.* British West Indies Study Circle (1973), 3–17; Steele (1986), 168–188; Staff, 27–31; Robinson (1964), 35–39.

75 Robinson (1964), 38–39. See also John McCusker, 'New York City and the Bristol Packet...', 177–189.

76 Robinson (1964), 93; Britnor, 39–43, 55–58.

77 Arnell (1980), 7–11, 17–18, 27; J.C. Arnell & M.H. Ludington, *The Bermuda Packet Mails and the Halifax–Bermuda Mail Service 1806 to 1886* (Great Britain, 1989), 15–17.

MAP 1. *Major Atlantic currents.*

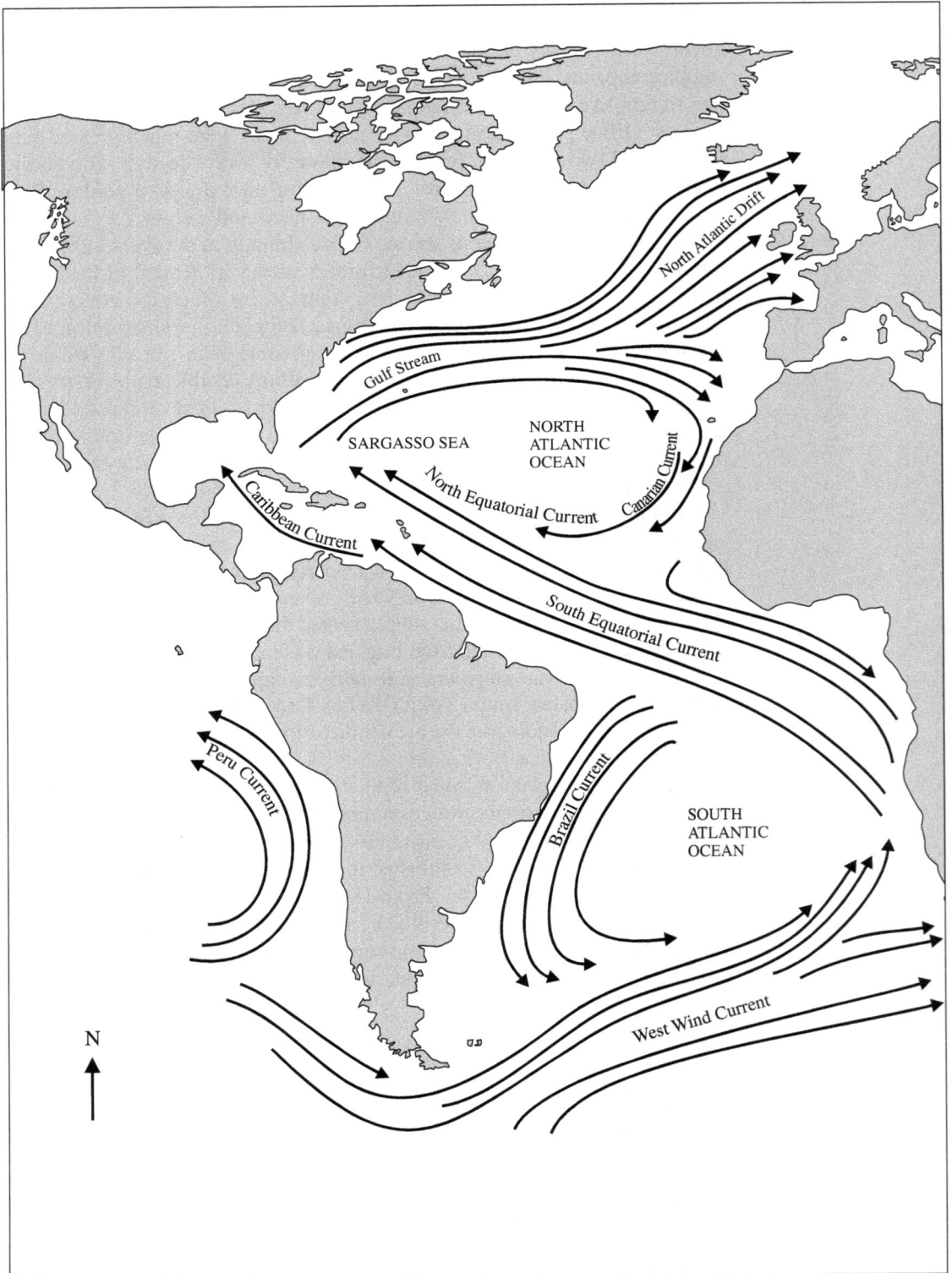

in 1808 and the service for Mexico in 1824.[78] Many of these routes were reorganized several times during their history.

The East India Company, or the EIC, had a long lasting monopoly in the East India trade until 1813 and on the China route until 1833, including a monopoly in the mail transmission between Britain and the Eastern trade ports.[79]

Background for the development of speed before 1815

From the early 18th century, not very much had happened to improve the speed of ocean going sailing ships. There were developments in cartography and hydrography, including the improvements in calculating the longitude, which made it possible to publish more accurate sea charts. A better knowledge of geography, as well as of prevailing winds and currents, helped the captains to take more advantage of them, and to avoid the most difficult sea areas.[80]

New technical equipment was slow in reaching ordinary ships. Unlike the exquisite but costly French chronometers, the English ones came gradually down in price until they were within the reach of ships' captains. By 1815, England had produced 4,000 or 5,000 chronometers, compared with France's 300, while in the 1790s only the EIC had equipped their ships with these costly devices. The company also had a hydrologist in their service and published charts of the Bay of Bengal. The Royal Navy did not issue chronometers to all its ships until 1825. In 1833 the French Navy had 44 chronometers for its 250 vessels, and the United States Navy had 54 in 1835. Not until the 1840s did the supply of chronometers catch up with the demand.[81]

Ship building improved slowly. One important invention was the copper sheathing of the planking beneath the waterline of vessels, which sheltered the bottom from the teredo worm. The wooden vessels were liable to be damaged by worms and they collected barnacles and 'a kind of musillagenous stuff', particularly in the West Indies, which retarded their sailing, while nothing could cling to a copper sheathing; it kept clean and resisted worms.[82] The gradual modification of the ship's hull finally created the large and efficient, extremely beautiful, fast clipper model – the ships which would make record sailings on the world's longest sea routes from the mid-19th century.[83]

---

78 Arnell & Ludington, v–vi; J.N.T. Howat, *South American Packets. The British Packet Service to Brazil, the River Plate, the West Coast (via the Straits of Magellan) and the Falkland Islands. 1808–1880* (York, 1984), 1–4; Robinson (1964), 111.

79 Robertson, B 29, B 30; Staff, 58.

80 For early hydrographic work by the French Dessiou family in 1770–1851, see Paul Hughes & Alan D. Wall, 'The Dessiou Hydrographic Work: Its Authorship and Place' in *International Journal of Maritime History, Vol. XVII*, No. 2 (St. John's, 2005), 167–192. In the 1840s, the American hydrographer, Lieutenant M.F. Maury published sailing instructions which covered widely the sea routes of the whole world.

81 Daniel R. Headrick, *When Information Came of Age. Technologies of Knowledge in the Age of Reason and Revolution, 1700–1850* (Oxford, 2000), 108–115.

82 See Steele (1986), 44; Britnor, 40.

83 See Richard C. McKay, *Some Famous Sailing Ships and Their Builder Donald Mc Kay*

Even though heavy weather was always dangerous, sometimes even fatal, and caused long delays on the sea voyages, the other alternative was not much better. When it was calm, the ships did not move at all. The effect of prevailing winds was easily noticed in the duration of sea voyages across the North Atlantic, where the westbound journeys were always more difficult and the duration of sailings could be several weeks longer than on the eastbound journeys. In fact, a sailing vessel's journey from Liverpool to New York was nearly 500 miles longer than a vessel's journey from New York to Liverpool. This was due to the prevailing westerly winds. No sailing vessel could travel directly into the wind, and the extra 500 miles came from the tacking while the vessel tried to beat her way to the westward.[84]

During times of war, ship captures became everyday news. In May 1800, *Lloyd's List* reported 60 captures or recaptures of British ships. To avoid losses, large convoys were collected from trade ships sailing in the same direction, and escorted by men-of-war. Thus, e.g. on 27 June, 1800, *Lloyd's List* reported 69 ships arriving off Portsmouth in convoy from the different West Indian islands. Simultaneously, 30 ships arrived in Liverpool from the West Indies, and seven more at Lancaster. In total, the convoy had included more than 100 ships crossing the Atlantic together. The same day's paper told readers that 46 ships had arrived at Jamaica from London, Clyde, Liverpool, Newcastle and Cork, one of the ships having been captured by a Spanish privateer.[85]

From 1803, all ships – including armed merchantmen – were compelled to cross the Atlantic in convoy. The convoys were strictly scheduled and no delays were permitted. If the ships were not ready to sail, they had to wait for the next opportunity, even if their cargoes were perishable. Mails were carried equally slowly, independent on which of the ships actually carried them. The convoy was as slow as the slowest ship involved. Collecting large fleets of merchant ships took time, and the protection that could be given was limited anyway. Ships could be captured on their way to the rendezvous, gales and fog could separate them from each other, and there was always a risk that a superior enemy force could destroy the whole fleet.[86]

It was not only the merchant ships that could be captured during troubled times, but also the Falmouth packets, which carried important mails and sometimes bullion worth many times the ship's own value. Between 1793 and 1815, the packets were engaged by an enemy at least 128 times. Of the ships, 44 were totally lost to the enemy, and 31 were retaken or restored after a fight. 35 packets successfully fought off the attackers, and eight actually captured their attackers. As there were in total fewer than 100 Falmouth packets in service during those years, the record is quite impressive.[87]

(New York, 1928), passim.; and David R. MacGregor, *The Tea Clippers* (London, 1952), passim.

84   Albion (1938), 9.

85   *Lloyd's List* 27.6.1800.

86   Gerald S. Graham, *Empire of the North Atlantic. The Maritime Struggle for North America* (Great Britain, 1958), 232–235.

87   Pawlyn, 84. For complete lists of captured Post Office packets during the wars of 1777–

The duties of the commander of a mail packet in the event of enemy action were prescribed as follows: 'You must run where you can, you must fight when you can no longer run, and when you can fight no more, you must sink the mails before you strike.'[88] This was often done, and thousands of letters and other important mail never reached their recipients.

Perhaps due to the continuous troubles caused by wars and privateers, the speed of information transmission by the government packet service hardly improved at all during the 18th century, while all efforts were concentrated in keeping the service going. Edward Dummer's packets, in 1702–1711, made the trip between Jamaica and Falmouth in 42.8 days, on average,[89] and the Post Office packets of 1795–97, almost 100 years later, made the same trip in 41.7 days, on average.[90]

1782 and 1793–1815, see Robinson (1964), 308–314. There are several descriptions of the actions between the Falmouth packets and privateers, see e.g. Robertson, B 8, B 8 A–H; Robinson (1964), 69–74, 96–104; Pawlyn, 69–84. – For a complete list of the packets, see Robertson, B 2–B 7.

88   Robertson, B 1; Robinson (1964), 83.
89   Britnor, 9.
90   Calculated from 'Sailings and arrivals of Jamaica Packets, 1795, '96 and '97', Britnor, 75.

V   North Atlantic

The Great Innovation of Sailing on Schedule

The 'regular' Falmouth packets – New York–Liverpool becomes the main North Atlantic mail route – The line traffic starts – Effects on business information transmission

The 'regular' Falmouth packets

The war between Britain and the United States in 1812–1815 stopped the only official mail service which had been conducted between the Old World and New York. Due to the British trade blockade and the American counter actions, including privateering which was very common in the North Atlantic,[91] the British Post Office mail service between Falmouth and New York was discontinued for two years, 1813 and 1814, starting again in 1815. The Halifax and Bermuda service continued through the war, but not all of the monthly sailings could be conducted. As the same packet ships were used on the other Post Office routes for Lisbon, the West Indies and South America and no less than 17 of the vessels were captured during 1813–1815, the mail service met a continuous series of problems.[92]

By that time, the Falmouth packets primarily served the naval station and the merchants in Halifax, which had become an important *entrepôt* of trade and shipping during the previous few years. This was naturally an unsatisfactory situation from the point of view of those who had urgent business letters to send to and from New York.

Even if the packet service was called 'regular' it did not mean much more than that the ships departed monthly. Originally, the packets had sailed from Falmouth on the first Wednesday of each month and left from New York on the first Thursday of the month thereafter, but 'as time passed, the Falmouth departures had tended to be around mid-month', as Arnell puts it

---

91   About the war time arrangements for shipping in the North Atlantic region, see Graham, 237–261.
92   See Robinson (1964), 314.

TABLE 5. *Falmouth packet round trips and the consecutive information circles, Falmouth–New York, 1817.*

Packet	Departure from Falmouth	Arrival in New York (via Bermuda or Halifax)	Departure from New York	Arrival in Falmouth (via Bermuda or Halifax)	Ship's round trip, days	Minimum time to get an answer to a letter if sent by the first possible packet from New York > Information circle
Countess of Chichester	**29.1.17**	**28.3.**	**11.4.**[a]	**22.5.**	113	**113**
Francis Freeling	24.2.	16.4.	~10.5.	8.6.	104	104
Princess Elizabeth	25.3.	5.5.	6.6.	3.7.	100	75 by *Francis Freeling*
Lady Wellington	17.4.	20.5.	6.7.	5.8.	110	77 by *Pss Elizabeth*
Lord Sidmouth	19.5.	14.7.	**14.8.**	**12.9.**	116	116
Princess Elizabeth 2	**16.6.**	**12.8.**	6.9.	20.10.	126	**88** by *Lord Sidmouth*
Grace	18.7.	30.8.	10.10.	9.11.	114	94 by *Pss Elizabeth 2*
Swiftsure	20.8.	11.10.	**13.11.**	**5.12.**	107[b]	107
Lady Wellington	**20.9.**	**5.11.**	7.12.	5.1.	107[b]	76 by *Swiftsure*
Countess of Chichester	7.10.	26.11.	~6.1.18	29.1.	114[b]	90 by *Ly Wellington*
Princess Elizabeth 2	18.11.	18.1.18	15.2.	20.3.	122[b]	122
Grace	**22.12.**	**8.2.18**	10.3.	15.4.	114	88 by *Pss Elizabeth 2*

Source: Sailing lists of Arnell & Ludington, 23. – The figures in **bold** show the consecutive information circles enabled by the service if the first letter was sent from Falmouth on 29.1.1817.

~ Estimated departure date from New York.

[a] The earlier ship, *Queensbury*, had already departed on 17.3.1817.

[b] Direct homeward sailings from New York to Falmouth.

in the *Atlantic mails*.[93] For example in 1816, the sailing day from Falmouth was only once a Wednesday, while it was four times a Monday, twice a Tuesday, three times a Thursday and twice a Sunday. The departure dates

93   Arnell (1980), 63.

varied between the 8th and 18th of the month. From New York the ships sailed between the 2nd and 18th of the month.[94]

In 1816, the average trip from Falmouth to Halifax took 25 to 41 days, the stay at Halifax three to 13 days and the trip from Halifax to New York four to nine days. A merchant who sent a letter to New York could not know whether it would be received in 33 or 64 days. He could not even know when a ship would leave from New York carrying the answer to his letter. The stays at port in New York varied between 20 and 51 days.[95]

There was a major difference from the information transmission point of view whether the replies were bound to one ship's round trip, or whether they could be sent by a vessel which departed earlier from New York.

When there was another mail packet leaving from New York to England before the last arrived ship's departure, the time to receive an answer to a letter sent by the latter ship shortened markedly. The difference between a ship's round trip and an information circle, in which the minimum time was used to send an answer by the next packet, can clearly be noticed in Table 5, which depicts the Falmouth packet service in 1817.

It can also be noticed that the number of consecutive information circles enabled by the system was only three if calculated from the beginning of the year, and three also if calculated from the February departure. However, if the first letter of the chain was sent on 25 March, it connected with a series of reliable sailings, which enabled four consecutive information circles within the year, the last one ending on 20 March, 1818.

The earlier packet had already departed from New York before the next mails arrived from England no less than five times out of twelve, thus causing long delays in replies. A letter sent by *Princess Elizabeth* on 25 March, 1817, from Falmouth could receive an answer on 8 June in 75 days, as the *Francis Freeling* was still at port in New York and departed a few days after the arrival of the English mails. But the answer to another letter sent by the *Princess Elizabeth (2)* from Falmouth on 18 November missed the *Countess of Chichester's* departure in New York and was carried to England by the *Princess Elizabeth (2)* on her return voyage, arriving in Falmouth on 20 March, 1818, in 122 days.

The problem was also well-known at the other end of the journey. While the mail ships arrived at Falmouth very irregularly, the leaving packets did not wait for them. Therefore, when e.g. the *Countess of Chichester* arrived on 22 May, 1817, the *Lord Sidmouth* had departed just three days earlier. The next opportunity to send letters to New York by official mail was on 16 June, 3.5 weeks later. In England, the dates of mail arrivals and the next departures were somewhat better-coordinated than in New York, however.

The examples show that the speed of information transmission across the Atlantic could have been improved by several weeks by more careful schedule planning even in the days of slow sailing ships. It can also be asked, why this

94 See the sailing lists of Arnell & Ludington, 15–19.
95 The winter sailings via Bermuda were even longer and more unpredictable. The trip from Falmouth to Bermuda took 28 to 54 days, the stay at Bermuda three to four days and the trip from Bermuda to New York six to 18 days. Calculated from the sailing lists of Arnell & Ludington, 21.

planning was not done. The answer was probably mainly in the complexity of the sailing packet system, as will be shown in Chapter VI.1.

The Falmouth packet service to Halifax, Bermuda and New York was an administrative compromise which should have served everybody, but which made nobody happy. It did not serve the British well due to its slowness and irregular schedules, and several days had to be added for the inland journey between Falmouth and London (or any other place) both outwards and homewards.[96] The New York merchants felt that the stops at Halifax or Bermuda unnecessarily lengthened the duration of the journeys. The mails for Bermuda were carried most of the year from Halifax by naval sloops after the European mails had arrived, and the answers did not always reach Halifax in time to catch the packet leaving for England. Finally, the Halifax merchants were often in a situation where, because a packet departed for England a few days before another packet arrived from there, the answers to the mails could not be sent until three or four weeks later.[97]

In 1816, the average duration of the westbound sailings was 34 days between Falmouth and Halifax, and 39 days between Falmouth and Bermuda. The average stop at Halifax or Bermuda was five days, after which the rest of the trip to New York took about seven days. An average eastbound journey to Falmouth took 23 days from Halifax and 24 days from Bermuda. The speed of the government packet sailings did not improve during the following years. In 1816–1820, the average duration of the trip between Falmouth and Halifax was 34 days, and between Falmouth and Bermuda 39 days.[98] The Falmouth packet system, with all the mail routes included, will be discussed further in Chapter VI.1.

New York–Liverpool becomes the main North Atlantic mail route

Falmouth had originally been chosen as the primary port for the government's mail sailings in the 17th century due to its good geographical advantages for shipping. It was sufficiently far away from the French coast to prevent seizure of the packets by privateers and it offered good shelter from the weather and wind. The location was sufficiently well fortified to deter enemy raids and, due to being at the eastern end of the shortest Atlantic sea route, the port enabled the fastest passages and reduced the risks of shipwreck.[99]

---

96 Falmouth is located on the southwest coast of England, some 270 miles from London. The 'Great Post Road' from Cornwall to London was not much more than an old ridgeway keeping to the drier high ground whenever possible. Despite the mostly poor condition of the road, 'strategic staging' had reduced the duration of mail transport between Falmouth and London to three or four days by the mid-18th century, and by 1798 to 2.5 days, which remained the norm for several decades. See Pawlyn, 9–16. Before the railways were built, about two more days had to be added for the mail service to places like Liverpool in northwest England.

97 For example the June packet arrived in Halifax on 26 July while the packet to England had left four days earlier. The September packet arrived on 21 October, while the packet to England had left three days earlier. See the sailing lists of Arnell & Ludington, 21.

98 Calculated from the sailing lists of Arnell & Ludington, 21–29.

99 Pawlyn, 9–10.

In peace time, the advantages of Falmouth were less evident. The owners of the newly established American sailing packet companies hardly considered that port as an alternative when they decided to start regular sailings between New York and England. These decisions were made on a purely commercial basis, and the primary port of trade for them was Liverpool – although sailings were later added to London, and to Havre on the French side of the Channel.

Before looking at the regular line service started by the American shipping companies from 1818, a few words need to be said about the reasons why these two ports, New York and Liverpool, could play such an important role in the history of transatlantic trade as they did between 1820 and 1860.

Although New York had already become the leading port for American exports and imports by 1797, the city lost the lead once more to Boston. According to Albion, the first step in New York's significant rise after the war was the British decision to 'dump' the bulk of their manufactures there instead of some other city. It seemed better for the purpose than Boston, where the British tolerated a reasonable amount of leakage in the blockade and which consequently had not been deprived of European goods to the extent of New York, where imported goods were scarce and prices high. Anticipating the peace news, the British sent a large number of well-laden merchantmen to Halifax, Bermuda, and other nearby places ready to sail for New York with the lifting of the blockade and take full advantage of the situation.[100]

Two years later, when it seemed probable that the British would turn their shipments from New York's over-stocked market to somewhere else, New York took several steps to maintain its lead in the import business. Within a few years, it had drawn to itself three major trade routes: from Europe, from the southern ports and from the West. New auction legislation, aiming to attract more buyers, was passed at Albany on the same day as the Erie Canal bill. During the years when the canal was being constructed, a 'cotton triangle' – following the model of the old 'flour triangle' of the seventeenth century and the 'sugar triangle' of the later colonial period – was formed on the southern route. It diverted the commerce between Europe and the cotton ports some two hundred miles out of its normal course, in order to collect toll and at the same time to provide eastbound cargoes to Liverpool. These cargoes mainly included cotton, rice and naval stores.[101]

Without producing many articles of commerce itself, New York became an *entrepôt* where goods of every sort from every place were exchanged in the early 19th century. As Albion puts it in his history of the port of New York, 'the New Yorkers grew rich from the profits, commissions, freights, and other excuses for levying toll upon that volume of the business'.[102]

---

100 Robert Greenhalgh Albion, *The Rise of New York Port 1815–1860* (New York, 1939), 10–12.
101 Albion (1939), 3–15, 95–121; Albion (1938), 50–52. – Part of this cargo was transported forward to the Baltic. See Ahonen, 318, 328.
102 Albion (1939), 10. – According to Ahonen, perhaps a half of the re-exports were traded via New York and a fifth via Boston in 1821–1860. Britain was the major trading partner of both the United States and Russia over the whole period discussed. Its central role in

In 1800, Philadelphia had been the largest city of the United States with a population of 69,000 compared with around 60,000 in New York. Ten years later, New York's population was already 96,000 compared with Philadelphia's 91,000.[103] In his study of urban growth and information circulation, Allan Pred came to the conclusion that, by 1817, New York had clearly outdistanced Philadelphia and all other competitors by establishing an informational hegemony which led to complete domination of the entire American system of cities. According to Pred, this superiority was mainly based on the information and shipping frequency advantages of the city.[104]

Only shortly before the rise of New York, Liverpool had overtaken Bristol, which had long stood second only to London in terms of population and commerce. In the mid-1810s, Liverpool was a fast growing port town of around 100,000 inhabitants.[105] In 1817, more than 6,300 vessels entered the port, their total tonnage being almost 693,000.[106]

Until the abolition of the British slave trade in 1807, Liverpool had been Britain's centre of that business. Between 1795 and 1804, the Liverpool sailings accounted for 85% of the almost 1,300 slave voyages undertaken from British ports.[107] Towards the end of the era, other trading activities were growing and it did not take many years to find new business for the former slave ships.[108] Goods produced by slave labour in the Americas were imported via Liverpool in increasing amounts. For example, between 1810 and 1850, imports of raw cotton increased from 40,000 tons to just under 360,000 tons, American wheat from just over 8,000 tons to nearly 75,000 tons, flour from 900 tons to 103,000 tons, sugar from 46,000 tons to 52,000 tons and rum from 578,000 gallons to 726,000 gallons.[109]

In 1802, half of Britain's cotton imports had arrived through Liverpool, mainly to supply the needs of the nearby cotton manufactories of Lancashire. By 1812, nearly 70% of Britain's cotton imports arrived via Liverpool, and by 1830 Liverpool's share of the imports had reached 90%.[110] The city's

Atlantic trade can be illustrated by the fact that around 1830 it produced about 45% of European pig iron and consumed 66% of its cotton wool. In the years 1821–1860 between 41% and 53% in value of U.S. domestic exports went to Britain. See Ahonen, 40–41.

103 Albion (1939), 419. – According to Pred, there were over 100,000 inhabitants in New York and 87,000 in Philadelphia in 1810. Philadelphia's population equaled the size of Boston's and Baltimore's population together. See Pred (1973), 5.

104 Pred (1973), 43, 203, 223, 270.

105 Liverpool had over 94,000 inhabitants in 1811, an increase of almost 17,000 in the previous ten years. Liverpool Street Directories, 1818, Appendix, 160.

106 Liverpool Street Directories, 1818, Appendix, 161.

107 Williams, David M. 'Abolition and the Re-Deployment on the Slave Fleet, 1807–1811' in *Merchants and Mariners: Selected Maritime Writings of David M. Williams. Research in Maritime History No. 18* (St. John's, 2000), 1. – A detailed analysis of the volume and tonnage of the Liverpool slave trade, including annual clearing ratios etc. can be found in D.P. Lamb's 'Volume and tonnage of the Liverpool slave trade 1772–1807' in Roger Anstey & P.E.H. Hair (ed.), *Liverpool, the African Slave Trade, and Abolition. Essays to illustrate current knowledge and research.* (Chippenham, 1989), 91–112.

108 See Williams, 'Abolition and the Re-Deployment...', 6–11.

109 Francis E. Hyde, *Liverpool and the Mersey. The Development of a Port (An Economic History of a Port) 1700–1970* (Devon, 1971), 41.

110 Gail Cameron & Stan Crooke, *Liverpool – Capital of the Slave Trade* (Liverpool, 1992),

hinterlands included major industrial areas such as Lancashire, Yorkshire, the Midlands and the Black Country. Liverpool exported piece-goods – coal, iron bars, rails, hoops, rods and pigs, linen, manufactured goods, pottery and copper – to all parts of the world.[111]

During the period between 1815 and 1860, Liverpool had a somewhat larger volume of trade than New York, while New York had a somewhat larger ownership of shipping. In population the two ports were relatively equal. The cargoes which travelled the Liverpool–New York shuttle in the course of a year were doubtless the most valuable of any route in the 'seven seas'.[112]

The line traffic starts

As the lively traffic between New York and Liverpool ensured that there was always cargo for the return voyage, shipowners were encouraged to start regular line traffic between the two ports. There would naturally have been no need for all the trouble involved in starting a packet line just to carry one's own goods. The potential profits depended on how successfully the operators could fill up the rest of a packet's hold with fine freight (instead of bulk) belonging to other merchants who had goods to ship. Most of the major commercial houses in New York had their own vessels, but the dry goods merchants, auctioneers and manufacturers' agents were not interested in shipping itself. They only wanted to receive their goods from abroad as soon as possible.[113]

According to Albion, this service provided for shippers was the most important aspect in the development of the packets, and the main explanation for the success of the line principle. The rapid delivery appealed to the recipient and meant quicker financial returns for the shipper. While it had been necessary earlier to study the sailing notices of the various regular traders and transient ships and guess which one would be most likely to sail first, the packet service obviated that difficulty. Not only were the sailing dates known in advance, but the goods could be forwarded to one of the small group of operators or agents instead of a large and varying number of them.[114]

In addition to the merchant goods, mails and passengers, the American sailing packets soon carried large quantities of specie in both directions across

31. In addition to the transatlantic trade, Liverpool quickly took its part from the East India sailings after the abolition of the EIC monopoly in 1813, and instead of the former triangular slave trade, started direct imports of gum, ivory and palm oil from West Africa. See Cameron & Crooke, 33; Williams, 'Abolition and the Re-Deployment...', 10–11.

111 Hyde (1971), 29–30, 41. See also Adrian Vaughan, *Railwaymen, Politics & Money. The Great Age of Railways in Britain* (Cambridge, 1997), 44–47.
112 Albion (1938), 30.
113 Albion (1938), 37.
114 Albion (1938), 37.

the Atlantic. At that time, gold or silver coins were shipped in great amounts back and forth to balance inequalities in international trade, for the alternative was an excessive discount of premium in bills of exchange. This business – earlier taken care of by the Falmouth packets – was soon undertaken almost exclusively by the American packets and it was not uncommon for a ship to carry in her 'strong room' boxes or casks full of minted coins worth a quarter, or even a third, of a million dollars. If the Bank of England needed major amounts of specie or bullion to balance its reserves and meet the London bankers' balances, it was shipped in several instalments by successive packets to reduce the risk of shipwreck.[115]

The New York packets began to draw business away from the less regular vessels for shipments not only to New York but also to other American ports. If a Manchester manufacturer wanted to send a consignment of woollens to Boston, Charleston or New Orleans, it was easier and generally quicker to ship it by packet to New York and have it sent to the final destination by one of the coastal packets than to search for vessels which might, sooner or later, sail directly to the other port.[116]

The importance of the American sailing packets may have been overestimated by American maritime historians like Albion, Cutler, or Lubbock,[117] but it has certainly been underestimated by British scholars. For example, Francis E. Hyde hardly mentions the packets in his important study of the Liverpool Port.[118]

Compared with the slow and unpredictable Falmouth packet service, a direct regular line between New York and Liverpool was a most welcome improvement from the business information transmission point of view. The American packets sailed (mostly) regularly on the date announced, regardless of weather, and without waiting for a full cargo. The captains, as well as nearly all the seamen of the American packet lines, had learned to handle sail in the fast American privateers during the war and had developed techniques for speed. The first packets were small, about 400 tons, regular traders which had already been in service under the same ownership, or purchased second-hand. In the mid-1820s they were replaced by a larger and more uniform type, which increased gradually from about 500 to 800 tons.[119]

The first American sailing packet line – later known as the Black Ball Line due to the black ball on the company's red house flag and a large black ball painted on the vessels' topsail – started sailing simultaneously from New York and Liverpool in early January 1818. The line was owned by five New York merchants, all textile importers. Jeremiah and Francis Thompson were sons of a prosperous woollens manufacturer, Benjamin Marshall was in the textile importing business, while Isaac Wright and his son William were also

---

115 Albion (1938), 39; A. Andréadès, *History of the Bank of England 1640–1903*. (London, 1909), 224–225, 320–327.
116 Albion (1938), 37–38.
117 See Basil Lubbock, *The Western Ocean Packets* (Boston 1925).
118 See Hyde (1971), passim.
119 Staff, 59; Albion (1938), 79; Carl C. Cutler, *Queens of the Western Ocean*. The Story of America's Mail and Passenger Sailing Lines (Annapolis, Maryland, 1967), 99–100.

in the importing and shipping business. They chose two old firms of the first rank – Cropper, Benson & Co. and Rathbone, Hodgson & Co. – to act as the Liverpool agents, each being responsible for two ships.[120] This allowed the owners to send their own shipments by the fastest possible way, and take full advantage of the information their ships carried from Europe before it became public property.[121]

During the first year of their existence, the 'Black Ballers' sailed on the first day of each month from Liverpool and on the fifth day of the month from New York. This service marked the beginning of the practical application of the 'line' to ocean navigation, with several vessels under co-ordinated private management, sailing in regular succession on specified dates between specified ports.[122]

In keeping with their claim that the ships would leave on schedule 'full or not full', the owners went to great lengths to ensure that the first packet would sail punctually. Despite a heavy snow storm in New York on 5 January, the *James Monroe*[123] slid into the stream on time as advertised. However, the owners apparently failed to convince their Liverpool agents of the importance of such initial punctuality, for the *Courier*, which should have departed on 1 January, was three days late in leaving.[124] The delay might have been caused by the chronic Liverpool complaint, the prevailing north-westerly winds, which often prevented ships from getting under way in winter. In fact, only a few packets sailed from Liverpool on their appointed days until towing became general.[125]

For an unknown reason, the scheduled departures of Black Ball Line vessels from New York were changed in the first year of operations from the 5th of each month to the 10th. The actual departures of the first year took place as follows: 5 January, 5 February, 5 March, 6 April, 11 May, date missing in June, 10 July, 12 August, 10 September, date missing in November, and 11 December. The sailing dates from Liverpool are totally missing because *Lloyd's List* did not report them that year, but at least the *James Monroe* put back into port on 6 March, probably damaged by heavy weather, and arrived in New York as late as 30 April.[126] Due to the late arrival, the vessel was again six days behind schedule when departing from New York on 11 May, 1818.[127] This could even have been the reason for the overall change

---

120 Albion (1938), 112–114; Cutler (1967), 99.

121 Albion (1938), 112. – This was not always positive, however. In 1828, cotton speculations caused Jeremias Thompson's crash and bankruptcy, and he had to sell his share in the Black Ball Line to his brother Francis. See Albion (1938), 114.

122 Albion (1938), 20.

123 A full list of the American sailing packets, 1818–1858, including their names, measurements, builders, years of launching and starting the service, years when service ended, total packet service years, each ship's average westbound sailings and longest and shortest trips, and remarks on each ship's subsequent service or faith at sea, is given by Albion (1938), 276–287. He also lists the respective coastal line ships. See Albion (1938), 288–295. For other, less regular and often short-lived sailing lines, see Cutler (1967), 371–413 for the transatlantic lines, and 414–548 for the coastal lines.

124 Albion (1938), 20–22.

125 Cutler (1967), 101; Albion (1938), 237; and the data collected for this study.

126 *Lloyd's List* respectively. – For the *James Monroe*, see *Lloyd's List* 10.3.1818; 5.6.1818.

127 *Lloyd's List* 12.6.1818.

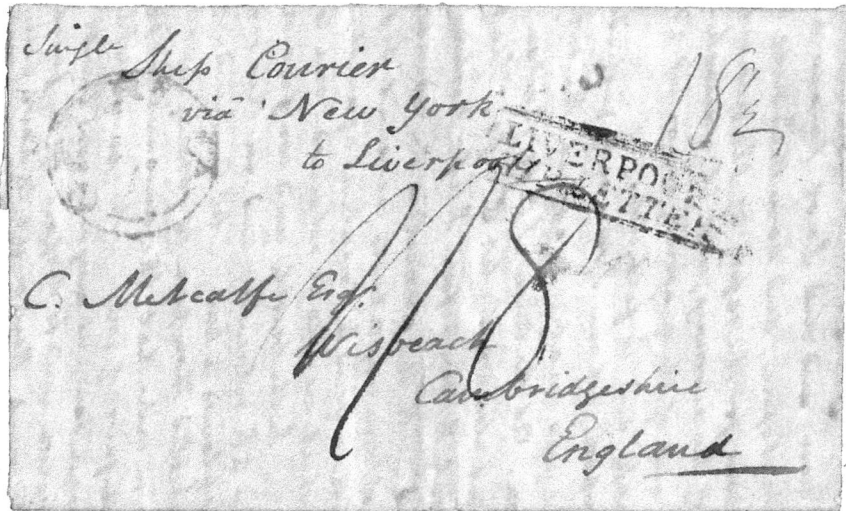

FIG. 4. *The letter sent from Georgetown on 4.12.1819 to Cambridgeshire, England, was carried from New York to Liverpool by the pioneering Black Ball Line packet* Courier *on her sixth round trip. She departed from New York on 10.12.1819 and arrived in Liverpool on 5.1.1820, in 26 days.*

of sailing dates, if the company really wanted to show for PR reasons that their ships were sailing on schedule.

Although not a complete success, the new American packet line was far more regular than the British government mail service and, due to the direct sailings with no time-consuming call at Halifax, the American packets were remarkably faster. An average eastbound sailing took 24.4 days from port to port. The fastest sailings took only 20 days, while the slowest took 29 days.[128] The average duration of westbound trips was 43 days.[129]

Interestingly, the fastest eastbound trips of the Falmouth packets, in cases when they sailed directly from New York to Falmouth (the November–February departures from New York in 1816–1822), were sometimes even quicker than those of the Black Ball Line packets. The Falmouth packet *Francis Freeling* sailed from New York to Falmouth in 17 days in November 1818 and the *Montague* in 19 days in February 1819.[130] But the average eastbound sailing from New York via Halifax or Bermuda took 38 days – a huge difference compared with an average Black Ball Line trip of 24 days,

---

128 *Lloyd's List* 1818. According to Cutler, who has used American sources, there were two 18-day sailings eastwards in 1818. This can not be verified by *Lloyd's List* maritime intelligence but it is not impossible as three departure dates from New York are missing from the data. See Cutler (1967), 105.

129 Cutler (1967), 105; Albion calculated for his book *Square-Riggers on Schedule* the durations of all westbound journeys using the maritime intelligence of New York daily newspapers 1818–1857, but never published the exact sailing dates. See Albion (1938), 318–323, 349.

130 Sailing lists of Arnell & Ludington, 25.

even if the Falmouth packets stayed seven days on average in Halifax or Bermuda before proceeding to Europe. An average westbound Falmouth packet trip all the way to New York took 50 days, including a three days' stop at Halifax or Bermuda.

It is not known by how many days the Falmouth packet departures were delayed in each case from their original schedule, as there seems to have been no fixed sailing dates on the Halifax route. In the case of the Black Ball Line packets, it can easily be calculated. If the packets had really sailed on schedule, the mails would have been transmitted from New York to Liverpool in about 25 days. As they did not always do so, the average duration of mail transmission from the original sailing date in New York to the actual arrival date in Liverpool was almost 28 days. Letters could, of course, be processed for the packet's mail bag as long as the ship stayed in port, but the bulk of the letters were written in order to leave at the scheduled time, and these mails naturally suffered from the delay. Westbound, the difference between theory and practice must have been even greater.

During the coming years, the speed and regularity of the new American packet line improved. According to Staff, an average sailing by the Black Ball Line packets during the first nine years of the company's existence took 23 days eastwards, and 40 days westwards.[131] The benefits for business information transmission were remarkable, especially because the success of the pioneering company soon attracted competitors to the same route.

The first sailings of the new line traffic were not noticed by *Lloyd's List,* but Lloyd's agents who always tried to find the fastest possible ways for their information transmission, started to use the Black Ball Line's packets as their primary means of communication in the autumn of 1818.[132] This can be verified by following the thread of incoming maritime intelligence published by *Lloyd's List.* The New York port lists of ship arrivals and departures were still carried by merchantmen (not Falmouth packets!) in August and September.[133] From then on, the lists were sent by the Black Ball Line packets if they were sailing rather soon – one monthly sailing was not enough for the newspaper's needs, however.

Thus, the Black Ball Line packet *James Monroe* brought for *Lloyd's List* the maritime intelligence of the New York port regarding the time period 27.8– 10.9.1818. The ship departed from New York on 10 September and arrived

131 Staff, 61.
132 This was no wonder, as the sailing lists of Liverpool port were sent to Lloyd's in London by the Liverpool underwriters' agents who were soon deeply involved in the American sailing packet business. The Liverpool underwriters had started an agency system of their own in 1815, but whenever possible they appointed as their agents men who were already acting as Lloyd's agents. About the cooperation between Lloyd's and the Liverpool underwriters, see Wright & Fayle, 285, 340.
133 The maritime intelligence regarding arrivals and departures 15–27.7.1818 at the port of New York was sent to England by the merchantman *Carolina Ann.* The ship departed from New York on 29 July, 1818, and arrived in Liverpool 30 days later, on 28 August. The sailing lists were published in *Lloyd's List* 1.9.1818. – The maritime intelligence regarding the period 29.7–3.8.1818 was sent by the merchantman *Fair Cambrian,* which departed from New York on 7.8.1818 and arrived in Liverpool 28 days later, on 4 September. The sailing lists were published in *Lloyd's List* 8.9.1818.

in Liverpool 26 days later, on 6 October. The intelligence was published in *Lloyd's List* on 9.10.1818.[134] The *Amity* brought the intelligence for the period 25.9–10.10.1818 (exact sailing date from New York not published by *Lloyd's List*), while the *Courier* brought the intelligence for 6–9.11.1818 in 21 days, and the *Pacific* the intelligence for 5–9.12.1818 in 24 days.[135] The lists in between were sent by the fastest merchantmen. For example, the 9–19.10.1818 list was sent by the *Hercules* in 24 days, the 21–27.10.1818 list by the *Ann* in 26 days, and the 30.10–4.11.1818 list by the Falmouth packet *Francis Freeling*, which sailed from New York to Falmouth in 17 or 18 days.[136]

The examples show clearly that there was no real difference between the existing options concerning the speed of transport. Even if the speed of the Falmouth packets also improved during the coming years, while new and faster ships were built for the purpose, the American sailing packet line service became the most important means of business information transmission especially because of its frequency and regularity.

Even if the Black Ball Line's performance in 1818 cannot be reconstructed accurately by using the sources available, a theoretical construction can easily be made based on the line's general schedule. It was built in a safe way to enable exact sailing dates. A departure from both sides of the Atlantic on the first of each month allowed a two-month sailing westwards and a one-month sailing eastwards – targets which could be met in almost any circumstances. During the period 1818–1832, only 11 out of 521 journeys took more than 60 days on the Liverpool – New York route.[137] Even if the ship left a few days late, which sometimes happened, it could easily come back on schedule at the other end, and there would be enough time for the merchants to answer their letters before the next packet departure from the port.

By this simple organizing of regular line traffic, with the same number of annual sailings as the Falmouth packets made, and with the same problems with prevailing winds and rough weather, the tiny American sailing packet line was able to notably improve the transatlantic information transmission from its very first year. Instead of the three consecutive information circles enabled by the Falmouth packets, information could now circle four times back and forth across the Atlantic during a year. However, to achieve the full benefit of the regular traffic, more ships were needed on the route – and they would be there soon.

The first announcement of new competition for the Black Ball Line came in early January, 1822, from Byrnes, Trimble & Co., a New York firm engaged

---

134 The inland mail from Liverpool to London by daily mail coach before the opening of the railway took about 24 hours in the mid-1820s (Wright & Fayle, 340).or 30 hours 'by the new stage coach' which 'carries but four insides, and only one night on the road' ('Coaches' in *Post Office*, Liverpool Street Directories, 1818, Appendix, 85). As *Lloyd's List* was published only twice a week before 1837, there were at least two obvious causes of delay between the ship arrival and the publishing of the intelligence.

135 These sailing lists were published in *Lloyd's List* 6.11.1818; 4.12.1818; 8.1.1819.

136 *Lloyd's List* 20.11.1818; 27.11.1818; 1.12.1818. According to the sailing lists of Arnell & Ludington, the *Francis Freeling* departed from New York 9.11. instead of 8.11. as reported by *Lloyd's List*, thus making the trip in seventeen days. (Arnell & Ludington, 25)

137 See the records of Albion (1938), 318–319.

principally in the Chesapeake flour trade. The partners had been operating regular traders to Liverpool for several years and now started line traffic with four packet ships from 25 January. The monthly service included sailings from New York on the 25th and from Liverpool on the 12th of each month. In 1823, the dates were changed to the 24th and 8th respectively. The line was soon named the New Line or Red Star Line[138], while the Black Ball Line became the Old Line. The Black Ball owners quickly met this first challenge with an announcement of doubled service. They expanded the line from four to eight ships and stated that they would maintain sailings twice instead of once a month, departing on the 1st and 16th of the month from each port. This service started in mid-March, 1822.[139]

For the Black Ball Line, the new competitor was not the only blow that year. In April, their packet *Albion* was dashed to pieces on the Irish coast with heavy loss of life[140] and in July, their *Liverpool* sank on her maiden voyage after striking an iceberg, though no lives were lost. Despite the threatened loss of public confidence from these disasters, and the expense involved just at the very time when they were expanding their service, the Black Ball Line managed to survive the year with its prestige intact.[141]

Five days after the sinking of the *Liverpool*, the newspapers of 30 July published an announcement concerning another new Liverpool line. This would be known as the Swallowtail Line, or the Fourth Line, as the added Black Ball service had already been considered as the third line. The agents in whose name the advertisement appeared were Fish & Grinell, who, under the later names of Fish, Grinell & Co., and Grinell, Minturn & Co., would become the foremost packet and general shipping house in New York. Two years later, in 1824, the company started a packet service to London by the same name. For recognition, the Liverpool line packets carried a blue and white swallowtail house flag, while the London line packets carried a red and white one, thus giving the following names to the lines: the Blue Swallowtail Line and the Red Swallowtail Line. Additionally, another packet line to London was established in 1824, the Black X Line. Both London lines operated via Portsmouth. Three packet lines were also established for the New York–Havre route in 1822–1823: the Old Line, or later Union Line, the Havre-Whitlock Line which was later merged with the Union Line, and the Havre-Second Line.[142]

After some readjustments, the traffic was organized as follows: the Black Ball Line packets departed from both New York and Liverpool on the 1st

---

138 There was a red star on the company's house flag to distinguish it from the Black Ball.
139 Albion (1938), 30–31; Cutler (1967), 149–150, 377.
140 Of the 54 people on board, 46 perished. In addition to the April mail, the ship carried a considerable amount of gold and silver, as well as normal freight. One box of £5,000 in specie was recovered, and the shores were strewn with commercial letters in large amounts from the mailbags. See Albion (1938), 202–208.
141 Albion (1938), 31.
142 The names of the lines are somewhat confusing and mixed, as their organizations and owners changed during the years. The classification above is adequate for what has been used by Albion and Staff, while Cutler's is slightly different. See Albion (1938), 276–286; Staff 121–126; and Cutler (1967), 376–380, 389–391, 394–396.

and 16th of each month, while the Red Star Line packets departed from New York on the 24th and from Liverpool on the 8th of each month. The Blue Swallowtail departures used an opposite schedule, sailing on the 8th from New York and on the 24th from Liverpool. Thus, there was a weekly sailing from both ports all year round. All the packets made three round trips per year, compared with only two of most merchantmen. There was a great difference in efficiency, as the American packet owners could share their capital costs between three instead of two annual voyages, and some extra income could also be gained during the winter months when most other transatlantic vessels lay idle.[143] In 1824, an average packet round trip on the New York – Liverpool route took fewer than 84 days, while the Falmouth packets made their Falmouth – New York round trip in 118 days, on average.

By 1824–1825, the regularity of the line sailings had improved markedly. Hard competition made the companies try their best to keep to their schedules, and speed records were followed intensively by the public on both sides of the Atlantic. Table 6 shows how punctual the packet departures from New York – the ships' home port where a good reputation was most important – were in these years.

As can easily be noticed by one glance at the table, the departure dates from New York were very punctual in the mid-1820s. Of the 76 departures published by *Lloyd's List* 1824–1825,[144] only 17 sailings were delayed or changed, while 59 departures were made exactly on the date announced. The delay was usually only one day. To compare with the Liverpool departures, see Table 7.

The losses of the Black Ball Line packets *Amity* in April 1824 and *Nestor* in December 1824 caused a gap in the schedule only for the January 1825 departure.[145] Timetables were reorganized and both wrecked ships were soon replaced by new, larger vessels. The 520 tons *Florida* sailed for her first voyage already in early November 1824 and the 560 tons *Manchester* in May 1825. The *Silas Richards* replaced the Blue Swallowtail Line's smallest vessel *Robert Fulton*, which was sold in 1824.[146]

Departures from Liverpool were never as punctual as those from New York. At least 23 out of 47 departures were delayed in 1825.[147] The autumn and winter sailings in particular could be delayed by several days due to bad weather. It

---

143 Albion (1938), 27.

144 The dates in Table 6 do not cover exactly the two calendar years, but for technical reasons the intelligence published by *Lloyd's List* during those years. – There are normally two reasons for a missing date: it was not reported by *Lloyd's List,* or the particular issue is missing from the microfilm available.

145 Albion notes that 'had it not been for the high reputation of the Black Ball owners and their natural desire to preserve the prestige of the line after the loss of the *Albion* and *Liverpool* two years before, there might be grounds for suspecting an attempted marine insurance fraud in thus bringing in a new captain who disposed of their two oldest vessels, wrecking both of them at low tide where they would be constantly awash and consequently much more difficult to salvage'. See Albion (1938), 220.

146 Staff, 123; Cutler (1967), 378.

147 The Liverpool sailing dates of 1824 are not available. *Lloyd's List* did not publish them and the issues of the *Liverpool Customs Bills of Entry* of that year are missing from the MMM archives.

TABLE 6. *Mail carrying American sailing packets, dates of departure from New York, 1824–1825.*

ship (* = new)	company	1 outw NY	2 outw NY	3 outw NY	4 outw NY	5 outw NY	6 outw NY
New York	BB	**16.12.23**	3.5.24	**16.8.24**	**16.12.24**	**16.4.25**	**16.8.25**
Panthea	RS	**24.12.23**	9.5.24	**24.8.24**	25.12.24	27.4.25	- -
Columbia	BB	**1.1.24**	**16.4.24**	**1.9.24**	**1.1.25**	**1.5.25**	**1.9.25**
Cortes	BSw	**8.1.24**	**8.5.24**	- -	9.1.25	**8.5.25**	**8.9.25**
Orbit	BB	**16.1.24**	- -	sold	–	–	–
Meteor	RS	**24.1.24**	- -	- -	**24.1.25**	**24.5.25**	- -
Amity	BB	- -	wrecked	–	–	–	–
Corinthian	BSw	- -	**8.6.24**	**8.10.24**	**8.2.25**	**8.6.25**	12.10.25
Pacific	BB	**16.2.24**	**16.6.24**	**1.10.24**	**1.2.25**	**1.6.25**	**1.10.25**
John Wells	RS	**24.2.24**	**24.6.24**	**24.10.24**	- -	25.6.25	**24.10.25**
William Thompson	BB	**1.3.24**	**1.7.24**	**16.10.24**	**16.2.25**	- -	- -
Leeds	BSw	**8.3.24**	**8.7.24**	**8.11.24**	- -	**8.7.25**	**8.11.25**
Canada	BB	**16.3.24**	**16.7.24**	**16.11.24**	17.3.25	**16.7.25**	**16.11.25**
James Cropper	BB	**1.4.24**	**1.8.24**	3.12.24	**1.4.25**	**1.8.25**	- -
Manhattan	RS	- -	22.7.24[a]	25.11.24	27.3.25	**24.7.25**	- -
Nestor	BB		17.5.24	**16.9.24**	wrecked	–	–
Robert Fulton	BSw		- -	sold	–	–	–
Florida*	BB			2.11.24	**1.3.25**	**1.7.25**	2.11.25
Silas Richards*	BSw			**8.12.24**	- -	**8.8.25**	- -
Manchester*	BB					19.5.25	17.9.25

Source: Lloyd's List 1824–1825. BB = Black Ball Line, scheduled sailing dates 1st and 16th of each month; BSw = Blue Swallowtail Line, sailing date 8th; RS = Red Star Line, sailing date 24th. Sailings which took place on the scheduled date are marked in **bold.**

 - - = data missing   – = not sailed

[a] This date may be incorrect. The packets hardly departed before scheduled date.

often happened that the clearing at the Customs House of Liverpool was done in time for sailing on schedule, but the ship departed several days later. There were also second or, in later years, even fifth clearances before the ship really sailed, probably caused by the late arrival of important freight.[148]

148 *Liverpool Customs Bill of Entry* 1825, 1834, 1835.

TABLE 7. *Delays of the American sailing packets at the port of Liverpool, 1825.*

Packet and shipping line	Scheduled sailing date	Clearing date	Factual sailing date	Delay, days
Canada, BB	1.1.	1.1.	4.1.	3
Manhattan, RS	8.1.	8.1.	10.1.	2
James Cropper, BB	16.1.	15.1.	22.1.	6
Silas Richards, BSw	24.1.	24.1.	26.1.	2
New York, BB	1.2.	1.2.	- -	- -
Panthea, RS	8.2.	(8.2.); 2nd clear. 10.2.	13.2.	5
Columbia, BB	16.2.	16.2.	**16.2.**	0
Cortes, BSw	24.2.	23.2.	**24.2.**	0
Meteor, RS	8.3.	8.3.	**8.3.**	0
Pacific, BB	16.3.	16.3.	**16.3.**	0
Leeds, BSw	(16.3.)	(14.3.); 2nd clear. 15.3.	**(16.3.)**	- -*
Corinthian, BSw	24.3.	24.3.	**24.3.**	0
William Thompson, BB	1.4.	31.3.	- -	- -
John Wells, RS	8.4.	8.4.	**8.4.**	0
Florida, BB	16.4.	16.4.	17.4.	1
Canada, BB	1.5.	30.4.	- -	- -
Manhattan, RS	8.5.	7.5.	10.5.	2
James Cropper, BB	16.5.	16.5.	**16.5.**	0
Silas Richards, BSw	24.5.	24.5.	**24.5.**	0
New York, BB	1.6.	1.6.	8.6.	7
Panthea, RS	8.6.	8.6.	9.6.	1
Columbia, BB	16.6.	16.6.	**16.6.**	0
Cortes, BSw	24.6.	24.6.	27.6.	3
Manchester, BB	1.7.	1.7.	- -	- -
Meteor, RS	8.7.	8.7.	**8.7.**	0
Pacific, BB	16.7.	16.7.	**16.7.**	0
Corinthian, BSw	24.7.	23.7.	**24.7.**	0
William Thompson, BB	1.8.	1.8.	**1.8.**	0
John Wells, RS	8.8.	8.8.	11.8.	3
Florida, BB	16.8.	16.8.	- -	- -
Leeds, BSw	24.8.	24.8.	**24.8.**	0
Canada, BB	1.9.	1.9.	**1.9.**	0
Manhattan, RS	8.9.	8.9.	9.9.	1
James Cropper, BB	16.9.	16.9.	**16.9.**	0
Silas Richards, BSw	24.9.	24.9.	28.9.	4
New York, BB	1.10.	1.10.	**1.10.**	0
Panthea, RS	8.10.	8.10.	12.10.	4
Columbia, BB	16.10.	15.10.	23.10.	7
Cortes, BSw	24.10.	24.10.	5.11.	12
Manchester, BB	1.11.	1.11.	8.11.	7
Meteor, RS	8.11.	- -	10.11.	2
Pacific, BB	16.11.	16.11.	17.11.	1
Corinthean, BSw	24.11.	24.11.	29.11.	5
William Thompson, BB	1.12.	1.12.	**1.12.**	0
John Wells, RS	8.12.	8.12.	**8.12.**	0
Florida, BB	16.12.	16.12.	21.12.	5
Leeds, BSw	24.12.	- -	27.12.	3

Table 7, sources: Lloyd's List 1825; Liverpool Customs Bills of Entry, 1825. – Sailings which took place on the scheduled date are marked in **bold.**

* The *Leeds* had sailed from Liverpool on 4.1. but ran on the Banks (at Mersey) and sustained great injury. (See *Lloyd's List* 7.1.1825, 11.1.1825, 14.1.1825.) She was now leaving after repairs, having stayed in port for over three months. This was probably the reason why there was no Blue Swallowtail Line departure on 24.4.

As can be noticed from Table 7, it should never be assumed that clearing dates were automatically the same as the final sailing dates. A comparison between the official sailing dates published by the companies, the dates of clearing at customs and the final sailing dates shows significant differences. This is also a good example of the diversity of information received when using different sources in calculating the duration of information transmission.

A calculation based on Tables 6 and 7 gives the result that the average delay of the departure of an American sailing packet at the port of Liverpool in 1825 was about two days, while the delay in New York was just a half day. As can be noticed from Table 7, the ships were in each case cleared at customs at the right time for a scheduled departure, but the delays took place when the ship was due to leave the port. During the worst winter months, only two vessels managed to leave on the scheduled date from Liverpool.

Despite these delays, there was now more frequency and regularity in North Atlantic communications than ever before. The speed of the packets varied, especially on westbound trips, but the averages were extraordinary: 24 days eastwards and 36 days westwards in 1825.[149]

Effects of the regular sailing packet service on business information transmission

What did all this mean from the business information transmission point of view? It can be illustrated by examining the consecutive information circles enabled by the service.

As can be seen from Table 8, a letter sent from Liverpool by the Red Star Line packet *Manhattan* on 10 January (the ship was delayed two days from its original schedule), arrived in New York on 20 February, and if the recipient was in New York, he or she was able to answer quickly enough to send the letter by the same company's *John Wells*, which departed from New York on 24 February (or a few days later, but not earlier than that). This letter arrived in Liverpool on 20 March, only 69 days after the departure of the original letter from that port. If the recipient was in Liverpool, he could again answer this letter quickly enough to send it by the Blue Swallowtail packet *Corinthian*, which departed on 24 March. Within one year, five letters could be sent successively back and forth across the Atlantic, while a sixth one would already be on its way when the year ended.

149 Calculated from 37 trips of which enough data has been available.

TABLE 8. *Consecutive information circles enabled by the American sailing packets between Liverpool and New York, 1825.*

Letter sent by mail ship, company	Ship departure Liverpool	Ship arrival, New York	Next departing mail ship, company	Ship departure, New York	Ship arrival, Liverpool	Duration of getting answer, days
Manhattan, RS	10.1.	20.2.	John Wells, RS	~ 24.2.	20.3.	69
Corinthian, BSw	24.3.	18.4.	Panthea, RS	27.4.	21.5.	55
Silas Richards, BSw	24.5.	25.6.	Florida, BB	1.7.	28.7.	65
William Thompson, BB	1.8.	5.9.	Cortes, BSw	8.9.	3.10.	63
Panthea, RS	12.10.	10.11.	Canada, BB	16.11.	8.12.	56

Sources: Lloyd's List 1825; Liverpool Customs Bills of Entry, 1825. ~ = scheduled date.

By way of comparison, the information circulation enabled by the Falmouth packets in one year (1825) was as follows:

TABLE 9. *Consecutive information circles enabled by the Falmouth packet service in 1825, an example.*

Letter sent by mail packet	Ship departure, Falmouth	Ship arrival, New York	Next departing mail packet	Ship departure, New York	Ship arrival, Falmouth	Duration of getting answer, days
Marchioness of Salisbury	19.1.	10.3.	(Rinaldo) Marchioness of Salisbury	(10.3.) 9.4.	(20.4.) 12.5.	(91) 113
Lord Melville	21.5.	12.7.	(Queensbury) Lord Melville	(10.7.) ~10.8.	10.9.	112
Swallow	14.9.	26.10.	Kingfisher	9.11.	12.12.	89

Sources: Sailing lists of Arnell & Ludington, 37–39. ~ = estimate.

The example shows that the government mail service was not very well co-ordinated even in 1825, although the British merchants now seemed to have had better chances to answer the letters before the next packet departure. At the other end, there were still problems. The mails sent by the *Marchioness of Salisbury* arrived in New York on the same day as the packet to England departed. Somebody might have been able to send a quick answer immediately, but it is also possible that the mails were not handled and delivered from the Post Office before the deadline for answers to be brought in to catch the departing vessel.[150]

Thus the answers to the January mails could primarily be sent by the arriving packet, *Marchioness of Salisbury*, on her way homewards. The next round was inconvenient as well. The *Queensbury* had left from New York two days before the May mails arrived by the *Lord Melville*. But the September mails carried by the *Swallow* could be answered during the next two weeks and carried by the *Kingfisher*, which departed from New York on 9 November. Sending a letter and getting an answer to it took 105 days on average and only three consecutive information circles could be achieved within that year.

From this we can draw two important conclusions. Compared with the Falmouth packet service, the speed of information circulation across the North Atlantic was notably improved when the American packet lines started their better organized sailings. Instead of three round trips of letters by the Falmouth packets, information could be circulated more than five times within a year by the American sailing packets. A second conclusion is that Liverpool and New York enjoyed the cumulative advantage of faster communications compared with other ports due to slow inland communications. If further inland transmission was needed, the next packet had already sailed long before the answer was at the port of departure.

Even though there was also a packet service between New York and London, as well as New York and Havre, these services were never as effective as the weekly departures on the New York – Liverpool route. The service for London and Havre was most of the time only twice a month, and it was conducted by smaller ships – many of the Red Swallowtail Line packets had first served on the more important Liverpool line, and been replaced there by newer and larger vessels.[151] The average duration of westbound passages during 1818–1857 was 35 days from Liverpool (1,993 trips), 36 days from London (928 trips), and 38 days from Havre (1,239 trips).[152] Consequently, important outgoing letters were often sent from London by inland mail directly to Liverpool to be forwarded to the next departing packet, and incoming letters vice versa.[153]

Due to the superiority of the American sailing packet service, Liverpool became the de facto information centre for Britain on the Atlantic side without the government taking any measures. Instead, the Post Office closed up the

---

150 Even if the mails had been carried from New York by the *Rinaldo*, which departed on 10.3 (see Table 9) the next packet from Falmouth would have been the same *Lord Melville*, which departed on 21.5.1825.

151 See the list of mail-carrying packets in Staff, 125.

152 Albion (1938), 197, 317. The averages are rounded here into full figures. – The London line mails were landed at Portsmouth, from where they were taken to the City by mail coach, a one day's voyage.

153 For example, a letter was sent from New York on 22.11.1823 to the Fredrick Huth banking house in London by the Red Star Line packet *John Wells,* which sailed from New York precisely on schedule on 24.11.1823 and entered Liverpool on 15.12.1823. The letter arrived in London on 17.12.1823 – only 25 days after leaving the sender. Johan Snellman, *North Atlantic Mail* (2004). Postal historical collection. (JSC).

TABLE 10. *Number of mail-carrying American packets from New York, 1820–1855.*

Destination	1820	1825	1830	1835	1840	1845	1850	1855
Liverpool	4	16	16	16	20	24	24	24
London	–	4	8	10	12	12	16	16
Havre	–	12	12	14	16	16	12	16

Source: Albion (1938), 274. – The number of vessels varied within these frames due to replacements, etc.

Falmouth packet mail service to New York at the end of 1826. The American ships had literally driven the Falmouth packets from the route, and even the official mail of the General Post Office in London, destined for the Canadian General Post Office, was carried by the American packets instead of their own mail service.[154] Yet the Falmouth packet service for Halifax and Bermuda continued until the Cunard Line steamers took it over in 1840.

The American sailing packets accepted letters from England to the United States at two-pence a letter, irrespective of the weight or number of enclosures. The packet line agents provided mail bags in their Liverpool and London offices, and the bags were sealed when the vessel was due to sail, and taken on board. The same procedure was usual at Havre and Bordeaux on the French side. In England the practice was widespread and used by the majority of merchants throughout the kingdom. Special messengers of the different companies would carry their bags to Liverpool, and although this was a direct infringement of the Post Office monopoly for the carriage of mail within Britain, little could be done about it. The practice had become so usual and was done so openly that it became an accepted procedure. In the late 1830s it was revealed by Roland Hill, the Secretary of the Post Office, when advocating his postal reform, that the American sailing packets carried some 4,000 letters each westbound voyage, none of which had passed through the Post Office.[155]

On their arrival at New York or Boston, letters for the United States went into the Ship Letter Office to be rated for postage. If addressed to a place at the port of arrival, six cents was charged. For anywhere beyond, a ship letter rate of two cents plus the inland postage was levied. The letters for Canada were sent to the New York Post Office or via Boston, and then forwarded

154 See Arnell & Ludington, viii; 43; Staff, 62.
155 Staff, 54; Robinson (1964), 114–115. – Even the arriving letters were often delivered directly to the merchants without going through the Post Office. The Secretary of the Treasury wrote a letter to the American Chamber of Commerce in Liverpool 8.4.1837 to remind the merchants about the fact that it was required by law to send the arriving letters via the Post Office. Between 14.2.1836 and 28.2.1837 no less than 2,371 letters and packages 'beyond the privilege allowed to consignees' had been found by the Liverpool Customs and sent to the Post Office. In one instance alone, 530 letters were discovered, and out of 111 packages of newspapers opened between 29.9.1836 and 20.2.1837, containing 822 newspapers, there were also found concealed 648 letters. – In the ACC Minute Book, February 1842 – December 1866, related to the meeting on 13.4.1837. 380 AME/2. Liverpool Public Record Office (LPRO).

to the exchange office at the Canadian border, where the Canadian Post Office accepted them. The postage charge was made up of the ship rate, the United States postage to the border, and then the Canadian inland postage. By this means, a letter to Quebec would cost 47 cents instead of 92 if it was brought by the Post Office packet. Likewise, the postage on a letter from London to Montreal and York, instead of being 96 cents, and one dollar 12 cents respectively, would cost 31 cents, and 47 cents. Apart from the notable benefits to the merchants, this cheap means of communications was a blessing to the emigrants who could thus more easily keep in touch with their relatives at home.[156]

A letter from a Bible Society member in Montreal to a colleague in London gives a good example of the general thinking: 'I would again recommend your writing us by the New York and *not* the English packets as by it much time will be saved as well as the saving in postage of the value of two or three Bibles.'[157]

Indeed, the British Post Office's losses of postage rates were a major reason for the decision to start subsidizing transatlantic mail steamship services in the coming years.

There is one more important and rather confusing aspect to be discussed regarding the American packets and their central role in business information transmission during their heyday: the unpredictability of the duration of sailings. As already noticed, the actual sailings did not always take place accurately on schedule, but that was a minor problem compared with the discomfort caused by the common unawareness of the duration of each voyage. The passengers on board were normally betting upon the length of the voyage, with a ten-day range. That was about the normal spread.[158]

The unknown length of the voyage was not only an inconvenience to the passengers. While the date for outgoing mail was set in advance at the ports of New York and Liverpool, no one knew the date when the mails would arrive from overseas. The staff in the Post Offices on both sides of the Atlantic had to be ready for emergencies, for sometimes several packets could arrive on the same day due to delays caused by rough weather or other problems at sea.

For example, one day in August 1827 the New York Post Office received two incoming Black Ballers, one line packet from London and Havre each, as well as a few regular traders. Two years later, more than 17,000 letters came in on a single week, three Black Ballers and some other packets having arrived at the port during the same time. Some of the mails were for New York, while the rest were to be handled and forwarded to other parts of the country.[159]

When the well known New Orleans packet line owner Edward Knight Collins started his Dramatic Line between New York and Liverpool in 1837, the rush in the Post Offices became even more frequent as the line decided

---

156 See Staff, 54.
157 A letter to Joseph Jarn, Esq. in London, dated in Montreal 8.10.1829. Published in the catalogue of Charles G. Firby Auctions, *British North America Stamps and Postal History. Dr. Kenneth M. Rosenfeld Collection, June 18, 2005* (Waterford, MI, 2005), lot 722.
158 Albion (1938), 200, 244.
159 Albion (1938), 187.

TABLE 11. *Consecutive information circles enabled by the American sailing packets between Liverpool and New York, 1838.*

Letter sent by mail ship, company	Ship departure, Liverpool	Ship arrival, New York	Next departing mail ship, company	Ship departure, New York	Ship arrival, Liverpool	Duration of getting answer, days
Orpheus, BB	2.1.	8.3.	Orpheus, BB	~ 16.3.	10.4.	98
England, BB	20.4.	12.5.	Europe, BB	~ 16.5.	9.6.	50
Siddons, DL	16.6.	19.7.	Shakespeare, DL	~ 1.8.	19.8.	64
England, BB	20.8.	23.9.	Sheridan, DL	~ 1.10.	19.10.	60
North America, BB	22.10.	4.12.	Hibernia, BB	9.12.	27.12.	66

Sources: *Lloyd's List 1838.* – If the exact departure days from New York have not been recorded by *Lloyd's List*, the line's general sailing date has been used as an approximate. This does not affect the calculation of the information circles.
~ = scheduled.

to use the same sailing dates (the 16th from New York and the 1st from Liverpool) as the Black Ball Line. The race between the two companies' ships at sea often ended with both packets arriving on the same day.[160] From a business information transmission point of view, this arrangement was not really satisfactory. Even if the competition between the two companies might have shortened the duration of a single trip by a few days, it gave no possibility to send mail across the Atlantic more often. Even if the monthly Dramatic Line sailings increased the number of regular transatlantic sailing packet journeys from 48 to 60 per year, the number of annual information circles remained at five, as it had been since the early 1820s.

Another problem which caused stagnation in the development of transatlantic mail services was that the speed of an average trip could not really be improved. Despite the rather punctual departures and hard driving, better knowledge about sea routes and currents, or technical improvements, the packet arrival dates always depended heavily on the winds at sea. Even if the eastbound sailings were more predictable, the westbound trips could take anything between three and eight weeks, or even more.

The slow trips generally occurred in the winter when gales or ice sometimes stretched out a trip even to ten or 12 weeks. The slowest passage of all was the 89-day crossing of the Blue Swallowtail Line's *Patrick Henry* late in the sailing packet period. Another slow passage, depicting the effects of

160 In 1838, this happened at least on 5.1.1838, 19.3.1838, 16.4.1838, 12.5.1838, 22.10.1838, and 30.11.1838 in New York; and on 27.1.1838, 24.4.1838, 20.6.1838, 21.7.1838, and 19.10.1838 in Liverpool. See *Lloyd's List* 1838, respectively.

prevailing winds, was the 69-day crossing of the Black Ball Line's *South America* in the winter of 1833–1834. Although she had one of the fastest general averages of all packets, and her Captain Robert H. Waterman later set up a series of all-time speed records as a clipper commander, there were only about a dozen packet journeys slower than that in the whole 40 years.[161]

Diagram 1 clearly illustrates this key problem of the sailing packet service. The average length of a westbound journey was 34 days, but it varied very much from one journey to another. Even though there were slower and faster vessels,[162] one and the same ship could make a westbound trip in 41 days and the following one in 22. It was not unusual that the vessels arrived in another order than they had left from the port of departure, even if there was one or two weeks difference between the sailing dates. Though it was true that winter sailings were harder and often longer than those of the spring or autumn[163] (summer sailings often suffered from fog on the North American coast), even the winters were variable.

The mid-1830s until 1838 were the heyday of the American sailing packets. In 1834, all three companies on the Liverpool route again replaced one of their older and smaller ships with a new one: the Black Ball Line replaced the *New York* of 516 tons with the *Columbus* of 663 tons, the Blue Swallowtail Line replaced the *Silas Richards* of 454 tons with the *Independence* of 732 tons, and the Red Star Line replaced the *John Jay* of 502 tons with the *England* of 729 tons. The new vessels were not necessarily faster than the old ones, as can be seen from Diagram 1, but they were certainly more attractive from the passengers' point of view. The wage costs did not seem to be a major problem during this phase. While the old ships of 450 to 500 tons had sailed with 18 to 26 men on board, the new ones needed 30.[164].

As it was always impossible to predict the duration of each trip, duplicates of letters were often sent to ensure the fastest possible dispatch of the information. For example in 1837, the Dramatic Line's *Sheridan* sailed from Liverpool on the same day as the Black Ball Line's *Columbus*. Both ships were delayed – according to the original schedules, the *Sheridan* should have sailed on the 12th or 16th and the *Columbus* on the 16th March[165] – and they both sailed on the 19th. Johan Snellman's philatelic collection includes a cover with two separate letters written in Liverpool on 17 and 18 March 1837, sent by the *Sheridan*. According to the hand marking made by the writer of the letters, they were duplicates, while the originals were sent by the *Columbus*. The duplicate cover arrived faster than the original, and was handstamped in New York on 16 April, while the *Columbus* arrived in

---

161 Albion (1938), 52.
162 See the records of Albion (1938), 320–321.
163 For the monthly averages of 1818–1827, see the records by Albion (1938), 322.
164 Records of the number of personnel on board when the ship cleared outwards, *Liverpool Customs Bills of Entry*, 1834. – The ship weights are from Staff's packet lists, 121–123.
165 According to Cutler, the Dramatic Line's sailing dates were 'eventually' fixed at the 25th from New York and the 12th from Liverpool, but this system did not work for a long time. At least from the beginning of 1838, the Dramatic Line sailed from both ports on the same day as the Black Ball Line. See Cutler (1967), 377, 380; *Lloyd's List* 1838, passim.

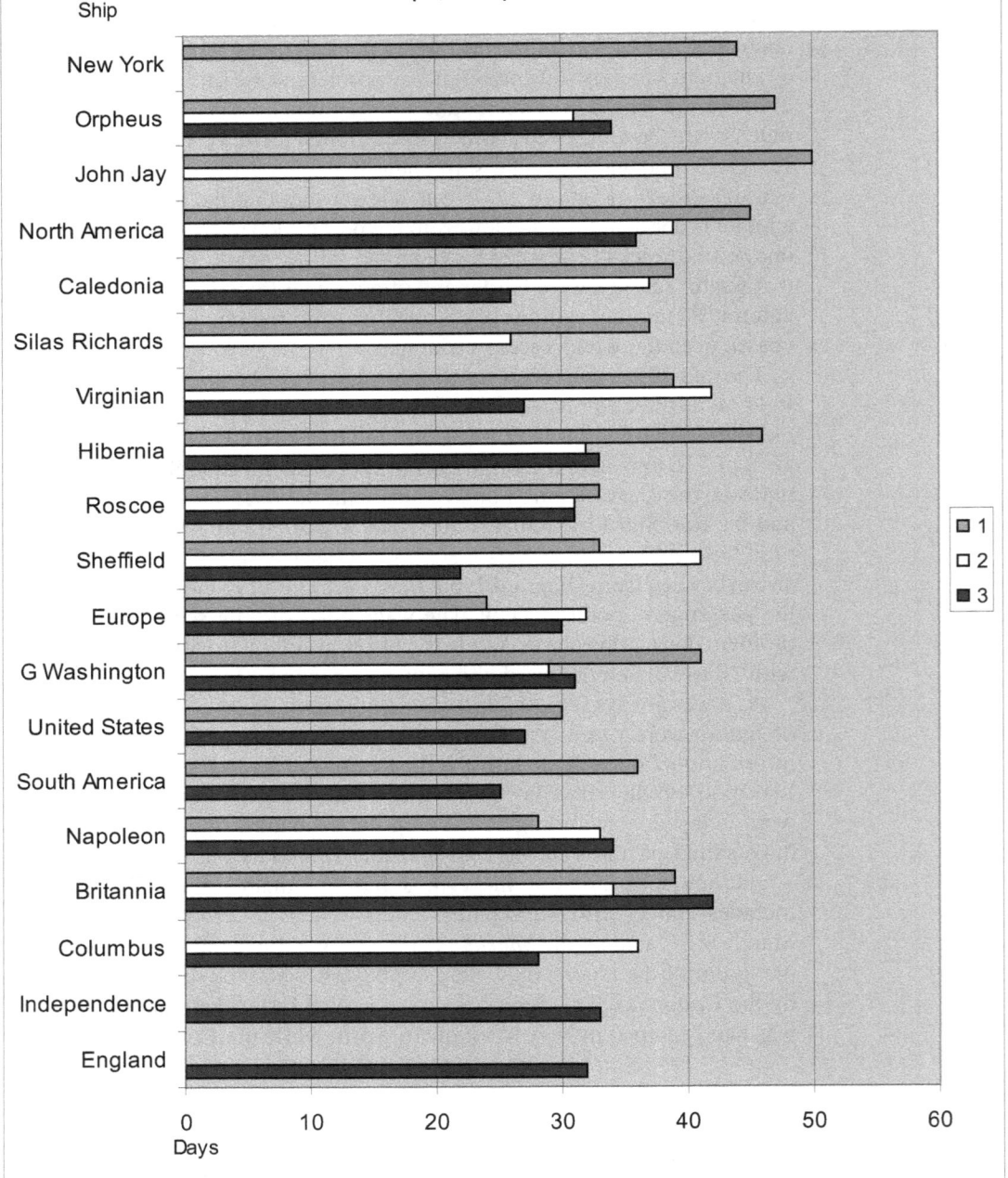

Diagram 1. Mail carrying American sailing packets, duration of westbound trips, Liverpool - New York, 1834

Sources: Lloyd's List 1834; Liverpool Customs Bills of Entry, 1834. All scheduled sailings were made, but in some cases the sailing data is missing from the sources. The selection of which regular traders have been included in the figures as mail-carrying packets is based on the list published by Staff, 121–127.

New York on 17 April. The recipients have not marked the arrival date in Richmond, but the letter was answered already on 21 April.[166]

The example shows again how useful it was to be involved in business at the main port cities. The latest information could be written or added to existing letters even after the ship's scheduled sailing date. Also, by using duplicates, the fastest possible answer was ensured.

Until the introduction of ocean-going steamships, the American sailing packets offered a superior mail service compared with any other world trade route. Surprisingly, they could also keep their position for one more decade during the shift period from sail to steam, as can be noticed in the following chapter.

Wind vs. Steam – a Decade of Struggle

Early experiments – The start of the transatlantic steamship service – The origins of the North Atlantic mail contract – The early years of the Cunard Line – Competition between early transatlantic mail carriers – Wind vs. steam – the finale

Early experiments

Steam technology was transferred from land to sea in the early 19th century. The earliest commercially successful steamboat was built by Robert Fulton in 1807. His 18-horsepower engine steamer made the passage from New York to Albany in 33 hours. In Britain, the first steamboat was launched on the Clyde in 1811. In 1814 there were still only two steamboats in Britain, in 1816 there were 15, in 1825 there were 163, in 1835 there were already 538 and in 1839 as many as 840. A similar development was seen in the United States, where approximately 1,300 steamboats were built during 1808–1839.[167]

Steamboats replaced sailing packets in the British Post Office coastal services in the early 1820s. The mails for Ireland were carried by steamboats from Holyhead to Dublin over the Irish Sea from May 1821 and the mails for the continent from Dover to Calais from the end of the same year. The Milford station was converted to steam in 1824, though the receipts from mail and passengers were rather slight. The Bristol Chamber of Commerce bombarded the Post Office with reasons for transferring the Milford packets to the port of Bristol, which could easily become a busy packet station due to the demands of commercial activities. The Post Office ignored these demands, but added Liverpool as a new packet port on the west coast of England.[168]

---

166 Ship letter from Liverpool on 17.3. and 18.3.1837 to Messrs John & Dan K. Stewart, Richmond, Virginia. (JSC); *Lloyd's List* 21.3.1837; 9.5.1837.
167 Peter Allington & Basil Greenhill, *The First Atlantic Liners. Seamanship in the Age of Paddle Wheel, Sail and Screw* (London, 1997), 12.
168 Robinson (1964), 120–121.

The steam packet service from Liverpool to Dublin started in 1826. Previously, the Liverpool letters to Ireland had gone first to Chester and from there joined the London mails on their way to Holyhead. This was rather inconvenient as the mails had to leave from Liverpool before the business day was over, and the letters were on their way for 24 hours. The direct steam ship traffic between Liverpool and Dublin reduced the time to some 12 hours. Liverpool also had a steam-powered mail service to the Isle of Man.[169]

Even though there were already private steamship companies serving on the coastal routes, the British Post Office ignored them and built a competing steam packet service. The reason was, according to Francis Freeling, the Secretary of the Post Office, that private owners 'would have no inducement to avoid delay or irregularity, and that the safety of the mails was so important that it could not be left in private hands'. Due to these investments, the annual expense for the services, which had been about £78,000 in 1817, more than doubled during the next ten years.[170]

A report by the Commissioners of Revenue in 1830 showed that the expenses for the first eight years of the Post Office steam packet service had amounted to over £620,000 while the receipts were less than £243,000.[171] It seemed to be a poor business for the Post Office to build steamboats and run the mail service. These figures, together with the public pressure to reduce the high postage rates,[172] were among the most important reasons when the Post Office later decided to change its policy and 'outsource' the overseas mail services to private, subsidised steamship companies.

Before any transatlantic steamers became reality, steam vessels were already in use for a regular foreign mail service on shorter sea routes, such as crossing the North Sea between London and Holland or Hamburg. The steamship service shortened the trip notably compared with the horse-drawn mail coach to Harwich and crossing of the North Sea by sailing packets. The 170-year-old Harwich mail service was given up, and mails to Holland were carried by the General Steam Navigation Company. This line, founded in 1824, received its first mail contract in 1831. The steam packets would depart regularly from London for Rotterdam and Hamburg, reaching Rotterdam in 28 hours and Hamburg in 54. By the mid-1830s, steam packets were leaving

---

169 Robinson (1964), 121.
170 Robinson (1964), 118–122.
171 Robinson (1964), 122.
172 Roland Hill, Secretary of the Post Office, published his well-known pamphlet *Post Office Reform: Its Importance and Practicability* in 1837. Hill's calculations about the benefits of reducing the high inland postage rates to a uniform one penny rate caused a furious debate in public and in the Parliament. The uniform inland rate was introduced in 1840, together with the first prepaid postage stamp in the world, the Penny Black, as well as the prepaid stationery covers, known as Mulready covers according to their designer. These inventions supported the decision to adopt the one penny postage, as the stamps and stationery covers could be bought in quantities before use, and prepaid letters were easier and quicker to handle in the Post Office. See Robinson (1948), 258–320; Gavin Fryer & Clive Akerman (ed.), *The Reform of the Post Office in the Victorian Era, Vol. 1* (London, 2000), 79–139. For the pamphlet, see Fryer & Akerman, 1–46. For the parliamentary debate, see the Reports of the Select Committee on Postage in *BPP, Transport and Communications, Posts and Telegraphs, 1 and 2*, passim.

from London twice a week. The mails for Sweden were sent across the North Sea via Hull from 1840.[173]

In France, the first regular steam packet service was established on the Saône in 1826, after many fruitless attempts. In 1833 there were only 75 steamboats in France; in 1835 there were 100; and in 1838 still only 160. The French started their Mediterranean mail steamship service between Marseilles and Constantinople in 1837.[174]

The first steamship to cross the Atlantic was the American *Savannah* in 1819. Her trip from Savannah, Georgia, to Liverpool took 29 days, and the engine was used for only 100 hours of the total of 700 spent at sea. The ship had no passengers or cargo on board during the trip, despite advertising in the local press before the voyage. Even though the trip could be called nautically successful, the result clearly indicated that ocean-going steamships were not yet economical.[175]

The *Royal William* was another vessel which crossed the North Atlantic eastbound once. She even carried passengers on her voyage. The ship was originally built for Quebec–Halifax–Pictou traffic in 1831, but in 1833 the owners decided to send her across the Atlantic to be sold in Europe. The eastbound trip took 22 days to Cowes and 25 days to London, including all the stoppages due to a problem common for the early steamers: the fires under the boilers had to be put out for hours several times during the trip to remove the salt crystals which came from the sea water that was used for cooling.[176]

A few more transatlantic trips at least partly under steam were recorded during the 1820s and 1830s on the southern route: the *Conde de Patmella* from Liverpool via Lisbon to Brazil in 1820; the *Rising Star* to Valparaiso, Chile, in 1822; and the *Curaçao* from Antwerp to the Dutch West Indies in 1827, after which she probably made two or three more round trips before becoming a man-of-war in Belgium in 1830. The *City of Kingston* sailed from London for Madeira, Barbados and Jamaica in 1837, continuing later to New York but ending up in Baltimore due to a heavy storm.[177]

---

173 Robinson (1964), 123; Moubray & Moubray, 105–106.
174 Allington & Greenhill, 12. For the early French Mediterranean service, see Raymond Salles, *La Poste Maritime Française, Historique et Catalogue, Tome II, Les Paquebots de la Méditerranée de 1837 à 1935* (Limassol, Cyprus, 1992), 9–34.
175 About Savannah's trip, see Albion (1939) 314; John A. Butler, *Atlantic Kingdom: America's Contest with Cunard in the Age of Sail and Steam* (Washington D.C., 2001), 41–44; Arnold Kludas, *Record Breakers of the North Atlantic. Blue Riband Liners 1838–1952* (London, 2000), 33–36; Staff, 63; and Tyler, 1–17.
176 Lawrence Babcock, *Spanning the Atlantic. A History of the Cunard Line* (New York 1931), 24–29; Bonsor (1975), vol. 1, 51–52; Kludas, 35–36; Robinson (1964), 125–126; David Tyler, *Steam Conquers the Atlantic* (New York, 1939), 25–27.
177 Albion (1939), 316; Allington & Greenhill, 14; Babcock, 24; Bonsor (1975), vol. 1, 45–46; Stuart Nicol, *Macqueen's Legacy. A History of the Royal Mail Line*, vol. 1 (Gloucestershire, 2001), 31; Robinson (1964), 125; Tyler, 22–23. Some transatlantic voyages were obviously made also by the Royal Navy at least partly under steam. See Allington & Greenhill, 14; Tyler, 23–25.

The start of the transatlantic steamship service

A discussion about the possibility of making a westbound voyage across the North Atlantic by steamship continued in Britain throughout the 1830s. It was asserted by sceptics that the boiler would be completely clogged by using sea water for such a long time, the vessel could not carry enough coal for a trip of over 3,000 nautical miles while still leaving enough room for passengers, crew, freight and stores, and the necessary fuel, when loaded, would destroy the trim of the vessel. The Atlantic crossing might be done only if the shortest possible distance between the two continents was used, from the west coast of Ireland to Halifax.[178]

The famous race between the steamers *Sirius* and *Great Western* from Britain to New York in April 1838 was finally the start of a commercial transatlantic steamship service. The *Sirius* was a wooden paddle steamer of 700 tons and a substitute for the British and American Steam Navigation Company's (B&A) *British Queen*, a much larger vessel designed for regular North Atlantic service. The launching of the *British Queen* was delayed by several months due to the bankruptcy of the company that should have delivered the engines, and the B&A decided to charter the *Sirius* for a transatlantic journey to save the honour of the company, as they had already announced the commencement of this traffic.[179]

According to Stephen Fox, the voyage of the *Sirius* was 'just a headless, dangerous publicity stunt, a desperate gambit by sore losers, and hardly worth the historical attention it had received ever since'.[180] Even so, the 'publicity stunt' was very successful, as the amount of attention paid to it shows. This was not the first time, and would not be the last time, that shipping companies took risks in the North Atlantic for publicity and reputation – and not all cases had a happy ending.

The rival *Great Western* was a much larger and more efficient ship of 1,340 tons. She was owned by the Great Western Steamship Company and was built together with the Great Western Railway, which was opened in its full length between London and Bristol in 1841. Isambard Kingdom Brunel, the well-known chief engineer, was responsible for both these projects.[181]

In April 1838 both steamers were ready for their first Atlantic crossing. Due to damage caused by a fire in her engine, the *Great Western* did not sail from Bristol as scheduled. She finally left on 8 April, four days after the *Sirius*, which departed from Cork, Ireland, on 4 April. The *Great Western* was so much faster that she arrived in New York on 23 April, only a few

---

178 Robinson (1964), 126; Tyler, 39–41. Both refer to Dr. Dionysius Lardner's article in *Edinburgh Review* of April 1837.

179 Kludas, 36–37; E. Le Roy Pond, *Junius Smith: A Biography of the Father of the Atlantic Liner* (New York, 1927), 100.

180 Stephen Fox, *The Ocean Railway* (London, 2003), 78. – Bernard Edwards describes the risks of the *Sirius* voyage in *The Grey Widow Maker. The true stories of twenty-four disasters at sea* (London, 1995), 27–33.

181 For its origins, see e.g. Pond, 98; Robinson (1964), 127; Bonsor (1975), vol. 1, 60; Butler, 45. For the Great Western Railway, see Vaughan, 178–192.

hours after the *Sirius's* wildly celebrated arrival.[182] The *Sirius* brought with her 94 passengers but the *Great Western* only seven, while 50 others had cancelled their bookings when they heard about the engine fire and the beaching on a sand bank on the way to Bristol. On the way back, people crowded onto the faster and larger vessel, and the *Great Western* carried home 68 passengers.[183]

Both steamers were equipped with an important innovation made in 1834, a circulating freshwater cooling system that eliminated any need for stoppages to scrape the caked salt from the boiler's interior.[184] The *Great Western* took 600 tons of coal when departing from Bristol, and still had 155 tons a board upon arrival, having burnt an average of 29 tons of coal per day.[185] The *Sirius* ran short of coal and was forced to burn wooden fittings and a good deal of resin to keep her engines going. On the eastbound voyage she had to make an extra call at Falmouth for coal, and it was from there that her mails were forwarded by land to the recipients.[186]

FIG. 5. *The letter sent from Baltimore on 28.4.1838 was carried by the* Sirius *on her first voyage on the way back home. She left from New York on 30.4. and had to make an extra call at Falmouth on 18.5. for coaling. The mails were sent from there by land to London. 'PAID' and the rate marking have been struck out, and only the inland 5s postage has been charged from the recipient. On the reverse, 'SHIP LETTER FALMOUTH' (used in 1835–1840) and the London arrival handstamp of 21.5.1838.*

182 A comparison of the ships' logs has been published by Tyler, 384–387.
183 Bonsor (1975), vol.1., 60–61; Kludas, 37; Nicholas Fogg, *The Voyages of the Great Britain. Life at Sea in the World's First Liner* (Wilts, Great Britain, 2002), 9; Staff, 68.
184 Butler, 45–46; Bonsor (1975), vol. 1, 55.
185 Allington-Greenhill, 9.
186 The story about the *Sirius* coal varies in different sources. See Albion (1939), 318; Butler, 46; Babcock, 32; Tabeart, 16; and Pond, 113; Robinson (1964), 127; Tyler, 58–59, 384–386.

FIG. 6. *The letter sent from Baltimore on 11.6.1839 was carried by the* Great Western *on her 8th round trip. She left from New York on 13.6. and arrived in Bristol on 27.6. The letter arrived in London on 28.6., in 17 days.*

Both ships carried mail on board. These letters are usually regarded as the first transatlantic steamship letters in postal historical collections.[187] There are no records of the number of letters carried on the ships' westbound journeys, but on the way back the *Sirius* carried some 17,000 and the *Great Western* some 20,000 letters.[188] According to a newspaper columnist of the *Albion* in New York on 5 May, 1838, no charge was taken for the mails.

The loss of profit this caused for the *Sirius* owners was calculated at up to $4,000 – or £1,000 – a sum that would have paid for a large part of the costs of the voyage. According to the paper, the letter bags would

187 Robertson shows a very early cover sent as private ship letter by the *Savannah* in 1819. It is the only one known from the experimental period. See Robertson, B.48/C.

188 Pond, 113; Staff, 68; Robinson (1964), 127.

have been more profitable for the company than the 28 cabin passengers carried.[189]

According to Tyler, the *Sirius* brought with her some Liverpool newspapers of 3 April and Cork newspapers of 4 April, while the *Great Western* brought London newspapers of 6 April and one from Bristol of 7 April. An employee of the New York *Courier & Enquirer* found the *Great Western's* mails on arrival and managed to get off with the newspapers and mail bags. The *Courier's* editors kept them for several hours, went through the contents and published a special foreign news edition. The other newspapers were greatly annoyed, and so was the British Minister in Washington, whose mail was thus delayed.[190]

Although somewhat unplanned, this was the start of the regular steamship mail and passenger service between Britain and New York. As a mail carrier, the *Great Western* took letters westward at ship letter rates. From New York the rate was the same as on the American sailing packets, 25 cents each, and her captain received 2d from the British Post Office for each single letter he landed at Bristol.[191]

The *Sirius* made only two round trips across the Atlantic, and then returned to coastal service. The *Great Western* made more than 40 North Atlantic round trips during 1838–1846, and was then sold to the Royal Mail Steam Packet Company for the British – West Indian service. In 1855, she was used as a troop carrier in the Crimean War, and in 1856 was finally sold to be scrapped.[192]

The *Sirius* and the *Great Western* were soon followed by other transatlantic pioneers. The *Royal William* of the City of Dublin Steam Packet Co. entered the traffic in July 1838 and the *Liverpool* of the Transatlantic Steam Ship Co. in October 1838. The British and American Steam Navigation Company's *British Queen*, which had chartered the *Sirius* for the first Atlantic voyage, entered the traffic in July 1839 (see Fig. 7).[193]

In 1838–1839, these five steamers made 26 transatlantic round trips in total. While the average westbound trip of the American sailing packets between Liverpool and New York took 34.3 days during 1833–1847,[194] the average trip by the pioneering steamers was made in 17.7 days during 1838–1839 – in about half of the time.[195]

Despite the good start and great publicity, several of the pioneering steamers appeared to be non-profitable and they had to be taken out of service after a few trips. The *Royal William* ended her last voyage in February 1839. The *British Queen* was also short-lived in this service, primarily due to the financial problems caused to the company by the loss of its new flagship the *President,* which sailed from New York for Liverpool in March 1841 with 136 people on board and was never heard of again.[196]

---

189 Staff, 155.
190 Tyler, 56.
191 Robinson, 128; Staff, 155–156.
192 Tabeart (1997), 16–19; Bonsor (1975), vol. 1, 60–66.
193 Tabeart (1997), 16–17. The *Royal William* should not to be confused with the earlier Canadian namesake.
194 Albion (1938), 317.
195 Calculated from the sailing lists of Tabeart (1997), 17.
196 Tabeart (1997), 18. For the loss of the *President,* see e.g. Pond, 210–222; Bonsor (1975),

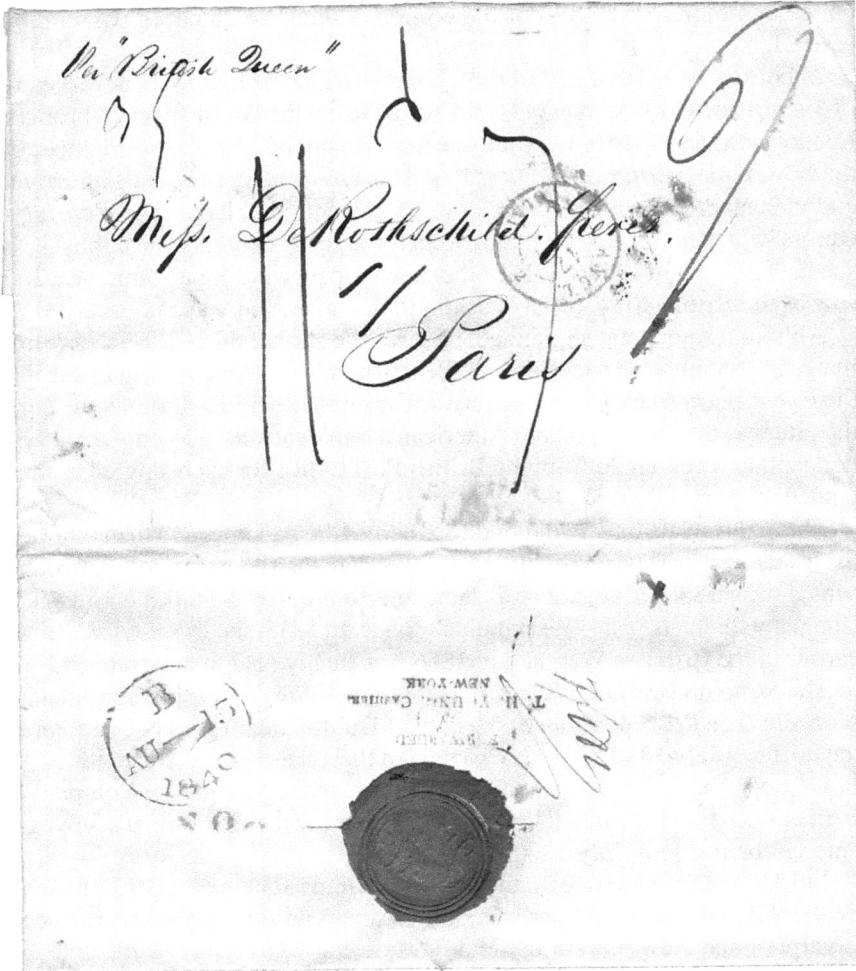

FIG. 7. *The letter sent from New York on 31.7.1840 to the Rothschild banking company in Paris, was carried by the* British Queen *on her 6th round voyage. She departed from New York on 1.8. and arrived in Portsmouth on 15.8. The letter was forwarded to the ship in New York by 'T. H. Young, Cashier'. It was carried across the English Channel on 17.8.1840 and must have arrived in Paris within a couple of days, in about 19 days in all.*

vol. 1, 56–58; Staff, 77–78; Robinson (1964), 129–131; Butler, 46–47; Albion (1939), 320; Fox 99–101. – The shipowning company B&A announced to their shareholders in December 1841 that the total receipts for the nine voyages of the *British Queen* had been £82,000 and the total expenses less than £71,000. This would have meant an average profit of over £1,200 per voyage, compared with £1,350 of the ill-fated *President*. Bonsor notes that the figures most probably did not take into account interest charges, depreciation, insurance or management expenses, which turned the profit into a substantial loss and forced the company into liquidation. Bonsor (1975), vol. 1, 58. In 1837, the company's prospectus had optimistically estimated that the profits of the *British Queen* would be

The only long-lived pioneering steamer in the North Atlantic service was the *Great Western.*

The *Great Western* was clearly the fastest of all the pioneering steamers. She made her westbound trips in 15.8 days on average in 1838–1842, and in 16.4 days in 1843–1846. Her eastbound trips took 13.7 days on average in 1838–1842, and 14.8 days in 1843–1846.[197]

It has been argued that steamships offered 'a huge advantage of independence from the wind' and that they maintained a regular schedule regardless of the weather.[198] Even if this was very much true compared with the sailing ships, the pioneering steamship traffic was not regular in the sense of line service. The *Great Western* sailed from both ports at about seven-week intervals, staying approximately ten days at port, on average.[199] The duration of the trip was still unpredictable, even if the journeys were generally faster than by the sailing packets. Winds and streams also affected the steamers. Diagram 2 shows the difference between the duration of the *Great Western's* westbound and eastbound sailings between 1838 and 1846.

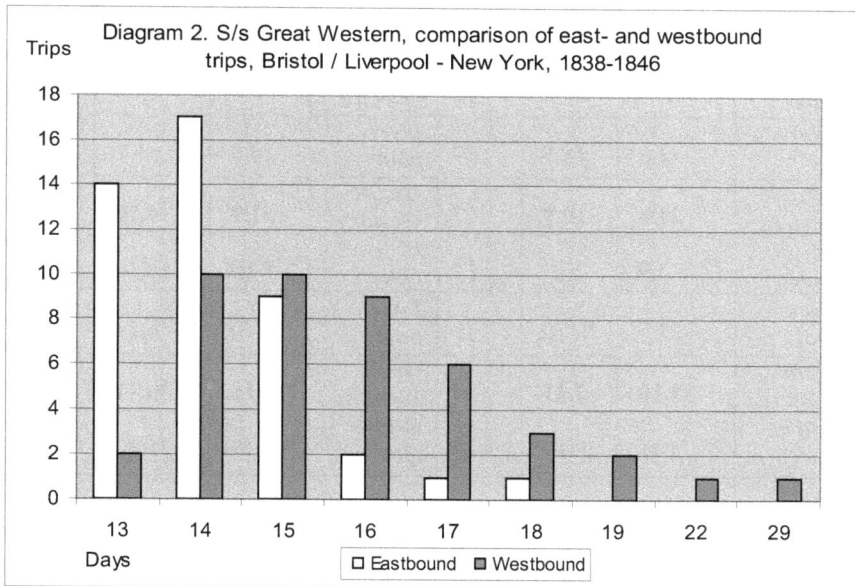

Diagram 2. S/s Great Western, comparison of east- and westbound trips, Bristol / Liverpool - New York, 1838-1846

Source: Sailing lists of Tabeart (1997), 17–19.

over £4,500 per round trip or about £27,000 for a whole year. See Tyler, 44.

197 See sailing lists of Tabeart (1997), 19. – The Great Western changed her home port from Bristol to Liverpool in 1843, but this was not the reason for the longer trips during the later period. The vessel was able to make 13-day voyages from New York to both ports in 1842 when she sailed a triangle while testing the port of Liverpool.

198 E.g. Kludas, 38; Talbot, 133; Pond; 1–3; Babcock, 80.

199 Her actual sailing dates in 1838 were 8.4., 2.6., 21.7., 8.9. and 27.10. from Bristol; and 7.5., 25.6., 16.8., 4.10., and 23.11. from New York. See Tabeart (1997), 17–19.

TABLE 12. *Consecutive information circles enabled by the pioneering transatlantic steamers in 1839.*

Letter sent by steamer	Ship departure England	Ship arrival New York	Days	Next departing steamer, company	Ship departure New York	Ship arrival England	Days	Information circle, days
Great Western	**28.1.**	**16.2.**	19	Great Western	**25.2.**	**12.3.**	15	43
Liverpool	*6.2.*	*25.2.*	19	Liverpool	*9.3.*	*25.3.*	16	47
Great Western	**24.3.**	**15.4.**	22	Great Western	**23.4.**	**7.5.**	14	44
Liverpool	*20.4.*	*7.5.*	17	Liverpool	*18.5.*	*2.6.*	15	43
Great Western	**18.5.**	**31.5.**	13	Great Western	**13.6.**	**27.6.**	14	40
Liverpool	*13.6.*	*30.6.*	17	Liverpool	*6.7.*	*20.7.*	14	37
Great Western	**6.7.**	**22.7.**	16	Great Western	**1.8.**	**14.8.***	13	39
British Queen	12.7.	28.7.	16	British Queen	1.8.	14.8.	13	33
Liverpool	*1.8.*	*18.8.*	17	Liverpool	*24.8.*	*8.9.*	15	38
Great Western	**24.8.**	**10.9.**	17	Great Western	**21.9.**	**4.10.**	13	41
British Queen	3.9.	20.9.	17	British Queen	1.10.	15.10.	14	42
Liverpool	*21.9.*	*10.10.*	19	Liverpool	*19.10.*	*6.11.*	18	46
Great Western	**19.10.**	**2.11.**	14	Great Western	**16.11.**	**30.11.**	14	42
British Queen	3.11.	23.11.	20	British Queen	2.12.	25.12.	23	52
Liverpool	*16.11.*	*5.12.*	19	Liverpool	*15.12.*	*11.1.40*	28**	56
Average, Great Western			16.8				13.8	41.5
Average, all			17.5				15.0	42.9

Source: Tabeart (1997), 17. The consecutive information circles enabled by the sailings of the *Great Western* are marked in **bold** and those enabled by the *Liverpool* in *italics*. The *Great Western* sailed from Bristol; the *Liverpool* from Liverpool; and the *British Queen* from Portsmouth.

* The date is corrected here according to Fox, 82–83; Pond, 180–181. Tabeart's date is 15.8.

** This was the *Liverpool's* last transatlantic voyage. She ran short of coal and had to replenish at Fayal, Azores, which caused a notable delay. See Tabeart (1997), 17.

The *Great Western* made most of her westbound voyages in 14, 15 or 16 days, a notable difference compared with the sailing ships. Not all the trips were fast, however. While a record voyage was twice made in 13 days, the longest trip took 29 days in February–March 1843. In the 1840s, the *Great Western* was not in use all year round but stayed at port during the mid-winter months. The eastbound trips normally took 13 to 15 days, with only a few exceptions. There is a visible difference in the duration of east- and westbound voyages.

How did the pioneering steamship service affect the duration of business information transmission? Table 12 shows the flow of the consecutive information circles during 1839. Compared with the five consecutive circles enabled by the American sailing packets in 1838, with an average information circle of 64.4 days (varying between 50 and 98 days),[200] the pioneering steamers enabled six consecutive circles, the average being 41.5 days if the letters were carried by the *Great Western* and 44.5 if carried by the *Liverpool*. The shortest information circle was conducted by the *British Queen*, which carried the answers to letters sent from England in only 33 days. She stayed in New York for only four days on her maiden voyage, so as to be able to rush away simultaneously with the *Great Western*. They arrived at Bristol and Portsmouth within two hours of each other.[201]

As can be seen in Table 12, both the *Great Western* and the *Liverpool* made six round trips to New York during 1839. Each of the two vessels alone enabled six consecutive information circles for the letters and answers of the British merchants. The port stays were short at both ends, and the length of one information circle varied between 33 and 56 days.

The speed of communications was clearly improved by the introduction of the pioneering steamers. The westbound trips in particular were made faster than ever. The steamers made 11 North Atlantic round-trips in 1838 and 15 in 1839. Winter sailings were avoided. For example, between 16 November 1839 and 20 February 1840, no steamer left from British ports on the North Atlantic route.[202]

There were now four independent shipping companies running the service to New York from several British ports, and the sailings were mostly organized in ways that complemented each other. Yet there were no regular sailing dates, and the unpredictability of the system was still a problem. The next step would be similar to that which had made the American sailing packets so revolutionary two decades earlier: the organizing of line traffic across the ocean.

The origins of the North Atlantic mail contract

From the early 1820s, the superiority of the American sailing packets had been a cause of harm to the British Post Office, not only due to lost postage income but also lost prestige. The government packets were a subject of continuous complaint in the media. Not only were they slower and less

---

200 See Table 10.
201 See Fox, 82–83; Pond, 180–181.
202 See the sailing lists of Tabeart (1997), 17.

regular than the American sailing packets, but their seaworthiness was also publicly suspected, and not without reason.[203]

The problems dated from the period after the Napoleonic wars, when the Admiralty took over the Falmouth packet service. In connection with the establishment of peace there was a need for a considerable reduction in the number of ships and men in the Royal Navy. By transferring the Post Office packet service to the Admiralty, the surplus men and ships could be kept in use, and they would – at least in theory – be ready for active service in the future. The Treasury supported the plan in the hope of financial savings, and despite the strong opposition by the Post Office, the transfer took place in April, 1823. The contracts and agreements made between the Post Office and the individual Falmouth packet captains were transferred to the Navy Board, and as each contract expired, a naval packet took the place of the privately owned hired vessel. This was a long process, and the last hired packet remained in service until 1839.[204]

The sailing ships that the Admiralty brought into use in the packet service were ten-gun brigs and sloops, later packet brigs. The first category of packets was small men-of-war, mainly 230–240 tons, and built for general naval purposes in the 1820s. These ships were not designed for the packet service, and each vessel had to be modified and re-equipped, including a reduction in armaments to six guns in many cases. The packet brigs were built in the 1830s for the packet service. They were bigger, about 360 tons, and more seaworthy than the older ones.[205]

Between 1827 and 1840, no fewer than nine of the 25 naval packets of the first category were lost at sea for varying reasons, mainly a combination of the ships' poor sailing qualities, bad weather and ice. Several ships just disappeared. Public concern was strongly expressed in the newspapers. The Admiralty packets were called 'the very refuse and ridicule of the navy', 'the lowest vessels that swim the seas', 'these official bum-boats', 'death ships' and 'coffin ships'. In 1827–1828, a total of 102 officers and crew were lost in three different packet disasters, as well as 19 passengers and all mails and bullion carried.[206] The press advised the Admiralty that '…it would be better if we cannot build safe vessels ourselves to buy a score or two of the New York packets.'[207]

After 1826 there was no British packet service to New York, only to Halifax and Bermuda, from where the mails to the British Ambassador in Annapolis, Maryland, were carried by a mail boat. The service had been conducted by Samuel Cunard of Halifax since 1827, this being his first mail

203 Howat, 30; Staff, 62.
204 Howat, 27–28; Staff, 61. For details of the transfer, see Britnor, 141–146.
205 Howat, 29.
206 Howat, 30. The quotations are from *The Times* 1824–1834, picked out by Howat. – Some details of the packet losses are described by Arnell (1980), 89–90. – The Falmouth packets had larger crews than the American sailing packets as they were Admiralty-governed ten-gun brigs instead of trade ships.
207 Staff, 62. The quotation is from *London Courier* of 1834, cited by Staff. – In fact, foreigners were not permitted by American law to participate in the ownership of American vessels. (Albion 1938, 130)

STEAM VESSEL SIRIUS Lieutenant RICH? ROBERTS: R.N. off NEW YORK.
The first BRITISH Steam Vessel that ever crossed the Atlantic (performed her Voyage from Cork in 18 Days)

FIG. 8. *Meeting the* Sirius *in mid-Atlantic on her first voyage ensured the people a board the Admiralty packet* Tyrian *that it was time to establish a regular steamship mail service across the Atlantic.* © *National Museums Liverpool (Merseyside Maritime Museum).*

contract with the British government. Later during the same year the service was altered to carry the British mails from Halifax to Boston, and in 1833 the contract expanded to provide a second mail boat service between Halifax and Bermuda.[208]

In May 1838, when the *Sirius* steamed homeward on her first transatlantic trip (see Fig. 8), she met the Admiralty mail brig *Tyrian* at sea, which was returning from Halifax. As the *Tyrian* was rolling in the flat calm several hundred miles from her home port, the captain decided to send his mails by the steamer. A distinguished Nova Scotian by the name of Joseph Howe was on board and evidently the meeting in the middle of the ocean made a deep impression on him as immediately after arriving he started to press the Colonial Secretary for steam communication between Britain and the North American colonies. New Brunswick and Quebec joined with Nova Scotia, asking for twice-monthly communications with British North America.[209]

The purpose of these suggestions was mainly political. There were open rebellions in Canada at that time, and information reached England slowly and incompletely. The Admiralty felt uncomfortable about the fact that the British mail transmission depended so largely on the American sailing

208 Arnell, 21–23; Arnell & Ludington, viii–xi.
209 See Robinson, 131–132; Hyde (1975), 4. Some authors give the honour of being fathers of the idea also to Sir Thomas Chandler Haliburton, better known under his pen-name Sam Slick, and William Crane, both 'prominent citizens of the Maritime Provinces'. All three men were on board the *Tyrian*, when she met the *Sirius* at sea. See Tyler, 71; Staff, 69; Pond 116–117; Babcock, 33.

packets.[210] The outcome of the debate and the positive experiences of the pioneering steamers was an advertisement by the Admiralty in November 1838 asking for tenders for a steamship mail service between England and Halifax, with an additional link between Halifax and New York. The service was to be performed by steamers of no less than 300 hp. Voyages should be monthly, and the home port should be Liverpool, Bristol, Plymouth, Falmouth or Southampton.[211]

Two tenders were submitted in response. The first one was from the St. George Steam Packet Company, which owned the *Sirius*, offering a service from Cork and connected to a feeder service from Liverpool by smaller vessels. There would also be a similar link between Halifax and New York. The other tender was from the Great Western Steamship Company, offering a monthly service between Bristol and Halifax by 1,000-ton iron steamers or 1,500-ton wooden steamers. The service was to Halifax only, with no further link to New York.[212]

These tenders were not exactly what the Admiralty wanted to receive, and negotiations were opened with Samuel Cunard of Nova Scotia, who had arrived in Britain with a new suggestion.[213] Cunard, born in Halifax in 1787, was well known in the shipping business also in Britain due to the mail services between Halifax–Boston and Halifax–Bermuda at that time. The family had been involved in the shipbuilding business in Halifax, and Samuel Cunard had also worked for a time in Boston, learning the business of ship-broking before joining his father's and brothers' company.[214]

Samuel Cunard had been a shareholder in the first *Royal William* before she crossed the Atlantic in 1833. He also had interests in the General Mining Association, which ran the Cape Breton coal mines in Sydney, Nova Scotia, and was the Halifax agent for the company. Due to this arrangement, Cunard's ships could later be supplied with relatively cheap coal from this source.[215]

In 1839, Samuel Cunard spent several months in Britain searching for partners and collecting capital for a new steamship company that could fulfil the Admiralty's needs. With the help of friends, he was introduced to some Cabinet members. He was also introduced to Robert Napier, a marine engineer who already had a well-known shipbuilding company in Glasgow; to two Glasgow merchants, David and Charles MacIver; and to James and George Burns, who operated a small fleet of coastal steamers to Liverpool. These men became the main partners of the new British and North American Royal Steam

---

210 Tyler, 75–77; Fox, 88.

211 Robinson (1964), 132; Hyde (1975), 5; Tabeart (1997), 16; Babcock, 34.

212 Hyde (1975), 5; Robinson (1964), 132; Staff, 70; Tyler, 77–78.

213 See Hyde (1975), 5; Staff, 69.

214 For Samuel Cunard's family background and early businesses, see Babcock, 3–14; Hyde (1975), 1–4; Butler, 71–74; Fox, 39–49.

215 Hyde (1975), 3; Tyler, 78–80. Coal supplies were a key element in the steamship traffic. The coal problem was not that easily solved, however. According to Tyler, Cunard mainly used Welsh coal as the American quality was not good enough, and the anthracite was not easily obtainable before the railways and canals had been built in the interior of Pennsylvania. The owners of the *Great Western* tried Nova Scotian coal but found it 'soft and full of dirt'. As a result they continued to send a supply of English coal to New York, even though they had to pay duty on it. See Tyler, 27–128, 187–188.

Packet Company shipping line, soon to be known as the Cunard Line.[216]

In May 1839, the first contract was made with the Admiralty for carrying mail regularly 'with all possible speed' from Liverpool to Halifax by three steamships of at least 300 hp each, and also taking care of the mail transport to Boston. In addition, the company carried mails from Halifax to Quebec twice a month in smaller steamers to connect with the transatlantic ships, when the St. Lawrence River was free of ice. The mail contract was to last for seven years with an annual subvention of £55,000.[217]

This was not exactly what the Admiralty had originally wanted either. However, Samuel Cunard was aware that a line between Liverpool and Halifax alone would probably not get enough passengers and freight to be profitable, as Halifax had already lost a lot of its commercial importance to American cities. The rapid development of Boston made that port a good choice for a new steamship connection. Moreover, the run from England to New York via Halifax was much longer than to Boston, and this route would have placed Cunard at a disadvantage in competition with the ships that crossed the Atlantic directly to New York without calling at Halifax. The change was approved by the Admiralty without major problems.[218]

But suspicions surfaced among the Cunard Line's shareholders concerning the profitability of the new business. The company had bound itself to pay the Admiralty £500 in addition to other fines for every 12 hours that the ships might be late from their prescribed fortnight schedule, on each side of the ocean. This meant that an average of only one day's delay for each sailing during the year would practically cancel all revenue to be derived from the subsidy. Such a commitment was considered to be a heavy risk in the unpredictable North Atlantic conditions.[219]

The contract did not mean that all trips should be made in 14 days. For example, the *Great Western* had been able to manage only three of her eleven westbound journeys in a fortnight or less in 1838–1839. None of the other steamers had made it even once. But, according to the schedule, the ships should leave twice a month from both ports. Even this was considered too risky, if only three vessels were involved in the service, as it would have meant continuous running with about two weeks at sea and one at port – rather unrealistic at that time.

There was no assurance that the Cunard Line would win passengers and freight from the competing steamship companies or the popular sailing packet lines, which would be necessary for profitable business. The counter

216 For the foundation, capital structure and control of the Cunard Line, see Hyde (1975), 7–15.
217 For the whole contract, see Arnell (1986), 265–273. Copies of several contract versions are held by the Sydney Jones Library Archives in Liverpool. See CP, PR 3/1/12a (SJ).
218 Babcock, 42–43; Hyde (1975), 8; Robinson (1964), 133; Bonsor (1975), vol. 1, 72–73.
219 Babcock, 45–46; Hyde (1975), 10.

MAP 2. *North Atlantic mail steamship routes in the mid-19th century.*

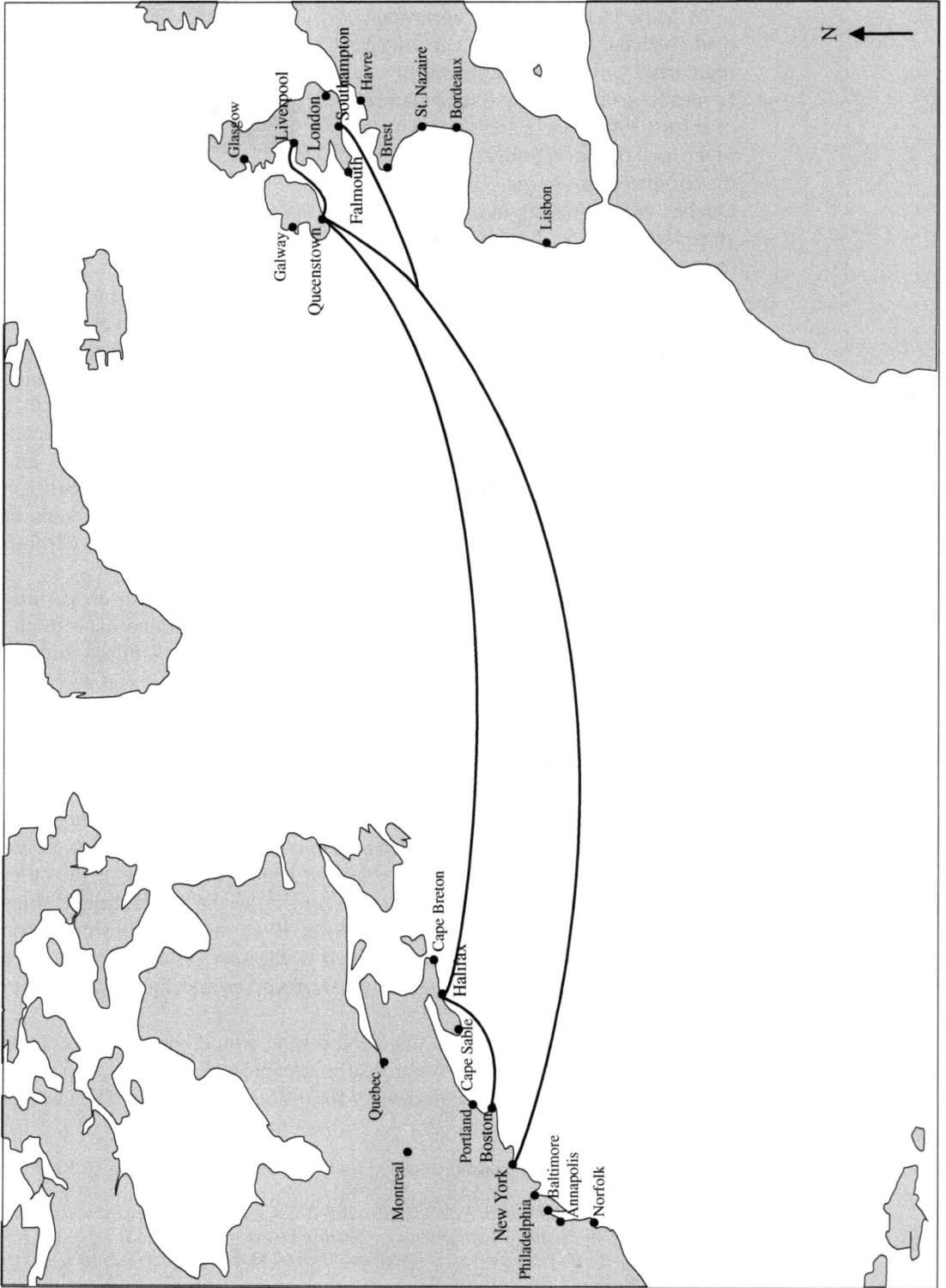

arguments stressed the fame of Robert Napier's reliable engines, as well as the fact that America was rapidly expanding westward, starting new industries and attracting more emigrants and travellers from Europe. The company did not have to win business from the sailing packets; it could create business of its own.[220]

The Cunard shareholders were finally convinced that the opportunity was worth the risk, and the company obtained much more capital than had been planned when the original ships were ordered from Napier. With four ships instead of three they could ensure a bi-monthly sailing from each side of the ocean, and extend the regular service all the way to Boston, making only a call at Halifax, as the chief merchants and businessmen of Boston had strongly desired. They considered that the new line was of great importance for the city's trade, and had been extremely disappointed to learn that Boston would only be served by a branch from Halifax. This would have meant that passengers and freight to and from Europe would have to be transhipped at extra cost by small steamers at Halifax.[221]

The Canadians were naturally unhappy with the change in final destination. From their point of view, it showed that Cunard was, strictly speaking, an American packet line instead of a Canadian one.[222] The Admiralty approved Cunard's suggestion however, and a new agreement on government subsidies totalling £60,000 was signed in July, 1839.[223]

The Admiralty also made a similar contract with the newly established Royal Mail Steam Packet Company for carrying mails between Britain and the West Indies in 1839, to Mexico in 1842 and to South America in 1851. A third contract was made with Peninsular and Oriental Steam Navigation Company, or P&O, for carrying mails between Britain and Alexandria in 1840, via Suez to Calcutta in 1842, and to Penang, Singapore and Hong Kong in 1845. From 1852, P&O also carried mails to Australia.[224] Additionally, a steamship mail route was opened to Cape Town, South Africa in 1850.[225] These mail routes and their development will be examined in Chapters VI and VII.

The early years of the Cunard Line

The Cunard Line's first Atlantic crossing was made by the *Unicorn*, a small steamer that was purchased for feeder service between Pictou, Nova Scotia, and Quebec on the St. Lawrence River during the months when the river was navigable. The *Unicorn* also carried mail during her trip, thus starting the

---

220 Babcock, 46.
221 Babcock, 49; Hyde (1975), 10–12.
222 Arnell (1980), 94.
223 See Arnell (1986), 265–273. In 1841, the subsidy was increased to £80,000 due to the need for a fifth vessel. See Robinson (1964), 134.
224 Robinson (1964), 148–149, 165; Nicol, vol. 1, 44–45; Tyler, 98–99. The first P&O contract was made for mail service between Britain and the Iberian Peninsula in 1837. See Cable, 6; Kirk (1987), 5–8.
225 See Philip Cattell, *The Union Castle Ocean Post Office*. British Maritime Postal History, Vol. 3 (Heathfield), 11.

Cunard mail service across the Atlantic. The first contract steamer *Britannia* started on the route on 4 July, 1840.[226]

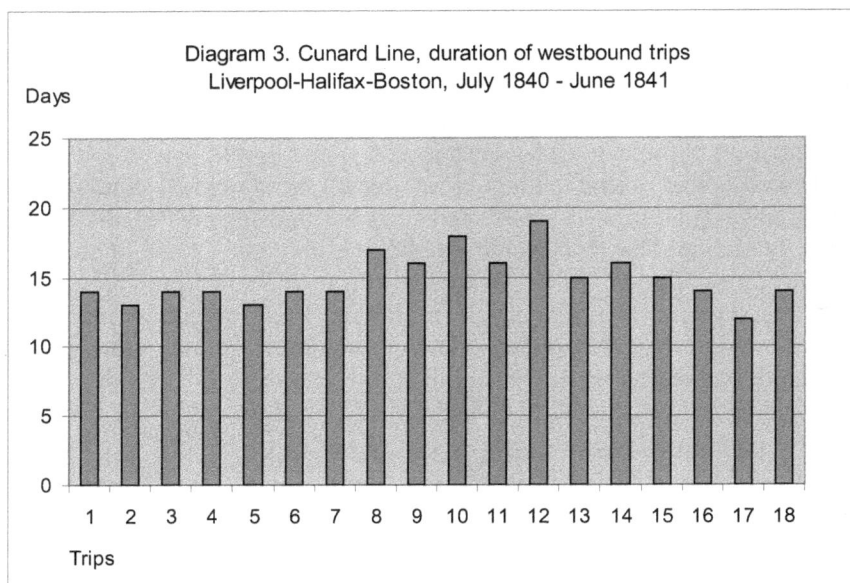

Diagram 3. Cunard Line, duration of westbound trips
Liverpool-Halifax-Boston, July 1840 - June 1841

Source: Sailing lists of Hubbard & Winter, 17–18.

During the first year of the company's transatlantic mail business, the Cunard Line's ships made the westbound trip from Liverpool to Boston in 13 or 14 days in summer conditions. This included the required stop at Halifax. In November–March, there was only one trip per month in each direction. During the most difficult winter season from early December to the end of March, the westbound journey took 16 to 19 days.

All the eastbound trips except one were made in 13 to 15 days. In May 1841, the *Britannia* ran upon the rocks off Halifax, which caused a ten-day delay to that journey, as can be noticed in Diagram 4.[227]

All the four Cunard steamers in the North Atlantic service – the *Britannia*, *Acadia, Caledonia* and *Columbia* – were new and equal in size, each of them ca. 1,150 tons. They were wooden paddle steamers with a clipper bow, one funnel and three masts. They all had a two-cylinder side-lever engine of 420 hp, and an average speed of nine knots. The ships accommodated 115 first class passengers each. In accordance with the Admiralty agreement, gun platforms and bases were also installed on the ships' decks to be prepared for military purposes in case of war.[228]

226 Hubbard & Winter, 17; Bonsor (1975), vol. 1, 73–74.
227 Sailing lists of Hubbard & Winter, 17–18.
228 Bonsor (1975), vol. 1, 140–141. Kludas, 40–42. Robinson (1964), 134.

Diagram 4. Cunard Line, duration of eastbound trips
Boston-Halifax-Liverpool, July 1840 - June 1841

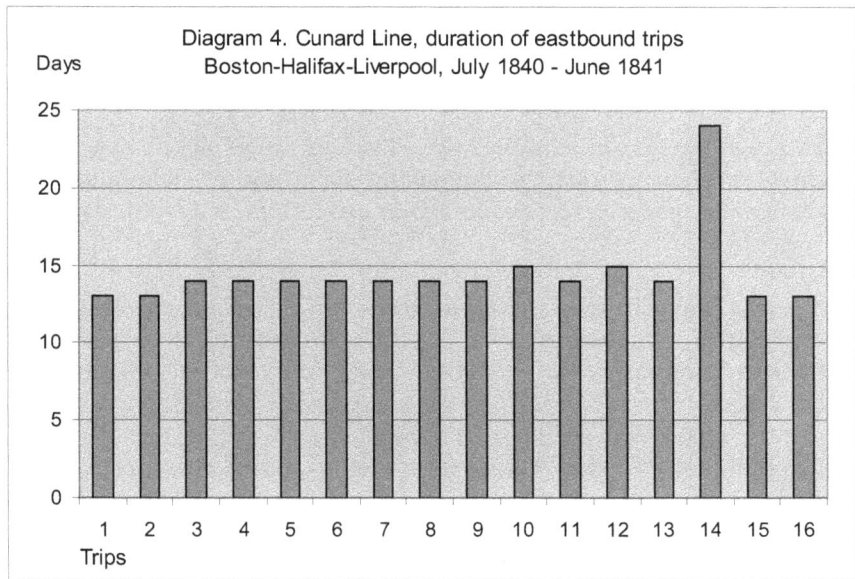

Source: Sailing lists of Hubbard & Winter, 17–18. – The similarity of the four vessels was an obvious advantage. All the voyages could be conducted within the same schedule, which made the service more regular and reliable.

Due to the ships' identical size and efficiency, they were able to make comparable voyages, which was convenient for the shipping management as well as for the mail service. Their performance was more predictable and reliable than if they had all been different – one of the obvious benefits of giving the mail contract to one shipping line. The average westbound trip on the Liverpool–Halifax–Boston route took 14.9 days. The *Britannia* made a westbound trip in 15.0 days on average, the *Acadia* in 15.2 days, the *Caledonia* in 14.8 days and the *Columbia* in 14.3 days.[229]

In the eastbound direction, the differences were even smaller. The average duration of the voyages between July 1840 and June 1841 were as follows: the *Britannia* 13.9 days (excluding the ill-fated voyage of May 1841), the *Acadia* 13.8 days, the *Caledonia* 13.8 days and the *Columbia* 14.0 days.[230]

The agreement on a bi-monthly schedule caused no major problems for the Cunard Line. The departures from Liverpool regularly took place on the 4th and 19th of each month from April to October, and on the 4th during the winter months. In the eastbound direction the ships departed from Boston on the 1st and 16th of each month, and on the 1st in the winter.[231] The ships

229 The *Columbia* entered the service as the last vessel in January 1841.
230 Calculated from the sailing lists of Hubbard & Winter, 17–18. For the data on calls at Halifax, see Arnell (1980), 287.
231 Hubbard & Winter, 12, 17–18. – As the London Post Office did not make the mails on a Sunday, the departures were in these cases postponed to the following day. 'Tenders and

made 29 round trips during the first 1.5 years of the line's existence. Of the 58 departures, two from Boston were one day late with no reason given, and one from Liverpool was two days late due to an order by the British Postmaster General to wait for a late arrival of mail dispatches.[232]

This was the first time in the world that any shipping company could organize a relatively fast and punctually departing, reliable and rather predictable service in both directions between Europe and North America. Compared with anything else, the Cunard Line's performance was superior.

A Cunard round trip from Liverpool to Boston via Halifax and back home was normally run in about 40 days. The duration of the stay at the home port was normally approximately 20 days. In 1840, the schedule was tight, as not all of the four steamers had yet been launched. The *Britannia* stayed only five days in Liverpool between her two transatlantic voyages in October 1840, and so did the *Caledonia*.[233] It is worth noting that the steamers could be unloaded, loaded and coaled for a new transatlantic nautical voyage of 3,000 nautical miles within five days at the port of Liverpool, if necessary. The port had invested, and would invest, notable sums in new docks enabling the berthing of steamships. The advantages of Liverpool soon became so obvious that even the *Great Western* made the port her regular terminus.[234]

The Cunard steamers were mainly built for passenger and mail service, but they also carried freight, and the coaling took time as well. It was proposed that the ships would carry twice the amount of coal necessary for the Atlantic crossing.[235] The economic balance of the three different businesses – passengers, mail and freight – varied during the years. On eastbound trips, the steamers met hard competition from the American sailing packets. While Cunard ships were able to charge £7 a ton for freight from Liverpool to New York, it was only on rare occasions that cargo could be obtained for carriage homewards, and during the winter months there was very little cargo to carry at all.[236] The early years of the line saw a series of financial crises and the contract with the Admiralty was modified several times. Only after a few years' service could the line turn profitable.[237]

Contracts for Carrying the Mails…N:o 10. Return of the Dates of Sailing…', 28–29. CP, PR 3/1/12. (SJ).

232 Sailing lists of Hubbard & Winter, 17–18.

233 See the sailing lists of Hubbard & Winter, 17.

234 For the development of the Liverpool Dock system, see Adrian Jarvis, *Liverpool Central Docks 1799–1905. An Illustrated History* (Bath, Avon, 1991), passim. A brief introduction to the early steamship period docks can be found on pages 8–9, 144–145. See also Hyde (1971), 79. For the *Great Western*, see Bonsor (1975) vol. 1, 61–62.

235 Hyde (1975), 9. This was probably not always the practice, as coal took space from the freight carried. Yet the Cunard ships were seldom obliged to make extra calls for coaling. The examples known are mainly from the time Cunard served on the Liverpool–New York route non-stop and the ships sometimes had to make an extra call at Halifax due to lengthened trips in heavy gales, or during the American Civil War. See Arnell (1980), 310–311, 318, 320. – According to the Cunard coaling records, the ships normally had about 100 tons of coal left from the previous trip when they arrived for the next coaling. See *Cunard Passage Book I,* in CP, GM2/1–4 (SJ).

236 Hyde (1975), 80.

237 Fox, 102–105.

Competition between early transatlantic mail carriers

Maritime historians have criticised the Cunard Line's mail contracts for killing the competition and making rival businesses non-profitable.[238] However, many opinions are based on aspects that were only relevant some 20 years later, when there were competing companies that really could afford a similar service. Occasional trips by various steamship companies were not an answer to the requirements of a fast, regular and reliable mail service.[239]

The only pioneering steamship that could compete with the Cunard steamers in speed was the *Great Western*. Diagram 5 depicts her performance compared with Cunard's *Britannia* during 1840–1846, when they both were in regular North Atlantic service.

As can be noticed, the performance of the two ships was almost equal, even though the *Great Western* was a somewhat larger ship of 1,340 tons compared with the 1,150-ton *Britannia*. Both ships made only one westbound trip in 13 days during 1840–1846. The *Britannia* made a few more voyages in 14 or 15 days than the *Great Western*. Eastbound, the *Britannia* made three voyages in 12 days, while the *Great Western* made none. In total, the *Britannia* made 23 eastbound voyages in 14 days or less, while the *Great Western* made 20.

It is obvious that the *Great Western* would have been able to carry the mails under Government contract as well as the Cunard steamers. But the Admiralty wanted a regular bi-monthly service across the Atlantic, and the Great Western Steamship Company could not afford that. In modern terms, the Admiralty had organized a competitive bidding to outsource some of their services – mail transport, as well as building and maintaining fast steamers, and a competent crew for a potential crisis situation – and chosen one company to take care of it. A fast and reliable service would also draw postage income from the American ships, thus bringing in more revenues to the British Post Office. As the Cunard vessels sailed under a mail contract, letters could be sent by them only via the official post organization.

As there was no co-ordination between the official mail service and the pioneering steamers on the same route, the new potential of faster business information transmission could not always be used in an optimal way. The post offices were not able to handle this kind of situation. In November 1842,

238 See Allington & Greenhill, 17; Robinson (1964) 137–138; Fogg, 20; Hyde (1975), 34–36; Milne (2000), 170–174; Jeffrey J. Safford, 'The decline of the American merchant marine, 1850–1914. An historiographical appraisal'. In Lewis R. Fischer & Gerald E. Panting (ed.) *Change and Adaption in Maritime History. The North Atlantic Fleets in the Nineteenth Century* (Newfoundland, 1985), 73.

239 This was later admitted even by Alfred Holt of Liverpool, who was one of the bitter competitors concurring with subsidized ships on different trade routes, mainly in the West Indies and China: 'Postal subsidies were originally granted in aid of lines of communication which, it was supposed, could not live, or at any rate be maintained with regularity, without them. No doubt the ends aimed at were realised. Communication was opened at an earlier date, and maintained more regularly, than it would have been without subsidies; and some most imposing fleets have come into existence under the system.' Alfred Holt, *Review of the Progress of Steam Shipping during the last Quarter of a Century*. Institute of Civil Engineers. Minutes of Proceedings, vol. 51. (Liverpool, 1877), 9–10.

Diagram 5. Great Western vs. Britannia, duration of westbound trips, July 1840 - December 1846

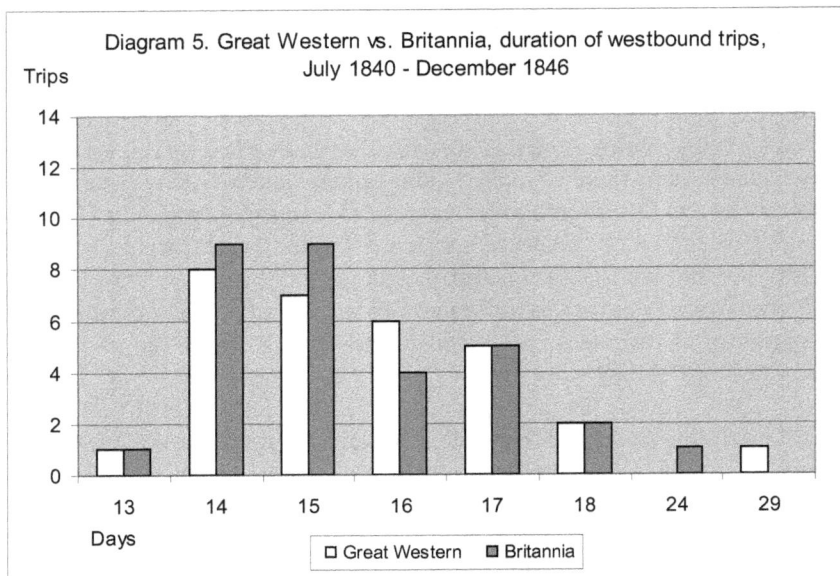

Sources: Sailing lists of Tabeart (1997), 17–19 and Hubbard & Winter, 17–21. – The *Great Western* served on the Bristol / Liverpool–New York route and the *Britannia* on the Liverpool–Halifax–Boston route.

the problem was discussed by some leading cotton importers at a Committee meeting of the American Chamber of Commerce in Liverpool, and as a result, a memorial was sent to the Postmaster General representing 'the grievance and praying' that arrangements would be made to secure the posting of letters to a departing mail steamer as late as possible.[240]

The memorial depicts the problem: 'For example, on the 4th November instant, the day of the departure of the *Acadia* Steamer for Halifax, the letter box was closed at 8 a.m. but on payment of a small fee, letters were received until 9, after which all letters were refused, although the letter bags did not leave the Post Office until a quarter before 12, and the Packet did not get under weigh until 20 minutes past 12. Thus nearly four hours elapsed of the Mail from the Post Office, and the Packet remained in Port upwards of three hours after the latest period of which letters were received at the Post Office upon any terms. It not infrequently happens, especially when the Halifax packet leaves early in the day, that letters which it is of greatest importance to despatch cannot be delivered at the Post Office until within a short time of the departure of the Packet, such for instance as Foreign letters addressed to persons in Liverpool to be forwarded to Correspondents in America received from London or elsewhere by the Morning's Post.'[241]

240 The American Chamber of Commerce (ACC), Liverpool, Minutes of the Committee meeting on 22.11.1842. 380 AME/2. (LRO).
241 The ACC to the Postmaster General 23.11.1842. (380 AME/2, LRO)

The memorial continues with an example: 'In illustration, we would state that the letters by the *British Queen*, which had been some days due, reached Liverpool on the morning of the sailing of the *Acadia* but as the delivery of the letters at the Post Office did not commence until a quarter before nine, it was impossible to answer them or even to acknowledge the receipt before the final closing of the Halifax Mail at nine. Under these circumstances, as the Post Office refused to receive letters, there was the strongest completion, amounting in some cases to an overpowering necessity to send letters in the only way in which they could be conveyed, by the hands of Passengers, and even those who were most anxious to conform to the law were in a manner compelled to evade it.'[242]

According to the memorial, the number of clerks employed in the Liverpool Post Office was inadequate, even for ordinary business, and on packet days the increased influx of letters was quite overwhelming. 'In cases where the tide is so early as to make it necessary for the packet to leave the port at or about noon, the merchants would gladly pay any reasonable fee for the privilege of an extra hour. We would respectfully request that your Lordship will cause such arrangements to be made as may afford the public the advantage of posting letters within the shortest practicable period before the sailing of each packet for Halifax,' the merchants suggested.[243]

Unfortunately this was not the only occasion when the American Chamber of Commerce in Liverpool had to contact the Postmaster General for better ship mail service. In September 1840, two queries were made about the mails that were sent from Liverpool to Southampton for the *British Queen* to be carried to New York. There were serious doubts about the faith of those letters.[244] In February 1846, there were complaints about 'the delay which exists in the despatch of business in the Liverpool Post Office owing to the want of a sufficient number of clerks and particularly calling attention to the delay in the delivery and despatch of ship letters...'[245]

There were obviously things to improve in the logistics of overseas mail transmission. Not only was it important that the sea voyages were as fast as possible and frequent enough, but the inland network should also enable the best possible use of the potential. If the answers to the letters sent from New York on 8 October were not taken on board the *Acadia,* which departed simultaneously with the incoming mails on 4 November, the next option was to send them by the *Columbia*, which departed 15 days later on the 19th. While the *Acadia* made the trip in thirteen days, the *Columbia's* trip took

242 The ACC to the Postmaster General 23.11.1842. (380 AME/2, LRO). – The *British Queen* had been sold to Belgium in September 1841, but she completed three more transatlantic voyages under the Belgian flag. She had departed from New York for the last of these voyages on 8 October 1842, made an extra call at the Azores for coal and arrived at Southampton after a 26-day journey on 3 November. See Bonsor (1975), vol. 1, 58–59.
243 The ACC to the Postmaster General 23.11.1842. (380 AME/2, LRO)
244 The ACC to the Postmaster General 7.9.1840 and 11.9.1840. (380 AME/1, LRO)
245 Resolved at the General Meeting of the American Chamber of Commerce, Liverpool, 12.2.1846 that a memorial would be prepared for the Postmaster General. (380 AME/2, LRO)

17 days, thus causing an extra four days delay.[246] The answers to the letters of 8 October would have arrived in New York in 40 days by the *Acadia* but in 59 days by the *Columbia*. Thus, one or two hours flexibility in the Post Office routines could make an almost three weeks difference in the speed of information without any changes in the speed of the vessel or the frequency of ship departures.[247]

The Cunard Line sailings improved the number of consecutive information circles from five by the American sailing ships and six by the pioneering steamers to almost eight per year in 1841, the first whole calendar year of the company's operations. An example from the mid-1840s shows the strong and weak points of the service:

One of the obvious strengths in the Cunard Line's performance was the punctuality of the departures throughout the year. Yet the early steamers were not able to run equally long voyages, even if their independent averages were very close to each other. This meant that the unpredictability of one single voyage was still a problem, although hardly considered as such by contemporaries, who had never experienced anything better. As can be seen in Table 13, the duration of the westbound voyages included in this particular chain of consecutive information circles varied between 11 and 20 days. Eastbound the duration varied between 12 and 17 days.

As can be noticed by comparing Tables 12 and 13, the pioneering steamers could sometimes enable shorter one-time information circles than the Cunard Line, as they did not need to wait for a fixed sailing date before leaving from New York. Thus, the regularity could also be an obstacle to faster information circulation.

There was no co-operation with the Great Western Steamship Company steamers but instead they were sailing almost side by side. From the business information transmission point of view this naturally meant a series of lost opportunities compared with a situation where the sailings would have complemented each other. From this angle the pioneering steamers (See Table 12) were better organized during the time before government sponsored mail sailings. It seems that the Great Western Steamship Company's strategy was to induce as many passengers and freight customers as possible to use their direct sailings from New York instead of the Cunard Line's sailings from Boston. The *Great Western* and the *Great Britain* typically departed one or a few days before the Cunard sailings. However, their sailings were so much slower that the benefit was not great, as can be noticed in Table 13.

246 See the sailing lists of Hubbard & Winter, 19.
247 The next sailing packet, Dramatic Line's *Sheridan*, would have departed from Liverpool on 15.11.1842. She arrived in New York on 25.12.1842. (*Lloyd's List* 17.1.1843) By this means, the New York letters of 8 October would have received an answer even more slowly, in 78 days.

TABLE 13. *Consecutive information circles enabled by the transatlantic mail steamers in 1845.*

Letter sent by mail ship /company	Ship departure, Liverpool	Ship arrival, New York /Boston	Days	Next departing mail ship, company	Ship departure, New York / Boston	Ship arrival, Liverpool	Days	Information circle, days
Cambria	4.1.	24.1.	20	Cambria	1.2.	13.2.	12	40
Cambria	4.3.	18.3.	14	Cambria	1.4.	13.4.	12	40
Hibernia	19.4.	6.5.	17	Hibernia	16.5.	31.5.	15	42
Caledonia	4.6.	19.6.	15	Caledonia	1.7.	14.7.	13	40
Cambria	19.7.	30.7.	11	Great Western, or Britannia	31.7. / 1.8.*	18.8. / 15.8.	(18) / 14	(30) / 27
Caledonia	19.8.	3.9.	15	Caledonia	16.9.	28.9.	12	40
Hibernia	4.10.	19.10.	15	Great Britain, or Hibernia	28.10. / 1.11.	18.11. / 18.11.	(21) / 17**	(45) / 45
Cambria	19.11.	4.12.	15	Cambria	16.12.	28.12.	12	39
Average, days			15.3				13.4	39

Sources: Sailing lists of Hubbard & Winter, 20–21; and Tabeart (1997), 19. All the other vessels were owned by the Cunard Line, except the *Great Western* and the *Great Britain* owned by the Great Western Steamship Company.

* See note.[248]

** *Hibernia* run aground off Cape Race, Newfoundland, and had to put into St. John's for about two days. (Hubbard & Winter, 21.)

248 The departure date 1.8. was mainly possible if the recipient was in Boston and not in New York. The *Cambria* arrived in Boston on 30.7. at 5.10 p.m. and the *Britannia* departed from there on 1.8. at 2.10 p.m. ('Tenders and contracts for carrying…', 28–29. CP, SJ) The *Great Western* sailed from New York on 31.7., being another uncertain option for a New York business partner to answer the English mail. If the letters had been late for these ships, they would have been carried by the *Cambria* on 16.8. and arrived in Liverpool on 28.8. The rest of the circle would have been changed as follows: *Britannia*, CL, 4.9. from Liverpool, arrived in Boston 19.9., departure by the same ship 1.10. (the *Great Western* sailed from New York 18.9.), arriving in Liverpool 14.10. Departure from Liverpool by the *Caledonia*, CL, 19.10. and arrival in Boston 3.11., departure by the *Great Western* from New York 6.11. and arrival in Liverpool 21.11. – two days after the Cunard steamer *Cambria* had departed. The letter would have then been carried by the *Acadia*, CL, which sailed from Liverpool on 4.12. and arrived in Boston on 19.12. She departed on 1.1. and arrived in Liverpool on 15.1.1846. Thus there was very little help from the other steamships in traffic as there was no cooperation between the sailings. Sometimes a delay of a few hours could make a two-week delay in the information transmission with a chain effect for the rest of the year. See the sailing lists of Hubbard & Winter, 20–21; Tabeart 19.

The Cunard Line's privileged position as the official mail line was often claimed to be the reason for the financial problems of its competitors. But the company's success was not due to the government subsidies alone. It was based on the same qualifications that had made the American sailing packets successful two decades earlier: the regularity and frequency of their sailings, the speed and reliability. These requirements would not have been fulfilled without good shipping management, regardless of government subsidies.

To counter the competition from Cunard, the Great Western Steamship Company had launched a new iron-screw steamer in July 1845, the 3,450-ton *Great Britain*, which was three times larger than any of the Cunarders. The ship's performance did not fill the high expectations, however. She met continuous difficulties and, in September 1846 on her fifth outward voyage, went aground off Ireland and was only refloated the following summer. The company was not in a financial position to recondition her and she was sold for £24,000 – about one-fifth of her original cost.[249]

The Cunard mail contract was renewed in 1846, despite all claims to the Halifax and Boston Mails Committee, which was investigating the issue. Cunard's plan to make New York the western terminus for their transatlantic service was complained of as ruining the Great Western Steamship Company, which had served on the route carrying mails for eight years without government subsidies. A member of the Select Committee proposed that the contract for the New York mails would be opened to public tender, but this was not acceptable to the majority of the Committee.[250]

The Great Western Steamship Company would, of course, have been financially more successful had they received at least part of the government subsidies, but the contract was for regular mail service and some naval readiness, and the Admiralty had already received what they needed. Why should the government have provided subsidies to every company who wanted to carry mail across the Atlantic?

In the light of the early experiments by the Post Office as an owner of mail steamboats, it was not a poor idea to outsource the service to a private company. In the absence of government support, there would have been no regular mail steamship service across the Atlantic for years. Small companies with one or two steamers departing from different ports when they had full cargo could not be called a line service. The situation would later change dramatically, due to technical improvements that enabled emigrant transport by steamships in the late 1850s, as will be described in Chapter V.3.

The Cunard Line's new contract included two routes, one to New York and another one to Halifax and Boston. The sailings would be bi-monthly from each port on alternate Saturdays eight months in the year, and monthly during the winter. The New York service began in January 1848, in good time before the Americans would start their own mail steamship service on the same route.[251]

---

249 See Bonsor (1975), vol. 1, 62–64; Fogg, 12–20.
250 Robinson (1964), 138; Hyde (1975), 35; Babcock, 88–90; Tyler, 161–164.
251 Until September 1850, the New York ship also made a call to Halifax, in both directions.
     The trip between New York and Halifax took approximately 48 hours. See Arnell (1980),

Four new steamships – *America, Niagara, Europa* and *Canada* – were built for the purpose, at a final cost of about £90,000 each. As Fox notes, most of the capital for these steamers came from private investors, while the mail subsidy mainly provided 'seed money' and the prestige of a government contract.[252] As with all the other companies, the mail contract lines built ships on private risk capital, and new investments were continuously needed to meet the requirements of faster and more reliable voyages. During the coming years, many shipping companies would fail, even if they were mail carriers on behalf of their national governments.

For the Cunard Line, the decision to invest in the New York service seemed to be right from the beginning. In 1848, the duties collected on Cunard cargoes in New York averaged $10,500 and in Boston $29,500. In 1850 the respective figures were $118,000 in New York and $63,000 in Boston.[253]

The Great Western Steamship Company gave up the struggle and sold the *Great Western* to the Royal Mail Steam Packet Line for the West Indian service. The *Great Britain* started a new career on the Australian route.[254]

Wind vs. steam – the finale

The start of the Cunard Line's New York service has been called the final end of the period of importance for the American sailing packets. Even if there had already been steamers on the North Atlantic route for ten years, their schedules had mainly been those of regular traders, not of liners. As long as Cunard was sailing to Boston instead of New York, the packets could hold their own in the competition, but the line's coming to New York was too much for them. The packets could compete rather successfully against steamships that operated singly, but when the steamships adopted the line principle, the old 'canvasbacks' had to give way.[255]

The steamships' speed alone had not been enough to displace the sailing packets from the North Atlantic traffic. Even if the most important mails as well as bullion and specie had been transferred to steamers from the very beginning,[256] they were not able to carry much freight, and the passengers preferred the comfort of the sailing ships. Also the bulk mail, especially eastbound, was still carried in great amounts by the sailing packets.

The size of the sailing packets reached their peak during the early 1850s in conjunction with the boom in the emigrant business. The first sailing packets

---

308–310; Hubbard & Winter, 23. In 1852 the service was made weekly throughout the year, the ships leaving from Liverpool on Saturday of each week alternately for the two American ports. Hyde (1975), 35. – For the timing of the contract, see Fox, 114–115.

252 See Fox, 115, 121.

253 Albion (1939), 325.

254 Robinson (1964), 138; Tyler, 165–166. The *Great Britain* made 32 round trips to Australia between 1852 and 1876. Later on she was sold, her engines were removed and she became a full-rigged sailing ship. She was beached at the Falkland Islands in 1937 and was towed back to Britain for restoration in the 1970s. The ship can now be visited in the old Great Western Dock in Bristol as a historical monument. See Fogg, 29, 177, 182–186; Bonsor (1975), vol. 1, 64–65.

255 Albion (1938), 253.

256 Albion (1938), 258.

of over 1,400 tons were built in the late 1840s. In 1860 the average size of the packets on the New York – Liverpool route was 1,320 tons – three times the size of the first Black Ballers in the 1820s. Some of these ships had a capacity for 800 or 900 steerage passengers. The largest of all regular packets was the *Amazon* of 1770 tons, built in 1854.[257] Even though this was the period when the American clippers were world famous for their speed, the Chinese tea race and various adventures in distant waters, the information transmission on the North Atlantic route was steadily being transferred to the steamers.

TABLE 14. *Average size of the mail-carrying American sailing packets, in tons.*

	1820 (n)	1830 (n)	1840 (n)	1850 (n)	1860 (n)	1870 (n)	1880 (n)
Liver-pool	420 (5)	538 (17)	745 (20)	1,074 (28)	1,320 (21)	1,400 (5)	–
London	–	416 (10)	593 (12)	912 (19)	1,087 (17)	1,013 (5)	1,029 (4)
Havre	–	428 (12)	604 (16)	893 (13)	1,030 (10)	–	–
All, on average	420 (5)	471 (39)	662 (48)	984 (60)	1,175 (48)	1,207 (10)	1,029 (4)

Source: Calculated from the lists of mail-carrying packets published by Staff, 121–127. – The number of packets differs somewhat from Albion's figures in Table 10 as the table above also includes replacements made during that particular year.

Even if the size of the sailing packets grew markedly, their service speed did not follow the trend after the introduction of steamships on the route in the late 1830s. As can be seen in Diagram 6, the proportion of 20–29 days and 30–39 days for westbound packet trips was about the same – even somewhat smaller – in 1845 than in 1835, and the proportion of the longest trips of 40–49 or 50–59 days had grown correspondingly.[258] There seems to be no signs of speed improvements after 1835.

Another phenomenon which indicates that the sailing packets were losing their hold on the first class business – mail, fine freight and cabin passengers – was that they no longer cared about the punctuality of the sailing dates as much as they did in the 1830s. If the reliability of a mail ship service is measured by the regularity of sailings and the safety records, the performance of the American sailing packets in the mid-1840s was noticeably below such expectations.

257 Staff, 121–127; Cutler (1967), 377–392.
258 In 1825, 11 dates are missing from 48 sailings; in 1835 one date is missing from 48 sailings; and in 1845 four dates are missing from 70 sailings.

Diagram 6. American sailing packets, duration of westbound trips (% of all), Liverpool - New York, 1825, 1835, 1845

trips

70
60
50
40
30
20
10
0

20-29 days | 30-39 days | 40-49 days | 50-59 days

■ 1825 □ 1835 ■ 1845

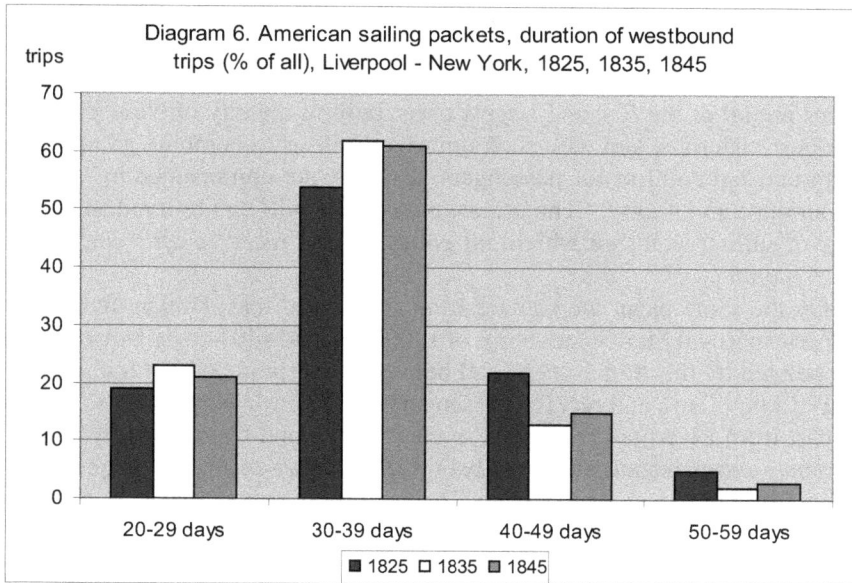

Source: *Lloyd's List 1825, 1835, 1845; Liverpool Customs Bills of Entry, 1825, 1835.*
The number of sailings included is 37 in 1825, 47 in 1835 and 66 in 1845.

As can be seen in Table 15 (in the end of the book, p. 426), the departures from Liverpool were mostly delayed from their scheduled sailing dates in 1844–1845. Only 25 sailings out of 147, or 17%, took place on the scheduled date. The number of disasters at sea had also grown alarmingly.

Despite one of the poorest records in sailing regularity, the Red Star Line advertised in the *Liverpool Mercury* in January 1845: 'Sails on the 26th of every Month… These ships are all of first class, recently built in the city of New York, and for strength, beauty of model, punctuality and swiftness of sailing, as well as for extent and comfort of cabin accommodations, are not surpassed by any in the trade, and their commanders are men of great experience… To insure punctuality in sailing, no goods can be received onboard unless they are down two days before the day of sailing.'[259]

The Black Ball Line and the New Line did not mention punctuality in their advertisements, despite being the most punctual of all the sailing packet lines in 1844–1845. The sailing dates were naturally expressed. Also their ships were 'of first class' and commanded by 'men of character and experience' or 'men of experience and ability'. Each sailing packet line offered the Atlantic crossing in their 'elegant and commodious' cabins for £25, everything included except wines and spirits, which could be procured from the steward.[260]

The Dramatic Line, managed by Edward K. Collins, later to be an important steamship line owner, had appeared in the transatlantic traffic in 1836. Albion

259 *Liverpool Mercury* 24.1.1845.
260 *Liverpool Mercury* 24.1.1845.

calls the line 'a group of splendid ships that momentarily threw most of the others in the shade'.[261] So did the company's advertisement, too: 'Line of Packets for New York. Sailing of the eleventh of every month... These ships are all of the first and largest class, built in the city of New York, of the best materials, and with such improvements as to combine great speed with unusual comfort for passengers, and they are commanded by men of experience and ability... The utmost punctuality will be observed as on the day of sailing to insure which, *no goods can be received after the 9th of each month...*'[262]

On the same page, the Cunard Line announced that 'British and North American Royal Mail Steam Ships of 1200 tons, and 440 horses' power each, Appointed by the Admiralty to sail between Liverpool and Boston, calling at Halifax to land and receive passengers and Her Majesty's Mails' would depart from Liverpool on the 4th of each month and from April (when the summer season began) additionally on the 19th. Passengers' luggage should be on board the day prior to sailing. The price for the passage was 38 guineas, including provisions but without wines and liquors, which could be obtained on board. The steward's fee was one guinea, and dogs were charged £5 each. At the end of the advertisement, there was an important note: 'All *Letters and Newspapers* intended to be sent by these vessels must pass through the Post-office, and none will be received at the Agent's Offices.'[263]

Cunard's advertisement did not mention comfortable accommodation or experienced commanders, even though each captain's name was well pointed out in the advertisement, and they were in fact very experienced.[264] The accommodation on the early steamers was again one of their greatest disadvantages and nothing to advertise when compared with the sailing packets.

The advertisements in the *Liverpool Mercury* on that day[265] included two sailing packets that had sailed from Liverpool on 26 November and 1 December 1844, and were never heard of again. The *United States* of the Red Star Line and the *England* of the Black Ball Line met a tremendous storm and were lost with several other ships, including the Havre Line packet *Normandie* as well as the Boston Line packet *Dorchester*, the crew of which was saved by the New Line packet *Rochester* on her way to New York.[266] The

---

261 Albion (1938), 43–44.

262 *Liverpool Mercury* 24.1.1845. Italics are in the original text. – It should be noted that none of the American sailing packet lines used their well-known nick names (Black Ball Line, etc.) in their advertisements in 1845, but the names Old Line; New Line; New York Line; Line of Packets for New York, etc. Only in the 1850s would the corporate identity, built on easily recognizable symbols of the company flags, become marketable commodities and give 'an air of solidity and reliability to what were often *ad hoc* arrangements', especially in the emigrant business. See Milne (2000), 165.

263 *Liverpool Mercury* 24.1.1845.

264 According to Babcock: 'The officers were picked from men of long experience at sea. Mates generally had to have served before as masters of other ships. The later captains had to have served as mates on Cunarders. The engineers were experienced in the profession and their assistants were bred in the trade. In short, the primary injunction of safety was carried out with a thoroughness hitherto unknown to the sea.' (Babcock, 54)

265 *Liverpool Mercury* 24.1.1845.

266 *Lloyd's List* 3.2.1845; 10.4.1845. Missing ships were always awaited for several months as their voyages could have been seriously lengthened by bad weather or other

companies kept the schedules of the *United States* and the *England* in their advertisements until 21 March. By then, the Red Star Line had replaced the *United States* by a transient ship called the *Empire* and the Black Ball Line had replaced the *England* by its own packet named *Oxford,* which should have sailed two weeks later and arrived in Liverpool on the same day as the newspaper was published.[267]

The Cunard Line's advertisement also included a replacement. One of the company's original steamers, the *Columbia,* had been wrecked off Nova Scotia in July 1843, fortunately without loss of life or mail.[268] Her replacement, the *Cambria,* mentioned in the advertisement, had just left on her maiden voyage and was now advertised as departing for the following one.[269] Cunard had also purchased a fifth vessel for the transatlantic route; the *Hibernia* was launched just before the loss of the *Columbia* and took her place until the new ship was ready for the route.[270]

In the pressure of hard competition, packet schedules were tightened when reorganizing sailings due to disasters, new launchings, etc. In 1844–1845, several ships made three-month round trips instead of the traditional four months, calculated from one Liverpool departure to the following one. All these ships – the *Virginian* and *Waterloo* of the Red Star Line as well as the *Independence* and *Patrick Henry* of the Blue Swallowtail Line[271] – were among the fastest on the North Atlantic route.[272] However, these short round trips did not depend on speed, which was in all cases average, but just changes in the schedule. The efficiency of the packet sailings could apparently have been improved by tightening schedules, but it would also have increased the risk of problems and delays.

As can be seen in Table 15 (in the end of the book, p. 426), westbound sailings involved a high risk of disasters. Of the 143 recorded trips of 1844–1845, at least a dozen ended in reported losses or other problems. Additionally, one loss of 'main top-mast etc.' was also reported from an eastbound voyage.[273] Interestingly, five of these misadventures happened to the same ships, the *Virginian* and the *Independence*, which were among the speediest of all in packet history, and made the three-month round trips.[274] Also the lost *England* was one of the fastest vessels. They had all sailed from Liverpool to New York in three weeks or less. The *United States* was in the medium speed class in packet records of 1818–1858.[275]

According to Albion's calculations, nearly one packet in six was totally lost in service. The figure could also be put more nicely: only 22 of nearly

difficulties.
267 *Liverpool Mercury*, January–March, 1845.
268 See Bonsor (1975), vol. 1, 75; Babcock, 73–74.
269 *Liverpool Mercury* 24.1.1845.
270 See Bonsor (1975), vol. 1, 75; Babcock, 75.
271 See Table 14.
272 Albion (1938), 276–281, 318–319.
273 The arrival of the *Independence* off Liverpool on 2 September 1844 was reported in *Lloyd's List* 3.9.1844; arrival at port 4.9.1844.
274 The *Independence* actually took back her own place in the schedule in the spring of 1845, having lost it due to repairs after storm damage in December 1844.
275 Albion (1938), 278–279.

FIG. 10. *In case of a disaster at sea, the only hope for saving the people on board and the mails was that another ship would pass by and pick them up before it was too late. – An old German postcard 'Rettung naht' (by E. Schneider).*

6,000 packet crossings ended in such wrecks.[276] It seems, however, that the hard competition between the sailing packet lines as well as between sail and steam made the packet captains take more risks than they did in the earlier years. Most of the wrecks took place during the period when the competition between sail and steam was hardest.

From a mail transmission point of view, the trend was most alarming. Between 1838 and 1847 no less than 21 mail-carrying ships were lost on the North Atlantic route – two each year on average. Two of the ships were Falmouth packets and two were steamers, while 17 were American sailing packets. Eight were on the New York–Liverpool route, two on the Boston–Liverpool route, two on the New York–London route, and five on the New York–Havre route. Six of the ships just disappeared, and were lost with all hands.[277] It is notable that two out of every three wrecks took place in November–February, indicating that the packet captains took too heavy risks, especially during the rough winter sailings.

The only precautionary measure to ensure solid business information transmission across the Atlantic was to send duplicates. This was very typical

276 Albion (1938), 202.
277 See Staff, 121–128; Bonsor (1980), vol. V, 1888–1897; Pawlyn, 132–133. – In total, more than 600 British ships, including all kinds of coastal vessels, were lost each year in 1833–1835 and 1841–1842. The loss of lives varied between 1,450 and 1,560. See *BPP, Shipping Safety 3,* First and Second Reports of the Select Committee on Shipwrecks in 1843, Appendix 4, 52.

during the shift period. The duplicates also ensured the fastest possible dispatch of information.

It is not easy to find relevant numbers of North Atlantic merchant correspondence from this period. For example, there is almost nothing in the Liverpool archives. Fortunately, the huge correspondence of the London-based banking firm, Frederick Huth Co., was partly saved from being burnt during the wartime energy crisis by a philatelist, and these letters can easily be discovered in the philatelic exhibitions of today.[278] A sample of Huth's correspondence from the period 1836–1850, including 74 transatlantic letters to London, interestingly depicts the change from sail to steam:[279]

As can be seen in Table 16, business information transmission by sailing ships did not end in 1838 when the mail-carrying steamships started their regular trade across the Atlantic. The sample here is naturally too small to give any reliable figures on the share of each means of communications during the period. It is too small even to tell anything about these shares in the incoming mail of Frederick Huth Co. However, it clearly demonstrates

TABLE 16. *From sail to steam. A sample of Frederick Huth's correspondence, 1836–1850.*

Year	Merchant ship	American sailing packet	Steamer	Total
1836	–	3	–	3
1837	1	4	–	5
1838	–	4	1	6
1839	1	2	3	6
1840	1	3	2	6
1841	–	5	5	10
1842	–	4	2	6
1843	–	2	1	3
1844	–	1	2	3
1845	2	1	1	4
1846	–	1	3	4
1847	–	1	5	6
1848	–	–	3	3
1849	–	–	3	3
1850	–	–	7	7
total	5	31	38	74

Source: Letters received by the Frederick Huth & Co. in the following postal historical collections: SRLC, JSC, JAC, STC, and RWC.

278 Other well-known company names of this period in philatelic collections are e.g. Morrison, Cryder & Co. in London, Rothschild & Sons in London and Paris, Louis Roederer in Reims, August Martell in Cognac, Abraham Bell & Co. in New York and Daniel Gibb in San Francisco.

279 This sample is compiled from letters exhibited in five philatelic collections: SRLC; JSC; JAC; Seppo Talvio, *North Atlantic Mail* (2006) (STC); and Richard F. Winter, *Transatlantic Mails. Steamship* (1988) (RWC). Photocopies of each cover with relevant postal historical descriptions are held by the writer.

that a great part of the bulk mail – especially eastwards – was still carried by sailing ships during the first decade after the launching of the transatlantic steamship service.

There is no reason to believe that any part of this material would have been preferred in the philatelic collections. They are all bulk mail and carry no prepaid postage stamps, which would make them especially attractive or valuable. The letters are collected because of their postal markings: routes, ship names, rates and forwarding markings, and none of them should have caused distortion in the sample. Even if the proportions might be slightly different in a larger sample, it seems obvious that the American sailing packets dominated the mail route until the steamship traffic started and that they kept a good share of it for several years before the steamers finally took over the business.

The sample also shows that merchant ships were still used for information transmission on the North Atlantic seaway, even if this was uncommon. One of the letters was sent from Buenos Aires by a merchant ship instead of a government packet, and another one was sent directly from New Orleans instead of using the coastal route to New York, from where the letters were normally forwarded to Liverpool by the American sailing packets.

Interestingly, most letters were sent via Liverpool, even if Frederick Huth Co. was located in London and there would have been direct packet services to London as well. Three of the five merchant ship letters, 25 of the 31 packet letters, and 32 of the 38 steamship letters arrived via Liverpool – 57 of 74 letters in all. Additionally, it happened twice that the original routing was via Liverpool, but the forwarding agent in New York had sent the letter by an earlier departing London packet instead.

Regarding the steamship letters, the reason is naturally that Liverpool was the home port of the Cunard Line as well as of the short-lived pioneering steamer *Liverpool,* and that the *Great Western* had also used Liverpool as her home port since 1843. For most of the sailing packet arrivals, there is no explanation other than the more frequent schedules of the Liverpool packets, and maybe the reputation for faster sailings. Since the railway was opened for the whole distance between Liverpool and London in 1838,[280] the letters usually arrived in the City on the following day after the ship had entered the port at Liverpool. If the ship arrival fell on a Saturday, the letters were dispatched in London on Monday.[281]

At least 19 of the 74 letters were duplicates, or originals of which a duplicate had been sent by another vessel. In some cases, it is mentioned in the letter by which ship another one of the letters had been sent. In several cases it remains unknown, however.

Up to 1838, duplicates of letters were normally sent by two different sailing packets from New York. None of the duplicates mentions merchantmen, and

---

280 The London–Birmingham railway was opened in 1837, while the Birmingham–Liverpool connection already existed. After finalizing the work the trains were able to run to their permanent terminus in Birmingham in late 1838. See J.H. Clapham, *An Economic History of Modern Britain. The Early Railway Age 1820–1850.* (Cambridge, 1930), 387; Vaughan, 89–90.

281 Arrival postmarks of the letters in the Huth correspondence.

none of the letters by merchant ships indicates that it would be a duplicate. It seems that merchant ship letters were not alternatives to normal mail on the North Atlantic route but were used on special occasions, probably as consignee's letters in cases where their own cargo was sent by the same trader. As the Falmouth packet service to New York had been closed down in the 1820s, this alternative as a duplicate was out of the question.[282]

From 1838, it was common to send one of the letters by a steamship and the other one by a sailing packet. From 1844, in all cases where a duplicate records a ship name, both letters were sent by steamers.

A particularly interesting duplicate was the one of which the original, dated 23 November, 1850, in Havana, Cuba, had been sent on the day of writing by the Royal Mail Line's steamer *Conway* to St. Thomas, where it arrived on 2 December. The letter proceeded on the next day by the same company's mail steamer *Avon*, which arrived at Southampton on 22 December, 1850. Meanwhile, the duplicate letter was continued by the writer in Havana on 2 December, and sent by another route to Frederick Huth & Co. in London. The letter was carried by the United States Mail Steamship Company's steamer *Georgia*, which departed from Havana on the day of writing the continuation, and it arrived in New York on 7 December. From there, it was forwarded by an agent, A.C. Rossire & Co., to the Cunard Line steamer *Europa*, which departed from Boston on 11 December and arrived at Liverpool on the 21st. The letter was received in London on the 23rd – probably simultaneously with the original, which had departed from Havana nine days earlier.[283] This can indeed be called professional use of existing international mail steamship services at that time.

As many of the letters arrived from distant places like Havana or New Orleans, forwarding agents were often used to ensure that the information was sent by the fastest possible means.[284] If the writer was not sure of the ship schedules, he could write 'per first Packet' or 'per first Steamer' on the cover and the forwarding agent, often a well-known merchant house, took care of the rest. In these cases the letter was sometimes addressed to the forwarding agent, who struck off his name and address and sent the letter forward to the final recipient.

New York agents in the Huth correspondence were, for example, Aldrick & Kruger, William W. De Forest & Co., Goodhue & Co. and Meyer & Stucken.

---

282 There was one Falmouth packet connection in the sample from the Mexico route: a duplicate letter sent from Tampico on 26.7.1836 via New Orleans, New York and Liverpool to London.It arrived in 69 days. The original was sent by the Falmouth packet *Seagull*, which sailed from Vera Cruz on 7.8. and from Havana on 26.8.1836, arriving at Falmouth on 26.9.1836. This letter arrived in London in 64 or 65 days. For the sailing dates of the *Seagull*, see *Lloyd's List* 30.9.1836.

283 A German language merchant letter from Havana 23.11. & 2.12.1850 via New York and Boston to Fredrick Huth & Co., London (STC); Phil J. Kenton & Harry G. Parsons, *Early Routing of the Royal Mail Steam Packet Company 1842–1879* (Surrey, England, 1999), 122, 126; Theron J. Wierenga (ed. Richard F. Winter), *United States Incoming Steamship Mail 1847–1875* (Austin, TX, 2000), 341; Hubbard & Winter, 28.

284 For the forwarding system, see Kenneth Rowe, *The Postal History of the Forwarding Agents* (Kentucky, 1984), 1–22. A useful Internet link related to this source can be found (summer 2006) at the address http://www.pbbooks.com/webfa.htm

FIG. 11. *The port of Boston.* *(Ballou's Pictorial, 1856.)*

Letters could also be forwarded by Hale's Foreign Letter Office or Gilpin's Exchange, Reading Room and Foreign Letter Office. In New Orleans at least Hermann & Co. was one of the used forwarding agents; in Boston, Shelton Brothers & Co. and J. Winslow & Sons.[285]

In addition to the Frederick Huth Co. correspondence, a sample of transatlantic business letters from the same period can be found in the collection of Rathbone Bros & Co. This small portion of letters, only 23 from the period 1841–1849, gives rather similar results to the sample above. Ten of the letters are from the years 1841–1842. Two of them were sent by sailing packets, and the rest by steamers. Of the 13 letters from 1848–1849, 11 were sent by Cunarders and two by other mail-carrying steamships.[286]

At least five of the ten earlier period's letters refer to duplicates in one way or another. William Rathbone Jr., the writer of the letter dated New York, 30 April 1841, notes: 'Dear Sirs, I wrote on the 28th instant pr *Columbia* with such information as I could collect of your friends here, which however was not definite enough to make it worthwhile to send a duplicate...'[287] Three of the letters are duplicates or enclose duplicates, and in one case the writer tells that he will write 'more fully by the steamer which will probably reach you before this'. This letter was sent by a sailing packet and received on 28 July, while the steamer *Britannia* arrived in Liverpool one day later, on 29 July.[288]

285 Frederich Huth Co.'s correspondence 1836–1850 in JAC.

286 Letters to Rathbone Bros & Co., Liverpool, 1841–1849 in Rathbone Collection (RP XXIV.2, SJ). – Rathbone Bros & Co. was a well-known merchant house, at that time especially engaged in cotton imports from America. See Williams, David M., 'Liverpool Merchants and the Cotton Trade 1820–1850'. In Merchants and Mariners: Selected writings of David M. Williams, 42–51. In *Research of Maritime History No. 18*. (Newfoundland, 2000).

287 William Rathbone Jr. to Rathbone Esq., Liverpool, from New York 30.4.1841. (RP XXIV.2, SJ).

288 William Rathbone Jr. in a letter addressed to Rathbone Esq., Liverpool, from New York 7.7.1841. Arrival marking of the recipient 28 July. (RP XXIV.2, SJ). – The *Britannia's* sailing dates, see Hubbard & Winter, 18. – Some of the Rathbone letters were forwarded

Although it caused much trouble in the company routines to send duplicates and even triplicates of letters across the Atlantic, and the postage rates were rather high, the cost was considered acceptable because of the general unpredictability of the sailings.[289] The examples above were all from eastbound journeys. The difference between sailing packets and steamers was more evident westbound.

In 1845, there were no less than 102 mail ship departures from Liverpool to New York / Boston. All mail-carrying North Atlantic steamships departed from Liverpool that year, in addition to no less than five American sailing packet lines.[290] Compared with the situation ten years earlier, the improvement in the scale of options in business information transmission was remarkable.

In addition, some of the regular traders called themselves 'packets' or were hired as transients by the packet lines for a few voyages, and they could and often did carry letters and newspapers on board as well. 'News and Observations, American News' in the *Liverpool Mercury* of 31 January 1845 gives a good example: 'The New York packet ship *Sea*, Captain Edwards, arrived on Monday, bringing New York papers to the 11th inst. Their contents are unimportant both politically and commercially...'[291]

Even though most 'American News' of that time was carried by Cunard steamers, a fast sailing packet could still be a news-bringer eastbound in 1845, especially in winter when there were not many steamship sailings. The *Sea* is not listed as a line packet by Albion or Staff, but Cutler mentions her as one of the New Line's vessels that year.[292]

It can easily be noticed in Diagram 7 why the sailing packets lost the competition against steamers in mail transmission, especially westwards. The benefits of steam power in the struggle against the westerly winds were so obvious that there was practically no reason to send letters by sailing ships any more. There were few situations where the next sailing packet would have had an even theoretical chance of arriving in New York before the next steamer. Instead of sending an original by a steamer and a duplicate by a packet, or vice versa, duplicates were now being sent by two successive steamers to ensure solid information transmission, even in the case of misadventures at sea.

---

by an agent: two by T.W. Ward in Boston and one by the Gilpin's Exchange, Reading Room and Foreign Letter Office in New York.

289 Hargest notes that the 'Cunarders' made additional savings possible: 'Their relatively fast crossings, together with the regularity and certainty of their sailings, were obviating the necessity for sending many duplicate copies of the same letter by different ships in order to be certain that a copy would arrive as early as possible, or would arrive at all.' See Hargest, 2. – Duplicates played no further role in Rathbone's correspondence in the 1850s.

290 In addition to the Dramatic Line, there was also another later established packet company on the New York – Liverpool route: the Red Cross Line, established in 1844. A well-known mail-carrying packet company on the Boston – Liverpool route was also Enoch Train's White Diamond Line, which began operations in the same year. See Staff, 127; and Cutler (1967), 371–373.

291 *Liverpool Mercury* 31.1.1845.

292 Cutler (1967), 381

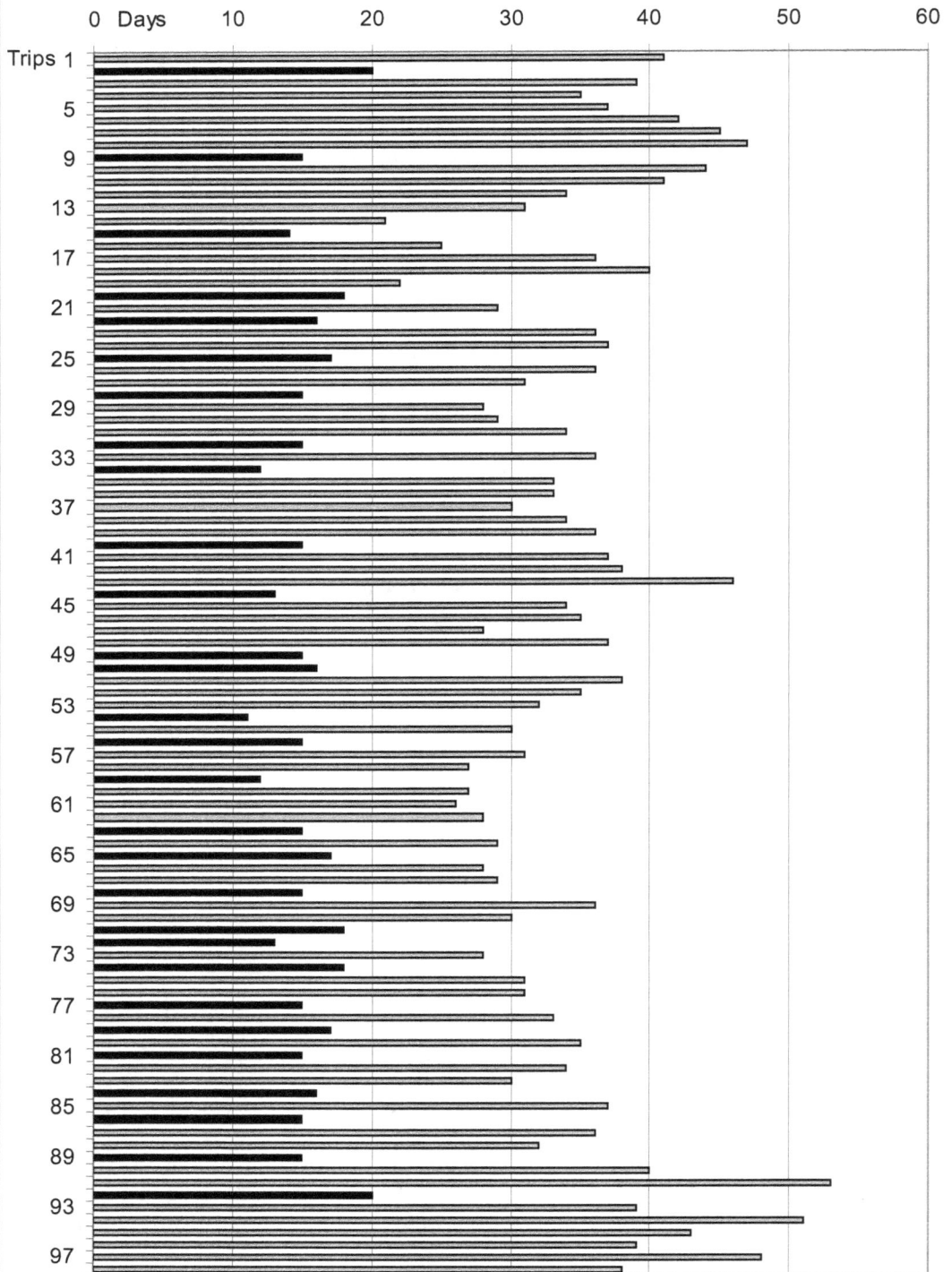

Diagram 7. Duration of westbound trips, the American sailing packets and the mail carrying steamers, Liverpool - New York / Boston, 1845

Source: Lloyd's List 1845; sailing lists of Tabeart, 19. – The difference between sail and steam was remarkable on westbound voyages. The **black** pillars depict the sailings of the mail-carrying steamers from Liverpool to New York or Boston in 1845: the Cunard vessels and the pioneering steamers *Great Western*, *Great Britain* and *Massachusetts* (an American steamer, which only made two round trips). The **light** pillars depict the sailing packet voyages. Their departures on 18.2.1845, 22.9.1845, 29.10.1845 and 7.11.1845 are missing from the table. They should have been placed between trips 11 & 12, 73 & 74, 82 & 83 and 84 & 85.

Even though the Cunard Line's monthly winter sailings were the only ones conducted by steamers in the mid-1840s, using them in business information transmission was notably faster than using the sailing packets.

Table 17 shows the different options for business communications from November 1844 to February 1845. During those four winter months, at least 30 mail-carrying line vessels sailed from Liverpool to New York or Boston. In November there were eight ships, in December seven, in January seven and in February seven – approximately two each week.

The duration of the New York packets' westbound sailings varied between 27 and 51 days, and the duration of eastbound sailings between 16 and 31 days. The respective figures for the Cunard Line steamships were 15 to 20 days westbound and 12 to 16 days eastbound. The steamers were so much faster that it was normally better to keep the letter or its duplicate waiting for the next steamship departure instead of sending it by any sailing packet that would leave before that date.

If, for example, a letter had been sent from Liverpool to New York by the Cunard steamer *Britannia* on 5 November 1844, the answer to it would have arrived in Liverpool on 16 December. An answer to that letter could have been sent by the *Cambria* on 4 January, 1845, and the answer to that letter would have been in Liverpool on 13 February. If the sender had instead used the sailing packet *Queen of the West* for carrying the original letter, he would have received the first answer to it only on 13 February, 1845, by the same vessel.[293] The steamship service enabled two consecutive information circles for correspondence compared with only one by the sailing packets.

This can be called the 'leverage effect' of steamship communications. It was not only the single fast crossing of the ocean that counted. As communication is basically a two-way activity, this effect doubled the impact of the regular steamship mail service, being thus even more revolutionary than has generally been estimated in historical research. And, as will be demonstrated later, not only could the technology be improved but also the whole system of communications.

293 The *Queen of the West* was one of the finest sailing packets of the time. She was a new 1,160-ton vessel (the Cunarders were 1,150 tons) that had sailed from New York to Liverpool in 15 days in February of the same year. According to Cutler, packets of that size and finish – 'floating palaces' – cost $100,000 and upwards, which was nearly double the cost of the average packets of the thirties. See Cutler (1967), 254–257, 378.

TABLE 17. *Mail sailings on the Liverpool–New York / Boston route, winter 1844–1845.*

ship	line	sailed from Liver-pool	arrived in NY (B)	days	sailed from NY (B)	arrived in Liver-pool	days
Yorkshire	BB	1.11.44	29.11.44	28	16.1.45	8.2.45	23
s/s Britannia	**CL**	**5.11.44**	**22.11.44** (B)	**17**	**1.12.44**	**16.12.44**	**15**
Queen of the West	NL	8.11.44	11.12.44	33	- -	13.2.45	- -
Sheridan	DL	14.11.44	30.12.44	46	29.1.45	14.2.45	16
Cambridge	BB	17.11.44	7.1.45	51	1.2.45	24.2.45	23
s/s Caledonia	**CL**	**19.11.44**	**7.12.44** (B)	**18**	**16.12.44**	**29.12.44**	**13**
Patrick Henry	BSw	22.11.44	9.1.45	48	8.2.45	26.2.45	18
United States	RS	26.11.44	'went missing'	–	–	–	–
England	BB	1.12.44	'went missing'	–	–	–	–
s/s Acadia	**CL**	**4.12.44**	**21.12.44** (B)	**17**	**1.1.45**	**14.1.45**	**13**
Rochester	NL	6.12.44	11.1.45	36	- -	22.3.45	- -
Garrick	DL	12.12.44	15.1.45	34	- -	26.3.45	- -
Oxford	BB	18.12.44	20.1.45	33	- -	21.3.45	- -
George Washington	BSw	- -	- -	- -	6.3.45	26.3.45	20
Independence	BSw	25.12.44, put back	–	–	–	–	–
Virginian	RS	28.12.44	14.2.45	48	- -	8.4.45	- -
Montezuma	BB	3.1.45	13.2.45	41	8.3.45	8.4.45	31
s/s Cambria	**CL**	**4.1.45**	**24.1.45** (B)	**20**	**1.2.45**	**13.2.45**	**12**
Hottinguer	NL	8.1.45	16.2.45	39	- -	13.4.45	- -
Roscius	DL	12.1.45	16.2.45	35	27.3.45	22.4.45	26
Europe	BB	17.1.45	13.2.45	27	1.4.45	26.4.45	25
John R. Skiddy	RS	22.1.45	5.3.45	42	1.4.45	26.4.45	25
Independence	BSw	28.1.45	14.3.45	45	8.4.45	28.4.45	20
Samuel Hicks*	RS	29.1.45	?	?	- -	- -	- -
s/s Hibernia	**CL**	**4.2.45**	**19.2.45** (B)	**15**	**1.3.45**	**17.3.45**	**16**
New York	BB	4.2.45	23.3.45	47	- -	11.5.45	- -
Liverpool	NL	7.2.45	23.3.45	44	- -	26.4.45	- -
Siddons	DL	11.2.45	24.3.45	41	- -	26.4.45	- -
Columbus	BB	18.2.45	- -	- -	- -	3.6.45	- -
Ashburton	BSw	25.2.45	31.3.45	34	- -	11.5.45	- -
Stephen Whitney	RS	28.2.45	31.3.45	31	- -	4.6.45	- -

Source: *Lloyd's List 1844–1845.* – Steamship departures are marked in **bold**. Only the Cunard Line had winter sailings at that time.
* The sailing of *Samuel Hicks* 29.1.1845 was advertised by the company in the *Liverpool Mercury* as one of the line's regular sailings. She might have been a transient. (*Liverpool Mercury* 24.1.1845)

Benefits of Competition

New mail contract lines – Cunard Line vs. Collins Line – Ocean Line and Havre Line, the forgotten contract companies – Competition and business information transmission – Changes in the transatlantic mail services in the late 1850s – Emigrant lines take their share of mail transport – Effects on business information transmission – Open competition, the new deal on mail contracts – In search of glory - reputation and real life – What happened to the speed of business information transmission?

New mail contract lines

Actually, the Cunard Line never had a monopoly in the North Atlantic mail transmission. Until the late 1840s, the company competed with the American sailing packets and the pioneering steamers, and after that with foreign contract mail carriers.[294] As letters carried by the competitors in the 1840s are not considered rarer in philatelic collections than those carried by the Cunard steamers, the amount of mail carried must have been large by all these means of communications. One reason for using alternatives to mail contract vessels was the high postage rates, which could be partly avoided by private shipments.

It did not take long before other governments adopted the British model for their transatlantic mail services, not so much for faster communications but for the commercial interest and the prestige of the country, as the French Minister Thiers put it in the French Parliament in 1840.[295] In April 1847, after a few years' hesitation, the French Government announced that it had made a ten-year contract with Compagnie Générale des Paquebots Transatlantiques, or the Hérout & de Handel, for a mail service from Havre directly to New York. The Government also provided the use of four paddle-wheel transport steamships of the French Navy and a substantial financial subsidy.[296]

The line planned to start its operations from Havre on 31 May 1847, but the basin at Havre had to be dredged before it could support steamships. As a result, the first voyage had to be delayed, and the next seven voyages started from Cherbourg. The company's small steamships proved to be unsuitable for

---

294 The *Great Western* was in non-regular North Atlantic service up to December 1846; the American ship *Massachusetts* made two round trips in 1846; and the *Sarah Sands* was in traffic 1847–1849, making three more round-trips in 1852. See Tabeart (1997), 19–20. The *Sarah Sands* was the second ocean-going iron screw steamer after the *Great Britain*, and was chartered by the Red Cross Line, one of the New York packet lines of the later period. According to Bonsor, 'it can certainly be said that they [her trips] were a success as nearly all her passages were considerably faster than those of contemporary sailing packets, which were what she was intended to compete with rather than with the Cunard wooden paddle-steamers'. The *Sarah Sands* was also the first steamer to carry emigrants. For example, in August 1848, she was reported to have departed from Liverpool with 60 first class, 46 second class and 200 steerage passengers. In 1852 she arrived in New York with 124 cabin and 238 steerage passengers. See Bonsor (1975), vol. 1, 184–185; and Arnell (1986), 205.

295 Marthe Barbance, *Histoire de la Compagnie Générale Transatlantique. Un Siècle d'Exploitation Maritime* (Paris, 1955), 30.

296 See Barbance, 30; Staff, 85.

the North Atlantic route. They were slow, had frequent machinery problems, and often ran short of coal before the intended voyages were completed. Later historians have not found much positive to say about the company's performance. According to Staff, 'the line was so ill managed and its ships got themselves into so many ludicrous situations that it lasted less than a year. Its effect in the field of competition cannot be said to have been serious.'[297]

It was not only the speed that was important. Albion describes the Hérout & de Handel Line's performance as a comedy of errors: 'The first trip was almost the only one completed in a satisfactory manner. Ship after ship ran out of coal and had to finish the trip under sail, while the New York–Havre sailing packets sped past them. Some clumsy accidents occurred in New York harbor, where the helmsmen, not knowing English, did not understand the pilots' orders. French pride was hurt by the constant jokes on the subject; some eighty of New York's most prominent French residents held a meeting to inquire into the matter. The hearing revealed one shortcoming that was regarded as more unforgivable than running out of coal or bumping brigs. It was at least to be expected that Frenchmen could feed their passengers well, but that was apparently not the case. Lieutenant Maury [the well known oceanographer] told the tale of one of the French liners putting to sea without sugar; when this was discovered, the captain offered to put back to New York but, as Maury remarked, it was too late: the passengers had already become *sour*. This sugar business broke up the line.'[298]

Of the sailings conducted, the average westbound journey took 18.1 days, and the eastbound 17.0 days.[299] In February 1848, the Hérout & de Handel Line suspended operations having lost the government subsidy due to the poor performance. The service was not restarted, and it was 16 years before another French steamship company would be established on the North Atlantic route for mail service.[300]

There was aroused interest in the United States, too, in establishing their own steamship mail services, when it became evident that the sailing packets had lost their superiority on the North Atlantic route to the British steamers. In October 1845, the U.S. Postmaster invited tenders for a mail steamship service from New York to various European ports. Encouraged by Cunard's example six ship operators wanted to start a transatlantic mail service. Of these tenders, three were accepted. The mail route from New York via Southampton to Bremerhaven – or Havre on alternate voyages – would be taken care of by Edward Mills, a promoter unknown in the shipping world. The contract with the Ocean Steam Navigation Company, or the Ocean Line, required four vessels and bi-monthly mail service. This was changed to a monthly service to Bremerhaven with only half of the subsidy appropriated. The service started in June 1847 and the contract was later extended for a second five-year period.[301]

297 Staff, 85; see also Barbance, 30.
298 Albion (1939), 324. For more stories about the line's performance, see Tyler, 149; Barbance, 30.
299 Sailing lists of Hubbard & Winter, 93. Tyler has come to similar averages in his calculations. (Tyler, 149)
300 Hubbard & Winter, 91; Barbance, 30–31.
301 Hubbard & Winter, 81–84; Butler, 99–100; Albion (1939), 323–324; and Tyler, 143–144.

The mail contract for the Havre route was signed with the New York & Havre Steam Navigation Company, or the Havre Line. It was a monthly service with a call at Southampton on each voyage. The line started operations in October 1850.[302]

The most important mail service between New York and Liverpool was granted to Edward K. Collins, whose Dramatic Line had been running sailing packets on the same route since 1836 and earlier packets between New York and Vera Cruz, Mexico, as well as between New York and New Orleans.[303] The ten-year contract with the New York & Liverpool United States Mail Steamship Company, or the Collins Line, was made to construct and equip four steamers for a bi-monthly mail service at least eight months a year, with a monthly service during the winter. In 1852 the contract was changed to a bi-monthly service throughout the year.[304]

In the autumn of 1850, the North Atlantic mail and passenger steamship service looked very different from what it had been only a year earlier. The American mail steamship tonnage clearly beat the Cunard Line's, whose seven vessels in traffic were rather small compared with the new rivals.

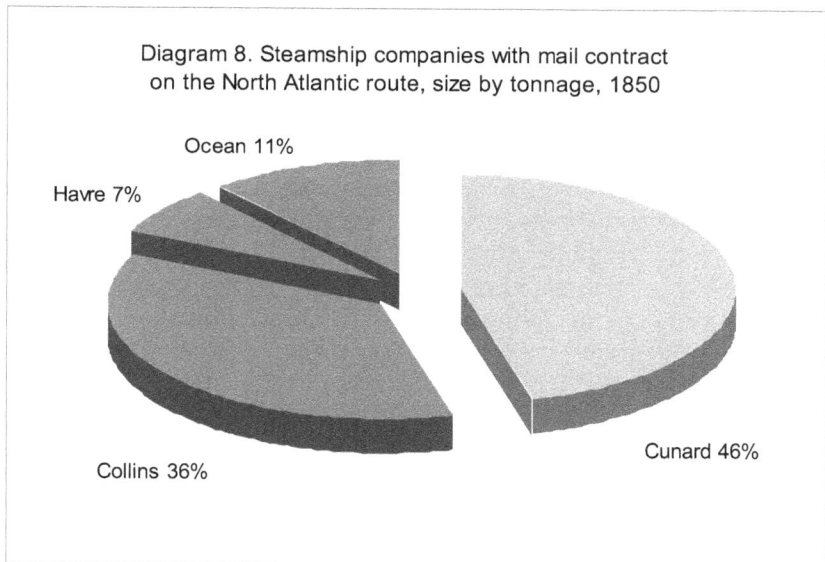

Diagram 8. Steamship companies with mail contract on the North Atlantic route, size by tonnage, 1850

Ocean 11%
Havre 7%
Collins 36%
Cunard 46%

Source: Staff, 129–131. The total tonnage of the mail-carrying steamship lines on the North Atlantic route in late 1850 was 31,824 tons.

302 Hubbard & Winter, 109–111; Albion (1939), 325.
303 The history of the rise and fall of the Collins Line has been told by dozens of maritime historians. See for example Tyler, 181–246; Albion (1939), 325–330; Arnell (1986), 191–204; Staff, 86–90; Kludas, 44–46; Babcock, 91–106; Hubbard & Winter, 95–108; Bonsor (1975), vol. 1, 201–208; Butler, 89–103, 199–224; Fox 116–139; and Hyde (1975), 37–39. About the Dramatic Line, see Butler, 95–97; Cutler (1967), 198, 210–211, 380; and Staff, 123–124. About the Vera Cruz Line, see Cutler (1967) 401, and about the New Orleans Line, Cutler (1967), 500. Even a fictitious story about the company, based on historical events, has been written by Warren Armstrong, *The Collins Story* (London 1957).
304 Hubbard & Winter, 95–96.

Cunard Line vs. Collins Line

Edward K. Collins started his mail steamship service between New York and Liverpool in late April, 1850. The competition between the two shipping companies, the Cunard Line and the Collins Line, has aroused more passionate feelings among contemporaries and maritime historians than probably any other period of transatlantic history. Not only was it a contest between two popular companies, but there were also strong political passions and national prestige involved.[305]

This study will focus on the effect of the Cunard-Collins contest on the speed of business information transmission. Both companies were generously subsidised by their governments and carried mail on the same route, but only one of them survived.

According to several maritime historians, it was agreed from the outset that the Collins service should beat the Cunarders.[306] At the time when the Collins Line started its service, the Cunard steamers could occasionally make the westbound trip between Liverpool and Boston in 12 days, including the stop in Halifax. In 1850, Cunard's new steamship *Asia* made the voyage to New York in 11 days.[307] This was the starting point for Edward Collins, who promised that his vessels would make the trip faster than any others.

The Collins steamers were notably larger than Cunard's – wooden paddle-wheelers of about 2,850 tons with excellent accommodations including, for example, the first steam heating system on board.[308] The Collins Line's first steamship, the *Atlantic,* entered service in April and the *Pacific* in May 1850. The two other ships, the *Arctic* and the *Baltic,* made their first voyages in October and November of the same year. They were all sister ships and carried 200 cabin passengers each.[309]

Calculations from the sailing lists show that the Collins Line could reach its target of being faster than any other – crossing the Atlantic in 11 days or less – only occasionally in 1850–1851. In fact, 43.2% of the line's westbound and 32.4% of its eastbound voyages lasted 12 days or more. The Cunard

---

305 The Collins Line's contract was a political question from the very beginning. In the U.S. Congress it was strongly opposed by Senators from Ohio and Missouri as being only a waste of money, but warmly supported by Senators from New England, and especially from New York. One of the strongest arguments for the contract was borrowed from the British: government-controlled vessels could be transformed into warships if needed. At the time of the discussion, the United States was at war with Mexico, and the relationship with Britain had its critical moments in the 1840s. (Tyler, 136–138, 145–146) There was a new discussion in the Congress about the Collins contract in 1852 and once more in 1855. See *Speech of Mr. Edson B. Olds, of Ohio, on the Collins Line of Steamers, delivered in the House of Representatives, February 15, 1855* (Washington, 1855), passim. – Edson B. Olds was the Chairman of Committee on Post Office and Post Roads in the U.S. Congress.

306 See e.g. Albion (1939), 325–326; Kludas, 45; Butler, 99; Babcock, 92; and Hyde (1975), 37.

307 Hubbard & Winter, 28.

308 For further descriptions, see Bonsor (1975), vol. 1, 202; Bonsor (1980), vol. 5, 1859; Staff, 86; and Tyler, 182.

309 Bonsor (1975), vol. 1, 202–207; Hubbard & Winter, 98.

Line's figures on the Liverpool–New York route were 72.5% and 35.0% respectively.[310]

Despite misfortunes and delays in the beginning, Edward Collins' PR efforts impressed his contemporaries, who believed that the Cunard Line was playing a losing part in the contest by clear figures. Even Lawrence Babcock, the latter company's historian, wrote in the 1930s: 'From this time on, the fastest passages were made by the Collins ships without a single Cunard victory to even the contest.'[311]

In fact, the speed of the two companies was more identical than could be expected, but the public image was different. From the beginning, PR and reputation at the home port was considered more important than the image on the other side of the Atlantic. Thus, the Collins steamers always strove to sail fast voyages westbound towards New York, their home port, even though it caused them problems in the form of broken machinery and major disasters. Too hard or careless driving was said to be typical of the Collins Line's captains, many of whom were former sailing packet commanders. The vessels achieved high speed at the cost of abnormally heavy wear and tear on the engines, and it was not unusual that the mechanics worked day and night on repairs during the time spent in New York.[312]

The Cunard steamers made a few more fast eastbound trips than the Collins Line, although the larger Collins vessels would probably have been able to beat them in that direction as well, if the company had felt it was important.

As can be seen in Diagram 9, the Collins Line made several faster westbound voyages than Cunard in 1850–1851. However, the spread of the duration of voyages was notable. The Collins Line made most trips in 10 to 12 days and the Cunard Line in 11 to 13 days, but the voyages could sometimes last even 17 or 18 days. The average westbound Collins Line voyage took 11.9 days, while the Cunard Line took 12.5 days.

Eastbound, Cunard made a few faster trips than Collins. During the first 1.5 years of the contest, Cunard's ships made seven eastbound trips in ten days versus the Collins Line's four and almost as many 11-day voyages as the Collins Line. All trips were made in 10–13 days. The average eastbound voyage of both shipping lines took 11.3 days.

The complementing services of the British and American mail contract lines now enabled a well-working communications system across the Atlantic.[313] In addition to the remarkable improvement in speed, the business world derived benefit from the markedly increased frequency of mail ship departures. The circulation of business correspondence in 1851 is depicted in Table 18, the starting point being a letter sent from Liverpool to New York on 1.1.1851.

While the regularity of the Cunard Line vessels and their winter sailings had enabled an improvement in information circulation from six times per

---

310 Calculated from the sailing lists of Hubbard & Winter, 28–30; 98–99.
311 Babcock, 93.
312 See Albion (1939), 326–328; Babcock, 94–95; Butler, 202; Bonsor (1975), vol. 1, 204.
     – For background on the Collins Line's captains, see Albion (1938), 170–171.
313 For the Ocean Line and the Havre Line, see under the sub title 'Ocean Line and Havre Line – the forgotten contract companies'.

Diagram 9. Cunard vs. Collins, duration of westbound trips Liverpool - New York, May 1850 - Dec 1851

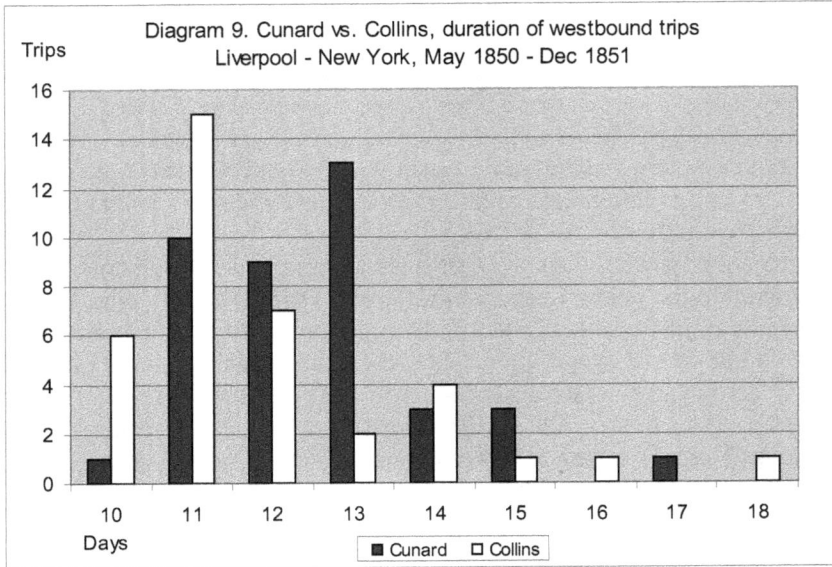

Source: Sailing lists of Hubbard & Winter, 28–30; 98–99.

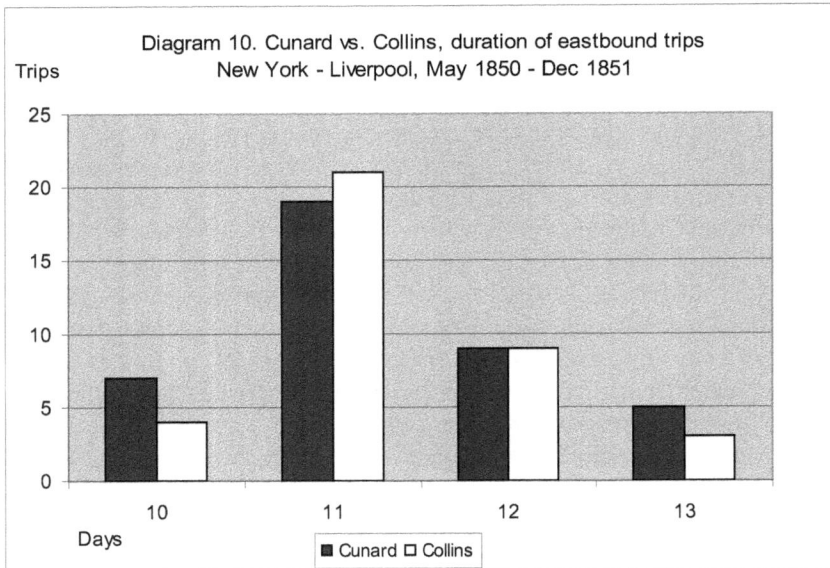

Diagram 10. Cunard vs. Collins, duration of eastbound trips New York - Liverpool, May 1850 - Dec 1851

Source: Sailing lists of Hubbard & Winter, 28–30; 98–99.

year by the pioneering steamers to eight times, the frequency of sailings was the following step. From 1848, when the Cunard Line started the additional mail route directly to New York, the combination of the line's services

118

– 22 annual round trips to Boston and 22 to New York – alone enabled ten consecutive information circles between Liverpool and New York, whether via Boston or directly to New York. However, these sailings were not coordinated in the best possible way. It often happened that the ship for England had only just departed when the next one arrived, or she departed on the same day.[314]

The tight competition with the Collins Line also forced the Cunard Line to improve its service. At that time, the Cunard Line operated with seven vessels of various sizes. Of the original four ships built in 1840, the *Columbia* was wrecked in 1843 and the others were sold abroad at the end of the decade. When the Collins Line started its transatlantic service, Cunard still had in traffic the old 1,420 tons *Hibernia*, which had replaced the *Columbia* in 1843, *Hibernia's* sister ship the *Cambria* from 1845, the four sisters' series of 1848 – the *America*, the *Niagara*, the *Europa* and the *Canada,* all approximately 1,830 tons – and the new 2,230-ton *Asia*, which made her maiden voyage in May 1850.

The *Asia's* sister ship *Africa* started the service in October 1850, replacing the *Hibernia*, which was sold to Spain. All the seven ships in traffic served both mail routes, Liverpool–New York and Liverpool–Halifax–Boston. Compared with the Collins Line's four new, large steamers sailing only the direct Liverpool–New York route, the Cunard Line's position was really challenging.[315]

Cunard did not perhaps 'trim' its vessels to move faster like Collins did, even if this has been doubted. The company's main doctrine was clearly expressed as safety first,[316] and the records are superior to any other company. To date, the Cunard Line – still afloat – has lost no passengers' lives and hardly any mail during its 165-year history, excluding the two world wars.

Several arrangements were made by the Cunard ship management in the early 1850s to improve the company's position in the competition. Originally, all Cunard ships had served on both routes evenly, except the old *Hibernia,* which served only on the Boston route, and the new *Africa,* which served only on the more important and visible New York route.[317]

In 1851, the new ships *Asia* and *Africa* made 65% of the New York trips, while the other five ships only made 35% in total. The speed of the new vessels was thus utilized on the New York route in the maximum way. These two ships were the only ones that could compete with the Collins Line's vessels and make the westbound trip in 12 days or less, while the other Cunard

---

314 See the sailing lists of Hubbard & Winter, 24–25.

315 Until September 1850, the Cunard Line's ships also made a call at Halifax on the way to and from New York. See Arnell (1980), sailing lists, 308–310.

316 See Hyde (1975), 73; Fox 106–109, 113, 138, 187, 276. Several innovations for safety at sea were taken in use by the Cunard Line, e.g. the white light at the masthead at night, the green light on the starboard side and the red light on the port. Another remarkable innovation was the use of safe tracks for the ships to avoid ice and icebergs or collisions with other vessels. See Bonsor (1975), vol. 1, 78; Hyde (1975), 45–47.

317 Sailing lists of Hubbard & Winter, 28.

TABLE 18. *Consecutive information circulation enabled by transatlantic mail steamers in 1851.*

Letter sent by mail ship, company	Ship departure, Liverpool / South- ampton (S)	Ship arrival, New York/ Boston (B)	Next possible departing mail ship, company	Ship departure, New York / Boston (B)	Ship arrival, Liverpool	Infor- mation circle, days
Franklin HL	2.1. (S)	16.1.	Pacific ColL	22.1.	3.2.	33
Baltic ColL	8.2.	20.2.	Africa CL	26.2.	9.3.	29
Canada CL	15.3.	28.3. (B)	Arctic ColL	2.4.	14.4.	30
Niagara CL	19.4.	1.5. (B)	Asia CL	7.5.	17.5.	28
Washington OL	21.5. (S)	2.6.	Africa CL	4.6.	15.6.	26
Hermann OL	18.6. (S)	2.7.	Arctic ColL	5.7.	15.7.	26
Niagara CL	19.7.	31.7.	America CL	6.8. (B)	17.8.	29
Atlantic ColL	20.8.	1.9.	Canada CL	3.9. (B)	14.9.	25
Baltic ColL	17.9.	28.9.	Europa CL	1.10. (B)	12.10.	25
Pacific ColL	15.10.	26.10.	America CL	29.10. (B)	9.11.	25
Atlantic ColL	12.11.	23.11.	Cambria CL	26.11. (B)	8.12.	26
Baltic ColL	10.12.	23.12.	Niagara CL	24.12. (B)	4.1.52	25
Average duration						27.3

Sources: Sailing lists of Hubbard & Winter, 29–30, 87, 99, 111. ColL = Collins Line, CL = Cunard Line, HL = Havre Line, OL = Ocean Line. – An average westbound journey took 12.3 days, varying between 11 and 14 days, while the average eastbound journey took 11.1 days, varying between 10 and 12 days. – Note that one extra day has been added to the information circle in those cases where the ship departed from Southampton, as this caused an extra one-day inland journey from Liverpool.

ships made it in 13 to 15 days on average.[318] These arrangements enabled an improvement in the speed of the company's westbound voyages.

In 1852, the Collins service was at its best and the line's ships averaged the westbound crossing nearly a day faster than the Cunarders. While the enthusiasm over the line's speed performance was still high, Collins

318 Sailing lists of Hubbard & Winter, 28–29.

determined to take full advantage of it. In the summer of 1852, after what Albion calls 'his masterpiece in lobbying', the United States Congress raised the line's subsidy from the original $385,000 to $858,000 a year.[319] In comparison with the $33,000 a voyage received by the Collins Line, the Ocean Line received only $16,666 and the Havre Line only $12,500. Pleading penury, they refused the Postmaster General's request to increase the number of their voyages to 26.[320] And Congress did not increase their subsidies, on the grounds that no national interest was involved, since they had no foreign competitors.[321]

Even in the new situation, the Cunard Line carried most of the mail: 2,613,000 letters in 1851, compared with 843,000 carried by Collins, 313,000 by the Ocean Line, and 139,000 by the Havre Line. But passengers preferred the Collins ships' prestige, speed, comfort and meals. During the first 11 months of 1852, the Collins liners carried 4,300 passengers, and the Cunarders nearly 3,000.[322]

This was a successful period for the Collins Line. No major problems were met at sea. The good luck continued until the autumn of 1854, when the *Arctic*, which had been driven ashore off Liverpool in November 1853 without damage and struck a submerged object off the Irish coast and been obliged to put back in the summer of 1854, collided with the French steamer *Vesta* in fog near Cape Race, Newfoundland, at the end of September and sank in four or five hours. Only two lifeboats with 35 of the crew and 14 passengers were rescued, plus one survivor from a raft from which 75 others had been washed overboard in a heavy gale. Among the more than 300 lives lost were the wife, the only son and a daughter of Edward Collins, as well as five family members of the Collins Line president and financier James Brown.[323] The crew's behaviour was later strongly criticized; instead of attempts to save the vessel, there had been panic and lack of discipline that led to the abandonment of floundering women and children. The rush to the lifeboats caused serious injury to some of them during the launching.[324]

In 1855 there was no contest on the Liverpool–New York route as the Cunard Line was obliged to provide several of their vessels for Crimean War troop transport and could only serve the Liverpool–Halifax–Boston mail route. By January 1856, the line was able to resume the weekly sailings to New York and Boston.[325]

---

319 Albion (1939), 327–328. An opposing Congressman declared that the Collins application was sustained 'by the most powerful and determined outside pressure I have ever seen brought to bear upon a legislative body'. (Tyler, 210)
320 In 1852, the Ocean Line and the Havre Line made only 11 round trips each. See the sailing lists of Hubbard & Winter, 87, 111–113.
321 Tyler, 215. The only competitors on the Havre route were the American sailing packets. On the Bremen route there were no competitors at all, excluding merchant ships.
322 Albion (1939), 328.
323 Butler, 202–206; Albion (1939), 328; Bonsor (1975), vol. 1, 204; William Henry Flayhart III, *Perils of the Atlantic. Steamship Disasters 1850 to the Present*. (New York, 2003), 19–38. Descriptions of the disaster were widely published by the contemporary newspapers, including *Lloyd's List* 12.10.1854 and *Liverpool Mercury* 13.10.1854.
324 Butler, 206; Albion (1939), 328; and Fox, 128–132.
325 Hubbard & Winter, 13.

The Collins Line recovered from the loss of the *Arctic* and continued their service with the three remaining vessels. However, another catastrophe soon occurred. On 23 January 1856, the company's *Pacific* departed from Liverpool, and was never heard of again. It was generally thought that she had foundered after colliding with an iceberg. Nearly 200 perished.[326]

The loss of the *Pacific* so soon after the *Arctic* was a blow from which the company never fully recovered. An additional reason for the Collins Line's difficulties was the delay in launching the new 4,150-ton steamer *Adriatic*, which had been ordered after the loss of the *Arctic*.[327] The new vessel cost $1,200,000. In August 1857 the Collins Line was given six months' notice of their government subsidy being reduced from the annual $858,000 to the original figure of $385,000.[328]

The Congress decision to reduce the Collins Line subsidy was the subject of furious debate and it has been regarded by some historians as one of the most serious mistakes ever made in U.S. maritime history. Some others have stated that the unfortunate events affecting the American merchant fleet were mainly related to the Civil War and its consequences.[329]

Whatever the consequences of the decision, it was obvious that the Collins Line did not meet expectations as a mail contract company. Diagram 11 shows the difference between the last good years of the line compared with the two years after the loss of the *Pacific*. No nine or ten-day voyages were made in 1856–1857, and only eight 11-day voyages, compared with 17 in 1853–1854. Almost 50% of the trips took 14 days or more.

The company also lost its grip on the service eastbound. The number of short ten to 11-day trips decreased from 36 to 18, and ten journeys were made in two weeks or even more.

The reason for the company's poor performance during the last period can easily be noticed from Diagram 12. Since the loss of the *Pacific*, the Collins Line had had to use chartered vessels to keep the service going. The company's own two ships, the *Atlantic* and the *Baltic*, could not make all the voyages, especially because the *Baltic* was out of traffic from 5 February to 16 August 1857 due to prolonged repairs – as was the *Atlantic* from 5 March to 20 June. Between 1 April and 27 May no ship under the Collins flag departed from Liverpool, as there were no ships to run.[330]

The chartered steamships were the *Ericsson* of 1,920 tons, the *Alps* of 1,275 tons and the *Columbia* of 1,900 tons. Of these, the *Ericsson* made nine trips during the period presented in the diagram, the *Alps* made one and the *Columbia* two. One trip (trip 20 in Diagram 12) was not made at all, apparently due to lack of capacity.[331]

326 Hubbard & Winter, 107; Albion (1939) 329–330; Butler, 217–218; Bowen, 192. See also Fox 135–136.

327 According to Staff, the *Adriatic* was 3,670 tons. (Staff, 131)

328 Albion (1939), 330; Hyde (1975), 39; Bonsor (1975), vol. 1, 205. For the Congress debate, see *Speech of Mr. Edson B. Olds...,* 3–56.

329 The discussion about the decline of the American merchant marine has been described and analyzed by Safford in 'The decline of the American merchant marine....', 60–79.

330 See Hubbard & Winter, 108; Bonsor (1975), vol. 1, 205.

331 Delayed mails also caused Collins Line extra troubles in the form of penalties. See Tyler, 237.

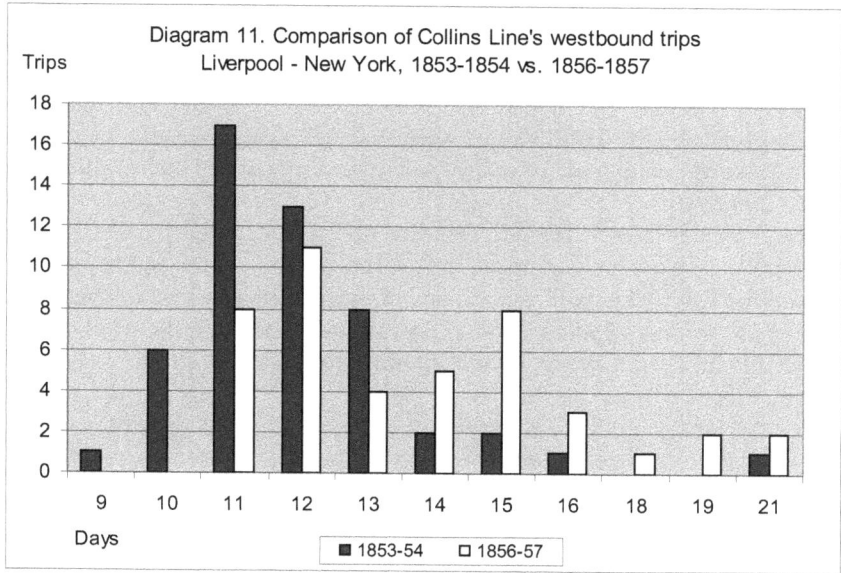

Diagram 11. Comparison of Collins Line's westbound trips Liverpool - New York, 1853-1854 vs. 1856-1857

Source: Sailing lists of Hubbard & Winter, 101–103 and 107–108. – The profile of Collins Line's westbound sailings changed remarkably during the last difficult years. The number of trips included in the calculation was 51 in 1853–1854 and 44 in 1856–1857.

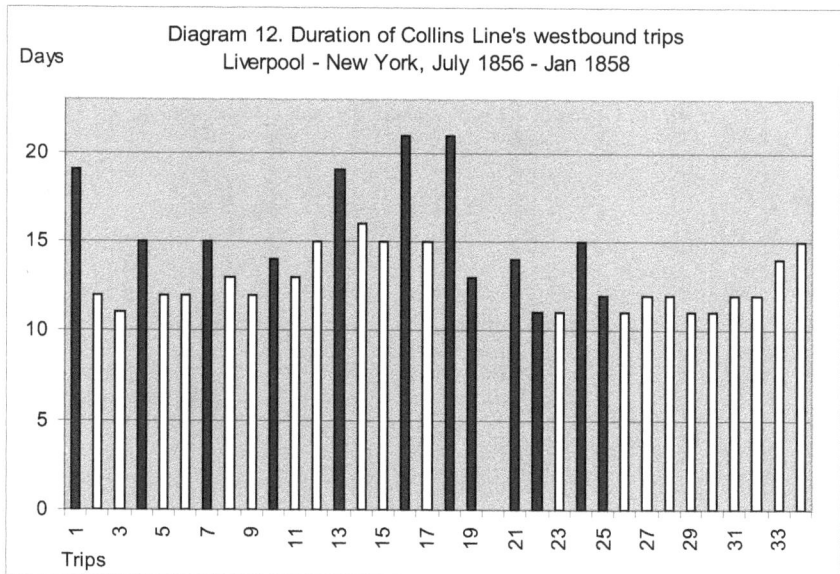

Diagram 12. Duration of Collins Line's westbound trips Liverpool - New York, July 1856 - Jan 1858

Source: Sailing lists of Hubbard & Winter, 107–108. – The dark columns depict trips made by chartered vessels. It is easy to notice their negative impact on the profile of the Collins Line's sailings.

It can be noticed in the diagram that most of the delays were caused by the chartered ships, while the company's own vessels' performance was still acceptable even in these abnormal circumstances. On the other hand, not all the voyages made by the chartered vessels were slow, and not all the voyages made by the Collins ships were fast. An average westbound voyage by a chartered vessel took 15.6 days, while an average trip by a Collins ship took 12.7 days.

The company's new *Adriatic* was scheduled to start service in February 1857. In April, however, her trials were rescheduled for June and her maiden voyage for July. New valves and condensers, the main cause of the delay, were in the process of being fitted. In July, it was stated that she was unlikely to be ready until the autumn, if then. At this point, the U.S. Congress decided on the reduction of the subsidy.

The *Adriatic,* one of the finest wooden paddle steamers ever built for the North Atlantic service, sailed from New York in late November with only 37 passengers. Her maiden voyage homewards is illustrated in Diagram 12 as trip 32. This was the only voyage that the *Adriatic* made for the Collins Line, which closed down in January 1858. Trip 33 in the diagram was the *Atlantic's* and trip 34 the *Baltic's* last voyage in the company's service.

It is interesting to compare the performance of two vessels, the Collins Line's *Atlantic* and the Cunard Line's *Asia,* during the years of tight competition. The *Atlantic* was the Collins Line's first steamer, brought into use in April 1850. She was in traffic until the final closure of the company in 1858. Her west- and eastbound transatlantic sailings are depicted in Diagrams 13 and 14. As can be seen, her performance did not change very

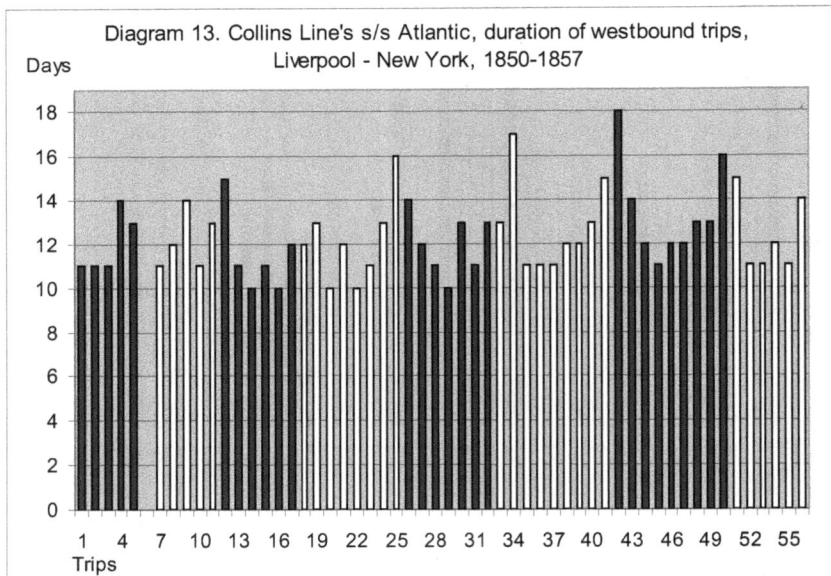

Diagram 13. Collins Line's s/s Atlantic, duration of westbound trips, Liverpool - New York, 1850-1857

Source: Sailing lists of Hubbard & Winter, 98–108. Even years are shown in dark colour to make it easier to distinguish the different years from each other.

much during the years, except the temporary lengthening of trips in 1856 after the loss of the *Pacific*.

While the westbound sailings were more prolonged during the winter months, the differences in the eastbound sailings were smaller. But the eastbound sailings were also approximately one day longer in 1856 than in any other year. The extra care followed the company's second total loss within two years. The line's reputation, as well as the government subsidy, was seriously endangered. In 1857, the *Atlantic* made shorter voyages – maybe to balance the poor performance of the chartered vessels.

Interestingly, the *Atlantic* was able to make nine round trips in 1856–1857, when she did not make a single ten-day voyage, whereas her service was limited to six to eight round trips, or even less, during the years when she made her speediest averages. Saving the engines would have made the ships more efficient and profitable, and probably saved the company.

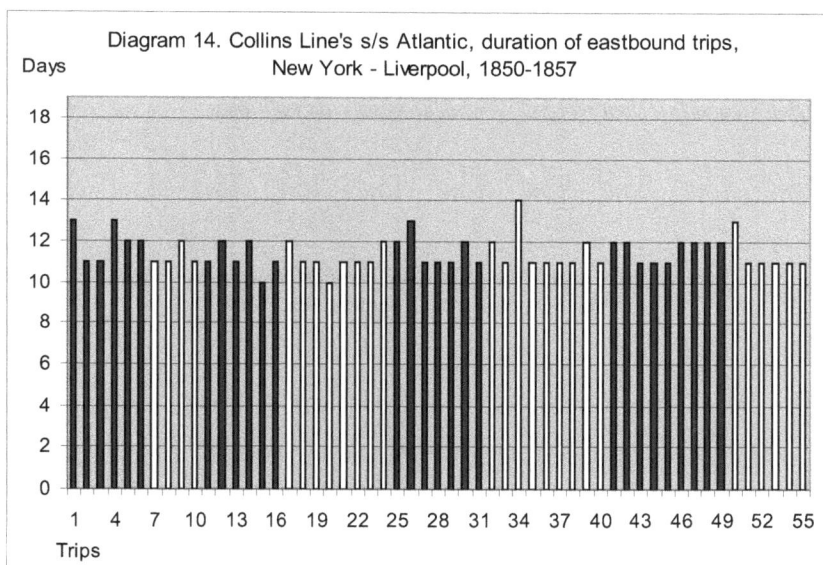

Diagram 14. Collins Line's s/s Atlantic, duration of eastbound trips, New York - Liverpool, 1850-1857

Source: Sailing lists of Hubbard & Winter, 98–108.

As can be seen from Diagram 14, the *Atlantic* only made two ten-day voyages eastbound during her lifetime, compared with five such voyages westbound, although they were more difficult to achieve. Each company's public image was chiefly measured at the home port, which can also be noticed in Diagrams 17 and 18.

The Cunard Line's steamship *Asia* made her maiden voyage in May 1850, and continued in service until 1867, making 120 round voyages. Her west- and eastbound trips in 1850–1857 are depicted in Diagrams 15 and 16.

FIG. 12. *The letter sent on 22.12.1857 from Manchester to New York, was carried by the Collins Line's* Atlantic, *which sailed from Liverpool on 23.12. and arrived in New York on 6.1.1858. This was the ship's last voyage under the company's flag, and the second last voyage of Collins Line before its collapse.*

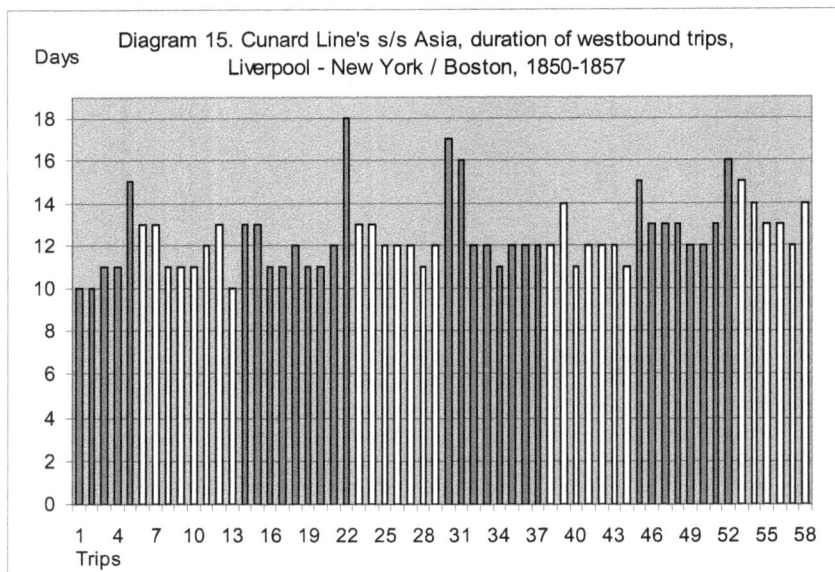

Source: Sailing lists of Hubbard & Winter, 28–41. – Trips 1,2,13 and 37–44 were made to Boston instead of New York.

It is worth to notice that the *Asia* made no 10-day voyages after 1851, and only two 11-day voyages after mid-1854. Eastbound, there was also a great

FIG. 13. *The letter sent from Liverpool on 16.2.1867 to New York, was carried by the Cunard Line's* Asia *on her 119th, or second last, westbound Atlantic crossing. She arrived in Boston on 3.3. and the letter was received in New York on 4.3.1867.*

difference between the performances of the two competing vessels. Compared with only two 10-day voyages eastbound by the *Atlantic*, the *Asia* made 14 such voyages. Note the clear change also on the eastbound voyages from

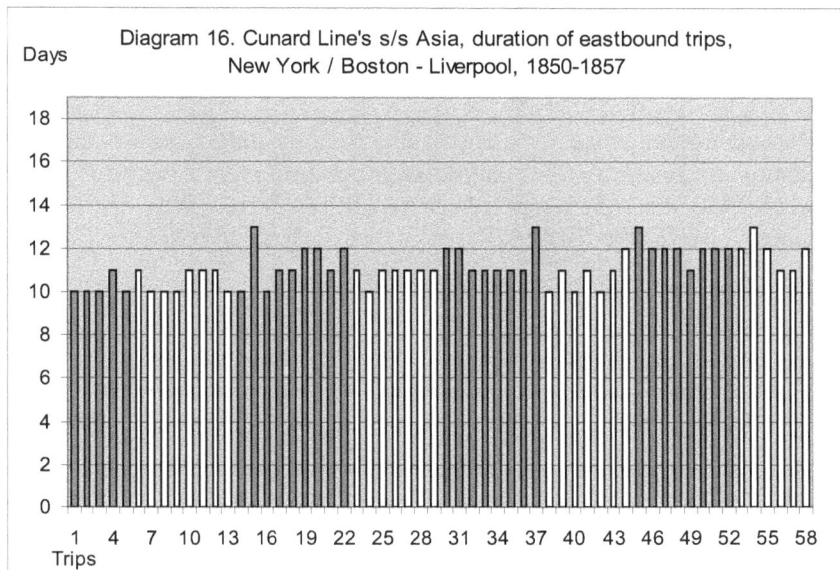

Source: Sailing lists of Hubbard & Winter, 28–41. – Trips 1, 2, 13 and 37–44 were made to Boston instead of New York.

127

10-day trips in 1850–1851 to 11-day trips in 1852–1855 and 12-day trips from 1856.

Did the Cunard Line race? Yes, very clearly in 1850–1851. But in 1852 the company seems to have changed its policy. The trips became slower, and in 1856 and 1857 the *Asia* was about two days behind her records of 1850.

The trend should not be examined independent of the historical context. The losses of the Collins Line's *Arctic* and *Pacific* were not the only serious disasters at sea during those years. The Havre Line lost both their original vessels in 1853–1854; the *Humboldt* was wrecked in dense fog off Halifax in November 1853 and her sister ship the *Franklin* went aground in similar conditions at Long Island in July 1854. The Inman Line lost two of their three ships, the *City of Glasgow* and the *City of Philadelphia*, during the same year 1854. The *City of Glasgow* 'went missing' in March 1854 with 480 lives lost. Additionally, the emigrant ship *Powhatan* of Baltimore was lost in the spring of 1854 on her way from Havre to New York along with about 250 lives. Several other serious disasters took place during the latter part of the 1850s.[332]

The Cunard Line kept to its 'safety beyond speed' policy, even in the time of tight competition, with the possible exception of the years 1850–1851, while other companies constantly took more risks at sea. The weather conditions were the same for all ships and the Cunard's vessels were also involved in several incidents during these years,[333] but their captains did not take unnecessary risks for a faster journey. In addition to their risk-averse policy, the Cunard Line management avoided extra costs wherever possible.[334]

The Cunard Line's annual subsidy from the British Admiralty had increased to £188,040, or $940,200, after the opening of the New York route, including a weekly service to New York and Boston on alternate voyages all year round. Collins received $858,000 for 26 annual round trips from New York to Liverpool.[335] It has been estimated that in 1855, a year before the loss of the *Pacific,* the company's possible fate without the subsidy would have been bankruptcy.[336] As Tyler has pointed out, the winner of the North Atlantic contest required not only the best record for speed and regularity, but also a low level of costs.[337]

The average expense for a round trip by a Collins Line steamer had constantly increased over the years. Coal prices were reported as having risen between 1852 and 1855 – partly because of the Crimean War – by 50% in Britain and by 75% in the U.S. Seamen's wages had increased by 33%, the

---

332 Bonsor (1980), vol. 5, 1888–1889; Hubbard & Winter, 113–115; Bonsor (1975), vol. 1, 213–215, 220, 238; *Liverpool Mercury* 9.5.1854. – It was also stated that the Collins Line's *Pacific* was racing with Cunard's *Persia* when she went missing. (Butler, 217). The *Persia*, having sailed on her maiden voyage from Liverpool three days later than the *Pacific*, also hit an iceberg during her voyage, but managed to limp to New York in 14 days from Liverpool. Yet the *Persia* departed from New York on schedule 11 days later, which indicates that her damage was rather easy to repair. See Fox, 163; sailing lists of Hubbard & Winter, 37.
333 See Bonsor (1975), vol. 1, 85.
334 Hyde (1975), 47–49.
335 *Speech of Mr. Edson B. Olds...*, 3 and 10; Robinson (1964), 139–141.
336 *Speech of Mr. Edson B. Olds...*, 30, 47–49.
337 Tyler, 178.

cost of provisions by 25%, and repairs to machinery by 30%.[338] In February 1855, when the House of Representatives dealt with the continuation of the Collins Line subsidy, the reasons given for the huge sums of money needed for the service were the extra cost of coal (400 more tons per voyage at $7 per ton, making $2,800) and the cost of repairs ($5,000 per voyage) that were needed for higher speeds.[339]

The speed certainly caused extra costs in coal consumption. It was calculated for the U.S. Congress that, given calm winds and smooth sea and a distance of 3,060 nautical miles westbound, a Collins steamer would consume 850 tons during a ten-day voyage, 700 tons during an 11-day voyage, 590 tons during 12 days, 500 tons during 13 days and 440 tons during 14 days. Thus, lengthening the voyage from ten to 12 days would have saved about 30% in coal costs. It was argued by the Americans that the Cunard steamers saved costs by running at slower speeds, and, as they replenished their coal supply in Halifax, they could leave Liverpool with less coal on board and consequently take that much more freight, earning more revenues.[340]

The Cunard Line's capital costs were obviously lower than the Collins Line's. American shipbuilding was highly priced compared with their British counterparts, and, in contrast to the Cunard Line, Collins and his associates had borrowed two-thirds of their capital. The operating costs of the two companies also differed remarkably. In total, the cost of an average round trip by a Collins Line steamer was claimed to exceed $42,300, while a Cunard vessel made a similar trip for less than $13,300.[341]

The British Post Office received notable revenues from postage, compensating for the subsidy paid to the Cunard Line. According to the postal treaty signed in London in December 1848, the postage on mail between Britain and the U.S. was to be shared, depending on the nationality of the mail-carrying ship. The basic postage remained at one shilling, or 24 cents, per half-ounce. This was split into three parts: ocean postage 16 cents, the U.S. inland postage five cents and British inland postage three cents. Exchange

---

338 *Speech of Mr. Edson B. Olds...*, 16.

339 Letter from Edward K. Collins, January 19, 1855. In *Speech of Mr. Edson B. Olds...*, 26.

340 Statement of Daniel B. Martin, Engineer in Chief, United States Navy, 12.1.1855, included in *Speech of Mr. Edson B. Olds...*, 28. In fact, at that time the Cunard Line had not made a scheduled call at Halifax on the way to New York for over four years. On four occasions during 1851–1853, a Cunard vessel had put into Halifax for coal after an extra long voyage due to westerly gales. (See sailing lists of Arnell (1980), 310–312) – Regarding the Boston route, what was said was principally correct. – On the whole, these calculations regarding coal consumption should perhaps not be taken too literally. The Cunard Line's *Asia* coaled 850 tons on average for a westward trip in 1851–1853, normally having an average 125 tons left from the eastbound passage. Thus a trip to New York was started with an average amount of 975 tons of coal. The *Asia* was 600 tons smaller than the Collins vessels and made her westbound trips in about 12 days on average. (Calculated from *Cunard Passage Book 1*, years 1851–1853, in CP, GM 2/1, SJ)

341 Tyler, 209. The Collins Line's own figures for the round trip cost were even higher, from $63,000 to over $65,000. (*Speech of Mr. Edson B. Olds..*, 16; Tyler, 209) – There is no evidence that the figures of the two companies are strictly comparable, but the Cunard Line could certainly manage their operations with less expense than the Collins Line.

offices were established at the ports used by the liners of both countries, and letters were stamped with special postmarks denoting the postage due to either the U.S. or the British Post Office.[342]

Thus, from the one shilling paid on a single letter carried by a Cunarder, the British Post Office received ocean postage of 16 cents plus inland postage of three cents, making a total of 19 cents, and leaving the American inland postage of five cents to be credited to the U.S. Post Office. When carried by an American ship, the U.S. Post Office received 16 cents plus five cents, leaving three cents for the credit of the British Post Office. Double weight had double costs.[343]

TABLE 19. *Postal income from letters carried by the Cunard Line and the Collins Line 1851–1854.*

Company	Year ending June 30, 1851	Year ending June 30, 1852	Year ending June 30, 1853	Year ending June 30, 1854
Cunard	$537,000	$565,600	$578,000	$589,200
Collins	$205,800	$228,900	$233,300	$265,200

Source: *'Revenue received by the United States under the Postal Treaty with Great Britain of the 15th of December, 1848', in Speech of Edson B. Olds... 18–19.*

Of this postage, the British Post Office received a total of $1,913,800, while the US Post Office received $1,279,400.[344] In addition to this, there were the 'closed mails', e.g. to Prussia by an American mail steamer. The mail bags containing these mails were guaranteed to be sealed and delivered directly to the Prussian Post Office. The postage on closed mails carried by Collins Line steamers amounted to $3,900 during the first year mentioned, $11,900 during the second year, $30,700 during the third year and $33,600 during the last year mentioned. The newspapers are missing from the table above. The postage on newspapers carried by Collins Line steamers amounted to $4,500 during the first year mentioned above, $5,600 during the second year, $6,100 during the third year and $8,900 during the last year mentioned.[345] The Cunard Line's respective figures are not included in the report.

It was claimed by the Americans that the British Post Office not only held letters over for the Cunard Line, but also arranged its schedules so that it could bring all letters from the continent to the Post Office just in time to meet the sailings of the Cunard steamers.[346] Whether this was meant to be a restriction on competition or just wise logistics – or both – cannot be answered in this connection.

342 Staff, 82. For a detailed explanation of the rather complicated system of postage rates under different postal treaties, see Hargest, 27–39.
343 Staff, 82–83.
344 Calculated from the records published in *Speech of Mr. Edson B. Olds..*, 18–19.
345 *Speech of Mr. Edson B. Olds...*, 18–19. For the Prussian closed-mail, see Hargest, 85–98.
346 *Speech of Mr. Edson B. Olds...*, 21.

Another restriction on competition was carried out by the companies themselves. A modern-day discovery of key documents has proved that the two shipping lines had had a secret working arrangement for the pooling of earnings on the carriage of passengers and cargo from the beginning. The agreement did not obviate the competition in service between the companies, but it did help to maintain the levels of rates and to balance the fluctuations in earning capacity. The 'grey eminences' behind this arrangement were the two brothers – James Brown, the senior partner of Brown Brothers & Co. in New York and the most important investor in the Collins Line, and William Brown, the senior partner of Brown, Shipley & Co. in Liverpool and a major investor in the Cunard Line. After the loss of the *Pacific,* the agreement was not renewed in 1856, as Collins could not adhere to the terms before the new *Adriatic* would be ready for service.[347]

The cartel only included freight and passenger rates, while the postal agreements with the governments gave the economic frames for mail transmission. But what happened to the speed of information transmission during this colourful and historically strongly emphasized period? Did the contest between the two shipping lines improve the speed of the mail service on the North Atlantic? Actually, no.

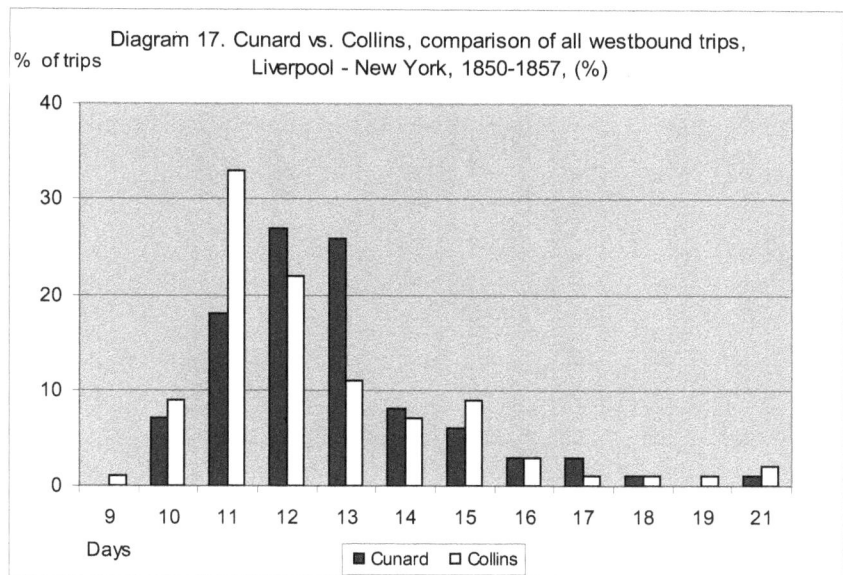

Diagram 17. Cunard vs. Collins, comparison of all westbound trips, Liverpool - New York, 1850-1857, (%)

Source: Sailing lists of Hubbard & Winter, 28–41, 98–108.

---

347 For details of the arrangement and how it worked, see Hyde (1975), 39–45. For background, see Edward W. Sloan, 'The First (and Very Secret) International Steamship Cartel, 1850–1856', in David J. Starkey & Gelina Harlaftis (ed.), *Global Markets: the Internalization of the Sea Transport Industries since 1850. Research in Maritime History, No. 14* (St. John's, 1998), 29–52. See also Fox, 121–123.

During the whole period of 1850–1857, the Collins ships clearly made faster westbound voyages than the Cunarders, as can be seen in Diagram 17. The company made 43% of their westbound voyages in 11 days or less, while Cunard's ships managed to do this on every fourth trip. The average westbound voyage by Collins ships took 12.4 days compared with the Cunard Line's 12.7 days.

Eastbound, the Cunarders made the Atlantic crossing 33 times in ten days or less, while the Collins ships only made it 17 times. In other words, 20% of Cunard's trips were made in ten days or less, while the percentage of Collins trips was only nine. An average Collins trip took 11.5 days and a Cunard trip 11.2 days.

This makes the comparison of all Atlantic crossings look somewhat different from the common expectations. The percentage of the Cunard Line's fast voyages to the company's total number of sailings was larger than that of the Collins Line.[348] But in the long run, their performance was rather similar. An average trip was made in 12 days by both companies. The weakened performance of the Collins Line during the last years of the company's existence naturally negatively affected the statistics for the whole period.

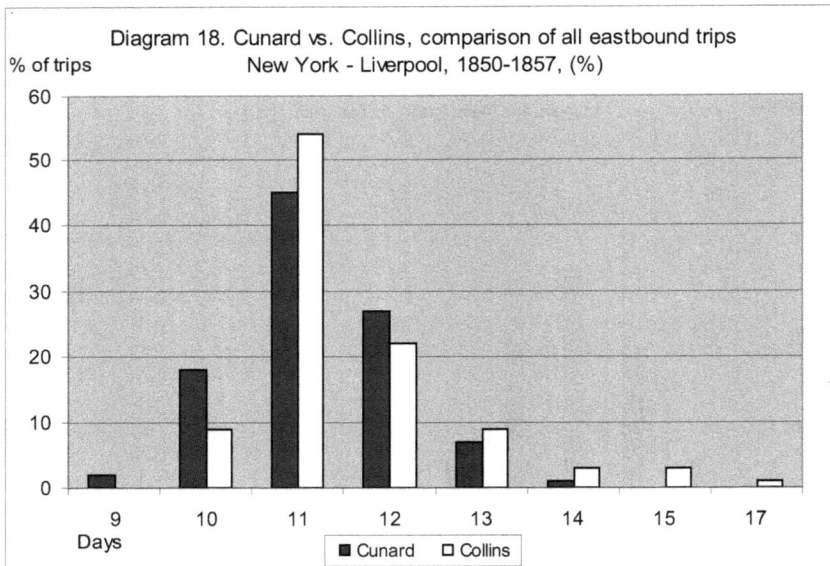

Source: Sailing lists of Hubbard & Winter, 28–41, 98–108.

348 Percentages are used in the comparison of crossings in 1850–1857 as the numbers of sailings were rather different. The Collins Line made 370 Atlantic crossings in total while the Cunard Line made 336 voyages between Liverpool and New York during this period. In 1855 the Cunard Line did not have a service to New York as several of the ships had been conscripted as troop carriers in the Crimean War. See the sailing lists of Hubbard & Winter, 28–41, 98–108.

TABLE 20. *Duration of all transatlantic voyages of the Cunard Line and the Collins Line, Liverpool–New York / New York–Liverpool, 1850–1857, (%).*

Company	10 days or less	11 days	12–13 days	14 days or more
Cunard Line	13.4%	31.5%	43.6%	11.3%
Collins Line	9.5%	43.8%	31.9%	14.9%

Source: Sailing lists of Hubbard & Winter, 28–41, 98–108.

While in 1850–1851 the Collins ships had made more than 50% of their westbound trips in 11 days or less, in 1857 the figure dropped below 30%. The percentage of eastbound trips made in 11 days or less dropped from 70–80% to about 50%.

Although the Cunard Line's westbound performance was weaker in 1857 than in 1850–1851, their eastbound performance was stronger. The improvement followed the entrance of the company's new steamship *Persia*, which immediately made new speed records in both directions in 1856, keeping the Blue Riband for the next seven years.[349]

It can be said that the tight competition between the two shipping lines cost much extra money for the respective governments, and the lives of several hundred people who perished in disasters at sea, but caused no remarkable improvement in the general speed of communications. Even though the competition forced both companies to build larger and faster ships – the *Persia* for the Cunard Line and the *Adriatic* for the Collins Line – their specific influence cannot be noticed in the annual records. Actually, a much more important factor than the speed was that the number of mail sailings doubled, generating real benefit from a business information transmission point of view. And it should be noted that in the shadow of the struggle of the Titans, three other American steamship lines were also conducting a mail service to Europe under a U.S. Government contract.

Ocean Line and Havre Line – the forgotten contract companies

The Ocean Line, which was established in 1847, carried mail between New York and Bremen, via Southampton, monthly throughout the year.[350] In the late 1840s Bremen was already the main continental port for the U.S. trade, handling about one third of German tobacco and one quarter of its rice, whaling oil and cotton imports. It had held a trade agreement with the United States since 1827, with an American consul in Bremen, and Bremen had established consulates in New York (1815), Baltimore (1818), Philadelphia (1827) and New Orleans (1840). Additionally, Bremen had become an important hub in the emigrant trade. The required capital for

349 Kludas, 146, 148. – The Blue Riband holder was the record keeper of the fastest westbound Atlantic crossing.
350 Excluding the worst winter months during the first years, but since 1851 all the year round. See Hubbard & Winter, 82.

the new shipping company was collected with the help of some influential German-Americans, while Bremen and other German states offered to lower transit duties for American goods in Germany, improve navigation on the Weser, speed up railway construction in north-west Germany and build a new dock with a wider lock so that paddle steamers had access to the new harbour.[351]

When the mail contract with the U.S. Government had been signed and the traffic started, the Bremen City Post was named the U.S. Postal Agency on the continent, through which all mails on the New York–Bremen route, and later also the routes to and from Russia and Scandinavia, would be sent at postal rates below those via England. However, not all the German states were included, while Baden, Württemberg and the Thurn und Taxis posts did not join in with the transit rate reductions, requiring higher postal rates for them.[352]

The Ocean Line's steamers, the *Washington* and the *Hermann*, built in the United States, were described as the ugliest (by the Americans as 'the most beautiful' and by the Germans as 'the largest') ships ever put to sea, and they were slower than the Cunard's old *Britannia*. Despite the drawbacks, the service was conducted for two five-year periods until the U.S. Government changed their subsidies policy in 1857 along with the closing of the Collins Line.[353]

The first arrival of the *Washington* in Bremerhaven in June 1847 raised great excitement and interest, even though the ship could not bring her passengers or mails closer than that. Due to the inappropriateness of the port, everything had to be off-loaded onto auxiliary steamers for a 3.5-hour trip up the river Weser to the city of Bremen. On the way back home, the *Washington* had machinery problems and had to put back to Southampton. She finally arrived back from her maiden voyage 35 days after her departure from Bremerhaven.[354]

In Britain, the reception of the first American mail steamer arriving at Southampton was very cool, and the Government indeed took measures to protect the British Post Office services against competition. By direction of the Lords of the Treasury, all letters carried to England were charged as if they had been conveyed by British steamers, thus making the postage rate double. The discrimination against American mail steamers continued for several months and led to a counter-action by the U.S. Congress. The new law, generally known by postal historians as the 'reprisal' or 'retaliatory' act, led to a situation where all packet mail between the two countries

---

351 See Edwin Drechsel, *Norddeutscher Lloyd Bremen, 1857–1875*, volume 1, (Vancouver, 1994), 3–4; Lars U. Scholl, 'New York's German Suburb: The Creation of the Port of Bremerhaven, 1827–1918' in Lewis R. Fischer & Adrian Jarvis, (ed.) *Harbours and Havens: Essays in Port History in Honour of Gordon Jackson*. Research of Maritime History No 16 (1999), 201–205; Butler, 99–101.

352 Drechsel, 5. Hubbard & Winter, 126.

353 Staff, 80; Tyler 154–156; Drechsel, 4. There was also a German company carrying mails between Bremen and New York during 1853–1857, W.A. Fritze & Company, with two wooden paddle steamers, *Hansa* and *Germania*. The vessels should have run alternately with the Ocean Line steamers to achieve semi-monthly trips throughout the year. However, only eight voyages were made during 1853–1854 and one final voyage in 1857 after the Crimean War. See Hubbard & Winter, 125–128.

354 Hubbard & Winter, 82–84; Butler, 100–101; Tyler, 155–156; Drechsel, 4.

FIG. 14. *The letter sent from Liverpool on 23.9.1848 was carried by the Cunard Line's* Cambria *during the retaliatory period. She sailed from Liverpool on 23.9. and arrived in Boston on 6.10.1848. The letter was prepaid by a one shilling postage stamp, equivalent to 24 cents. Another 24 cents (note the handstamp) has been charged in Boston for the same letter due to the Reprisal Act.*

required double sea postage (see Fig. 14). After a period of strong reactions and protests, negotiations were opened and a postal treaty between the two countries was signed in December 1848.[355]

Although one could say that the Ocean Line's performance did not warrant all the measures taken, the British government reacted as they did because they knew that more American competition would appear in the North Atlantic very soon. The service of the two Ocean Line ships was filled with engine problems, incidents and extra calls for coaling due to lengthened voyages. The line's performance, especially westbound, was far from regular, and it was not satisfactory in the other direction, either. The average westbound trip took 15.9 days and the eastbound 14.6 days. Two to four days should be added for the trip between Southampton and Bremen, including the stay in Southampton, for the duration of the whole voyage.[356]

As Scholl has put it, Bremen in effect became America's continental post office. In 1848 the Ocean Line ships carried 80,000 letters to Bremen, and five years later the number had risen to 350,000.[357] Not all mails were carried by the line's vessels however. From late 1849 the United States took

355 Hargest, 23–28.
356 Hubbard & Winter, 84–90. The performance of W.A. Fritze & Company's ships was even inferior. Their average sailing from Bremen to New York took 21.9 days and the return voyage took 19.9 days. Although the sailings were meant to be direct, the ships had to put in at other ports for coaling three times (once at Halifax, twice at Boston) and they also called at Southampton twice for reasons not given. See sailing lists of Hubbard & Winter, 127.
357 Scholl , 'New York's German Suburb...', 206.

Diagram 19. Ocean Line, duration of westbound trips
Southampton - New York, 1847-1857

Days

Trips

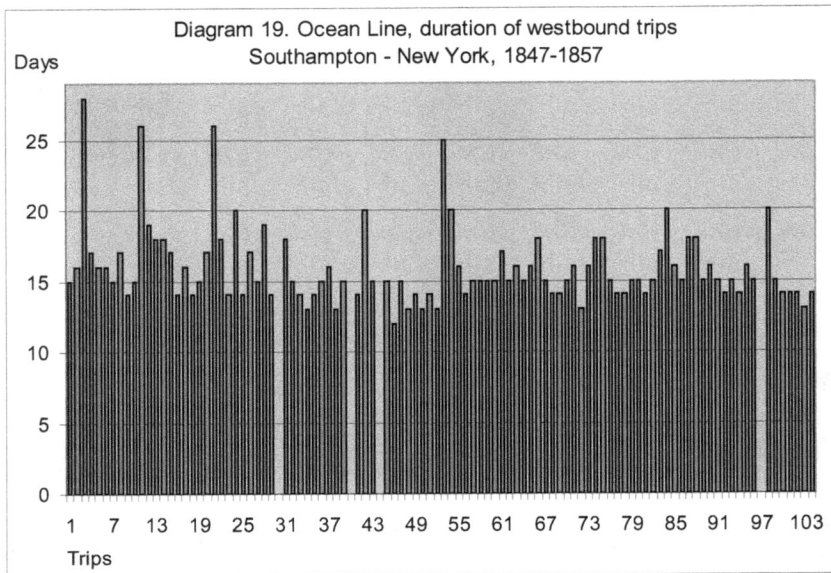

Source: Sailing lists of Hubbard & Winter, 84–90. – The profile of the Ocean Line's westbound sailings clearly illustrates the unpredictability of the company's service.

advantage of the U.S. British Postal Convention of 1848 to send closed mails via England to Bremen when regular Bremen packets were not available. In addition to the Bremen Closed Mail, there was also the Prussian Closed Mail carried by contract ships other than the Ocean Line's. In 1849 and 1850 five closed mails were sent to Bremen by Cunard and Collins vessels; in 1851 there were 11 extra mails, most of them carried by the Havre Line; and in 1852 there were no less than 34 extra mails to Bremen by other mail ships – mainly by the American contract lines the Collins Line and the Havre Line – while the Ocean Line only conducted 12 sailings during the year.[358]

The Havre Line started the transatlantic service between New York and Havre via Southampton (Cowes) in October 1850. The company's two original steamships, the *Franklin* and the *Humboldt,* were both wrecked in 1853–1854. They were replaced by chartered vessels until the new ships, the 2,240-ton *Arago* and the 2,300-ton *Fulton,* were ready for service in June 1855 and February 1856. They both had berths for a total of 350 passengers in first and second class, and they could also carry 800 tons of cargo.[359]

As Bonsor notes, the *Arago* and the *Fulton* were probably the most successful of the American transatlantic wooden paddle steamers. Even though they both lost one round voyage in 1859 due to machinery breakdowns, they normally sailed with commendable regularity until the

358 See Hubbard & Winter, 409–414.
359 Hubbard & Winter, 110; Bonsor (1975), vol. 1, 213–214.

end of 1861, when the U.S. War Department took them up during the Civil War. They were returned to the North Atlantic in late 1865.[360]

In 1866, the company restarted its service between New York and Havre via Falmouth, but gave up in 1867 due to several reasons, 'not the least of which' was 'the bad commercial policy of the United States Government, which has already caused so much American tonnage to slip into foreign hands'.[361] Of the three ocean steamship lines established under the U.S. Government subsidy in the late 1840s, the Havre Line was the only one to survive ten years after the subsidies were removed, thus showing that the service was not impossible without it, if the company's business was on somewhat healthy grounds.[362]

Compared with all the prestige and publicity that followed the Collins Line from beginning to end, the Havre Line has certainly not received all the attention it would have deserved. It was owned by Messrs. Fox & Livingston, who had extensive experience with sailing packets running between New York and Havre as owners of the Old Line, one of the Havre sailing packet pioneers from the early 1820s.[363]

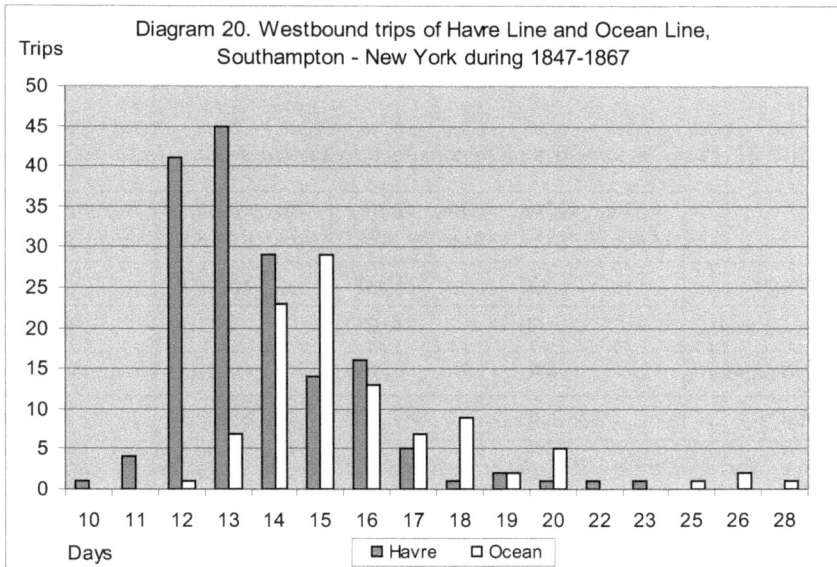

Diagram 20. Westbound trips of Havre Line and Ocean Line, Southampton - New York during 1847-1867

Source: Sailing lists of Hubbard & Winter, 84–90, 111–120.

360 Bonsor (1975), vol. 1, 214.
361 *The Times* 3.1.1867, cited by Bonsor (1975), vol. 1, 214.
362 Bonsor (1975), vol. 1, 213–214. Hubbard & Winter, 109–110.
363 About their sailing packet business, see Albion (1938), 126–127, and Cutler (1967), 394–396. For a list of their ships, see Albion (1938), 284; Staff, 125–126.

As can be seen in Diagram 20, the Havre Line's performance was very different from the Ocean Line's. The company made most of their westbound sailings in 12 or 13 days, some even faster. The spread of the duration of sailings was broad, however, so that the service could not be called regular by any means.

The Havre Line had originally received half of the Government contract originally meant for the Ocean Line, which was not able to organize the alternate trips to Havre. Of the original contract of $350,000 per year, the line to Bremen received $200,000 and $150,000 was left for the Havre Line.[364] In June 1857, when the contracts for these two lines expired, only temporary one-year contracts were offered by the Postmaster General, based on the compensation for sea postage only.[365]

The Ocean Line's ships were in service from June 1847 to July 1857 and the Havre Line's from October 1850 to December 1861, and again from November 1865 to December 1867. After the American Civil War, the Havre Line's ships called at Falmouth instead of Southampton in 1866–1867. In 1867 the company sailed in a joint venture with the New York Mail Steamship Company.[366] In total, the Havre Line made 161 and the Ocean Line 100 westbound trips.

The quantity of mail carried by the Havre Line steamers was rather humble compared with the big contract mail lines. The published figures are from the early 1850s. In 1851, the Cunard Line carried 2,613,000 letters, the Collins Line 843,000 letters, the Ocean Line 313,000 letters and the Havre Line 139,000 letters.[367] From that year on, postage for mail carried by the Havre Line varied as follows:

TABLE 21. *Postal income from letters carried by the Havre Line 1851–1854 .*

	Year ending June 30, 1851	Year ending June 30, 1852	Year ending June 30, 1853	Year ending June 30, 1854
Postage	$37,300	$80,800	$53,400	$63,300
Closed mails	$1,100	$6,500	$5,400	$10,600
Newspapers	$80	$100	$100	$2,200
Total	$38,420	$87,400	$58,900	$76,100

Source: 'Revenue received by the United States under the Postal Treaty with Great Britain of the 15th of December, 1848' in Speech of Mr. Edson B. Olds...18–19.

During 1852–1854, the Havre Line and the Ocean Line carried almost similar quantities of mails. The postage on mails carried by the two companies decreased in 1853 compared with 1852, and did not return to that level even in 1854, while the postage for the Cunard Line and the Collins Line steadily

364 Bonsor (1975), vol.1, 212.
365 Hubbard & Winter, 110.
366 Hubbard & Winter, 120.
367 Albion (1939), 328.

increased.[368] Undoubtedly, the mails arrived faster in Havre or Bremen by the more frequent ships via Liverpool and from there by railway than if they had waited in New York for the next direct shipping to those countries.

Competition and business information transmission

The frequency of steamship mail sailings from New York and Boston to Europe was now really satisfactory compared with anything earlier. There were two weekly departures by steamers, which normally made the trip in less than two weeks, even in ten days.

As can be seen in Table 22, the American contract mail sailings departed from New York each Saturday and the Cunarders every Wednesday from New York or Boston alternately. The eastbound sailings in April–May 1853 mostly took about 11 days, with the exception of the Ocean Line's *Washington*, which sailed to Southampton (Cowes) in 14 days.

TABLE 22. *Frequency of mail steamship sailings from New York and Boston (B) to Europe, April–May 1853.*

Ship	Shipping line	Departure	Arrival
Baltic	Collins Line	April 2 Saturday	April 14, Liverpool
Asia[1]	Cunard Line	April 6 Wednesday	April 17, Liverpool
Franklin	Havre Line	April 9 Saturday	April 20, Cowes April 21, Havre
Niagara	Cunard Line	April 13 Wednesday (B)	April 25, Liverpool
Atlantic	Collins Line	April 16 Saturday	April 27, Liverpool
Europa	Cunard Line	April 20 Wednesday	May 1, Liverpool
Washington	Ocean Line	April 23 Saturday	May 7, Cowes May 10, Bremen
America	Cunard Line	April 27 Wednesday (B)	May 9, Liverpool
Arctic	Collins Line	April 30 Saturday	May 11, Liverpool
Arabia	Cunard Line	May 4 Wednesday	May 14, Liverpool
Humboldt	Havre Line	May 7 Saturday	May 18, Cowes May 19, Havre
Canada	Cunard Line	May 11 Wednesday (B)	May 22, Liverpool
Pacific	Collins Line	May 14 Saturday	May 24, Liverpool
Asia	Cunard Line	May 18 Wednesday	May 29, Liverpool
Hermann	Ocean Line	May 21 Saturday	June 2, Cowes June 4, Bremen
Cambria	Cunard Line	May 25 Wednesday (B)	June 6, Liverpool
Baltic	Collins Line	May 28 Saturday	June 7, Liverpool

Source: Hubbard & Winter, 33, 87, 101, 113, 383. – Within a few years the sailings of the various mail contract companies had been organized into a perfectly matching combination of services.

368 *Speech of Mr. Edson B. Olds…*, 19.

How did the sailings serve business? One of the companies that could really benefit from fast business communications was Rathbone Bros & Co. which had the advantage of being located at both ends of the best working sea connections of the time. The correspondence between Rathbones in Liverpool and their New York agency, opened in 1851,[369] was very active. A sample of 113 incoming letters from Henry Wainright Gair, an agent and partner in Rathbone Bros & Co. in New York in 1853[370], shows that national priorities had very little influence when choosing the mail-carrying ship. Instead, reputation and the expected speed of the carrier seem to have most affected the choice.

Of the letters, 77 were sent by the Cunard Line's ships, 44 via Boston and 33 directly from New York, while 31 of the letters were sent by the Collins Line's vessels. Only three letters were sent by the Havre Line and two letters by the Ocean Line, which both operated via Southampton.

The average delivery time from the date of the letter to its arrival in Liverpool was 12.3 days from New York, independent of the mail-carrying company – the Cunard Line or the Collins Line. The inland journey via Boston or via Southampton added an extra day to the delivery time. Thus the trips via Boston by the Cunard Line and via Southampton by the Havre Line or the Ocean Line took 13.3 to 13.5 days on average.[371] All the letters were carried on eastbound trips, which were less challenging for seafaring; more differences would probably have been seen on the westbound run.

Some details from the sample can be selected for further examination. Six letters written between 24 February and 4 March, 1853 were sent by two different steamers, the *America* of the Cunard Line from Boston on 2 March and the *Arctic* of the Collins Line on 5 March directly from New York. The letters, which were written between 24 February and 1 March, were dispatched in Liverpool 12 days after the *America* had departed from Boston. Their total delivery time from writer to recipient varied between 13 and 18 days due to different waiting times at port, without the shipping line having anything to do with it.

Two letters, dated 1 and 4 March, were sent by the *Arctic,* which sailed from New York on 5 March and arrived in Liverpool on the 16th. The total delivery time of the letters varied between 12 and 15 days, showing that the whole duration of information transmission still depended on the sender as well, not only the mail-carrying vessel.

The Rathbone practice shows that letters were regularly written to be sent by the next day's ship and last-minute information was sent on the sailing day. Of the 113 letters, 68 were written the day before ship departure – 21 of them via Boston – and ten letters were written on the same day as the ship departed. An express service took care of the urgent letters to the Boston

369 See Sheila Marriner, *Rathbones of Liverpool, 1845–73* (Liverpool, 1961), 14.
370 Letters to Rathbone Bros & Co., Liverpool, 1853. In Rathbone Collection, RP XXIV.2. (SJ). – H.W. Gair was related to Rathbones by marriage. (Marriner, 6).
371 The averages of the Havre Line and the Ocean Line may be somewhat too positive due to the small number of cases and the fact that all the letters involved were written on the day before or even on the same day as the ship departed, while the averages of the Cunard Line and the Collins Line include cases where the letters had been written earlier and stayed in port for several days before the actual sailing.

steamer, and indeed, one of the letters was written on the same day as the ship departed from Boston.[372]

TABLE 23. *Examples of differences in total delivery time depending on the sender, letters from New York to Liverpool, 1853.*

Ship	Shipping line	Date of letter	Date of ship departure	Date of ship arrival. Liverpool
America	Cunard	24.2.	Boston 2.3.	14.3.
America	Cunard	28.2.	Boston 2.3.	14.3.
America	Cunard	28.2.	Boston 2.3.	14.3.
America	Cunard	1.3.	Boston 2.3.	14.3.
Arctic	Collins	1.3.	5.3.	16.3.
Arctic	Collins	4.3.	5.3.	16.3.

Source: Letters to Rathbone Bros & Co. in Rathbone Collection, RP XXIV.2. (SJ)

Changes in the transatlantic mail services in the late 1850s

During the Crimean War, while the Cunard Line was withdrawn from the New York route, 'Commodore' Cornelius Vanderbilt, a well-known shipowner in the New York region, submitted a low bid to the Postmaster General. His ships would carry mail between New York and Liverpool semi-monthly, alternating with the Collins Line, to form a weekly communication. His company would conduct the service for $15,000 each round trip, with a contract to exist for five years. No contract was made, but Vanderbilt started the traffic at his own expense. His steamers *North Star* and *Ariel* served the route between New York and Havre, including a call at Southampton, with departures every third week, starting from April 1855.[373]

Although Vanderbilt's service was not really regular when examined in the sailing lists, it easily beat the Ocean Line in both directions.[374] In June 1857, when the second five-year contract with the Ocean Line for monthly voyages to Bremen expired, the Postmaster General awarded a temporary contract to Vanderbilt for service on the Bremen route for one year, 13

---

372 One of the urgent letters for a next-day departure had been marked 'Express New York' to Boston. Letter to Rathbone Bros Co. 20.12.1853. (Rathbone Collection, RP XXIV.2., SJ).

373 Hubbard & Winter, 161–162; Butler, 211. – The line was called the Vanderbilt European Line to differentiate it from the Vanderbilt Line on the Nicaragua route, see Chapter VI.3. – For details of Vanderbilt's earlier life and career, see Butler, 121–134.

374 An average Vanderbilt voyage between New York and Southampton took 13.1 days westbound and 12.5 days eastbound during 1855 and 1857, while the corresponding figures for the Ocean Line were 15.1 days and 14.5 days respectively. Calculated from the sailing lists of Hubbard & Winter, 89–90, 163–165.

round voyages. Compensation was U.S. inland and sea postage on the mails carried. Temporary contracts were continued after the Collins Line suspended operations.[375]

The Ocean Line declined this type of compensation, which was considerably less than it had received under the previous contract, and desired continuation of the former subsidy. When this was rejected, the company suspended operations in July 1857.[376] The vessels were sold for what was said to be about a tenth of their original value for use on the Pacific coast, and the stockholders only received about a third of their investment. However, in contrast to the Collins Line, the company had at least paid dividends in 1853 and 1854 of 7% and 10% respectively.[377]

The Vanderbilt Line continued with temporary contracts in 1858, when also the Collins Line had suspended operations. From May 1858 Cornelius Vanderbilt was awarded temporary contracts for single trips for the Havre route as well.[378] At the end of 1858 an Act was passed that foreign overseas mails should be carried for the postage – i.e. the inland and sea postage if by an American ship, or the sea postage only, if by a foreign ship.[379]

The Vanderbilt Line would hardly be remembered in maritime history without their steamer *Vanderbilt,* which entered the traffic in May 1857, immediately challenging the Collins Line's *Atlantic* and the Cunard Line's new iron paddle wheeler *Persia.* The *Vanderbilt* could accommodate 400 first and second class passengers, and carry 1,200 tons of cargo and 1,400 tons of coal, her consumption of which was 100 tons per day.[380]

The *Vanderbilt* created a sensation on her third eastbound voyage by steaming from New York to the Needles (on the Isle of Wight) in nine days and eight hours at an average speed of 13.87 knots. The company claimed that this was faster than the *Persia's* record trip, but due to claimed errors in the method of comparison, the *Vanderbilt* could not obtain the Blue Riband from the *Persia.* This was one of the three voyages which the *Vanderbilt* ran in head-on competition with the Collins Line's *Atlantic,* leaving New York on the same day. During all these three trips, the *Vanderbilt* called at Southampton and arrived at Havre on the same day as the *Atlantic* arrived at Liverpool. According to Hargest, the U.S. Postmaster General 'appears to have been extremely co-operative with Vanderbilt, for despite the fact that a heavy subsidy was being paid to the Collins line for carrying the mail, nevertheless, mails were sent to Southampton and Havre by the *Vanderbilt.*'[381]

The speed of the *Vanderbilt* was equal to the Cunard Line's new *Persia* while in service during 1857–1859, calculated from May 1857,

---

375 Hubbard & Winter, 161–162. For the change from subsidized mail steamship lines to compensation in the form of sea postage only, see Hargest, 113–115.
376 Hubbard & Winter, 83, 161.
377 Tyler, 242.
378 Hubbard & Winter, 161.
379 Robinson (1964), 141.
380 Bonsor (1975), vol. 1, 330.
381 See Hargest, 117.

when the latter entered the traffic. The *Persia's* average westbound trip took 11.4 days, while the *Vanderbilt's* average was 11.0 days. Eastbound, the figures were 10.1 and 10.5 days respectively. Again, both vessels steamed homewards faster than their competitors in the same direction.

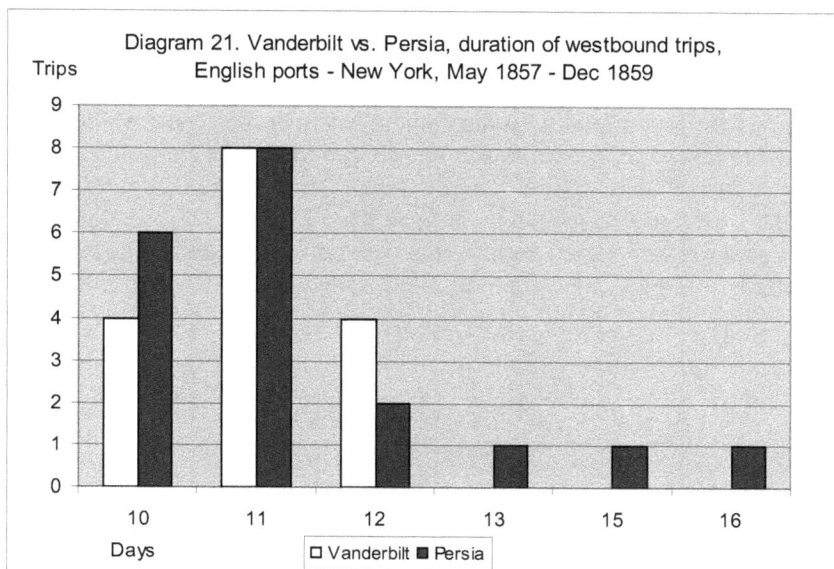

Source: Sailing lists in Hubbard & Winter, 38–44, 163–165.

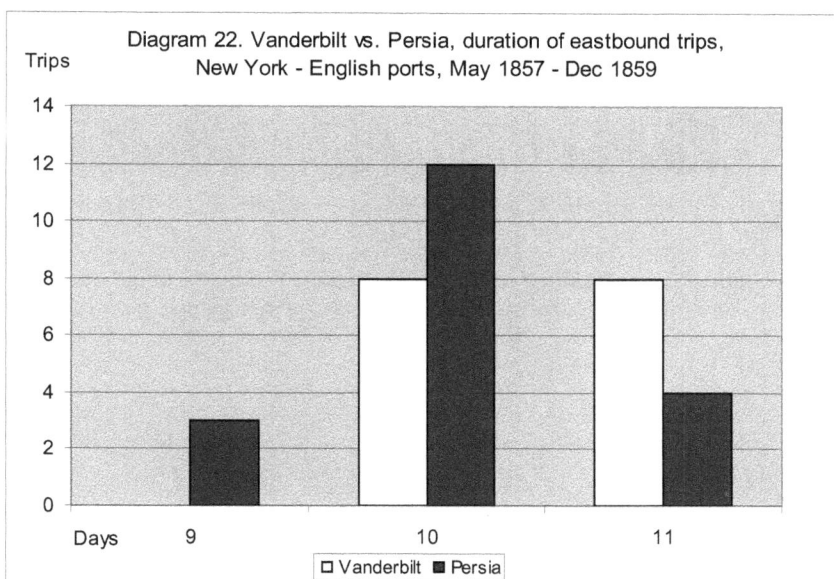

Source: Sailing lists in Hubbard & Winter, 38–44, 163–165.

As can be noticed in the diagrams, the performance of the two vessels was clearly better than any other ships before that date. The *Persia* even made three nine-day crossings eastbound, from port to port. The regularity of the ships was excellent compared with anything ever seen on the Atlantic. During her career as a mail steamer, the *Vanderbilt* never took more than 12 days for an Atlantic crossing. It should be noticed, however, that she was out of traffic during the worst winter months.[382]

Cornelius Vanderbilt showed that it was possible to run a mail service without government subsidies and even conquer the best performance of a subsidized vessel. The competition between the *Vanderbilt* and the Cunard Line service was parallel with the contest between the *Great Western* and the Cunarders ten years earlier. But one speedy vessel was not sufficient for a regular and reliable mail service if the other ships of the company did not meet the expectations. As can be noticed from Diagram 23, the Vanderbilt Line's performance varied a great deal depending on which ship made the journey.[383]

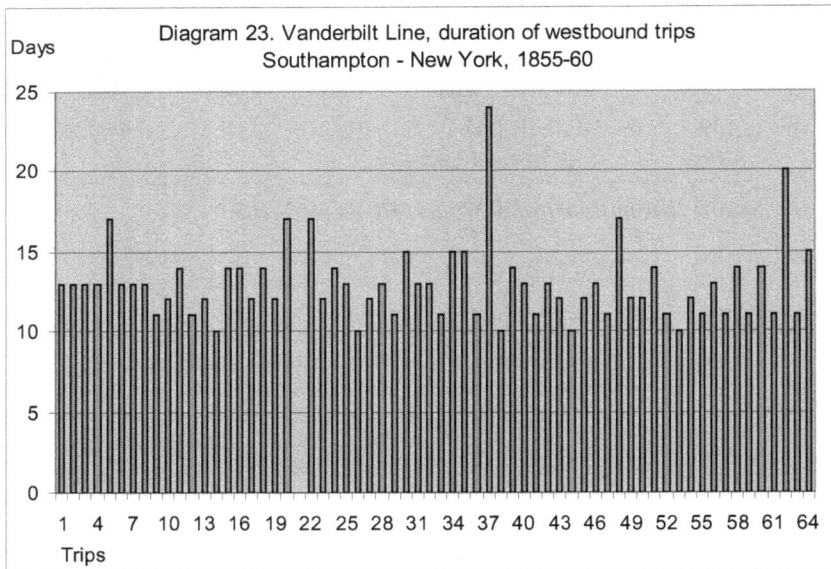

Diagram 23. Vanderbilt Line, duration of westbound trips Southampton - New York, 1855-60

Source: Sailing lists of Hubbard & Winter, 163–165. – The profile of the westbound sailings of the Vanderbilt Line looks very different to the flagship's performance.

382 The remark also includes the *Vanderbilt's* performance in 1860. See the sailing lists of Hubbard & Winter, 165.
383 The company's service was ceased in 1858 for months due to problems with two vessels, the *Ariel* and the *North Star.* Two mail sailings were cancelled and a third was taken care of by the Inman Line. (Hargest, 116; Hubbard & Winter, 163–164.)

With the outbreak of the American Civil War, Vanderbilt's steamships were taken for charter by the Federal Government, and the Vanderbilt European Line's service was never started up again. Commodore Vanderbilt transferred his capital and interest to the railway business.[384]

Within about ten years, between 1857 and 1867, the American mail steamship companies disappeared from the North Atlantic service. Two of the original contract lines, the Ocean Line and the Collins Line, had to close down for lack of sufficient government subsidies, accompanied by poor management of ships and finances.

It has often been pointed out that the main reason for the collapse of the Collins Line was the cut in subsidy at a time when the company had just lost two of its four vessels. However, the Havre Line lost both its original vessels but could still continue in traffic, even after the Civil War. The line also lost its subsidies at the same time as all the other American shipping companies, only receiving compensation based on postage on the mails carried.

When comparing the Collins ships' and the *Vanderbilt's* performance, it can also be noticed that a fast, regular service did not necessarily mean continuous, long-lasting and expensive repairs. The *Vanderbilt* regularly stayed in New York for only seven to 14 days between her voyages, with the exception that the company had no service during the worst winter months, mainly January–February, even March, when all the line's ships stayed in the home port.[385]

The 3,350-ton *Vanderbilt* was somewhat larger than the *Atlantic* and her sisters, which were 2,850 tons each. The *Persia* was 3,300 tons. They were all wooden paddle steamers, except the *Persia*, which was Cunard's first iron ship built for the Atlantic service. The Collins ships and the *Persia* had two side-lever engines each, while the *Vanderbilt* had two beam engines. The American ships were built in their home country, the *Persia* in Britain.

The engines of the Collins ships (built in 1850) could produce 2,000 ihp, while those of the *Persia* (built in 1856) were already producing 3,600 ihp.[386] It seems that, among several other things that caused the collapse of the Collins Line, Edward Collins was somewhat ahead of his time and failed partly due to the same reason as the builders of the *Great Eastern* did on a larger scale.[387] The technology was not yet advanced enough to meet the expectations of the shipowners. Technological improvements would not only enable a faster service speed but would also reduce the machinery problems

384 Hubbard & Winter, 162; Butler, 241.
385 Sailing lists of Hubbard & Winter, 163–165.
386 Kludas, 45, 49.
387 The *Great Eastern,* of 18,915 tons, was Isambard Brunel's masterpiece, originally built for the Eastern route in 1860 but transformed for the North Atlantic service. She was about five times larger than any other ship in the world but never became an economic success. The technology of the time could not meet the challenges caused by the enormous size of the vessel – she was the largest ship in the world for the next four decades. The *Great Eastern* is best remembered for laying the Atlantic cable. See N.R.P. Bonsor, *North Atlantic Seaway* (New York, 1978), vol. 2, 579–585; John Steele Gordon, A Thread Across the Ocean. The Heroic Story of the Transatlantic Cable (London, 2002), 153–208. The *Great Eastern* never had a mail contract, although she may have carried letters privately like any merchant ship.

at sea. It did not seem possible, however, to speed up development too much. Neither the size and capacity, nor the speed of the vessels, could be increased before the technical solutions were in place, and that always took years, even though the engineers were working full days for further improvements.

Tyler has collected some interesting figures about technical efficiency development in steamships over 16 years, comparing the Cunard Line's first mail steamer *Britannia* with the *Persia*:

TABLE 24. *Comparison of technical development, the* Britannia *and the* Persia *of the Cunard Line.*

	Britannia	*Persia*
Built	1840	1856
Consumption of coal to New York	750 tons	1,400 tons
Cargo carried	224 tons	750 tons
Passengers	90	250
Indicated horse power (ihp)	710	3,600
Pressure per sq. in.	9 lbs	33 lbs
Coal per ihp / hour	5.1 lbs	3.8 lbs
Speed	8.5 knots	13.1 knots

Source: Tyler, 235.

What then did the Havre Line mean when it stated that the company closed down in 1867 for reasons 'not the least of which is the bad commercial policy of the U.S. Government, which has already caused so much American tonnage to slip into foreign hands'?[388] The company's steamers *Arago* and *Fulton*, built in 1855 and used in war service for several years, should have been replaced with new ones at the end of the 1860s. Why did the company not invest in new vessels? A major reason for the decline of the American merchant marine was the scarcity of capital. English investors considered American-built steamships inferior, and were reluctant to invest in them, while American investors put their money in sailing ships and, more often, in Western interior development – railways, telegraph, industrial enterprises and mines.[389]

American merchant shipping declined rapidly after the Civil War, a trend that was to continue for decades. In 1860 two-thirds of all export and import tonnage was carried on American ships, in 1866 only 30% and nine years later 27%.[390] When Britain passed the Navigation Laws of 1849 and opened its trade internationally, the Americans only moved to protect their shipyards,

---

388 Bonsor (1975), vol. 1, 214.
389 Safford, 72–73. Tyler, ix.
390 Later on, the figure was 16% in 1881 and less than 9% in 1910. See Safford, 53. Tyler gives different statistics, but a similar trend. See Tyler, 377.

doing nothing to encourage their shipping. This was partly seen as a political question: the southern pro-slavery leaders were against giving support to the northern shipping, as it would have strengthened the economic superiority of the northern states. The withdrawal of the Collins subsidy can also, at least partly, be seen against this background.[391]

Due to the legislation, American shipping companies had to use vessels built in the United States. The American shipyards were superior in building wooden vessels but they did not have much experience of iron, which was also expensive in America compared with Britain. Additionally, British mechanical skills and engineering were far beyond the American level.[392] The American steamship companies were left in the contest without support and in the new market situation the last American mail steamship companies closed down. In the view of regular business information transmission, this was not a problem however; several new European companies were eager to take the market share left by the Americans.

Emigrant lines take their share of mail transport

The Great Famine in Ireland, caused by several successive failed potato harvests in the mid-1840s, had started a new type of traffic across the Atlantic: mass transportation of emigrants fleeing from poverty to what they hoped would be a better life.[393] Between 1846 and 1875, more than 2.2 million Irishmen emigrated to the United States. The number of German emigrants was even larger, about 2.6 million, while the total number of English, Scottish and Welsh emigrants was 1.6 million during this period. The emigration of Scandinavians started later in the 1860s, followed by Italians and Russians as the largest groups at the end of the century.[394]

During the first peak of this mass transportation, almost 2.7 million people were carried across the Atlantic by sailing vessels, the main emigrant port being Liverpool. As long as the American sailing packets had better cargo to carry – mail, fine freight, specie and bullion – they were not interested in the steerage business and left it to the various emigrant lines.[395] Only after

---

391 This is one of the main conclusions made by Tyler, 226–229. See also Safford, 64, 74. – Junius Smith, whose pioneering steamer *Sirius* made the first transatlantic crossing in 1838, was mortally assaulted on his tea plantation in South Carolina in 1852 due to his anti-slavery opinions. See Pond, 266–279.

392 About the decline of the American merchant marine, see Safford, 53–81.

393 See Fox, 168–169; Kenwood & Lougheed, 63–64.

394 Maldwyn A. Jones: *Destination America* (New York, 1976), 16–17. – A useful analysis of the economic reasons for emigration and its effects on the labour markets on both sides of the Atlantic can be found in Kevin H. O'Rourke & Jeffrey G. Williamson, *Globalization and History. The Evolution of a Nineteenth-Century Atlantic Economy* (Massachusetts, 2000), 119–206. See also Kenwood & Lougheed, 66–69.

395 Several shipping lines were established for emigrant transport in the late 1840s. There

FIG. 16. *Emigrants departing from Liverpool. An illustration of the beginning of an emigrant trip in* Ballou's Pictorial, *published in Boston on 23.2.1856.*

TABLE 25. *Emigration to the United States from different areas, thousands of people, 1846–1875 (–1925).*

Area	1846–1855	1856–1865	1866–1875	1876–1885	1886–1895	1896–1905	1906–1915	1916–1925
England, Wales, Scotland	423	435	730	563	673	277	592	283
Ireland	1,288	416	535	487	537	345	277	123
Germany	971	537	1,063	1,170	891	285	302	200
Scandinavia	25	26	229	476	549	419	363	178
Russia	–	–	17	86	398	918	1,833	293
Italy	–	–	35	138	486	1,323	2,025	542
Total	2,707	1,414	2,601	2,919	3,534	3,567	5,391	1,620

Source: Jones, 16–17. – The figures of the five decades after 1875 are given to show how the early trends evolved over time. The American Civil War and WW1 caused a drastic reduction in the number of emigrants.

were more than a dozen of them operating between Britain and New York or Boston, often by chartered sailing ships of varying quality, in addition to the American sailing packets, which also started to carry emigrants at that time. See Cutler (1967), 371–392. – HAPAG was established for this purpose in 1847. The company carried German emigrants to America on sailing vessels for the first ten years and started their steamship service in 1856. For the sailing packet period, see Kurt Himer, *75 Jahre Hamburg-Amerika Linie. I Teil: Adolph Godeffroy und Seine Nachfolger bis 1886.* (Hamburg, 1922), 7–23.

the steamers took over the best business did emigrants become an interesting option for the sailing packets.[396]

By that time, technical developments had made it possible for steamships to carry more freight or passengers than earlier. Iron-built steamers with revolutionary screw propellers were more cost-effective in use than wooden paddle steamers. Later on, the compound engine would cause even more savings in coal consumption.[397]

The first steamship line to really take advantage of the screw steamers and start carrying steerage passengers was the Liverpool & Philadelphia Steamship Company, better known as the Inman Line, after the founder William Inman of Liverpool. The Inman Line started transatlantic traffic between Liverpool and Philadelphia in 1850. Having purchased an iron screw steamer, the *City of Glasgow*, in 1852, Inman converted her to an emigrant ship by preparing 400 temporary berths for westbound voyages and adapting them for cargo space eastbound. Apart from the fact that steamship voyages were notably faster than those of sailing ships – which was naturally convenient for passengers travelling uncomfortably in steerage – Inman's concept included cheap ticket prices compared with mail steamers and cooked meals on board for the less wealthy passengers as well.[398]

The Inman Line soon added two similar but larger steamers to its fleet, but it did not take long before the service was interrupted. The *City of Glasgow* sailed from Liverpool in March 1854 with 480 people on board, and was never heard of again. In September of the same year, the *City of Philadelphia* was lost near Cape Race. These misadventures made the public suspicious of the seaworthiness of screw steamers for several years.[399]

The only Inman ship remaining after the losses of 1854, together with the two replacements, were chartered to the British and French governments as troop carriers in the Crimean war. This saved the company financially, and the public had time to forget the disasters. After the war, the market situation on the North Atlantic route changed with the collapse of the Collins Line. Inman changed its American port from Philadelphia to New York and the company's name to the Liverpool, New York & Philadelphia Steam Ship Company. To replace the ceased Collins Line mail operations, the U.S. Postmaster General made individual trip contracts with steamship companies carrying mail to Liverpool and other European ports, offering compensation of sea postage only for the letters carried. The Inman Line thus started as a mail carrier between Liverpool and New York from early 1857, with a bi-monthly service.[400]

The Canadian Allan Line started a bi-monthly service on the Liverpool – Quebec route in 1856, sailing to Portland in the winter when navigation

---

396 Albion (1938), 247–251. – About the life on board, see Jones, 28–39.
397 About technical developments, see Fox, 140–167, 172–178.
398 The first iron screw steamer, the *Great Britain*, built in 1845, did not carry steerage passengers, but the second one, *Sarah Sands*, built in 1847, could carry 200. See Bonsor (1975), vol. 1, 63, 184–185. About William Inman and his business concept, see Fox, 178–181.
399 Bonsor (1975), vol. 1, 218–220; Fox, 182–185.
400 Bonsor (1975), vol. 1, 218–221, 238–239; Fox 181–185; Hubbard & Winter, 195–198.

up the St. Lawrence was impossible. Cornelius Vanderbilt started his line between New York and Bremen via Southampton in 1857, the same year as the Inman Line changed to the New York route. Additionally, two important German lines started their steamship service on the North Atlantic route: Hamburg-Amerikanische Packetfahrt Aktien Gesellschaft, or Hamburg-Amerika Linie (the Hamburg-American Line), usually shortened to HAPAG, between Hamburg and New York in 1856 and Norddeutscher Lloyd (the North German Lloyd), between Bremen and New York in 1858. Both German lines soon added a call at Southampton to their service.[401]

Of all these new lines, the Inman Line, HAPAG and the Norddeutscher Lloyd not only operated in the emigrant business, but also carried mail on behalf of the U.S. Post Office. The Allan Line started as a mail carrier under a Canadian government contract, but also carried emigrants from the very beginning. All these lines started their operations with iron screw steamers that had steerage accommodation for 300 to 400 passengers.[402]

Between 1860 and 1875 the traffic on the North Atlantic route grew enormously. In the early 1860s there were about two weekly sailings to New York from England, or from the German states via England. The slight growth during the American Civil War was mainly due to the increase in German sailings, especially those of the Norddeutscher Lloyd which replaced the Vanderbilt Line. In the late 1860s, the German companies grew strongly and during some years even took a larger market share on the route than the Liverpool companies. The unexpected and fast growth of the German lines is depicted in Diagram 24.

After the Civil War had swept all American competitors from the North Atlantic route, the market was divided between the two British and two German companies. The emigrant transports were the main reason for the remarkable growth in the number of sailings from the mid-1860s. The peak year of this period was 1873, when the four companies had a total of 279 New York arrivals.[403]

In Diagram 25, the Cunard Line's sailings to Boston and the Inman Line's service to Halifax (1867–1871) are not included.

---

401 Hubbard & Winter, 129–130, 161–162, 167–168, 235–236; Arnell (1980), 159–161. For the mail conventions between the United States and Hamburg & Bremen, see Hargest, 119–125.

402 There were also several other emigrant steamship lines established during these years: the Anchor Line between Glasgow and New York in 1856, the National Line between Liverpool and New York as well as London and New York in 1864, and the Guion Line between Liverpool & New York in 1866. These ships did not have mail contracts and are therefore excluded from this study. For these lines, see C.R. Vernon Gibbs, *British Passenger Liners of the Five Oceans*. (London, 1963), 222–232, 238–247; Bonsor (1975), vol. 1, 422–471; and Bonsor (1978), vol. 2, 599–615, 701–711.

403 Sailing lists of Hubbard & Winter, 44–45, 53–54, 200–201, 209–210.

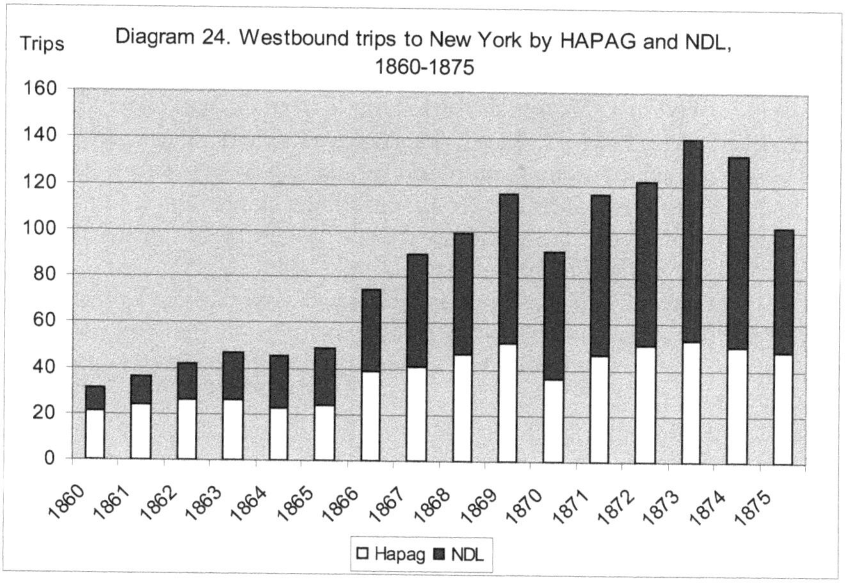
Trips
Diagram 24. Westbound trips to New York by HAPAG and NDL, 1860-1875
160
140
120
100
80
60
40
20
0
1860
1861
1862
1863
1864
1865
1866
1867
1868
1869
1870
1871
1872
1873
1874
1875
Hapag
NDL

Source: Sailing lists of Hubbard & Winter, 174–194, 242–262. – The number of German emigrants almost doubled in the mid-1860s, which correlates strongly with the growth in the number of sailings. See the emigrant records in Table 25.

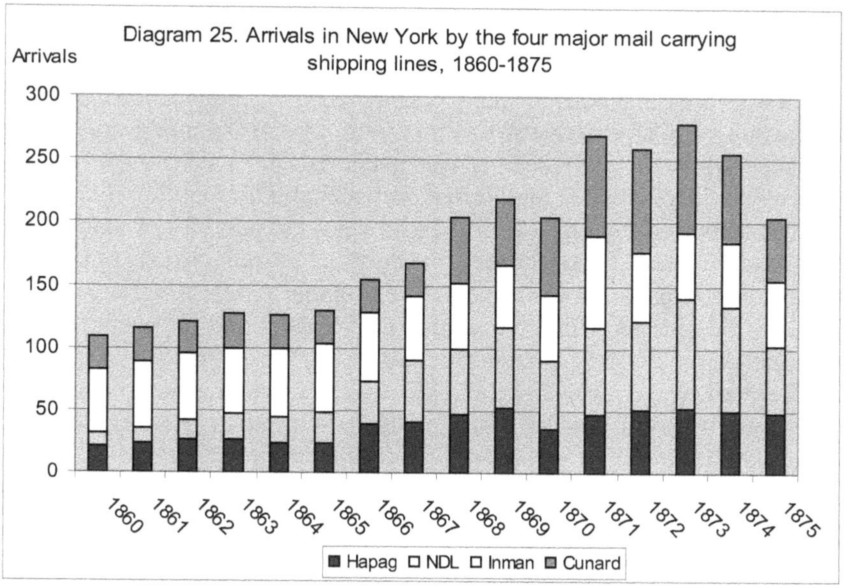
Diagram 25. Arrivals in New York by the four major mail carrying shipping lines, 1860-1875
Arrivals
300
250
200
150
100
50
0
1860
1861
1862
1863
1864
1865
1866
1867
1868
1869
1870
1871
1872
1873
1874
1875
Hapag
NDL
Inman
Cunard

Source: Sailing lists of Hubbard & Winter, 44–80, 174–194, 200–224, 239–262.

Effects on business information transmission

In addition to the leading shipping companies, there was the Irish Galway Line, established in 1858, which carried mails from Galway via Halifax, or alternatively via St. John's, to New York. After some changes in the company's mail contracts and continuous problems in meeting its commitments,[404] the line had to close down in early 1864. It has been stated that the decline of the company was due to the withdrawal of the government subsidy in 1861. Nevertheless, the abolition of the mail contract had a clear reason: the line's poor performance. Their westbound sailings took over 15 days on average. Half of the trips were conducted in 16 days or more, while the company's new *Adriatic* – purchased from the Collins Line – could make the same route in eight or nine days.[405]

During its short existence, the Galway Line introduced some new ideas to business information transmission. The company's contract included a plan that the ships would carry telegrams to St. John's, from where they could be transmitted to Canada or the United States, thus saving some time in information transmission. The transatlantic cable was not yet in regular operation, but telegraphic communications already existed from Newfoundland.[406] Due to the ships' slow voyages, this means of communications was not successful however; it was speedier to send the information by a mail steamer directly to New York.

An immediate effect of the Galway Line's service from Ireland was that the Inman Line started to make a call at Queenstown on the way to or from New York in 1859, thus ensuring its part of the lucrative Irish emigrant business. The Cunard Line, seeing the effect on the mail traffic, started the same practice later in the same year.[407]

In a way, the Inman Line actually did the Liverpool merchants a disservice by starting calls at Queenstown. From then on, the incoming mails were offloaded while the mail steamer was anchored off Queenstown, taken to Cork by auxiliary steamer and loaded onto the train for Dublin. Then a mail steamer conveyed the mails from Kingstown – the port city of Dublin – to Holyhead, England, from where they proceeded by train directly to London. Movements of mails and passengers in this manner saved about twelve hours of transit time. Meanwhile, the mails for Liverpool and the northern parts of England continued by the transatlantic mail steamer and were dispatched in Liverpool on the following day.[408] Thus, Liverpool businessmen lost the advantage of getting the American mails one day earlier than London. As

---

404 The company first had a contract with the government of the colony of Newfoundland, and then with the British government. See Hubbard & Winter, 263–264; Hargest 125–127.

405 See Timothy Collins, *Transatlantic Triumph & Heroic Failure – The Galway Line* (Cork, 2002), 151; sailing lists of Hubbard & Winter, 265–270.

406 Hubbard & Winter, 263–264. – This ship-telegraph route had already been used several years earlier by the New York Associated Press in connection with the Cunard Line's calls at Halifax. However, it had never been an official part of any mail contract. See Chapter V.4.

407 Hubbard & Winter, 44, 199–200; Collins, 149.

408 Hubbard & Winter, 14.

the most important news could be transmitted by telegraph from the first port of arrival in any case, the difference was probably no longer considered crucial in the late 1850s.

Liverpool had already started to lose its control over the North Atlantic mail transmission earlier. Several American and German mail-carrying steamers – the Vanderbilt Line, the Havre Line, HAPAG, the Norddeutscher Lloyd – called at Southampton instead of Liverpool on their way to Havre or Bremen, as the competition in shipping was very hard on the Mersey. In the late 1840s, the American Chamber of Commerce in Liverpool wrote 'to the Lords Commissioners of Her Majesty's Treasury' that '…whenever the (…) mails arrive late in the afternoon at Southampton, the letters for Liverpool are delayed twelve hours in London, always affording to the London Merchant decided advantage in all transactions – and moreover upon occasions when the arrival at Southampton happens to be late on a Saturday, the letters are not available in Liverpool until Tuesday morning as they do not arrive for delivery till after business hours on the previous Monday evening.' Therefore, the merchants 'humbly submitted' that the mails would be directly distributed to the country.[409]

There may have been some relevance in the claims of the Liverpool merchants, as the plan to abolish the mail contracts with the shipping lines carrying mails to Southampton was 'vigorously opposed' by London merchants in the 1860s,[410] even though they would have received their mails rapidly by train from Queenstown as well. It was not only important to get the news fast; it was also important to get it faster than the competitors.

Although all the mentioned shipping lines carried mails to and from England, it seems that British businessmen preferred ships with a reputation for being fast, and they also preferred short inland connections. The correspondence of Rathbone Bros & Co. lends some weight to this claim, even if it naturally represents only one company's aims, and especially one that was located in Liverpool.

A sample of letters from Rathbone & Bros Co.'s correspondence in 1864[411] shows that the company received mail from New York by almost every British mail steamer that arrived in Liverpool during the year. Of the 146 received letters, 77 had arrived by the Cunard Line and 64 by the Inman Line ships directly to Liverpool. Of the letters carried by the Cunard Line, 34 had arrived via Boston while 43 were sent directly from New York. Five letters had arrived by the German lines via Southampton.[412]

---

409 A Memorial to the Right Honorable the Lords Commissioners of Her Majesty's Treasury, resolved in a meeting of the ACC in Liverpool on 14.4.1849. (LRO, 380 AME/2). The memorial was written in cooperation with the West Indian Association, especially due to delays in the West Indies mails, but the problem was naturally the same whenever overseas mails arrived at Southampton.
410 Tyler, 341.
411 Rathbone Collection, RP XXIV.2.20, (SJ).
412 The Cunard Line had 27 arrivals from New York and 26 from Boston to Liverpool that year, the Inman Line had 54 arrivals from New York to Liverpool, the Norddeutscher Lloyd had 22 arrivals and HAPAG 23 arrivals from New York to Southampton. See the sailing lists of Hubbard & Winter, 50–52, 177–178, 241–242, 206–207.

All the Liverpool ships sailed via Queenstown. According to Hubbard & Winter, the Cunard Line's ships only stopped there for a short while, sometimes only for ten minutes, to dispatch the mail.[413] Especially westbound, the Inman Line must have used much more time getting all the hundreds of Irish steerage passengers on board.

It seems that by far the fastest alternative to sending business information from New York to Liverpool in 1864 was by a direct Cunarder. Cunard's ships sailed from New York to Queenstown in 10.5 days, while it took 11.1 days for the Boston vessels to arrive, even though the trip was about eight hours shorter. This was because, on the New York route, the Cunard Line had their newest and fastest vessels which sailed most of the voyages in nine or ten days. The Inman ships made the trip from New York to Queenstown in 11.7 days. About one day must be added to all these averages for the final trip to Liverpool. It was possible for a ship that had arrived at Queenstown early in the morning to reach Liverpool by the evening, but this did not happen very often. Even in these cases, it was too late to get the mails dispatched before the following morning.

Rathbone Bros & Co.'s agency in New York seemed to carefully follow the ship schedules. Most of the letters were written on the day before the ship's departure (68 cases) or on the same day (also 68 cases), while in only ten cases was a letter written two or three days – once even four days – before departure. Since 1853 there had been a supplementary service in New York for businessmen under pressure who wanted to get the latest information on board a ship that was departing on the same day. The arrangement consisted of a clerk stationed on the steamer's wharf after the official closing of the mails in the post office to receive the postage due and take care of the letters until ten minutes before the ship's departure. This service was advertised in commercial newspapers when available.[414] Several letters in the Rathbone correspondence of 1864 carry the handstamp 'Supplementary Mail'.[415] Although most of these letters were carried by the Cunard Line, the other lines were also included, which shows that the service did not depend on which flag the mail was carried under.

Due to the good business practices of the Rathbone agency, no unnecessary days were normally used in sending letters from New York. One extra day was normally needed for the inland transport of mails to Boston, however. Due to the Cunard Line's sailing schedule – Wednesday sailings from New York and Boston – the ship also quite often arrived in Liverpool on a Sunday. This happened 20 times in 1864, and it caused one day's extra delay for 35 Rathbone letters, as they were not dispatched before Monday. While the Inman Line sailed on Saturdays, this was not normally a problem for their ships, and it happened only twice during that year that the arrival occurred on a Sunday, causing an extra delay to three Rathbone letters.

All these details included, the duration of information transmission from the writer to the recipient was 12.2 days on average, if the letter was sent by

413 Hubbard & Winter, 14.
414 Hubbard & Winter, 7.
415 Rathbone Collection, RP XXIV.2.20, SJ.

a Cunarder directly from New York, and 13.6 days if it was sent via Boston. A letter sent by an Inman Line ship took 13.8 days on average – which made it a good alternative to Cunard's Boston sailings, but not to those from New York.

The sample of letters sent by the German lines, the Norddeutscher Lloyd or HAPAG, was so small (only five letters) that no conclusions can be drawn. However, all these sailings were made in 11 or 13 days, giving an average of 11.8 days. The letters were in Liverpool 13.6 days from the date of the letter on average. Even if the performance of the German ships seems to have been equal to the Inman Line's, they were only used in cases where the Inman Line ships that departed on the same day were only carrying mails to Ireland. Such arrangements were made by the Postmaster General for the Saturday sailings from New York; the U.S. mails were dispatched by more than one steamer each Saturday. Thus there could be two or even three mail ships leaving on the same day, one carrying the mails for Ireland, one for France and one for the rest of Europe.[416]

In light of the Rathbone correspondence, it seems that letters were not sent via Southampton and London if it could be avoided. In all the cases where a letter was sent by a German steamer, it arrived in Liverpool sooner than if it had been sent by the next Cunarder. The difference varied between three and five days. Three of the letters sent by the German steamers were forwarded by the supplementary service, indicating that something really important had to be communicated.

When comparing the services of the Cunard Line and the Inman Line, it was not exceptional that a Cunard ship that had departed from New York four days later than Inman Line's, arrived at Queenstown on the very same day, and their mails were dispatched in Liverpool simultaneously on the following day. Incidents like this naturally strengthened the Cunard Line's reputation as a reliable mail carrier, even if the Inman Line could also make fast voyages occasionally.

Sir Samuel Cunard – he had been knighted in 1859 – still insisted that the only safe means of mail transmission was by paddle-wheeler, and he kept this standard on the North Atlantic service until the 1860s.[417] The *Scotia*, built in 1862, was the last paddle-wheeler of the Cunard fleet sailing up to 1876. Samuel Cunard died in 1865, a few years after the launching of the *China,* the company's first iron screw steamer for the North Atlantic mail route, in 1862. This vessel adapted to the changed circumstances in many ways – in addition to 268 cabin passengers, she carried 771 in steerage. Until that date, Cunard had considered it inconsistent with the safety of the mails to carry emigrants, and therefore had refused to carry them. But times were changing.[418]

416 See Hubbard & Winter, 391–407.
417 The Cunard Line's Mediterranean service had used iron screw steamers since 1852. See Bonsor (1975), vol. 1, 78–79.
418 See Bonsor (1975), vol. 1, 142–147; Fox, 186–191.

Open competition – the new deal on mail contracts

By the late 1850s, the Inman Line, HAPAG and the Norddeutscher Lloyd were already sailing with iron screw steamers, which used less coal and were able to carry hundreds of emigrants. Although the Cunard Line had started to operate emigrant ships in their Mediterranean service,[419] they were still reluctant to use them on the North Atlantic service. As late as 1867, the company built the *Russia,* a fast iron screw mail steamer that carried 235 cabin passengers, but no steerage passengers. While the ship was under construction, the company learned that the British Post Office was not going to renegotiate their mail contract, which would expire at the end of 1867.[420]

The reason for this decision was clear. The British and American Post Offices were planning to reduce the existing postal rates by half, which would most probably increase the number of letters sent but decrease the postage revenues. Additionally, the British Post Office considered that the old kind of arrangement was not the most advantageous for its purposes. A reliable steamship service was now being conducted by several different companies. There would be a more frequent mail service to the United States if the steamship companies only had short, separate contracts. If the United States could make similar arrangements, communications between the two countries would be greatly improved.[421]

As the time for a new contract approached, the British Postmaster General advertised for offers to take the mails for the ocean postage alone – a practice that had already been in use in the United States for a long time. The Cunard Line refused to make any such offer and talked about retiring from the business. The Inman Line agreed to take the mails from New York to Queenstown and the German lines to Southampton at the rate of 1s. per ounce for letters and 3d. per pound for newspapers. In order to exclude the Cunard Line, Inman agreed to take the mails to Halifax as well as to New York.[422]

The Post Office had not expected the Cunard Line's refusal to tender and was caught in a difficult situation. There were four regular mails each week between Britain and the United States: Tuesday outwards from Southampton by the Norddeutscher Lloyd or HAPAG alternately; Thursday outwards from Queenstown by the Inman Line, sailing from Liverpool on Wednesday; and Sunday outwards from Queenstown by the Cunard Line, sailing from Liverpool on Saturday. The homeward mails from New York were carried by the Cunard Line on Wednesdays, by the German ships on Tuesdays, and by the Inman Line on Saturdays. Additionally, there were the weekly Allan Line mails to and from

---

419 The Mediterranean service was started in the early 1850s with traffic between Britain and the Mediterranean, and was separated from the North Atlantic business when a company named the British and Foreign Steam Navigation Company was formed in 1855. Both companies had the same owner families. Other prospects for a geographical enlargement of services were also considered at that time as the competition with the Collins Line was very tight. These considerations included a plan to start a steamship line to Australia. See Hyde (1975), 16–26.

420 See Bonsor (1975), 149; Hyde (1975), 51.

421 Tyler, 339; Hubbard & Winter, 14.

422 Tyler, 339; Hubbard & Winter, 225.

Canada. It was obvious that if Cunard withdrew from this pattern of services, the balance of regular mail deliveries would be greatly disturbed. Representations were accordingly made to John Burns[423] that the company should tender on the basis of a subvention rather than payment for sea postage.[424]

As always, the Cunard mail contract was also a political question. Before the new contracts with the Inman Line and the German companies had reached the Treasury, the Liberal government was replaced by a Conservative one. The new Postmaster General favoured acceptance of the Cunard Line's belated offer to take the New York mails for £95,000, or £120,000 if Halifax calls were required, in addition to the contracts of the Inman Line and the German lines. The Conservatives related positively to the Cunard Line and upheld the policy of subsidizing steamship lines. They had granted an increase to the Cunard contract in 1846 and an extension in 1858. On this occasion the Government made a compromise with the Cunard Line, permitting them to take the mails for a year and paying £80,000 for it.[425]

New arrangements were needed almost immediately as the United States had agreed to a convention that reduced the ocean postage by half.[426] The Postmaster General had to advertise for new bids. The National Line made the best offer, but was not given a contract due to its slowness – 14-day trips compared with less than ten by the fastest ones. By this time the Cunard Line had come to the conclusion that half a loaf was better than no bread and negotiated with Inman. The result was a private agreement whereby John Burns, speaking for both companies, confronted the Government with a request for £100,000 for the Cunard Line and £50,000 for the Inman Line. In a series of negotiations, these demands were reduced to £70,000 and £35,000 respectively, and the life of the contracts from ten to seven years. When these contracts expired, they were never renegotiated.[427]

From early 1869, the Cunard Line carried the British mails to New York, sailing from Liverpool each Saturday, and to Boston each Tuesday, via Queenstown. The Inman Line sailed to New York each Wednesday, also via Queenstown. Additionally, the German lines carried the Southampton mails for the postage only, as before.[428]

The postage rates for ocean letters were again reduced at the beginning of 1870. Instead of one shilling per letter in 1867 and six pence in 1868–1869, the postage rate for a transatlantic letter was only three pence in 1870.

---

423 After the death or retirement of the founders, the management of the Cunard Line was transferred to their sons, John & James Cleland Burns, Edward & William Cunard; and David & John MacIver. For the new capital structure and control of the company, see Hyde (1975), 12–23.

424 Hyde (1975), 52; Hubbard & Winter, 56–57, 149–150, 181–182, 212–213, 244–245.

425 Tyler, 339–340.

426 Tyler, 340. For the negotiations and details of the convention, see Hargest, 149–150.

427 Tyler, 340–341. – Milne gives a different view of the new contracts: 'Inman's co-operation with Cunard in 1868 was a subtle maneuver, gaining a new source of revenue for his own operation while greatly reducing the subsidy available to his key competitor. Cunard in turn had to co-operate because the alternative might have been worse: with official thinking turning in the direction of reduced subsidies, Cunard had to appear reasonable.' (Milne 2000, 174)

428 Hubbard & Winter, 15, 58–61, 212–213.

Simultaneously, the number of letters carried increased from 3.9 million in 1867 to 6.7 million in 1870. Despite the considerable growth in information transmission, the income for the Post Office declined markedly.[429]

After this, carrying mail was no longer a business for any steamship company. The British mail contracts with the Cunard Line and the Inman Line were far from the level the Cunard Line had started with. The United States held to its policy of paying only the sea postage. The steamship lines took the mails when convenient, on a weekly basis. In 1868 it twice happened that they did not bother to take the mails at all. When a further reduction in postage rates took place in 1870, the British lines refused to carry American mails and arrangements were made with the Guion Line and the Norddeutscher Lloyd.[430]

A couple of developments occurred on the North Atlantic route simultaneously – the traffic became more frequent and the sailings faster than ever. These two trends, combined with the drastic reduction in postage rates, increased the amounts of transmitted information markedly. Even if this must have been good for business on both sides of the Atlantic, it was not good for the shipping companies. Not only did the revenues from mails decline, but, due to the rapid increase in capacity, freight rates were also on the wane. Even the passenger rates were reduced due to the hard competition.[431]

In this business environment the transport of emigrants became an important part of shipping functions. The emigrant business was neither easy nor highly profitable,[432] but it added a considerable amount of income to the shipping companies during the good years. For example, the Cunard Line received £70,000 in mail subsidies from the British Government for 104 voyages during a year and an additional £16,000 for American mail postage carried from New York.[433] Leaving out the Boston route, it can be calculated that the income from the mails was £980 per round trip on average. If each emigrant paid the company £6 6s. for a trip from Liverpool to New York,[434] the additional income for 500 emigrants added £3,250 to the company's revenues on each round trip.

In 1870 the Inman Line carried 40,500 steerage passengers, the National Line 33,500 and the Guion Line 27,500. Although the Cunard Line carried fewer than 17,000 passengers in steerage, they carried an additional 7,500 cabin passengers, which was more than all the others together.[435] The effects

---

429 Tyler, 342.
430 Tyler, 343; Hubbard & Winter 169, 237. The Norddeutscher Lloyd did not always carry British mails westbound from Southampton, even if they carried German mails. (Hubbard & Winter, 248) HAPAG did not reapply for the British mail contract, but continued to carry U.S. mails. The company changed their port of call from Southampton to Havre, with some other adjustments included. See Hubbard & Winter, 169.
431 See Kenwood & Lougheed, 27; Tyler 197.
432 See Hyde (1975), 58–66.
433 Tyler, 355.
434 Hyde (1975), 64.
435 Bonsor (1975), vol. 1, 228. – Bonsor's statistics are based on a different logic and the number of voyages does not match with the lists of mail sailings by Hubbard & Winter. There may be other than Liverpool (– Queenstown) – New York mail sailings included in Bonsor's figures, e.g. the Inman Line's sailings via Halifax or the Cunard Line's sailings

of the Cunard Line's rethinking after the new deal on mail contracts can be seen in Diagram 26.

Until the end of 1868, the Cunard Line had 26 annual sailings to New York and as many to Boston. The new mail contracts required 52 sailings to both ports. But in the next few years, when emigrants were streaming over the Atlantic, the number of New York sailings was increased to 86. This meant heavy investments in new ships. The 2,500-ton *Siberia* and *Samaria*, with accommodation for 130 cabin passengers and 800 in steerage, were followed by a series of larger steamers in the late 1860s.[436]

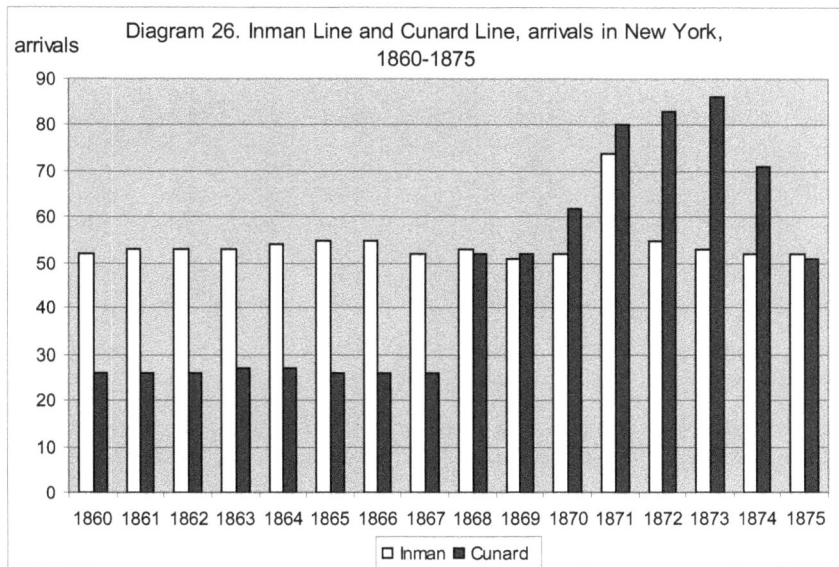

Diagram 26. Inman Line and Cunard Line, arrivals in New York, 1860-1875

Source: Sailing lists of Hubbard & Winter, 44–80, 200–224. – The Cunard Line service to Boston and the Inman Line service to Halifax are excluded.

Based on the claims of William Inman in the Parliamentary hearings, it has been assumed by historians that the two shipping lines had become essentially identical in both speed and service by the late 1860s.[437] However, in 1870 – even though the government subsidies were already being shared by these two companies – this was not yet true.[438]

from the Mediterranean.

436 The *Batavia*, the *Abyssinia*, the *Algeria* and the *Parthia*, all between 2,500 and 3,500 tons and with accommodation for 800 to 1,000 steerage passengers, were launched in 1870. Three more ships – the *Atlas* of about 2,500 tons and 800 in steerage, as well as the *Bothnia* and the *Scythia*, both of 4,500 tons and carrying 1,100 in steerage – were built for the North Atlantic route between 1873 and 1875. See Bonsor (1975), vol. 1, 150–152.

437 Fox, 192; Tyler 340; and Milne (2000), 173.

438 But the companies had had an agreement about fixed freight rates and minimum passenger rates to protect the British shipping lines against foreign competition since 1867 or early

As shown in Diagram 27, the Cunard Line made 21, or 34%, of its westbound trips in nine days or less, while the Inman Line made only five, or 10%. An average Cunard voyage took 10.2 days while an average Inman voyage took 10.6 days.

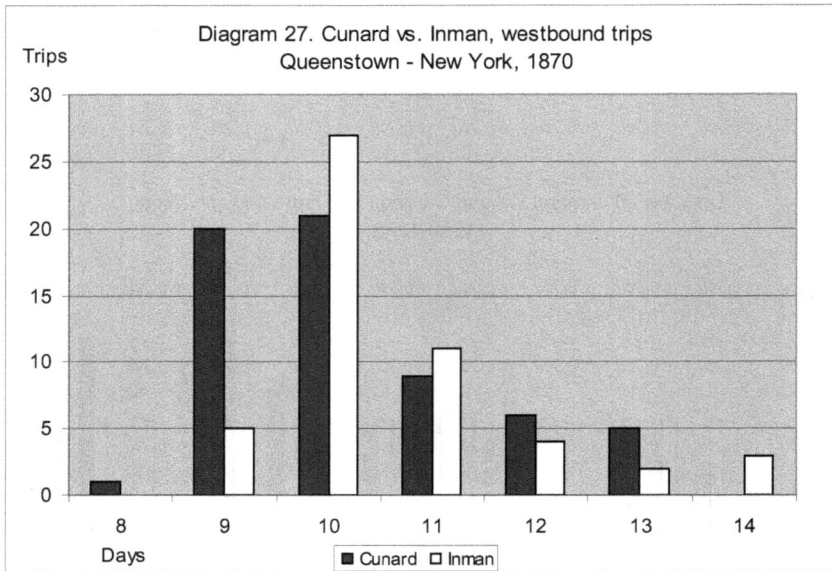

Diagram 27. Cunard vs. Inman, westbound trips
Queenstown - New York, 1870

Source: Sailing lists of Hubbard & Winter, 61–64, 215–217. – The total number of Cunard and Inman voyages was 61 and 52 respectively.

Eastbound the difference was even greater. While the Cunard Line made 43, or 70%, of their eastbound voyages in nine days or less, the corresponding figure for the Inman Line was only 20 voyages, or 38%. Additionally, the company had bad luck and two voyages were lengthened to 17 and 27 days.[439] An average Cunard voyage took 9.3 days while an average Inman voyage took 9.9 days.

The situation was quickly changing however. Instead of increasing the number of voyages like Cunard did, William Inman invested in larger and

1868. The National, Guion, Allan and Anchor lines also joined this agreement. See Hyde (1975), 94.

439 The length of the two unlucky voyages was originally given to Liverpool. To be comparable with the rest of the figures, these voyages have been calculated in the table as 16 and 26 days to Queenstown, even though the ships proceeded directly to Liverpool. One day has also been subtracted from the duration of the voyage in those cases where Hubbard & Winter only record the date of arrival at Liverpool. (In these cases, the ships have probably not been able to call at Queenstown due to bad weather or other reasons.) There was one such case in the Cunard Line's operations on the New York run that year (and five on the Boston run), and eight cases in the Inman Line's performance, including the two long voyages.

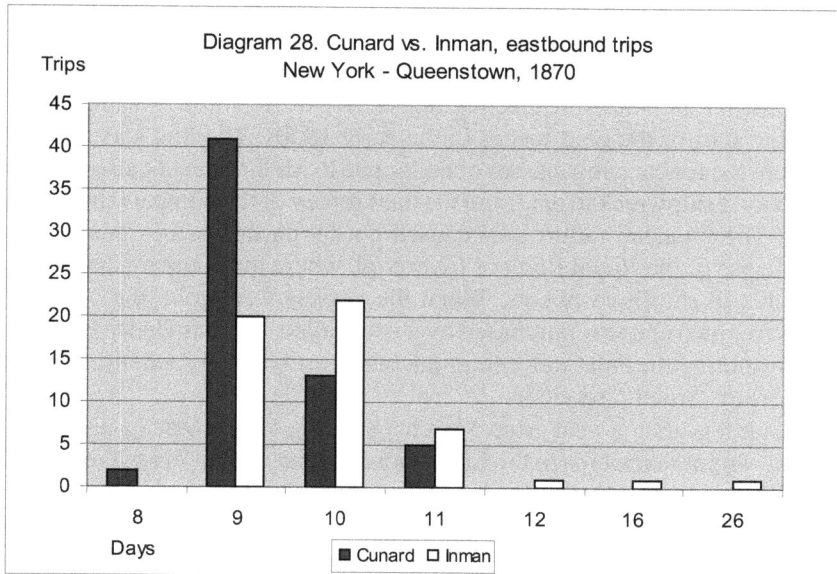

Diagram 28. Cunard vs. Inman, eastbound trips
New York - Queenstown, 1870

Source: Sailing lists of Hubbard & Winter, 61–64, 215–217. – The total number of Cunard and Inman voyages was 61 and 52 respectively.

faster vessels. After launching two new 3,000-ton vessels, the *City of Brooklyn* and the *City of Brussels,* with accommodation for 200 cabin and 600 steerage passengers, in 1869 the company launched three 4,500-ton vessels, each one able to carry 120 to 200 cabin passengers and 1,200 to 1,300 in steerage. The *City of Berlin*, launched in 1875, was a 5,500-ton steamer that could carry 170 first class, 200 second class, and 1,500 steerage passengers. She made a record passage in both directions on the North Atlantic route, steaming from Queenstown to New York in seven days, 18 hours and two minutes, and back home in 2.5 hours less.[440] The new ships were not only larger, but also faster than the Cunard Line's.

At this point two new mail-carrying steamship companies still need to be presented, one British and one French.[441] The transatlantic shipping boom

---

440 Bonsor (1975) vol. 1, 230–231.
441 These two were not the only important transatlantic steamship lines established in the early 1870s. The Holland-America Line (Nederlandsche-Amerikaanische Stoomvart Maatschappijj) established in 1872 and sailing between Hellevoetsluis and New York, the Red Star Line (International Navigation Company of Philadelphia) established in 1873 and sailing mainly between Philadelphia and Antwerp, and the American Line (American Steamship Company) established in 1873 and sailing between Philadelphia and Queenstown–Liverpool need to be mentioned. As they all served on different routes and in only a few years covered by this study, they are not examined here. Their sailing lists up to 1875 are available in Hubbard & Winter, 335–346. The history of the Red Star Line and the American Line, later merged with the Inman Line, is well covered by William Henry Flayhart III in *The American Line (1871–1902)* (New York, London, 2000). See also Bonsor (1979), vol. 3, 885–887 for the early years of the Holland-America Line, Bonsor (1975), vol. 2, 829–835 for the Red Star Line, and N.R.P. Bonsor, *North Atlantic*

of the early 1870s saw the establishment of a particularly important British mail-carrying steamship company: the Oceanic Steam Navigation Company Limited, better known as the White Star Line. The company name had been well known for conducting an emigrant service to Australia by sailing ships since the start of the gold rushes in the early 1850s. The line was not only remembered for carrying masses of emigrants to Melbourne but also because of the worst shipwreck to date, and the bankruptcy of the company in the late 1860s. The financial failure was caused not by unsuccessful trade, but by the collapse of the Royal Bank of Liverpool, where the company had heavy debts due to ship investments. When the vessels were sold, the company name remained and was purchased by a man called Thomas Henry Ismay.[442] After restarting the Australian emigrant business, Ismay turned his attention to the North Atlantic service.

Within less than a year from March 1871, the White Star Line brought five new large steamships to the Liverpool – Queenstown – New York route. The *Oceanic, Atlantic, Baltic, Republic* and *Adriatic* were all about 3,700 tons and carried 166 cabin and 1,000 steerage passengers. Ismay not only copied the names of his ships from the famous Collins Line of the 1850s, but also copied the business idea. His ships would not only be the fastest on the North Atlantic run, but also the most comfortable for passengers, with several new innovations – which would naturally soon be copied by other companies.[443]

Another long-lived shipping line to be mentioned here was the Compagnie Générale Transatlantique, or the French Line, which started a contract mail service for the French government between Havre and New York in June 1864. It was the first French mail line since the unsuccessful Herout & de Handel Line of 1847.[444] Contrary to the British government-subsidised mail system with different lines for the North Atlantic (the Cunard Line), the West Indies & South America (the Royal Mail Line), and the East India and Australasian routes (P&O), the French model was as follows: the North Atlantic and West Indies mails were taken care of by one shipping line (the French Line), while the South American and Asian routes were taken care of

---

Seaway (New York, 1979), vol. 3, 920–924 for the American Line.

442 See Robin Gardiner, *The History of the White Star Line* (Surrey, 2001), 25–66. – The emigrant ship *Tayleur*, chartered by the White Star Line for a trip to Australia, was wrecked off Ireland with the loss of 420 lives on her first voyage in 1854. See Gardiner, 26–28.

443 The ship names *Arctic* and *Pacific* were changed to *Republic* and *Celtic* (launched in 1872) due to the tragic associations the company believed the names might invoke among the public. See Fox, 241; Bonsor (1975), vol. 1, 733. – As if to continue the Collins traditions, the White Star Line's *Atlantic* was wrecked in April 1873 with the loss of 585 hands, thus adding new sad figures to the company's own record of worst disasters at sea – to be continued 39 years later when the White Star flagship *Titanic* sank with the well known consequences. For descriptions of the loss of the *Atlantic*, see Gardiner 86–89; Flayhart (2003), 39–55.

444 The company's early operations under the name Compagnie Général Maritime were affected by financial problems and the Crimean War. See Barbance, 31–48; and Bonsor (1978) vol. 2, 619–620. A short English résumé of the company's first years can also be found in Duncan Haws, *French Line. Compagnie Générale Transatlantic. Merchant Fleets* (Pembrokeshire, 1996), 7–8. For the mail service from 1864, see Hubbard & Winter, 275–276.

FIG. 17. *The* Lafayette *of the French Line was one of the two vessels which started the French mail service after a 16 years pause on the North Atlantic route in 1864. (Barbance: Histoire de la Compagnie Générale Transatlantique, 1955).*

by another company, best known by the name Compagnie des Messageries Maritimes, or Messageries Impériales during the Imperial period.[445]

The French Line started its North Atlantic mail service between Havre and New York in 1864. The company's ships were built following the model of the fastest Cunarders, while the paddle-wheelers were already doomed to be outdated by other transatlantic shipping lines. The French Line did not carry steerage passengers either.[446]

In 1865,[447] after a railway service had been established from Brest to Paris, the company's ships started to make a call at Brest *en route*[448] – a very similar arrangement to the Liverpool ships calling at Queenstown to pick up the latest mails from London. This probably gave some competitive advantage to the French Line against HAPAG, whose ships called at Havre on their way from Hamburg to New York. The sailings of the French Line were also transformed to a bi-monthly basis in 1866. HAPAG had changed Southampton to Havre as a port of call in 1869, but the arrangement saw several changes due to the Franco-Prussian war in 1870–1871. From 1872

---

445 For these companies' operations on the West Indian, South American and Asian routes, see the following chapters.
446 Considerable savings in fuel and increased cargo space made the company change this policy later, and they built new screw steamers and rebuilt the old paddle-wheelers. See Bonsor (1978), vol. 2, 619–625.
447 In the 1860s, the French Line services were limited by a series of wars: the American Civil war, the Mexican war and the Franco-Prussian war. See Barbance, 73–84; Haws, 8–9.
448 See Hubbard & Winter, 275–277.

the company had a weekly service from Havre on the way to and from New York.[449]

In January–June 1875 the average westbound voyage by a French Line ship from Havre to New York took 11.5 days, the same as the voyage by a HAPAG ship. For the whole year, the HAPAG average was 11.3 days.[450]

Thus the North Atlantic mail route to New York in the mid-1870s was dominated by three major British shipping lines, two German lines and one French line, in addition to a varying number of other major and minor shipping lines without a mail service. While the British and German companies' ships of the 1870s always had a large steerage capacity, the French Line ships typically did not have that kind of accommodation.[451] A comparison between the performance of different companies indicates that the number of people on board did not necessarily affect the speed after it had been accepted that emigrants could be carried in good new ships instead of those which no longer suited any better purpose. Bigger size and more effective machinery made it possible to keep the speed up – if preferred.

In search of glory – reputation and real life

The competition on the North Atlantic route was very hard during the whole period from the start of steamship traffic in 1838 to 1875, and did not decline after that. The public image of the shipping lines was largely based on the passenger comfort and record journeys, always highlighted by the press. They were also the most tangible advantages from the public's point of view. Even if the individual decision on travelling might have been based on current prices, the reputation of the shipping company played an essential role in decision making.[452]

Even though speed was probably not the most important element for passengers in practice, it was critical for mails and freight. The speed of mail steamers on the North Atlantic route increased steadily throughout the whole steamship era. The *Sirius* made her first voyage in 18.5 days, with an average speed of only eight knots. In the 1870s the *Germanic* of the White

---

449 See Hubbard & Winter, 169,180–189, 277. – The calls at Brest ceased in 1874 due to the continuous difficulty in navigating the approaches to the harbour. See Hubbard & Winter, 286.

450 Hubbard & Winter, 193–194, 286. The French Line records for July–December 1875 are not available.

451 Bonsor assumes that the company was not authorized to carry steerage passengers on board the New York mail steamers between 1871 and 1879. See Bonsor (1978), vol. 2, 628. – Additionally, the number of emigrants from France was rather low on the whole, compared with several other countries. See O'Rourke & Williamson, 155; Kenwood & Lougheed, 57–61; and Tyler, 362.

452 After a tolerable duration of a voyage had been ensured, the speed was not necessarily the most important aspect for the passengers. A passenger survey carried on Liverpool ships in 1882 and 1883 showed that faster ships attracted no more bookings than slower ones of the same line. In fact, the fastest express liners were not usually the most comfortable ships for travelling. Such White Star liners as *Oceanic* and *Celtic*, or later *Olympic* and *Titanic*, the HAPAG steamers *Amerika* and *Kaiserin Auguste Victoria*, or the French liners *France* and *Paris* are examples of luxurious ships that were not even built to be the fastest vessels on the route. See Hyde (1975), 74; and Kludas, 25–26.

Star Line doubled that speed to almost 16 knots. The speed record was improved 17 times from the *Sirius'* first trip to the end of 1875. The figure includes cases where a vessel was able to improve her own speed record, as the *Great Western* did several times during 1838–1843.[453]

As Samuel Cunard stated in his letter to Viscount Canning, the General Postmaster, in 1853, the mails could have been carried across the Atlantic by safe and good vessels of 400 hp, but 'effective and immediate measures [had to be taken] to meet our powerful opponents'.[454] These measures repeatedly meant larger and faster vessels to beat the competitors, not only for the public image of the company, but also for the prestige of the whole country.

The Blue Riband was an entirely unofficial contest for the fastest sea crossing of the North Atlantic. No one ever organized it, and in fact a physical emblem or trophy did not even exist at that time.[455] There were no official, written rules for the competition. The existing rules had been formulated over the decades, and maritime history has seen many kinds of interpretations of the records. As the contest for the Blue Riband was not organized by any authority, no official archive material has been left for historians. The information is mostly based on newspapers that enthusiastically followed the ship arrivals, as well as company records based on ships' logbooks and other corresponding material.[456]

In later historical research, the following rules have been accepted as putting an end to the confusion regarding the speed records of each time: The vessel should be in regular line traffic, westbound from Europe to North America. The eastbound records were considered to be of 'second class'. As the routes were different, only the average speed was calculated. The record sailing from coast to coast did not mean from port to port. In earlier times it was often measured between Daunt's Rock off Queenstown and Sandy Hook lighthouse off New York.[457]

There was typically a correlation between the size of the vessel and its speed. From 1838 until the end of the century almost all Blue Riband holders were also the largest ships in the world, excluding the *Great Eastern*.[458] She was never a Blue Riband holder but was definitely the largest passenger ship ever built until the 20th century.

Diagram 29 shows the development in size and speed of the fastest vessels on the North Atlantic mail route between 1840 and 1880. In the 1870s the size of vessels grew faster than the speed was improving, mainly due to the growing stream of emigrants. In the long run, these two elements – size and speed – would be tightly combined, as will be shown in the Epilogue.

---

453 The *Germanic* made the westbound trip at an average speed of 14.65 knots in 1875 and improved her record to 15.76 knots in 1877. See Kludas, 146–147.
454 Samuel Cunard's letter to Viscount Canning 11.3.1853, published by Staff, 140–142.
455 The 'Hales Trophy' was introduced as late as 1935. See Kludas, 16–18.
456 For a detailed analysis of the source material used in these calculations, see Bonsor (1980), vol. 5, 1867–1871.
457 Kludas, 10–16. Kludas' study of the Blue Riband contest is based on Bonsor's revised list of the record crossings. Bonsor was the first to provide separate lists for west- and eastbound record voyages, and he corrected many errors and omissions in press reports and company statements regarding the duration of the crossings. For these arguments, see Bonsor (1980), vol. 5, 1866–1887.
458 Kludas, 25; Staff, 103.

Diagram 29. Development of size and speed of the fastest mail carrying steamer on the North Atlantic route, 1840-1880

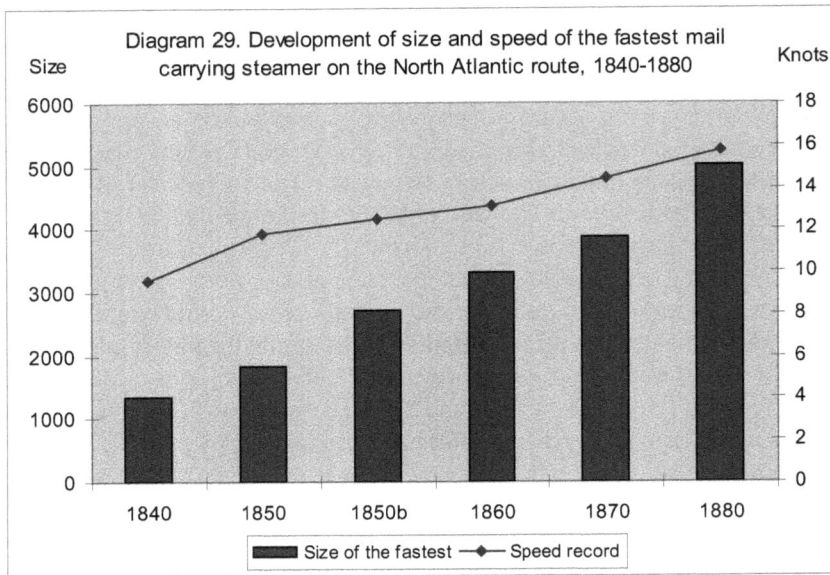

Source: Kludas, 36, 45, 49, 58, 60, 148. – The record ships were the following: *Great Western* (1840), the *Europa* of the Cunard Line (1850), the *Pacific* of the Collins Line (1850b), the *Persia* of the Cunard Line (1860), the *Scotia* of the Cunard Line (1870) and the *Germanic*, built in 1875, of the White Star Line (1880).

Maritime historians sometimes forget that one successful record crossing did not mean that all the North Atlantic traffic was conducted at the same speed. The newest, largest and fastest vessels were not at all representative compared with the rest of the Atlantic fleet. This dilemma characterized the transatlantic service during the whole steamship era, as can be seen in the following diagrams.[459]

In late 1850 (see Diagram 30), the fastest ship on the North Atlantic route was the Collins Line's *Pacific*. She made her record westbound, crossing with an average speed of 12.46 knots. Being one of Collins' four brand new liners, she represented an average vessel of that company but certainly not the rest of the North Atlantic shipping lines.[460] The *Pacific* was more than 1,000 tons larger than an average Cunarder, and more than three times bigger than the smallest ships in this traffic. The average size of vessels in the North Atlantic mail service was 1,946 tons.[461]

In 1860, however, the fastest ship in the North Atlantic mail service was not the largest one. As can be seen in Diagram 31, the short-lived American

---

459 Only companies with mail contracts are included in the diagrams. One major shipping line excluded for this reason is the Anchor Line, which had three ships on the North Atlantic route in 1860, 18 ships in 1870 and 25 ships in 1880 (Staff, 135). Chartered ships with only one to three round trips for the mail-carrying companies are also excluded from the figures.

460 See Staff, 130–132; Kludas, 45, 146.

461 The general average is weighted according to the number of ships in traffic by each company.

North Atlantic Steamship Company, which tried to start a regular mail service with the former Collins liners *Atlantic* and *Adriatic*, was statistically strong when measured by average ship size in tons. The company's *Adriatic* was clearly bigger than any other ship in traffic at the time, but she was never a Blue Riband holder.[462]

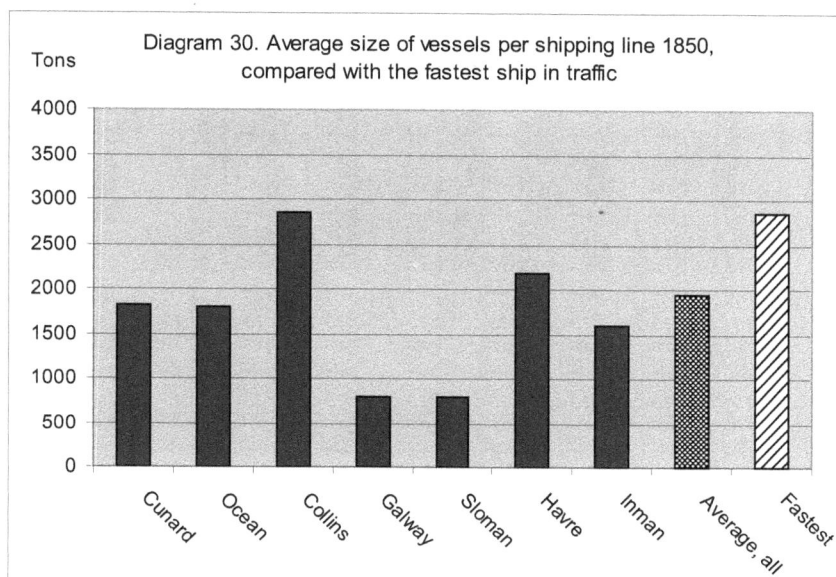

Diagram 30. Average size of vessels per shipping line 1850, compared with the fastest ship in traffic

Sources: Staff, 129–132; Kludas, 45, 146.

The average size of all ships in the North Atlantic mail service in 1860 was 2,225 tons, while the size of the fastest ship, the Cunard Line's *Persia*, was 3,300 tons. She was not a typical Cunarder of the time, but nearly 50% larger than the company's fleet on average, which was 2,260 tons.

In 1870, the fastest ship on the North Atlantic route was clearly larger than any company's average fleet. The Blue Riband holder was the Cunard Line's famous s/s *Scotia*, the company's last paddle-wheeler. Her size was 3,870 tons, while Cunard's fleet was only 2,670 tons on average.

At the beginning of the following decade the fastest ship on the North Atlantic route differed even more visibly from her average competitors. The White Star Line's 5,000-ton *Germanic* was 800 tons larger than the company's fleet on average, and 1,900 tons larger than an average vessel in the mail service.

462 The *Adriatic* made only one trip for the Collins Line before the collapse of the company. She was later owned and chartered by different shipping companies. She carried U.S. mail on five round voyages for the North Atlantic Steamship Company, which closed down in early 1861. During the Civil War she was used as a troop carrier. See Staff, 129–137; Hubbard & Winter, 271.

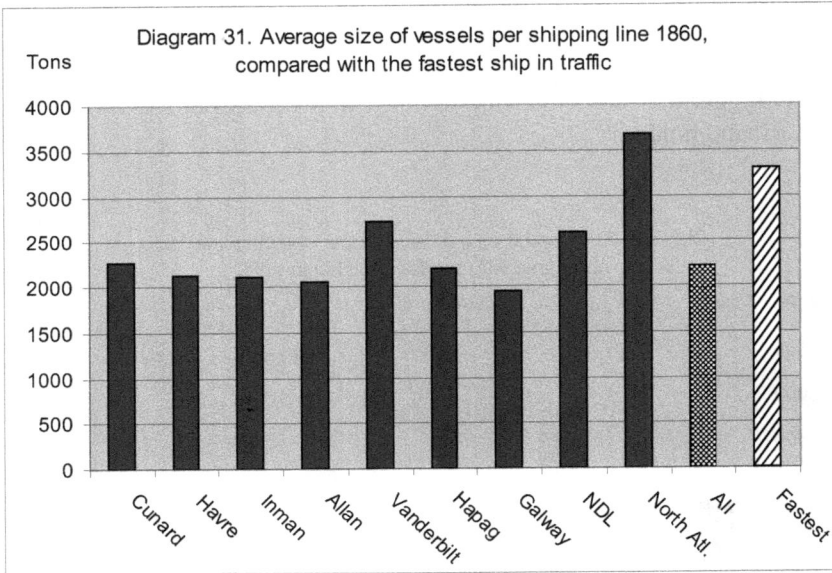

Diagram 31. Average size of vessels per shipping line 1860, compared with the fastest ship in traffic

Sources: Staff, 129–137; Kludas, 49, 146.

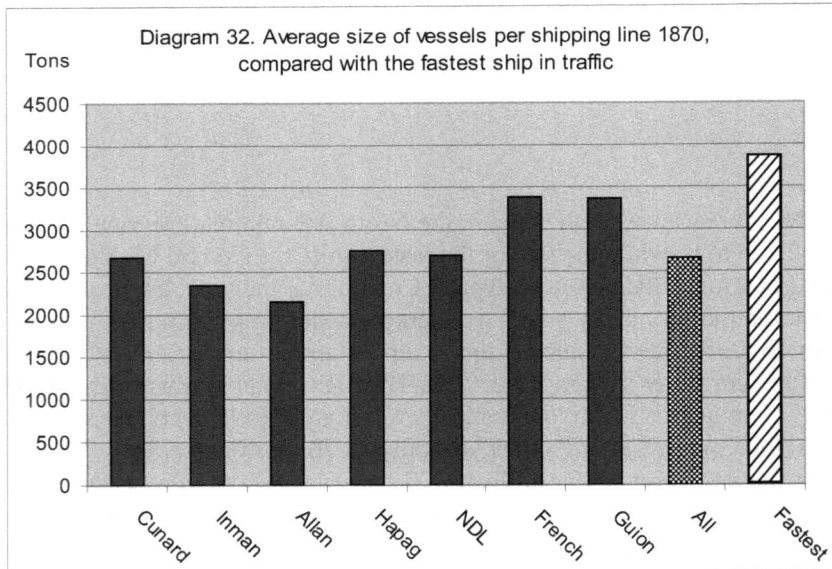

Diagram 32. Average size of vessels per shipping line 1870, compared with the fastest ship in traffic

Sources: Staff, 129–139; Kludas, 49, 146.

Thus the Blue Riband holders were extraordinary, brand new and fast ships, not representing average vessels in the traffic. When talking about speed in this context, it should be remembered that there was a major difference between the record voyages and the bulk of the sailings. The reality was not the same as the best possible performance.

Different strategies led to varying performance between the major mail-carrying companies in 1875. The durations of westbound journeys between Queenstown and New York by the three major British mail-carrying companies are compared in Diagrams 33, 34 and 35.

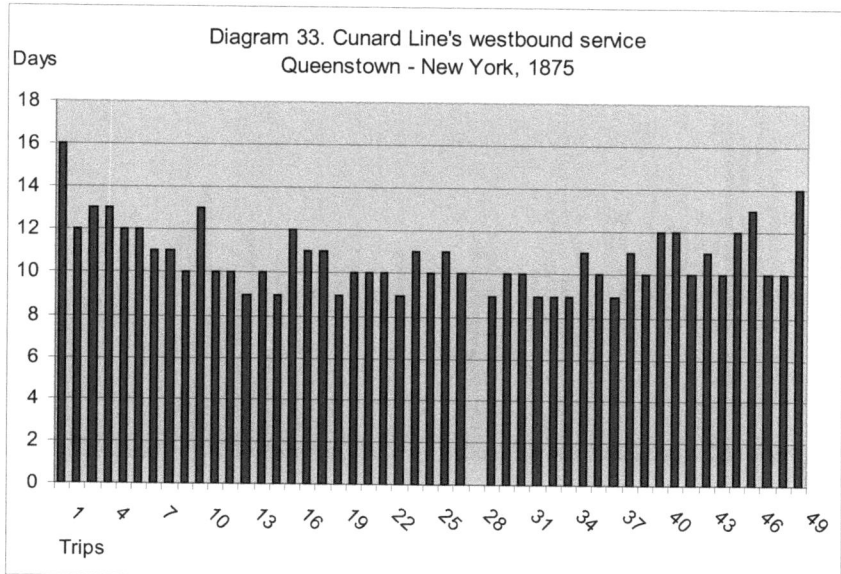

Diagram 33. Cunard Line's westbound service Queenstown - New York, 1875

Source: Sailing lists of Hubbard & Winter, 78–80. – Sailings after 12 December are missing from the records. – The profile of the Cunard Line sailings in 1875 clearly shows that fast and regular mail sailings were no longer the company's main priorities.

While investing in middle-size steamers for frequent emigrant sailings, the Cunard Line lost their former superiority on the North Atlantic mail run. In 1875, their journeys lasted from nine to 13 days, and two winter trips were even longer, taking 14 and 16 days. The average duration of the line's voyages was 10.8 days. This was not very impressive, remembering that the company's steamer *Asia* made an average westbound voyage on the one-day-longer route from Liverpool to New York in 11.4 days in 1850. In addition to the long average duration of the trips, the length of a single journey was quite unpredictable.[463]

As we have already seen, regularity was quite an inaccurate concept in the 19th century and the world was used to irregularities, especially regarding

463 This unfortunate period ended in the 1880s after long internal discussions and, finally, a change in the company's policy. To start a major shipbuilding programme for larger and faster vessels able to compete in the North Atlantic business, the company was publicly listed in 1880 with the name Cunard Steam Ship Co Ltd. See Hyde (1975), 24.

ship arrivals. The vessels were not expected to arrive punctually, as it was considered almost impossible. However, Diagrams 33 and 34 illustrate very clearly that both official British mail carriers had serious problems in meeting any expectations of regularity. After 35 years of steamship line service in the North Atlantic, forecasting the duration of the journey was still difficult.

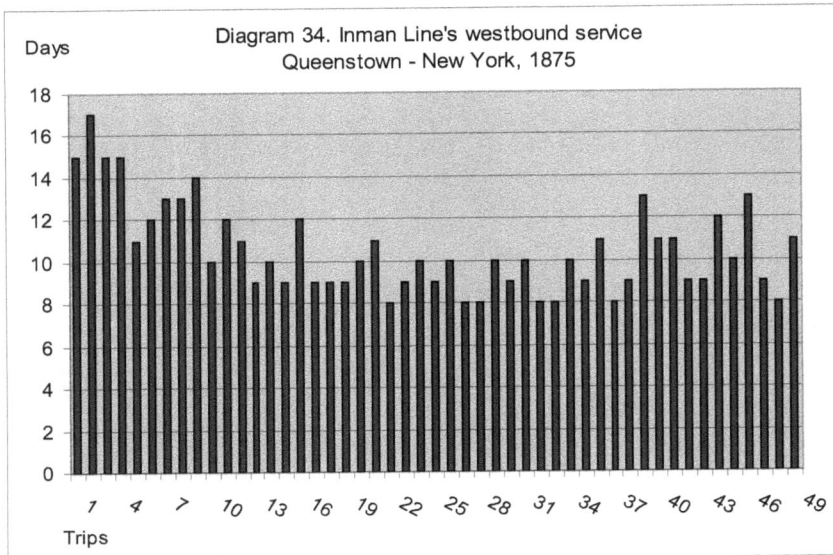

Source: Sailing lists of Hubbard & Winter, 223–224. – Sailings after 10 December are missing from the records. The sailing from Queenstown 2.1.1875 is not included in the diagram due to scale problems. The 23-day-long voyage has been included in the average sailing figure, however. – The profile of the Inman Line's sailings in 1875 clearly shows the problem of having a mixture of different vessels on the same route. Some of the ships were really fast, but the company's performance as a whole was not balanced.

Once again it was shown that a fleet with various kinds of vessels, old and new, large and small, was not ideal for a regular mail service. And history repeated itself – the performance of a newcomer with a fleet of similar, newly launched, effective vessels was superior. Diagram 35 shows the White Star Line's performance on the same route.

After divesting their oldest vessel, the *Oceanic,* and getting the new *Germanic* into traffic instead of the chartered *Belgic,*[464] the White Star Line had a fleet which could make the North Atlantic run in eight to ten days without a single exception during the whole year. Compared with Cunard and Inman, the difference was notable. The average duration of the Inman Line's westbound voyages was 10.8 days – exactly the same as Cunard's,

---

464 Trip one in Diagram 35 was the *Oceanic's* last voyage, and trip four was the *Belgic's* last voyage.

even if some of their ships were clearly faster. The White Star Line had taken the leading role; their average westbound trips took only 9.3 days during the whole year.

Although the White Star Line's regularity – only two days margin in arrivals – was very good compared with the competitors of the time, their sailings were still far from punctual. The *Vanderbilt* had already been able to operate with similar margins 18 years earlier.[465]

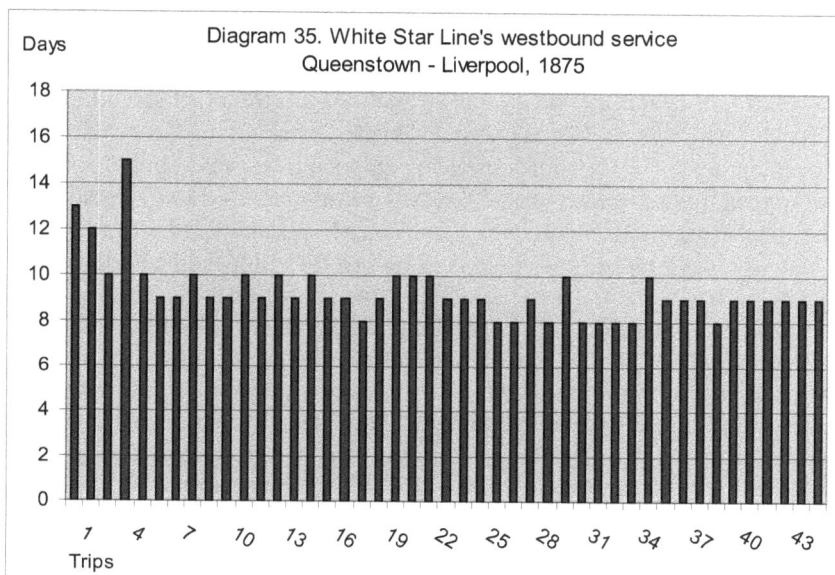

Source: Sailing lists of Hubbard & Winter, 331–333. – Departures after 3 December are missing from the records. – As can be noticed, the White Star Line's performance clearly beat the competitors in speed and regularity of sailings.

A shipping line's reputation did not consist of just passenger comfort, speed and regularity, but of safety as well. In view of the fact that safety was critical for the shipping business, one would have expected the shipping lines to pay more attention to the losses and different delays caused by continuous mishaps. But even if safety regulations were included in the rules of all steamship companies, only the Cunard Line really extracted routine obedience to these regulations.[466]

465 See Diagrams 21 and 22.
466 See Fox, 106–109. – The companies generally paid more attention to regularity than safety, as the mail contracts often included monetary sanctions in case of delays. For concrete examples, see e.g. Arnell (1980), 181–182. – The passengers were naturally worried about their safety and some measures were taken to calm them. 'These steamers carry Phillip's Patent Fire Annihilators. An experienced Surgeon is attached to each steamer', announced the Inman Line in an advertisement in the *Liverpool Mercury* 13.10.1854. In 1874, after several fatal shipwrecks in the Atlantic within a short period, the American Line announced: 'All steamers are fitted with Life Rafts, in addition to the extra number

In fact, it was considered that a certain number of shipwrecks each year were natural and unavoidable. Even if disasters at sea caused unwanted negative publicity for the companies, the incidents were soon forgotten. For a historian of our time, it is somewhat difficult to understand how a shipping company could continue their business after losing nine steamships in mail service over eight years, with a total loss of 556 lives.[467]

During 1838–1875, more than 50 mail-carrying steamships were lost on the North Atlantic run, many of them with all mails and sometimes with considerable loss of human lives.[468] In addition to these ill-fated voyages, a great number of trips were interrupted by mechanical problems, as well as damage caused by gales or collisions with other ships. The steamship machinery was not advanced enough to withstand heavy weather and hard driving: broken shafts, rudders, side-levers and cylinders, as well as lost screw blades, were among the troubles most often mentioned.[469] All steamships were equipped with canvas until the 1880s, and, especially in the early years, the sails were often used to give additional speed or prevent rolling. Moreover, if a steamer lost its rudder or screw, or broke a shaft, she lost steerage and could only be saved by proceeding under sail.[470]

Hargest has collected a notable list of irregularities in the mail sailings, caused by different problems.[471] Hubbard's & Winter's sailing lists, covering the years 1840–1875, are even more informative, although no records are complete in this regard. According to the notes of the latter source, not counting the trips where vessels were lost, more than 90 trips were interrupted due to machinery problems and 16 due to storm damage. Additionally, ships ran aground more than 20 times, needing repairs in half of the cases. Collisions caused damage in 12 cases – often to both parties involved in the incident. In a few cases the ship struck something – an iceberg, a whale or a reef. One ship caught fire.[472]

---

of Life Boats and Life Preservers.' See *Lloyd's List* 9.10.1874.

467   The Allan Line lost the following vessels in shipwrecks on the Liverpool – Quebec/Portland mail route: *Canadian (I)* 1857, *Indian* 1859, *Hungarian* 1860, *Canadian (II)* 1861, *North Briton* 1861, *Anglo-Saxon* 1863, *Norwegian* 1863, *Bohemian* 1864 and *Jura* 1864. Most of the disasters took place off the rocky and foggy Canadian coast, but the line even managed to lose one of their vessels as a result of a mishap in the River Mersey at Liverpool. See Bonsor (1980), vol. 5, 1888–1889; and Hubbard & Winter, 131–144.

468   The total number of lost passenger steamers was 65. Of these, 36 were lost while carrying mails under government contract. In addition, 14 of these ships carried mail occasionally. For example, the Anchor Line, not listed by Hubbard & Winter but mentioned as a potential mail carrier by Staff, lost 11 passenger ships on the North Atlantic run during that period. The Inman Line lost six ships during the period, but two of the disasters took place before the company had a mail contract. The loss of the pioneering steamer *President* in 1841 has been added to the figure as she carried American mails. See Bonsor (1980), vol. 5, 1888–1890; Hubbard & Winter, 195–196; and Staff, 135. Hubbard and Winter have listed all the sailings of steamship lines with a mail contract. Staff has also listed a few other lines that carried mails occasionally.

469   Hubbard & Winter, passim.

470   There are several examples of mail sailings that ended in returning to port under canvas. The sails were used in these kinds of situations as late as the 1870s, 40 years after the invention of ocean steam power. See Hubbard & Winter, 18, 49, 62, 80, 98, 113; 277, 278, etc.

471   Hargest, 127–133.

472   Total wrecks, caused by any of these problems, are not included in these statistics. Of all the passenger steamship losses between 1841–1875, no less than 41 were wrecked, mainly off the coasts of North America and Ireland, two were abandoned, four destroyed

In addition to machinery troubles and problems caused by stranding or collisions, more than 50 voyages were lengthened due to the need for coal. Even though ships normally carried extra coal to manage delays caused by heavy weather, it sometimes happened that they had to call at Halifax – or the German and French ships in England – for coal before the end of the trip. Delays due to fog, ice and snowstorms were common on the North Atlantic route as well: Hubbard & Winter report about 80 cases.[473]

The management of all companies could have done much to prevent unnecessary delays, problems and loss of money, as well as loss of vessels and human lives. It was not by chance that some companies were continuously in trouble and had to cease their operations within a few years, or even less, due to general mismanagement. Typically, the shipping lines that had introduced the latest technology first, especially the screw steamers, had more engine troubles than the more conservative Cunard, which was accused by competitors of letting others do the expensive experiments and just collecting the benefits.[474] The cautious attitude of the company can also been seen in the number of delays caused by fog or ice. Even though the Cunard Line's vessels ran aground or collided, and even though they were not immune to mechanical trouble, almost half of their ships' recorded delays were caused by cautious waiting in bad weather.[475]

On the whole it can be said that the speed of mail steamers improved notably during the period 1838–1875. The frequency of the mail service grew from a monthly or bi-monthly service to almost daily traffic from England and at least bi-weekly sailings from the German and French ports. The regularity of the departures did not really improve on the early days of contract mail sailings, as the departures were generally regular from 1840 onwards. Bad weather, mechanical problems and other misfortunes caused delays and heavy losses in the service throughout the period. The size of the ships was steadily growing, and so was the speed. Yet the record holders were lonely examples of the latest technology. The bulk of the mail steamers in everyday service consisted of smaller and slower vessels as the fleets were only gradually modernized in the most economic way.

by fire, five lost in collision, three foundered, one collided with an iceberg, and nine went missing without trace. See Bonsor (1980), vol. 5, 1888–1890.

473 Hubbard & Winter, passim.

474 Hyde (1975), 33. – A lively discussion about the technological progress versus government mail subsidies has been published in Holt, *Review of the Progress...* Institute of Civil Engineers. Minutes of Proceedings, 2–94.

475 During 36 years, Cunard Line's ships ran aground at least eight times in addition to the two shipwrecks. However, no repairs were needed in four of the eight times. The ships were involved in at least two collisions and once struck a submerged object, thought to be a whale. Two delays were caused by non-detailed storm damage and ten delays by broken machinery. At least 23 major delays were caused by fog, ice or snowstorms. Additionally, Cunard ships were reported to have passed Queenstown without calling in due to heavy weather at least five times during the period. See Hubbard & Winter, 17–80. – Even if these lists are far from perfect, they give an overall picture of the reasons for delays in the mail service and the different shipping company profiles. During the first 75 years of its existence, Cunard Line made thousands of round trips across the Atlantic and lost only three ships, no passengers, and almost no mail.

What happened to the speed of business information transmission?

Although so many new speed records had been made and so many lives lost in an unnecessary speed contest during the two decades between the mid-1850s and mid-1870s, it is surprising to notice how little the efforts to improve the speed of ships actually affected business information transmission after a certain level of performance had been achieved. This level was achieved during the contest between the Cunard Line and the Collins Line in 1851, as can be noticed in Diagram 36.

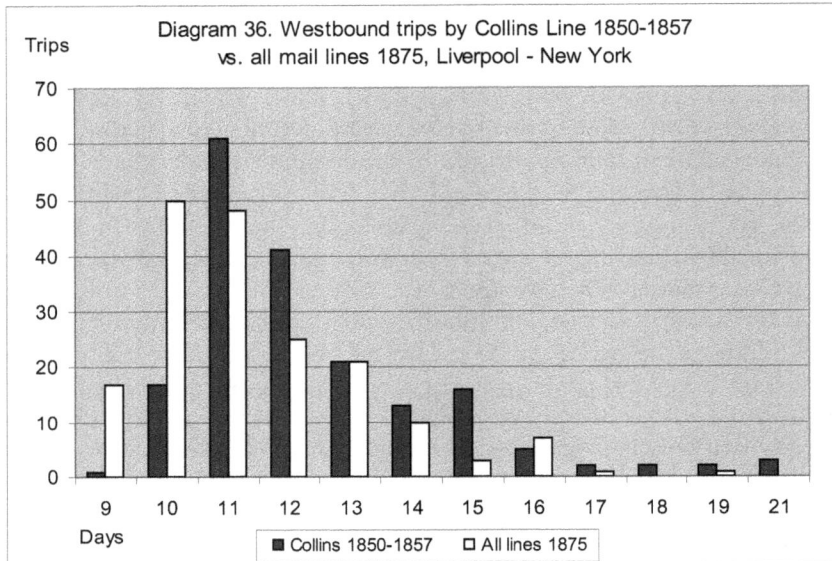

Diagram 36. Westbound trips by Collins Line 1850-1857 vs. all mail lines 1875, Liverpool - New York

Source: Hubbard & Winter, 78–80, 98–108, 223–224, 315–316, 331–333. – 'All mail lines' include all the contract mail steamers on the Liverpool–New York run in 1875: the Cunard, Inman, White Star and Guion Lines. The number of Collins Line trips during 1850–1857 was 184, and the number of mail steamer voyages in 1875 was 183.

The diagram, even if somewhat artificial, shows that during the two decades, the duration of an average westbound crossing of mail steamers had only been reduced by one day.[476] Simultaneously, the spread of the duration of all voyages was about the same. In 1875, the trip could still take anything between nine and 19 days, while about half of the journeys, or 53.6%, were conducted in ten to 11 days. In 1850–1857 the duration of Collins Line trips varied between nine and 21 days, and 55.4% were made in 11 to 12 days.

---

476 An average Collins Line trip westwards – including the *ad hoc* voyages by chartered steamers in 1857 – took 12.4 days, while an average westbound voyage of all contract mail steamers on that route in 1875 took 11.3 days.

Table 26 shows the information circulation between Liverpool and New York enabled by the mail contract lines in 1875. The starting point is a letter sent from Liverpool on 1.1.1875.

As already noted, the westbound trips were shortened by approximately one day (0.9) on average between 1851 and 1875. The mail contract lines made 296 round trips on the North Atlantic run in 1875. Additionally, there were 49 eastbound trips by HAPAG, which did not call at the English ports westbound. Nevertheless, this large network could not enable more than 14 consecutive information circles within a year. The improvement was not impressive, compared with the 12 information circles made by the Cunard Line and Collins Line ships during 70 round trips in 1851. The duration of one information circle had been reduced somewhat more. While it had taken 27.3 days on average to get an answer to a letter from Liverpool to New York in 1851, the figure was 26.1 days in 1875.

The ships had been technologically improved since the early 1850s, which enabled more efficient use of the vessels in service. For example, the Cunard Line's *China* made ten round trips in 1875 and her average westbound trip from Liverpool to New York took 10.9 days.[477] The White Star Line's new *Adriatic* made ten round trips in 1875 as well. Her average westbound trip from Liverpool to New York took ten days. Compared with the 1850s, the Cunard Line's *Asia* made seven to nine annual round trips during her best years.[478]

Since there were almost 300 annual round trips conducted in 1875 by ships that were more efficient than ever before, why did the information circulation not reach the maximum, which would have been 17 consecutive circles per year instead of 14?[479] The answer is that there was no need for it. Since the final introduction of the Atlantic cable in 1866, the mail steamers had lost their important role as the first news bringers, just like the American sailing packets in 1838. It was not considered necessary to organize ship departures in the most efficient way from the mail system's point of view. The transmission of the bulk of the mails – even if still very important – was not so urgent any more. This was probably one of the ideas behind the radical changing of the mail contracts that occurred at the end of the 1860s, even though it has not been clearly pointed out by postal historians.

If the sailing dates, especially from New York, had been organized more evenly, there would have been a mail ship departure from that port almost every day of the year. Instead, four lines organized their departures on Saturdays, while there were no departures at all on several days of the week.[480]

---

477 Between 5.1.1875 and 9.1.1876, both dates from Liverpool. (Sailing lists of Hubbard & Winter, 78–80) She served mainly on the Liverpool–Boston route. Built in 1862, she was one of the oldest ships the company had in transatlantic service. See Bonsor (1975), vol. 1, 146–147.

478 Sailing lists of Hubbard & Winter, 28–41.

479 The estimate of the maximum is based on an average ten-day westbound and nine-day eastbound crossing, allowing one day for the writer at both ends of the journey.

480 In 1875, the Inman Line, the White Star Line and Norddeutscher Lloyd all sailed from New York on Saturdays, which was also the departure day of the Cunard Line's ships from Boston. See the sailing lists of Hubbard & Winter, 78–80, 193–194, 223–224, 260–262, 315–316, 331–333.

TABLE 26. *Consecutive information circles enabled by transatlantic mail steamers in 1875, an example.*

Letter sent by mail ship, company	Ship departure, Queenstown / Southampton (S)	Ship arrival, New York	Next possible departing mail ship, company	Ship departure, New York	Ship arrival, Queenstown / Plymouth (Pl)	Infor- mation circle, days
Parthia CL	3.1.	19.1.	Pommerania HPG	21.1.	31.1. (Pl)	30
Neckar NDL	2.2. (S)	14.2.	Abyssinia CL	17.2.	28.2.	28
Hermann NDL	2.3. (S)	13.3.	Cuba CL	17.3.	26.3.	26
Mosel NDL	30.3. (S)	10.4.	China CL	14.4.	24.4.	27
Rhein NDL	27.4. (S)	8.5.	Scotia, CL	12.5.	21.5.	26
Donau NDL	25.5. (S)	4.6.	Germanic WSL	5.6.	14.6.	22
Wisconsin GL	17.6.	27.6.	Russia CL	30.6.	9.7.	24
Main NDL	13.7. (S)	23.7.	City of Berlin, IL	24.7.	2.8.	22
Wyoming GL	5.8.	14.8.	Wisconsin GL	17.8.	27.8.	24
Rhein NDL	31.8. (S)	10.9.	Britannic WSL	11.9.	20.9.	22
City of Richmond IL	24.9.	3.10.	Scythia CL	6.10.	15.10.	23
Oder NDL	19.10. (S)	30.10.	Dakota GL	2.11.	11.11.	25
Abyssinia CL	14.11.	26.11.	City of Chester IL	27.11.	6.12.	24
Wyoming GL	9.12.	20.12.	Russia CL	22.12.	31.12.	24
Average, days						24.8
Comparable average to Liverpool						26.1

Sources: Sailing lists of Hubbard & Winter, 78–80, 193–194, 223–224, 260–262, 315–316, 331–333. CL = Cunard Line, GL = Guion Line, HPG = HAPAG, IL = Inman Line, NDL = Norddeutscher Lloyd, WSL = White Star Line. – Although the home port of most vessels was still Liverpool, Hubbard & Winter only give records as far as Queenstown for the year 1875. The average duration from Queenstown or Southampton to New York was 10.9 days, and if calculated from Liverpool, it was 11.4 days. The respective averages of eastbound voyages were 9.4 days and 10.3 days.

As can be seen in Table 26, there were sometimes four-day intervals between arrivals and departures, while there could also be a mail steamship departure on the very next day after a letter's arrival.[481]

The date of arrivals at the destination was still unpredictable. A few examples of the variation in length of the Saturday sailings give an idea of the problem.

As shown in Tables 27a–c, the duration of information transmission by the Saturday sailings could last anything between ten and 15 days. One extra day has been added to the examples for the inland trips between New York and Boston, as well as from Queenstown or Southampton to Liverpool. In practice, a letter could sometimes reach the Boston departure, even if written in New York on the same day as the ship was sailing. The improved inland connections, especially railways, had streamlined the whole chain of communications, giving more equal opportunities to the cities outside New York.

481 In the example, 13.3.–17.3.1875, 10.4.–14.4.1875 and 8.5.–12.5.1875; and 23.7.–24.7.1875, 10.9.–11.9.1875 and 26.11.–27.11.1875.

TABLE 27 A–C. *Duration of some Saturday mail sailings from New York, 1875.*

Ship, line	Departure date from New York / Boston (B)	Arrival date in Queenstown /Southampton (S)	Duration of journey from New York to Liverpool, days
Mosel, NDL	6.3.1875	17.3.1875 (S)	12 (11 + 1)
China, CL	6.3.1875 (B)	15.3.1875	11 (1 + 9 + 1)
Celtic, WS	6.3.1875	16.3.1875	11 (10 + 1)
City of New York, IL	6.3.1875	20.3.1875	15 (14 + 1)

Ship, line	Departure date from New York / Boston (B)	Arrival date in Queenstown /Southampton (S)	Duration of journey from New York to Liverpool, days
Oder, NDL	3.4.1875	14.4.1875 (S)	12 (11 + 1)
Atlas, CL	3.4.1875 (B)	13.4.1875	12 (1 + 10 + 1)
Adriatic, WS	3.4.1875	12.4.1875	10 (9 + 1)
City of Brooklyn, IL	3.4.1875	15.4.1875	13 (12 + 1)

Ship, line	Departure date from New York / Boston (B)	Arrival date in Queenstown /Southampton (S)	Duration of journey from New York to Liverpool, days
Rhein, NDL	15.5.1875	25.5.1875 (S)	11 (10 + 1)
Algeria, CL	15.5.1875 (B)	24.5.1875	11 (1 + 9 + 1)
Celtic, WS	15.5.1875	24.5.1875	10 (9 + 1)
City of Berlin, IL	15.5.1875	24.5.1875	10 (9 + 1)

Source: Sailing lists of Hubbard & Winter, 78, 223–224, 261, 332. CL = Cunard Line, IL = Inman Line, NDL = Norddeutscher Lloyd, WS = White Star Line.

Table 28 shows the main changes in business information transmission by sail and steam on the North Atlantic route 1815–1875, starting from the Falmouth packets and ending with the international steamship companies. In addition to giving some rough estimates of changes in speed and regularity, the table shows the number of round trips conducted by vessels with a mail contract and the number of consecutive information circles their services enabled each year in question. Additionally, there are a few comments on the reasons for improvement or stagnation of services.

TABLE 28. *Business information transmission by sail and steam on the North Atlantic route, 1815–1875.*

	Period in mail service	Speed	Regularity		Frequency – round trips per year	Consecutive information circles per year*	Reason for improvement / stagnation
			Departures	Arrivals			
Merchant ships	(Continuously)	– –	– –	– –	n.a.	n.a.	No importance for information transmission on this route during this period.
Falmouth packets (NY route)	1815-26	– (–)	–	– –	12	(1816: 2.5) 1826: 3	In 1826 departures were better coordinated in New York.
American sailing packets; Black Ball Line only	1818-22	–	+	–	12	1818: 4	Regular sailings.
American sailing packets; all Liverpool – New York	1822-47	–	+	–	1825: 48 1838: 60	1825: 5 1838: 5	In 1825, more frequent sailings. In 1838, sailings of the new ships were not coordinated.
Pioneering steamers	1838-49 (& 1852)	+	+	–	1839: 15	1839: 6	Faster speed, especially westwards.
Mail contract steamers; Cunard Line	From 1840 –	+ (+)	+ +	+	1845: 20	1845: 8	Regular sailings.
Mail contract steamers; Cunard, Collins, Ocean & Havre Line	1848-57	+ (+)	+ +	+	1851: 92 (70 by Cunard Line & Collins Line)	1851: 12	Improvement in speed; more frequent and well coordinated sailings.
Steamers in competition; Cunard, Inman, White Star, Guion, NDL, HAPAG	From 1858-75	+ (+)	+ +	+	1875: 296 (+ 49 by HAPAG eastbound only)	1875: 14	Slight improvement in speed; departures should have been more effectively organized for maximum benefit.

– – = very poor; – = poor; + = rather good; + + = good
n.a. = not applicable – this question has not been examined as merchant ships were not a primary or even a secondary means of information transmission on this route during the period.
* An information circle is the time between sending a letter and getting an answer to it. For example, in 1826 it was possible to send a letter and get an answer to it, send an answer to that letter and get an answer to it, etc. in three consecutive information circles per year by using the Falmouth packets. In 1875 fourteen such circles could be made per year by using the mail steamers.

Business Information and the Telegraph

It has generally been assumed that all overseas information transmission was slow and stable before the time of the telegraph, and that it was then suddenly catapulted into the modern age. As has already been shown in the earlier chapters of this study, the improvement in business communications by sea was continuous throughout the period from sail to steam, as was the development of the telegraph and its use in business information transmission. Instead of a fast jump from one era to another, the shift from information transmission by ship to telegraph took its time and included both progression and setbacks.

Throughout history there have been situations where it has been necessary to send messages faster than a man alone could move from one place to another. Messengers on horseback and carrier pigeons were used as early as Ancient Egyptian times. Early visual systems of communication, using smoke by day or the glow of fires by night to send signals from one hill to another, are well known in different parts of the world.[482]

The early methods of signaling messages from one place to another were generally used for military purposes, such as in the Roman Empire and by Napoleon during his many wars. The first really successful optical telegraph was developed by Claude Chappe, a French clergyman, during the years of the revolution. His invention was introduced in France in the 1790s and soon adapted in Sweden by Abraham Niclas Edelcrantz[483] to be used for royal messages around Stockholm, and between Grisslehamn and Eckerö on the important mail route from Sweden to Finland. Contrary to Napoleon, who successfully used the optical telegraph during wartime, the Swedes neglected to maintain the system and it failed during the time of greatest need during the war between Sweden and Russia in 1808–1809. Finland was incorporated into Russia and the optical telegraph was forgotten for years. During the Crimean war, however, new optical lines were built by the Russians along the Finnish shores and successfully used for military purposes.[484]

Although the French optical telegraph system had aroused enthusiasm in the German states from the very beginning, it took 38 years before the invention was adapted by neighbours. The first line was erected in Prussia in 1832. The main reasons for the delay were related to decision making on the most practical system, as well as political problems between the states. The British developed their own system based on Chappe's idea, and rather close to the one developed by Edelcrantz. Lord George Murray's

---

482 A general overview of early communications systems has been presented in several telegraph histories, independent of their more or less local focus. See e.g. Frank Large, *Faster than the Wind. The Liverpool to Holyhead Telegraph* (Great Britain, 1998), 8–9; Einar Risberg, *Suomen Lennätinlaitoksen historia 1855–1955* (The History of the Telegraph in Finland) (Helsinki, 1959), 15–22; and James D. Reid, *The Telegraph in America. Morse Memorial.* (New York, 1886), 2–6.

483 Despite being called a Swede in many history books, A.N. Edelcrantz was of Finnish origin. He was born and grown up in Turku, and moved to Stockholm for high administrative posts in his later years. (Risberg, 33)

484 Large, 10–11; Risberg, 23–27, 30–49.

FIG. 18. *Early pre-telegraph communications off Liverpool. The Bidston lighthouse was erected in 1771 as a navigational aid for vessels in the Rock Channel. Bidston Hill provided a fine point to spot vessels approaching the port and convey news of their arrival to their owners in town. The flag of the shipowner was raised when one of their vessels was identified. Additional signs informed how many ships were approaching, as well as whether they were snows, brigs or ships. A flag flying at half-mast indicated a vessel in distress. By 1825, there were some 50 flagpoles stretching both north and south of the lighthouse. © National Museums Liverpool (Merseyside Maritime Museum).*

optical telegraph was used between London and Dover, Portsmouth and Great Yarmouth. Due to the usual fog and poor visibility at the coasts of England, the optical telegraph was never a great success on the Channel. The London – Portsmouth semaphore telegraph was in Admiralty use until 1847, however.[485]

The optical telegraph was normally exclusively used by the authorities, especially for military purposes. In Sweden, exceptionally, it was suggested as far back as 1810 that the lines could be used for commercial purposes. The proposal seems to have been ahead of its time, as it did not arouse notable interest among either the administrative decision makers or the commercial associations. Nevertheless, private announcements and maritime intelligence were transmitted by the optical telegraph during later years, and from 1837 this service was subject to a fee.[486]

The noteworthy exception to all the other optical systems in the world was the telegraph, which was introduced between Liverpool and Holyhead off the west coast of Wales in 1827 (for an earlier system, see Fig. 18). Built

485 Risberg, 27–30; G.R.M. Garratt, *One Hundred Years of Submarine Cables* (London, 1950), 2.
486 Risberg, 49.

by private capital and operated by the Trustees of the Liverpool Docks, the system was especially planned for commercial use.[487] In these circumstances, it could indeed shorten the duration of important information transmission by several days.

The system was developed and partly owned by Barnard L. Watson, probably a former lieutenant of the Royal Navy. It included 11 stations at Liverpool, Bidston, Hilbre Island, above Prestatyn, near Rhyl, above Colwyn Bay, on the Great Orme, Puffin Island, above Point Lynas, on the west side of Anglesey, and on Holyhead Mountain. It was originally a one-mast system, overhauled and improved in 1841 as a two-mast system, and was replaced by the electric telegraph as late as 1861.[488]

The stations were located within 3.3 to 12.5 miles, or about five to 20 kilometres, distant from each other in places where there would be the fewest problems with visibility. Even if the duration of message transmission varied greatly depending on weather conditions, the system normally worked rather well and the signals were seldom stopped for a whole day. The message was generally transmitted through the whole chain of stations within a few minutes.[489]

The signal system was based on numbered codes covering the alphabet, compass signals, time signals, words and phrases, auxiliary verbs, merchant names, telegraph stations and gazetteers, ship names and signals between pilot boats. The words and phrases included e.g. lists of different kinds of hazards met at sea to be forwarded to the shipowner or Lloyds. There were also references to various cargoes – useful knowledge for the shipowners who could start selling the freight before it had physically arrived in port.[490]

The Liverpool–Holyhead telegraph was used in business information transmission from the very beginning. Its origins date back to the period, when the port of Liverpool had started to grow and was the most important destination for the American sailing packets. Once it was known that a vessel was approaching, arrangements could be made for the disposal of the cargo, and it was also possible to start planning the next voyage. They could also learn the state of the wind at Holyhead, and important political or commercial information from Ireland or America could be transmitted by the homeward bound vessels.[491]

---

487 Large, 3, 18–19, 109–111; Risberg, 30.
488 Large, 3, 19, 109–111, 115–117.
489 Large, 83–89, 97.
490 Large, 92–93, 99–100. In fact, there were two different code books. Large explains the differences, as well as the control codes used by Chappe and Edelcrantz, 90–107.
491 Large, 18. – *Lloyd's List* commonly reported that ships were arriving 'off Holyhead' or 'off Liverpool'. Especially after the railway had been opened for the whole distance between Liverpool and London, the news of a ship's arrival off Holyhead was published in London before the vessel was in the port of Liverpool. Another news service speeded up by the telegraph was the 'Vessels spoken with' also published in *Lloyd's List*. It included information about vessels met at sea: the name of the ship and her captain, port of origin and destination, as well as the longitude and latitude where met at sea. When comparing the contents of 'Vessels spoken with' and the published information on ship arrivals, it seems evident that many of the reports were sent by the optical telegraph system while the ship was still at sea.

In a report in 1836, Barnard L. Watson gave a brief summary which shows the scale of operations: 'In the year 1828 there were about 847 vessels reported by name inward and outward bound; in 1831 there were 1712; in the present year, up to 30th Nov., there were upwards 2440, besides several hundred without numbers, upwards of 500 reports respecting Pilot boats, about 200 communications respecting wrecks, accidents and casualties, and the state of the wind and weather reported upwards of 700 different times. Telegraph Office, Liverpool, Dec 12, 1836.'[492]

On average, this meant that about eight ships were reported outwards or inwards each day, as well as one or two pilot boat movements. Additionally, there was news about problems at sea at least every second day. Weather conditions were reported twice every day. As there were naturally periods with less traffic at sea, especially in the winter, some days during the best sailing season must have been rather busy at the telegraph stations.

Thus, the semaphore telegraph was used in business communications in this particular area between merchants, their ships at sea, and Lloyd's – and spread by these parties to other stakeholders when needed – from the 1820s.

In the 1830s, the electric telegraph was invented more or less simultaneously in several countries and developed into different forms. The needle telegraph, developed by the British W.F. Cooke and Charles Wheatstone from the original invention made by the Danish Hans Christian Oersted would be used especially on the railways. It appeared to be very important for safety reasons to have a warning system for approaching trains and the electric telegraph grew very fast especially in countries were the railway network was quickly built.[493]

In 1845, Cooke installed an electric telegraph between London and Portsmouth, soon rendering the semaphore obsolete. In the same year negotiations were begun with the government to lay a telegraph on the Chester to Holyhead railway line. The total length would be 300 miles linking London to Holyhead via Birmingham, Manchester and Liverpool, and thus giving Lloyd's 'every facility for shipping purposes'.[494] It remains somewhat unclear what happened to this plan. The electric telegraph between Holyhead and Liverpool seems to have been completed just fifteen years later, in December 1860.[495] Although much discussed, the Committee of the Liverpool Docks 'did not see any need to change the system'.[496]

492 Large, 19.
493 J. V. Kieve, *Electric Telegraph. A Social and Economic History* (Devon, 1973), 18–35. See also Risberg, 54–64; Reid, 71–75.
494 Large, 14; Kieve, 38.
495 Large, 116; Kieve, 55–56, 62, 64.
496 Large, 115. – According to Large, there were also many practical problems to be solved. Land owners were unhappy with the wires crossing their fields, and submarine cables caused constant difficulties even in the 1860s. Additionally, the communications between ships at sea and the telegraph on land was still based on flags and other good old-fashioned systems which needed eye-sight. The wireless telegraph later used by ships would be invented only at the end of the century. (Large, 115–117) The existing semaphore system probably also gave some advantage to the Liverpool merchants in receiving news from the sea before it was forwarded to London. This benefit was not long-lived, however. In

FIG. 19. *One of the early commercial uses of the electric telegraph was to inform the results of race courses to the betting rooms in town. The Electric & International Telegraph Company had their office at the race course in Newmarket from 1860.*

An experimental electric line was laid between Paris and Rouen in 1845, and, as it was a success, the French government decided in 1846 to replace all the optic lines with electric ones. Wheatstone & Cooke also built a telegraph between Brussels and Antwerp in 1846. The lines used to transmit marine news between Bremen and Bremerhaven in 1847, as well as between Hamburg and Cuxhaven in 1848, were similarly built by private entrepreneurs. In Sweden the optical telegraph stations were replaced by electrical stations one by one from 1853, and the line between Moscow and St. Petersburg was brought into use in 1858.[497]

the early 1850s, an electric telegraph line was built between Holyhead and Chester along the railway. In addition, a direct telegraph line existed between London and Liverpool from 1851. (Kieve, 49, 55, 82)

497 Large, 14; Risberg, 64. – According to Reid, the Hamburg–Cuxhaven telegraph line, built by two Americans, Charles Robinson and Charles L. Chapin by using relay technology, worked better than the Wheatstone system. (Reid, 85)

The early electric telegraph was mainly of state interest, and not even meant for commercial use (see Fig. 19). The lines were opened for public use in the late 1840s or early 1850s, or even later depending on the country in question. One of the first such companies was the Electric Telegraph Company in Britain in 1848. The costs of sending messages were very high at the beginning, but they reduced notably in the coming years. Connections between different countries were opened in the late 1840s.[498]

The number of messages sent by telegraphs increased fast during the first 15 years in public use. The following comparison illustrates the progress made on the European continent, in Britain, France, Belgium and Austria.

TABLE 29. *Number of electric telegraph messages sent, 1851–1866.*

Country	1851	1856	1861	1866
Austria	45,000	252,000	846,500	2,507,500
Belgium	14,000	99,000	269,000	1,128,000
France	9,000	360,000	920,000	2,842,500
Britain*	99,000	812,000	1,201,500	3,150,000

Sources: BPP, Transport and Communications, Posts and Telegraphs 3. Reports from Select Committees on the Electric Telegraphs Bill with the Proceedings, etc. 1867–1868, Appendix 1, 17–18; Kieve, 68.

Due to differences in sources, the British figures cover only the messages sent by the Electric & International Telegraph Company, which held approximately 60% of the market share in Britain in 1868. The main competitor, the British & Irish Magnetic Telegraph Company was about half the size of its main rival, measured by miles of lines or sent messages, whether they were inland or including the Atlantic and continental cables. Together the 'Electric' and the 'Magnetic', as they were popularly called among the public, transferred 96% of the overseas telegrams to and from Britain in 1868.[499]

498 Risberg, 64–65.
499 Kieve, 68, 73. –The Electric Telegraph Company had been established in 1846 on the basis of Cooke's and Wheatstone's patents to build the telegraph in cooperation with the railway companies, while the English & Irish Magnetic Telegraph Company was established in 1851 to provide links between England and Ireland by submarine telegraph. It was merged with the British Electric Telegraph Company in 1856, forming the British & Irish Magnetic Telegraph Company. Its technology was based on magnetic electricity. The company's head office was in Liverpool, and there was a strong provincial and commercial interest among the local shareholders and directors. (Kieve, 43–44, 54, 269) – Britain nationalized the telegraph companies in 1868–1869 and the Post Office took over the businesses. See Kieve, 138–175. The new arrangements included a uniform one shilling rate for 20 words, independent of the distance, following the model of the uniform one penny postage rate. As a result, the number of sent telegrams increased in Britain from about 6,500,000 in 1869 to 19,250,000 in 1875 (calculated from mid-1874 to mid-1875). Such expansion was not seen in any other country. See Kieve 162–163, 183. The maximum inland rates had been reduced from ten to four shillings in the early 1850s, and one shilling rates had

While the Europeans were building their technologically different electric telegraphs, the Americans chose a further option. Samuel F.B. Morse, originally an American artist, invented an electro-magnetic telegraph, which was based on experiments by the German professor Georg Simon Ohm and the American engineer Joseph Henry. Morse introduced his system publicly in 1837 and after a few years of improvements it was brought into public use in the United States in 1845.[500]

As the U.S. Government refused Samuel Morse's offer to sell his invention for the sum of $100,000, private capital was collected to establish the Magnetic Telegraph Company. In early November 1845 its first line was opened between Philadelphia and Norristown, Pa. As if to point out the basic difference between the European and the American systems, the office in Philadelphia opened on the second floor of the Merchants' Exchange.[501] It would become typical that the European telegraph companies were mainly state-owned, while the Americans were private. Between the late 1840s and the 1860s, the American continent saw tremendous growth of telegraph networks operated by local companies under the Morse patent, and cooperating with the railroad.[502]

The spread of the new technology met difficulties in most places. Several problems had to be solved – both technical and practical. None of the early lines could boast about their transmitting capacity, and therefore much business had to be done at night. There were also continuous breaks in the lines. During the first five months in public business, the Magnetic Telegraph Company's lines were down for 36 entire days. The direct telegraph line between Philadelphia and New York was delayed for years due to the latter city's geographical location; the gutta-percha that was needed for submarine cables had not been introduced yet, and the messages had to be sent to New York by ferry over the Hudson from Newark, where the telegraph line from Philadelphia ended. In the New Orleans and Ohio Company in 1854, the problems were manifold. Yellow fever swept through the south and almost every operator fell ill. The line was kept going with great difficulty and business almost stopped. When the winter set in, a storm ruined miles of the line, and business was again suspended for a long period. Creditors became alarmed. In fact, many of the local companies had to be merged or leased during the first decade of the telegraph.[503]

been introduced by minor competitors already in the early 1860s. (Kieve, 53, 64)

500 The technological solutions varied greatly in different countries. Instead of the different needle systems, the line opened between St. Petersburg and Helsinki in 1855 was based on Morse's invention. (Risberg, 75–84). About Morse's discoveries and the development of his electro-magnetic telegraph, see Reid, 48–111.

501 Reid, 112–117.

502 The main historical American telegraph companies are listed by Reid, vii–xiii. About the cooperation with the railway companies, see e.g. Reid 244–245, 479–481. Reid's book covers probably all the important telegraph companies in North America during the first four decades of commercial telegraph.

503 Reid, 120–121, 128–130, 139, 173–175, 207–209. – Gutta-percha was the coagulated latex of certain rubber trees growing in the Malay Peninsula. Even if known in Europe by the mid-17th century, its excellent insulating and underwater conductor qualities were only discovered in the late 1840s. It was used for the insulation of submarine cables for

Interestingly, New York was not very eager to get in touch with its neighbours by telegraph. The metropolitan city had its own interests and was mainly focused on overseas communications. Therefore the original line to that city was actually drawn from Springfield, Mass., to Buffalo, N.Y., via Albany and Utica. Springfield was designed to be the connecting point with the New York and Boston Company, the absurdity of which soon became apparent and the eastern terminus was changed to the city of New York. The first pole of this line was planted on the corner of Wall Street and Broadway in August 1845. The office of Poughkeepsie was opened in October 1846, almost a year later than the first line was opened in Philadelphia, while Hudson was opened at the end of the same month.[504]

The telegraph line between Boston and New York was completed somewhat earlier, in late June 1846. However, the line had been cheaply and carelessly constructed. As a storm was setting in, the wires broke in numerous places. In one of these, 170 breaks were reported in a section of 30 miles. The breaks occurred so often that during the first year of the company's existence, the line did not work for half the time. Even if the wires did work, delays were the rule. Not even the passing trains could be reported perfectly.[505] J. S. Brown and Paul Duguid hit the nail on the head when they claimed that the myth that the telegraph was the start of the information age ('People travelled at the speed of the train. Information began to travel at the speed of light.') was built on a merely technological approach. Instead of celebrating just the speed and separation, more attention should be paid to the way information and society was intertwined.[506]

The first to fully recognize the value of the telegraph for news purposes were the newspapermen in New York. In 1847–1848, the newly established New York Associated Press ran a steamer between Digby, N.S., and Portland, Me., to carry the news received by transatlantic steamers at Halifax. The European news was sent overland by express riders to Digby, 149 miles, to be dispatched from there by steamer to Portland and telegraphed to New York in advance of the arrival of the Cunard steamer at Boston. When the telegraph line was continued to St. John, N.B., the steamer took the shortest route from Digby to St. John, from where the news was telegraphed via Boston to New York.[507]

In 1851, it was possible to send messages by telegraph from Halifax to Portland, where they were re-telegraphed to New York. According to the

---

almost a century until challenged by modern synthetic plastics based on polyethylene by 1950. See Garrett, 6; Kieve 101–102.

504 Reid, 300–304.

505 Reid, 358–359.

506 John Seely Brown & Paul Duguid, *The Social Life of Information* (Boston, 2000), 17–18.

507 Reid, 343–346, 362–364.; Bonsor (1975), vol. 1, 77. – In Europe, *The Times* in London had been the first newspaper to use 'the electric telegraph' already in 1844. See Oliver Woods & James Bishop, *The Story of The Times* (London, 1983), 90. This use must have been mainly experimental, however, as the telegraph lines were mainly built a few years later. – According to Kieve, it was Julius Reuter who was 'probably the first man to see the immense advantages of the use of the telegraph for newspapers and had established an office in London 1851'. (Kieve, 71)

Canadian postal historian J.C. Arnell, the system continued even after the Cunard steamers did not officially call at Halifax on their way to New York after 1850. They often heaved-to off Halifax to drop dispatches and mail to a waiting boat, so that the telegraphic news service could continue to operate. Thus, the Cunard steamers' call at Halifax, combined with the gradual introduction of telegraphic communications between different areas in North America, enabled messages to reach Boston and New York considerably before the arrival of the steamers at their destination.[508]

In this way, the combination of mail steamers and telegraph could at least temporarily be used for speeding up the most important news on both sides of the Atlantic for more than 15 years – the semaphore telegraph between Holyhead and Liverpool even longer – before the Atlantic cable was in permanent use. Thus the telegraph was not born out of nothing, but was already a part of overseas communications. However, the steamships were still the most important part of the information chain, and the existing options of speeding up news transmission at the end of the journey by telegraph were quite marginal.

During the first ten years that the electric telegraph was in common use, the network of inland telegraph lines had been extended throughout the European continent and the British Isles, as far as the Western coasts of Ireland. On the other side of the Atlantic, telegraph lines had been extended throughout the Eastern states and provinces, and across Newfoundland, although there was a gap between the coasts of Newfoundland and the mainland. It was natural that dreams should arise of linking the Old and New Worlds by an Atlantic cable.

The first attempts to lay submarine cables in the 1840s failed due to problems in the insulation of the conducting wire. The first cable which was laid successfully in the English Channel in 1850 was cut by a fisherman's anchor, and anchors were indeed a problem for submarine cables also in the following years, around the Merseyside in England as well as in the Mediterranean.[509] However, permanent cables were established linking England with Ireland in 1853 and with the Continent, between Dover and Ostend, in the same year. Anglo-Dutch and Anglo-German cables were laid, and by 1857 there were electric communications with Holland, Germany, Austria and St. Petersburg. In the Mediterranean, several cables were laid for the French and Italian governments. Not all attempts were successful, however. Several costly failures were encountered in laying a cable in the deep waters between Sardinia and the coast of North Africa, as well as between Malta and Alexandria.[510]

The history of the Atlantic cable had its roots in the building of the electric telegraph in Newfoundland, a difficult task because the line traversed more than 400 miles of wild and desolate country. As the available capital became

---

508 Bonsor (1975), vol. 1, 77; Arnell (1986), 190. Arnell does not mention any source for his statement, however. This kind of arrangement may have been only temporary, as Cunard vessels hardly sailed that northern route all year round.

509 Robinson, 271; Garratt, 6–11; Large, 115–117; Kieve 103–104, 115.

510 Garratt, 13; Kieve, 105, 115.

exhausted before the work was complete, the English engineer F.N. Gisborne who was mainly responsible for the project, traveled to New York for support. He was fortunate in meeting Cyrus W. Field, a wealthy merchant who had recently retired from commerce in his early thirties. Field soon took an active interest in the project, but was of the opinion from the outset in 1854 that the Newfoundland project was just a link to a larger one, the Atlantic cable. During the next twelve years, Field would be the soul of the Atlantic project, a man of tireless energy and courage who never lost his faith in the undertaking. Samuel F.B. Morse was also originally involved in the project on the American side. But a great deal of the science, mechanical skills and capital came from Britain.[511]

The Atlantic cable was a huge project and included several risks. The problems were partly technical and practical, and partly financial. The depth of the Atlantic Ocean was unknown and a survey of the route had to be made by deep-sea soundings. No single ship was large enough to carry and lay the cable, which would be more than 2,500 nautical miles long and weigh 107 lb. per mile. The elementary theory of electrical transmission was still in a very primitive state, causing costly mistakes. And the estimated capital needed was £350,000, of which about two thirds was for the production of the cable.[512]

The first attempt to lay the Atlantic cable in 1857 became a failure. The cable, laid by two vessels, the H.M.S. *Agamemnon*, lent by the British Government, and the frigate *Niagara* of the U.S. Navy, was technically ill-suited to the deep waters of the Atlantic. The first expedition was not able to lay the cable at its whole length, as it was broken in heavy seas and several hundreds of miles of it was lost in the depth of the ocean. The ships had to return to Plymouth, and the rest of the cable was discharged and coiled on the wharf, where the gutta percha insulation then deteriorated in the sun while waiting for the following attempt. The next expedition in 1858 ended with equally poor results.[513]

In August of the same year, the third effort was successful, and congratulatory messages were exchanged between Queen Victoria and James Buchanan, the President of the United States, across the Atlantic by

---

511 To get a good overall idea of the building of the first Atlantic cable, Garratt's short history is very useful. See Garratt, 14–22. Two recent books give very different perspectives: Gordon's *A Thread Across the Ocean...* highlights Cyrus W. Field's role in the project, while Gillian Cookson's *The Cable. The Wire that Changed the World* (Gloucestershire, 2003) gives a more balanced picture of the development that led to the final breakthrough of fast Atlantic communications. See Gordon and Cookson, passim. See also Kieve, 105–115. About Morse's role in the project, see Cookson, 56–57, 60–63, 69–70, 72. Reid put it this way: 'Faraday and Morse encouraged the American projector [Cyrus W. Field]. But scientific and practical men were so divided, that it was difficult to inspire the degree of confidence necessary to success.' He continued: 'In face of all these obstacles, Mr. Field went to London, and succeeded in 1856 in organizing the first Atlantic Telegraph Company, and raising the necessary money to carry out the project, subscribing himself for more than one-quarter of the entire capital.' (Reid, 519) British sources give a rather different picture of Field's role as an investor in the project. See Kieve 107, Cookson 63.

512 Garratt, 14–15; Cookson, 23–24, 52–54, 62–63.

513 Garratt, 15–17. Cookson, 81–96.

the new means of communications. Unfortunately, the cable – technically poor already from the beginning – was not in good condition after all the handling in difficult circumstances. Messages could be transmitted only at a very slow rate and with much unreliability and repetition. Within a few weeks, the signals became unintelligible and in October, the cable was completely dead. The failure of the cable was never fully explained. According to Garratt, there were so many contributory causes that the wonder is not that it failed, but that it ever worked at all.[514]

During its short existence, the first Atlantic cable had showed its usefulness. Although only a few hundred messages were sent through it, many were extremely important. For example, the British government saved an estimated £60,000 while being able to halt the mobilization of two British regiments in Canada, as an urgent message could be sent by telegraph that the Sepoy Mutiny in India had been put down.[515]

The failure of the cable – and the consequent loss of some £500,000 by the shareholders who had subscribed for it – discouraged any further attempt to lay an Atlantic telegraph connection for some years. The undertaking was further discouraged in 1859 by the failure of the Red Sea Cable, in which some £800,000 had been invested.[516]

A great part of the capital had come from British merchants in London, Liverpool, Manchester and Glasgow. In the first meeting to raise money for the Atlantic cable, held in Liverpool in November 1856, Cyrus W. Field had put an outstanding argument to the investors: the information about changes in market prices, especially cotton, could be dispatched immediately by the electric telegraph. While it now took 40 days to send a letter and get an answer from New Orleans, a telegram would be in America – due to the time difference – before they had even sent it. In addition to the capital from American and British investors, national governments also took part in the project.[517]

When the project failed, the disappointment was intense. The need for a new cable was widely expressed, but investors were now more careful. The American Chamber of Commerce in Liverpool wrote a memorial to the Earl of Derby, the First Lord of Her Majesty's Treasury:

> '…having witnessed and also to a certain extent experienced the great national as well as individual importance of the temporary success of electric communications between this country and the continent of America, your memorialists have learned with deep regret that the communication by the present Atlantic cable has become inoperative and that considerable further capital will be required to restore it and lay such additional wires as may be requisite to render the communication

514 Garratt, 18. Cookson, 96–105. – Kieve, referring to the report of the Joint Committee appointed by the government, explains that the faults were on the electrical side and also the core, and that especially the conductor was too small. See Kieve, 110–111.

515 According to Cookson, 271 messages were forwarded from Trinity Bay, Newfoundland to Valentia, Ireland and 129 telegrams passed in the other direction, at an average of ten words each. Unfortunately the author does not give any reference to the sources used. See Cookson, 102.

516 Garratt, 19.

517 Cookson, 62–63; Garratt, 15; Large, 14.

certain; the impossibility of which is no longer doubted...

...that your memorialists are informed that the funds subscribed by the originators of this great undertaking have already been exhausted and they believe that it will be impossible to obtain the necessary capital for completing this great work without the aid of such guarantee as would secure a moderate return upon the investment to those subscribing...

... that your memorialists would submit that looking at the magnitude of the work, its vast national importance, consolidating as it will when the chain is properly completed the various colonies and dependencies of this country into one vast Empire; that considering the entire capital and labour already expended without any return, and that without extraneous aid the work can never be accomplished, as it would tend much to the national welfare, if Her Majesty's government were to extend their aid in such form and manner as they may feel justified by precedent and would enable the Atlantic Telegraph Company to obtain the requisite capital to complete their vast and noble undertaking.'[518]

A few years passed before the capital was again raised for a new attempt. Meanwhile, technical progress and new arrangements in cable production improved the prospects of success. In the maritime historical context, the first enthusiastic attempts to lay an Atlantic cable in the late 1850s were contemporary with the collapse of the Collins Line and the entrance of several new steamship lines – the Vanderbilt Line, the Inman Line and the German lines – with only sea postage mail contracts. Even though the telegraph is seldom mentioned in this connection, the expectations of fast Atlantic communications in the near future must have affected the decisions to cut the American mail subsidies.

Nevertheless, the British government continued the Cunard contract for ten years in the summer of 1858, just a few weeks before the brief success and the failure of the first cable. The renewal of the contract was strongly opposed by competitors, especially the Inman Line, but even the British Post Office was in opposition. The Admiralty which still had the mail contracts under their control thought that the service had national importance and preferred the continuation.[519]

While the U.S. Congress had been suspicious about supporting a telegraph line which would start and end on British territories on both sides of the Atlantic, the American Civil War stimulated attempts to raise new capital to continue the project.[520]

In 1865, when the Civil War was finally close to its end, President Abraham Lincoln was assassinated in Washington. The news of the President's death

---

518 'Laying of the Atlantic Cable'. Memorial of Liverpool Merchants Trading with America and Associated as the American Chamber of Commerce, 2.12.1858. (LRO, 380 AME/2)

519 Robinson (1964), 143–144. In 1860, a parliamentary committee saw so little need for these arrangements that it recommended the return of power to contract for sea-going mail services from the Admiralty to the Post Office. This happened by an Act of Parliament in the same year. See Robinson (1964), 144.

520 About the American discussion on the possibility of moving the western terminus of the Atlantic cable to the United States from the British territories, see Cookson, 64–67. See also Kieve, 112.

on 15 April was rushed across the ocean by the steamship *Nova Scotian,*
reaching a telegraph station in Londonderry on 26 April. The despatch
arrived in London two hours later and appeared in the British newspapers
on the following day, 12 days after the assassination. Julius Reuter, first
with the news, was later accused of having personally profited on the stock
market through holding back his early knowledge. The shock value of the
report was somewhat muted as so much time had passed since the event,
but the value of Reuter's coup gives some perspective to the proposed costs
of Atlantic telegrams.[521]

The case is a good example of coordination between ships and telegraph.
The Allan Line ship *Nova Scotian* was on her winter route between Portland
and Liverpool, which included a call at Londonderry in North Ireland instead
of Queenstown used by other companies, due to her northern route. The Allan
Line's vessels did not usually make a call at Halifax or Newfoundland, but
the captain of the *Nova Scotian* may have heard about the assassination,
which took place already on 14 April, by telegraph in Portland before the
ship departed, and thus heaved to at Halifax for the freshest news.

The *Nova Scotian,* leaving from Portland on 15 April, was ahead of her
competitors, the *Etna* of the Inman Line and the *Teutonia* of HAPAG, which
both departed from New York on 15 April, certainly carrying the same news.
The importance of the news was well understood on board all the vessels.
The *Etna* made an exception and did not call at Queenstown at all, but rushed
directly to Liverpool, while the *Teutonia* headed to Southampton. They both
arrived on 28 April – too late as the news had already been published in the
newspapers on the day before.[522]

By the time of the next Atlantic cable expedition in July–August 1865,
several improvements had been made both in the production arrangements
and the technical qualities of the cable. The newly established telegraph
construction and maintenance company also subscribed the remaining
capital required. During the time that had passed, a suitable ship had also
been constructed. The gigantic *Great Eastern*, built by the famous Isambard
Brunel for passenger service on the Eastern route, had become an economic
failure and was lacking employment. In her absence, it would have been
necessary to employ three ships to lay the cable, and the hazards caused by

---

521 Cookson, 140–141. – The news was published by *The Times* 27.4.1865 with the remark
     that the report had arrived 'via Greencastle, per *Nova Scotian*'.
522 Sailing lists of Hubbard & Winter, 178, 208. – The Electric and the Magnetic had contracted
     with Reuter's in January 1859 for the exclusive rights to supply foreign telegrams to
     all towns in the UK. Reuter's retained the exclusive right of supplying commercial and
     shipping news within 15 miles of London (the former were prohibited from passing it on
     to newspapers or public rooms). In February 1865 the telegraph companies (including
     the minor United Kingdom Electric Telegraph Company) formed a combined news and
     intelligence department under the direction of a joint committee and managed by Charles
     Boys of the Electric. As the companies had a monopoly of the telegraph communications
     of the UK, newspapers requiring news by telegraph were compelled to resort to them for it,
     and take what they were willing to supply. The smaller newspapers were possibly satisfied,
     but the larger ones were not as they continually attacked the telegraph companies. This
     dissatisfaction would be one of the major factors in the nationalisation of the telegraph
     system. (Kieve, 71–72)

the participation of even two ships in the laying operation had been amply demonstrated in the late 1850s.[523]

After one more failed attempt, a working Atlantic cable was finally laid in late July 1866. A few weeks later, the lost end of the earlier cable was found in the mid-Atlantic and the second cable was safely landed at Trinity Bay, Newfoundland in September.[524] The Old and the New World were now finally connected with electric telegraph, which had been in common use on both sides of the Atlantic already for two decades.

The commercial use of the Atlantic cable started immediately, although not without problems. Sheila Marriner describes Rathbone Bros & Co.'s experiences of the early Atlantic telegraph: 'There were two serious disadvantages... the possibility of costly errors arising through genuine mistakes, since orders by cable could be fulfilled and shipped before they were confirmed by letter. The danger of loss arising from this was minimized by limiting the amount of orders entrusted to any one cable to £40,000. The other serious difficulty was that of deliberate fraud. This could be overcome by the use of cipher which would prevent 'enterprising people connected with the telegraph all through this country' from selling 'the contents of your messages to your neighbours'.'[525] The telegraph company refused at first to take messages in code because of the great advantages to be gained by being able to read any important message. Finally the company agreed to the use of cipher, but when it did, this became accepted practice.[526]

A year after the opening of the Atlantic cable, Rathbone Bros & Co.'s agent in New York concluded desperately: 'It seems almost impossible to get the cable honestly managed.' The following month, the agent wished that the cable had never been laid. There was 'not the slightest doubt' that the news about corn prices was falsified in the interest of speculators who had combined to keep up the price of the article.[527] Despite practical problems, the Rathbones were in almost daily telegraphic communication with New York, sending orders and keeping the agency advised on sales, of the market and of the reasons for anticipated price rises and falls.[528]

Graeme J. Milne has also examined the usual complaints by British merchants concerning the electric telegraph: only the briefest of messages

523 See Garratt, 19–21.
524 See Garratt, 21–22; Kieve 114–115; Cookson, 142–150. – The success in laying the Atlantic cable ended another ambitious project, the building of the Russian-American overland route telegraph across the Siberia and via Alaska. The losses of this unfinished attempt reached $3,000,000, mainly to be paid by the American Western Union Telegraph Company. See Cookson, 150; Reid 508–517.
525 Marriner, 114.
526 Marriner, 114. Each company had their own code books, and the telegrams had to be interpreted on both sides of the Atlantic: first to the cipher language and then back to English again. Examples of telegrams with opened cipher codes can be found e.g. from C.K. Prioleau's correspondence in the business records of Fraser, Trenholm & Co. at the MMM (B/FT, box 2). – The use of codes also caused confusion and delays: 'What is penance in Charleston code. Telegraph at once. Orleans March April paid 91. Dufour.' (Telegram from H. Dufour & Co. at Havre to C.K. Prioleau & Co. in London, 5.1.1875. (MMM, B/FT, box 2)
527 Marriner, 114–115.
528 Marriner, 115.

could be sent and there was a great deal of suspicion about the reliability of foreign lines and the honesty of their operators. Technical problems were common. Even the greatest asset of the telegraph – speed – could not always be relied upon due to backlogs of messages piled up in the chain of telegraph offices. Larger documents, samples and the like had to go by sea in any case. Traders therefore needed reliable mail *and* telegraph services, which doubled the cost.[529]

The contents of the telegrams had to be very short, not only for security but due to the very high price of the transmission. The original rate was £20 for the 20 first words plus £1 for each additional word. By 1872, the price had been drastically reduced to four shillings per word, and in 1888 further to one shilling.[530]

In fact, transatlantic communications became a mixture of steamship letters and telegraphs which complemented each other. Short orders were sent by the telegraph, but the explanations were written and documents sent in letters carried by the mail steamers.[531] Rathbone's New York agents Busk & Jevons wrote to Liverpool 6.1.1869 in a letter sent by the Cunard steamer *Russia*: 'Dear Sirs, on 31st Dec. we telegraphed you 'write' Schwinds Leed worth ten quarter encourage 'shipment', this you no doubt forwarded by Messrs Lamport & Holt's steamer of 2nd Jan. The shipment of 2610 bags coffee p. *Catharine Leed* referred to above as being worth 10 ¼ *costs 9 ¼* & consequently promises a fair profit. Thinking of the tone of Messrs Schwind, McKinnel & Co.'s letter that they are likely to be somewhat backward in shipping & facing ourselves a very good opinion of operations in coffee this year, we added our message 'encourage shipment' which will we hope induce them to act more boldly…'[532]

529 Milne (2000), 129–130. There were similar problems in the United States, see Reid 136–137, 308, 327–328, 357–358. To reduce costs, the operators sometimes employed young girls with small salaries. They made free translations and left out what they could not read. Commercial terms were unknown to them and they gave new terms to trade. (Reid, 780)

530 Garratt, 38. – JoAnne Yates has compared the information costs by ordinary mail and telegraph in American companies. According to her, the companies could exert more central authority over their agents by insisting e.g. that no unauthorized price cuts should be made or that rush orders had to be confirmed with the headquarters. In such cases, the high cost of sending a telegram was justified as the use of the telegraph led to savings in the company's business. The study does not cover overseas information transmission. See JoAnne Yates, 'Investing in Information: Supply and Demand Forces in the Use of Information in American Firms, 1850–1920' in Peter Temin (ed.) *Inside the Business Enterprise. Historical Perspective on the Use of Information.* (Chicago, 1991).

531 Richard B. Kielbowicz has noticed the same in the inland news-gathering of American newspapers: only hard facts were transmitted by telegraph while the rest was sent by ordinary mail. Also the U. S. newspaper exchange system needed physical transmission of documents. See Richard B. Kielbowicz, 'News Gathering by Mail in the Age of the Telegraph: Adapting to a New Technology' in *Technology and Culture*, Vol. 28, No. 1, Jan. 1987, 26–41.

532 Busk & Jevons in New York to Rathbone Bros & Co. in Liverpool 6.1.1869. In the Rathbone Collection, RP XXIV.2.28. (SJ). – Schwind, McKinnell & Co. was a Rio merchant house which sold flour and bought coffee for the Rathbones. (Marriner, 21, 71)

As the quote describes, the tones of ordinary letters could also express feelings which could not be caught in a short telegraph message. And important documents should naturally be sent only by mail: 'Dear Sirs, we have balanced the books & closed our accounts for the year but we have not time to dissect them for this mail. As we know you are anxious to receive them at the earliest moment possible we send you now the only essential documents, viz. Balance Sheet and Agency Assets... By next mail we will hand you our customary statements of the year's business...'[533]

The growing use of the telegraph and speedier carriage of cargoes by steamship had fundamental effects on the organization of the produce markets in Britain. It reduced the need for carrying stocks, since fresh supplies in producing centres could be quickly conveyed to the markets and the level of prices in the markets could be made known in the producing areas so that it was no longer necessary to try to forecast conditions months ahead on inadequate information. Fluctuations in prices tended to narrow as up-to-date information about current business conditions and markets in all parts of the world became more readily available. Consequently, operations in produce markets became subject to international rather than to local and national influences. The spread of the telegraph killed the consignment business in cotton and in grain, but instead inspired the futures market.[534]

From the 1840s, there was a growing tendency for people to buy and sell goods 'to arrive'. The essence of the 'arrivals' business was that the news should travel faster than the goods, and with the development of fast mail steamers this became possible. The establishment of telegraphic communications from New York to Nova Scotia and Newfoundland further increased the disparity between the speed of news and cargoes. This led to the development of the arrivals business in the cotton trade. During the American Civil War, a good deal of speculative activity took place in cotton and in buying and selling 'to arrive'. According to Nigel Hall, in this kind of forward market it was a common practice for specific lots of a commodity to be contracted for before they were available for delivery. The Liverpool cotton market was the first in Europe to develop further to a futures market, in which contracts were highly standardized and did not refer to a particular cargo. The quality and quantity of the product set was fixed, and the only negotiable part of the contract was the price. Arrival and future delivery markets were separated in the early 1870s, following the opening of the Atlantic cable.[535]

The development of the telegraph from the Napoleonic wars to the Atlantic cable is depicted in Table 30.

---

533 Busk & Jevons in New York to Rathbone Bros & Co. in Liverpool 7.1.1870. In the Rathbone Collection, RP XXIV.2.29. (SJ)

534 Marriner, 54, 115–116. Earlier, all cotton handled by a merchant, whether as owner or consignee, was sold through his selling broker to a buying broker who acted for the spinner. The few powerful spinners who imported cotton themselves employed brokers. The cables facilitated the spinner-importing, and also produced a fusion of broker-merchant, who both imported and sold, thus leaving the middlemen out. See J.H. Clapham, *An Economic History of Modern Britain. Free Trade and Steel 1850–1886* (Cambridge, 1932), 315–316.

535 Marriner, 115–117; Hall, 99–107.

TABLE 30. *Development of business information transmission by telegraph.*

Time period	Geographic area	Type of telegraph	Owner-ship	Use	Benefits
Napoleonic wars	Especially in France & countries occupied by the French; also Sweden-Finland, etc.	Optical telegraph	State owned	War ships, warfare	Military and administrative use only; after 1810 also private use possible in Sweden
1827–1861	Liverpool - Holyhead	Optical telegraph	Private	Merchant ships; era of the American sailing packets, mail steamers	Commercial use, speeding up business information transmission
1845 –	Britain and continental Europe	Needle-telegraph	Mostly state owned	Railways; Admiralty	Administrative use; safety; speeding up information transmission
1845 –	USA	Electro-magnetic telegraph	Private	Railways; inland business; connections to mail steamers	Commercial use; safety; speeding up business information transmission
Late 1840s, or 1850s	Europe	Needle or electro-magnetic telegraph	Mostly state owned (Britain nationa-lized in 1868-69)	Railways; inland business; connections with mail steamers	Commercial use allowed; safety; speeding up business information transmission
1851 –	English Channel; Irish Sea; Mediterra-nean	Submarine cable	Private	Overseas communi-cation	Commercial use; speeding up business information transmission
1858, failed	North Atlantic	Submarine cable	Private	Transatlantic communi-cation	Commercial use; speeding up business information transmission for a short while
1866	North Atlantic	Submarine cable	Private	Transatlantic communi-cation	Commercial use; speeding up business information transmission; enabling the 'futures' market

VI The West Indies and South America

Wind vs. Wind

Choosing between private and public mail services, a micro case – Merchant ship communications between Britain and Guiana in 1840, a general view – The West Indian and South American mail services as parts of the whole Falmouth packet system – The South American route – The Mexico route – The last years of the Falmouth packet service, a conclusion.

While business information transmission in the North Atlantic was mainly taken care of by fast and regular sailing packets owned by commercial shipping lines from the early 1820s, the communications on two other important trade routes – the West Indies and South America – were dominated by merchant vessels. Additionally, the Falmouth packets were an important means of communications on both these routes.

The West Indian mail route followed the old sugar route between Britain and the colonies in the Caribbean including ports on the northern coast of South America. Over the years, other than British colonies were also included, and auxiliary ship services were started between several colonies and the British packet stations.[536] In addition to the Caribbean islands, the Falmouth packets normally sailed to British Guiana and Mexico. The South American route consisted of sailings from Falmouth to Rio de Janeiro, and down to Buenos Aires and Montevideo either by the same packet or by an auxiliary ship.

Choosing between private and public mail services – a micro case

In view of the importance of the West Indian trade route in the early 19th century, surprisingly small numbers of merchant letters can be found in public collections, compared with the amount of correspondence kept in archives from other regions. One of the explanations given is that the descendants

---

536 For different West Indian route descriptions and auxiliary ship services between 1820 and 1842, see Britnor, 129–140, 149–154; and John L. L. DuBois, Jeremiah A. Farrington and Roger G. Schnell (eds), *Danish West Indies Mails* 1754–1917 (Snow Camp, USA, 2000), 32–33.

of merchants involved in the West Indian businesses did not preserve these documents because they wanted to forget the period of slave trade.

A handful of letters from Demerara and Berbice, British Guiana, to the Liverpool merchant houses Sandbach, Tinne & Co. and Thomas and William Earle & Co. in 1825–1841, discovered in the Merseyside Maritime Museum Archive's collections, give a very homogeneous picture of information transmission. These 15 letters were carried by merchant vessels. The average time between writing and receiving them was 51 days.[537]

In addition to these general letters, a more variable case can be found in the correspondence between Thomas and William Earle & Co. and their sugar plantation at Berbice in 1840.[538] This interesting sample consists of ten letters from 1840, each of them carrying a monthly return of the plantation's business activities. Written by the same person to the same recipient and sent by different means of communication by various routes from a minor colonial county across the Atlantic in the age of sail makes the sample extraordinary in postal historical research.[539]

The letters portray the practical options and choices made by an individual, giving a picture of how efficiently the different means of information transmission served the merchants conducting regular business with the colonies. Comparing the micro case with shipping records gives an idea of the effectiveness of merchant ships as mail carriers, as well as the effectiveness of the government mail service between Britain and Guiana in 1840.[540]

At that time the government service included a variety of British, Danish, Dutch, French and Spanish colonies – a difficult service as the ports of call were so widely spread and not easy to navigate. By 1810, six local West Indian mail boats had supplemented the sailing packets that crossed the Atlantic, and by 1840 there were a dozen. The communications from England were twice a month.[541]

Thomas and William Earle, a father and son who were merchants and shipowners of Liverpool, were former slave traders who well knew the opportunities of the Caribbean area and were familiar with the organization

---

537 Bryson Collection, Records of Sandbach, Tinne & Co., D/B/176; Earle Family and Business Archive, correspondence of Thomas and William Earle & Co, D/Earle/5/2 (MMM, Liverpool). Additionally, three letters to Sandbach, Tinne & Co. (dated 26.11.1825, 6.2.1826 and 2.3.1836) are included in the calculation from a private philatelic collection: Heikki Hongisto, *Sugar in the life of Mankind.* (2005) (HHC). – Even though all the letters were carried by private ships, one of them was a duplicate of which the original had been sent by a government packet from Berbice to Thomas and William Earle & Co, dated 18.10.1841.

538 See the correspondence of Thomas and William Earle & Co, D/Earle 5/1–11 (MMM).

539 In 1837, the amount of postage charged by Postmasters in the colonies was only £410 from Berbice for the whole year, while e.g. the figure from Canada was a hundred times greater, £38,977. *BPP, Transport and Communications. Post and Telegraphs 2, (1838).* Select Committee on Postage, Appendix E, 221.

540 For a more detailed description, see Seija-Riitta Laakso, 'Managing the Distance: Business Information Transmission between Britain and Guiana, 1840' in *International Journal of Maritime History*, XVI, No.2 (December 2004), 221–246.

541 See Robinson (1964), 93; and 'A List of Packets at Present, Employed in the Service of the Post-Office' in *Lloyd's Register* 1840.

of commerce there.[542] In the 1830s, the company had acquired a plantation in Berbice, Guiana as a part of a bad debt.[543] The Plantation Hanover, with 'Sugar, Rum, Molasses, Cane, Livestock and Negro Labour',[544] was run by a manager, J.M. Houston, whose preserved correspondence with Liverpool includes the ten monthly returns of Plantation Hanover in 1840, two reports apparently being missing.

This specific year was crucial from the owners' point of view, due to the recent abolition of slavery, which after a few years' transition period had given full freedom to the plantation workers in 1838. British Guiana, together with Jamaica and Trinidad, was one of the colonies that suffered most from the changes. Many estates, earlier prosperous and productive, were now cultivated at a considerable loss, and several were abandoned.[545]

J.M. Houston, the manager, calculated the return of the plantation's activities at the end of each month and sent the report by ship to the Earles of Liverpool. The letters, carrying the sender's remarks on the means of transport as well as postal handstamps, enable us to follow the process of business information transmission in practice. What happened to the letters between writing and receiving them? Who took care of them, and how long did it take in each case to deliver the information?

The January report of Plantation Hanover was sent by the merchant ship *Goshawk*, which departed from Berbice on 13 February and arrived in Liverpool on 11 April.[546] The report was dispatched to Thomas and William Earle & Co.'s office in Liverpool on the arrival day. The letter was carried fully privately, having no post office markings. The Earles learned about their plantation's economic progress 71 days after the month in question had ended.

The February and March reports were sent by the British government's packets, with postal markings by the Berbice Post Office respectively. The February report was sent from Berbice on 18 March and received by the Earles on 13 May. The report was carried either by the *Ranger* packet, which arrived at Falmouth on 10 May, or by the *Penguin* packet, which arrived on 8 May.[547] As the letter was delivered in Liverpool on the 13th, the most probable arrival date at Falmouth was the 10th.[548]

---

542 For the changes in Liverpool merchants' interests in the Caribbean area, see Williams, 'Abolition and the Re-Deployment...' 1–17; Milne (2000), 51–53; and Dawn Littler, 'The Earle Collection: Records of a Liverpool Family of Merchants and Shipowners', *Transactions of the Historic Society of Lancashire & Cheshire*, Vol. 146 (Liverpool, 1996), 97–102.

543 Littler, 96.

544 J.M. Houston to Thomas and William Earle & Co in his Monthly Return of Plantation Hanover, Berbice, for January, 1840. Earle Correspondence, D/Earle 5/7/1 (MMM).

545 *BPP, Colonies. West Indies 1,* (1842), Report of Select Committee on West India Colonies, iii–v. – Some estate owners may have been better prepared for the changes than others. For example, John Gladstone of Liverpool, who had purchased several plantations in Demerara in the 1820s, sold his assets properly by 1849 without major losses. S.G. Checkland describes Gladstone's business ideas and networks in the West Indies in his article 'John Gladstone as Trader and Planter' in *Economic History Review*, v. 7, 1954/55, 222–228.

546 *Lloyd's List* 13.4.1840.

547 *Lloyd's List* 11.5.1840; 12.5.1840.

548 At that time, the mails were sent by coach from Falmouth via Exeter to London and from

The West Indian packets usually sailed directly from Falmouth to Barbados, from where the local mail boats (at this period mostly steamers) delivered the mails to the islands. On the way back home, the packet sailed via several of the islands collecting the mailbags for Britain. The system was slow and complicated, and the schedules often changed due to weather conditions or other reasons.

As the sources are not clear in this matter,[549] we cannot know for certain to which island the mails from Berbice were forwarded in the spring of 1840. Table 31 shows the dates on which the two alternative packets stopped at the islands during their home voyage. As the monthly return of the plantation was sent from Berbice as late as 18 March, Barbados could not have been the place where the mails from Guiana were collected at the time. Tobago[550] was out of the question for the same reason. The local mail boat could have carried the letter to Trinidad, were it would have been taken to the *Ranger*, but the *Penguin* had already passed the island.

The Guiana mails could also have been sent by a separate local mail ship to the rather distant St. Thomas, which was the other main interchange point of mail, together with Barbados. Why this would have been done, when the Falmouth packets also sailed via Trinidad, Grenada etc. on their home voyage,[551] remains unclear. None of the monthly returns bear transit markings from the West Indian Islands, but this was rather typical.[552] Independent of whether the Guiana mails were carried to St. Thomas by a mail steamer or by the Falmouth packet, they had to be sent from Berbice and Demerara more than ten days before the packet would proceed from St. Thomas to Puerto Rico, Haiti and England. To use a fixed reference, it is assumed here that, at the latest, St. Thomas was the island where the Guiana mails were collected.

The table clearly depicts the problem of carrying the West Indian mails, and makes the complaints of merchants understandable. The *Ranger* packet had sailed from Falmouth on 5 February and arrived at Barbados on 13 March – on the very same day as the *Penguin* packet, which had left from Falmouth on 17 February.[553] The packets delivered the mails and proceeded to Tobago, the *Ranger* on the 14th and the *Penguin* one day later. There was a longer stay at Trinidad or Grenada before continuing the journey. Both ships departed from Grenada on the same day, as well as from several other islands, visiting different ports at Haiti, however. The ships' inter-island journeys between Barbados and Cape Henry, or Cape Haitien alternatively,

there by railway to Liverpool. It normally took a couple of days. See *BPP, Transport and Communications. Post and Telegraphs 2, (1838)*. Appendix E, 227–232; and Clapham (1930), 387.

549 See Britnor, 150, 154; and DuBois (etc.), 32–33.
550 Tobago has been mentioned as one of the places where the Demerara and Berbice mails were forwarded. See e.g. Britnor, 154.
551 *Lloyd's List* normally published the dates of departures of all the islands visited, as can be noticed from Table 31.
552 About the use of postal handstamps on the 'loose packet letters', see DuBois (etc.), 34–36.
553 *Lloyd's List* 7.2.1840; 19.2.1849; and 25.4.1840.

TABLE 31. *Departure dates of the* Ranger *and* Penguin *packets, of Falmouth, from the West Indian islands and arrival in England, February–May 1840.*

Port	Ranger packet	Penguin packet
Falmouth	5.2.	17.2.
Barbados	13.3. / 14.3.	13.3. / 15.3.
Tobago	15.3.	16.3.
Trinidad	21.3.	17.3.
Grenada	23.3.	23.3.
St. Kitts	29.3.	29.3.
Tortola	31.3.	31.3.
St. Thomas	1.4.	1.4.
Puerto Rico	2.4.	1.4.
Cape Henry		5.4.
Cape Haitien	5.4.	
Falmouth	10.5.	8.5.
Duration of the round trip	95 days	81 days

Source: Lloyd's List 11.5.1840, 12.5.1840.

had taken three weeks before they turned back to England, and the crossing of the Atlantic an additional five weeks.

The *Ranger,* carrying the February report, made the journey back home from St. Thomas two days slower than the *Penguin,* in 40 days. The report arrived in Liverpool on 12 May,[554] and was received by Thomas and William Earle & Co. on the 13th, 74 days after the end of the financial reporting period.

The March report was sent on 9 April – rather soon after the end of the financial reporting month. It was carried by the *Hope* packet, which sailed from Falmouth on 4 March, arriving at Barbados on 4 April, and proceeding on the same day to Tobago and from there on 6 April to Trinidad, where she stayed for several days, then continuing as depicted in the note below.[555] The trip from Barbados to Falmouth with all the stops at the islands took 52 days. The packet arrived on 26 May carrying a remarkable freight of 150,000 dollars.[556] The March report was delivered to the plantation owners in Liverpool a few days later, approximately 58 days after the end of the reporting period.[557]

---

554 Date of the Liverpool Post Office arrival handstamp on the letter.

555 The departure dates of the *Hope* from different ports were as follows: Falmouth 4.3.; Barbados 4.4.; Tobago 6.4.; Trinidad 12.4.; Grenada 14.4.; St. Kitts 18.4.; Tortola 19.4.; St. Thomas 20.4.; Puerto Rico 21.4.; Cape Haitien 26.4. and the arrival at Falmouth 26.5.1840 (*Lloyd's List* 28.5.1840).

556 *Lloyd's List* 28.5.1840. It was not unusual for the armed Falmouth packets to carry high-value freights of bullion and specie when arriving from Mexico or the West Indies. Arrivals of treasury were usually reported by *Lloyd's List.*

557 The exact date of the letter's arrival in Liverpool is missing. It has been assumed here that it was 28 May, allowing two days for the mail transport from Falmouth to Liverpool.

The April report was sent privately by the merchant ship *Ann & Jane*. The ship had arrived in Berbice on 30 March from Liverpool, but after some unexplained delays she departed on 20 May, having stayed 51 days at port. The report arrived in Liverpool by the *Ann & Jane* in 32 days, being dispatched to William and Thomas Earle & Co. on the next day after the ship's arrival, 22 June.[558] Despite the fast sea journey, it took the report 53 days to reach the owners.

Another alternative for J.M. Houston would have been to send the report by the *Lapwing* packet, which sailed from St. Thomas on 6 June and arrived at Falmouth on 15 July. The letter would have been dispatched in Liverpool around 17 July – 25 days later than by the private vessel.

The May report was sent from Berbice by the merchant ship *Laidmans*, of Liverpool. No date of sending the letter is available, as J.M. Houston did not date these documents, and the letter is missing departure markings of any post office. According to *Lloyd's List*, the *Laidmans* arrived 'off Salcombe' on 12 August and entered Gravesend, London, on 16 August from Demerara.[559]

As the ship was not sailing for Liverpool, the captain dispatched the mailbag to a local boat off Salcombe, while the ship proceeded to London. The letter was posted from Kingsbridge, a small village in the inland, and marked by the post office handstamp used for private ship letters.[560] It also bears the arrival handstamp of the Liverpool Post Office of 14 August, and the recipient's note on 15 August. The postal markings, together with the information published by *Lloyd's List*, prove clearly that the letter was carried by the *Laidmans*. As the vessel's exact departure date from Demerara is unknown, it is not possible to calculate precisely the duration of the sea journey. However, the letter arrived in Liverpool two days before the ship entered London, and was received by Thomas and William Earle & Co. 76 days after the end of the financial reporting period.

The use of the official mail service would have shortened the delay markedly. Even if J.M. Houston had not finalized his calculations quickly enough to get them on board the *Star* packet, which stopped at St. Thomas on 18 June and arrived at Falmouth as early as on 18 July, he could have had them ready for the *Reindeer* packet, which called at the island on 24 June and arrived in Falmouth on 7 August.[561] The first alternative would have shortened the waiting time by more than three weeks, and the latter by about one week.

The June report was sent by the merchant ship *John Horrocks*, of Liverpool. The new 294 tons vessel had arrived in Berbice on 12 April, probably on her first voyage as she was built in the same year.[562] She departed for Liverpool on 30 July, carrying J.M. Houston's calculations of the plantation's financial results for June. When the ship left the port, more than four weeks had passed since the end of the financial period.

---

558 *Lloyd's List* 22.6.1840. The letter bears no postal markings, only the recipient's note about the arrival date.
559 *Lloyd's List* 15.8.1840; 17.8.1840.
560 'SHIP LETTER KINGSBRIDGE', see Tabeart (1997), 132.
561 *Lloyd's List* 20.7.1840; 10.8.1840.
562 *Lloyd's Register*, 1840.

The vessel arrived in Liverpool on 10 September, and the letter was delivered to Thomas and William Earle & Co.'s office on the same day. The sea voyage took 42 days, and the letter was in the owners' hands 72 days after the end of the financial month in question. No postage fees were paid for this direct, private service. If the official mail service had been used, the *Mutine* packet would have picked up the June report from St. Thomas on 22 July and brought the letter to Falmouth on 21 August. By this means, the letter would have arrived at the Earles' office about 18 days earlier than it did,[563] taking into account the couple of days needed for the trip from Falmouth to Liverpool.

The July report was sent by government mail, and it bears the Berbice Post Office handstamp of 21 August. The mails were picked up by the *Hope* packet at the port of St. Thomas on 4 September, and the ship arrived in Falmouth on 23 October.[564] The trip across the Atlantic alone took 44 days – the longest eastbound West Indian packet journey of the year. The July report was 86 days old when received by the plantation owners in Liverpool on 25 October.

What if J.M. Houston had sent the July report by a merchant ship instead of the government packet? There were several regular traders leaving from Demerara for Britain during the month of August: the *Isabella* (of Glasgow) for London on 13 August, arriving at Gravesend on 2 October, the *Marquis of Chandos* (of London), departing on the same day and arriving at Gravesend on 17 October, the *Sandbach* (of Liverpool), also departing on the same day and arriving at Liverpool on 22 September, as well as the *Thistle* (of Glasgow), departing on 23 August and arriving at Clyde on 22 September.[565] All these vessels would have carried the July report to the owners much faster than the mail packet. By the *Sandbach*, the report would have been in Liverpool 33 days earlier than it was.

Common to the sailings above was that they all departed from Demerara. The only sailing[566] from Berbice was that of the *Richmond Hill* on 1 August,[567] too early for the July report to be finalized by the plantation manager.

It would have been curious if no contacts had existed between Demerara and Berbice for private mail sending, although sailing between those two ports was rather difficult due to the prevailing winds and currents of the river.[568] An overland route existed and the Post Office planned to use it, according to a statement given in that specific year.[569] How long and in what condition

---

563 *Lloyd's List* 23.8.1840.

564 The departure dates of the *Hope* from different ports during the trip were as follows: Falmouth 17.7.; Barbados 16.8.; Tobago 17.8.; Trinidad 26.8.; Grenada 29.8.; St. Kitts 2.9.; Tortola 3.9.; St. Thomas 4.9.; Puerto Rico 5.9.; Cape Henry 9.9. and Falmouth 23.10.1840 (*Lloyd's List* 26.10.1840).

565 *Lloyd's List* respectively.

566 The only sailing departure reported by *Lloyd's List*, but the reports possibly did not include all of them.

567 *Lloyd's List* 12.9.1840.

568 Britnor, 136. For the Atlantic and Caribbean winds and currents, see Map 1.

569 'Sketch of the New Arrangements for the Conveyance of Her Majesty's Mails in the West Indies. To Commence in October, 1840', Britnor, 153–154. During the steamship era, Berbice mails were often taken overland from Demerara. See Kenton & Parsons, 14.

the route was, is not known. As the manager's reports generally consisted of formal remarks about the work at the plantation only, no evidence about such communications problems has been preserved.[570]

The August Report was sent by the merchant ship *Guiana*, of Liverpool. The ship had arrived at Berbice from Glasgow on 10 July,[571] and was loading for London. There is no information about the departure date of the *Guiana* from Berbice, but she arrived at Deal on 9 November. The letter bears the private ship letter handstamp of London[572] and a date handstamp of 10 November. The report arrived in Liverpool on the 11th, being dispatched on the same day.[573] It took the report 72 days after the end of the reporting period to reach the hands of the owners.

If not sent by the *Guiana*, the letter could have been picked up by the *Pandora* packet from St. Thomas on 18 September, arriving at Falmouth on 27 October – about two weeks earlier than by the Berbice–Liverpool merchantman.

The September report arrived in Liverpool on 1 December by the merchant ship *Ann & Jane*, the same vessel that carried the April Report. *Ann & Jane* was one of the regular traders between Liverpool and Berbice, making 2.5 round trips during 1840. She had arrived at Berbice on 8 September, and departed for Liverpool on 25 October. Her home trip took 37 days, and the report entered Thomas and William Earle & Co.'s office on the date of the ship's arrival, 62 days after the end of the reporting period. The letter bears no postal markings.

Even if this was a relatively fast delivery, the *Peterel* packet would have brought the report from St. Thomas, departing from there on 18 October, to Falmouth on 26 November. The report would have been in Liverpool a few days earlier than it was by the private ship.

Finally, the November report – the October and December reports are missing – was sent from Berbice by the merchant ship *Camerons*, of London. According to *Lloyd's List*,[574] the ship sailed for London on 13 November and arrived at Deal on 5 March and the letter, posted from Deal on the following day,[575] arrived in Liverpool on 8 March, 1841 – 98 days after the end of the financial reporting period. It is clear that the ship did not sail on the date mentioned, with the November report on board. The departure must have

---

570 However, J.M. Houston mentions in his June Report something that may describe the rural conditions: five sheep had been killed by a tiger on plantation Op Hoop Van Beter, a nearby coffee plantation earlier owned by the Earle family. J.M. Houston to Thomas and William Earle & Co in his Monthly Return for June, 1840. Earle Family and Business Archive, D/Earle 5/7/6, (MMM).

571 *Lloyd's List* 25.8.1840.

572 The handstamp 'SHIP-LETTER' on the cover was used in London 1840–1857. Deal would have used the handstamp 'DEAL SHIP LETTER' and Gravesend 'SHIP LETTER GRAVESEND' in 1840. See Tabeart, 63–64, 102, 182.

573 *Lloyd's List* 10.11.1840. Liverpool Post Office arrival handstamp and the recipient's note on the letter.

574 *Lloyd's List* 14.1.1841; 6.3.1841.

575 'DEAL SHIP LETTER' and handstamp of Deal 6.3.1841, Liverpool Post Office arrival handstamp 8.3.1841. The recipient's note 7 March 1841 cannot be correct, as the postal markings clearly indicate a later arrival.

been several weeks delayed. The *Camerons* arrived at Deal on the same day as the *Euterpe*, which had sailed from Berbice on 6 January, 1841.

Why the manager did not choose another alternative, remains unclear. There were several vessels sailing directly from Berbice for Liverpool and Glasgow before the departure of the ships for London. The best choice would have been the *Favorite* for Glasgow on 7 December, arriving on 19 January, 45 days before the November report was finally at Deal.[576]

Two Falmouth packets sailed home before the *Camerons*, both arriving on 12 February, 1841. The *Swift* and *Ranger* packets had left St. Thomas on 30 December and 1 January respectively, sailing again together, each of them carrying high-value freight, the *Swift* 100,000 dollars and the *Ranger* 80,000 dollars.[577] The packets would have taken the November report to England more than three weeks earlier than it actually arrived.

J.M. Houston used private merchantmen in seven cases out of ten to send his monthly returns to Liverpool. In six cases out of the seven, the government mail would have been a faster alternative. Eight of the ten reports would have been quicker in Liverpool if sent by a Falmouth packet instead of a merchant ship. In two cases, a private vessel was faster than the official mail.

The figures in Table 32 give a 72 days' average duration of information transmission between the end of the financial reporting period and the arrival of the results in Liverpool. The shortest time between the end of the reporting period and the arrival of the monthly return in Liverpool was 53 days, when sent by a merchantman, and the longest time 98 days. By government packets, the figures were 58 days and 86 days respectively.

Not all the time was spent at sea. By cutting the transmission of each letter into slices, it has been shown here that even several weeks could pass after the end of the reporting period before the merchantman chosen by the manager *de facto* departed with the letter on board. This waiting time varied from a couple of weeks to over a month, in some cases probably more, even though it cannot always be completely reconstructed.

The small sample of letters gives a clear and versatile picture of the communication conditions between the plantation and its owners on the two sides of the Atlantic. Compared with the on-line financial reporting and management systems and strict information obligations of today's business life, the ownership and management of distant plantations in the early 19th century was not very systematic. The communications were not only slow, but entirely unpredictable.

In many cases, the letters from Berbice would have been in England much faster by a government packet than by a merchant ship, but sometimes it was vice versa – making it difficult for J.M. Houston to decide on the means of communications. He could have sent duplicates to ensure that at least one of them was carried by the fastest possible transport but none of the letters bear any markings indicating that.[578]

576 *Lloyd's List* 20.1.1841; 15.2.1841.
577 *Lloyd's List* 16.2.1841.
578 The other sample of letters from 1826–1841 show that both merchant houses, Sandbach, Tinne & Co. as well as Thomas and William Earle & Co., usually often received duplicates

TABLE 32. *Monthly returns of Plantation Hanover, Berbice, in 1840. Duration before the information was available to the owners in Liverpool after the end of each financial period.*

Monthly Return	Days elapsed before information was available to owners after financial reporting period	Ship type: Merchant vessel (M) Falmouth Packet (F)
January	71	M
February	74	F
March	58	F *
April	53	M *
May	76	M
June	72	M
July	86	F
August	72	M
September	62	M
November	98	M

The alternative options (private / government mail) were checked in each case. The best possible choice at the date has been marked in the table with an asterisk (*).

By sending duplicates, the average time between the end of each reporting period and the fastest arrival of the information in Liverpool would have decreased from 72 days to 56 days without any changes in the transports. This would naturally have increased costs and the manager may have thought that the reports were not important enough for the extra expense. The owners may have thought that they were important, however, as most of the reports have been preserved among the company papers until this day.

from their plantations in Guiana. Seven of the 15 letters in this sample are duplicates, five of them in Sandbach's correspondence and two in Earle's. Interestingly, both duplicates in the latter collection are from 1841, as if the practice would then have been introduced at the plantation. Subsequently, at least three letters out of 11 in Earle's correspondence from 1842 are duplicates. As the whole sample consists of only 36 letters from 1825–1842, they can naturally only give examples of business practices and can by no means be interpreted as full evidence of the companies' policies in this question. See Records of Sandbach, Tinne & Co., D/B/176; Correspondence of Thomas and William Earle & Co, D/Earle/5/2. (MMM). – There could naturally also be other reasons for sending duplicates than just getting the message through as fast as possible. For instance, something new could have happened since the original letter was sent: 'I have already written to you to this packet but since posting my letter, I have seen W.B. Chisholm. I had a long & interesting conversation with him…' (William Carter to William Earle, Berbice 23.1.1842, 'p. Packet'. Correspondence of Thomas and William Earle & Co, D/Earle/5/8/4b, MMM).

When comparing the alternatives in sending the report each month, one can also ask whether J.M. Houston really did his best to finalize the figures as quickly as possible to get them shipped by the earliest possible means. The rhythm of life and business was not very busy at that time, and the overall economic situation in Guiana was hardly motivating either. Perhaps there were good reasons to delay sending bad news to the owners.

Complaints of slow communications were usual everywhere in the world, but as long as the transport was dependent on winds, not very much could be done to ensure a fast voyage. If the owners had comments or instructions regarding the financials or management of their overseas businesses, it would take another two to three months before the manager would have them in hand. Typically, the owners had to rely on their managers' abilities to make decisions without specific advice, and he had to have authority, when needed. If things went wrong, the manager could be changed, of course.[579]

In the case of Plantation Hanover, the owners were clearly anxious about the plantation's financial condition. The Earle correspondence includes several letters from John Ross, Attorney, written to the company management in Liverpool. According to him, Hanover had a reputation for being one of the most unproductive estates in the colony. He discussed the possible selling price and the balance of accounts. A couple of weeks later, in another letter, he points out errors in the accounts.[580]

Furthermore, the owners were not at all happy with the plantation's management in Berbice. In addition to mentioning the problems that arose from the emancipation of the slaves and the subsequent discontent regarding notes to pay, John Ross also criticized the agent for running high expenses. In October he called it mismanagement and suggested some names of new possible managers for Hanover.[581] And indeed, a few months later the manager had been changed to another person.[582]

In conclusion it can be noted that instead of the government mail service, the plantation manager preferred to send his financial reports to Liverpool by familiar merchant vessels. If possible, he chose a ship with Liverpool as the home port. He did not bother to send mail by vessels sailing from Demerara but preferred to wait until a ship was leaving from Berbice, even though it would take more time. He did not want to ensure

---

579 Brown & Duguid have pointed out that it was finally the telegraph, linking the European capitals to their overseas colonies, which radically reduced the independence of the overseas administrators. With rapid communications, decision making could be centralized and the financial and executive autonomy of the overseas partners was quickly absorbed. See Brown & Duguid, 30.

580 John Ross of Inverness to Thomas and William Earle & Co., Liverpool, 30.12.1839; 10.1.1840. He continues about the possible sale of the plantation 20.1.1840. D/Earle 5/1–11, (MMM)

581 Ross to Thomas and William Earle & Co., Liverpool 16.8.1841; 30.10.1841. D/Earle 5/1–11, (MMM)

582 The Earle correspondence includes a letter from Mr. Nash, Manager of Plantation Hanover, to William Carter, Attorney, in Liverpool, 12.4.1842. (D/Earle 5/1–11) Despite several attempts, the plantation was not sold in the 1840s but abandoned as unprofitable, and closed up decades later by William Earle's descendants. Earle Family and Business Archive Records. Thomas Algernon Earle's interview, September 1939. (MMM)

the fastest possible transmission of the monthly returns, as he did not send duplicates.

The manager should have sent the mails by official mail as such a service existed, but this regulation was widely ignored. On arrival, letters were forwarded to the post office if inland transport was needed. A private ship letter arriving in Liverpool was dispatched directly to Thomas and William Earle & Co.'s office, not a single time to the Liverpool Post Office.[583]

Merchant ship communications between Britain and Guiana in 1840, a general view

As has been noted above, there were two different means of business information transmission in use between Britain and Guiana in 1840. Several questions remain open: How lively was the commercial traffic between the mother country and the colony at that time? Which British ports had the most traffic to Guiana? Was there a great difference in the number of sailings for Demerara and Berbice? How long did it normally take for a merchantman to sail from Guiana to Britain? How long did the ships stay at port? How well did the British government's West Indian mail service work as a whole? This chapter will focus on the merchant shipping on the Guiana route.

The statistics of British Parliamentary Papers concerning the trade and commerce of the West Indies do not include a return of ships sailing to or from the West Indian ports in 1840. However, the existing figures for the years 1822–1830 show a great variety in annual sailings. The number of importing British merchant ships arriving at the port of Demerara varied between 128 in 1824 and 184 in 1829, while the number of exporting ships varied between 145 in 1826 and 212 in 1829. Respectively, the number of importing merchant ships arriving at the port of Berbice varied between 25 in 1822 and 1826, and 33 in 1827, while the number of exporting ships varied between 20 in 1826 and 31 in 1822, 1824 and 1827.

Thus, during the 'good old times' before the abolition of slavery, an average of 162 importing British merchant ships arrived annually at the port of Demerara, while 180 sailed to Britain with exports. Another 28 ships arrived in Berbice, and 27 exported from that port. A large number of other vessels also used these ports, but despite their number, the average size was

---

583 This practice was well known by the General Post Office and the Treasury, and became part of a lively parliamentary debate in 1838 in connection with the General Post Master's plan to uniform the inland postage rates, which were based on miles carried, to one penny. Simultaneously with this reform in 1840, the rates of incoming private ship letters were uniformed to 8d per oz., covering the transmission from the exit port of the country of origin to the addressee anywhere on the British Isles. See Robertson, C2; and *BPP, Transports and Communications, Posts and Telegraphs 1 and 2* (1838). Select Committee on Postage, passim. – In the sample of 1825–1841, six letters had arrived via the Post Office: two via Glasgow, two via Deal, one via Plymouth and one to Sandbach, Tinne & Co. through the Liverpool Post Office, carrying the 'LIVERPOOL SHIP LETTER' handstamp. Six letters were forwarded to the recipient by the captain, two duplicates privately, and one remained unknown as the cover was not included in the records. There were paid and non-paid letters in both companies' correspondence. See D/B/176; D/Earle/5/2 (MMM) and HHC.

small, usually less than 100 tons, indicating mainly transports between nearby colonial islands. The average size of British ships for Demerara was over 280 tons, while that for Berbice was somewhat less than 240 tons.[584]

To find answers to the questions outside the statistics, the number and duration of commercial sailings between Britain and Guiana in 1840 were calculated using the maritime intelligence published by *Lloyd's List* during that year. Irish ports and Channel Islands were left out, for work economic reasons. The number of these sailings was not remarkable. In practice, there were three British ports which dominated the Guiana trade: London, Liverpool and Glasgow.[585]

The calculation of merchant ship traffic between Britain and Guiana in 1840 gave somewhat confusing figures. Some 245 ships were reported by *Lloyd's List* to have arrived at or departed from a port in either end of the route.[586] The total includes all ships that sailed in at least one direction during the calendar year. Even though some of the vessels made two or three round trips during the year, only 184 sailings were reported by the ports of London, Liverpool and Glasgow for Demerara or Berbice, while these ports reported 177 arrivals from the British ports. Only 104 sailings from Guiana for London, Liverpool and Glasgow were reported, and 130 arrivals from Guiana at these ports.

Part of this phenomenon can be explained by the fact that not all ships made direct journeys between Britain and Guiana. Many vessels were tramp ships, proceeding from the West Indies to somewhere else, loading or unloading part of the cargo *en route*. In this case the ship could have been reported to sail for or from Barbados, Jamaica etc. – or not reported at all, as sometimes happened – instead of mentioning a British port. At the arrival port in Britain, however, the ship was reported as having arrived 'from Demerara', leaving it open when she actually sailed, and from where. Sometimes a ship could also arrive e.g. in Ireland and suddenly appear to be loading in London. However, the total figures for 1840 were close to the annual average of 1822–1830, and the shipping to and from Berbice had even increased.

Another and probably more interesting aspect from the business information transmission point of view is the remarkable difference between the numbers of reported sailings, regarding the home voyage vs. trips in the other direction. Only some 60% of the ships reported to have arrived in Demerara or Berbice (177) were reported to have ever sailed back for Britain (104). Even though the production volumes were low in Guiana that year, the ships must have sailed back home, or somewhere else, during the year.

---

584 The figures are calculated from the statistics in *BPP. Colonies. West Indies 2* (1806–49), Select Committee Reports and Correspondence on the Trade and Commerce of the West Indies. Appendix, 306–307. For comparison, the largest vessels of the East India Company, trading with India and China, at that time were 1,200–1,300 tons, even 1,400 tons. *Lloyd's Register* 1826.

585 The total number of other British ship departures and arrivals was approximately 10% of the whole. Of these other ports, Bristol and Plymouth had the most traffic to Guiana but still less than 20 sailings in total.

586 An exact number of vessels cannot be given, as there were several ships by the same name and insufficient other details.

An explanation for the missing intelligence might be that the sailing lists were published in *Lloyd's List* basically to inform the underwriters, shipowners and other stakeholders about the safe arrival or departure of vessels at foreign ports. The long distance communications were so slow that the ship in question had often arrived in Britain before the news about her departure from Guiana had been published by *Lloyd's List* in London. The maritime intelligence gives several examples of this kind of delay.[587]

Publishing out-dated news was in no-one's interest. Stakeholders did not need the information about the ship's departure from Guiana, if the vessel was already at the home port. Most probably *Lloyd's List* normally just left out this information, which explains at least partly the difference mentioned above. This observation depicts an overall problem of business information from the colonies in the era of sailing ships: the information received could be totally out-dated when it finally arrived.

TABLE 33. *Number of ships reported by Lloyd's List to have sailed between the British ports London, Liverpool and Glasgow, and the Guianian ports Berbice and Demerara, 1840.*

Reported in	sailed for			arrived from		
	Berbice	Demerara	B + D	Berbice	Demerara	B + D
London	16 (15)	54 (43)	70 (58)	14 (8)	45 (24)	59 (32)
Liverpool	16 (16)	54 (53)	70 (68)	10 (12)	32 (37)	42 (49)
Glasgow	3 (3)	41 (47)	44 (50)	2 (4)	27 (19)	29 (23)
L + L + G	35 (34)	149 (143)	**184 (177)**	26 (24)	104 (80)	**130 (104)**

In brackets are the corresponding figures from the other side of the Atlantic. E.g. Lloyd's List reported that 54 ships had sailed from London for Demerara during the year, and that 43 ships had arrived in Demerara from London.

Of the 595 records included in Table 33 a great part is overlapping as the figures include both ends of a single trip. As the dates of arrivals or departures

587 E.g. the *Lady Campbell's* arrival in Liverpool 6.5.1840 was published by *Lloyd's List* on 7.5.1840. Her departure from Demerara (14.3.1840) was published almost a week later, 13.5.1840. The *Palmyra's* arrival in Liverpool 1.7.1840 was published by *Lloyd's List* 2.7.1840 and her departure from Demerara (26.5.) a week later, 9.7.1840. It could also happen that the news of the ship's departure from the colonial port and arrival at the homeport were published in the same issue, and even on the very same page, like when *Lloyd's List* published the departure of the *Thistle* from Demerara (23.8.) and her arrival at Clyde 22.9.1840, on 23.9.1840. Quite often this problem has been avoided by a note in the arrivals: 'sailed ...' thus combining the two different news types.

are missing from many journeys, it has only been possible to calculate the duration of 148 sea voyages.

London and Liverpool were the main British ports for the Guiana trade. Glasgow was the third important one, while the others played a minor role. About 20% of the sailings were for Berbice, while the majority was for Demerara. Glasgow's trade was almost entirely focused on Demerara. Only three ships sailed from the Clyde for Berbice during the year.

Despite the well known difficulties in Guiana, it seems that a few more British merchant ships were sailing to or from its ports in 1840 than a decade earlier. This meant that, despite decreasing trade figures, the opportunities for information transmission had actually increased since the 1820s.

An average sailing from Britain to Guiana took some 43 days, and an average home voyage 51 days. The duration of sailings varied a lot, 30 to 49 days being the most usual on the way to Guiana, and 40 to 59 days on the home voyage. The shortest sailing was from Glasgow to Demerara, 26 days, and the longest from Demerara to London, 77 days.[588]

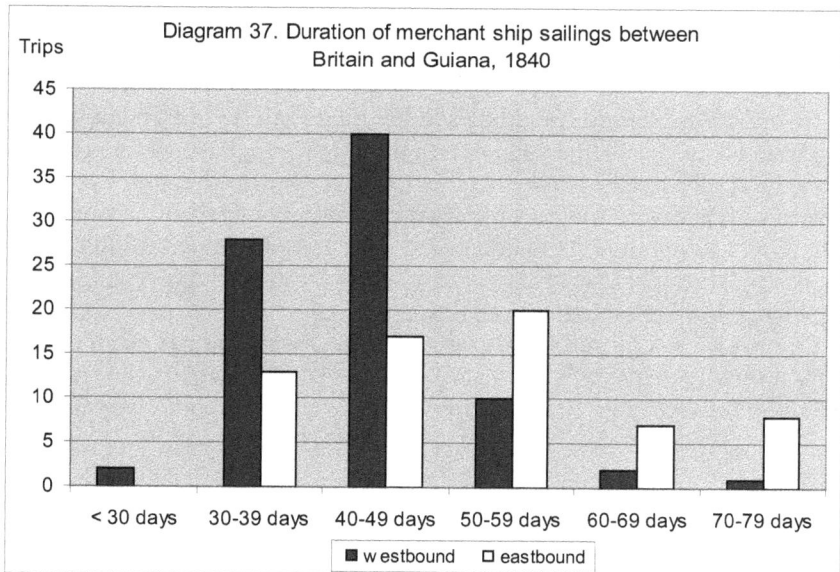

Diagram 37. Duration of merchant ship sailings between Britain and Guiana, 1840

Source: Lloyd's List, 1840. – The total number of westbound sailings included in the records was 83 and the number of eastbound sailings 65.

The rather big difference in duration of westbound and eastbound sailings may have been caused by the imbalance of trade between Britain and Guiana. The estimated value of imports from the mother country to Demerara was about £480,000 on average in 1822–1830, while the value of exports from

588 Three trips with durations between 82 and 97 days have been left out of the calculation, as they most probably were not direct sailings.

Demerara to Britain was about £1.4 million on average. The figures of Berbice were about £70,000 and £200,000 respectively.[589] The imported British industrial products were typically of higher value than the exported colonial bulk products, thus causing even more difference in the weight of cargo inwards and outwards.

The port stays varied between 12 and 120 days, without any reasons given. The stays of more than two months may have included major ship repairs, or even a non-reported trip somewhere else in between. The large British ports worked more efficiently than the colonial ports, even though their functions were also still very labour intensive, as Sarah Palmer has shown in her studies of the economics of the 19th century port of London.[590] In Liverpool, a dramatic dock planning and building process took place with the advent of steam in the 1840s and 1850s, but had not yet started by 1840.[591]

Regular Guiana traders normally spent roughly four weeks unloading and loading in London or Glasgow, and more than five weeks in Liverpool, on average. The port stays in Demerara and Berbice were longer, from six to seven weeks on average. It is not mentioned in the documents whether labour shortages in Guiana were just as problematic at the ports as they were at the plantations. However, the delays in production at the plantations alone must have also caused extra waiting time for the exporting ships at ports.[592]

Of the 245 merchant ships sailing between the ports in question during 1840, about ten percent could be called regular traders. They made at least two round trips during the year, one of the ships being fast enough to make three. Of these vessels, 13 were on the London–Demerara route, five on the Liverpool–Demerara route and four on the Glasgow–Demerara route. One ship from Liverpool and London sailed regularly to Berbice. Unlike tramp ships, regular traders normally sailed directly between the two ports, being somewhat more reliable mail carriers.

Due to the slow and crowded passage up the River Thames, the merchant ships normally delivered their mailbags at Deal one or two days before their arrival in London. The Gravesend Post Office was also commonly used, as

589 *BPP, Colonies. West Indies 2* (1806–49), Select Committee Reports and Correspondence on the Trade and Commerce of the West Indies. Appendix, 307.

590 Sarah Palmer, 'Port Economics in an Historical Context: The Nineteenth-Century Port of London', *International Journal of Maritime History*. Vol. XV No. 1 (June 2003), 27–67.

591 Jarvis *(1991), 68–102;* Graeme J. Milne, 'Port Politics: Interest, Faction and Port Management in Mid-Victorian Liverpool', in Lewis R. Fischer & Adrian Jarvis, *Harbours and Havens Havens: Essays in Port History in Honour of Gordon Jackson. Research in Maritime History No. 16* (St. John's, 1999), 35–62.

592 The plantation owners claimed that after abolition, having been able to purchase their own land, the former slaves were not willing to work at the plantations for more than 'three or four days in a week, and from five to seven hours in a day'. *BPP, Colonies. West Indies 1* (1842), Report of Select Committee on West India Colonies, iii–v. – Modern research has examined more critically the reasons for these problems. See e.g. Douglas Hall, 'The Flight from the Estates Reconsidered: The British West Indies, 1838–1842' and O. Nigel Bolland, 'Systems of Domination After Slavery: The Control of Land and Labour in the British West Indies After 1838' in Hilary Beckles & Verene Shepherd (eds): *Caribbean Freedom. Economy and Society from Emancipation to the Present* (Princeton, 1996), 55–63, 107–123.

well as places off the southern coast, e.g. Salcombe in the micro case of this study. The law required the incoming ship's captain to forward the letters to the nearest post office at the first port of call in Britain. In many cases the first port of call depended on the weather, the need for water or stores, etc., and could be wherever it was most convenient to put in.[593]

While many of the other merchantmen on the Guiana route were rather small vessels – not much over 200 tons and some even below that – the regular traders were mostly bigger, near 400 tons or even above. However, the fastest vessel on the route was the 214 tons *Thistle* of Glasgow, making three full round trips despite suffering a heavy gale 'with loss of boat, bulwarks, spars &c.' during one of the journeys in January 1840.[594] The *Thistle* was obviously a fast-sailing ship but, due to her smaller size, her loading and unloading were also faster than some larger vessels. Especially her port stays in Glasgow were rapid: 14, 19 and 27 days.

Not many round trips can be fully reconstructed due to missing dates. One good example of a regular trader with almost three round trips is the *Parker*, with sailings and port stays as follows:

TABLE 34. *Duration of sailings and port stays of the regular trader* Parker *on the Liverpool–Demerara route, 1840.*

Ship	Departure		Arrival		Duration, days	
	British port	Guianian. port	British port	Guianian. port	at sea	at port
Parker		Demerara 11.12.1839	Liverpool 17.1.1840		37	
	Liverpool 17.2.			Demerara 19.3.	31	31 Liverpool
		Demerara 5.5.	Liverpool 4.6.		30	47 Demerara
	Liverpool 25.7.			Demerara 26.8.	32	51 Liverpool
		Demerara 13.10.	Liverpool 28.11.		46	48 Demerara
	Liverpool 26.12.			Demerara 22.1.1841	27	28 Liverpool

Source: Lloyd's List, 1840.

The example shows the great differences in the time spent at sea – or at port – even by the same vessel. It was rather impossible to forecast the duration of a voyage. On average, the *Parker* spent 34 days at sea and 32 days at port during the period. In other words, the first round trip from Liverpool included

593 Robertson, A1, C5.
594 *Lloyd's List* 22.1.1840.

61 days at sea and 47 days at port in Demerara, i.e. 44% of the time spent at port. The second voyage included 78 days at sea and 48 days at port in Demerara, i.e. 38% of the time spent at port. The exceptional efficiency of the *Parker* becomes evident when comparing these figures with the general average of time spent at port during the period. It was usually 53–55%.[595]

The records, even if not so representative as one would hope, give an impression that the merchant ships between Liverpool and Demerara were the best options to send private mail from the colony to the mother country. There were four to five ships leaving for Liverpool from Demerara each month, on average, but only one or two from Berbice.

Due to the nature of the business, i.e. trading colonial plant products, more than 40% of the recorded ship departures from Guiana fell in November–January. In addition, many ship captains most probably have wanted to avoid the hurricane season, which lasted from June to November, being worst from August to October.[596] Thus, there were months when no ships departed for London or Glasgow, and only one or two for Liverpool. Even if there were ships loading at the port, the mail sender could never be certain of their schedules.

Due to the many missing dates in *Lloyd's List's* maritime intelligence, a perfect information circulation by using merchant ships as mail carriers on the Guiana route cannot easily be reconstructed. Table 35 depicts one example of how to send letters to and from Demerara, starting from Liverpool at the beginning of the year 1840.

TABLE 35. *Consecutive information circles enabled by merchant ships between Liverpool and Demerara in 1840, an example.*

Letter sent by merchant ship	Ship departure, Liverpool	Ship arrival, Demerara	Next possible departing merchant ship	Ship departure, Demerara	Ship arrival, Liverpool	Infor-mation circle, days
Leonora	4.1.	~ before mid-February*	*James Ray*	16.2.	7.4.	94
Hardware	8.4.	17.5.	*Rapid*	28.5.	1.7.	84
Parker	25.7.	26.8.	*Mary*	7.9.	28.10.	95
Stormont	10.11.	18.12.	*Victory*	19.12.	Jan.–Feb. 1841	- -

Sources: Lloyd's List 1840.

---

595 Ojala (1999), 238, 435.

596 *Lloyd's Maritime Atlas* (London 1964), Map 1. This variation of voyages was also noticed by Steele, although he looks at it from the perspective of English ports. As he also remarked, the West Indian mail packets demonstrated that ships could safely sail on the route regardless of the seasons. See Steele (1986), 23, 286, 290.

* The exact arrival date has not been reported. In this table, 42 days are allowed for the trip, compared to 39, 32 and 38 of the other westbound trips. – The duration of the last round trip has not been calculated as it continues for a great part to the following year.

As can be noted from table 35, less than four consecutive information circles could be implemented on the West Indian route within a year, if only merchant ships were used as mail carriers. Guiana is naturally an example of a distant colony, compared to e.g. Jamaica, but the information transmission between the plantations and their owners in the mother country was of course equally as important for these owners as for any others having businesses in the colonies.

In two cases (7.4.1840 and 18.12.1840) the table gives a very tight schedule for answers to the letters. It could have been implemented only if the locals had frequent contacts with the Coffee House, or the Post Office service was quick enough with the dispatches. Good luck was sometimes needed for the most rapid information flows.

The West Indian and South American mail services as parts of the whole Falmouth packet system

Apart from the merchant ships, there was the official channel for sending business letters to Britain, or via Britain, to be forwarded to other places in Europe: the Falmouth packets. As already depicted in the micro case of Plantation Hanover, the government's mail system was rather slow and complicated. However, it would still have been a better option for the plantation manager in most cases, compared with the private ship dispatches.

The mail packets sailed from Falmouth for the West Indies on the 3rd and 17th of each month.[597] Although delays of one or two days due to heavy gales were not exceptional, most departures from England were made on time. The round trips of the packets consisted of three parts: the westbound Atlantic crossing, the inter-islands journey, and the eastbound crossing on the way back home. Each of these parts depended on the earlier one, and the duration of them all was rather unforeseeable.

In 1840,[598] the packets' westbound crossing of the Atlantic varied between 20 and 45 days, nine of the journeys being made in less than 30

---

597 *Lloyd's List*, 1840. The mails had earlier been sent on the first and third Wednesday of each month from London, the packets leaving from Falmouth on the following Saturday, but this somewhat confusing system had been adjusted in 1834. The mails were now made in the London Post Office on the 1st and 15th of each month. If these dates happened to be Sundays, the departure from Falmouth consequently took place on the 4th and 18th. See Britnor, 149–152.

598 To be consistent, this calculation is based on data concerning packets by which it was possible to send mail to Britain from the West Indies in 1840. Thus, the *Tyrian* was the first packet included. She departed from Falmouth on 4 December, 1839 and arrived at Barbados on 16 January, 1840. The *Ranger* was the last packet of the next 12 months, departing from Falmouth in November, 1840. She was back in Falmouth on 12 February, 1841.

MAP 3. *Falmouth packet routes during the first half of the 19th century.*

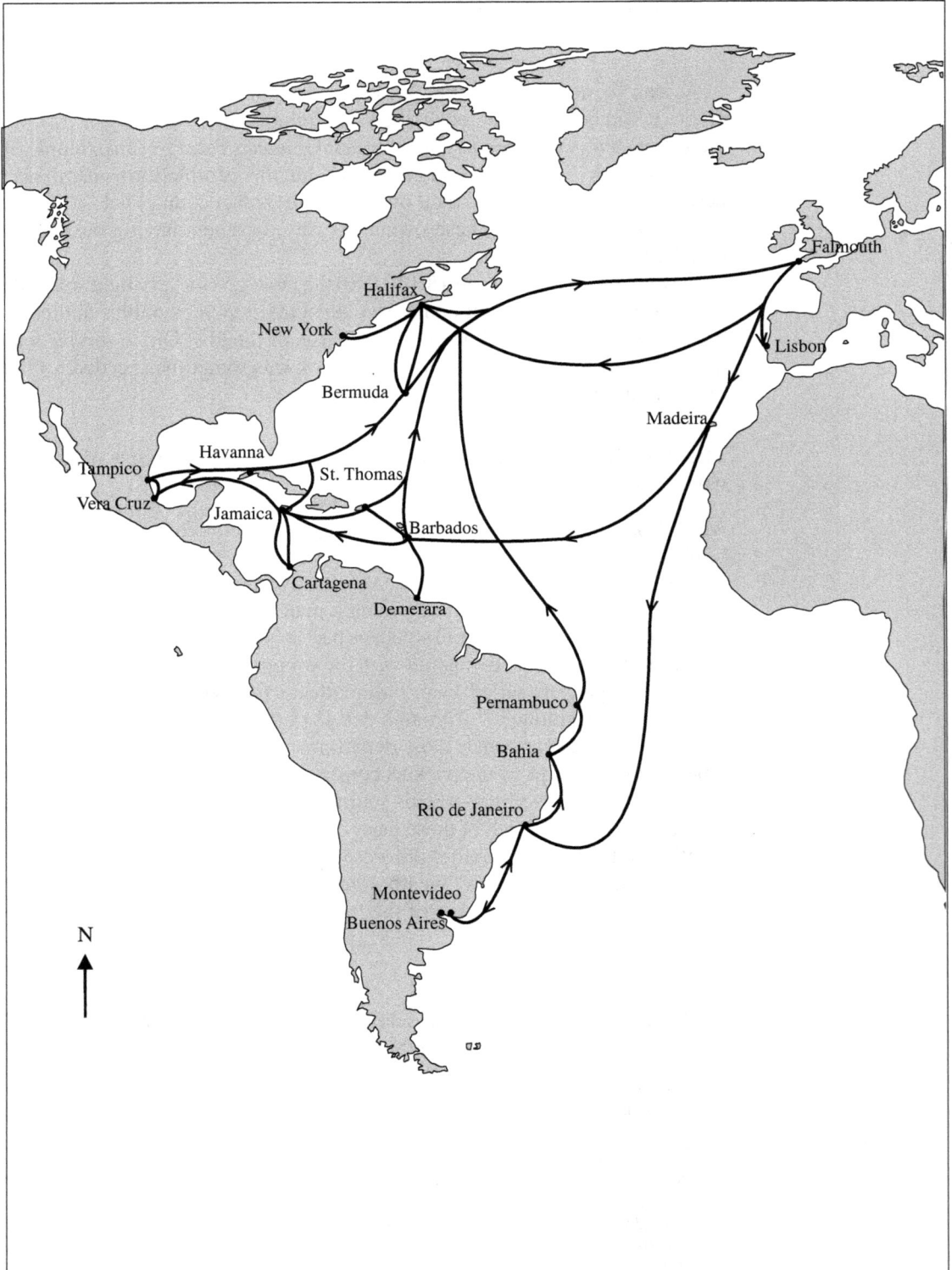

days.[599] The average westbound trip from Falmouth to Barbados took 31 days.

The duration of the inter-islands journey between Barbados and Cape Henry or Cape Haitien at Haiti varied between 20 and 30 days, being 23 days on average. The inter-islands journey started within 24 hours of the packet's arrival at Barbados. If one packet was delayed, arriving simultaneously with the following one, which had departed two weeks later from Falmouth, the two ships sailed together for virtually the rest of the voyage.

The eastbound trip from Haiti to Falmouth took 33 days on average. The shortest sailing took only 25 days, and the longest 44 days. The average eastbound sailing was thus considerably faster than an average merchant ship sailing. The packet ships were approximately the same size as the merchant ships, near 300 tons on average,[600] and they sailed with no cargo. Without the time-consuming cruising among the islands, the mail packets could have constituted a really competitive means of communications.

Yet the duration of the West Indian mail packet sailings had not changed much since the pioneering times of Edmund Dummer. His packets sailed from Channel ports, mainly Falmouth or Plymouth, to Barbados during 1702–1711 in 32.7 days on average, being only two days slower than the Falmouth packets of 1840.[601] At the same time, however, it looks like the merchant ships would have sailed from British ports to Guiana clearly faster in 1840 than to Barbados in 1698–1700. According to Ian K. Steele, an average merchantman of the earlier period sailed from the Channel ports to Barbados in 62.9 days (20 cases) and from the west coast of England in 80.2 days (26 cases).[602]

We should probably not assume that merchant shipping developed so much faster than mail sailings. It seems that the customs-to-customs calculation method used by Steele may have added a number of extra days to the duration of voyages. The ships did not always leave on the same day as they were cleared from the customs, due to bad weather conditions or other reasons.

Despite generally faster sailings, the West Indian mail transmission – even if conducted bi-monthly – was organized in a way that gave no advantage to the government mail service compared with the merchant ships in terms of business information circulation. Table 36 gives an example of the best options, starting from Liverpool at the beginning of the year 1840.

599 In three cases, the date of the stop at Barbados is missing, making it impossible to calculate the duration of the westbound and inter-islands journeys. Normally, the Falmouth packet departures and arrivals were well reported in *Lloyd's List* compared to the merchant vessels.

600 'A List of Packets at Present Employed in the Service of the Post-Office', *Lloyd's Register*, 1840.

601 Britnor, 9.

602 Steele (1986), 283.

TABLE 36. *Consecutive information circles enabled by Falmouth packets for correspondence between Liverpool and Demerara in 1840, an example.*

Letter sent by packet	Ship departure Falmouth	Ship arrival at Barbados > Demerara	Next possible departing packet	Ship departure, Haiti	Ship arrival, Falmouth	Information circle, days
Sheldrake	3.1.	3.2.	Sheldrake	4.3.	6.4.	98
Lapwing	17.4.	21.5.	Lapwing	12.6.	15.7.	93
Pandora	3.8.	31.8.	Pandora	22.9.	27.10.	85
Swift	4.11.	- -	Swift	4.1.	(12.2.41)	(100)

Source: Lloyd's List 1840.

As can be seen in table 36, the information circulation enabled by the Falmouth packets on the West Indian mail route was not at all faster than what could be achieved by merchant ships (see table 35). The only good thing in the service was the regularity in sailing times from England. The arrivals at Barbados varied considerably, and there seems to have been no fixed departure dates from Haiti. From a Liverpool merchant's perspective, at least four extra days had to be added for the inland connections to and from Falmouth. The mails were made in London two days before the departure of the packet, and they arrived via the London Post Office.

When looking at the West Indian route only, it seems strange that the Falmouth packets did not adopt the practice that had already been used by the American sailing packets in the North Atlantic for 20 years. The American packets made three round trips each year, not more or less, independent of contrary winds and other mishaps. Thus they could generally sail on the published date from both sides of the Atlantic. As already discussed, this punctuality made the North Atlantic business communications the best existing at the time.

The Falmouth packets made the West Indian round trip in 87 days on average. The longest round trip took 107 days and the shortest only 73 days. Within these limits, it would have been rather easy to organize a better working system, similar to the North Atlantic line traffic model. As there was a packet leaving from England regularly bi-monthly, there could have been one leaving from the other end correspondingly. Now there was a packet leaving regularly from Falmouth, but the time between two packet departures from Haiti at the other end of the voyage could vary between two and 34 days, not to mention the two ships that departed on the same day in April 1840.

Unfortunately, the system was too complicated to allow simple solutions. The same packets that carried the Guiana mails to Barbados and the answers ome to England also carried mails for Halifax and Bermuda until mid-1840, when the Cunard Line took over the North Atlantic route by its new steamers.[603] In addition, they sailed the long mail routes to Vera Cruz and Tampico as well as to Bahia, Pernambuco and Rio de Janeiro. The last mentioned route was so long and therefore unpopular among packet captains that the ships were not normally sent there twice in succession. The stormy Halifax route with its raw winter winds was a similar case. As the mail routes were not equally long, scheduled mixed round trips were not easy to organize.

Although the South American packet route was the longest, it was not actually very much longer than the route to Mexico. The average duration of the round trip to Rio de Janeiro was 133 days and to Vera Cruz 126 days in 1840.[604]

The South American route

The South American route had existed since 1808 as part of the good relationship between Britain and the Portuguese Royal family living in exile in Brazil during the war time. The sailings were originally only to Rio de Janeiro, with a call at Madeira and Tenerife on the way outwards, but as the trade developed between Britain and Brazil, demand arose for an additional port of call in South America. In April 1817, the 'merchants of Liverpool and London' represented to the Postmaster General that Pernambuco as well as Bahia should be included as ports of call 'as it would be a great convenience to the Trade'. A committee of captains at Falmouth considered that the voyage out and home to Rio would not be lengthened by touching Pernambuco by more than a week to ten days.[605]

The service on that route was certainly not easy, and the customers were not happy either. The coast of Pernambuco was reported by packet captains to be dangerous in the extreme, having neither lighthouses to direct vessels by night nor a port in which a packet could take shelter by day, and not the smallest assistance could be rendered from the shore. Strong gales were not the only problems during the early packet voyages. Captures by privateers and pirates caused several serious losses, and sometimes the ships had such a lack of crew that they were not able to sail on schedule. Heavy loss of life was not only due to action on board during the wartime captures, but at least 99 men were killed by yellow fever between 1780 and 1828 on board the packets.[606]

---

603 See the sailing lists of Arnell & Ludington, 69.
604 The figures are calculated from the sailing lists of Howat, 81; and from *Lloyd's List* 1840.
 – The official length of the round voyage Falmouth – Rio de Janeiro – Falmouth was 18 weeks. See Howat, 5.
605 See Howat, 1–6. – In practice, the system was more complicated. On those journeys starting from Falmouth in January–June each year, the packets called at Bahia and Pernambuco on their homeward voyage. On the journeys commencing from Falmouth in the second half of the year, Bahia and Pernambuco were touched at the outward voyage. And in 1832, when the Post Office service to South America was totally taken over by the Admiralty, this was adjusted once more so that the respective months were February–July and August–January. See Howat, 65. The reason for the odd six-month arrangement was simply that the running order of the South American ports of call depended on the prevailing winds. See Pawlyn, 111.
606 Howat, 5, 10, 16–18; and Pawlyn, 54–56, 66–68.

The merchants trading between Pernambuco and Britain complained a year or so after the arrangement had been made that the packets did not stay long enough to enable them to reply to the letters brought from Britain. In a number of instances, the packet had only remained a day or less. It was essential for the merchants to have sufficient time to receive their mail, absorb the contents and write replies to their trading contacts in Britain. As a result of the representation made, instructions were issued by the Secretary of the Post Office that packets should stay at Pernambuco for 48 hours, as they did at Bahia, unless it was detrimental to their safety.[607]

The sailing lists of Howat do not enable the calculation of all voyage lengths during the first years of packet service, as the arrival dates in Rio are not recorded. A comparison between the length of the home trips from Rio to Falmouth gives us the following results:

TABLE 37. *Average duration of packet sailings from Rio de Janeiro to Falmouth, 1820–1850.*

	1820	*1830*	*1840*	*1850*
Days on average	62.2	60.1	58.7	51.9

Source: Sailing lists of Howat, 13, 77, 81, 86. – The packets called at Bahia and Pernambuco on six homeward voyages out of 12 each year.

It is interesting to note that the average sailings shortened by about ten days from the 1820s to the 1850s even if the route arrangements remained the same and all these trips were conducted by government sailing packets.[608] Here the difference was clearly in the technical improvements of the vessels.

As already described in connection with the Falmouth packet sailings to Halifax (see Chapter V.2.) the Admiralty took over the Post Office administration of the mail packets in 1823 as part of the post-war arrangements. The ships which the Admiralty introduced in packet service were slow ten-gun brigs and sloops, later packet brigs. The first category packets were small men-of-war, mainly 230–240 tons, and built for general naval purposes in the 1820s. The ships were modified and re-equipped for mail service, mostly including the reduction of the armament to six guns, but they were never really suitable for this duty. The later packet brigs were built in the 1830s especially for the mail service. They were larger, about 360

---

607 Howat, 6.

608 In 1830, there was a double service to South America, conducted by both the Post Office and the Admiralty. The Post Office packet sailings covered the route Falmouth – Rio de Janeiro – Montevideo – Buenos Aires – Montevideo – Rio de Janeiro – Falmouth and did not make a call at Bahia or Pernambuco. Their average home voyage from Rio took 51.3 days. (Howat, 61) In three cases, the mails were transferred from the packet to a man-of-war in Rio, however. These changes caused serious protests among the local merchants as well as the Post Office in England due to confusion in sailing schedules and differences in postage rates. See Howat, 54–55.

tons, and more seaworthy than the older ones. Before these rearrangements took place, nine of the 25 naval packets of the first category were lost at sea between 1827 and 1840. Several of them just disappeared.[609]

In table 37, the year 1840 happens to be in the middle of the shift period, when the Admiralty had already replaced part of the old men-of-wars with new-model packet brigs. Five of the monthly trips from Rio were conducted by the newer, purpose-built vessels. Their average sailing time was 51 days, while the trip by the old vessels took 64 days on average. In 1850, only newer ones were left in service, and the average sailings had reduced to less than 52 days.[610]

As mentioned, an average packet round trip between Falmouth and Rio de Janeiro took approximately 133 days. This was not the same as the information circle, however. By 1840, the packet system had been organized in a way which in four cases out of 12 made it possible to send an answer to a letter by the packet which was leaving from Rio earlier than the one which had carried the mails from England. Even this small arrangement reduced the length of an average information circle by eight days, from 133 to 125 days, without any changes in the duration of sailings. Table 38 shows how this worked. For an example of the alternative Rio de Janeiro–Falmouth–Rio de Janeiro, see Fig. 20.

Despite the varying length of sailings, the information circulation could have been clearly faster during the period of Post Office sailing packets, if the arrivals and departures had been better coordinated. Only four times out of 12 were the merchants in Rio de Janeiro able to reply to their letters immediately, while in the rest of the cases, the earlier packet had already left the port when the next one arrived with the latest news. In these four cases, the information circulation enabled by the combined service of two packets was several weeks shorter than the single vessel's round trip.

Calculating from the beginning of 1840, the Falmouth packet service could offer fewer than three consecutive information circles between England and Rio de Janeiro that year. The first circle started by the departure of the *Alert* on 10 January 1840, the second by the *Delight* on 5 June and the third by the *Express* on 9 October. As can be noticed in Table 38, two of the circles clearly benefited from the possibility to send the answer from Rio de Janeiro by an earlier packet.[611]

Even if the information circulation to Rio de Janeiro can be considered rather fast compared with e.g. the much nearer located Demerara, the situation

---

609 Howat, 29, 32–35.
610 See the list of Admiralty packets in Howat, 32–35. It is a more complete list than the one in *Lloyd's Register* 1840. – The longer route via Bahia and Pernambuco on homeward sailings half of the year did not explain the difference. There were new and old vessels on both routes, and the new ones were typically faster on both routes throughout the year. See the sailing lists of Howat, 81. – As an exception to the rule mentioned, the *Seagull* which was the last Falmouth packet in service was of middle-size, 280 tons.
611 This opportunity remained occasional even in 1850, when it was possible only three times out of 12 to send an answer to a letter by an earlier departing packet. Additionally, one packet left on the same day when the packet from England arrived, thus giving only a slight opportunity to somebody close to the port to send an answer to a letter by that vessel. See sailing lists of Howat, 85–86.

was worse if the letters proceeded to Argentina or Uruguay. The mail sailings to Buenos Aires started in 1824, and as long as the Post Office packets served on the route, they continued from Rio to Montevideo and Buenos Aires on their trip from Falmouth. The long sailing seemed to be too much for the Navy officers, as the system was changed when the Admiralty gradually replaced the private contract packets. Starting from late 1832, there was a branch packet service between Rio and the southern ports.

In 1830, the Post Office packets made the round trip from Falmouth via Rio and Montevideo to Buenos Aires and back again in 170 days on average. In two cases it was possible to send the answers from Buenos Aires by an earlier packet. This reduced the length of one information circle by ten and another by 23 days. The average duration of one information circle was thus 168 days.[612] The system enabled two full information circles with Buenos Aires during that year, starting from Falmouth on 23 January and ending at the same port on 11 December 1830. The third circle started from Falmouth on 24 December; this packet arrived at Rio on 18 February, 1831. At least two days at both ends need to be added for inland transmission to and from Liverpool.

TABLE 38. *Falmouth packet round trips and the length of information circles, Falmouth–Rio de Janeiro, 1840.*

Sailing packet	Departure from Falmouth	Arrival at Rio de Janeiro**	Departure from Rio de Janeiro	Arrival at Falmouth **	Ship's round trip, days	Information circle, England-Brazil-England, days	Information circle, Brazil-England-Brazil, days
Alert	10.1.40	28.2.	25.3.	13.5.	124*	124	126
Pandora	7.2.	31.3.	15.4.	1.6.	115*	115	134
Pigeon	6.3.	23.4.	**31.5.**	11.8.	158	158	147
Spey	10.4.	**22.5.**	21.6.	21.8.	133	> 123	126
Sheldrake	8.5.	26.6.	**31.7.**	26.9.	141	141	114
Delight	5.6.	**29.7.**	13.8.	17.10.	134	> 113	137
Alert	10.7.	27.8.	**27.9.**	20.11.	133	133	118
Magnet	7.8.	**24.9.**	18.10.	30.12.	145	> 105	etc.
Lapwing	4.9.	25.10.	**26.11.**	22.1.41	140	140	
Express	9.10.	**22.11.**	15.12.	11.2.	125	> 105	
Seagull	7.11.	28.12.	13.1.41	4.3.	117	117	
Penguin	8.12.	23.1.41	2.3.	13.4.	126	126	
Min.-max., days	- -	- -	- -	- -	115-158	105-158	114-147
Average, days	- -	- -	- -	- -	133	125	129

Source: Calculated from the sailing lists of Howat, 81.

---

612 Calculated from the sailing lists of Howat, 61.

– The options to send replies to the letters with an earlier packet are marked in bold.
– An average sailing from Falmouth to Rio de Janeiro took 48 days, varying between
42 and 54 days. The sailing to the other direction took 57 days on average, varying
between 42 and 73 days.
* February had 29 days in 1840.
** Six trips of the year were conducted via Pernambuco and Bahia.

FIG. 20. *The letter dated in Rio de Janeiro on 10.4.1843, was carried to England by
the* Swift *packet, which departed from Rio on 23.4. and arrived in Falmouth on 10.6.
The recipient, Frederick Huth Co. in London, has noted on the reverse that the letter
was answered to on 4.7. Thus the answer must have been carried by the* Penguin
*packet, which departed from Falmouth on 7.7. and arrived in Rio on 17.8. A concrete
case, where we know that the letter from Rio received an answer in 129 days of the
writing, or in 116 days after the mail-carrying packet had left the port of Rio.*

The Admiralty system for Bueros Aires was more complicated. Table 39 (in the end of the book, p. 428) depicts how it worked in 1840. The route consisted actually of several parts. Firstly, the outward sailing from Falmouth to Rio de Janeiro took 48.5 days on average, varying between 42 and 54 days. The branch packet was ready to sail for Buenos Aires within three to five days after the Falmouth packet had arrived. The sailing took about 12 days. The average waiting time in Buenos Aires was ten days, varying between seven and 22 days. The trip back to Rio was typically more difficult than the voyage down; it took 20 days on average. The next Falmouth packet took the mails and left within ten days on average. The delay varied between two and 19 days, however. The homeward trip from Rio to Falmouth took 57.3 days on average, nine days more than in the other direction.

As can be noted in Table 39, the departures of the Falmouth packets from Rio de Janeiro were organized so that the mails from Buenos Aires could always proceed by the next packet after the one which had brought the mails from Europe. This was a major improvement compared with other Admiralty ruled routes where the next ship had often just left when the auxiliary service arrived with the mails, but the system itself was rather slow with changes of ships and waiting at ports. Even if some vessels were apparently better than ten years earlier, the length of an average information circle did not reduce very much within a decade, only from 168 to 162 days.[613]

The Falmouth packets stayed at Rio for approximately 27 days on average, while it took almost 43 days on average for the branch service to make the round trip to Montevideo and Buenos Aires. With respect to the mail service between England and Brazil, it was obviously wise to organize the sailings to Argentina and Uruguay as a separate branch service and thus speed up the information transmission to and from Rio de Janeiro. One could say, however, that some more efficiency at the ports could easily have reduced the length of the information circles by at least one week. Now, two weeks were used on average for taking the European mails to the branch packet at Rio, and the branch packet mails to the leaving Falmouth packet at the same port on the way back home.

The Mexico route

The packet route to Mexico was established in 1826, and taken over by the Royal Mail Steam Packet Company together with the West Indian route in 1842.[614] As far as the writer of this study has been able to find out, no postal

---

613 Calculated from the sailing lists of Howat, 61, 81, 94.
614 See Howat, 27; Kenton & Parsons, 2–3, 8, 21. – There was also a French government mail packet line between Bordeaux and Vera Cruz in 1827–1835. The monthly service of the 'Paquebots Réguliers aux frais du Gouvernement' was ceased in mid-1835. The last ship was to sail from Bordeaux for Martinique, Haiti and Vera Cruz on 1.7.1835. A new service was started by Compagnie Général Transatlantique's steamers as late as 1862. The early French sailing packet service enabled about the same information circulation from Bordeaux to Vera Cruz as the Falmouth packet service did from England. A round trip normally took about five months and two information circles could be carried out in 11 months. Salles gives the departure and arrival dates from Bordeaux but no arrivals

historical research has been published about the Falmouth packet sailings on the Mexico route during the period. From Britnor we learn the following about the sailings on this route in 1832: The departure from Falmouth was on the third Wednesday of each month, and the packet proceeded via Jacquemel (Haiti), Jamaica, Belize (Honduras), Vera Cruz and Tampico (both in Mexico), back to Vera Cruz, Havana (Cuba) and home to Falmouth. On the arrival of the Mexico packet at Jamaica, a branch packet was dispatched to Cartagena (Colombia) and that vessel also brought the replies to Jamaica in time for the homeward bound Jamaica packet. A colonial boat conveyed the mails from Jamaica to Nassau (Bahamas), and took the replies to Crooked Island (Bahamas) to be picked up by the homeward bound Jamaica packet.[615]

As can be noticed from the list above, the Mexico route was actually a combined service for the North and West Caribbean islands, Central America and Mexico. In 1837, the Mexico packets, which had been calling at Belize, were ordered to sail directly from Havana to Vera Cruz and the Honduras mail had to be taken by a branch vessel from Jamaica.[616]

Several interesting details can be picked up from the *Lloyd's List* maritime intelligence on the Falmouth packet sailings for Mexico in 1840 (see Table 40). Probably the first thing to notice is that huge sums of bullion were carried by each of the packets from Mexico. During 1840, over $5 million arrived at Falmouth in the Mexico packets.[617] Vera Cruz and Tampico seem to have been the places where the Bank of England's bullion mainly came from, even if considerable amounts of money freight were also constantly arriving from the West Indies and other areas.[618]

Perhaps due to the importance of the Mexico route, the departures from Falmouth were strictly punctual throughout the year. That was where the punctuality ended, however. It is hard to find any logic in the departure dates at the other end of the trip.[619] Due to the delay of the *Opossum* in

and only a few departure dates from Vera Cruz, which makes it impossible to reconstruct the information circles enabled by the service on that route at the period. Apart from the possibility to send a message by an earlier leaving packet, which remains unknown, the missing intelligence makes it impossible to compare any options to send mail to Europe by the French *or* the British service. See Raymond Salles, *La Poste Maritime Française, Tome IV, Les Paquebots de L'Atlantique Nord, Antilles – Amérique Centrale et Pacifique Sud, États-Unis* (Limassol, 1992), 9–14.

615 Britnor, 150. – In 1840, the Falmouth packets for Mexico departed on the 17th of each month (*Lloyd's List* 1840).

616 Britnor, 150. – As can be seen in table 40, several Falmouth packets called at Belize again in 1840. Continuous changes were typical on these routes.

617 In addition to the packets mentioned in this table, the *Pigeon* arrived from Vera Cruz at Falmouth on 15.1.1840 with $200,000; the *Reindeer* on 15.4.1840 with $580,000; and the *Delight* on 30.4.1840 with $250,000. (See *Lloyd's List* 1840, respectively). They had all departed for their round trip in 1839.

618 For example, the American sailing packet *Columbus* arrived at Liverpool on 15.6.1840 with $50,000 from New York; and the Philadelphia packet *Monongahela* with 'upwards 500,000 dollars'. (*Lloyd's List* 17.6.1840)

619 For some more dates, the October, November and December 1839 sailings proceeded as follows: the *Pigeon* sailed from Vera Cruz on 28.11.1839, Tampico on 10.12. and Havana on 19.12. arriving at Falmouth on 15.1.1840; the *Reindeer* sailed from Vera Cruz on 11.2., Tampico on 17.2. and Havana on 6.3. arriving at Falmouth on 15.4.1840; and the *Delight* sailed from Vera Cruz on 6.3., from Tampico on 10.3. and Havana on 27.3. arriving at

TABLE 40. *Falmouth packet sailings for Mexico and consecutive information circles enabled by them, 1840.*

Packet	Dep. from Fal-mouth	Dep. from Cr. Island	Dep. from Belize	Dep. from Vera Cruz	Dep. from Tam-pico	Dep. from Vera Cruz	Dep. from Hava-na	Arrival, Falmouth
Opossum[a]	(17.1.) **29.1.**			**23.4.**	**30.4.**		**13.5.**	**12.6.** ($760,000)
Linnet	17.2.				21.4.	2.5.	13.5.	11.6. ($380,000)
Lyra	18.3.	19.4.	1.5.	20.5.	28.5.		15.6.	17.7. ($230,000)
Tyrian	17.4.					7.7.	22.7.	21.8. ($350,000)
Seagull	17.5.				24.7.	2.8.	19.8.	23.9. ($808,650)
Penguin	**17.6.**		**29.7.**	(arr. 8.8.)	**16.8.**	**24.8.**	**11.9.**	**18.10.** ($170,000)
Skylark	~17.7.							2.12.[b] ($440,000)
Crane	17.8.		2.10.	~12.10.	18.10.	29.10.	10.11.	7.12. ($95,200)
Star	17.9.				13.12.	23.12.	5.1.41	12.2.41[c] ($800,000)
Spey[d]	17.10.	–	–	–	–	–	–	–
Sheldrake	**18.11.**							spring 1841
Pandora	17.12.							spring 1841

Source: *Lloyd's List, 1840–1841.*
[a] The *Opossum* departed from Falmouth already on 17.1. but put back on 28.1.
[b] The *Skylark* arrived at Cork already 28.11.1840. Her exact departure date from Falmouth in July is missing.
[c] On the same day as the *Star* arrived from Mexico with a considerable freight of $800,000, two other Falmouth packets arrived from the West Indies, the *Swift* with $100,000 and the *Ranger* with $80,000. Thus the mail coach from Falmouth to London was responsible for the safe transport of almost one million dollars on a single day. (*Lloyd's List* 13.2. and 16.2.1841)
[d] Wrecked at the Bahamas Channel 24.11.1840; crew, passengers, mails and stores saved (*Lloyd's List* 16.1.1841). The vessel was abandoned but later brought to Nassau by *HMS Thunder.* (*Lloyd's List* 16.2.1841)

Falmouth on 30.4.1840. (*Lloyd's List* 1840, respectively)

January, the February packet *Linnet* was in Tampico before the January mails arrived, departed on the very same day from Havana as the *Opossum* and arrived at Falmouth one day earlier. These two ships shared a freight of $1.14 million and there may have been good reasons to sail together, but from the information transmission point of view this was naturally not an ideal arrangement.

The system gave the Vera Cruz merchants about two weeks time to answer their mails. During that time the English packet sailed for Tampico and returned. The departure from Havana to Falmouth was most often on a Wednesday, Thursday or Friday at around mid-month, although the date varied between the 5th and the 27th. The home trip was made in 32.6 days on average.[620] As can be noted from table 40, only two full information circles were possible between the trade partners in Britain and Mexico in that year. The next packet for Mexico departed on 18 November and would be back in Falmouth sometime in April 1841.

The Admiralty seems to have preferred to send the Mexico packets from Falmouth exactly on schedule instead of enabling the British merchants to answer their arriving letters. The *Skylark* departed on 17 July, the same day as the *Lyra* arrived from Mexico, and the answers had to wait for the next vessel for a whole month. The *Crane* departed from Falmouth for Vera Cruz four days before the *Tyrian* arrived with the mails from Mexico, the *Star* departed six days before, and the *Spey* just one day before the mails arrived.

Even if it was naturally important to keep the timetables, it might have been useful to reconsider them as it frequently happened that the duration of the Mexico sailings – the length of an average round trip was 126 days – was such that the mails from Vera Cruz arrived just after the monthly packet departure had taken place. If the service had been bi-monthly, this problem would not have existed – something to keep in mind when comparing the American sailing packets' weekly service in the North Atlantic with anything the Admiralty was able to do on any route.

The last years of the Falmouth packet service, a conclusion

In conclusion, it can be noted that the varying length and the complexity of the Falmouth packet routes as well as their auxiliary services made the organizing of the mail system a challenging task. The Admiralty had 24 packet vessels for four different routes and monthly services, except the West Indies, which was bi-monthly. Of the packets, 13 were small (about 230 tons) and rather unsuitable for the service, two were middle-size (280 and 320 tons) and only nine were purpose-built, around 360 tons vessels. Additionally, there were several branch services: between Halifax and Bermuda; widely at the Caribbean and the northern parts of South America; and between Rio de Janeiro and the southern ports. This puzzle was supposed to function perfectly during the age of sail, when prevailing winds and storms could ruin any plans, and often did.

---

620 Calculated from the dates of 11 arrivals in 1840, as the sailing date of the *Skylark* from Havana is missing. See *Lloyd's List* 1840–1841, respectively.

Diagram 38 illustrates the sailings of the Falmouth packets on different mail routes in 1840. It starts from 1 January and shows on which routes and for how long each ship was sailing during the year. The service for Halifax ended in the summer of 1840, when the Cunard Line's mail steamers started their operations. For this reason, three ships were left unemployed in the middle of the year. Additionally, the *Spey* packet struck on a coral reef in the Bahamas Channel and was lost in November 1840.[621]

Each of the packets could sail on any route, and no difference was made on the basis of their slowness or other disadvantages.[622] Basically, as was noticed when examining the South American route, a great part of the differences in duration of voyages were due to the varying quality of the packet vessels. As already discussed in Chapter V, it caused a dilemma, even on the North Atlantic route, if the shipping companies used very different steamers, while it was a great advantage if the fleet consisted of similar types of vessels. Although the problem was obviously well known by the Admiralty, nothing was done about it – in addition to economic reasons, it was probably thought that the vessels would soon be replaced by steamers anyway.

The general popularity of the American sailing packets was based on the idea of regular departures from both ends. Their schedules were built so that the targets could usually be met without problems and even if the duration of sailings varied a lot, the departures were on fixed dates from both Europe and New York. This was rather easy to manage due to the frequency of sailings. The longest waiting time between a ship's arrival and the next one's departure was one week only and generally just a few days. The number of vessels in service enabled sufficient time for loading and unloading at ports at both ends of the voyage.

The regularity of the Falmouth packets was limited to the departures from England only, and the rules varied between the routes. In 1840, the West Indian packets departed quite regularly on the 3rd and 17th of each month; the Mexico packets very accurately on the 17th (with the exceptions caused by Sundays); the South American packets on a Friday nearest to the 10th of each month with a couple of exceptions; and the Halifax mails on the first or second Saturday of each month.[623] As a whole, the departure dates from England can be called regular within their own logic.

The philosophy used for the departures from the other side of the ocean was different. The schedules were calculated from each arrival of the Falmouth packet from England – regardless of whether the trip had taken three or six weeks. Strict orders regulated how many days or hours after the ship had arrived at Barbados the auxiliary ships should depart for the colonial islands, and by which date the mails should be collected to Havana, Cape Haitien or some other place selected for the purpose during the years. The advantages

621 *Lloyd's List* 16.1.1841; 16.2.1841.
622 Leaving out the Lisbon packets that had already been replaced by steamers in 1840, the Falmouth packets took their turns for the various voyages according to the time of their arrival at the home port. See Robinson (1964), 111.
623 For the West Indies and Mexico routes, see *Lloyd's List* 1840; for the South American route, see the sailing lists of Howat, 81; and for the Halifax route, see the sailing lists of Arnell & Ludington, 69.

of this system were that the mails were carried home as fast as possible, and the vessels were back in England as soon as they could be.

Unfortunately the advantage of knowing in advance when the next mail ship would leave from Falmouth was in several cases cancelled out by the fact that the packet from abroad arrived shortly after another one for the

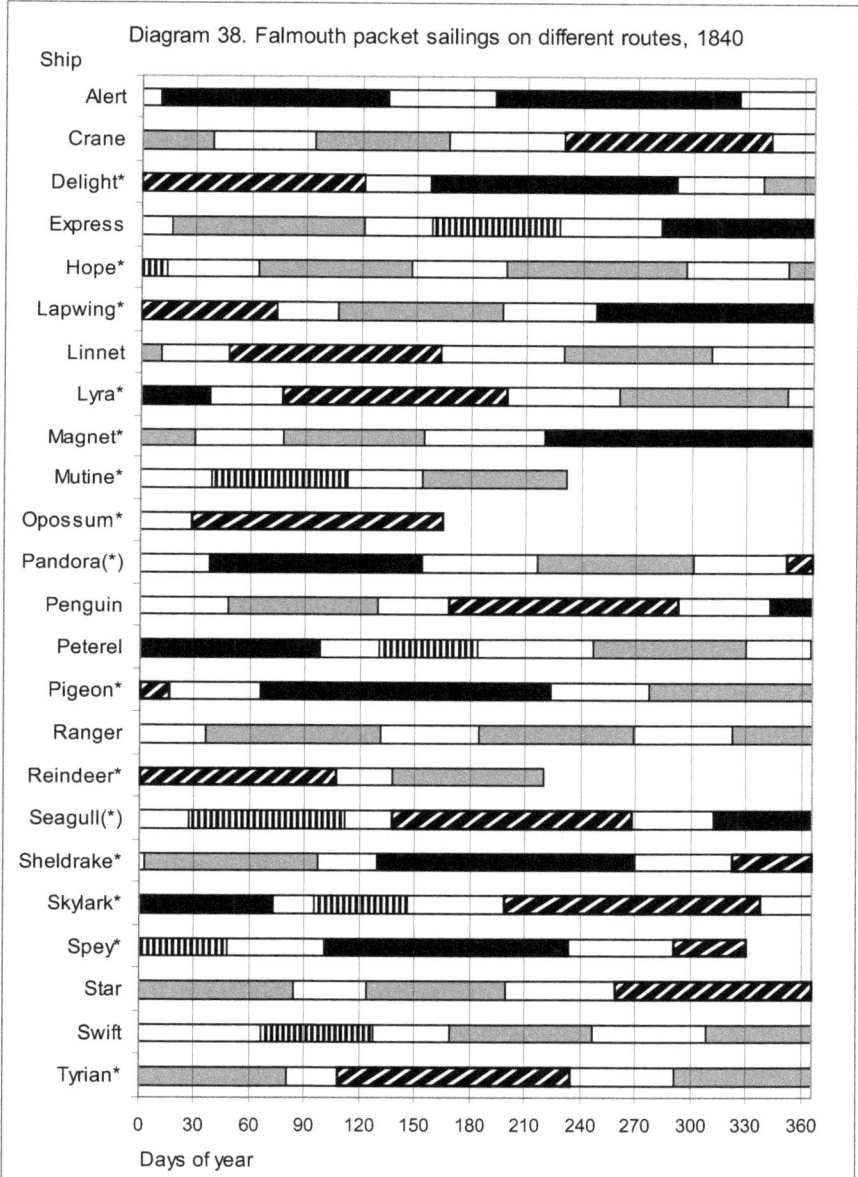

Diagram 38. Falmouth packet sailings on different routes, 1840

Source: Lloyd's List 1840. – The small-size ships are marked with an asterisk*, and the medium-size ships with (*). The black parts of the pillars depict a trip to South America, and the grey parts a trip to the West Indies. The vertically striped parts of the pillars depict a trip to Halifax, and the diagonally striped parts a trip to Mexico. The white parts of the pillars depict the time each ship stayed at the home port between sailings.

same place had left the port. Even at the risk of slowing down the arrival of letters from the colonies, it might have been useful from the information circulation point of view to adjust the sailing dates to avoid such incidences. This would have been a difficult task in the long run, however, in view of the requirement for regularity of sailings. There would also have been the risk that the expected ship might never arrive.

The era of the Falmouth sailing packets ended on the Halifax route in mid-1840, when the Cunard Line started the steamship service from Liverpool via Halifax to Boston; and on the West Indian and Mexico routes in early 1842 when the Royal Mail Steam Packet Company took over these routes with its new purpose-built steamers. Six sailing packets continued on the long South American run until the end of 1850, when the *Seagull* took home the last mails from Rio de Janeiro, arriving in Falmouth on 30 April 1851.[624]

Overnight Change from Sail to Steam

By Royal Mail to sixty ports – The long way to South America

By Royal Mail to sixty ports

While there was a ten-year-long shift period in the North Atlantic when mails were being sent by all possible means – American sailing packets, pioneering private steamers and government contract steamers – the complicated Falmouth packet system on the West Indian route was changed overnight to an even more complicated Royal Mail Line (Royal Mail Steam Packet Company, or RMSP) system. Even if the government subsidy was as huge as £240,000 (compared to the Cunard Line's much discussed £81,000), no competitors were struggling for the contract. In fact, the government did not even ask for bids but just accepted the proposal made by a man called James MacQueen.[625]

MacQueen was a Scotsman who had spent years in the West Indies, working as a sugar plantation manager in Grenada, and travelling a great deal around the Caribbean area and the Spanish Main. He returned to Glasgow at the age of 35 and earned his living as a newspaperman and merchant, also showing much interest in topography and African geography. He was the first person to plot the exit of the Niger into the Bay of Benin. In identifying the Niger's course he was helped by his slaves on Grenada, some of whom were Mandingos, who had once lived on the river banks.[626]

This background gave him the ability to plan a network of steamship communications, which would serve the merchants in Britain as well as the West Indies, and several other places. His 'General Plan for a Mail Communication between Great Britain and the Western and Eastern parts

624 See sailing list of Howat, 86.
625 See Gibbs, 322.
626 Nicol, vol. 1, 33–35.

FIG. 21. *The Royal Mail Line paddle steamer* Dee *was one of the 14 original vessels built for the West Indies service in 1841. They were all produced to the same basic design and were named after British rivers. The* Dee *remained in service until 1860. (Painting by William Clark, 1841.) © National Museums Liverpool (Merseyside Maritime Museum).*

of the world; also Canton and Sydney westward of the Pacific' included operations around the world: from Falmouth to Halifax; North America, the West Indies and Brazil; to Canton in China and Sydney in New South Wales (Australia) via Panama; the Mediterranean and East India by the Red Sea; and the eastern world by the Cape of Good Hope.[627] The distances from port to port and the days of departures and arrivals were all carefully calculated. As MacQueen believed that a canal through the Central American isthmus (he preferred the Nicaraguan route instead of Panama) would be opened 'at no distant date' he boldly planned some of his routes to take advantage of direct access to the Pacific by such a canal, being thus some eighty years ahead of his time. Also his proposals for rapid bunkering of the steamers would have been considered advanced even in later decades.[628]

The plan was obviously too much to be implemented by one company. Vernon Gibbs states in his book about British passenger liners that both the Cunard Line and P&O actually owed their birth to MacQueen's

627 MacQueen was also involved in the affairs of the Pacific coast of South America and worked towards a line of steamers for a service along the coast. This resulted in the formation of the Pacific Steam Navigation Company in 1840. The company became closely linked with the Royal Mail Line in the coming years. See Nicol, vol. 1, 39.

628 T.A. Bushell, *Royal Mail. A Centenary History of the Royal Mail Line 1839–1939* (London, 1939), 4; and Nicol, vol. 1, 37.

representations. His proposals to the British Government in June 1837, strongly supported by the West India Committee, led to the establishment of the Royal Mail Company in September 1839, and to the Caribbean mail contract in March 1840.[629] The huge amount of capital needed – £1.5 million – was collected with the help of bankers involved in West Indian affairs, including the well known Barings Bros in London. The first Chairman was John Irving, MP and merchant, who was also the Chairman of the Colonial Bank.[630]

MacQueen himself took on the role of an expert in Caribbean circumstances, which he undoubtedly was. His plan for the West Indian mail system was indeed very ambitious. While fourteen new steamers and three schooners were being built for the purpose, MacQueen set up a final tour to prepare the service. Over a period of eight months and covering a distance of over 18,000 miles, he studied the best options for the mail services, including ports, routes and schedules. His final plans consisted of the transatlantic service and ten branch lines covering the area between Halifax in the north and Demerara in the south, Barbados in the east and Tampico in the west. The routes covered some sixty ports and required the steamers to travel over 547,000 miles a year.[631] The routes are well covered in earlier studies and do not need to be repeated here in detail.[632] The transatlantic passage started and ended at Southampton, which had just been connected with London by railway. The Admiralty, which was still responsible for mail transport at sea, insisted that the Royal Mail ships had to carry the mails via Falmouth even though the inland mail was much slower than it would have been from Southampton. The mails were made up in London and the ships left from Southampton on the 1st and 16th of each month, while the departure from Falmouth was on the 3rd and 18th. Falmouth was finally left out from the service in September 1843.[633] This was naturally a great disappointment to the port, which had been Britain's main packet station for over 150 years.

The local routes between the Caribbean islands and Central America formed a complicated network where everything depended on something else. There were separate routes from Barbados to Guiana; from Grenada to Curacao; from Barbados to Turks' Islands, by Antigua; from Turks' Islands to the Jamaica district, to the Cartagena and Santa Martha district, and to the Havana and Honduras district; from Havana to the Mexico district, and to the North American stations; and to the Madeira district.[634]

The new traffic started on 1 January 1842, thus changing the West Indian mail system from sail to steam in a single night. By that date eight Royal Mail steamers had already sailed for the West Indies to take up stations.

---

629 Gibbs, 323.
630 Nicol, vol..1, 40; and Bushell, 7–9.
631 M.H. Ludington & Geoffrey Osborn, *The Royal Mail Steam Packets to Bermuda and the Bahamas 1842–1859* (London, 1971), Preface.
632 See especially Kenton & Parsons, 2–7, 80–81, 116–119, 222–226, 322–323; and Ludington & Osborn, 3–23.
633 Kenton & Parsons, 2, 36. For the early arrangements in Southampton, see Bushell, 36–40.
634 For more details, see Kenton & Parsons, 2–3.

The first vessels to leave from England were the sister ships *Lee* and *Larne,* which left from Southampton on 3 December 1841. These small vessels of 250 and 300 tons would be used for the inter-island services. The first large Royal Mail vessel to cross the Atlantic was the *Forth*, 1,939 tons, which departed from Southampton on 17 December to be ready at St. Thomas for the mails carried by the *Thames*, which sailed from Falmouth on 3 January directly to Demerara, and the *Tay*, which left on the same day with the first regular mails for Barbados.[635]

The first sailings were fast compared with the earlier standards. The *Thames* arrived in Demerara from Falmouth in 20 days and the *Tay* at Barbados in 18 days. In 1840, the average westbound trip from Falmouth to Barbados by a sailing packet had taken 31 days, varying between 20 and 45 days.[636] During the first nine months of 1842, the average trip between Falmouth and Barbados by a Royal Mail steamer took 19.2 days, varying between 17 and 24 days. More than 70% of the trips were made within 18 to 20 days. Not only were the steamers faster, but their arrivals were much more predictable. They also sailed punctually from Falmouth without exception.

There were problems, however. The service was not only to Barbados and back home. Cooperation between the network of different routes proved difficult, and this added too many days to the time required for mail transmission.

Thus, even if the mails were carried from England to Barbados in fewer than 20 days on average, the sailing back via St. Vincent, Grenada, St. Croix, St. Thomas, Turks' Islands, Nassau, Bermuda and Fayal to Falmouth took about 38 days on average, varying between 33 and 45 days.[637] And even worse than that, the ships arriving in Barbados from Falmouth often continued their journey on the same day, leaving no time for answers. The next packet would leave some two weeks later.

In practice the circulation of information to and from Demerara was as fast as to and from Barbados, even though the latter was several days closer to England, because the system served all the colonies during one West Indian round trip. The merchants at Barbados received their news from Europe earlier than those in Demerara, and their letters arrived somewhat faster in England than those from Guiana, but the information circulation was equally long from the British merchant's point of view.

The duration of the homeward transport of mails was normally almost twice the length of the voyage westbound. The consecutive information circles enabled by the service between Liverpool and Demerara in 1842 are illustrated in table 41.

635 Sailing lists of Kenton & Parsons, 10; and Duncan Haws, *Merchant Fleets. Royal Mail Line & Nelson Line* (1982), 26–30.
636 See chapter VI.1.
637 Calculated from the voyages which started from Falmouth in January–September 1842. See the sailing lists of Kenton & Parsons, 10–12. Several dates are missing from the lists.

TABLE 41. *Consecutive information circles between Liverpool and Demerara enabled by the Royal Mail Line service in 1842.*

Depar-ture from Falmouth	Arrival at Barbados & depar-ture for Demerara	Arrival in Demerara & depar-ture for Barbados	Arrival at Barbados & depar-ture for Grenada	Arrival at Grenada & depar-ture for Nassau	Arrival at Nassau & departure for Falmouth	Arrival, Falmouth (or South-ampton)	Infor-mation circle, days
3.1.	21.1. 26.1.	30.1. 4.2.	5.2. 21.2.	22.2. 22.2.	- - 13.3.	2.4.	93
17.4.	5.5. 5.5.	6.5. 14.5.	17.5. 24.5.	25.5. 25.5.	3.6. 4.6.	22.6.	70
17.7.	4.8. 5.8.	8.8. 17.8.	21.8. 22.8.	23.8. 25.8.	3.9. 6.9.	4.10.*	83
17.10.	5.11.** 8.11.	14.11. 16.11.	22.11.** 24.11.	–	–	20.12.	68

Source: Sailing lists of Kenton & Parsons, 10–14, 26–28.
* The ship was about ten days late. She called at Corunna on 1.10. due to strong easterly gales.
** The station was changed to St. Thomas. Barbados was visited on the way to and from Demerara.

As can be noticed, the system enabled only four information circles within a calendar year – not very impressive compared with the 3.5 information circles carried out by the Admiralty's old sailing packets two years earlier. One of the Royal Mail steamers' circles was even longer than the average Falmouth packet circle, which was 92 days.

The Royal Mail route system soon proved to be impractical and was changed for the first time in October 1842, after only nine months' experience. As can be noticed from the table, the fourth circle was conducted via St. Thomas instead of Barbados. The trip homewards now included only calls at Bermuda and Fayal. This arrangement shortened the trip notably and the length of the information circle reduced from an average of 82 days during the three first trips to only 68 days on the fourth voyage.

The average trip from Falmouth to St. Thomas in 1842 took 22.7 days, compared to 19.2 days to Barbados. Additionally, the merchants of Barbados had to wait three to four days before the mails arrived from St. Thomas at their island. For these merchants, the route change was clearly a disadvantage, in terms of arriving news from England. However, they now had approximately six days time to answer their letters while the inter-island ship made her trip to Demerara. This was much better than answering on the same day or waiting two weeks for the next steamship – clearly an improvement.

While the businessmen in Demerara certainly felt that the new arrangement was an improvement in their communications, those in Berbice had an extremely busy schedule if they wanted to answer immediately to the letters received. The Royal Mail steamers usually went only as far as Demerara, while Berbice, Surinam and Paramaribo were served by local vessels or the mail was taken overland.[638] Sometimes the ships stayed at Demerara only for one or two days, which made it rather impossible for the Berbice businessmen to write immediate answers to the arriving letters.[639]

A concrete example from early 1842 shows how the mail system worked via Barbados. A letter by William Earle from Liverpool to William Carter, Attorney, who was visiting Berbice at the time, was sent on 15 February by the Royal Mail steamer *Teviot*. She departed from Falmouth on 17 February and arrived at Barbados on 8 March. The letter proceeded by the *City of Glasgow,* which arrived in Demerara on 11 March, and was finally received by the Attorney in Berbice on 13 March, according to the handwritten marking. He wrote an answer on the same day and it was carried by the same steamer from Demerara on 15 March. The letter arrived at Barbados – the steamer had been damaged at Tobago but was able to continue – on 18 March. The *Medway* took then the letter from Barbados, departing on 4 April. She arrived at Nassau on 16 April. The *Clyde* sailed with the mails for Europe on 17 April, arriving at Falmouth on 8 May. The mails arrived in London on 10 May, and the letter was received by William Earle in Liverpool on the same day.[640] The duration of this concrete information circle was 84 days.

The first letters from Liverpool to Berbice in January and February 1842 arrived surprisingly quickly, in 24 and 26 days. A delay with the next mail caused immediate alarm. Carter wrote to Earle: 'I waited in Berbice for the steamer from Barbados with the 1 March mail from England until the 28th, but nothing was heard of her. I determined to go down to Demerara, where I arrived in a small schooner with several other passengers to England... There I heard that the mail had <u>not</u> reached Barbados on the 26th, that the steamer I had been looking for was disabled! I immediately made inquiries for a vessel going to Barbados... From Barbados I shall go to St. Thomas where I hope to receive letters...'

Carter sent his letter on 7 April from Barbados by the merchant ship *St. Vincent.* The letter was received by William Earle in Liverpool on 21 May

---

638 Kenton & Parsons, 14.
639 Sailing lists of Kenton & Parsons, 28.
640 Earle Correspondence, D/Earle 5/8/8, 5/9/8. (MMM); and the sailing lists of Kenton & Parsons, 10–11, 14.

in 44 days. Carter also sent a duplicate on the following day, on 8 April by official mail. The letter carries the handstamp of Barbados Post Office 18 April, and it arrived in England by the Royal Mail steamer *Solway* on 28 May.[641] The steamship letter was on the way 50 days – almost a week longer than the letter by the traditional merchant ship.

William Carter sent one more letter from Barbados before the Royal Mail steamer departed. The merchant ship *Alice* took the letter, dated on 22 April, to Liverpool in 35 days.[642]

The huge difference between the West Indian and North Atlantic mail routes was concretely demonstrated in Carter's following letters from his trip to the north. He continued from Barbados to St. Thomas, from where he sent a letter to William Earle on 28 April. It arrived in England by the same Royal Mail steamer than the duplicate sent from Barbados 20 days earlier. A letter from New York on 14 May was sent by the Cunard steamer *Caledonia,* which departed from Boston on 16 May and arrived in Liverpool on 29 May[643] – on the same day as Earle received all the Royal Mail letters from the West Indies, the oldest of which had been sent 36 days before the letter from New York!

The shipping management of the Royal Mail Line – including routes, schedules, coaling, and repairs – was obviously much more challenging than the back and forth sailing between Liverpool and New York across the North Atlantic. The original routing via Barbados, which was reminiscent of the old system used by the Falmouth sailing packets, was changed in October 1842. St. Thomas in the Danish West Indies became the hub of all mail routes. The main reason for the change was that the route via Turks' Islands was too dangerous and one of the Royal Mail steamers, the *Medina,* had already been lost there in May 1842.[644] Figure 22 gives an example of how the new system worked.

641 William Carter to William Earle from Barbados 7.4. and 8.4.1842. Earle correspondence, D/Earle 5/8/8;10. (MMM); See also sailing lists of Kenton & Parsons, 10–12.
642 William Carter to William Earle from Barbados 22.4.1842. In Earle correspondence, D/Earle 5/8/11. (MMM)
643 William Carter to William Earle from St. Thomas 28.4.1842 and New York 14.5.1842. In Earle correspondence, D/Earle 5/8/12–13. (MMM)
644 Kenton & Parsons, 10. – Indifferent sea charts, uncertain compasses and unlit coral reefs were mentioned as reasons for a number of disasters during the first decade of Royal Mail services. For further descriptions, see Bushell, 41–53.

FIG. 22. *Royal Mail Line's steamers at St. Thomas 23.11.1842.*

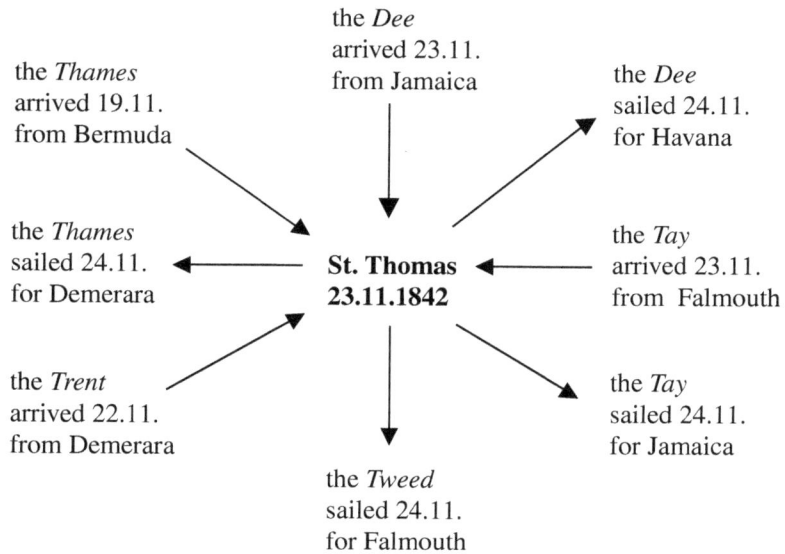

the *Dee*
arrived 23.11.
from Jamaica

the *Thames*
arrived 19.11.
from Bermuda

the *Dee*
sailed 24.11.
for Havana

the *Thames*
sailed 24.11.
for Demerara

St. Thomas
23.11.1842

the *Tay*
arrived 23.11.
from Falmouth

the *Trent*
arrived 22.11.
from Demerara

the *Tay*
sailed 24.11.
for Jamaica

the *Tweed*
sailed 24.11.
for Falmouth

On 23 November, there were five large Royal Mail Line's steamers simultaneously at the port of Charlotte Amalie, St. Thomas. The steamer *Tay* arrived with the European mails from Falmouth on 23 November. On the same day, the *Dee* arrived with the Jamaica mails, while the *Thames* was already there, having arrived from Havana, Nassau and Bermuda a few days earlier, and so was the *Trent*, which had arrived from Demerara on the 22nd. All the mails were quickly sorted and on the following day the *Tay* sailed for Jamaica, the *Dee* for Havana and the *Thames* for Demerara. The *Tweed* took all the mails which had been collected from the islands and proceeded for Falmouth, via Bermuda, on the same day.[645]

645 See the sailing lists of Kenton & Parsons, 26–32. The respective intelligence of *Lloyd's List* varies somewhat from these lists. According to *Lloyd's List*, the *Thames* arrived from Bermuda on the 19th and not the 18th. According to Kenton & Parsons, it was the *Tay* which sailed for Jamaica 24.11. while according to *Lloyd's List* it was the *Trent*. *Lloyd's List* does not report the *Dee's* trip to Jamaica between 8.–23.11. None of the sources tell from where the *Tweed* arrived at St. Thomas on 23.11. or where the *Trent* proceeded after 23.11. Kenton & Parsons' sailing lists are largely based on maritime intelligence published in Caribbean newspapers, which were nearer the scene but might be less reliable for other reasons – *Lloyd's List* again was published far away in London and changes were possible after the intelligence was sent by the Lloyd's agent. For the references, see Kenton & Parsons, 415–417. (Also *Lloyd's List*, *The Times* and *Illustrated London News* are among their sources.) – Without knowing the original plans for sailings – if any – it is impossible to interpret from the sailing lists whether the inter-island vessels were on schedule or not. For example, Nicol mentions that the *Clyde* was at Nassau on 17 February nine days behind schedule. (Nicol, vol. 2, 25) The sailing lists can only tell that the ship arrived at Nassau on 16 and departed on 20 February. Thus, we can only see from the sailing lists where the ships have been, not where they *should* have been at that time.

MAP 4. *Royal Mail Line routes to the West Indies, January 1842.*

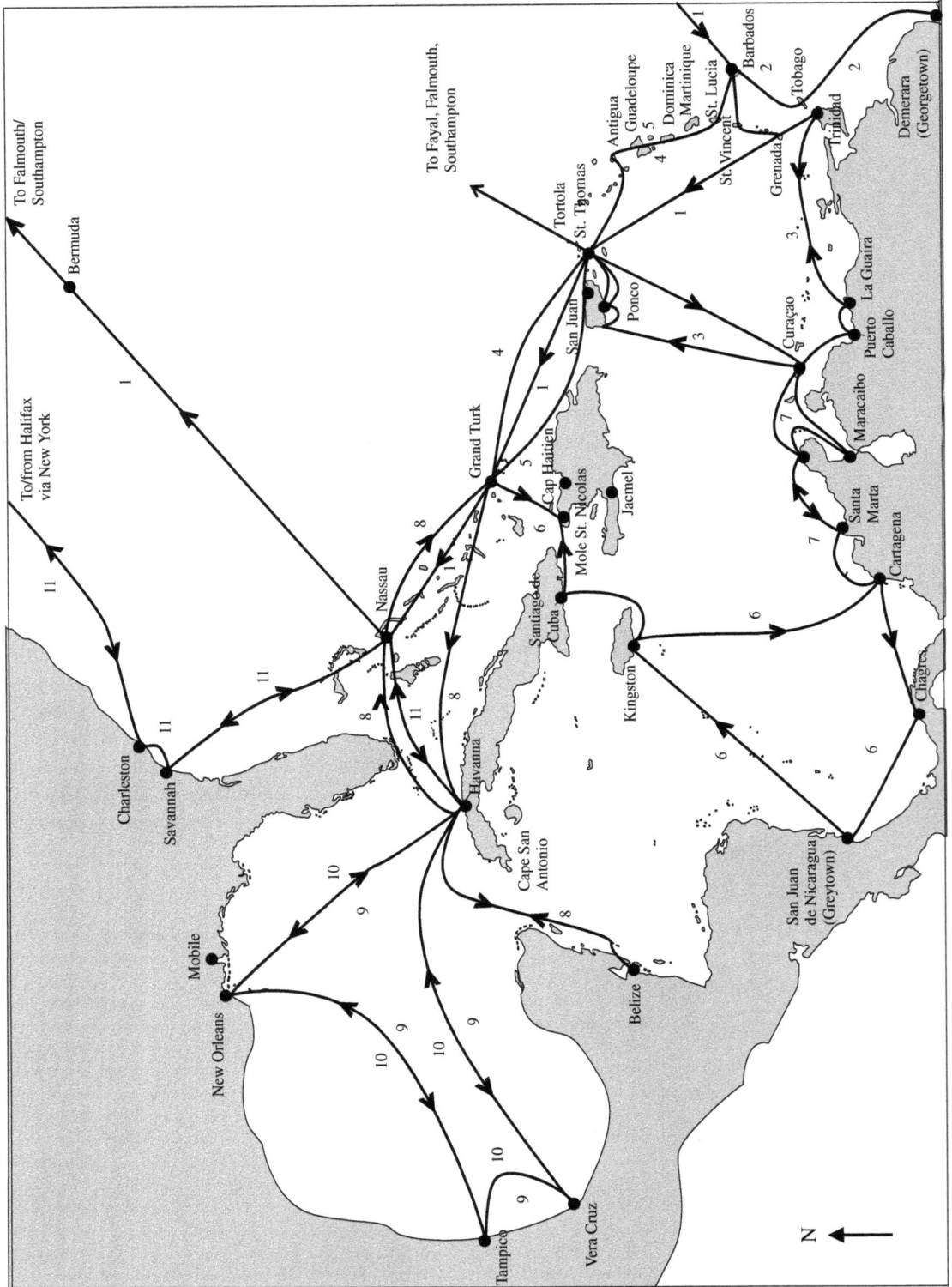

It is easy to imagine that everything did not always work that punctually. A few notes from *Lloyd's List* as well as the sailing lists of Kenton & Parsons give some idea of the difficulties: The *Tay* grounded at Havana in February, but without major harm. The *Medina* was in quarantine in Nassau for ten days in March 1842. She was totally lost on a reef at Turks' Island in May. Crew, passengers and mails were saved, however. The *City of Glasgow* was damaged in March. The *Clyde* struck a reef near Nevis and had to return to St. Thomas in July. There was a fire on board the *Teviot* in July. The *Thames* was damaged while striking a reef at Nevis (between St. Thomas and Antigua) in August, and had to proceed to London for repairs. The *Solway* lost sails and gib boom in a hurricane in September. In April of the following year she ran onto a reef off Corunna, Spain, and was lost. The *Isis* was damaged on a reef near Puerto Rico in September, and totally lost near Bermuda in October of the same year. All passengers and crew, except for a boy, were saved.[646]

In addition to the disasters at sea, many kinds of minor incidents followed each other. One of the often mentioned problems was coaling. The steamers required some two thousand tons of coal per week, and the whole supply had to be shipped to the depots in sailing vessels charted for the purpose. Bad weather in the Atlantic inevitably caused delays to the colliers and there were occasions when the local services had to be curtailed in consequence. In March 1842, the *Medway* and *Tweed* were reported to be delayed due to a shortage of coal. A report on the *City of Glasgow* noted further: 'Negroes were on strike in Demerara which made coaling difficult – took 24 hours to ship 52 tons, which was all that was available. Chief Engineer and a coal trimmer suspended for 'misbehaviour'.' Also the *Thames* reported shortage of coal in April.[647]

The crews of the steamers were not always of the best quality. Another report on the *City of Glasgow* writes: 'March 1842. The surgeon was sent home because he was insane. Ship's crew described by Captain Boxer was 'absolutely very little short of savages'. The third engineer was imprisoned at Barbados for attacking the saloon cook – 'he is a notorious character having been flogged and dismissed from Her Majesty's service'.' The Havana authorities complained about the *Clyde's* crew's 'rowdyism'; they wanted a stone wall built around the depot to keep them in. On the other hand, also the circumstances on the islands were primitive, and sometimes violent.[648]

For obvious reasons the mails did not always arrive 'just in time'. The captains had to improvise, as a report on the *Thames* describes: '23 April. Captain Hast will attempt to complete Table 3 on schedule but doubts it will be possible – if it becomes evident the ship is falling behind, they will return via Trinidad, coal at Grenada and thus be ready to receive the mails for the

---

646 *Lloyd's List* 11.6.1842; 29.8.1842; 5.11.1842; and sailing lists of Kenton & Parsons, 10–21, 26.
647 Bushell, 27; Nicol, vol.2, 26; Kenton & Parsons, 16, 19. – St. Thomas was probably the most reliable place for coaling. For example the *Medway* had to sail from Curaçao to St. Thomas for coaling, which made an extra ten days sailing. (Kenton & Parsons, 16)
648 Nicol, vol. 1, 54–56; Nicol vol. 2, 25–26.

western area. If *City of Glasgow* is still disabled he will take the mails for Guiana.'[649]

All shipping companies with Admiralty contract also had to carry on board their vessels a Naval Agent who had complete jurisdiction over the mails 'with full authority in all cases to require a due and strict execution of the contract... and to determine every question whenever raising relative to putting to sea, or putting into harbour, or to necessity of stopping to assist any vessel in distress, or to save human life...' This officer was 'to be provided with a first-class cabin and suitable accommodation for his servant and a properly equipped boat for his use.' As Gisburn notes, this was not a bad appointment for an ex-Naval officer who (as frequently was the case) had been of decidedly second-rate calibre during his active service days.[650]

With two masters on board a vessel, the system led to inevitable friction. In March 1842, when the *Forth* and *Tay* of the Royal Mail Line were simultaneously at the port of Nassau, the two Naval Agents failed to agree on which of the two vessels should carry the homeward mails and which one would continue on the inter-island routes in the West Indies. They compromised by sharing the mailbags and both sailing home to England. The *Forth* won this unbelievable race, arriving at Falmouth on 20 April with six passengers and a few bags of mail. The company was already embarrassed by the non-delivery of two ships which were under construction at Bristol, and such occurrences just added to their difficulties.[651]

The sailing lists of 1842–1843 report at least 14 cases where the ships had arrived somewhere without the mails they should have had with them. Additionally, it frequently happened that the vessels did not call at all ports, which naturally ended with the same result. In several cases, the Navy vessels took care of the mails which had been left after.[652]

The reports published in England regarding the Royal Mail service were not encouraging. For example, at the end of April 1842 it was reported that no mails had arrived from Jamaica for two months. They were later brought by HMS *Spitfire*, a Navy vessel. In August, it was reported that while the *Forth* was on her way homewards, the 'mails from Bermuda were forgotten and put ashore at Fayal'. In November, it was reported that the *Trent* proceeded to St. Thomas without Barbadian mails. They were forwarded by a hired sailing vessel. In May 1843, when the *Thames* arrived at Barbados with no English mails, a Barbadian newspaper wrote that this was the fourth time that had happened recently.[653]

649 Nicol, vol. 1, 54; Nicol, vol. 2, 27.

650 See Harold G.D. Gisburn, *The Postage Stamps and Postal History of the Bahamas* (London, 1950), 22.

651 Gisburn, 22; Bushell, 27. – The *Tay* arrived on the following day. The *Forth* sailed back to the West Indies on 1 May taking a direct route to Demerara via Barbados, while the *Tay* departed on 16 May, also proceeding to the Demerara route. See the sailing lists of Kenton & Parsons, 10, 12.

652 See for example Kenton & Parsons, 13–17.

653 Sailing lists of Kenton & Parsons, 13, 28. – The Jamaica mails in April should have been carried by one of the two steamers, *Forth* or *Tay*, which both decided to sail home instead.

When examining the improvement in speed of communications between Europe and the Caribbean or Central American area, it must be noted that many advances were due to mail route adjustments rather than changes in the speed of vessels – even though technological improvements also took place during those years.

Between January 1842 and January 1875, the Royal Mail Line's West Indian contract was changed four times and the routes 11 times. The scale of operations was continuously declining. The original 11 routes were decreased to five or six by the end of the 1840s. The original system included six different communications hubs: Barbados, St. Thomas, Curaçao, Turks' Islands, Havana, and Nassau. All these ports were places where two to four different mail routes met. Already in October 1842, several routes and ports of call were omitted and the number of hubs was decreased to four or five. After the loss of the *Medina* at Turks' Islands, the area was avoided and these routes were redirected via St. Thomas.[654]

The lessons from the practical experiences in the Caribbean and Central American area, as well as the inevitable financial problems meant continuous streamlining of the Royal Mail Line services. Systems were also changed back and forth. For example, Barbados was originally the station for incoming mails from Europe, while Nassau was the station on the way out. In October 1842, it was changed so that all mails came in via St. Thomas and out via the same island, or alternatively via Havana–Nassau. In July 1843 the mails came in via Barbados and out via St. Thomas or Havana–Nassau. From 1850, St. Thomas was the main station both on the way in and out – until it was changed in 1872 so that St. Thomas and Barbados were the stations for both the incoming and outgoing mails alternatively.[655]

It is not possible here to go through the development of the speed of information transmission on all the different routes. Keeping the Guiana route still as an example, one can follow the improvement in mail transport by steamship up to the 1870s. As already noted from Table 41, the start of the steamship service in 1842 did not bring major changes to the information circulation compared to the sailing packet period. Ten years later, the

---

654 From October 1842, the Royal Mail mail steamers would 'no longer touch at New Orleans, Savannah, Charleston, New York, Halifax N.S., Curacoa, Paramaribo in Surinam, Maracaibo, Bahia Honda, San Juan de Nicaragua, Mayaquess in Porto Rico, Ponce in Porto Rico, Turks' Island, Cape Nichola Mole in Haiti, or Santa Cruz'. The mails for Mexico, Honduras (Belize), Chagres and the Isthmus of Panama, Cartagena, Santa Martha, La Guayara and Puerto Cabello would be made only once in a month instead of a bi-monthly service. Mail transmission by schooner between Madeira and Fayal would also be omitted. ('Notice to the Public and Instructions to all Postmasters... General Post Office 12th September, 1842', reprinted by Kenton & Parsons, 24.) – In June 1843, the system was adjusted again. The packets would no longer touch at Cape Haitien, St. Domingo, but instead at Jacmel on the same island. On the home voyage, Bermuda and Fayal would be touched only alternatively. ('Notice to the Public and Instructions to all Postmasters... General Post Office, June 1843', reprinted by Kenton & Parsons, 34.) With these changes, the company managed to conduct the mail service until the end of the first contract in 1847, except for the several months of 'emergency plans' caused by the loss of the *Tweed* in February 1847, as there was no vessel to replace her. See Kenton & Parsons, 73–78.

655 See the route maps 1–12 in Kenton & Parson, passim.

MAP 5. *Royal Mail Line routes to the West Indies, June 1852.*

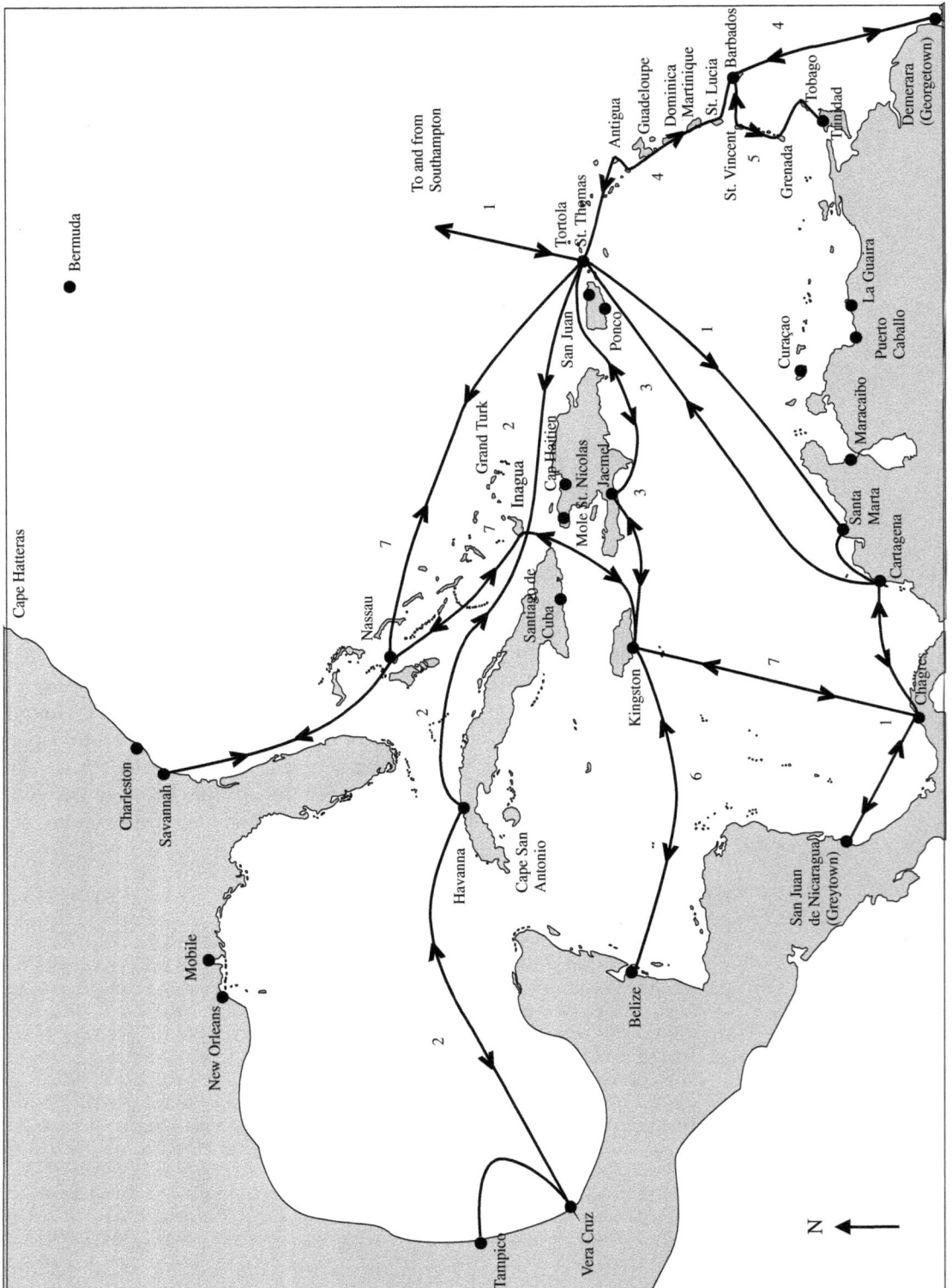

Bermuda

Cape Hatteras

Charleston
Savannah
Mobile
New Orleans

Nassau

Grand Turk
Inagua

Havanna
Cape San Antonio

Tampico
Vera Cruz

Belize

San Juan de Nicaragua (Greytown)

Chagres

Kingston

Santiago de Cuba
Mole St. Nicolas
Jacmel
Cap Haïtien

San Juan
Ponce

Tortola
St. Thomas

To and from Southampton

Antigua
Guadeloupe
Dominica
Martinique
St. Lucia
Barbados

St. Vincent
Grenada
Tobago
Trinidad

Demerara (Georgetown)

Curaçao
La Guaira
Puerto Caballo
Maracaibo
Santa Marta
Cartagena

N

number of consecutive information circles between Liverpool and Demerara within a calendar year had increased from four to six. This happened at the same time as the Cunard Line and the Collins Line were competing on the North Atlantic route and the number of consecutive information circles there had increased to twelve, compared with six at the time of the pioneering steamers.

Between 1842 and 1852, the duration of an information circle between Liverpool and Demerara was reduced by some three weeks on average, from more than 70 to approximately 50 days. Apart from the confusion caused by the tragic loss of the *Amazon* in January 1852, a reliable information circle within two months could be counted on. The mails were made in London on the 1st and 16th of each month, and the Royal Mail steamers sailed from Southampton on the following day.

An average journey from Southampton to St. Thomas took 17.5 days and the trip homewards 16.9 days. The average round trip between St. Thomas and Demerara, via Barbados, took 11.4 days. A few days were lost in waiting at ports, but most arrangements worked fluently: the ships were ready to depart even on the same day once the mails had arrived. The problem was clearly in Guiana. The inter-island steamer – which normally was one of the large transatlantic vessels but not the same one which had just arrived from Europe – left from Demerara on the same or next day after arrival. The merchants in Berbice had to wait about two weeks for the next steamer to send answers to their letters. If they were in a hurry, they could of course take a trip to Demerara in wait for the arriving mails, as William Carter did in the earlier example in 1842. This was not very practical, however, as it was not known beforehand which day the steamer would arrive.

TABLE 42. *Consecutive information circles between Liverpool and Demerara enabled by the Royal Mail Line service in 1852.*

Trans-atlantic steamer	Departure from South-ampton	Arrival at St. Thomas and departure of inter-island steamer for Demerara	Arrival in Demerara and departure for St. Thomas	Arrival at St. Thomas and departure for South-ampton	Trans-atlantic steamer	Arrival date at South-ampton	Infor-mation circle, days
Amazon*	2.1.	–					
Avon	11.1.	4.2. 8.2.	15.2. 15.2.	20.2. 25.2.	Great Western	18.3.	69
Great Western	2.4.	23.4. 23.4.	28.4. 29.4.	3.5. 7.5.	Parana	22.5.	52
Parana	2.6.	17.6. 20.6.	25.6. 25.6.	30.6. 2.7.	Parana	17.7.	47
Parana	2.8.	19.8. 19.8.	24.8. 25.8.	30.8. 3.9.	Parana	22.9.	53
Medway	2.10.	22.10. 22.10.	28.10. 28.10.	2.11. 4.11.	La Plata	17.11.	48
Parana	2.12.	19.12. 22.12.	29.12. 29.12.	1853: 3.1. 3.1.	Parana	18.1.	49

Source: Sailing lists of Kenton & Parsons, 131, 136. – The figures in 'Information circle, days'' include one extra day at both ends for the Liverpool – Southampton – Liverpool inland route.

* The *Amazon* caught fire at sea in the Bay of Biscay on her maiden voyage. She was lost with 115 lives and all mails. Until this disaster, the Admiralty had not approved iron steamers in the mail service, but preferred wood as it was thought it would be better in war service. Now the attitudes changed under the pressure of public opinion, and all mail steamers could be built of iron. See Bushell, 63–71; Nicol, vol.1, 45.

While the peak of the development in mail transmission by steamship was almost reached in the North Atlantic in the 1850s and only minor improvements would take place within the next two decades, there was still much to be done in the West Indian service. A decade later, information circulated between Liverpool and Demerara like this:

TABLE 43. *Consecutive information circles between Liverpool and Demerara, enabled by the Royal Mail Line service in 1862.*

Trans-atlantic steamer	Depar-ture from South-ampton	Arrival at St. Thomas & depar-ture of inter-island steamer for Deme-rara	Arrival in Deme-rara & depar-ture for St. Thomas	Arrival at St. Thomas & depar-ture for South-ampton	Trans-atlantic steamer	Arrival at South-ampton	Infor-mation circle, days
Atrato	2.1.	16.1. 16.1.	21.1. 23.1.	28.1. 31.1.	Atrato	14.2.	45
La Plata	17.2.	7.3. 7.3.	12.3. 13.3.	17.3. 17.3.	La Plata	30.3.	43
Seine	2.4.	16.4. 16.4.	21.4. 23.4.	29.4. 1.5.	Seine	14.5.	44
Shannon	17.5.	31.5. 31.5.	5.6. 8.6.	12.6. 13.6.	Shannon	28.6.	44
Atrato	2.7.	16.7. 16.7.	21.7. 23.7.	28.7. 30.7.	Atrato	13.8.	44
Tas-manian	18.8.	1.9. 1.9.	6.9. 6.9.	12.9. 14.9.	Tas-manian	28.9.	43
Seine	2.10.	16.10. 16.10.	21.10. 23.10.	28.10. 29.10.	Seine	13.11.	44
Shannon	17.11.	1.12. 2.12.	7.12. 8.12.	13.12. 15.12.	Shannon	29.12.	44

Source: Sailing lists of Kenton & Parsons, 209, 212. – The figures in 'Information circle, days' include one extra day at both ends for the Liverpool–Southampton–Liverpool inland route.

MAP 6. *Royal Mail Line routes to the West Indies, March 1860.*

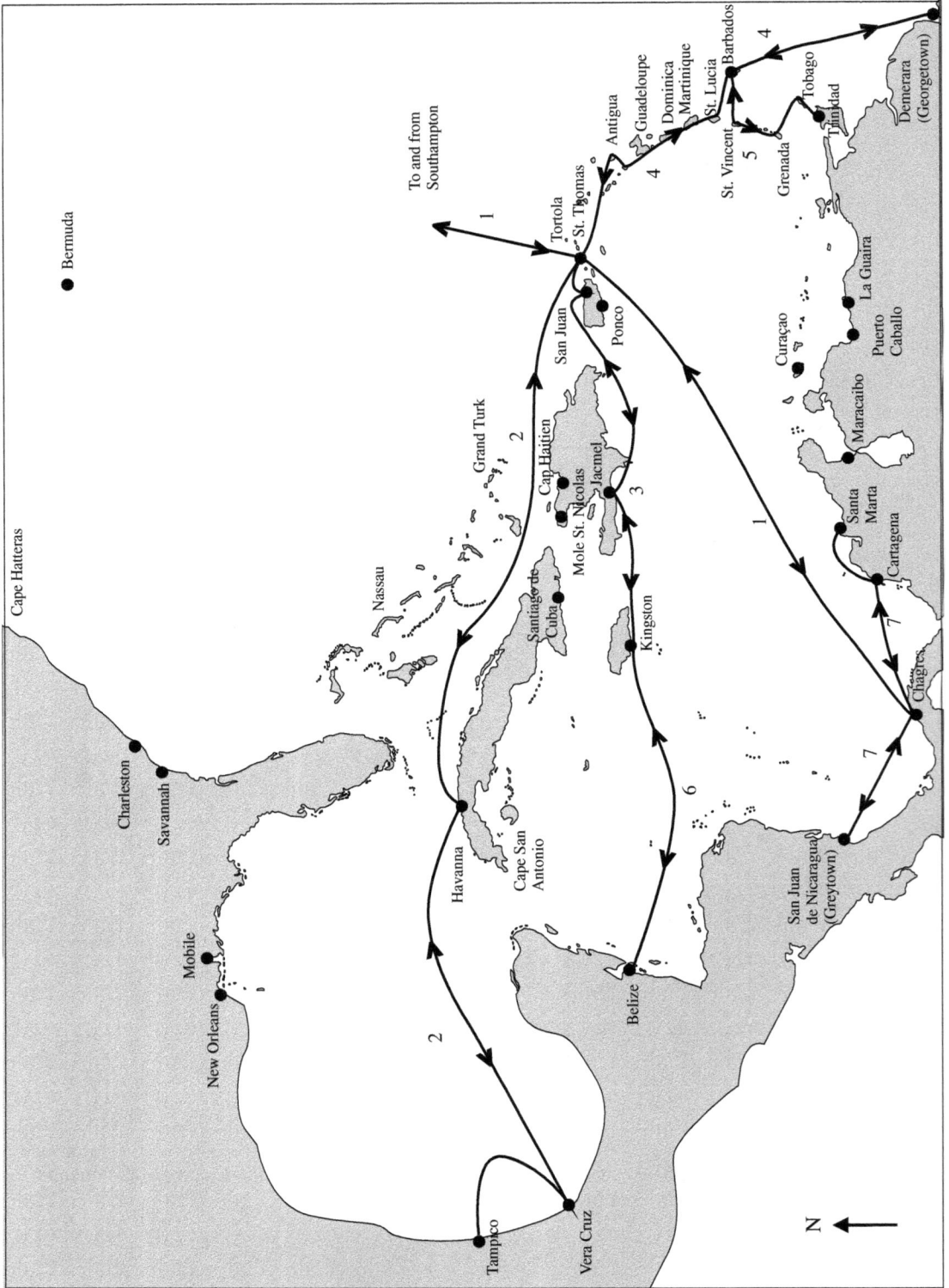

Eight, rather than six, consecutive information circles could now be conducted within a year. The average duration of an information circle was 42 days. The ships departed punctually from Southampton and rather regularly from St. Thomas, depending on the mail arrivals from the different inter-island routes. The arrivals in Southampton were regular within one or two days margin only, and there was at least three days to reply to the letters – a tight schedule, but not impossible.

Merchants could keep contact with their trading partners in the West Indies within 1.5 months rather than two months. The schedules of the Royal Mail Line were nicely organized: the same vessel which took the mails from Southampton sailed back with the answers. While she stayed at St. Thomas, the inter-island vessels collected the mails from the other colonies. Those from Barbados and Demerara could be sent to England by the same vessel, while those from more distant places were sent by later arriving steamers.

The length of an average trip between Southampton and St. Thomas had been shortened by three days to 14.5 days. The duration of the voyage was approximately the same in the other direction. The inter-island trip was about as long as it had been a decade earlier, but the ship now stayed in Demerara for one to three nights, which was a clear improvement.

It can be said that this was the peak of the improvement in information transmission by steamship between Liverpool and Demerara, if measured by information circles. But as in the North Atlantic, some progress could perhaps still be seen in the early 1870s. The number of consecutive information circles did not increase, and in 1872 one sailing was missed in Southampton due to the late arrival of the ship from St. Thomas.[656]

An interesting change from the shipping management point of view took place in April 1872, when the Royal Mail decided to organize the sailings to and from the West Indies via St. Thomas and Barbados alternately. At that time there was no major difference in the length of sailings to these places, the trip outwards took 13.5 days and homewards less than 13 days on average. For those who lived on the islands, there was naturally a difference whether they received their mails directly or indirectly, which might have been a reason for this arrangement.[657]

For the business partners in Demerara and Berbice, the arrangement was good news. As can be seen in table 44, there was now finally enough time to answer their letters. The inter-island trip was lengthened by the arrangement but as the steamers were somewhat faster than a decade earlier, the duration of the information circle was approximately one day shorter than in 1862.

656 The next ship to the West Indies departed on the same day.
657 There were also other reasons to reduce the number of calls at St. Thomas. Despite its excellent harbour and ideal geographical situation, St. Thomas had some serious disadvantages. It was situated in the middle of the hurricane region. In 1867, when the Royal Mail Line used the island as the hub where its steamers entered simultaneously for the mails, several of the vessels with some 150 men were lost in a hurricane, which sank 58 of the 60 vessels anchored at Charlotte Amalie that morning. An earthquake, followed by a huge tidal wave – tsunami – caused additional damage at the same port only a few weeks later. St. Thomas was furthermore avoided because of the frequent yellow fever and cholera epidemics. See Bushell, 115–124; Kenton & Parsons, 246–250.

TABLE 44. *Consecutive information circles between Liverpool and Demerara enabled by the Royal Mail Line service in 1872.*

Trans-atlantic steamer	Depar-ture from South-ampton	Arrival at St. Thomas (S) / Barbados (B) and departure of inter-island steamer for Demerara	Arrival in Demerara and departure date	Arrival at St. Thomas (S) / Barbados (B) and departure for South-ampton	Trans-atlantic steamer	Arrival at Ply-mouth*	Infor-mation circle, days
Moselle	2.1.	(S) 17.1. 18.1.	23.1. 24.1.	(S) 29.1. 29.1.	Nile	10.2.	41
Tas-manian	17.2.	(S) 2.3. 3.3.	8.3. 10.3.	(S) 14.3. 20.3.	Nile	2.4.	46
Nile	17.4.	(B) 30.4. 30.4.	3.5. 8.5.	(S) 14.5. 15.5.	Tagus	27.5.	42
Moselle	3.6.	(S) 16.6. 17.6.	23.6. 26.6.	(B) 30.6. 30.6.	Elbe	13.7.	42
Tas-manian	17.7.	(B) 30.7. 30.7.	2.8. 7.8.	(S) 13.8. 14.8.	Nile	27.8.	43
Tagus	2.9.	(S) 15.9. 17.9.	23.9. 26.9.	(B) 29.9. 29.9.	Moselle	12.10.	42
Elbe	17.10.	(B) 30.10. 30.10.	2.11. 7.11.	(S) 13.11. 14.11.	Tas-manian	26.11.	42
Nile	2.12.	(S) 16.12. 17.12.	23.12. 26.12.	(B) 29.12. 30.12.	Tagus	13.1.	43

Source: *Sailing lists of Kenton & Parsons, 288–289, 295.* – The figures in 'Information circle, days' include one extra day at both ends for the Liverpool–Southampton –Liverpool inland route.
* Plymouth became the arrival port of the mails in England from October 1867.
(Kenton & Parsons, 247)

A brief look at the merchant correspondence of Sandbach, Tinne & Co. and Thomas & William Earle & Co. in 1875–1876 tells that the Demerara letters were normally in Liverpool within 23 days on average, while those from Berbice took a few days longer. Of this small sample of 18 letters, all covers are missing. Not much more information than the dates of writing and the recipient's markings are available. Most letters are from Demerara, and only two from Berbice. A few interesting details can be picked up, however.[658]

Firstly, it seems that the letters were not always written while the mail steamer was already waiting at port. Two of the letters were written three days before the steamer arrived, and one letter one day before. Most typical was that the letters were written on the same or the following day after the ship's arrival, after incoming letters had been received. This happened in 11 cases. The rest of the letters were written just before the steamer departed. In one case the steamer did not stay at port overnight but the incoming letters had to be read and answered during the same day, which was done. And in three cases, the letter had been started on one day and continued on the following one or two days while waiting for the ship's departure.

At that time, the inter-island service worked rather regularly. The senders in Demerara could know quite exactly when the next mail steamer would depart. The ship to St. Thomas normally departed on the 5th or 6th of each month, and the one for Barbados on the 25th or 26th. The arrivals were more varying. The ships from St. Thomas arrived between the 2nd and 6th, and the ones from Barbados between the 22nd and 26th of the month in question. This factor – as well as the length of each month – may at least partly explain the slight difference between the theoretical and practical information circles.

An interesting thing is that not all the letters arrived by the Royal Mail steamers. At least one of the letters was sent by a merchant steamship ('per *Annan*')[659]. The letter was written in Demerara on 2 February 1876, just three days before the Royal Mail inter-island steamer *Corsica* arrived, and departed on the following day. The letter was received by Sandbach, Tinne & Co. in Liverpool on 28 February and answered on the 29th – the same day as the Royal Mail transatlantic steamer *Nile* arrived at Plymouth. As the cover of the letter is not preserved, no information about the *Annan's* arrival port is available but one could expect that she sailed directly to Liverpool or some other nearby port on the west coast of Britain.

There are three more cases where two almost simultaneously sent letters probably have been transmitted by different means. In one of them, the writer states: 'We enclose copies of our letter yesterday by direct steamer...'[660]

---

658 Bryson Collection, Records of Sandbach, Tinne & Co., D/B/176; Earle Family and Business Archive, correspondence of Thomas and William Earle & Co., D/Earle/5/11. (MMM)

659 The *Annan* was an iron screw steamer of 662 tons and 98 hp, built in 1872. She was owned by a Jacob Lohden, West Hartlepool, who had three ships in *Lloyd's Register* in 1882. The ship represents an average merchant vessel among those mentioned in Sandbach, Tinne & Co. correspondence in the mid-1870s.

660 Letter to Sandbach, Tinne & Co. in Liverpool from Sandbach, Parker &c. dated in Demerara 25.3.1876. Bryson Collection, Records of Sandbach, Tinne & Co., D/B/174. (MMM)

As there is no sender's note about a ship's name and the covers with postal markings are missing, these cases remain unsure. At least one can state that the British government mail was not the only means of communications from Guiana even in the mid-1870s.

One could assume that, as late as in the 1870s when the ships were so much faster than earlier, it would have been possible to organize the schedules to allow enough time to answer the letters at least in Britain. However, there are two cases in the sample of 1875–1876 where the letter arrived in Liverpool on the same day as the next ship departed for the West Indies from Southampton. Additionally, there was one case where the letter had not been answered at all, probably due to the tight schedule.

The phenomenon is familiar from the North Atlantic route. Carrying mail in the 1870s was not as important for the shipping companies as it had been when no other means of communications existed.

As a conclusive example of the development of business information transmission on the West Indian route, one can state that the number of information circles between Liverpool and Demerara, conducted mainly by the British mail services, grew as follows:

TABLE 45. *Development of business information transmission by sail and steam between Liverpool and Demerara, 1840–1862.*

	Period in mail service	Speed	Regularity		Sailings per year	Information circles per year	Reasons for improvement / stagnation
			Departures	Arrivals			
Merchant ships	Continuously	– –	– –	– –	hundreds	1840: 3.5	Direct sailings.
Falmouth packets	Before 1842	– –	–	– –	24	1840: 3.5	Time-taking inter-island service in the Caribbean.
Royal Mail Line	From 1842–	+ (+)	+(+)	+	24	1842: 4 1852: 6 1862: 8	In 1842: More regular; faster speed. In 1852: Reduced inter-island service, faster speed. In 1862: Better coordination, faster speed.

– – = very poor   – = poor   + = rather good   + + = good

The international mail services in the Caribbean region, which started in the early 1860s, will be presented in Chapter VI.3.

The long way to South America

Even if the Royal Mail Line had been ready to take care of the South American mail service in addition to the West Indian mail route right from the beginning, the Admiralty had been wise enough not to give everything to the company simultaneously. A new steamship route to Rio de Janeiro, Montevideo and Buenos Aires was finally included in the company's mail contract in July 1850. Of the £270,000 government subsidy, £30,000 was related to the Brazil and River Plate route starting from the beginning of 1851. This was the final end of the Falmouth sailing packet service – a decade later than regular steamship service replaced the packets on the North Atlantic and the Caribbean routes.[661]

The Royal Mail Line had learnt a lot from its earlier experiences, and the technology had improved enough for new challenges. Most of the problems met in the Caribbean could be avoided, timetables could be kept and it frequently happened that the ships arrived at port several days before schedule. This was naturally due to the fact that the company had learnt how to plan the schedules so that the result was positive performance instead of bad reputation. The mail contract also included penalties for delays, which may explain the need for rather loose timetables. And even though the South American route was very long, the system of branch services was simple and easy to manage compared with the West Indian routes.

A Royal Mail steamer left from Southampton for South America on the 9th of each month, or the 10th if the 9th fell on a Sunday. According to schedule, the ship arrived in Lisbon on the 14th or 15th, Madeira on the 18th, Tenerife on the 19th, St. Vincent at Cape Verde between the 23rd and 25th, Pernambuco on the 2nd or 3rd of the following month, Bahia on the 4th or the 5th, and Rio de Janiero on the 8th. She stayed at Rio for approximately four days, departing for the home voyage on the 12th, and was back in Southampton on the 12th of the following month.[662] In real life, there were naturally differences in the performance.

661 For the contract, see Howat, 103–104.
662 Howat, 105.

TABLE 46. *Royal Mail steamship round trips and the length of information circles, Southampton–Rio de Janeiro 1851.*

Steamer	Departure from Southampton	Arrival in Rio de Janeiro	Departure from Rio de Janeiro	Arrival in Southampton	Information circle, England–Brazil–England, days	Information circle, Brazil–England–Brazil, days
Teviot	**9.1.**	**7.2.**	**11.2.**	**14.3.**	64	87
Tay	10.2.	11.3.	14.3.	15.4.	64	86
Medway	10.3.	6.4.	12.4.	14.5.	65	87
Teviot	**9.4.**	**9.5.**	**12.5.**	**8.6.**	60	87
Tay	9.5.	8.6.	11.6.	11.7.	63	89
Severn	**9.6.**	**8.7.**	**15.7.**	**12.8.**	64	84
Teviot	9.7.	7.8.	14.8.	10.9.	63	84
Tay	9.8.	8.9.	14.9.	14.10.	66	86
Severn	**9.9.**	**7.10.**	**15.10.**	**13.11.**	65	81
Teviot	9.10.	6.11.	14.11.	11.12.	63	etc.
Tay	10.11.	9.12.	15.12.	15.1.52	67	
Severn	**9.12.**	**4.1.52**	14.1.	15.2.	68	
Min.–max.	- -	- -	- -	- -	60-68	81-89
Average	- -	- -	- -	- -	64	86

Source: Sailing lists of Howat, 129. – The consecutive information circles enabled by the Royal Mail sailings in 1851 are market in bold. An average outward trip took 29 days, varying between 26 and 30 days, while the homeward trip took 30 days on average, varying between 27 and 32 days.

The improvement in the speed and regularity of the information transmission on the commercially important South America route was notable. While the average voyage from Rio de Janeiro to Southampton by a Falmouth packet had taken 52 days in 1850, the Royal Mail steamers made the same trip in 30 days on average in 1851.[663] This was probably one of the most notable improvements in the speed of one-way information transmission during the shift period from sail to steam.

Instead of only three information circles enabled by the Admiralty packets in 1850, the Royal Mail steamers could facilitate 4.5 consecutive information circles between England and Rio de Janeiro in 1851. But this performance was still far from ideal. Even if the sailings were now organized so that the merchants in Rio de Janeiro could reply immediately to their letters, the system did not work in the same way at the other end. As can be seen in Table 46, the

663 Calculated from the sailing lists of Howat, 85–86, 129.

FIG. 23. *The paddle steamer* Magdalena *was one of the five new vessels built by the Royal Mail Line, when they extended their contract to South America. They were then the largest wooden vessels afloat. After the dramatic fire which destroyed the* Magdalena's *sister ship* Amazon *in 1852 with heavy loss of life, the Admiralty finally admitted that iron hulls might be a safer option. © National Museums Liverpool (Merseyside Maritime Museum).*

steamer to South America had usually just departed a few days before another steamer arrived from there. For this reason, the information circles were three weeks longer from the Brazilian perspective than from the English.

The duration of the voyage from Buenos Aires to Southampton was shortened by more than a month from 76 days in 1850 to 44 days in 1851. The whole round trip between Falmouth and Buenos Aires had taken 150 days by a Falmouth packet, while the average round trip between Southampton and Buenos Aires by the Royal Mail steamers took 95 days.[664] A letter sent from England in the early January got now an answer from Argentina in mid-April instead of late May.

Why was the difference between the round trips by sail and by steam not more than 55 days, even though the duration of the homeward voyage alone had shortened by 32 days? Firstly, the prevailing winds and currents made the sailing homewards from Buenos Aires longer than in the other direction. By sailing ship the difference was nine days on average, as it had been in 1840, but it was only two days by a steamer. Thus the benefit of using steam instead of canvas was greater on the way homewards than in the other direction. Even if the difference was not as notable as on the North Atlantic route, it definitely was relevant.

The mails remained two or three days in Rio de Janeiro before the departure of the branch steamer to Buenos Aires. The ship stayed there one

664 Calculated from the sailing lists of Howat, 85–86, 99–100, 129.

or two weeks to give the merchants time to receive the letters and answer them.[665] Back in Rio, there was an approximately four days' wait before the transatlantic steamer departed with the mails for Europe.[666] There were thus three major port stays in South America on the round trip to Buenos Aires (in Rio, in Buenos Aires and again in Rio) while there was only one on the round trip to Rio. The fewer port stays there were, the more efficiency could be achieved by using steam power. The benefits of steam could best be seen on the round trips to Rio de Janeiro. While an average Falmouth packet made a round voyage to Rio in 122 days, the same voyage took an average Royal Mail steamer only 64 days.[667]

The new route was an immediate success with steadily climbing passenger and freight figures already from the first year. The value of specie carried outwards between June and November 1851 reflected the trend: £35,000, £47,090, £88,000, £73,000, £115,000, and £232,000. In today's terms, the figures were enormous. The November figure, for example, was four times greater than the value of the steamship carrying it. The valuable freights were mostly investment infusions supporting economic development in South America, in which British business was heavily involved. Nearly £200,000 from the November figure was gold contributed by British business houses towards the foundation of a commercial bank in Rio de Janeiro.[668]

Although coal still took most of the space, general cargo was also carried from England, mainly in the form of manufactured goods. Homewards, the ships carried gold and silver in minor quantities, diamonds (often to the value of £20,000 to £30,000) as well as coffee and tropical fruits. The number of passengers was normally between 30 and 70 southwards, but rose steadily. In 1855, the totals approached 200, which was close to the limits of the vessels. Already from the start, the homeward lists were better, about one hundred passengers or more. Many of them disembarked at Lisbon, all classes from ambassadors to deported slave-traders.[669]

---

665 The duration of the port stay was originally one week but it was lengthened already in mid-1851 to give more time for the answers. Due to poor inland connections the additional time was really needed and was not even enough in many cases. The change did not affect the schedule homewards from Rio de Janeiro. See the sailing lists of Howat, 129.

666 See Howat, 105, 129.

667 Calculated from the sailing lists of Howat, 85–86, 99–100, 129. – According to the official schedule, the round trip to Rio would take 62 days and sixteen hours. It should be remembered that calculations based on dates do not give exact figures. Nevertheless, one can say that the company kept the schedules admirably.

668 Nicol, vol. 1, 64.

669 Nicol, vol. 1, 64. – The trip was not too comfortable for the first years' passengers. Apart from the normal disadvantages of being at sea during that time period, the South American port facilities were not in place yet. Bushell describes the conditions: 'The well-planned Avenidas, the fine buildings, hotels, warehouses and quays which have made Rio de Janeiro into one of the fairest cities in the world, had not yet come into being. The 'Esk's' [Royal Mail Line's first steamer to arrive, she would become the branch steamer between Rio, Montevideo and Buenos Aires] passengers stepped ashore into a town of narrow, evil-smelling streets, of stagnant pools, rotting garbage and foul drains which are said to have repelled even the hard-bitten British seamen of those days. After a brief stay, the 'Esk' set off again southward, called at Monte Video and entered the muddy waters of the River Plate... In the early days, the Royal Mail steamer anchored about 7 miles off the city

In addition to the lack of comfort, the South American ports suffered from political unrest between Brazil, Uruguay and Argentina. In the early 1860s, England and Brazil were close to war, and the port of Rio was blockaded for some time. But the economy of the South American countries grew with the help of foreign capital, mainly British and American, and also French to some extent. Both the ports and the railways were built by foreign funds.[670]

Some statistics exist on the number of letters carried during the first years. In April 1852, one mail outwards included 3,414 letters to the Brazilian ports (Rio de Janeiro, Pernambuco and Bahia); 1,020 letters to Buenos Aires; 996 letters to Montevideo; 925 letters to the ports on the European side of the Atlantic (Madeira, Cape Verde, Teneriffe, St. Vincent and Lisbon); and 833 to the British Admiral in Rio. Homewards, there were 5,668 letters from the Brazilian ports; 1,794 from Buenos Aires; 1,136 from Montevideo; and 918 from the other ports. In total, the mail steamer carried 7,188 letters on the way to South America and 9,516 letters on the way back home. As this was the only existing mail service to the eastern parts of South America, other countries than the British also used it constantly. In fact, 44.7% of the letters outwards were of foreign origin, and 56.9% of the letters on the home voyage were addressed to other countries than Britain.[671]

In 1856, the Royal Mail steamers carried 66,252 letters outwards and 80,076 letters homewards on the South American route, as well as 123,408 newspapers outwards and 60,084 homewards. The total number of letters carried via Britain was 146,328 in 1856, and it increased to 242,000 in 1863.[672]

The Royal Mail steamship service was a great improvement in the communications between Europe and South America. How did the business connections work in practice then? In contrast to the mostly disappeared West Indian correspondence of the British merchant houses, several archives preserve business letters from South America. Eliminating those with no postal markings left, a sample of 253 transatlantic letters from Brazil, Uruguay and Argentina were examined for this purpose.

The letters come from three merchant houses of Liverpool. Daniel Williams was involved in shipping animal products such as salted hides, horsehair and meat from South America to Liverpool, as well as shipping outward cargoes of salt, coal and ironmongery. The letters from six different places in South America have been sent to the company's office in Liverpool, or to the Artigas villa in Ormskirk, Lancashire, some 15 kilometres outside Liverpool. Most

---

[Buenos Aires]. The passengers and mails were transferred to a tiny steamer which took them to a point about two miles off shore. Here a second transhipment took place into a whale boat which was sailed, or rowed, close in-shore. When about 200 yards off the beach, the long-suffering passengers were again transferred, this time to a horse-drawn cart which finally landed them at a tiny wooden jetty. If the weather were at all unpropitious, the landing at Buenos Aires must have been the most formidable experience of the whole passage.' See Bushell, 58.

670 Pekka Valtonen, *Latinalaisen Amerikan historia* (Helsinki, 2001), 208–209, 617.
671 Howat refers to the Post Office statistics. (Howat, 150)
672 Howat refers to the Post Office statistics. (Howat, 116)

letters of the sample, 211 in total, are from this correspondence between 1854 and 1872.[673]

Of the other letters, 23 come from the Rathbone Bros & Co.'s correspondence already referred to in the North Atlantic connection. Even if most of the Rathbones' businesses were connected with trade between Liverpool and New York, they were also involved in the coffee trade from South America to Europe and the United States, and tea shipments to Brazil. The letters are from Rio de Janeiro, Montevideo and Buenos Aires between 1854 and 1872. The third merchant correspondence comes from Henry Eld Symons, of Kirkdale, who was concerned in general trading principally with South America and Australia. The sample includes 19 letters from Rio de Janeiro and Buenos Aires to Liverpool in 1857–1858. Henry Eld Symons died in March 1858, and the correspondence ends in the summer of that year.[674]

Due to some significant changes in the postal services on the South American route in the late 1850s and 1860, the material has been divided into two: 1854–1859 and 1860–1872. The following table shows the origins of the letters and the time period.

TABLE 47. *Origins of the merchant correspondence from South America 1854–1872.*

Merchant house	Buenos Aires	Herbi-dero via Monte-video	Salto via Monte-video	Monte-video	Rio Grande via Rio de Janeiro	Rio de Janeiro	Total # of letters
DW	1859–1870	1854–1858	1861–1867	1855–1872	1854–1860	1854–1865	211
HES	1857–1858	–	–	–	–	1857–1858	19
RB	1854–1856	–	–	1855–1872	–	1856–1871	23
Total # of letters	54	20	27	102	21	29	253

The total numbers of letters from different ports Buenos Aires 54, Montevideo 149 and Rio de Janeiro.50. DW= Daniel Williams, HES = Henry Eld Symons, RB = Rathbone Bros & Co.

673 Correspondence of Daniel Williams, DB/175 (MMM). For the Williams records, see Dawn Littler, *Guide to the Records of Merseyside Maritime Museum, Volume II* (St. John's, 1999), 13.
674 Correspondence of Rathbone Bros & Co., RT XXIV.2.36. (SJ); Accounts and papers of Henry Eld Symons, 380 MD (LRO). For Rathbone's businesses in South America at that time, see Marriner, 21, 44–46.

Of the 93 letters from 1854–1859 in the sample, 13 were sent from Buenos Aires, 20 from Herbidero via Montevideo, 25 from Montevideo, 21 from Rio Grande via Rio de Janeiro and 14 from Rio de Janeiro. 89 of them were sent by Royal Mail steamers and four by merchant ships.

This sample raises an interesting problem, not widely touched on by historical research. Instead of just concluding that communications was slow at that time, it should be noticed that it was much slower from some places than from others. Daniel Williams could receive several letters in the same day's mail from South America: for example, one from Herbidero, Uruguay; one from Rio Grande, Brazil; one from Buenos Aires, Argentina; and perhaps one from Rio de Janeiro, Brazil. All these letters had arrived by the same transatlantic steamer from Rio de Janeiro, but it had taken the letter from Herbidero 35 days to arrive in Rio via Montevideo by land and branch steamer, while it had taken the letter from Rio Grande 18 days to arrive in Rio by land, and the letter from Buenos Aires 13 days to arrive in Rio by branch steamer. The letter from Rio de Janeiro had been posted on the same day or the day before the transatlantic steamer departed and it was thus bringing the freshest news.[675]

In other words, the letters arriving by the same mail steamer could vary very much in age: the letter from Herbidero was more than two months old (in one case in 1855 it was 3.5 months old), the letters from Rio Grande and Buenos Aires were both about 1.5 months old, but the latter was at least a few days fresher; while the letter from Rio de Janeiro was received about one month after it had been written. And this was not the worst aspect of the issue. The letters which had travelled the longest times were answers to letters which had been on the way in the other direction equally long times. Thus, Daniel Williams would have received on 13 April 1856 from Rio de Janeiro an answer to a letter he had written on 10 February, but from Herbidero an answer to a letter he had written on 8 November of the year before.[676]

It must have been rather confusing to deal with different business partners with different time lags. One can also imagine that some merchants would

---

675 These are average figures calculated from the sample. Additionally, it took 31 days on average for the letters to arrive by the transatlantic steamer from Rio de Janeiro in Liverpool.

676 This example is partly based on the Williams correspondence, partly on the sailing lists of Howat, 131. There are practically no outward letters at all preserved in the archives, and letter books are not useful as they lack all postal markings, as well as notes of arrival dates. – In fact, Daniel Williams did not receive on 13 April any of the letters which arrived in Southampton on the 12th although he should have received them if they had been addressed to Liverpool. His villa address in Ormskirk was a continuous problem for the local post offices. For instance the letter from Herbidero had circulated an extra three days in the surroundings before its final arrival. It bears the following post office handstamps and markings: arrival in London 13.4.; Liverpool 14.4.; Birkenhead 14.4.; New Brighton 15.4.; note by hand: 'not known at New Brighton'; and finally the recipient's note 15.4.1856. Another point to note is that all the mails were not handled in London on the same day. While the contents of the Montevideo mailbag – with the letter from Herbidero – had been handstamped there 13.4., the letter from Rio Grande, which was in the Rio de Janeiro mailbag, was handstamped in the London Post Office already 12.4. and in Liverpool 13.4. Daniel Williams received that letter in Ormskirk already on 14.4.1856. (Daniel Williams correspondence, D/B/176, MMM)

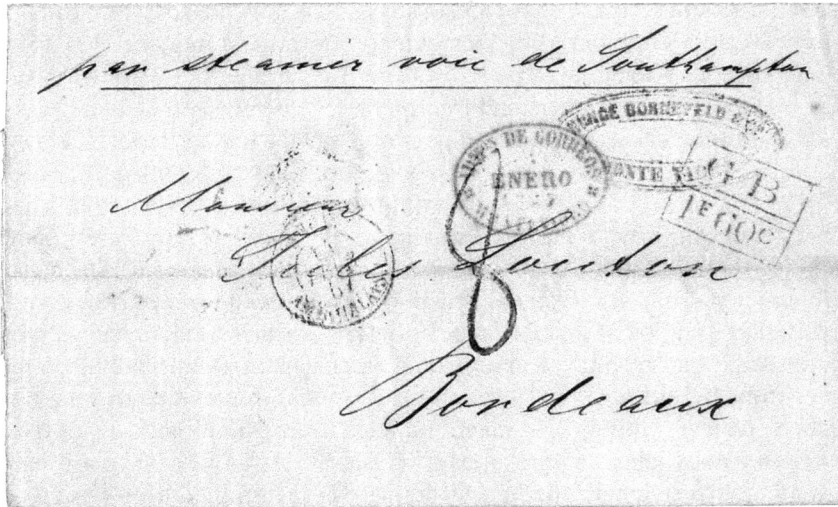

FIG. 24. *The letter from Montevideo, Uruguay, dated on 4.1.1857, departed on 5.1. by the Royal Mail Line branch steamer* Prince *to Rio de Janeiro, and from there on 14.1. by their transatlantic steamer* Avon, *which arrived in Southampton on 13.2. The letter then continued via Calais and Paris to Bordeaux, arriving there on 16.2.1857 (two of the French handstamps on the reverse). – The rate 'GB 1F 60C' was based on the British-French convention which came into force on 1.1.1857.*

have been in a clearly better position if they had carried on business with New York, for example, where they could have expected to get answers to their letters in about 25 days at that time. By speedier communications, also capital moved faster in the North Atlantic region than in the South American trade. No doubt, this made the contribution of agents in such places as Rio de Janeiro and Montevideo particularly valuable. They could deal with the inland producers and organize shipping while the letters were on their way to and from Europe.

Even if there was such an improvement in the speed of communications between Europe and South America in the early 1850s, the users of the postal services were not happy. The merchants and bankers from London and Merseyside wrote several memorials to the Post Office about the Royal Mail Line's schedules. The problem was that, while the incoming letters arrived before mid-month, answers from Britain could be sent no sooner than the 9th of the following month.[677] This delayed the information flow by about three weeks. In fact, an information circle from Rio de Janeiro to London and back to Rio took three weeks more time than the circle from London to Rio and back to London despite the fact that the letters were carried by exactly the same vessels.[678]

The entrepreneurial Liverpool merchants soon made proposals to start a monthly packet service to South America directly from Liverpool. As the

677 Howat, 147.
678 See Table 46.

Post Office was already paying a subsidy for one such service, it was not eager to make new mail contracts. However, the South American & General Steam Navigation Co. began its operations by four new iron screw steamers between Liverpool and the South American ports in August 1853. These vessels did not carry packet letters, but undoubtedly ship letters to Rio de Janeiro, Montevideo and Buenos Aires. One of the Rathbone letters of the sample of Liverpool correspondence was carried by a 'Liverpool steamer' in late 1854, but the service does not seem to have taken any greater role in the mail transport.[679]

In the following summer, the Post Office finally made a contract with the South American & General Steam Navigation Co. for monthly mail sailings, which would depart from Liverpool on the 24th of each month to avoid conflict with the Royal Mail Line's sailings. Only four round trips – and those with machine problems and other delays – were made under the mail contract before the company's ships were chartered to the Crimean war for troop transports, and the service ended without ever starting again. In total, the company undertook only 12 sailings to South America. But as Bonsor puts it: 'Perhaps this was just as well, however, as no fewer than eight other concerns established lines of iron screw steamers to Brazil between 1854 and 1859 and not one of them remained in operation for more than a year or two.'[680]

By 1858, perhaps partly due to the pressure of potential competition, the Royal Mail Line could finally offer an accelerated service to the West Indies and South America in a new mail contract. The company agreed to introduce a faster service to Brazil from 9 May 1858 and to the West Indies no later than from 14 September 1859. It also agreed to provide four new iron paddle steamers, three to the West Indian and one to the South American route.[681]

The faster journeys to South America were achieved by leaving out the stops at Madeira and Tenerife, which were already being served by contract packets on their way from Plymouth to the west coast of Africa, and by increasing the average speed of the steamers to 9.5 mph on the transatlantic route, and to 9.0 mph on the branch route. The ships were now coaling in every port on the route except for Pernambuco and Buenos Aires, instead of

---

679 Howat, 147–151. Correspondence of Rathbone Bros & Co., RT XXIV.2.36. (SJ) For the shipping company's history, see N.R.P. Bonsor, *South Atlantic Seaway* (1983, Jersey, C.I.), 34–38.

680 Bonsor (1983), 36. – The list of these companies show the wide interest in the South American trade at that time: Compagnie de Navigation Mixte (French, 1853–1858); Companhia de Navegação a Vapor Luso-Brasileira (Portuguese, 1854–1857); Compagnie Franco-Américaine (French, 1856); Union Line (British, 1856–1857); Compagnia Transatlantica (Italian, 1856–1857); Hamburg-Brasilianische Packetschiffahrt Gesellschaft (German, 1856–1858); European & American Steam Shipping Company (British, 1857); and Real Companhia de Navegação a Vapor Anglo-Luso-Brasileira (Portuguese, 1859–1860). See Bonsor (1983), 39–63.

681 See Howat, 116. – On the West Indian route, matching arrivals and departures from England were not a reality before April 1860. The nicely working new schedule, which enabled eight consecutive information circles instead of six on that route, is presented in Table 48, the example being from 1862. For the change, see the sailing lists of Kenton & Parsons, 184, 193.

carrying heavy loads of coal at the beginning of the journey, and they were thus able to proceed faster.[682]

One of the main reasons for accelerating the service to Brazil by seven days was to ensure that the correspondence from South America reached Britain in time for a reply to be sent by the Southampton steamer on the 9th of the same month. This improvement in the mail communications was effective for all dispatches for the following 137 months, except for only two occasions when the homeward steamer suffered an accident.[683]

Table 48 shows the effects on the information circulation in the early 1860s, when the system had been taken fully into use. The duration of the one-way voyages was reduced by only four to five days from the early 1850s, but the number of consecutive information circles increased from four to six per year. The letters could now be replied to within a few days after arrival at both ends of the journey.

TABLE 48. *Royal Mail Line steamship round trips and length of information circles, Southampton–Rio de Janeiro, 1862.*

Steamer	Departure, Southampton	Arrival, Rio de Janeiro	Departure, Rio de Janeiro	Arrival, Southampton	England– Brazil– England, days	Brazil– England– Brazil, days
Oneida	**9.1.**	**2.2.**	**8.2.**	**5.3.**	55	54
Tyne	10.2.	7.3.	11.3.	6.4.	55	53
Magdalena	**10.3.**	**3.4.**	**8.4.**	**4.5.**	55	56
Oneida	9.4.	3.5.	9.5.	2.6.	54	60
Parana	**9.5.**	**3.6.**	**8.6.**	**4.7.**	56	55
Magdalena	9.6.	8.7.	11.7.	6.8.	58	53
Oneida	**9.7.**	**2.8.**	**8.8.**	**2.9.**	55	57
Tyne	9.8.	2.9.	9.9.	2.10.	54	53
Magdalena	**9.9.**	**4.10.**	**9.10.**	**3.11.**	55	55
Oneida	9.10.	1.11.	8.11.	2.12.	54	56
Tyne	**10.11.**	**3.12.**	**9.12.**	**2.1.63**	53	etc.
Magdalena	9.12.	3.1.63	9.1.	4.2.	57	
Min.–max.	- -	- -	- -	- -	53–58	53–60
Average	- -	- -	- -	- -	55	55

Source: Sailing lists of Howat, 134. – Royal Mail steamers sailed from Southampton on the 10th, if the 9th was a Sunday. An average outward trip took now 25 days, varying between 23 and 29 days, while the homeward trip took 25 days on average, varying between 23 and 26 days.

682 Howat, 117.
683 Calculated by Howat, 117.

Table 49 shows a conclusion of the development on the South America route, combining the information of Tables 38, 46 and 48.

One of the interesting details is that the change from sail to steam in 1851 cut the duration of an average information circle by 61 days when looked at from England, but by only 43 days when looked at from Rio de Janeiro. In other words, the length of an average information circle by the very same Royal Mail steamers on the very same voyages was 64 days from England to Brazil and back to England, but more than three weeks longer from Brazil to England and back to Brazil. The problem was caused by poorly matching schedules in England.

By the early 1860s, the length of one information circle could finally be reduced to 55 days on average from the earlier 64 or 86 days. This was possible as the Royal Mail Line steamers could now make their round trips to South America in less than two months. This improvement enabled a system where the next ship for Brazil was still waiting in the port, when the one from there arrived.

This clear change is an extraordinary example of how information transmission could be speeded up without new technological innovations or increasing the frequency of sailings. The new arrangement of the existing schedules increased the number of consecutive information circles per year by no less than one-third.[684]

TABLE 49. *Development of the speed of information transmission between England and Brazil, 1840–1862.*

Year	Ship type; size; freq- uency of service	One way England– Brazil, days on average	Diff.	One way Brazil– England, days on average	Diff.	Infor- mation circle, England– Brazil– England, days on average	Diff.	Infor- mation circle, Brazil– England– Brazil, days on average	Diff.	Conse- cutive infor- mation circles per year
1840	Sailing packet; 230–360 tons; monthly	48		57		125		129		2.5
1851	Steamer; 1,700– 1,800 tons; monthly;	29	(–19)	30	(–27)	64	(–61)	86	(–43)	4.0– 4.5
1862	Steamer; 2,200– 2,900 tons; monthly	25	(–4)	25	(–5)	55	(–9)	55	(–31)	6.0

Diff. = Difference in days.

684 Calculated from the sailing lists of Howat, 131–133.

The change can also easily be noticed in the Liverpool merchant correspondence. Instead of the average 31 days before May 1858, letters from Rio de Janeiro were arriving three or four days faster after that date. And the letters from Rio Grande, which had earlier been transmitted in 50 days on average, were delivered in 40 days. Most probably, the inland connections between Rio Grande and Rio de Janeiro had also been improved at that time.[685]

International Competition and the Influence of the Telegraph

The French postal services, the West Indies and the Spanish Main – The French postal services, South America – The Panama route – International competition and the introduction of the telegraph in the West Indies – International competition and the introduction of the telegraph in South America

The French postal services, the West Indies and the Spanish Main

As was noted in the context of the North Atlantic mail services, the French model of a government-subsidised mail system was based on different geographical thinking from the British. Instead of one shipping line operating on the North Atlantic route (the Cunard Line), one on the West Indian & South American routes (the Royal Mail Line), and one on the East Indian and Australasian routes (P&O), the French model was the following: the North Atlantic and West Indian mails were taken care of by one and the same company, Compagnie Générale Transatlantique, or the French Line, and the South American and Far Eastern routes were taken care of by another, Compagnie des Services Maritimes des Messageries Impériales. Later, other companies also joined the system.

The French Line started their contract mail service for Vera Cruz in the early 1860s urged by the government during a military expedition to Mexico.[686] The first French mail steamship service of 1862–1865 operated between St-Nazaire, close to Nantes on the western coast of France, Fort-de-France at Martinique, Santiago de Cuba, and Vera Cruz. The service was carried out once a month by a fleet of four iron screw steamers of 1,700 to 1,900 tons. Two of them, the *Tampico* and the *Vera Cruz*, were purchased from the former South American & General Steam Navigation Co. of Liverpool.[687]

---

685 Correspondence of Daniel Williams, DB/175 (MMM). Correspondence of Rathbone Bros & Co., RT XXIV.2.36 (SJ); Accounts and papers of Henry Eld Symons, 380 MD (LRO).

686 The earlier French attempts to run a mail service between Bordeaux and Vera Cruz in the 1830s have been explained in Chapter VI.1.

687 See the sailing lists of Salles, Tome IV, 25; and the fleet lists of Haws (1996), 23–24. – There was also a branch service between Martinique and Guadeloupe and further to St.

Even though the French started their mail operations by steamship in the Caribbean 20 years later than the Royal Mail Line, they could not at once build a well working schedule for information transmission. A pick-up from the sailing lists of Salles gives us the following results for the first whole year of operations on the new route:

TABLE 50. *Round trips and consecutive information circles on the St-Nazaire– Martinique–Vera Cruz–St-Nazaire route enabled by the French Line service, 1863.*

Steamer	Departure from St-Nazaire	Arrival in Martinique	Departure from Vera Cruz	Departure date Martinique	Arrival in St-Nazaire	Information circle, Martinique, days	Information circle, Vera Cruz, days
Vera Cruz	16.1.	2.2.	16.2.	**3.3.**	20.3.	63*	63
Floride	16.2.	**1.3.**	16.3.	27.3.	12.4.	**32**	55
Louisiane	16.3.	30.3.	16.4.	27.4.	14.5.	59	59
Tampico	16.4.	2.5.	17.5.	30.5.	15.6.	59	59
Vera Cruz	16.5.	4.6.	17.6.	1.7.	17.7.	62	62
Floride	16.6.	2.7.	16.7.	28.7.	12.8.	57	57
Tampico	16.7.	5.8.	18.8.	1.9.	19.9.	65	65
Vera Cruz	18.8.	4.9.	18.9.	**3.10.**	20.10.	63	63
Louisiane	16.9.	**1.10.**	15.10.	26.10.	9.11.	**34**	54
Floride	16.10.	31.10.	14.11.	26.11.	15.12.	60	60
Tampico	16.11.	3.12.	15.12.	26.12.	14.1.	59	59
Vera Cruz	16.12.	3.1.64	15.1.	28.1.	14.2.	60	60

Source: Sailing lists of Salles, Tome IV, 25. – In most cases, the ship homewards had already departed from Martinique when the mail steamer from St-Nazaire arrived. * The *Louisiane* had departed from Martinique on 28.1.1863 and the answers for the letters which arrived on 2.2. had to wait until 3.3. – if not sent by e.g. the Royal Mail Line from some other island.

For military operations it was probably enough that a regular service was conducted by fixed monthly departure dates from both terminal ports. In fact, an average trip from Vera Cruz to St-Nazaire by the French Line – 29.4 days – took just about two days longer than the trip from the same port to Southampton by the Royal Mail Line.[688] As the average round trip to Vera Cruz by the French Line took almost exactly 60 days, the risk of missing the

Lucia, St. Vincent, Grenada and Trinidad in 1863–1865. See Salles, Tome IV, 27–29.
688 The sailing north to Southampton was somewhat longer than to St-Nazaire but the Royal Mail Line had a shorter route in the Caribbean, where they proceeded homewards from St. Thomas while the French Line sailed more eastwards for Martinique.

opportunity to send an answer from France by the following steamer was great. In several cases the ship had already departed when the letters from Mexico arrived. The Royal Mail Line made the round trip to Vera Cruz in 57.5 days on average, which allowed the merchants two to five days time to send their answers by the next steamer – a rather tight schedule, but obviously possible to manage during the time of the railways.[689]

Even though the difference in speed was not remarkable between the two shipping companies, the Royal Mail Line could afford six annual information circles to Vera Cruz, while the French Line enabled only five.

The merchants at Martinique – and those in France who traded with that colony – were in an underprivileged position. Even if the sailings to Martinique were made in 16.5 days on average in both directions, the answers had to wait for three to four weeks at the island and more than two weeks on average in France due to the schedules. The unpredictability of the service must have been even more irritating from the businessmen's point of view. At Martinique, the average waiting time was 26.6 days. In two cases the earlier ship was delayed and the answers to France could be sent within two days of the mail's arrival. In St-Nazaire, the time available for answers could be anything between one and 32 days – and it was.[690]

The information circles between Martinique and the mother country depended on the sailings from Vera Cruz, and most often the information circulation was equally slow to both places. The average length of an information circle to Vera Cruz was 59.7 days, and to Martinique 56.1 days, thanks to excessively delayed ship departures. The Royal Mail Line did not have sailings to Martinique at that time but the nearby Barbados could be reached almost as quickly, in 17.3. days on average. Due to the bi-monthly service and matching schedules, the Royal Mail Line could afford eight annual information circles to Barbados compared with the French Line's five to Martinique. Even if the Royal Mail Line had had a monthly service only, it would have enabled six information circles between Britain and Barbados.[691]

What did the merchants on Martinique do in this situation? They sent their letters by the Royal Mail Line steamers, as they had done earlier. A letter in the writer's collection was sent from St. Pierre, Martinique, on 10 September 1863 to Agen, France by the Royal Mail steamer *Tasmanian*, which departed from St. Thomas on 13 September and arrived in Southampton on the 28th. It was carried by train from Paris to Bordeaux and from there to Toulouse on the 29th, and it arrived in Agen on 30 September – three days before the French mail ship would even have departed from Martinique.[692]

It did not take long, however, before the French rearranged their mail service. In August 1865, the system was thoroughly changed and the main problems solved. This was a similar overnight change to the Royal Mail Line's a few years earlier. One can only wonder why the system was not

689 Calculated from the sailing lists of Salles, Tome IV, 25; Kenton & Parsons, 215–216.
690 See Table 50.
691 Calculated from the sailing lists of Salles, Tome IV, 25; Kenton & Parsons, 215, 218.
692 SRLC; sailing lists of Salles, Tome IV, 25; Kenton & Parsons, 215.

better organized from the very beginning. According to Salles, the mail route was improvised in a hurry to serve the military operations in Mexico.[693] The new system included several mail routes. There were two monthly sailings from St-Nazaire: one for Vera Cruz and the other for Colon–Aspinwall. Additionally, there were several branch routes. At least the sailings to the terminal ports were now organized *comme il faut*.[694]

The new arrangements on the Mexico route included the transformation of the French mail centre from Martinique to St. Thomas, which was located further westwards and thus closer to Vera Cruz. All the three steamers were changed to new and larger ones. The *Impératrice Éugenie* and the *Panama* were iron paddle steamers of 3,400 tons each, and the *France* was an iron screw steamer of 3,200 tons.[695] These changes shortened the sailing time in each direction by a couple of days and enabled earlier departures from Vera Cruz. The length of the round trip was thus reduced from 59.7 to 54.4 days. The extra five days gave the French merchants time to answer their letters immediately and by this means increased the number of consecutive information circles between France and Vera Cruz from five to six per year. By these changes, the French mail service achieved the same efficiency and speed on the route as the British.

TABLE 51. *Round trips and consecutive information circles on the St-Nazaire–Vera Cruz–St. Thomas–St-Nazaire route enabled by the French Line service, 1866.*

Steamer	Departure from St-Nazaire	Departure from Vera Cruz	Departure from St. Thomas	Arrival in St-Nazaire	Information circle, Vera Cruz, days
Louisiane	**16.1.**	**13.2.**	**22.2.**	**10.3.**	53
Panama	16.2.	13.3.	24.3.	7.4.	50
Imp. Eugénie	**16.3.**	**13.4.**	**28.4.**	**12.5.**	57
France	16.4.	13.5.	22.5.	7.6.	52
Panama	**16.5.**	**13.6.**	**26.6.**	**11.7.**	56
Imp. Eugénie	16.6.	13.7.	24.7.	8.8.	53
France	**16.7.**	**13.8.**	**24.8.**	**8.9.**	54
Panama	16.8.	13.9.	25.9.	8.10.	53
Imp. Eugénie	**16.9.**	**13.10.**	- -	**13.11.**	58
France	16.10.	13.11.	22.11.	10.12.	55
Panama	**16.11.**	**13.12.**	**19.12.**	**9.1.**	54
Imp. Eugénie	16.12.	13.1.	- -	12.2.	58

Source: Sailing lists of Salles, Tome IV, 105. – The **bold** figures show an example of how the six consecutive information circles could be achieved during the calendar year.

693 Salles, Tome IV, 17.
694 The routes, their schedules, mail steamers, and postal handstamps used on the specific routes are explained by Salles, Tome IV, 30–223.
695 Fleet lists of Haws (1996), 26–28.

As the sailing date of the Royal Mail Line was on the 2nd of each month and the French Line's on the 16th, the frequency of business communications with Mexico actually doubled. There were now 24 annual mail sailings in total from Britain and France. This did not increase the number of matching information circles, however. The voyage was so long, and the stays at port in Europe as well as Mexico so short, that the other shipping company could never offer a faster alternative to send a letter. An example: a Royal Mail steamer departed from Southampton on 2 April 1866, arriving at St. Thomas on the 16th. The branch steamer for Mexico left on the next day and arrived in Vera Cruz on 28 April. She departed with answers to the letters on the 30th. The fact that also a French Line steamer visited Vera Cruz in the mid-month and would be there again in mid-April did not affect the British communications in any way. The same was evident in the French communications respectively.[696]

Thus there were two simultaneous information circulation processes which never met each other. However, the positive effect of more frequent service was undoubtedly greater than the harm caused by the slow sailings. The concrete advantages of such a double system on a long mail route will be presented in connection with the introduction of the French services on the South Atlantic run, where a similar arrangement had taken place a few years earlier with good results.

The French branch services suffered from mismatching internal schedules just like the British services had done years ago. Martinique is a good example. The island was now served as part of the other long mail route from St-Nazaire to Colon–Aspinwall.[697] Since the railway between Colon and Panama had been opened in 1855, several shipping companies had been willing to take their part of the business. The Panama mail route will be examined more closely later in this chapter. In this connection, it is probably enough to state that the round trip between St-Nazaire and Colon via Martinique took 50 days on average, which was an appropriate time to enable six consecutive information circles per year. The ships called at Fort-de-France *en route* in both directions. And more than that, there was a branch steamer operating between St. Thomas and Fort-de-France to facilitate a bi-monthly service to Martinique. When the transatlantic steamer for Vera Cruz arrived from St-

---

696 Sailing lists of Kenton & Parsons, 240–243; and Salles, Tome IV, 105.

697 The new route was called Ligne A, and the Mexico route Ligne B. The branch services had similar alphabetically organized names, which were also used in the postal handstamps on the mail carried by these services. Ligne C operated between Fort-de-France and Cayenne, French Guyane, Ligne D between St. Thomas and Kingston, Jamaica, Ligne E was the branch line between St. Thomas and Fort-de-France, Ligne F was a branch line between Vera Cruz, Tampico and Matamoros in Mexico, Ligne G was the branch line between Fort-de-France and Point-de-Pitre on Guadeloupe; and Ligne L was the line between Fort-de-France and Venezuela. The missing letters between G and L and after L were used in other parts of the world: for example, Ligne H was the Havre – New York route, Ligne J and K were the South American routes, and Ligne Z was a Mediterranean branch line. This postal line system was developed by the French Post Office, and included several shipping companies' operations. See Raymond Salles, *La Poste Maritime Francaise, Tome VII, Index Alphabétique des Cachets Postaux et Marques Maritimes* (Cyprus, 1993), 98–102.

Nazaire to St. Thomas, the mails were taken to Martinique and Guadeloupe by an auxiliary ship, and the answers were carried to St. Thomas two or three days before the main steamer's return.[698]

The transatlantic steamers departed from St-Nazaire on the 8th and 16th of each month.[699] According to the new schedule, Martinique received the mails from St-Nazaire on the 3rd as well as the 22nd or 23rd of each month, and the mail steamers left towards St-Nazaire from the island between the 7th and 9th, as well as on the 18th of each month.[700] This was somewhat impractical as there were now two incoming mails after each other without any outgoing, and vice versa. Table 52 shows the problem clearly.

Even if a bi-monthly service now existed for Martinique, it was only a partial improvement from the business information transmission point of view. The earlier 56 days long information circles were now reduced to 46 days on average. But the length of the circles varied between 37 and 57 days, and even the average lengths of them varied from 41 to 50 days depending on the original departure date – the 8th or 16th. The letters sent from St-Nazaire on the 16th by the French Line steamer to Vera Cruz could be answered rather quickly at Martinique by sending the letters to France by the steamer which was on its return voyage from Colon. This did not work vice versa, however. The company made the needed changes in the schedules as late as 1872, thus finally enabling eight consecutive information circles by the French service between St-Nazaire and Martinique.[701]

The French mail services mainly overlapped with those of the British instead of complementing them. Yet the departure from St. Thomas for St-Nazaire on about the 24th of each month was appropriately between two Royal Mail Line departures (which took place at about the middle and end of the month) thus speeding up the correspondence from St. Thomas to Europe by a few days.[702]

In 1872, the French Line changed its departure dates from St-Nazaire to Colon from the 16th to the 20th of each month. This also caused a change at the other end: the ships started to leave from St. Thomas later in the month, almost simultaneously with the Royal Mail Line.[703] As a result, the French Post Office probably lost many of their British customers as the service was of no use for them any more. This was the price paid for getting the mail system to work better at Martinique. It was a never-ending problem in the Caribbean to keep everybody satisfied on the different islands.

698 See the sailing lists of Salles, Tome IV, 79, 168.
699 The earlier sailing date from St-Nazaire was originally the 6th but was changed to the 8th from April 1866. See Salles, Tome IV, 79.
700 See Salles, Tome IV, 79, 105, 168.
701 Sailing lists of Salles, Tome IV, 80, 106, 168.
702 Sailing lists of Kenton & Parsons, 240; and Salles, Tome IV, 105.
703 Sailing lists of Kenton & Parsons, 289; and Salles, Tome IV, 106.

TABLE 52. *Round trips and information circles enabled by the French Line service to Fort-de-France, Martinique, 1866.*

Departure from St-Nazaire	Arrival at Fort-de-France	Departure from Fort-de-France	Arrival in St-Nazaire	Round trip, days	Information circle, days
6.1.	22/23.1.	**9.2.**	27.2.	52	52
16.1.	**3.2.**	18.2.	10.3.	53	42
6.2.	22/23.2.	**16.3.**	31.3.	53	53
16.2.	**3.3.**	18.3.	7.4.	50	43
6.3.	22/23.3.	**10.4.**	26.4.	51	51
16.3.	**3.4.**	18.4.	12.5.	57	41
8.4.	22/23.4.	**9.5.**	24.5.	46	46
16.4.	**3.5.**	18.5.	7.6.	52	38
8.5.	22/23.5.	**9.6.**	22.6.	45	45
16.5.	**3.6.**	18.6.	11.7.	56	37
8.6.	22/23.6.	**9.7.**	25.7.	47	47
16.6.	**3.7.**	18.7.	8.8.	53	39
8.7.	22/23.7.	**10.8.**	3.9.*	57	57
16.7.	**3.8.**	18.8.	8.9.	54	49
8.8.	22/23.8.	**9.9.**	24.9.	47	47
16.8.	**3.9.**	18.9.	8.10.	53	39
8.9.	22/23.9.	**9.10.**	26.10.	48	48
16.9.	**3.10.**	18.10.	13.11.	58	40
8.10.	22/23.10.	**13.11.**	2.12.	55	55
16.10.	**3.11.**	18.11.	10.12.	55	47
8.11.	22/23.11.	**14.12.**	28.12.	50	50
16.11.	**3.12.**	18.12.	9.1.	54	42
8.12.	22/23.12.	**9.1.**	25.1.	48	48
16.12.	**3.1.1867**	18.1.	12.2.	58	40

Source: Sailing lists of Salles, Tome IV, 79, 105, 168. – All the arrival dates at Fort-de-France (the 22nd /23rd & 3rd) as well as the departure dates of the 18th from the same port are scheduled dates published by Salles, not the implemented sailing dates. This has no relevance in the issue, however. The arrivals and departures printed in bold are those where a faster departure could have been of benefit: the letters which arrived on the 3rd could have been answered already on the 9th of that month by the other route's service homewards.

* The delayed arrival was due to the *Louisiane* being quarantined in Corunna during the home voyage. (Salles, Tome IV, 79)

The French postal services, South America

On the South American route, the French Post Office's invasion started already in 1860 – in reverse order compared with the British mail services which had started on the West Indian route a decade earlier than they entered South America. The contract was given to the well known French shipping company, Messageries Impériales, which already operated from Marseilles on the Mediterranean mail routes with no less than 57 ships. The new route to Rio de Janeiro, with a branch service to Montevideo and Buenos Aires, used Bordeaux as the terminal port instead of Marseilles, however. For this service, the company received an annual subsidy of 4,700,000 francs.[704]

The service started in May 1860 with no major problems. The first four steamers employed on the transatlantic route were all purpose-built and new: The *Béarn*, *Estramadura*, *Guienne* and *Navarre* were all 1,900 to 2,400 tons iron paddle steamers, later converted to screw. The branch steamer *Saintonge* carried the mails from Rio to Montevideo and Buenos Aires. The system was copied from the British, without unnecessarily repeating their mistakes, as the French Line had done in the Caribbean. From the first year, Messageries Impériales operated in a very proper way, departing from both Bordeaux and Rio on the 25th of each month, and arriving at the other port on about the 20th of the following month. The departures were punctual, and the arrivals at Bordeaux were more often early than late.[705]

A comparison between the Royal Mail Line (see Table 48) and Messageries Impériales services to Rio de Janeiro, with the year 1862 taken as a random example, shows that there was no major difference in their operations.

It can easily be noticed that, by the early 1860s, technological development and the ability to set up effective logistic networks had reached a point where regular, relatively fast and reliable communications were the norm. Both companies made their round trips in 55 days on average, which was in line with their contracts.[706]

This did not mean that all uncertainties had been washed away. The arrival dates were not always as scheduled, but varied to some extent in both directions. For example, in 1862, the duration of the journey from Rio de Janeiro to the European terminal ports varied between 24 and 27 days if

704 Duncan Haws, *Merchant Fleets. Messageries Maritimes* (Pembroke, 1998), 3–4; Raymond Salles, *La Poste Maritime Française, Tome III, Les Paquebots de l'Atlantique Sud; Brésil–Plata de 1860 á 1939, Cote Occidentale d'Afrique de 1889 à 1939* (Cyprus, 1992), 9. – The company's name followed the political history of the country. Being originally Messageries Nationales it was changed to Messageries Impériales during the time of Napoleon III, carrying this name during 1853–1870. In 1871, at the beginning of the Third Republic, the company was renamed Messageries Maritimes. See Haws (1998), 2–5. – The value of the subsidy was equivalent to about £190,000. In the mid-19th century, one pound was approximately 24 to 25 French francs. The estimate is calculated from the data given by Moubray & Moubray, 498; and Mario D. Kurchan, *Argentine Maritime Postal History* (Buenos Aires, 2002). 294.

705 Kurchan, 235; sailing lists of Salles, Tome III, 24.

706 About the Royal Mail Line contract effective in 1862, see Howat 116–117; about the Messageries Impériales fixed schedule of the same time period, see Salles, Tome III, 24.

TABLE 53. *Round trips and consecutive information circles enabled by Messageries Impériales service to Rio de Janeiro, 1862.*

Steamer	Departure from Bordeaux	Arrival in Rio de Janeiro	Departure from Rio de Janeiro	Arrival in Bordeaux	Information circle, days
Bearn	**25.1.**	**(20.2.)**	**25.2.**	**21.3.**	55
Navarre	25.2.	(20.3.)	25.3.	19.4.	53
Estramadure	**25.3.**	**(20.4.)**	**25.4.**	**19.5.**	55
Guienne	25.4.	(20.5.)	25.5.	18.6.	54
Bearn	**25.5.**	**(20.6.)**	**25.6.**	**20.7.**	56
Navarre	25.6.	(20.7.)	25.7.	19.8.	55
Estramadure	**25.7.**	**(20.8.)**	**25.8.**	**18.9.**	55
Guienne	25.8.	(20.9.)	25.9.	19.10.	55
Bearn	**25.9.**	**(20.10.)**	**25.10.**	**21.11.**	57
Navarre	25.10.	(20.11.)	25.11.	20.12.	56
Estramadure	**25.11.**	**(20.12.)**	**25.12.**	**18.1.**	54
Guienne	25.12.	(20.1.1863)	25.1.1863	20.2.	57

Source: Sailing lists of Salles, Tome III, 24–25. The arrival dates in Rio de Janeiro are scheduled, not necessarily applied arrivals. The normal variance can be seen when comparing these dates with the arrivals in Bordeaux.

made by Messageries Impériales, and 23 and 26 days if made by the Royal Mail Line.

Whereas many trips were made faster than scheduled, real delays were scarce. However, due to the long sea route across the stormy Atlantic and the fact that the average travel speed of the small vessels was still only nine or ten knots, variations obviously occurred.

Inland trips did not cause major delays to information transmission in Britain or Central Europe at that time, even if they certainly did in Uruguay or Brazil. The railways took the mails from Southampton to London or Liverpool on the same day, and from Bordeaux within two days. If the mail ship arrived in the evening, the dispatch of the letters took place on the following day.

Messageries Impériales organized their schedules from the beginning in the way that maximized the benefits of the doubled service from the users' point of view. As the Royal Mail Line steamers departed from both ends of the voyage on the 9th, there was a good two weeks' difference between the French and the British services. For business communications it was sensible to use both of them, and the French mail steamers soon carried a good proportion of mails also to Britain.

The Liverpool merchant correspondence gives concrete evidence for this. Of the 160 letters sent from South America between 1860 and 1872, 84 were carried by the Royal Mail Line and 68 by Messageries Impériales.

In addition, eight letters were transmitted by two later established British mail contract lines.[707]

TABLE 54. *Merchant correspondence from South America by period and mail-carrying shipping company, 1854–1872.*

	RMSP	CMI	LH	PSNC	Merchant ships	Total
1854–1859	89	–	–	–	4	93
1860–1869	75	56	1	–	–	132
1870–1872	9	12	2	5	–	28
Total	173	68	3	5	4	253

Source: Correspondence of Daniel Williams, DB/175. (MMM); and Rathbone Bros & Co., RT XXIV.2.36. (SJ); Accounts and papers of Henry Eld Symons, 380 MD. (PRO).
RMSP = Royal Mail Steam Packet Co., or Royal Mail Line; CMI = Compagnie Messageries Impériales; LH = Liverpool, Brazil and River Plate Steam Navigation Co (better known as Lamport & Holt); PSNC = Pacific Steam Navigation Co.

It seems that, although the business contacts of the British used the French services in all the South American ports, it was especially the mails from Montevideo that were often carried by the steamers of Messageries Impériales. The Uruguayan business partners of Daniel Williams used the French mail service for letters sent not only from Montevideo, but also frequently from Salto, a city located up the River Uruguay, about one week from Montevideo. Additionally, the Rathbone Bros Co. received letters from Montevideo by French steamers.

TABLE 55. *Merchant correspondence from South America by port of departure and mail-carrying shipping company, 1854–1872.*

	RMSP	CMI	LH	PSNC	Merchant ship	Total
Buenos Aires	47	6	–	–	1	54
Montevideo	85	55	3	5	1	149
Rio Janeiro	41	7	–	–	2	50
Total	173	68	3	5	4	253

Source: Correspondence of Daniel Williams, DB/175. (MMM); and Rathbone Bros & Co., RT XXIV.2.36. (SJ); Accounts and papers of Henry Eld Symons, 380 MD. (PRO).
RMSP = Royal Mail Steam Packet Co., or Royal Mail Line; CMI = Compagnie Messageries Impériales; LH = Liverpool, Brazil and River Plate Steam Navigation Co. (better known as Lamport & Holt); PSNC = Pacific Steam Navigation Co.

707 Correspondence of Daniel Williams, DB/175. (MMM). Correspondence of Rathbone Bros & Co., RT XXIV.2.36. (SJ).

Due to the length of the journey, the double service did not improve the number of consecutive information circles within a calendar year. As on the Mexico route after 1865, the two mail services – even if working well separately and complementing each other in the best possible way – could not do more than they did.

During the years of the American Civil War, coastal services between South America and the United States were restricted and uncertain. The best way to send letters between e.g. Buenos Aires and New York was twice across the Atlantic.[708] The writer's collection includes two letters which have been sent by this means. A letter from Buenos Aires on 1 March 1862 to New York was late for the same day's Royal Mail sailing to Southampton, and was carried by the *Saintonge* of Messageries Impériales, departing on 14 March to Rio de Janeiro, and from there on 25 March by the same company's *Navarre*, which arrived at Bordeaux on 19 March. The letter was taken via London to Queenstown and on 24 April by the Inman Line's *Edinburgh* to New York, where it arrived on 6 May 1862.[709]

Another letter from Buenos Aires on 14 August 1862 to New York was carried by the *Saintonge* to Rio de Janeiro and from there on 25 August by the same company's *Estramadure*, which arrived at Bordeaux on 18 September. The letter was carried from Queenstown on 21 September by the Cunard Line's *Europa* to Boston and by railway to New York, where it arrived on the same day, 2 October 1862.[710]

The Panama route

The Panama route was a specific case from the very beginning. The interest in developing communications with the Pacific coast had arisen simultaneously with the recently achieved independence of the South American countries in the early 1820s. A six-month return of 1823 shows that 31 British and 33 American ships visited the port of Valparaiso, Chile, during the period. Additionally, several other ships calling at the port were British owned and manned, even if operating under the Chilean flag. Of the British ships, no less than 18 came from or sailed to Liverpool, and only one was bound to London. This trend continued in the following years. All the ships sailed to Britain via Cape Horn. The home voyage took four months on average.[711]

---

708 This idea was also used when sending important mail or specie from California to New York. Instead of loading them into a ship for New York in Colon at the Panama isthmus, they were taken by a Royal Mail steamer to Southampton, and then from Queenstown by a Cunarder to New York. Although slower, this was a safer route and the entire voyage was conducted under a neutral flag. See John Haskell Kemble, *The Panama Route 1848–1869* (Berkeley, 1943), 111.

709 SRLC; sailing lists of Howat, 134, and Salles, Tome III, 24, 29.

710 SRLC; sailing lists of Howat, 134, and Salles, Tome III, 25, 29.

711 A.R. Doublet, *The Pacific Steam Navigation Company. Its maritime postal history 1840–1853 with particular reference to Chile* (London, 1983), 17–18. Doublet also states that there was a line of packets from Liverpool to Valparaiso organized by the South American merchants of Liverpool since 1836. These packets were advertised to sail from Liverpool as follows: to Valparaiso, Islay and Lima (Callao) every three weeks, to Arica, Islay and Lima every two months and to Lima direct every six weeks. The Vice Consul

Doublet records several options for mail routes in the 1820s or early 1830s between the west coast of South America and Europe. Undoubtedly, all these routes were slow and the communications were unreliable. Letters from Chile in particular could be sent by the following ways:

- northwards by sea, usually by private ship, to Panama, taken over the isthmus to Chagres to connect with the West Indian service of the Falmouth packets
- southwards by private ship via Cape Horn to Buenos Aires and then by ship to Rio de Janeiro to connect with the South American service of the Falmouth packets
- by private ship all the way. If the ship was from the United States, the letters were usually transferred at an American port to a ship bound for Britain
- by British warships of the Pacific squadron returning to or coming from Britain. French and American naval vessels were used similarly by their own nationals.
- overland via Mendoza to Buenos Aires and then by private ship or packet to England.[712]

The connection with the Falmouth packets at the West Indies has not been examined by historians and very little is known about it. Pawlyn mentions that the Jamaica service was extended to include Cartagena 'near Panama' in 1825, and Britnor notes that in 1838 H.M.B. *Hornet* was employed as a branch packet boat between Jamaica and Chagres.[713] Whether there was any other service between Cartagena and Chagres than private ships before 1838 is not known.

The route via Panama was apparently not much used by the countries south of Callao (near Lima in Peru) due to the very long voyage and the strong Humboldt stream. The passage from Falmouth to Chagres took 45 days. No less than 23 days were counted for unloading the goods, procuring mules for the land journey to Panama, and the reloading and detention of vessels due to the dilatoriness of the Custom House officers and people. The voyage from Panama to Callao took 35 days and to Valparaiso against the monsoon 22 more days – in total 125 days.[714]

The Panama overland route, although much shorter than its eastern counterpart between Alexandria and Suez, presented far greater difficulties. Instead of the flat country of a river delta, the Isthmus of Panama consisted of a rugged central mountain range with outlying hills, densely covered with

at Tacna (Peru), referred to this service in a letter to Foreign Office in October 1842: '...I would recommend all the official despatches to be sent by the direct ships from Liverpool to Arica...' Nothing more seems to be known about this service. See Doublet, 24. The ships must have been regular traders without government contract. The timing matches with the overall increase of activity by the Liverpool merchant ships, e.g. in East India and Australasia (see Chapter VII.1.) The line model itself was a copy of the American sailing packets on the Liverpool – New York run.

712 Doublet, 18.
713 Pawlyn, 95, 111; Britnor, 150. Also Doublet states that there was a monthly mail service by British men-of-war between Jamaica and Chagres in the 1830s. (Doublet, 20)
714 Doublet, 24.

tropical forest, gradually descending to sea level. Rivers were shallow and there were no roads. The ravines and luxuriant undergrowth were breeding grounds for fever-carrying mosquitoes. Mails, goods and travellers used dugout canoes on the waterways, and mules where the water courses were not available. The less than fifty miles passage over the isthmus took an average of four days from Chagres to Panama and two days in the reverse direction, but in the rainy season the journey could take much longer.[715]

The other existing connection with the official mail service was not much easier. The Falmouth packet branch route from Rio de Janeiro to Buenos Aires included a leg over the Andes to Chile and Peru from 1824, when Buenos Aires and Montevideo were included in the South American service. The route across the Andes would take 14 to 18 days from Buenos Aires to Santiago depending on the season. In early 1829, the service was totally closed following 'clashes between conflicting parties and predatory Indians'. The route was not re-opened before 1832, and it was still reported to be 'very irregular' in 1837.[716]

In addition to these arrangements and the use of men-of-war, merchant ships were continuously used as mail carriers. As Doublet puts it, 'merchants, private or persons in official positions used any available ship to convey mail to Europe'.[717]

In these circumstances the Pacific Steam Navigation Company started its operations between Panama and the young states on the west coast of South America. The aim was to arrange monthly communications between Panama and Valparaiso by two steamers, calling at the somewhat exotic intermediate ports of Coquimbo, Huasco, Copiapo, Arica, Islay, Pisco, Callao, Huanchaco, Lambayique, Payta, Guayaquil and Buenaventura. The company, established in London in 1838 and granted a Royal Charter in 1840, was given a mail contract by the British Post Office for five years in 1845, with a fixed annual subsidy of £20,000.[718]

This was the only mail contract in the history of the British Post Office for vessels which actually had nothing to do with Britain – they did not touch any British or imperial colonial port. The value of the postage was so small that it covered only a fifth of the subsidy. A Committee Report inspecting contract packets stated in 1853: 'The extension of British influence and British commerce appears to have been the chief inducement for supporting this communication between the republics of New Grenada, Bolivia, Peru and Chile...'[719]

The mail service of the Pacific Steam Navigation Company was closely connected with the Royal Mail Line's service to Chagres, which started in 1842 along with the other new West Indian routes. Cartagena, Chagres and San Juan de Nicaragua were served by the same branch steamer from

---

715 Bushell, 87; Robinson (1964) 154; Doublet, 35. – Water ways could not be used in the same way in both directions due to currents etc., which may have been the reason for the different length of the inland voyage.
716 Doublet, 20; Howat, 48–50.
717 Doublet, 25.
718 Doublet, 25–33.
719 Robinson (1964), 154. – Panama belonged at that time to New Grenada (Columbia).

Kingston, Jamaica. Cartagena was also a part of another branch line from Curaçao, which was served by a triangle line from Barbados–Grenada as well as St. Thomas. The mails for Chagres could thus arrive at Cartagena by two different routes, but as they all arrived from Europe by one and the same ship, this was no particular benefit. In October 1842, this overlapping service was deleted from the company's route map.[720]

The published sailing lists do not enable any deeper examination of the early schedules of the Royal Mail Line's service to the isthmus. One round voyage of early 1843 can be picked up as an example:

TABLE 56. *Royal Mail Line, round trip Falmouth–Chagres, January–April 1843, an example.*

Port	Arrival	Departure	Comments
Falmouth		4.1.	Falmouth–St. Thomas (main route out)
St. Thomas	27.1.	27.1.	St. Thomas–Kingston (route 6)
Kingston, Jamaica	30.1.	1.2.	Kingston–Chagres–Kingston (route 10)
Chagres	12.2.	16.2.	
Kingston, Jamaica	28.2.	2.3.	Kingston–Havana–Bermuda (routes 6 & 6b)
Havana, Cuba	6.3.	9.3.	
Bermuda	15.3.	18.3.	Bermuda–Falmouth (main route return)
Falmouth	2.4.		

Source: Sailing lists of Kenton & Parsons, 25–27, 31–33.

The trip from Falmouth to Chagres by the Royal Mail steamers, using a combination of four different mail routes, took 39 days – six days less than by the Falmouth sailing packets. The journey from Chagres to England was even longer, taking 45 days. In addition to the transit ports named in the table there were several others where the ships called at briefly on the way. The following ports were called at during the round trip: (Southampton –) Falmouth – Madeira – St. Thomas – Jamaica – Santa Martha – Cartagena – Chagres – Cartagena – Jamaica – Cape San Antonio – Havana – Bermuda – Fayal – Falmouth (– Southampton). The mails waited at different ports for ten days in total, in addition to the four days stay at Chagres waiting for the mails from the Pacific. Thus, of the 88-day-long round trip on the Atlantic side of the voyage, 14 days were spent at port and 70 at sea.[721]

There is no published maritime intelligence on the Pacific Steam Navigation Company's early sailings. A record from 1846 notes that the new *Ecuador* sailed from Panama on 25 May and arrived at Callao on 6 June, proceeding

720 Kenton & Parsons, 9, 19, 25, 33.
721 Sailing lists of Kenton & Parsons, 25–27, 31–33.

on 18 June and arriving at Valparaiso on 24 June. Thus the sailing down to Chile took no more than a month with the stops included.[722] The Postmaster General's announcement of the PSNC contract in 1846 informed the public that mails for the ports at New Grenada, Ecuador, Peru, Bolivia and Chile would be made in London on the 17th of each month, and that the steamship from Panama would be ready to leave with the mails on the Pacific side approximately on the 23rd of the following month.[723]

At that time, it took the Royal Mail steamers 33 to 35 days to arrive at Chagres from Southampton. The *Ecuador's* sailing matches well with the Postmaster General's announcement. The Atlantic mails arrived at Chagres on 20 May and it seems that they were taken across the isthmus in five days – quite an improvement compared with the description of earlier times. Probably the explanation is that mails and passengers were easier to take across the isthmus than any normal cargo. Loading and unloading did not take much time and the customs officials had less to say. It was also easier to organize the inland trip on a regular basis.

To conclude, it seems that the steamships operating jointly on the Atlantic and Pacific mail routes managed to reduce the duration of information transmission from England from the earlier four months (or more) to 50 days for Callao and 68 days for Valparaiso. Instead of the fewer than 1.5 consecutive information circles that were possible earlier, two full circles could now be conducted each year with rather good regularity.

There was a growing interest in the isthmian route also in the United States. The west coast of North America had been part of the United States from the mid-1840s after the Oregon boundary dispute with Canada and the war against Mexico, and the gold rush to California started in 1849. As the transcontinental railway was not yet built, the easiest way to reach San Francisco was along the two water routes on both sides of the isthmus.[724]

The traffic across the isthmus increased rapidly, so much that in 1850 a group of New York investors began the construction of a railway from Chagres to Panama City. According to Bushell, the Royal Mail Line also contributed with a remarkable sum. The railway was completed in 1855. Chagres was replaced by a more modern port slightly to the east, named Aspinwall by the company which built it, but later known as Colon.[725]

The American coastal services by steamship consisted of four principal routes: the Panama route to California from New York and New Orleans via Cuba or direct to the isthmus; the New Orleans and Vera Cruz route; the Charleston and Havana route; and the New York and Brazil route which was inaugurated as late as 1865.[726]

The service between New York and Chagres was started in December 1848 by a U.S. Postmaster General mail contract. The purpose-built steamers entered the service in September 1849 and January 1850. The United States

722 Doublet, 33.
723 The announcement is reprinted by Doublet, 34.
724 Robinson (1964), 154–155.
725 Robionson (1964), 155; Bushell, 88.
726 Wierenga, 73–81.

Mail Steamship Company mail contract was for ten years and was extended for one year in 1858. At the conclusion of its contract, the company withdrew from the Panama route and it was taken over by the Pacific Mail Steamship Company and the Panama railroad, which formed the North Atlantic Steamship Company to operate a line between New York and Colon.[727]

The Pacific Mail Steamship Company – not to be confused with the British Pacific Steam Navigation Company which operated from Panama southwards – operated between Panama City and San Francisco, with various calls at Acapulco, Manzanillo, San Blas, and Mazatlan in Mexico and San Diego and Monterey in California. The service started in February 1849. After 1851, usually only one stop was made at either Acapulco or Manzanillo. This speeded up the voyage.[728]

An interesting comparison can be made from the report of the U.S. Postmaster General in 1853. The different mail routes between New York and Colon, a distance of 2,000 miles with twice-a-month service, received a total annual subsidy of $290,000. The service between Panama City and San Francisco, a distance of 4,200 miles with a twice-a-month service in each direction, received $348,250. And the Panama railroad, even if not yet fully completed, received an annual subsidy of $95,335. Thus the whole service between New York and San Francisco cost the U.S. government $733,585 in total. This payment covered a twice-a-month (24 round trips) mail service along a route of no less than 6,200 miles by steamship plus the railway costs. In the same year, the Collins Line received $858,000 on the North Atlantic route for 26 round trips between New York and Liverpool, a distance of 3,100 miles.[729] The extra cost for showing national pride on the North Atlantic route was high indeed.

How did the American mail service work between New York and San Francisco in the early 1850s? Table 57 shows the consecutive information circles enabled by the combined service in 1851.

TABLE 57. *Consecutive information circles enabled by the American mail service from New York to San Francisco via Panama, 1851.*

Dep. from New York	Arr. in Chagres	Dep. from Panama	Arr. in San Fran- cisco	Dep. from San Fran- cisco	Arr. in Panama	Dep. from Chagres	Arr. in New York	Infor- mation circle, days
11.1.	24.1.	2.2.	27.2.	5.3.	26.3.	29.3.	~9.4.	88
11.4.	24.4.	1.5.	20.5.	31.5.	19.6.	26.6.	6.7.	86
11.7.	~24.7.	1.8.	19.8.	1.9.	19.9.	24.9.	6.10.	87
7.10.	~22.10.	4.11.	16.11.	5.12.	18.12.	22.12.	6.1.52	91

Source: Sailing lists of Wierenga, 321–322, 341–342. ~ marked are estimates.

---

727 Wierenga, 74.
728 Wierenga, 74, 319–326. Pacific Mail Steamship Company operated also to Callao and Valparaiso in South America. (For some inadequate sailing lists, see Wierenga, 336–337.)
729 The U.S. Postmaster General's report is reprinted by Wierenga, 81.

The mail service between New York and San Francisco via Panama was quite efficiently organized in 1851, when taking into account that it was a combination of two different steamship services and a non-completed railway. It took 88 days on average to receive an answer from San Francisco to a letter written in New York. The schedule seems tight at the New York end, but it probably worked as the system was not changed.

Within a few years, business information transmission by this route improved in a most admirable way:

TABLE 58. *Consecutive information circles enabled by the American mail service from New York to San Francisco via Panama, 1856.*

Dep. from New York	Arr. in Colon	Dep. from Panama	Arr. in San Francisco	Dep. from San Francisco	Arr. in Panama	Dep. from Colon	Arr. in New York	Information circle, days
5.1.	16.1.	16.1.	30.1.	5.2.	~19.2.	19.2.	27.2.	53
5.3.	13.3.	14.3.	28.3.	~5.4.	- -	21.4.	30.4.	56
5.5.	13.5.	- -	1.6.	5.6.	18.6.	19.6.	28.6.	54
5.7.	- -	- -	29.7.	5.8.	19.8.	20.8.	29.8.	55
5.9.	- -	16.9.	29.9.	6.10.	20.10.	20.10.	28.10.	53
6.11.	18.11.	- -	30.11.	5.12.	18.12.	19.12.	28.12.	52

Source: Sailing lists of Wierenga, 325–326, 352–354. ~ marked are estimates.

Instead of 88 days in 1851, an information circle could now be accomplished in 53.5 days on average. The service enabled no less than six information circles per year instead of only four a few years later.

The length of the sailings had been shortened by reducing the number of the ports of call and by replacing old steamers with new ones. The completion of the Panama railway in 1855 was an important part of the achievement. The *New York Herald* noted on 17 April 1855 under the headline 'Efficiency of the Panama Railroad' that the captain of the steamer *John L. Stephens*, off San Francisco on 16 March, had sent the following message for Messrs. Forbes and Babcock, Agents Panama Mail Steamship Company, San Francisco: 'I left Panama with my command at 7 30 P.M. of the 20th inst. With 266 (256?) mailbags, 421 passengers, 620 packages of freight, and three horses, all of which were on board and the ship under weigh in ten hours from Aspinwall. R.H. Pearson.'[730]

European letters to California could be sent by a Royal Mail steamer from Southampton via St. Thomas to Colon, across the isthmus and by the American mail service to San Francisco. Another option was to send the

---

730 Wierenga, 324.

Fig. 25. The letter sent from Glasgow, Scotland, on 30.3.1858 to San Francisco, was carried via Liverpool and New York by three different mail steamers and across the Panama Isthmus by the newly established railway, from sender to recipient in 46 days. (See the text.)

letters across the North Atlantic by a Cunarder or by some other mail service, and then by the American coastal services via Panama.

Also the second alternative seems to have been in use. The writer's collection includes a letter from Glasgow on 30 March 1858 to San Francisco (see Fig. 25). It was carried across the Atlantic by the Inman Line's *City of Washington*, which sailed from Liverpool on 31 March. The letter arrived in New York on 13 April and proceeded for Colon on the 20th by the United States Mail Steamship Company's *Star of the West*. It continued over the isthmus by railway and was carried from Panama by the *John L. Stephens* of the Pacific Mail Steamship Company, arriving in San Francisco on 15 May in 46 days.[731]

The letter could have been carried by the Royal Mail steamer *Parana*, which left Southampton on 2 April and arrived at St. Thomas on the 22nd. The steamer *Trent* departed on the next day and arrived at Colon on 28 April.[732] From Colon the letter would probably have been sent to San Francisco by the same ship as it was sent by, anyway. The British-American connection did not work in the best possible way. If a letter was sent via the North Atlantic route, it had to wait in New York almost a week, and if it was sent via the West Indies, it waited in Colon. It was obviously not in the British interests to change their schedules according to American needs, and vice versa.

The British services via Panama to the west coast of South America also naturally benefited from the Panama railway. Although there are no sailing

731 The letter bears the 31.3.1858 transit handstamp of Liverpool port, used on outgoing North American mail. – no markings from London or Southampton. (SRLC; for this handstamp, see Tabeart, 165–166.)
732 Sailing lists of Kenton & Parsons, 176–177.

lists available from the west coast traffic in the 1860s, a letter in the writer's collection gives evidence of the improvement. The letter, sent on 15 January 1866 from Havre was carried by four different steamships: first by a branch steamer across the English Channel to Southampton and from there on 17 January by the Royal Mail steamer *La Plata* to St. Thomas, where she arrived on 2 February. The same company's *Tyne* took the letter on the same day and sailed via Haiti and Jamaica to Colon, arriving on 8 February. From there the letter was taken by train across the isthmus to Panama on 9 February and by a Pacific Steam Navigation Company's steamer to Callao, where it arrived on 17 February.[733] The whole trip from Havre via England, the West Indies and Panama to Peru took only about a month – 33 days.

Simultaneously with the rapidly developing steamship services and railways, large sailing ships reached the peak of their development in both size and speed. The California and South American routes, as well as the tea trade from China to England, saw the expansion of the most beautiful clippers – fine, sharp and fast vessels designed to carry very heavy cargoes – built in American or British shipyards for companies still preferring sail to steam on the longest sea routes.[734] The clipper boom started in the late 1840s and continued until the depression of 1857, declining rapidly just before the American Civil War.

Even if very much admired for their speed, the clippers did not carry major amounts of mail to California or South America. The trip from New York via Cape Horn to San Francisco by the fastest clippers took at least three months, and an average sailing took 130 days.[735] However, the rapidly growing number of clippers on the long routes must have stimulated a need for fast mail services to carry out the trade. While the clippers were sailing around Cape Horn from New York to California, the mails were sent by fast mail steamers via Panama.

During the peak year 1853, at least 150 clippers sailed from the east coast of North America via Cape Horn to California. The sailings took place rather evenly throughout the year without seasonal variations. In practice, at least two ships left for San Francisco each week, and sometimes even four or five.[736] But the mail service by steamships via Panama was so much faster that there was no sense in sending letters by the clippers, even if the next steamer departure date was two weeks later.

The Panama route was not the only alternative for connecting the steamship traffic of the two oceans. In the early 1850s, there were strong opinions in the United States that the overland route should be drawn more north across

---

733 SRLC; sailing lists of Kenton & Parsons, 240, 243.

734 For the American clippers, see e.g. Cutler (1961), passim.; Mc Kay, passim.; and for the British clippers MacGregor (1952), passim. A recent paper by MacGregor gives a short and sharp analysis of the clipper period from the British point of view, see David R. MacGregor, 'The Tea Clippers, 1849–1869' in Richard Harding, Adrian Jarvis & Alston Kennerley, *British Ships in China Seas, 1700 to the Present Day* (Liverpool, 2004), 217–224.

735 Sailing lists of Cutler (1961), 476–520, covering the years 1848–1860. The average is calculated by Cutler.

736 Sailing lists of Cutler (1961), 487–493.

Nicaragua, thus shortening it by some 400 miles from New York, or 500 miles from New Orleans. The crossing itself was much longer at Nicaragua, some 170 miles, but most of it could be made by water along the San Juan River and Lake Nicaragua. The journey across the Isthmus of Panama was about 55 miles.[737]

So important was the position of the new route that Britain and the United States came close to war over Nicaragua at the beginning of the gold rush, when plans for digging a canal through the isthmus were drafted for the first time, and each of the two nations was eager to take control of it. A crisis was averted by a treaty specifically binding Britain and the United States to the joint control of any canal at Nicaragua or elsewhere in Central America.[738]

These lucrative overland routes to California also caused exciting and ruinous competition between the shipping companies. The chief element in the contest was the opening of a route over Nicaragua to rival that of Panama. The Nicaragua route was vigorously promoted by Cornelius Vanderbilt, the 'Commodore' who would later establish the Vanderbilt European Line for the North Atlantic service.[739] As the government had subsidised the mail routes between New York and Colon, and as Panama and San Francisco had already been occupied, Vanderbilt started an 'independent' line via Nicaragua, stating that his ships were faster and the rates cheaper than those of the 'monopolies'. While the Commodore and his associates were dominating the scene, several other competitors appeared, and the New York and San Francisco newspapers were often filled with lively descriptions and speculations concerning these businesses.[740]

Disregarding the financial ups and downs of the companies, caused by numerous rate wars and fluctuations in stock prices, which all led to uncertainties in operations, the competition had its positive sides as well. Low passenger rates attracted people to use the steamers when travelling to California, and, during the peak years, extra vessels were sent from New York so often that there actually was a weekly service to San Francisco.[741] The mail ship service was bi-monthly, but most probably other steamships were also used to carry letters privately. This may have speeded up the information circulation during those years, but the services were rather unpredictable. Several cases were reported where, for example, the passengers were left on their own at Panama without a ship to take them to San Francisco even if they had tickets for the whole journey.[742]

---

737 Kemble, 58–60.
738 David McCullough, *The Path Between the Seas. The Creation of the Panama Canal 1870–1914* (New York, 1977), 38. The importance of the Nicaragua route can also be seen in the fact that San Juan de Nicaragua, or Greytown as the British had renamed it, was one of the ports the Royal Mail steamers called at throughout the period, except a few months in 1842–1843. See the route maps of Kenton & Parsons, passim.
739 See Chapter V.3.
740 For details, see Kemble, 58–115.
741 See Kemble, 89. – For the different steamship services between New York and Colon, see the sailing lists of Wierenga, 340–364, between New York and San Juan del Norte (Nicaragua), 365–372; between San Francisco and Panama, 320–329, and between San Francisco and San Juan del Sur (Nicaragua), 331–335.
742 Kemble, 62–63.

The competition between the 'humbug steamship companies' was reflected in the popular ballads of the day. One of them began like this:

'The greatest imposition that the public ever saw,
Are the Californian steamships that run to Panama.
They have opposition on the route, with cabins very nice,
And advertise to take you for half the usual price:
They get thousands from the mountains, and then deny their bills,
So you have to pay their prices, or go back into the hills.'[743]

The Vanderbilt Independent Line was closed in 1856 after being mixed with the Nicaraguan revolutionary war.[744] The struggle between the different companies, also still involving Vanderbilt, continued on the Panama route until the late 1860s. When the mail contracts ended in 1859, new and different deals were made that resulted in the United States Mail Steamship Company, which had dominated the mail route between New York and Colon, discontinuing its operations. The company had never achieved the popularity of Pacific Mail and there were few regrets when it ceased its operations. The company was said to be in the hands of a 'number of heartless banking speculators, knowing little about maritime affairs, and less anxious about the multitudes who entrust their lives to their keeping, than of the semi-annual dividends'. Nevertheless, during its eleven years of operation the company suffered only one serious disaster, the loss of the *Central America* with 423 lives in a hurricane in September 1857.[745]

As this was the time when the American mail contracts on the North Atlantic route were transformed to cover only sea postage, the U.S. Postmaster General decided to invite bids for a new contract also on the Panama route. Both Vanderbilt and Pacific Mail bid on the contract, but it was awarded to a Daniel H. Johnson, who promised to carry out the service with $216,000 instead of the earlier $741,200 per year. It appeared later that he was totally unable to fulfil the contract and only acted as a 'broker' while the whole business finally ended in Vanderbilt's hands. The new 'mail line' Atlantic and Pacific Steamship Company started their operations in late 1859. The list of backers of the company showed that most of the old United States Mail organization had gone over to Vanderbilt as well.[746]

Thus the Vanderbilt steamers became the 'mail steamers' and the ships which carried the mails for more than a decade passed into the position of 'the opposition'. The Pacific Mail had carried the mails promptly and safely for a decade without losing a single mail. The new agreement again led to rate wars and hardly improved mail transmission – the sailing lists from the 1860s are not published anywhere. The Civil War caused additional safety problems regarding specie – the treasure shipments consisted mainly of gold from California – and there were times when the mail ships were protected by Navy vessels. During 1848–1869, over 400,000 people travelled from New

743 Kemble, 68.
744 For these events, see Kemble 74–76; Wierenga 368–372; and Valtonen, 326–328.
745 Kemble, 83, 86–88.
746 Kemble, 82–85.

York to San Francisco and more than 230,000 people in the other direction via Panama. The corresponding figures via Nicaragua were over 70,000 and more than 60,000 respectively. The shipments of specie via Panama were worth more than 710 million dollars and those via Nicaragua some 46 million dollars – huge sums of money in those days. For instance the whole fleet of Pacific Mail in 1859, consisting of seven ocean-going steamers, was offered two million dollars by Vanderbilt during one of the negotiations.[747]

Pacific Mail continued on the route, however, and was still operating at Panama in the 1870s, while the transcontinental railway had taken the mails and specie, as well as most passengers, to the inland route. Foreseeing the coming competition with the railway, Pacific Mail spread their operations to the Japan and China routes in the mid-1860s.[748]

The transcontinental overland mail route had already existed since the late 1850s. The letters were taken from the eastern coast of the United States to St. Louis in Missouri by railway, and then by mail coach via Fort Smith and El Paso to California. The latter service operated every second week under a very non-profitable mail contract from the government's point of view: the annual subsidy was $600,000 while the annual return was only a little more than $27,000. In the midst of the Civil War, the service was renegotiated and the 'Central Overland Route' for the northern territories was organized as follows: the first leg ran from St. Joseph, Missouri to Salt Lake City by the Central Overland Company; the second from Salt Lake City to Virginia City, Nevada by the Butterfield Company; the third to Sacramento was sub-let to the Pioneer Stage Company; and the final journey to San Francisco was completed by a river steamer service.[749]

The contract time was 35 days, but for example during the winter of 1861–1862 snowfalls were so heavy that only a light mail could be carried, and in the spring coaches sank up to their axles in mud. Summer conditions brought the unwelcome attention of the Indians. The conflicts continued through the 1860s. The road between Omaha and Denver was one of the worst affected. The contractor complained that between April and mid-August 1867, the Indians had robbed him of 350 head of stage stock, burned twelve of his stage stations, destroyed three coaches, severely wounding several passengers and killed 13 of his most reliable employees. The Indians also fought to prevent the railway from invading their land, and therefore attacked trains and destroyed railway property. During one attack in 1867, they derailed a train and scalped the people.[750]

Despite safety problems, the Panama route was rapidly superseded by the transcontinental railway after its opening in 1869. The difference in duration of information transmission was great, but not as huge as has been commonly supposed. Instead of comparing the several months trip around Cape Horn with the speedy railway, the right comparison would naturally be the three

---

747 Kemble, 86–93, 110–113, 254–255.
748 Kemble, 101, 114–115.
749 Moubray & Moubray, 248–249.
750 Moubray & Moubray, 249; Rudolph Daniels, *Trains Across the Continent. North American Railroad History* (Indiana, 2000), 52–53.

MAP 7. *Development of mail routes from New York to San Francisco in the mid-19th century.*

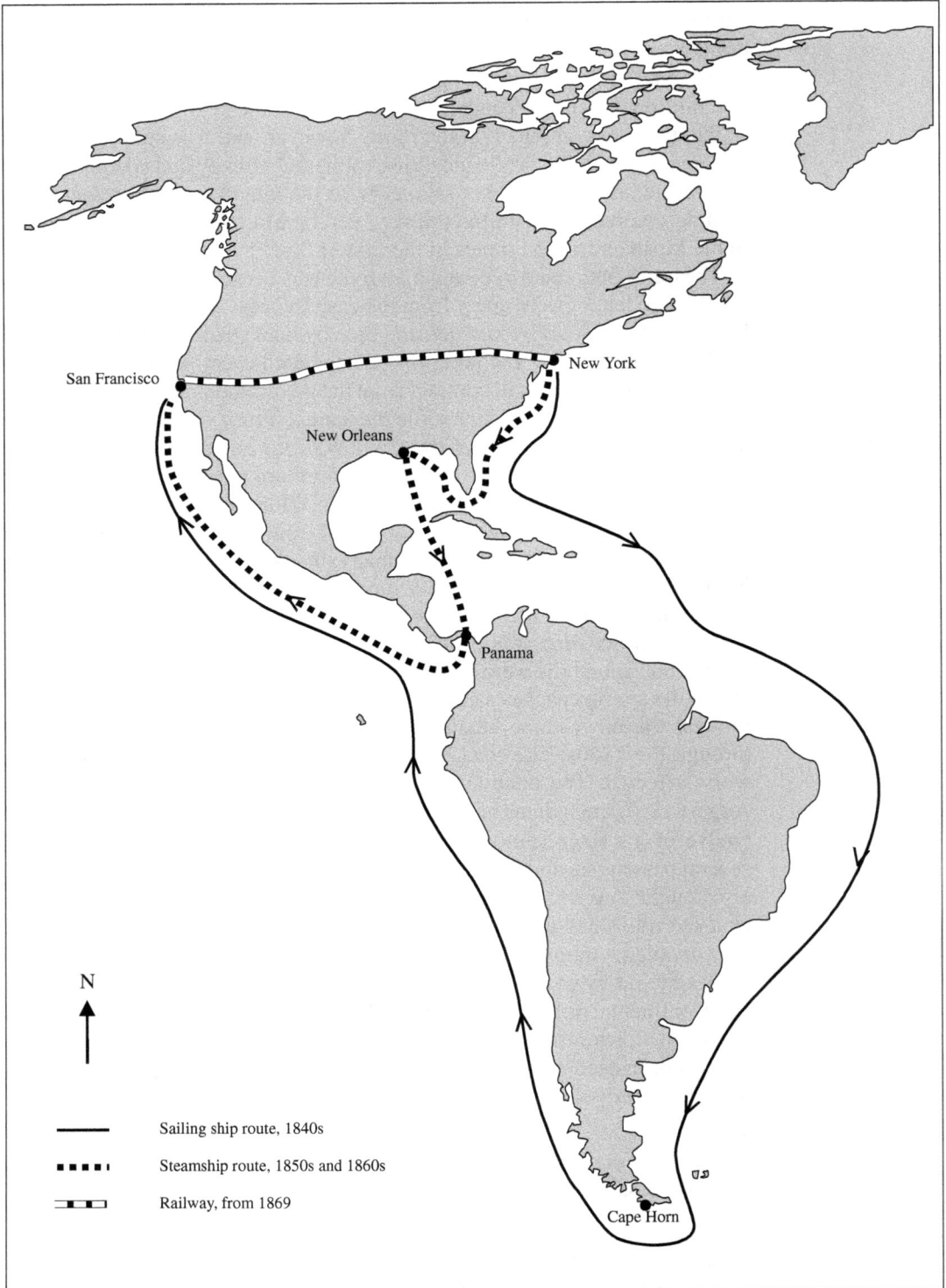

San Francisco

New York

New Orleans

Panama

N

Cape Horn

—————— Sailing ship route, 1840s

■ ■ ■ ■ ■ ■ Steamship route, 1850s and 1860s

▭▬▭▬▭ Railway, from 1869

week journey via Panama by steamer and the one week journey by train. A few years later, an express train could make the trip from New York to San Francisco in less than four days.[751]

While the transcontinental stage coaches had been less efficient in news transmission than the Panama steamers, the Pony Express (between St. Joseph, Missouri, and San Francisco in 1860–1861), together with the partially built telegraph, carried news between the coasts faster than the ships. From 1861, the telegraph alone made the mail steamers carriers of documents and confirmatory details instead of bearers of the first news of great events. When the mails were taken to the rails, the great time of the Panama steamers was over. Being a cheaper alternative, the Panama route was still popular among the less wealthy. Service was slower than in the old days, as the ships now made frequent calls at Central American and Mexican ports. The Pacific Mail Company was putting its best efforts into the transpacific service, and the Panama steamers suffered as a result. They were described as 'cheap and nasty', their awnings full of holes, the furniture shabby and the food bad.[752] Losing the mails and specie typically meant the loss of general interest. When the Panama Canal was finally opened on the same day as WW1 began in 1914, the benefits were in cargo shipping but not in information transmission.

TABLE 59. *Duration of information transmission by different means of communication between New York and San Francisco, ca 1850–1870.*

Means of communication	Time period	New York – San Francisco
Sailing ship (clippers)	1850s	~ 4 months
Steamer via Panama, no railway	– 1855	~ 6 weeks
Steamer via Panama, railway	1855–	~ 3.5 weeks
The Pony Express (152 westb. and 146 easb. trips in total, 11,500 / 23,500 letters in total)	1860–1861	~ 2–3 weeks (incl. 4 days for New York–St. Joseph)*
Transcontinental railway	1870s	~ 1 week

* Source: Richard C. Frajola, George J. Kramer and Steven C. Walske, The Pony Express. A Postal History (New York, 2005), 84-100.

The duration of information transmission has been estimated on the basis of the sailing lists of Wierenga and Cutler (1960) and they are just for a rough comparison. The sailing times of the clippers varied a lot and there is no intelligence on their sailings back to New York – many of them probably

---

751 After the opening of the transcontinental railway, also the Pacific mail steamship service from Australia and New Zealand was redirected via Honolulu to San Francisco to be carried by train to New York instead of using the Panama route. In the 1870s, the eastbound route enabled usually three consecutive information circles per year. For the sailing data, see Colin Tabeart, *Australia New Zealand UK Mails to 1880. Rates Routes and Ships Out and Home* (Fareham, 2004), 281–316.

752 Kemble, 114–115.

FIG. 26. *The letter sent from Rarotonga, Cook Islands, on 17.1.1874, to London was carried by a by-passing merchant ship to San Francisco, where it arrived on 9 April. The marking 'E.b.' down to the left indicates that the letter should be sent eastbound, i.e. via the United States and not via Australia and Suez. It took 82 days from the writing of the letter before it was in San Francisco, but only a week to bring it to New York by the newly opened transcontinental railway. The HAPAG's mail steamer* Holsatia *took the letter to Plymouth in ten days and it was received in London on 27.4. in 100 days. – Cook Islands, in the mid-Pacific, were a seldom visited place, where the only Europeans were missionaries and occasional ship crews.*

sailed on to China across the Pacific. As the clippers were not actual mail carriers on this route, they are included in Table 59 just as examples of the best possible performance by sailing ships. For exact figures, the steamship traffic on the Panama route should also be compared with the Nicaragua route and all the different companies, which would not give much that is new from the research point of view. Railway schedules are not easily found, and the difference would be in days only.

As a conclusion, it can be stated that information transmission between the east and west coast of North America included a paradox: the journey by sailing ship, which was the slowest means of communication, was also the longest in terms of miles. The combination of two steamship lines and an overland crossing at Panama or Nicaragua caused a double effect: the length of the journey was shortened markedly, while the speed was also greatly improved due to the change from sail to steam. The railway across the Panama isthmus made that part of the trip shorter and easier to manage, thus again speeding it up. And finally, when the shortest possible route and fastest possible vehicles were brought into use, the duration of the journey was reduced to less than a week compared with the original four monthsor more. This process was one of the most remarkable improvements in the duration of information transmission anywhere by traditional means of communication, even the telegraph included.[753]

---

753 The building of the Siberian railway in 1891–1904 might be another good example.

International competition and the introduction of the telegraph in the West Indies

The German Hamburg-Amerika Linie (HAPAG) started steamship operations between Hamburg and the West Indies, including inter-island services, in 1871. The German Imperial Post Office authorized HAPAG to organize the mail transportation on these routes similarly to the Royal Mail Line, and these two companies became 'friendly competitors', often visiting the same ports of call. Both companies also published postage stamps of their own for local use on the inter-island voyages. The Royal Mail Line used them only for a short while during 1875, but HAPAG's stamps were in use until the various countries wherein they provided mail services became members of the Universal Postal Union.[754]

Additionally, there were local steamship companies which took care of some branch routes. The most important was the company of Captain Robert Todd, who had an agreement with the Venezuelan government in the 1860s to carry out a mail service between La Guaira, Puerto Cabello and St. Thomas. This route was originally operated by the Royal Mail Line.[755]

The Royal Mail Line also lost several other mail routes to competitors, like the northern route to the Bahamas to the Cunard Line in 1859.[756] In early 1865, the West India and Pacific Steam Ship Company of Liverpool started a monthly service for Haiti, Jamaica and Mexico; and another route for Jamaica and Belize. The contract with the government remained short-lived, however, due to several alterations in sailing dates and occasions where no vessel was available. In April 1866, the contract was terminated and the letters carried by the company were treated by the Post Office as normal ship letters. The company was given another chance in 1868 with routes to Mexico and the northern coast of South America, but the contract was for one year only and the compensation was limited to the weight of the mail carried.[757]

In January 1875, the new mail contracts of the Royal Mail Line came into force. The annual subsidy was reduced by about £120,000. However, the company had already made the necessary improvements and modifications to meet this change in its fortunes. For the West Indian service the annual subsidy was now £86,750 and for the South American service payment was

---

754 Sigurd Ringström & H.E. Tester, *The Private Ship Letter Stamps of the World. Part 1. The Caribbean.* (Trelleborg, printing year missing), 126–128, 133–134; Bushell, 127–128. The Royal Mail Line histories by Bushell or Nicol do not comment on the German rival. – The Universal Postal Union (UPU) was established in 1875, but it was a few years before the countries involved in the West Indian mail services had joined. Letters with the HAPAG postage stamps of 1875–1877 are pictured in Ringström & Tester, 144–157.
755 See Ringström & Tester, 12–28.
756 See Gisburn, 23–25; Moubray & Moubray, 277–278. The Cunard Line had also had a service from Halifax to Bermuda from 1833 and further to St. Thomas from 1850. St. Thomas replaced by Kingston in 1880. This route was not much used for letters to or from Europe as it was slower than the Royal Mail Line connection. It mostly served the British administration at Bermuda. The Cunard service ended in 1886. See Arnell & Ludington, for introduction of the service x–xvi; for sailing lists between Halifax and Bermuda, 55–161. See also Moubray & Moubray, 280–281.
757 Moubray & Moubray, 276.

according to the weight of the mails carried. Several of the ports served in the West Indies were in fact non-contract ports. While other companies took parts of the Royal Mail Line's earlier routes, the opposite was also true. After Plymouth became the first port of call in England from October 1867, the West Indian ships started to call at Cherbourg on the French side before proceeding to Southampton from May 1869. In June 1873, a monthly service was inaugurated from Southampton to the West Indies calling at Bremen and Hamburg on the way home.[758]

Very little is known about the schedules conducted by the different mail lines during the 1870s, as no details have been published of them. It would be especially interesting to examine the 'friendly competition' between the Royal Mail Line and HAPAG on the West Indian route. That will remain for further examination by somebody else, however. From the business information transmission point of view, a detailed study of this time period is not crucial. The telegraph had already reached the Caribbean and the steamers were not urgent news carriers any more.

After a decade of negotiations, with several companies and governments being involved and numerous technical problems being solved, the first submarine telegraph was laid between Florida and Cuba in 1867 by the American International Ocean Telegraph Company. One of the difficult questions in developing the network was once again whether or not any country should have exclusive rights for communications via Panama, which would combine the Atlantic and the Pacific coasts by telegraph. As can be expected from the historical background, the British government was very adamant on this question. Although several countries and colonies were ready for grants and subsidies for the new telegraph network, International Ocean found it soon necessary to raise new capital under the name of a new company.[759]

West India and Panama Telegraph Company Ltd. was founded in London in 1869 and manned by directors mostly from Liverpool, which showed where the main interest in the area laid. By the early 1870s, a telegraph line had been opened between Santiago de Cuba and Kingston, Jamaica, while the one between Kingston and Panama was postponed due to technical difficulties. St. Thomas was combined with St. Kitts and onwards to Antigua, Guadeloupe, Dominica, Martinique, St. Lucia, St. Vincent, Granada and Trinidad. In early 1872, the line was continued to Barbados, and via Trinidad to Demerara.[760]

Instead of one cable telegraph company, there were in fact four of them involved in the Caribbean area. Two were British, (the West India and Panama Telegraph Company and the Cuba Submarine Company) and two were American (the International Ocean Telegraph Company and the Central

---

758 Bushell, 126–127; Ringström & Tester, 126. For the changes in the Royal Mail Line's contracts, see Kenton & Parsons, 222–227 for the fourth contract effective 2.1.1864, and 322–325 for the fifth contract effective 2.1.1875. The sailing lists of Kenton & Parsons cover the journeys only as far as Plymouth.

759 See Jorma Ahvenainen, *The History of the Caribbean Telegraphs before the First World War* (Helsinki, 1996), 9–22.

760 The Panama line was finally opened in 1875. See Ahvenainen (1996), 22–30, 42.

and South American Telegraph Company). Three of them formed an alliance and operated in competition with the Central and South American Telegraph Company, whose activities, as the name implies, were mainly in Central and South America. It did not operate in the West Indies and did not pose a threat to the monopoly of the Associated Companies.[761]

The companies soon found that things did not go according to their plans. The laying of cables and the initial establishment of services were much more arduous and expensive than had been calculated. As the original idea of extending activities to South America – the most lucrative part of the plan – did not come about, there was considerable unused capacity in the cable network. Another surprise was that demand for the telegraph remained much lower than had been estimated. The continuing depression in the sugar trade brought serious economic difficulties in most colonies, and the economic significance of the Caribbean area in world trade was on the decline. The social structure of the area was not favourable for the telegraph, as the large majority of the population was illiterate. The telegraph served members of the commercial community, manufacturers, plantation owners and various government officials, but beyond this it found little use. As the Caribbean islands belonged to different European powers, it was not surprising that the demand for traffic between the islands was not great.[762]

For the business in British Guiana, the telegraph seems to have been a useful tool, however. The Sandbach, Tinne & Co.'s correspondence gives several examples of how the combination of steamship letters and telegraph worked in practice:

> - 'We enclose copies of our letter yesterday by direct steamer… and have to acknowledge your telegram in answer to ours about the 'Malvina Shutte' for timber… We enclose a letter from Robert Smith about Ruimveld. It is of course what you would have anticipated when you did not send us a power of attr. Meanwhile we await your instructions – we do not wire 'Rotterdam' because it might mean so much we did not wish to say. The King Arthur is loading for London. Sugar is alongside @ 1s/9d…'
> - 'In your additions of 3 March you had the word 'avaria' – We substitute 'average' for the second 'avaria'.'
> - 'Dear Sirs. We have to acknowledge your P16 per mail with enclosures & your telegram 4/94… Harrisons. The reasons we telegraphed was… Glencorn. We will telegraph later on. We have heard from the owners.'
> - 'Dear John, the mail being late, we have 'nowt' to acknowledge, and little to say on our own account.'
> - 'Dear Sirs. We have your P38, 39, 40. Mexicans. Your telegram 4/119 duly received but the Government Secretary has not replied yet to us… Enclosures: letter for Crosby, letter for Olivieira, 3 telegrams, P/copies last mail.'[763]

761 Ahvenainen (1996), 196–197.
762 Ahvenainen (1996), 197.
763 Letters to Sandbach, Tinne & Co. in Liverpool from Demerara (Georgetown) 25.3.1876, 4.4.1876, 25.4.1876, 24.8.1876 and 5.9.1876. (Bryson Collection, Records of Sandbach, Tinne & Co., D/B/176, MMM)

The mixture of business information received by telegrams and steamship letters made communications between the sugar plantation in Demerara and the owner company in Liverpool rather complicated. For an outsider, it is almost impossible to understand what it was all about. Cross-references were necessary to keep the partner on the other side of the ocean informed about the status of knowledge of the writer at the time when he was sending the letter. Numbered letters and telegraph codes illustrate fairly standardized business communications. And more than that, the degree of independence at the plantation had been notably reduced. The owners, thousands of miles away, now controlled the distant plantation much more strictly than a few decades earlier.

International competition and the introduction of the telegraph in South America

In the late 1860s, the business environment of the old players like the Royal Mail Line and Messagerie Impériales changed markedly on the South American route. The introduction of the compound engine made it possible to carry more freight and passengers than earlier, instead of filling the ship holds with coal. This was particularly important on the long sea routes. While the royal mail services of Britain and France had enjoyed notable subsidies for their operations, new competitors could now start on the same routes without government support. The increasing space for cargo and passengers made the voyages profitable anyway, and in fact steamers now finally overtook sailing ships as long distance carriers. It did not take long before the government policy changed on the South American route as it did everywhere else, and the shipping companies were paid only according to the weight of the mails carried.[764]

The Liverpool-based company generally known as Lamport & Holt started their steamship service for South America in 1863 under the name Liverpool, Brazil and River Plate Steam Navigation Company. They sent two ships to South America in the first year, eight in 1864, 24 in 1865, and 41 in 1866. These vessels occasionally carried private ship letters for the Liverpool merchant houses.[765] In 1868, the company started as an official mail carrier under government contract on the route Liverpool–Lisbon–Bahia–Rio de Janeiro–Montevideo–Buenos Aires. A short-lived contract was also made with the London-based Tait & Company (London, Belgium, Brazil and River Plate Royal Mail Steam Ship Company).[766]

---

764 See Bushell, 125–127; Howat 164, 166, 169, 180, 189–190, etc. – The compound engine does not seem to have considerably affected the service speed of the vessels. For example, the speed of the Royal Mail steamers with compound engines in the 1870s was 11 to 12 knots, which was normal performance for ships with inverted engines, too. Technically, the 1860s were also the time when the old wooden paddle steamers were changed to iron screws. See the fleet list of the Royal Mail Line in Bonsor (1983), 21–24, Howat, 122.

765 Howat, 159. As an example of a private ship letter sent by a Lamport & Holt vessel, a letter from Montevideo 22.9.1863 to Rathbone Bros & Co. in Liverpool 'p. Str Kepler' (RT XXIV.2.36, SJ).

766 See Howat, 159–170, 175–181; Moubray & Moubray, 284–285.

An interesting phenomenon on the route was the entrance of the Pacific Steam Navigation Company on the east coast of South America. This was the same company that had been carrying mails under a British contract along the west coast from the mid-1840s. They now established a direct route from Liverpool via Bordeaux, Lisbon, Cape Verde, Rio de Janeiro, Montevideo and Punta Arenas to Valparaiso. Instead of sailing down to Cape Horn the steamers took the shorter route via the Straits of Magellan.[767]

In 1870, there were five regular mail steamship lines operating between the main West European ports and South America. The mails for Buenos Aires were sent to the departure ports from London on the 2nd, 9th, 19th and 23rd or 24th of each month, with Sundays sometimes changing the date by one day. The departure dates from Buenos Aires were on the 9th, 12th, 17th, and 27th of each month. The Pacific Steam Navigation Company, leaving on the 12th of each month from Liverpool, sailed via Montevideo to Valparaiso and Callao without going to Buenos Aires. Their ships departed homewards from Montevideo on the 26th.[768]

For natural commercial reasons, not all these companies operated on exactly the same routes. The Royal Mail Line, Lamport & Holt and Tait & Co. sailed to Buenos Aires from different British ports and Messageries Maritimes sailed to the same place from Bordeaux. The Pacific Steam Navigation Company sailed from Liverpool to Montevideo as mentioned above. The vessels also called at somewhat different ports during the voyage. As all shipping lines called at Rio de Janeiro and Montevideo, these ports actually kept more options for business communications than Buenos Aires. Communications with Uruguay benefited notably when Tait & Co. ceased its operations to Buenos Aires in 1870 and the Pacific Steam Navigation Company doubled its service to Montevideo and Valparaiso from July in the same year.[769]

---

767 See Howat, 185; Moubray & Moubray 285.

768 Howat, 187. – Additionally, the German Hamburg-Süd (Hamburg-Südamerikanischen Dampfschiffahrts Gesellschaft) started on the South American route two years later in 1872. See Bonsor (1983), 189, 200–201.

769 Royal Mail Line sailed the route Southampton–Lisbon–St. Vincent (Cape Verde)–Pernambuco–Bahia–Rio de Janeiro–Montevideo–Buenos Aires; Lamport & Holt sailed Liverpool–Bahia–Rio de Janeiro–Montevideo–Buenos Aires; Tait & Company sailed Falmouth–Rio de Janeiro–Montevideo–Buenos Aires; Pacific Steam Navigation Company sailed Liverpool–Bordeaux–Lisbon–St. Vincent (Cape Verde)–Rio de Janeiro–Montevideo–Valparaiso; Messageries Maritimes sailed Bordeaux–Lisbon–Dakar–Pernambuco, Bahia, Rio de Janeiro–Montevideo and Buenos Aires. See Howat, 123, 163, 180, 189–190; Salles, Tome III, 89.

TABLE 60. *Consecutive information circles between Liverpool and Montevideo in 1870, an example.*

Company	Port and date of departure	Date of arrival in Monte-video	Company	Date of depar-ture from Monte-video	Port and date of arrival	Infor-mation circle, days*
Tait & Co.	Falmouth 4.1.	8.2.	Lamport & Holt	~10.2.	Southampton 18.3.	73
Lamport & Holt	Liverpool 20.3.	19.4.	PSNC	28.4.	Liverpool 27.5.	68
Tait & Co.	Falmouth 3.5.	2.6.	Lamport & Holt	~10.6.	Southampton 13.7.	71
Lamport & Holt	Liverpool 20.7.	22.8.	PSNC	26.8.	Liverpool 23.9.	65
PSNC	Liverpool 29.9.	29.10.	Mess. Maritimes	2.11.	Bordeaux 26.11.	60**
PSNC	Liverpool 29.11.	~24.12.	PSNC	27.12.	Liverpool 3.2.71	66

Sources: Sailing lists of Howat, 137, 171, 183, 211; Salles, Tome III, 89, 91.
   * = information circles are calculated from the date of departure from the homeport to the date of arrival at the homeport, using the fastest possible change in Montevideo (not including those departures which took place on the same day when the mail from Europe arrived, however)
   ** = two days have been added for the trip between Bordeaux and Liverpool. From the other ports, the mails were principally sent on the same day by railway.

As the distance between Montevideo and Buenos Aires was just one sailing day, we do not know whether the difference was very remarkable in real life, however. There may have been local steamboat services which took the mails to Buenos Aires, although it should be remembered that there was a national border between the two cities. Table 60 shows the flow of consecutive information circles between Liverpool (or any other major English port with inland rail connections) and Montevideo in 1870. For Buenos Aires, one or two days should be added to the duration of the voyage.

By chance, the information circles starting from early January 1870 lead to a presentation without any Royal Mail sailings. Almost six consecutive information circles could be conducted on that route by using almost exclusively the newcomers, with one Messageries Maritimes sailing as an exception. An average information circle enabled by the service of the four companies took 67 days. As there were ships leaving rather often, the number of possible consecutive information circles rose to 5.5 per year. If the Royal Mail Line had sailed on the route alone, the length of an average information circle would have been almost the same, 68 days, but the monthly schedule would have enabled only four consecutive information circles within the calendar year.

The services of the different shipping lines were not identical. Interestingly, the old mail lines – Royal Mail, Messageries Maritimes and Pacific Steam Navigation Company – made constantly faster journeys than the newcomers – Tait & Company and Lamport & Holt. The Royal Mail Line had also finally abandoned the old branch service system between Rio de Janeiro and Buenos Aires, and the direct service shortened the duration of the voyage by a few days.[770] A fair comparison between all companies is difficult due to the different routes and the fact that not all the real dates are given in the sailing lists, but sometimes only the administrative schedules. Additionally, the sources sometimes disagree about the dates.[771] With these reservations, the average performance of the shipping lines was as follows:

TABLE 61. *Average duration of journeys between English/French ports and Montevideo, 1870.*

Shipping company	Average duration of the trip, home port – Montevideo	Average duration of the trip, Montevideo – home port
Lamport & Holt	30 days	35 days
Messageries Maritimes	30 days	26–27 days
Pacific Steam Navigation Co.	28 days	32 days
Royal Mail Line	28 days	30 days
Tait & Co.	33 days	35 days

Sources: Sailing lists of Howat, 137, 171, 183, 211; and Salles Tome III, 89, 91.

770 For the corresponding change in the Royal Mail Line's mail contract, see Howat, 122–123.
771 The factual dates of Messageries Impériales arrivals in South American ports are missing from the sailing lists of Salles, and the homeward sailing dates are given only from Buenos Aires. In a few cases, the comparison between the Daniel Williams correspondence (Bryson Collection, D/B 175, MMM) and the sailing lists give an unusually long transfer time between Bordeaux and Liverpool, four days instead of the normal two. This may indicate that the ship arrival dates in French newspapers could probably be incorrect, as the postal handstamps are to be considered more reliable. This is probable also because there is some non-correspondence between the sailing lists of Salles and Hubbard & Winter concerning the French Line sailings in the North Atlantic in the 1870s. Salles has used French newspapers and shipping company archives as sources, while Hubbard and Winter have used New York papers and *Lloyd's List* (Salles, Tome III, 4; Salles, Tome IV, 8, 238–239; Hubbard & Winter, 275, 284–286). But it is also possible that the sailing dates are right and the mail between Bordeaux and Liverpool has been delayed for some reason. In the Howat sailing lists, a few Tait & Co. and Lamport & Holt sailing dates are missing and estimates have been calculated by using Buenos Aires arrival or departure dates. In some cases, Howat has also used dates 'due to arrive or depart' instead of factual dates. Additionally, two Liverpool arrival dates have been corrected as the postal handstamps of letters in the Williams correspondence show clearly that the ship did not arrive on the day given. See Howat, 171, 183, 211.

Naturally, the British Post Office closely examined the duration of mail sailings. When Tait & Company was not able to improve its performance but instead asked for the possibility to lengthen the voyage to 42 days in a new mail contract, the Post Office turned to Pacific Steam Navigation Company for a better offer. Thus the latter company took over the contract in July 1870 while Tait & Company disappeared from the scene. Table 61 shows clearly the reason why Lamport & Holt was not asked to take the contract.[772]

In 1874, the Royal Mail Line started a bi-monthly service, thus following the example of Messageries Maritimes which had started a new commercial line in addition to their government mail service in 1872. The 'rapid' new line of Messageries Maritimes did not touch Bahia or Pernambuco, while the other line did. By 1875, the South American mail services by steamship had reached their peak in frequency and speed. In addition to the three mail-carrying lines from England and one from Bordeaux, there was the German Hamburg-Süd operating from Hamburg, the French Société Générale de Transports Maritimes (SGTM) operating from Marseilles, and the Italian Lavarello Line, operating from Genoa.[773]

Contemporary statistics by the Argentina Director-General of Posts and Telegraphs give interesting information on the numbers of letters carried by the shipping lines from Buenos Aires to Europe in 1876. Messageries Maritimes was the market leader with 100,000 letters (31%), while the Royal Mail Line carried 88,000 letters (28%). The Mediterranean companies had taken a considerable share of the transports within a few years of starting the service: SGTM carried 46,000 letters (15%) and Lavarello 45,000 letters (14%). Lamport & Holt carried 10,000 letters (3%); and 'various ships of the Pacific Steam Navigation Company and sundry German ships' carried 29,000 letters (9%). The total number of letters from Buenos Aires to Europe was 318,000.[774] In addition, the ships carried the mails from Montevideo and the Brazilian ports.

---

772 For the discussion about the renewal of the mail contract, see Howat, 181–190. – The Post Office also took a survey of the amount of British postage collected on the correspondence carried by the mail lines between South America and Britain during the six months beginning from June 1869. It was noticed that the earnings of the Royal Mail Line, the only company with a fixed subsidy (Messageries Impériales received subsidies from the French government), had not been diminished by the establishment of additional mail lines. Another survey showed that the payments by the Post Office to Lamport & Holt were only £4,834 in 1869 and £5,418 in 1870, which did not indicate large amounts of mails carried. The Pacific Steam Navigation Company's part was even somewhat smaller, but the company naturally had its role in the Pacific service. The actual earnings by the Royal Mail Line were still £33,100 in 1874, then declining rapidly to £20,828 in 1875, £16,976 in 1876 and being only £5,538 in 1880. See Howat, 128, 170, 181, 209.

773 See Howat, 123–126; Salles, Tome III, 91; Bonsor (1983), 102–105, 128–129, 135–136.. – No sailing lists exist of the operations of the German or the Mediterranean companies.

774 Howat, 126.

TABLE 62. *Consecutive information circles between Liverpool and Montevideo in 1875, an example.*

Company	Port and date of departure	Arrival in Monte-video	Company	Departure from Monte-video	Port and date of arrival	Infor-mation circle, days*
Mess. Maritimes	Bordeaux 5.1.	~3.2.	*Lamport & Holt* or *Mess. Maritimes*	11.2. 11.2.	Southampton 12.3. Bordeaux 9.3.	68 67
Mess. Maritimes	Bordeaux 20.3.	~18.4.	*PSNC*	27.4.	Liverpool 28.5.	71
PSNC	Liverpool 2.6.	1.7.	*Royal Mail Line*	2.7.	Southampton 31.7.	59
Mess. Maritimes	Bordeaux 5.8.	~3.9.	*Lamport & Holt*	10.9.	Southampton 10.10.	68
Lamport & Holt	Liverpool 18.10.	19.11.	*PSNC*	24.11.	24.12.	67

Sources: Sailing lists of Howat, 140, 174, 217; Salles, Tome III, 94. ~marked are estimates. – Two days have been added for the trip between Bordeaux and Liverpool. From the other ports, the mails could be sent on the same day by railway.

Table 62 gives an example of information circulation between the Atlantic mail ports and Montevideo, using Liverpool as the European terminal to be consistent – it could naturally be any major English port with railway connections.

There were no less than 86 mail sailings to and from Brazil and the River Plate ports in 1875, compared with 61 in 1870. However, the result from the business information circulation point of view was now poorer than earlier. Instead of 5.5, only five consecutive information circles could be carried out within the calendar year. The same result could have been achieved by using the Royal Mail Line's bi-monthly service alone.

The main reason for this outcome was that sailings could not be really coordinated due to the different contracts of the shipping lines. While Messageries Maritimes and the Royal Mail Line sailed bi-monthly, and Lamport & Holt monthly always on the same days (except for Sundays for the British lines), the Pacific Steam Navigation Company sailed every second Wednesday, thus altering the dates continuously.

The departures from the European ports were not evenly split but varied greatly. Even if there were seven to eight departures each month, the system did not work well from the business information transmission point of view. While there were sometimes four departures within a week's time, ten days could then pass without a single sailing.

The arrivals and departures were sometimes mismatched within the same shipping line, so that the next ship departed on the same day as, or one or two days before the arrival of the company's vessel from the other direction.[775] The Liverpool-based companies competed by sailing out on the same days as the old mail contract companies, or very close to them.[776]

For example in February 1875, Messageries Maritimes first sailed on the same day as their own vessel arrived at Bordeaux, so that no one could answer the arriving letters in Paris, to say nothing of England. The Pacific Steam Navigation Company then sailed out one day after the Royal Mail Line, which was not very useful for anyone. Lamport & Holt sailed a day after Messageries Maritimes had departed from Bordeaux, which meant that the mails for the sailings had to be sent from England almost simultaneously. And finally the Pacific Steam Navigation Company again sailed out on the same day as the Royal Mail Line. Instead of spreading the seven departures evenly on every fourth day, for example, three of the departures took place within six days between the 5th and 10th February, and four of them within five days between the 20th and 24th February. During the rest of the month, there were no sailings outwards at all.[777]

Additionally, answers to letters that arrived on a Pacific Steam Navigation Company ship on the same day as another of the company's vessels departed normally had to wait up to ten days for the following departure, while letters by the Royal Mail Line had to wait five days. After 1.5 weeks without sailings, there were again two on the same day.[778] Even if the sailings were somewhat faster in 1875 than five years earlier, the duration of specific voyages varied notably.

The Royal Mail Line's homeward sailings from Montevideo took 29.5 days (30.2 in 1870) on average, varying between 28 and 32 days. Lamport & Holt's sailings took 31.1 days (35) during the whole year, and 30.3 days under the new contract which began in April 1875. The duration of sailings varied between 26 and 37 days. Pacific Steam Navigation Company's sailings took 30.7 days (31.8) on average. The length of the sailings varied between 29 and 33 days. The express mail line of Messageries Maritimes made the home voyage in 25.1 days (25.6) on average, varying between 24 and 27 days, while the commercial line which visited several more ports used 30.3 days for the home voyage, varying between 26 and 35 days.[779]

As in the concurrent North Atlantic service, the speed and frequency of sailings was not utilized in the most efficient way. When the companies competed by sailing on the same day or very close to each others' sailing

---

775 For example the Messagerie Maritimes arrivals in early January, February, July, August, October and December 1875. See Salles, Tome III, 94.

776 For example the Lamport & Holt sailings in January–April (the schedule was changed from May 1875) and Pacific Steam Navigation Company sailings in late February and March, early May and mid-October. See the sailing lists of Howat, 139–140, 173–174, 216–217.

777 See the sailing lists of Howat, 139–140, 173–174, 216–217; and Salles, Tome III, 94.

778 See the sailing lists of Howat, 139–140, 173–174, 216–217; and Salles, Tome III, 94.

779 Sailing lists of Howat, 139–140, 173–174, 216–217; and Salles, Tome III, 94. The averages of 1870 are based on the sailing lists of Howat, 137, 171, 183, 211; and Salles, Tome III, 89, 91. When calculating the duration of the trips by Messageries Maritimes and Lamport & Holt, it has been estimated that the departures from Montevideo took place one day later than the given dates from Buenos Aires.

dates, the overlapping meant lost opportunities at least from the business information transmission point of view. When the transport of mails ceased to be the main purpose of the sailings and the needs of freight shipments and passenger traffic were preferred, information transmission was the loser.

From the mid-1870s, the British Post Office looked for economies in the overseas contract mail services. This led to a reduction in the sums paid to the companies per ounce of letters carried. The Post Office also wanted to economise by restricting the obligation to transport letters only to the outward mails from Britain. Overseas countries would then become responsible for making their own contracts with shipping companies for carrying the mails to Europe. Under these circumstances, Lamport & Holt's mail contract was cancelled in 1876, while the contracts with the two other British companies on the South American route, the Royal Mail Line and the Pacific Steam Navigation Company, were accordingly curtailed.[780]

The British Postal Agency in Buenos Aires, established in 1824, was also suppressed in June 1873 by an Argentina government decree, together with the French Agency. For decades, the British and French communities had enjoyed the privilege of being able to take their letters for their home countries and intermediate ports to their Consulate Packet Office for direct transmission without incurring the handling of the letters by the local Buenos Aires postal authorities or paying their charges. The letters would now be sent by the Argentine Post Office and be pre-paid by Argentine postage stamps. The mailbags would be delivered to the mail agents on board the English and French steamers 'on the day and hour fixed by the agents of those lines'.[781]

All the former privileges, subsidies and special arrangements were now removed from the information transmission services and no one coordinated the networks. This was undoubtedly cheaper for the governments and corresponded better with the principles of free competition, but it was definitely a step back from the business information transmission point of view. Even if the fastest messages could be sent by telegraph, the important bulk mails with documents, explanations to the telegrams and tone of voices in the letters were transported more slowly than earlier. Continuous improvement had been replaced by overlapping services, unhealthy competition which ruined tens of shipping lines, and the still rather unpredictable duration of information transmission.

The changes in the South American communications environment were also related to the introduction of the telegraph. But long and difficult distances, as well as the commercial and political interests of several countries involved in Europe, South America and the West Indies made the negotiations about laying the cables an extensive process. Several companies were established and capital collected, agreements were signed between governments and several thousand miles of gutta percha cables were manufactured for the purpose. Jorma Ahvenainen gives a detailed description of the early planning

---

780 See Howat, 170.
781 Howat, 121–122. For the French Consulates and their services in Lisbon, Gorée, Pernambuco, Bahia, Rio de Janeiro, Montevideo and Buenos Aires, see Salles, Tome III, 41–49.

period in his excellent study of the European cable companies in South America.[782]

The first working cable was laid between Uruguay and Argentine in late 1866. The River Plate Telegraph Company had been set up by two British men: John Proudfoot, a Liverpool merchant, and Matthew Gray, a Glasgow engineer, who was the Managing Director of the India Rubber, Gutta Percha and Telegraph Company. Proudfoot was primarily interested in trade between Britain and South America, while Gray's interest lay in the work these concessions would create for his company. The subscribers of the shares were mainly from Scotland and North West England, especially from Liverpool and Manchester.[783]

From the very beginning, the company proved to be a sound enterprise. When the line was connected with the land line between Argentine and Chile, established by the Transandine Telegraph Company in 1872, the River Plate Telegraph Company took the initiative by presenting itself as a quick carrier of messages between the western coast of South America and Europe. That was not exactly correct, but it is true that the telegraph shortened the duration of information transmission by several days at both ends of the journey. An urgent message could be sent from England or France to Lisbon by telegraph, and taken from there by a steamer to Montevideo, to be forwarded to Valparaiso or Santiago de Chile again by telegraph.[784] This was a similar system to the one used on the North Atlantic route in the earlier years, when the Atlantic cable did not yet work but there were telegraph lines from New York to Newfoundland and from Holyhead to Liverpool.[785]

The company advertised that 12 days could be saved in the duration of information transmission between Europe and Valparaiso by using its connections instead of the normal steamship service. In fact the effect of the combined services by mail steamers and telegraph was even greater. While the Pacific Steam Navigation Company sailed from Liverpool to Valparaiso in 42 days and in the other direction four days longer, the trip by their mail steamer between Lisbon and Montevideo took only 23 to 25 days. Thus the combined services shortened the duration of urgent information transmission by 19 to 21 days – even without the help of the Atlantic submarine telegraph cable, which was established between Portugal and Brazil by the Brazilian Submarine Telegraph Company in 1874.[786]

---

782 Jorma Ahvenainen, *The European Cable Companies in South America before the First World War* (Jyväskylä, 2004), 11–30. Also for further development of the international cable business in South America the book is highly recommended, passim.

783 Ahvenainen (2004) , 31–33.

784 Ahvenainen (2004), 35. – The inter-European lines were naturally used already in the 1860s.

785 See Chapter V.4.

786 See Ahvenainen (2004), 35, 92–96. The Pacific Steam Navigation Company's figures are factual average sailing times. The planned duration of sailings were 41 days to Valparaiso and 43 days back home. The planned duration of sailings between Lisbon and Montevideo were 23 and 24 days respectively. (Howat, 200) – The western coast of South America received telegraph connections between Valparaiso and Callao in 1875–1876, and the line between Panama and Callao was finally built by the Central and South American Telegraph Company in 1882. See Ahvenainen (2004), 111.

The early South American telegrams were expensive, however, and could certainly be used for urgent information only. The rate between Montevideo and Buenos Aires for ten words was Frs. 15.75 at a time when the Anglo-American company between Britain and the United States charged Frs. 50 for ten words. The tariff between Montevideo and Valparaiso was Frs. 21 for the first ten words and Frs. 13.10 for each further ten words. And the rate of a submarine telegram between Lisbon and Montevideo was Frs. 18,125 – per word.[787]

Researchers who are fascinated by the technical development expressed by the telegraph often overestimate its importance in overall information transmission. For example, Ahvenainen writes about the opening of the public cable between Europe and Buenos Aires in July 1875: 'Before this date a message sent as surface mail from Europe had taken one month to reach Rio de Janeiro, and a few days longer to reach Buenos Aires. Now, with the opening of the telegraph line, it took less than a day. This was a very great change in the speed of global communication.'[788]

It was of course a huge change, if the news could be received on the same or following day after being sent, and the value of the telegraph in transmitting news can certainly not be overestimated. Also in particular businesses it was important to receive the news in brief, or to send a 'buy' or 'sell' order as quickly as possible.

Yet the difference in information transmission to South America before and after the direct submarine telegraph line was opened was not as much as one month, but only about two and a half weeks. The duration of information transmission between the British ports and Rio de Janeiro had reduced constantly from 60–70 days by the Falmouth packets in the 1820s to 22 days by steamship from port to port in the 1870s.[789] If the already existing telegraph line between Britain and Portugal was used for part of the trip, the duration of information transmission between London and Rio de Janeiro was no more than 18 days.

As time is always measured in days and hours, one cannot actually talk about the speed increase in relative terms. Even if the use of telegraph undoubtedly was 20 times faster than the steamship service, it could seldom be utilized to such a degree in business communications. It naturally depended on the size of the business, but most companies probably did not have daily use for such new and expensive information systems. The decision on the acceptability of information costs depended each time on the issue at hand. In many cases, it was good enough to send the information by ordinary mail as usual. As bulk mail and telegraph were often used to complement each other, it is difficult if not impossible to calculate precise consecutive information circles after the intercontinental telegraph had been introduced.

Table 63 shows the reasons for the most remarkable changes in information transmission between Britain and Brazil between the 1820s and the 1870s.

787 Ahvenainen (2004), 33, 35, 122.
788 Ahvenainen (2004), 80. For a different view, see Kaukiainen (2001), 1–6, 21–23.
789 Royal Mail Line average between Southampton and Rio de Janeiro in 1875. Calculated from the sailing lists of Howat, 140.

The first notable reduction in the length of sailings took place in the 1830s, when the Admiralty changed part of the old men-of-wars to purpose-built packets in the Falmouth service. This change from one sailing ship type to another reduced the length of the voyage by ten days on average.

TABLE 63. *Duration of information transmission by sail, steam and telegraph between Rio de Janeiro and Falmouth / Southampton, 1820–1875.*

Year	Means of information transmission	Duration in days, average per year	Comments
1820	Falmouth packet	62.2	Original packets
1850	Falmouth packet	51.9	Part of the packets changed to new purpose-built vessels
1851	Royal Mail steamer	29.7	Change from sail to steam
1859	Royal Mail steamer	25.2	Streamlined route, new vessels
1872	Royal Mail steamer	22.0	Competition leading to a streamlined schedule
1872	Telegraph from England to Lisbon, steamer to Rio	~18	Combination of services was possible since the international telegraph lines were established in Europe in the 1850s and 1860s.
1875	Telegraph	~1	Information transmission depart from physical transport

Sources: The average numbers of sailing days are calculated from the sailing lists of Howat, 12–13, 85–86, 129, 132–133, 137–139.

The most striking change took place from the beginning of 1851, when the Royal Mail steamers replaced the Falmouth packets on the South American route. While the average packet sailing from Rio de Janeiro to Falmouth had taken 52 days, the steamers made the trip in less than 30 days. Calculated in days, this was an even more important overnight change than the opening of the submarine cable line in 1875.

The development in steamship technology did not reduce the length of the voyage remarkably between the early 1850s and 1870s. The duration of the trip was shortened by one week during that time, but it was caused by the streamlining of the route as much as by technological improvements. The reason for the humble progress in this respect is obviously that the Royal Mail Line started on the South American route 13 years later than the first pioneering steamers crossed the Atlantic. Most of the early problems in technology had already been solved, and the South American route could be served comparatively well from the very beginning.

The difference between the combined telegraph and mail steamship services, which had been in use for several years already, and the direct submarine telegraph line between Europe and Brazil was only 2.5 weeks.

Naturally the fast telegraph service enabled numerous information circles per year – in theory perhaps a hundred or more. Nevertheless, there were the time differences, and all kinds of technical delays could occur when sending the messages through different stations. The rates were high, and there was of course no need to send messages all the time. Although the telegraph did not perhaps revolutionise the South American trade, it was undoubtedly the fastest tool for those cases where delivery of urgent information was essential.

VII East India and Australasia

Breaking a Monopoly

Communications with the Asian trade ports by the East India Company – The development after the abolition of the EIC monopoly – Private merchantmen as mail carriers, the forgotten period in postal history – Merchant ships as news carriers – Steaming via the Cape of Good Hope vs. the Overland route – Fighting against the time of changes

Before the monopoly of the honourable East India Company (EIC) was abolished in 1813, nearly all information transmission between Britain and East India, or other Asian regions in which the British had trade interests, was carried by the East Indiamen. For China, this was the practice until 1833.[790]

It is not possible to describe here the whole story of the EIC. The archives of the India Record Office in the British Library in London keep 14 shelf kilometres of documents concerning the Company's history during three and a half centuries. A brief overview may still be necessary to understand the historical context.

The EIC was established in 1600 to take a share of the East Indian spice and textile trade then dominated by Portugal. In the mid-18th century the Company was purely a commercial enterprise which imported and exported goods from its factories, having trading posts in Calcutta, Madras and Bombay. By 1815, after a long period of wars, the Company ran the most powerful army in India, including the Bombay Marine, and ruled their

---

790 The EIC monopoly in the East India trade was modified by the British government in 1793 and abolished in 1813, with the aim of improving trade between Britain and India during the wartime. The company's commercial businesses ended with a further abolition of the China trade monopoly in 1833. The last trade vessels sailed back home in 1834. After that, up to the Sepoy Mutiny of 1857, the EIC activities in India were focused on the governmental duties of the presidencies, and then ceased. See Cain & Hopkins, 97, 282–288.

three presidencies from Fort William (Calcutta), Fort St. George (Madras) and Bombay Castle (Bombay & Surat). The Company's privileges in India included incomes from inland customs, tax on spirituous liquors, the salt and opium monopoly, administration of the Courts of Justice, police, etc. The EIC also had a trading post in Canton (Guangzhou), China, to trade tea for silver and later for Indian-grown opium. By the 1820s, when the British government had abolished the Company's monopoly on the other routes, the opium-tea trade was the only lucrative part of the business.[791]

There were also East India Companies in the Netherlands, France, Denmark, Scotland, Spain, Austria and Sweden. None of them gained as much importance in the whole Indian Ocean region in the long run, however, and the last companies were dissolved by the end of the Napoleonic wars.[792]

Until the 19th century, there was no other means to send mails to India or other trading posts east of the Cape than by ships of the different East India companies, which held their national monopolies on the Asian routes. All companies most certainly carried mails, but not much is known about the numbers of letters or any postal details. As only the British East India Company survived after 1815, this study will focus on its mail services, as well as on the use of private merchantmen as mail carriers after the abolition of the monopoly, and on the start of a government subsidised steamship service (see Chapter VII.2).

791 Lawrence James, *The Rise and Fall of the British Empire* (London, 2000), 24–26, 123, 129–138; Robertson, B 26. – Two recently published volumes of conference papers relating to the EIC and the China trade are worth further examination: H.V. Bowen, Margarette Lincoln & Nigel Rigby (eds): *The Worlds of the East India Company* (Suffolk, 2004); and Harding, Richard, Jarvis, Adrian & Kennerley Alston (eds.): *British Ships in China Seas: 1700 to the Present Day* (Liverpool, 2004). – For the EIC's privileges in India, mentioned above, see *BPP, Colonies, East India 3* (1812). The Fifth Report from the Select Committee on the Affairs of the East India Company, 1812, 12. – The military aspects of EIC activities are not discussed here, but to understand the specific role of the Company it may be useful to mention that the EIC's compensation for military expeditions at the Cape of Good Hope, Ceylon, Manila, Malacca and Molucca during the war was widely discussed in the Parliament. The Company wanted to get compensation for the shipowners for equipping the vessels with provision, wood, gun powder, and wages for the officers and seamen. Although the EIC played an important role in British expansion in Asia, the counterargument against compensation was that the company had also gained remarkable profits e.g. from the spice trade in Ceylon. See *BPP, Colonies, East India 2* (1810–1812). Third and Fourth Reports from the Select Committee of the Affairs of the East India Company. Appendix 47, 3–7. – The export of opium from India to China caused two Opium Wars between Britain and China, in 1839–1842 and 1856–1858. The importance of this trade can be verified from the export figures. Between 1848 and 1852, the earliest figures available, the export of opium from India was worth 61.5 million rupees on average, while the other exports were valued as follows: cotton 29.4 million, cotton manufactures 7.7 million, jute 1.3 million, jute manufactures 2.0 million, rice 7.6 million, and tea 0.4 million rupees. For the Opium Wars, see James, 236–238; for the statistics, see B.R. Mitchell, *International Historical Statistics. Africa, Asia & Oceania 1750–1988* (New York, 1995), 635.

792 The relationship between the British and Dutch East India Companies is well described by Femme S. Gaastra in 'War, Competition and Collaboration: Relations between the English and Dutch East India Company in the Seventeenth and Eighteenth Centuries', in Bowen, Lincoln & Rigby, 49–68.

Between 1761 and 1834, no fewer than 570 vessels sailed from London to East India or China on behalf of the British EIC. Some of them made only one 'double voyage', as the round trip was called on the East India route, while the long-lived ones in the early 19th century were able to make ten or 11 double voyages, the record being 14. Some 30 of them, mainly small 100–300-ton ships sailed as 'packets' for the company's important mails. They were sent out only once or twice a year, and thus did not form any regular service. The total number of voyages during the last 73 years of the company's commercial activities – the 'packets' excluded – was 2,451.[793]

The largest East Indiamen, built in the 1790s and early 19th century, were about 1,200 tons or even more. The vessels registered at 1,300 to 1,400 tons were mainly in service from 1817 until the disposal of the merchant fleet in 1834. The number of crew of the largest ships was standardized to 130. All the vessels were heavily armed, resembling men-of-war and, if necessary, took offensive as well as defensive action. Traditions were of the highest order, and the Marine Service was essentially a *corps d'elite*.[794]

Most ships sailed from London for the eastern waters during the spring, and returned within one or two years. The Company stated in a Parliamentary hearing in 1810 that the favourable season was considered to be mid-November to mid-March – no matter whether the voyage was from England or from India. As the homeward cargo was generally more valuable than the outward cargo, preference was given to sailing from India, rather than from England, in the favourable season.[795] In practice this meant that the ships often stayed in India and especially in China for several months before starting their homeward voyages. As Jean Sutton points out in a recent study,[796] the long stays in Canton were due not only to the monsoons, but also to the complicated and time-consuming trading system conducted by the Chinese authorities. There were consequent long delays in getting answers to mails sent from Europe.

The long passage normally started from England, with an East Indiaman being refitted and 'coming afloat' at her moorings in London. When the cargo

---

793 The figures are calculated from the lists published by Robertson. The 'packets' made 55 voyages to Asian ports, mainly to India, during 1761–1814. The lists originate from Hardy's last edition of 'Register of Ships Employed in the Service of the East India Company'. By extracting an analysis from many thousands of entries, Robertson has formed and published a very useful alphabetical list of all the East Indiamen that sailed during 1761–1834. See Robertson, B 31 – B 41.

794 See Robertson, B 29; Jean Sutton 'Lords of the East: the ships of the East India Company' in Harding, Jarvis & Kennerley, 25–31. A well known earlier study about the maritime service of the EIC, its ships, men and life on board, voyages and famous fights was published in the late 1940s by Sir Evan Cotton (ed. Sir Charles Fawcett): *East Indiamen. The East India Company's Maritime Service* (London, 1949). The political connections between the Parliament and the EIC during the last fifty years of the Company's commercial history are discussed by C.H. Philips in *The East India Company 1784–1834* (Manchester, 1968).

795 *BPP, Colonies, East India 2...* Appendix 47, 140. – It has also been stated that there was real reluctance at Lloyds to insure vessels going to India between June and January. See Geoffrey Eibl-Kaye, 'The Indian Mails 1814 to 1819. Negotiations between the Post Office and the East India Company' in *The London Philatelist*, Volume 113, April 2004, 113:86.

796 Sutton, 22–25.

FIG. 28. *The letter dated in Meerut, near Delhi in North India, on 22.4.1806 was handstamped (on the reverse) by the Bengal G. P. O. in Calcutta some five months later in September, to be carried to England by the* Tigris, *one of the East Indiamen. The* Tigris *was on her 2nd round trip (out of six) to India. After a rather normal five-to-six months sailing around Africa, the letter was received in London on 14.4.1807 – almost a year after being written.*

was stowed, she was taken down to Gravesend, where 'goods in private trade', supplies, water, livestock and finally most of the passengers were taken on board. In peace time she then proceeded to the Downs off Deal, to meet with the rest of the division of East Indiamen with which she was to sail. Passengers who had travelled by road to Deal embarked, and the convoy sailed on the first favourable wind. In times of war, the ships usually sailed to Portsmouth, assembled in convoy there and proceeded under the protection and orders of an escorting man-of-war.[797]

Before the Post Office Act of 1815, there was no packet mail service by the Post Office to the East. Letters were 'handed in' to the EIC ships – sometimes in Navy vessels – in bags sent from the Post Office or Government Departments or the EIC Office mainly at Gravesend, or they were brought on board by the passengers. Many senders, particularly the merchant community, waited until the last opportunity and then dispatched their letters to Deal or Portsmouth to be put on board there. The mails were only subject to the normal ship letter charges levied by the Post Office, and the inland postage. The EIC did not receive compensation for the service. The free transit was a great benefit to the Post Office, as a normal packet mail service on such a long route would have been very expensive. On the other hand, the service was very slow (see Fig. 28). The East Indiamen

797 Robertson, B 29.

were not designed to be fast mail carriers and their main interest was in trade.[798]

The departing convoy of East Indiamen normally took the course to Madeira and then with the N.E. winds towards the coast of Brazil, endeavouring to cross the equator at between 20° and 25° W. After slow progress in the Variables the next objective was to gain a latitude between 30° and 40° S. and take advantage of the strong westerly winds. The ships then steered to run down their easting in the 'roaring forties', eventually approaching the Cape of Good Hope from S. or even S.E. Most convoys called at the Cape for water and provisions, usually essential after two or three months at sea. Letters for St. Helena were normally landed at the Cape, to be picked up and forwarded by homeward sailing vessels.[799]

The ships bound directly for China continued on the forties until nearing the west coast of Australia. Then they continued on that latitude turning northward up the east coast of Australia, via New Guinea and the east coast of the Philippine Islands, then N.W. to Canton. Alternatively, they sailed northward at about longitude 100 E. for the Timor Sea, via 'Pitt's passage' and the Moluccas, then east of the Philippines to Canton. The convoys for India left the Cape on one of several routes depending on the season and prevailing monsoon, using the 'inner passage' by the Mozambique Channel, watering at Comoro Islands, and then the 'eight degree' or 'nine degree' passage to Bombay, or using the 'middle passage' to the east of Madagascar, watering at Mauritius. Ships for Madras and Calcutta sailed more N. or N.E., often calling at Ceylon before proceeding up the Coromandel Coast.[800]

Although navigation in the Indian Ocean offered its own problems, the critical part of any outward voyage from Europe was in the Atlantic. A ship which failed to make Cape Recife (in Brazil) could easily lose a further four or six weeks in making a second attempt, and would then need to water on the Brazilian coast before continuing. It was nearly impossible to sail directly from Europe to the Cape of Good Hope. Decisions regarding the three main turning points all had to be taken in the open ocean by the best means available: navigation by latitude, lead and lookout, lunar observations and later the chronometer. The effects of currents were especially difficult to calculate.[801] It sometimes happened that an East Indiaman or several of them parted the fleet and were never heard of again. Stranding on an unknown shore could be as

---

798 Robertson, B 30; Eibl-Kaye, April 2004, 113:78.
799 Robertson, B 29–30. Due to the prevailing winds and currents, sailing ships normally called at Madeira on the way outward and at St. Helena on the way home. Thus, letters from London to St. Helena were first carried twice across the Atlantic, via the coast of Brazil to South Africa and from there, after a varying delay at port, by another ship to St. Helena. This took at least four months, but if there were no homeward sailing ships available at the Cape, as often was the case, there could be a further delay of several weeks or even months. On the other hand, letters from St. Helena to London were carried directly in about two months. (Calculated from the maritime intelligence in *Lloyd's List* 1812–1813 and 1832–1833.)
800 Robertson, B 30.
801 For details of the development of navigation and knowledge of sea routes, see Andrew S. Cook, 'Establishing the Sea Routes to India and China: Stages in the Development of Hydrographical Knowledge' in Bowen, Lincoln & Rigby, 119–136.

fateful as a hurricane or an attack by the enemy. Due to the many uncertainties at sea, it was common to write duplicates and triplicates of letters to ensure that at least one of them arrived safely at the destination port.[802]

Before focusing on the time period after the Napoleonic wars, it may be useful to shortly examine the EIC's performance as a mail carrier in 1812, the last year before the abandonment of the monopoly in India. Table 64 shows the departure dates and the destinations of the East Indiamen leaving from England in 1812.

TABLE 64. *Departures and destinations of the East Indiamen, 1812.*

Departure from Portsmouth	# of ships	for Bombay	for Madras	for Bengal	for Ceylon	for China	for Bencoolen	for Penang	for Batavia
4.1.	7	5	-	1	-	6	1	-	-
1.3.	6	-	5	1	-	5	-	1	-
10.3.	7	1	4	7	-	-	-	-	-
25.3.	7	-	-	-	-	7	-	-	-
8.4.	8	1	7	8	-	-	-	-	
15.5.	8	1	-	5	2	-	-	-	2
4.6.	5	-	-	5	-	-	1	-	-
14.7.	2	-	-	2	-	-	-	-	-
21.9.	1	-	-	1	-	1	-	-	-
24.12.	6	5	-	-	-	6	1	-	-
total	57	13	16	30	2	25	3	1	2

Source: Lloyd's Register for Underwriters 1813. 'Ships in the East India Company's service &c.' – Several ships intended to trade in more than one port, making the total of destination ports more than 57. Additionally, there were two ships sailing for Australia.

As can be noticed from the table, even if there were 57 ships sailing to the East that year, there were in fact only ten occasions to send mail to Asia as the ships sailed in convoys. Additionally, there were only a few occasions to send mail to each destination. In five of the ten convoys there were ships sailing for

802 In 1780, the East Indiaman *Grosvenor*, homeward bound and full of passengers including many prominent members of Bengal society, ran ashore on the African coast 500 miles from the Cape. Although 135 persons reached shore, none was ever heard of again, except for four of the crew who eventually reached Cape Town by foot. Between 1761 and 1834, eleven of the 541 East Indiamen (the 'packets' excluded) disappeared without trace on the voyage. Additionally, 48 were lost at sea, four were condemned for other reasons, 15 were burnt, another 15 were captured by the French, three more were captured but recaptured, and one ship was blown up. Six vessels remained in India. Calculated from Robertson, B 31–41.

FIG. 29. *The East Indiamen usually sailed in convoy to minimize safety risks. The heavily armed vessels looked like men-of-war and also acted like them, if needed. This impressive fleet of East Indiamen in the China Seas was painted by William John Huggins, ca 1820–1830. © National Maritime Museum London.*

Bombay, 13 in total. The ships for Madras, 16 in total, sailed in three convoys in March–April. Almost every convoy included ships for Bengal (Calcutta), 30 in total. The 25 ships for China (Canton) sailed in five convoys.

There were also three ships sailing for Bencoolen, Sumatra, one for Ceylon, one for Penang off the Malayan coast, and one for Batavia in Java during the year. If the mail-carrying ship was not sailing directly to China but via India, as usually was the case, the duration of the mails for China lengthened remarkably.

Four of the convoys to the East departed within six weeks in March–April 1812, while there was a five-month period from mid-July to the end of December, when only one ship sailed to Asia.

The duration of sailings varied depending on the weather and navigation, as well as the size and load of the ships, etc. An average 'double voyage', i.e. the round trip from London to the Asian ports and back home, took one year and five months.[803] This included at least two to three months spent at ports in India, and even a longer time in China.

Only occasional trips were made to Southeast Asia. These journeys were for Batavia, Bencoolen, and Penang. At least two ships made a call at Malacca on their way to China.[804]

803 The figures referring to the voyages shown in Table 64 have been calculated from *Lloyd's Register for Underwriters 1813*, *'Ships in the East India Company's service, &c.'*; *Lloyd's List* 1812 and 1813, passim.
804 See *Lloyd's List* 14.5.1813.

There were no EIC 'packets' sailing to India between 1809 and 1814, and only one sailed during the last-mentioned year.[805] Thus, the East Indiamen were the only means of sending mail to Indian or other Asian ports in 1812, in addition to the men-of-war. All the EIC ships sailing for China were large, over 1,200-ton vessels, while the size of the ships exclusively for India varied between 500–950 tons. Of the 32 smaller ships, 14 were chartered by the EIC for one, four, six or eight voyages. Most of them departed together on 10 March or 8 April, 1812.[806]

As Lloyd's agents in various Asian ports did not normally report the exact sailing dates, and only seldom the arrival dates, even if the arrival itself had been announced in *Lloyd's List*, it is not possible to draw conclusions about the time spent at different ports, or the time between a mail arrival from London and the following ship departure. Thus, it is not possible to calculate information circles from the 1812 material. A couple of examples may clarify how business information transmission between Britain and the Asian trading posts worked at that time.

On 1 March, 1812, five large East Indiamen sailed from Portsmouth in convoy, protected by the Navy warship *Pique Frigate*. Of the East Indiamen the *Cuffnells*, the *David Scott*, the *Royal George* and the *Winchelsea* were on the way to China via Madras, at which port they arrived on 11 June, after a rather fast 102 days of sailing. The *Surat Castle* took a route for Penang and from there directly to China. According to maritime intelligence from Madras, the four ships 'were to sail for China about 25th July', but due to some unknown delays, they sailed on 16 September.

Further on, we only know about the movements of the *David Scott* and the *Royal George*. They were reported to have arrived together at Malacca on 25 October and in China, meaning Canton, on 13 January 1813. The ships were reported to be 'off Portsmouth' on 9 August of the same year, and they arrived at Gravesend on 13 August. The two other vessels *Cuffnells* and *Winchelsea* had arrived two months earlier, on 7 June, together with the fifth ship *Surat Castle*, probably having sailed together from China.[807]

The next vessels to sail for India departed from Portsmouth on 10 March, 1812. They sailed to Madeira in a huge convoy including about one hundred ships bound for the West Indies, South America, Africa, Madeira and East India, and were protected by the warship *Loire Frigate*. The ships *Asia, Astell, Bengal, Earl St. Vincent* and *Prince Regent* were bound for Madras and Bengal. The *Chapman* and *Lady Carrington* were on the way to Bombay and Bengal, while the *Coldstream* and *Larkins* were headed for St. Helena and Bengal. They were all chartered, medium size Indiamen between 550 and 950 tons.[808]

The *Asia,* together with the *Earl St. Vincent* and *Prince Regent*, probably also the *Astell*, arrived in Madras on 13 July, after 125 days of sailing. The

805 Robertson, B 27.
806 *Lloyd's Register for Underwriters 1813.*
807 *Lloyd's Register for Underwriters 1813; Lloyd's List* 23.10.1812, 9.2.1813, 14.5.1813, 4.6.1813, 8.6.1813, 10.8.1813 and 16.8.1813.
808 *Lloyd's Register for Underwriters 1813.*

Bengal had arrived four days earlier. They all sailed together for Bengal and arrived at St. Helena on their home voyage, being reported to have sailed on 26 November. They arrived at Gravesend on 16 May, 1813, with no reason for the delay given.[809]

The *Coldstream* and *Larkins* had arrived at St. Helena on 3 June and sailed from there for India on 7 July. They departed from Bengal on 27 December and arrived together at St. Helena on 16 March, 1813. Finally, the *Larkins* arrived at Gravesend together with a convoy including the *Cuffnells, Surat Castle* and *Winchelsea,* from China, on 7 June while the *Coldstream* was accompanied by the *David Scott* and *Royal George*, also arriving from China, on 13 August.[810]

Due to missing information and uncertainties in the newspaper intelligence as a whole, and especially at wartime, we cannot draw many conclusions from the details above. It seems clear that the sailings were conducted purely for trade purposes, including the administrative needs of the company in India, and that the mails arrived when they arrived. It is difficult to estimate whether the ships that sailed directly back to Britain from India without continuing to China could take with them answers to letters sent by earlier Indiamen. At least the ships *Asia, Astell* etc., which arrived at Gravesend on 16 May, 1813, must have carried answers to letters delivered by themselves on the outward journey as well as to letters delivered by the large Indiamen that had sailed earlier but continued to China. Even in this case the fastest answers were taken home by the same ships which took the letters in the other direction. An answer to a letter for India was thus received in somewhat over fourteen months, and the answer from China in somewhat over fifteen months.[811]

It was officially stated that it took 180 days on average to send a letter from Britain to India.[812] This did not mean, however, that the duration of an average information circle would have been approximately one year. The departures from the destination ports were seasonally limited and even the announced departure dates could be postponed by months. The sailing routes and ports of call varied, and several problems could delay the ship's voyage. When private traders entered the East Indian markets in growing numbers after emancipation, the slow and very unpredictable system of information transmission had to be reviewed. This took place between 1815 and 1819.

The development after the abolition of the EIC monopoly

The closing of the European ports by Napoleon and the long continuance of the war with France had led to a decline in British trade. For this and several other reasons, the Government made a decision to allow outside merchants admission to the Indian markets. After a hard struggle to postpone the evil day, the EIC finally lost the monopoly in India under the Charter Act of 1813.

---

809 *Lloyd's List* 6.11.1812, 9.2.1813, 16.4.1813, and 18.5.1813.
810 *Lloyd's List* 24.7.1812, 8.9.1812, 9.2.1813, 11.5.1813, 11.5.1813, 8.6.1813, 10.8.1813 and 16.8.1813.
811 Calculated from *Lloyd's Register for Underwriters 1813,* 'Ships in the East India Company's service, &c.'; *Lloyd's List* 1812 and 1813, passim
812 Eibl-Kaye, April 2004, 113:85.

Private traders, who had been allowed to ship goods only in the 'privilege' space of the EIC ships, were now able to use their own vessels, although they had to be at least 350 tons burthen. In addition, they had to obtain a licence for each voyage from the EIC upon payment of fee, and the ships could only use a few specific ports in India: Bombay, Madras and Calcutta, as well as the port of Penang. Private traders could not ship goods direct from India to the ports of continental Europe, and, to protect the West Indian sugar trade, an extra duty was charged on sugars imported from the East Indies over and above the duty levied on the West Indian sugars.[813]

Despite the restrictions, private trade proved to be more profitable and extensive than that of the EIC, and a consolidating Act of 1823 declared that this trade might be carried on by British vessels with all places within the limits of the EIC charter, except for China. Finally, the Charter Act of 1833 took away the exclusive privilege of trade with China, too, with effect from 22 April 1834, and by the end of that year the last of the East Indiamen had been sold to new owners.[814]

Although the war continued till 1815, the number of ships sailing for India more than doubled during the first years of free trade – from 57 in 1812 to 135 in 1815. In 1825, the number of ships sailing for India and other Asian destinations was 220 and in 1832, the last whole year of the EIC monopoly in China, the number of outgoing ships was 280. Additionally, there were an increasing number of ships sailing for Australia, frequently returning via Asian ports. Their number was six in 1815, 50 in 1825, and 114 in 1832.[815]

The opening up of the Indian market had several consequences and side effects. One was that imports from the mother country increased progressively. For example, whereas 30 British ships entered the port of Calcutta during the 1814–1815 sailing season, this increased to 91 in 1816–1817 and to 132 in 1817–1818. After the war, American traders also frequently visited Calcutta, but not usually the other Indian ports, which were further away. The lively traffic soon caused a glut in the market and the over-heated situation calmed down within a few years. Fluctuations would be typical in the future, too.[816]

813 K. Charlton, 'Liverpool and the East India Trade' in *Northern History. A Review of the History of the North of England. Volume VII. Reprint.* (University of Leeds, England, 1972), 54–55; Cotton, 125.

814 Cotton, 125. Many of the old East Indiamen continued in Chinese waters, however. According to the statistics from the port of Hong Kong, 11 former East Indiamen, about 1,200 tons on average, arrived at that port between August 1841 and December 1842, three of them even twice. Most of the vessels were carrying government stores from Britain, or from other colonies. See 'Ships arriving Hong Kong Aug. 41 – Dec. 42. From the 'Chinese Repository' for Jan. 1843' Appendix 41-B in Lee C. Scamp, *Far East Mail Ship Itineraries. British, Indian, French, American, and Japanese Mail Ship Schedules 1840–1880.* Volume I. (Texas, 1997), 398–406.

815 Calculated from the statistics of *Lloyd's Register for Underwriters 1813, 1816, 1826,* and *1833.* – The word 'Australia' is used here and further in this study for the geographic areas known then as New South Wales and Van Diemen's Land (equivalent to the current Australian states of New South Wales and Tasmania).

816 The Liverpool merchants who had led the campaign against the EIC were among the first to send their vessels to India. The first ship, mentioned also in the British Parliamentary Papers in 1831–1832, was John Gladstone's *Kingsmill*, which sailed for Calcutta in May

From the business information transmission point of view, one of the main consequences of the changes in market conditions was that the need for communications with Asia quickly increased manifold, while at the same time the only mail carrier, the EIC, withdraw its interests from merchandise in India and concentrated on the China trade. Basically this meant that, although the Company continued to sail to India for its own purposes, sailings were less frequent than earlier and the Company had no interest in carrying mails under the rule of the Post Office.[817]

Now the Post Office was facing a new situation. The mail service to Asia needed to be organized without high expense, but as fast and reliably as possible. The Post Office never planned to have its own vessels for the Indian route, as it had in the North Atlantic, the West Indies and South America. The Indian Packet Letter Act of 1815 enabled the use of private merchant vessels as packets during periods when there were no EIC ships sailing for the East. These ships had to be carefully chosen from the departing vessels, taking into account Lloyd's recommendations. Thus, between October 1815 and October 1816, 16 vessels carried official mail from Britain to India. Five of them were naval vessels, four were East Indiamen (with three of them sailing in a convoy together with one of the naval vessels) and seven were private merchantmen. Most of the mails (six out of seven) were carried by naval vessels from India to Britain.[818]

The system was not very successful. The naval vessels were warships and did not sail for business information transmission purposes. They did not call at all ports needed, but sailed directly from London or normally Portsmouth to Madras and Calcutta. There was also great difficulty in obtaining tenders from private ships for mail carrying, as they did not want any restrictions in their stay in India, the trade there being the main purpose of their voyages. For users, the postage fee for packet letters was considerably higher than for

1814. It was followed by two other Liverpool vessels in 1815 and no less than 17 more ships in 1816. In 1832, they already numbered 34. ('A List of Vessels that have cleared out from the Port of Liverpool for the East Indies, since the passing of an Act of Parliament 21st July 1813...' in *Liverpool Street Directories, 1818*. Appendix, 140–141.) For the statistics, see 'Number of Ships and Amount of Tonnage Entered Inwards at the Port of Calcutta between 1793 and 1831' in *BPP, Colonies, East India 8* (1831–1832). Appendix to the Report from Select Committee on the Affairs of the East India Company with an Index [II Finance and Accounts] Part II, Commercial, 772, 786. – Not all vessels under the British flag in Indian ports had arrived from England, however. There were dozens of Indian 'country ships', carrying the British flag and with British officers and lascar crews, sailing between India and other Asian ports. In addition to exporting cotton, they were also the main carriers of opium to China on behalf of the EIC. See Anne Bulley, 'The country ships from India' in Richard Harding, Adrian Jarvis and Alston Kennerley (eds.), *British Ships in China Seas: 1700 to the Present Day* (Liverpool, 2004), 35–41.

817 The value of the EIC's merchandise exports from England to India decreased from £710,700 in 1814–1815 to £71,900 in 1824–1825 and £2,600 in 1826–1827. Moreover, whereas the value of military stores carried by the Company to St. Helena and India was £944,100 in 1826–1827, it had decreased to £92,000 by 1830–1831. See *BPP, Colonies, East India 8*...An Account of the Exports by the East India Company for each Year, from 1814; distinguishing Military Stores from Merchandise. Appendix, No. 26, 767.

818 See Geoffrey Eibl-Kaye, 'The Indian Mails 1814 to 1819. Administration of the Packet Service and its Demise ' in *The London Philatelist*, Volume 113, May 2004, 113:114–119.

MAP 8. *Mail routes to Australasia in the mid-19th century.*

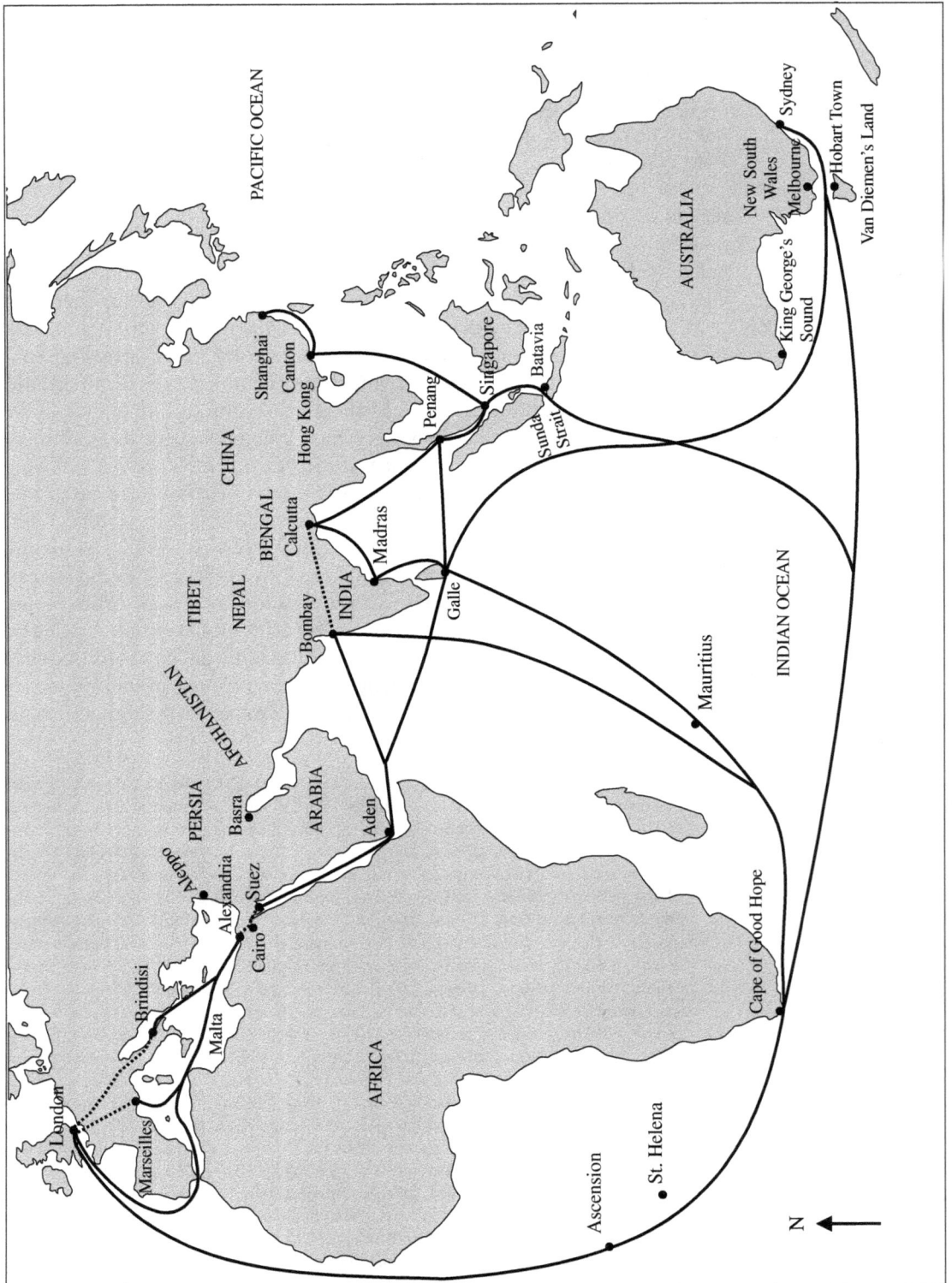

private ship letters. The Act of 1819 finally ended the confusion. All letters to and from India would be treated as ship letters, carried by any vessel, and the charge would be the same, 4d sea postage plus the inland letter rate for landing. Outgoing letters of less than 3 oz were charged sea postage of 2d.[819]

Private merchantmen as mail carriers – the forgotten period in postal history

The period from 1819 to the mid-1830s, when the overland route via Suez was gradually brought into use, has remained untouched in the history of communications. Those scholars who study the history of the EIC are generally not very interested in the late period, and postal historians have found it difficult to collect maritime intelligence on the hundreds or even thousands of private merchant vessels. Well known authorities in postal history have even claimed that 'before 1837 the only means [for letter communication with India] lay round the Cape of Good Hope in ships belonging to the East India Company'.[820]

John K. Sidebottom briefly mentions private merchantmen as mail carriers in *The Overland Mail*: '...the mail sent via the Cape to India amounted to only 150 bags a year, but, of course, very many more letters went to India without passing through the Post Office. The Cape service – operated by private ships including 'East Indiamen' – was roughly a weekly one...'[821] The present study is apparently the first attempt to find out how communications, especially from the business information transmission point of view, really functioned between British and Asian ports during that period.

The number of private vessels sailing for Indian ports grew steadily throughout the period between 1812, the last year of the EIC monopoly in India, and 1832, the last year of its monopoly in China. There were annual fluctuations, but the general trend was upwards. British ships dominated the Indian trade. After the Napoleonic wars, other nationalities also took a share of it, however. Vessels under American, French or Portuguese flags could be seen at the port of Calcutta although not often in the other Presidencies. In practice, most mails for Britain and other places in Europe were carried by British merchantmen, naval vessels here excluded.[822]

Table 65 shows how the number of departures from British ports for Asian destinations grew with the gradual abolition of the EIC privileges.

Although mail carrying was not a business for shipowners, the improved communications undoubtedly served trade, giving more frequent opportunities for information transmission. The more ships there were

---

819 See Eibl-Kaye, 'The Indian Mails...' May 2004, 113:114–124; Robertson, D 21 – D 25.

820 Moubray & Moubray, 180.

821 John K. Sidebottom, *The Overland Mail. A Postal Historical Study of the Mail Route to India* (Perth, Scotland, 1948), 48. He refers to General Post Office records.

822 The Americans were frequent visitors in Calcutta in the 1790s, but disappeared during the last war years. Detailed statistics of the major Indian ports in 1793–1830 can be found in BPP, *Colonies, East India 8,...* Appendix, No. 30, 772–839.

TABLE 65. *The departures of vessels from British ports to India, China & other Asian destinations during some selected years between 1812 and 1832.*

	1812	1815	1825	1832
January	7	11	15	11
February	–	10	18	19
March	20	2	11	22
April	8	26	13	16
May	8	26	27	28
June	5	8	26	36
July	2	5	22	35
August	–	4	6	24
September	1	10	18	21
October	–	4	15	27
November	–	3	12	15
December	6	–	2	3
total	57	109+26 =135	185+35 =220	257+29 =280

Source: Lloyd's Register for Underwriters 1813, 1816, 1826, 1833; Lloyd's List of the above-mentioned years, passim. The figures with a '+' are departures, which were published without an exact sailing date. The ships to New South Wales and Van Diemen's Land are not included in the figures. Their total number was 98 in 1832.

sailing on the route, the more even was the distribution of departures within a calendar year. While the former East Indiamen had carefully chosen the best winds for their sailings, growing competition forced shipowners to send their vessels out at any time of the year. This naturally meant that there were more ships arriving from and departing for India and other Asian ports throughout the year, and letters could be answered more often.

To get a clear picture of how communications worked, how long it took to carry mails from Britain to different Asian ports or to get answers to them, how frequent the traffic was on different routes and what the major problems were, one specific year has been examined in more detail. This year is 1832, the last 'normal' year when the large East Indiamen were still in the China service. At that time, merchant vessels offered the only means of sending letters to Asian ports, while steamers had not yet taken on their future role as mail carriers.

The ships sailing from Britain to India or other Asian trading posts, including Australia, in 1832 have been followed throughout their voyages for two and a half years until the end of June 1834, by which time most of them had returned home. Some vessels were still on their way at that time, and several would never return. Many vessels were fast enough to start – and in some cases even complete – a second voyage within the time period. Only the round trips which started in 1832 have been taken into account, however.

By 1832, the number of ship departures from Britain for the Asian and Australian ports – China still being the monopoly of the EIC – had increased to approximately 400 per year. Most of the ships were individually sailing private merchantmen and, as it was peace time, there was no need to sail in convoys. However, ship captains still preferred to sail in company with one or a few other vessels to avoid security risks.[823]

Due to insufficient data in some 20 cases, 378 of the approximately 400 merchant vessels have been included in this study. Of these ships, 128 sailed for Madras and Bengal and 76 for Bombay. In addition, 37 vessels, 20 of them being large East Indiamen on their last voyages under the flag of the EIC, sailed for China mainly via Indian ports but also directly via the Sunda Straits.[824]

The Indian trade ports were not the only places of interest east of the Cape of Good Hope. Equalisation of the duty on sugar from Mauritius in the mid-1820s had rapidly increased the export of sugar from that island.[825] In 1832, no fewer than 47 ships were reported to have sailed from Britain for Mauritius as their main destination port. But even though the Liverpool merchants often referred to the growing Mauritius sugar trade as an example of the positive consequences of trade emancipation,[826] only three of the 47 vessels were in fact from Liverpool. Seven vessels came from Bristol, Glasgow and Edinburgh, and the rest from London.

The Southeast Asian ports were growing rapidly as well. New business opportunities had opened up after the war. Since the EIC expedition to Ceylon in the early 19th century, Colombo had become a frequently used port of call on the way to Bengal. The former Dutch Batavia became an often visited port on the way to and from China and Australia, and the newly established colony of Singapore, 'founded' by Sir Stamford Raffles as late as in 1819 and belonging to the British crown from the early 1830s, was visited by no fewer than 62 British vessels in 1832. 17 vessels also sailed for Manila in the Philippines.[827]

There was fast development in the Australian colonies, New South Wales and Van Diemen's Land, too, even though there was not much basis for any serious trade yet. After the United States gained independence in 1775, Britain had started to transport convicts to Australia. By the 1820s, the number of penal transports had increased significantly, and in the census of 1833, no fewer than 40,000 people out of the total Australian population of 60,000

---

823 This can be noticed from the sailing dates published by *Lloyd's List* in 1832, passim. The East Indiamen continued their old tradition and generally sailed together.
824 Calculated from the maritime intelligence published by *Lloyd's List* 1832–1834.
825 See Charlton, 63. – Sugar production at Mauritius grew from 10,481 tons in 1825 to 20,485 tons in 1826, and to 32,750 tons in 1830. See Noel Deerr: *The History of Sugar. Volume I.* (London, 1949), 203.
826 See Charlton, 63.
827 The figures have been calculated from the maritime intelligence published by *Lloyd's List* 1832–1834. – Batavia, Singapore and Manila were not usually ports of destination but ports of call on the way to somewhere else. Therefore the figures in table 66 give a different picture of their role in the Asian trade than the text above.

were convicts. The rest consisted of free emigrants, 10,000 of them being children under 12 years old. Some British administrative and military groups need to be added.[828]

The Australian colonies did not offer attractive business opportunities compared with the Asian countries. The purchasing power of the population was very limited and there was little to export.[829] The growing need for manufactured articles from Britain and the export of wool, together with the continuing emigrant and convict transports, nevertheless increased the traffic considerably.[830]

There were thus several types of business going on in the Indian Ocean in the early 1830s. In addition to the traditional East Indiamen sailing for India and China, there were private merchantmen on their way to India or some of the Southeast Asian ports. There was the Mauritius sugar trade and the various ships for Australia, many of which were carrying emigrants or convicts and arriving back home via different Asian ports.[831]

To differentiate these businesses, it may be useful to examine the sailings by the homeports of vessels. Before the emancipation, the trade with India and other related Asian ports was dominated by London, as the city was the domicile of the EIC. After 1815, Liverpool took a notable share of the Asian trade. Glasgow participated with a smaller share, while the other British port towns only sent a few vessels to Asia each year, if any.

By 1832 London had lost approximately a third of the Asian shipping business to its rival ports. One quarter of the sailings now departed from Liverpool. The other British ports together accounted for less than 10% of the sailings.

Table 66 shows that Calcutta was considered the most important destination by the London merchants. The Bengal area was still the cornerstone of the EIC, and would be for 25 more years. But the Liverpool merchants and shipowners were now equal with London in the Bombay trade, and they had taken a remarkable share of the business in Madras and Calcutta. No fewer than 60 vessels from Liverpool sailed for India in 1832 – more than one per week on average.[832]

---

828 See *BPP, Crime and Punishment, Transportation 2,* 1837. Report of the Select Committee on Transportation. Appendix, No. 10, 261.

829 By comparison, the populations of India and China were approx. 260 million and 395 million respectively in 1830. See Mitchell, 55.

830 The value of Australian wool exports grew from £35,000 in 1830 to £849,000 in 1840, and to £2,305,000 in 1850. Although wheat exports had also started by 1850, they were worth little for decades. See Mitchell, 649.

831 Some vessels coming from Australia stayed in the Indian Ocean and China Sea for years as tramp ships without returning to England. Most of the 21 convict ships of 1832, having left their human freight at Sydney or Hobart Town, proceeded to the Asian trading posts. Strikingly often it was just these vessels that were wrecked in bad weather, the cargo being 'thrown over the board' or sold locally with the remains of the ship, far away from the sea assurance inspectors at home. Of the six vessels lost during a voyage to or from Australia, five were convict ships on their way back home, while one was an emigrant ship on the way to Australia, which was destroyed by fire off Brazil with heavy loss of life. (The tragic loss of the *Hibernia* was described in *Lloyd's List* 3.5.1833.)

832 Liverpool shipping expanded in several directions during the 1830s. For example, the Brocklebanks merchant house increased their sailings not only to Calcutta (from four in

TABLE 66. *Asian and Australian trade in 1832, number of departing British ships by home port and destination.*

Port	Ba-tavia	Bom-bay	Cey-lon	China	Madras, Calcutta	Ma-nila	Mau-ritius	Singa-pore	NSW, VDL	Total
London	4	26	7	25	61	3	36	6	79	247
Liver-pool	8	32	–	1	28	5	3	2	16	95
Glas-gow	–	10	–	–	8	1	2	2	–	23
Other*	–	–	–	1	1	1	6	1	3	13
Total	12	68	7	27	98	10	47	11	98	378

Source: *Lloyd's Register for Underwriters 1833; Lloyd's List, 1832–1834, passim.*
 * 'Other' includes three vessels from Edinburgh, four from Bristol, three from Greenock and one from Hambro. Two ships sailed from Plymouth and Portsmouth, originating probably from London.

London clearly dominated in terms of trade volumes, and even more in terms of values. The total tonnage of the vessels sailing from London to Madras and Calcutta in 1832 was 32,150 tons and to Bombay 12,740 tons. The corresponding figures of Liverpool were 9,350 tons and 12,740 tons respectively.[833]

The average vessels sailing from London to the different Australasian ports were nearly 400 tons on average, even if the large East Indiamen of over 1,200 tons are excluded. The average Liverpool vessels were approximately 330 tons, while the ships of other ports were even somewhat smaller. Typically, the ships for India were larger – over 400 tons on average – than those sent to Batavia or Manila, which were only 240–280 tons on average. The smallest ships of fewer than 200 tons were mainly for sailing to the Australian colonies or Mauritius, which probably showed that the trade carried on with these places was not at the same level of sophistication as that carried on with some more important areas.[834]

The difference in the value of imports was striking. On the India route, London dominated the trade in the very high valued silk and indigo – which had traditionally been part of the EIC monopoly, even after the gradual abolition in the 1820s – as well as most of the coffee, also importing two thirds of the saltpetre, three quarters of the sugar and 70% of the pepper. Liverpool thus had a minor share of these imports, and about half of the quantity of the

1830 to nine in 1840) and to Bombay (from none in 1830 to four in 1840), but also to 'Lima etc.' (from two in 1830 to seven in 1840) and to St. John's (from two in 1830 to five in 1840). The sailings for India must therefore be seen as a part of the general growth in trade and not as a separate phenomenon. For the Brocklebanks sailings, see John Frederic Gibson, *Brocklebanks 1770–1950,* Volume I (Liverpool, 1953), 88.

833 Calculated from *Lloyd's Register for Underwriters, 1833.*
834 Calculated from *Lloyd's Register for Underwriters, 1833.*

low valued rice and cotton. London's share of the official value of imports from India in 1830 was £2,681,730 and Liverpool's £333,710. Additionally, all bullion was shipped to London, worth some £815,000. In total, the value of imports to London was more than ten times that to Liverpool.[835]

Although the value of the Liverpool shipping for India was clearly inferior to that of its wealthy London rivals, communications with India benefited considerably from the fact that there were 147 ships sailing for India during the year instead of just 87. In addition, the ships from London often stayed for a long while at port in Portsmouth or Plymouth before sailing out, thus extending the length of the voyage. At least 36 vessels called at these ports on their way to India and stayed there for more than ten days on average before starting the voyage. Even if there was an 'express' mail from London to Portsmouth and Plymouth, the letters which were sent while the ship was at Gravesend or Deal were already two weeks old when she left the coast of England. Liverpool ships sailed out directly.[836]

The hard competition had considerably shortened the duration of sailings compared to the days of the EIC monopoly. The fastest journeys between Britain and India were made in fewer than 100 days, the records in 1832 being 83 days from London to Madras, 98 days from London to Calcutta, and 93 days from Liverpool to Bombay. The fastest sailings homewards were about two weeks longer in each case.

An average sailing from Liverpool to Bombay took 125 days and the home voyage 128 days in 1832–1834. An average sailing from London took 134 days while the home voyage took 130 days.[837] Even the slowest sailing, 174 days from Liverpool to Bombay, was shorter than the average sailing of 180 days two decades earlier. The figures include stops for watering and provisions.

The same improvement in speed could be seen in the round voyages. While the fastest East Indiamen had returned from India in about 14 months before the abolition of the monopoly, the fastest round trip was now made in somewhat over eight months, the record Liverpool–Bombay–Liverpool round trip taking 246 days.[838]

Due to the frequent traffic that had arisen between Britain and India, the information circle was easily shorter than the duration of a round trip by one specific vessel. In the best case, it could work in the following way:

835 The values of imports are based on the statistics published in *BPP, Colonies, East India 8... Part II Commercial, 1831–32.* Appendix No. 4. Imports – Calcutta, Madras and Bombay, 1830, 575.
836 Calculated from the maritime intelligence published by *Lloyd's List* 1832.
837 The averages are calculated from 13, 12, 10 and 18 voyages respectively.
838 Calculated from the maritime intelligence published by *Lloyd's List* 1832–1834.

TABLE 67. *An example of fast information transmission by private merchantmen between London and Bombay, 1832.*

Departure from London	Ship	Arrival in Bombay	Departure from Bombay	Ship	Arrival in London	Duration of the information circle
9.4.32	*Boyne*	16.7.32	18.7.32	*Hero*	16.11.32	221 days
			or 1.8.32	*Lady Feversham*	10.12.32	245 days

Source: *Lloyd's List, 1832.*

Thus the combination of faster sailings and more frequent departures at both ends of the journey enabled a major improvement in business information transmission. Although the record trip by the ship *Boyne* has been taken as an example on purpose, the homeward sailings were about average in length. A merchant who wrote letters to his business partners in Bombay in early April, now received answers in mid-November or early December – probably half a year earlier than before.

Due to missing dates, especially concerning the Bombay arrivals, it is not possible to calculate the average length of information circles. An average round trip – from home port to home port – was 309 days, i.e. some ten months, and remembering that all ships had to use about a month for unloading and reloading in Bombay, the average information circle must have been fewer than 300 days. Answers to letters left Bombay sooner than the ship in which they had been carried.

There was still plenty of variation in the duration of information transmission. Even if the system now enabled two information circles in 20 months or less, their length varied significantly, as can be seen in Table 68.

TABLE 68. *Consecutive information circles enabled by private merchantmen between British ports and Bombay, 1832–1833.*

Departure from Liverpool	Ship	Arrival in Bombay	Departure from Bombay	Ship	Arrival in Liverpool	Duration of the information circle
3.1.32	*Caledonia*	15.5.32	1.6.32	*Sir Francis Burton*	30.9.32	271 days
19.10.32	*Columbia*	March 33	1.4.33	*Ospray*	23.8.33*	308 days

Source: *Lloyd's List, 1832.*
* Arrival in Glasgow.

321

Not only had sailings become faster but port stays had also shortened radically. The average stay in Bombay – in the cases where both the arrival and departure dates were reported – was 30 days, if two extra long 76-day stays for unknown reasons are excluded. The ships also sailed quickly from Britain, some vessels being on the way back to Asian waters before the end of 1832. Not only information but also freight and capital moved faster than ever earlier.[839]

An average voyage from Britain to Madras took 118 days and back home in 126 days, while an average voyage to Calcutta took 137 days and back home in 141 days.[840] The differences were due to the varying lengths of sailing routes, and obviously the ships were also more heavily loaded on the way homewards.

While the ships often called at Madeira or the Cape on the way to the east, it was common practice to call at St. Helena on the home voyage. It was from there that most shipowners and merchants learnt that the vessel they were waiting for would soon be arriving. Even if the ships did not stay long at St. Helena – normally only a day or two – some of them sailed home faster and could tell news of the ships coming behind them. The last leg of the voyage from St. Helena to England took approximately two months on average – 59 days calculated from 124 voyages – but the variance was great, from 39 to 90 days.[841]

While information transmission with India had improved remarkably, the opportunities for communications with China still remained much the same as before. While the private merchantmen sailed to India in some four months on average, the record being less than three months, the trip to China via India took 7.5 months (224 days) on average.[842] As can be seen from table 69, there was no difference in the duration of information circles depending on the route in India.

In real life, information transmission from London to Canton probably did not take the eight months indicated above. For example, the *William Fairlie* arrived in Madras on 1 June and there were certainly country ships departing for China before the large vessel from Europe was ready to proceed.

---

839 For example, the *Caledonia* departed from Liverpool for Bombay on 3.1.1832 and again on 20.11.1832; the *Fortune* from Glasgow on 7.1.1832 and on 13.11.1832; and the *Sir Francis Burton* from Liverpool on 8.1.1832 and on 24.10.1832. There are plenty of similar examples of consecutive departures in 1833. (*Lloyd's List* 1832–1833).

840 Calculated from the maritime intelligence published by *Lloyd's List* 1832–1834. If the ship was sailing for Calcutta but called first at Madras, only the duration of the voyage as far as to Madras has been recorded. Due to the long distance, ships sailing for Calcutta often called at Madeira, the Cape or Mauritius for watering or provisions, which added a few days to the total length of the voyage. The stops are included in the figures. – The averages have been calculated from 36, 14, 43 and 38 voyages respectively. The reason for the low number of home voyages from Madras is that most ships sailed to Calcutta via Madras but home directly, or even if they called at Madras, it was left unreported.

841 Calculated from the maritime intelligence published by *Lloyd's List* 1832–1834. At least 160 ships of those which sailed from England in 1832 made a call at St. Helena on their home voyage. In 124 cases at least the departure date from that port was reported in *Lloyd's List*, and additionally 32 arrivals of which the departure date was not reported.

842 Calculated from the maritime intelligence published by *Lloyd's List* 1832–1834. – The averages have been calculated from 11 voyages.

TABLE 69. *An example of information transmission by the East Indiamen between London and Canton, 1832–1833.*

Depar-ture from London	Ship	Arrival in Canton	Departure from Canton	Ship	Arrival in London	Duration of the infor-mation circle
14.2.32	*William Fairlie,* via Madras	12.10.32	25.10.32	*Canning*	6.3.33	386 days
14.2.32	*Marquis of Camden,* via Bombay	20.10.32	25.10.32	*Canning*	6.3.33	386 days

Source: *Lloyd's List, 1832–1833.*

The problem, however, was that there were no ships leaving from Canton to Europe with answers before the sailing of the *Canning* on 25 October.

Starting from the late spring of 1832, the sailings of the large East Indiamen were rapid and direct, with no interruptions apart from the stop at St. Helena on the home voyage. The Company was in a hurry, and the duration of the round voyages of the last vessels sailing directly via the Sunda Straits to China was only a year on average, the record being 10.5 months only. The last four sailings from London to Canton took no more than 107 to 117 days. While the average home voyage directly from Canton to London took 125 days, the fastest sailing homewards took only 116 days.[843]

The main problems in business information transmission between Britain and China were the seasonal character of the sailings (most departures took place during the first half of the year), the complicated routes (most ships sailed via India, where they stayed at ports for weeks or even months) and the long passages.

The size of the vessel had surprisingly little to do with the duration of the voyage. The emancipation of the Asian trade had drastically increased the number of small ships on the Asian routes. Table 70 shows the change in ship sizes on the Asian trade routes from 1812 to 1832. As can be seen, almost all vessels on these routes were more than 500 tons in 1812, but 20 years later more than 70% were less than that. Simultaneously with this development, however, the average speed of information transmission increased remarkably, as has been shown above.

843 Calculated from seven voyages. The departure dates from China were not always reported.

TABLE 70. *Ship sizes on the Asian trade routes in 1812 and 1832, excl. Australia.*

Ship size, tons	% of vessels, 1812 (n=56)	% of vessels, 1832 (n=280)
100–499	1.8	71.0
500–999	55.3	22.0
1000–1499	42.9	7.0

Source: *Lloyd's Register for Underwriters, 1813 and 1833.*

Contrary to some earlier assumptions, the large East Indiamen of 1300 to 1400 tons were not slow, but sailed rapidly if there was a need for that. However, a small 294-ton merchant vessel from Liverpool could manage the route within approximately the same time, as can be seen from Table 71.

TABLE 71. *The fastest sailings from Britain via Anjer (Sumatra) to China, 1832.*

Departure port	Departure date	Ship, size	Arrival date in China	Days at sea
London	1.5.32	Lord Lowther, 1332 tons	16.8.32	107
London	25.5.32	Earl of Balcarras, 1417 tons	13.9.32	111
London	25.4.32	Edinburgh, 1335 tons	17.8.32	114
London	25.4.32	Berwickshire, 1332 tons	20.8.32	117
Liverpool	10.6.32	Walter, 294 tons	6.10.32	118

Calculated from Lloyd's List, 1832–1833.

Yet small ship size was not generally a special advantage either, even if mail packets were normally small compared to the large merchantmen. In fact, the main benefits of small vessels in mail service were probably mainly financial. They sailed with a smaller crew and were fast to load and unload.

On the route to Australia, all ships weighed less than 550 tons, and more than 40% of them were less than 300 tons. Of the smallest vessels, only two were among the 12 fastest, while six of the 26 largest ships of 401 to 500 tons were among the fastest. An average outbound voyage took 138 days and an average homeward voyage 156 days, probably due to different routes and stays at port.[844]

844 Calculated from *Lloyd's Register for Underwriters 1833* and *Lloyd's List* 1832–1834.
– The reporting from Sydney and Hobart Town was not very accurate. No fewer than 27 arrivals were reported in *Lloyd's List* without any date or giving just a 'previous to' date which could refer to any date within the previous few weeks. Only ten of the 53 vessels

TABLE 72. *The size and speed of vessels on the Australian route, from Britain to New South Wales and Van Diemen's Land 1832.*

Size, tons	Number of ships	Number of this size of ships among the 12 fastest
150–300	38	2
301–400	28	4
401–550	26	6
Total	92	12

Calculated from Lloyd's Register for Underwriters 1833 and Lloyd's List 1832–1834. The total number of vessels was 98, but the size of six remained unknown.

A few further records show even more variety. On the Calcutta route, the fastest sailing from London took only 98 days by the 1,333-ton East Indiaman *Macqueen*. The 650-ton *Duke of Northumberland* sailed from Portsmouth to Calcutta in 105 days and back to London in 116 days. The 360-ton *Samuel Brown* of Liverpool sailed for Calcutta twice in 1832. Her first sailing outwards took 113 days and the second 115 days. The 282-ton *Collingwood* sailed from Liverpool to Calcutta in 111 days.[845] The duration of the voyage seemed to depend less on the size of the vessel and more on factors such as the load, the skills of the captain and his men, and especially the weather.[846]

Merchant ships as news carriers

By 1832, *Lloyd's List* was publishing maritime intelligence from distant Asian ports more often and more accurately than earlier, partly because of growing interest but also as a consequence of improved communications. The intelligence was now received in London faster and more frequently than earlier, enabling a better news service for readers.

To illustrate how the news from different Asian ports reached British interest groups, a few cases have been picked out from the maritime intelligence published by *Lloyd's List* during the period in question.

The 666-ton *James Sibbald*, commanded by Captain Darby, had sailed from London for Calcutta on 14 June 1832, arriving at Bengal on 2 November. The news of the ship's arrival was brought to England by the *Duke of Lancaster*, which sailed from Sand Heads (off Calcutta) on 1 December. She arrived in Liverpool on 25 March and those who waited for news about the *James Sibbald* found the needed information in *Lloyd's List* on 29 March,

---

which were reported to have arrived were also reported to have sailed from Hobart Town and Launceston, while only 36 of the 70 vessels which were reported to have arrived were also reported to have sailed from Sydney.

845 Calculated from *Lloyd's Register for Underwriters 1833* and *Lloyd's List* 1832–1834

846 Also the qualities of the ship were naturally important: the rigging and the number and size of sails, the form of the hull, metal cover, technical equipment on board, etc. See e.g. Ojala (1999), 226–241, 435–436.

together with news about several other ships which had arrived in Calcutta before 1 December. It took the *Duke of Lancaster* 114 days to sail to England and the news about the arrival of the *James Sibbald* was 147 days old when published.[847]

By the time the owners in Britain learnt the good news about the ship's safe arrival in Calcutta, things had changed drastically in India. The following information about the *James Sibbald* arrived rather soon after, brought by an unknown vessel which had arrived at Bordeaux. The news, dated in Paris on 14 April, read shortly: 'The *James Sibbald*, Darby, from Bengal to London, is lost on Point Gordewain, entrance of the Coringa Bay. Crew and Passengers saved.'[848]

What had happened? Was the ship really a total loss? Where were the crew and passengers? There was news arriving by different ships from India, but it took almost two more months to learn the whole story.

The next news about the ship came by the *Lady Flora*, which had sailed from Madras on 10 January. She landed the mails off Margate on 27 April and arrived at Gravesend three days later after 110 days of sailing. The short news report, dated on 9 January, read: 'The *James Sibbald*, Darby, from Bengal to London, grounded on a Sand Bank off Coringa Point 29th ult. and there is but little hope of saving her either the ship or cargo. The Passengers had arrived at Masulipatam.'[849] This information was 112 days old when published. After this, nothing more was told about the passengers. However, the fate of the ship and cargo was important, and the reporting continued.

The following news came by the *Duke of Buccleugh*, which had sailed from Calcutta on 14 January. Dated two days earlier at that port, the story read: 'By last advices from the *James Sibbald*, which got on shore about 15 miles below Coringa 28th ult. she was being lightened, in the hope of getting her off.'[850] The *Duke of Buccleugh* sailed from Bengal via the Cape of Good Hope and St. Helena in 113 days and the news was 115 days old when published. However, it showed that the agent in Calcutta did not know well enough what happened at Coringa Bay. Although the news was the most up-to-date at the time, it would turn out to be too optimistic.

The following piece of news gave a different view: 'Madras, 3d Jan. The *James Sibbald*, from Bengal to London, on shore on the Coast, is full of water. About 1000 chest of indigo, with some other portions of cargo have been saved.'[851] The *London*, which carried the news, had sailed from Madras nine days later than the agent had dated his report. She was a large East Indiaman of 1,332 tons, probably heavy loaded. She was reported off the Wight on 5 May, but the news was published as late as on the 10th, 128 days old. For the owners, this was good news, however. One thousand chests

847 For maritime intelligence, see *Lloyd's List* respectively. – The news about ship arrivals were usually sent in long lists and it often happened that the earliest arrivals on the list could be weeks older than the latest, depending on how long ago there had last been communications from that port to London.
848 *Lloyd's List* 19.4.1833.
849 *Lloyd's List* 30.4.1833.
850 *Lloyd's List* 7.5.1833.
851 *Lloyd's List* 10.5.1833.

of indigo were worth some £45,000 while the value of the ship must have been considerably less.[852]

The fate of the vessel was clarified in *Lloyd's List* 11 days later: 'The hull of the *James Sibbald*, wrecked off Coringa, was to be sold 15th inst.'[853] This news, dated on 21 January in Madras, arrived by the *Coromandel*, which was reported arriving off the Wight on 18 May. The ship had sailed from Madras on 24 January and arrived at Gravesend on 24 May.[854] Despite the fact that *Lloyd's List* was published only twice a week at the time, news was often published before the ship carrying it had *de facto* arrived at the homeport. In this case, the news seems to have been landed 'off the Wight'.

And the final news about the wrecked vessel was reported in *Lloyd's List* on 14 June, two months after the first news about her accident, and 5.5 months after it happened: 'The cargo saved from the *James Sibbald*, wrecked off Coringa, has been reshipped per *Charles Eaton*, Fowle, arrived at Madras.'[855] This news had been sent by the *Wellington,* which sailed from Madras on 24 February, and it was 110 days old when published.

The story is a good example of how news arrived, not only slowly but sometimes also in a confusing order. The mails bearing news of the disaster were carried by six different ships which sailed from India within 1.5 months. The first piece of news, arriving from Paris, was short but quite correct, and the rest was additional information. *Lloyd's List* seems to have published everything they heard about the ship, even contradictory information. The paper never made a complete story about the disaster. There was no space or need to return to the matter. The readers could draw their own conclusions.

Another example tells about several British vessels which got into trouble in a severe storm at Bengal in May 1833. The interest groups – whether they were owners of the ships and their cargoes, underwriters, family members of the crew and the passengers, or anyone who had an interest in the ships' fortunes – received the bad news by a *Lloyd's List* report published on 1 October:

'Calcutta, 24th May. A severe Gale commenced here on the evening of the 20th instant, and continued with great violence for 24 hours. The *Duke of York*, Locke, from London & Madras, is high on shore about half a mile to the southward of Hedgellee Creek. The *Lord Amherst*, Hicks, bound to London, is stranded abreast of Kedgeree Light House, and reported to have broken her back. The *Eamont,* Nash, bound to Penang, Malacca and Singapore, is on shore and bilged a little below the same place, and within a cable's length of the *General Gascoyne*, Fisher, bound to Mauritius, which is said to be also bilg'd. The *Robert,* Blyth, bound to Liverpool, is high and dry above Kedgeree; and it is feared that they may all be considered as wrecks. – The *Sultan*, Mitchell, bound to Mauritius, it is hoped has got to sea, altho' there

---

852 The value of indigo is calculated from *BPP, Colonies, East India 8... Part II Commercial, 1831–32*. Appendix No. 4. Imports – Calcutta, Madras and Bombay, 1830, 575.
853 *Lloyd's List* 21.5.1832.
854 For maritime intelligence, see *Lloyd's List* respectively.
855 *Lloyd's List* 14.6.1832.

are apprehensions entertained of her either having foundered or gone on the Sand, in which case all hands must have perished.'

The report continues in the same *Lloyd's List* issue: 'Calcutta, 25th May. There is a probability of the *Robert* being got off; but the hopes of saving the other ships are very faint. No doubt a large portion of their cargoes may prove uninjured. Two people have been washed on shore from the *Sultan*, who report that they were blown from her at the instant after her masts went, but nothing is known of her afterwards. All concur that this Gale was more violent than any other in recollection.'[856]

The news must have been brought by the *Lord William Bentick*, which arrived from Bengal on 29 September.[857] She was a convict ship, which had sailed from Hobart Town via Batavia and Madras to Calcutta and was now on the way back home, having been out for 17 months. She sailed from Calcutta on 3 June, and was the first ship to enter Britain with the news about the storm damage. For information transmission, any vessel which was on the way homewards was good enough. The news was 130 days old when published, but the freshest available. A duplicate of the report might have been carried by the *Bengal*, which departed from Calcutta on 24 May, 1833, but the ship arrived in London as late as on 4 November.[858]

It took several weeks before any additional information about the disaster in Calcutta was received by arriving ships. On 8 November *Lloyd's List* reported:

'The *Duke of York*, Locke, from London; the *Lord Amherst*, Hicks, bound to London, and the *Eamont,* Nach, which were driven on shore near Calcutta in June, have been condemned. The *Robert,* Blyth, bound to Liverpool, and the *General Gascoyne*, Fisher, bound to Mauritius, which were driven on shore at the same time, would be got off.'

This news was carried by the *Hooghley* on her home voyage from a relatively efficient round trip to India. She had departed from London on 4 December, 1832 and arrived in Calcutta on 19 April 1833 from Madras. In June she departed homewards and on 6 November she was reported at Deal, where she also landed the mails.[859]

In November, more news arrived concerning the wrecked vessels: 'Mauritius, 26th July. The *Samuel Brown* brings accounts that the *Genl*

---

856 *Lloyd's List* 1.10.1833.

857 Her arrival was reported in *Lloyd's List* on the same day.

858 *Lloyd's List* respectively. – The wrecked *Lord Amherst* also carried mails for the East India Company. Five letters in the general correspondence of the EIC, dated between 27.12.1832 and 3.5.1833, give evidence that the *Lord Amherst's* mails were finally taken to London by the ship *Juliana*. She sailed from Bengal on 16.7.1833, having been delayed by loss of anchors and grounding in the Hooghley River, apparently without major damage. Her mails were landed at Portsmouth on 19.12.1833 and the letters were finally received by the EIC in London on 23.12.1833. The oldest letter was 361 days and the freshest 234 days old when received in London. – General Correspondence of the EIC, E/4/142 (BL, IRO). For the *Juliana's* incident, see *Lloyd's List* 10.12.1833.

859 For maritime intelligence, see *Lloyd's List* respectively. The ship also brought other sad news: 'The *Hooghley*, Reeves, arr in the Downs from Bengal, passed on the 20th August, in lat 35 S long 21 E during a hurricane, a vessel dismasted, also the contents of a ship's deck, mast, boats, batches, and topmast with rigging on.' (*Lloyd's List* 8.11.33)

Gascoyene, bound here, which was on shore in the [river] Hooghley 2d June, was proceeding to Bengal to be docked and repaired.'[860] 'Liverpool, 17th November. The *Robert*, Blythe, bound to Liverpool, ran on shore in the Hooghley, was got off previous to 23d June.' 'Kedgeree, 17th June. The *General Gascoyene*, Fisher, bound to the Mauritius, floated at high water.'[861] And 'Calcutta, 24th June. The *General Gascoyene*, Fisher, bound to Mauritius, which was on shore in the Hooghley, has put back here.'[862]

It remains somewhat uncertain by which ship the news from Mauritius was brought to England. The tiny *Clorinda*, only 183 tons, arrived from a long voyage to Hobart Town, Sydney, Singapore and Mauritius on 18 November. She had left Mauritius on 28 July, two days after the letter to *Lloyd's List* had been written, and probably landed the news on her way to Glasgow a few days earlier.[863]

Both the pieces of news published on 18 November were brought by the *Janet*, also on the way to Glasgow, on her way home from Manila, Singapore and Calcutta. The reports were received at Liverpool, maybe from Holyhead by the optical telegraph, and forwarded to London.[864] The carrier of the news published on 22 November cannot be identified due to a lack of maritime intelligence.

The final results of the incident could be read in *Lloyd's List* on 10 December, almost 2.5 months after the first distressing news about the incident had been published: 'Bengal, 23d July. The *Lord Amherst*, Hicks, has not been got off, being broken, bilged, totally dismasted, and filling with the tide.' And 'The *Eamont,* hence to Singapore, has been sold, with the cargo, as she could not be got off.'

This news had been dispatched by the *Patriot King*, a regular trader from Liverpool, already on her second voyage to India within the examined period. She left Calcutta on 2 August and was reported arriving at Milford on 7 December. She arrived in Liverpool on 16 December.[865]

The examples clearly show the great diversity of the mail-carrying ships, but also how useful it was from the information transmission point of view that there were many vessels sailing home from Asian waters throughout the year. Even though the length and routes of the sailings varied, the ships carried complementary news. Any ship could be a news bringer, if not for a specific merchant, at least for the business community as a whole. As all these ships were considered mail carriers by the Post Office, we can assume that important business letters were also carried by the same means as the Lloyd's agents' reports for the newspaper.

To highlight the difference between information transmission on the frequently sailed India route and on the China route (still the monopoly of the EIC), one more example might be useful. On 9 April, 1833 Lloyd's List published the following piece of news:

---

860 *Lloyd's List* 15.11.1833.
861 *Lloyd's List* 19.11.1833.
862 *Lloyd's List* 22.11.1833.
863 For maritime intelligence, see *Lloyd's List* respectively.
864 *Lloyd's List* 19.11.1833. The arrival of the ship was reported in the same issue.
865 For maritime intelligence, see *Lloyd's List* respectively.

'Singapore 8th Nov: The *Moffat*, Cromartie, [a smaller East Indiamen of 820 tons] from London to China and Halifax, put here 6th instant, with loss of main and mizzen masts, and having sustained damage during a Gale in the China seas, which commenced on the 22d and continued till 26th ult. (Mem. It was expected that the *Moffat* would be ready for sea about 28th Nov.)'

Four weeks later *Lloyd's List* reported that the *Moffat* had arrived in China on 10 January. Two weeks later the paper published contradictory news: 'The *Moffat*, Cromartie, from London, which put into Singapore and was stated in the List of 7th inst. to be arrived at China on the 10th January, had not arrived there on the 26th of that month.'[866] This was alarming, as the sailing from Singapore to Canton normally took only eight to ten days.

All these news items were carried to England by East Indiamen on their way back home. After the *Earl of Balcarras* had left Canton on 26 January without any information about the damaged *Moffat*, no vessels sailed from China for a month. In fact, the *Moffat* had arrived in Canton only three days after the departure of the *Earl of Balcarras* but the news about the happy turn of events did not reach England before the arrival of the following East Indiaman, the *Reliance*, in mid-June.[867]

The last example shows that even if the sailings from China by the large East Indiamen were not necessarily longer than by the ships from India, the long periods between the sailings caused unnecessary delays in information transmission. This would gradually change when trade with China was opened up in the following year.

The total number of mails carried by private sailing ships via the Cape was remarkable. In 1833, the Post Office statistics recorded 3,725 bags of mail for India, carried by 427 ships from 17 British ports.[868] Against these figures, it was not surprising that the pressure for faster communications with Asia would grow both in England and in the East

Steaming via the Cape of Good Hope vs. the Overland route

The first attempt to establish a steamship service between England and India took place in 1825, when the steamer *Enterprise* was taken from Southampton around the Cape of Good Hope to Bengal, sponsored by the wealthy merchant houses of London and Calcutta. The 479-ton ship was built especially for the venture. Her journey was made only six years after the first eastbound Atlantic crossing by the *Savannah,* with very similar results: although the trip was technically successful, the effort turned out to be a commercial failure. Instead of the planned 70 days, it took the vessel 113 days to reach Bengal. The ship ran out of coal and had to proceed under sail for more than half of the voyage.[869]

---

866 *Lloyd's List* 7.5.1833; and 24.5.1833.
867 *Lloyd's List* 14.6.1833.
868 See Sidebottom, 59–60. Obviously the figures also include mails for other Asian ports than India.
869 Daniel Thorner, *Investment in Empire. British Railway and Steam Shipping Enterprise in India 1825–1849* (Philadelphia, 1950), 23; Moubray & Moubray, 180.

The *Enterprise* was never taken back to Europe again. She remained in the Indian Ocean, mainly at Bengal, but was evidently also used by the EIC as a contemporary mail carrier between Bombay and Suez from 1826 to 1833.[870]

By chance, the *Enterprise* was piloted up the River Hooghly by a Thomas Fletcher Waghorn, a former naval officer now working for the EIC. He was convinced that the future of communications with Europe lay in steam propulsion, but soon realised that a shorter and more profitable route should be found for the service. Between 1826 and 1830, Waghorn was actively advocating, first in India and later in England, the idea of establishing a fast steamship service from England to Egypt to link up with a similar service from Suez to India.[871]

The overland route was not a new innovation; it had been in limited use since the early 17th century. There were in fact two alternative routes: one connecting the Mediterranean and the Persian Gulf via Aleppo, Baghdad and Basra; and another one connecting the Mediterranean and the Red Sea via Alexandria and Suez. By the late 1650s, the EIC had developed a custom to send overland letters from India to London every summer, usually in August, to advise of the safe arrival of ships, of the expected state of the market, of the plans for the next outbound fleet and of the amounts of Indian commodities to be purchased before the rains. The route may also have been used for sending duplicates of letters carried homeward by ships around the Cape of Good Hope. The Overland route was used in both directions.[872]

The EIC sent their own dispatches via the Persian route, from London via Marseilles (or Leghorn), Aleppo and Basra (or Gombroon) to Surat in India. The transit took at least six months, but eight months was more usual and over ten months was not at all uncommon. It was often difficult to find a safe means of communication through the different war arenas in Europe, while the Middle Eastern deserts rife with plague, invasions and raids were dangerous as well. Although the Red Sea route had been considered a number of times in the 17th century, nothing had happened by the end of the 18th century due to the resistance of the EIC, which wanted to stick to its old traditions. The Red Sea route was probably faster, but it was not safer or more regular, and it was generally condemned as hot, mysterious and distinctly unhealthy.[873]

When Thomas Waghorn advocated direct steamship communications between England and India via Egypt, he unwittingly aroused strong feelings

---

870 For the later years of the *Enterprise*, see Thorner, 23; Moubray & Moubray, 180; Sidebottom, 14; and Robertson, B 42. – The mail service was probably just an annual dispatch by the Bombay Government up the Red Sea to the EIC agent at Alexandria, to be forwarded to a Mediterranean steam vessel. The ship also carried dispatches for the Indian government during the first Burmese war. See Sidebottom, 8, 55.

871 Moubray & Moubray, 180; Sidebottom, 14. – For the background of Thomas Waghorn and his early attempts to find support for a steamship service around the Cape of Good Hope, see Sidebottom 15–19; for his career, see Cable, 53–64.

872 Holder Furber, 'The Overland Route to India in the Seventeenth and Eighteenth Centuries', first published in *Journal of Indian History,* 29 (Trivandrum, 1951). Republished in Rosane Rocher (ed.), *Private Fortunes and Company Profits in the India Trade in the 18th Century* (Variorum, 1997), see 116–117.

873 See Furber, 117–133; Moubray & Moubray, 180; and Cable, 56–57.

among the different parties. The EIC offered limited support but little financial backing, while the British Post Office rejected most of his proposals out of hand. The Anglo-Indian merchants had differing opinions. The Bombay Government and mercantile community had nothing against the idea, as the Overland route would have brought Bombay, on India's west coast, 1,000 miles closer to England than either of the east coast ports of Calcutta and Madras. The merchant houses in London and Calcutta, then the hub of India's political, economic and military life, were for a direct steamship service to Bengal, via Suez or around the Cape.[874]

Fighting against the time of changes

The EIC was naturally not very interested in supporting anything that would mean better business communications for its rivals who had actively fought against the Company's privileges in India and elsewhere. The Government of Bombay, in close intimacy with the Bombay mercantile interests, pressed the EIC in the 1820s to open up a steamship route from Suez to the Red Sea and eastward across the Arabian Sea to Bombay. The Company finally agreed to supply the engine for a wooden steamer built in the Government shipyard at Bombay. The ship, tactfully named *Hugh Lindsay* after the Chairman of the Court of Directors of the EIC, was launched late in 1829. She made her maiden voyage in the following March from Bombay to Suez in 33 days. The costs of this and later voyages by the vessel were so high that the EIC forbade any further steam trips to the Red Sea.[875]

In fact, the Company was not interested in improving even its own information transmission. A deeper look at the EIC's General Correspondence from Bengal, Madras and Bombay to London, sent in 1832–1833, presents a striking picture of the Company's general attitude towards communications between East India and the mother country.

C.H. Philips has examined the communications process of the EIC in his general study of the Company in 1784–1834. According to him, Lord

---

874 Thorner, 25–28; Moubray & Moubray, 180. – More than a dozen pamphlets were published in Britain for and against the different shipping and route plans. For a useful list, see Thorner's bibliography, 184–186. – Even as late as 1838, one of the hopeful advocates of the longer sea route, Sir John Ross, Captain of the Royal Navy, published a plan to collect £500,000 capital for a new India Steamship Company for steam communications to India via the Cape. The service was planned to reach only as far as Point-de-Galle in Ceylon, probably to get support from both the Bombay and Calcutta merchants. The continuation of the trip by local means would have made the duration of information transmission equally long to both the main trade ports. Ross calculated that the trip between England and Ceylon would be made in 46 days. The plan included three steamers and two store ships for coaling. See Sir John Ross, *On Communication to India in Large Steam-Ships, by the Cape of Good-Hope* (London, 1838), 3–44. For the different interests, see Cable, 68–69.

875 See Thorner, 25–26; Sidebottom, 61–62. – How long it took for the mails to arrive in England by this trip remains unclear. According to Thorner, it took 59 days in grand total, 'an impressively brief period for that age'. According to the Moubrays, however, the estimated time taken for the whole trip would have been 61 days 'had there been a steamship to take the mails from Alexandria'. See Moubray & Moubray, 181.

Ellenborough, President of the Company's Board of Control from 1828, made several efforts to improve the speed of communications between India and London. Having been appointed President, Ellenborough was shocked to find that the home government was only dealing with events that had taken place in India over two years before. In his view, London had abandoned effective control over the Indian Governments, and he 'determined to remedy the evil without delay'. As Philips puts it, 'the first and obvious step was... to establish steam communication between India and England via the Red Sea... The 'chairs' adopted his suggestion and within ten years a monthly service by this new route was established.'[876]

Ellenborough also turned his attention to the system of preparing dispatches in reply to the letters of the Company's Governments in India. Under the existing system the latter sent home all information in huge, general letters, which took a considerable time to prepare and included both trivial and important matters. No attempt was made in London to deal with the more important matters first. Instead, all subjects were replied to paragraph by paragraph in strict numerical order. The system was certainly slow and clumsy. Simultaneously, the number of folio volumes received from India grew every season, without any increase in the staff which would take care of preparing the drafts.[877]

Ellenborough estimated that one year would be time enough to send and receive an answer to a dispatch between London and India. He made four suggestions, namely that 1) both the Board and the India House should increase their staff, 2) the method of conveying information through huge general letters should be replaced by one in which each subject was to be dealt with in a separate letter, 3) an abstract of each letter should be written on the cover so that the home government could deal with the more important letters first; and 4) all consultations to be sent home should be lithographed, thus saving the time involved in copying them by hand at the India House. According to Philips, Ellenborough carried through his proposals despite strong opposition by the 'chairs', achieving a beneficial increase in efficiency and dispatch in the system of correspondence.[878]

A closer look at the Company's General Correspondence of 1832–1833 in the India Record Office, British Library, gives a rather conflicting picture of the overall efficiency by which the improvements were carried through. A portion of 1,422 letters from Bengal, Bombay and Madras show clearly that there were major differences in the communications culture of the three presidencies. Calcutta was the most phlegmatic in its communications. Letters written in Fort William frequently waited for months at port before a ship to England took them on board. E.g. the ship *Isabella* dispatched 31 letters written in Calcutta between April and November 1832 when arriving in London in early April 1833. The *Georgiana* dispatched 29 letters written in Calcutta between July 1832 and March 1833 when arriving in London in

876 Philips, 264–268.
877 Philips, 264–265.
878 Philips, 266–267.

early September, 1833.[879] Even if these are extreme examples, it is hard to understand why the letters were not put on board earlier departing vessels.

As can be seen in Table 73 (in the end of the book, p. 429), most ships carried letters which had been written over a period of several months. On the other hand, it can be noted that letters written during one and the same month were carried by several ships; e.g. the letters written in Calcutta in December 1832 were taken to London by 12 different vessels. In reality, the number of letters was larger than can be observed from the table. The correspondence in the EIC records includes first copies, duplicates or triplicates of letters, depending on which one arrived first. In most cases, there is a handwritten note 'Read in Court' with a date close to the date when the letter was received, indicating that this was the first copy that arrived.[880]

The EIC preferred to send the letters by ships which were chartered by the Company, or which had formerly been in its service. Of the 24 ships in Table 73, no fewer than 18 were or had been chartered by the Company. Letter copies sent by several vessels proved to be a useful system, as two of the ships were wrecked during the home voyage. As can be seen, the vessels often sailed close to each other, due to safety reasons and old tradition. As a result, there were long periods when no letters arrived from Bengal with EIC correspondence: two months in the spring, another two months in the summer and several one month periods in the autumn.

The table shows that the letters (both originals and copies) were collected in ships which were loading at port, without any knowledge of their actual departure dates. Many vessels carried letters to London which had been written even before the ship had arrived in Calcutta. The 'ranking' of how the first, second and third copies were divided between the ships for England seems to have depended on the expected departure date, as well as the reputation of the ship, its Captain and its owners in the eyes of the EIC officials in Calcutta.

The latter principle meant that e.g. the Liverpool ships were excluded. Of the nearly 700 received letters in the EIC General Correspondence, sent from Bengal in 1832 and 1833, only one was carried by a Liverpool vessel. This was the *Hindoo,* owned by the prosperous Brocklebank family of Liverpool. The letter, an original dated on 25 June, 1833, must have been important as it was sent by the next possible vessel. The *Hindoo* sailed on 8 July.[881]

Even in the best case, there was usually at least one week's lag between the date of the freshest letter and the ship departure from Bengal, probably due to the time-consuming trip in the river Hooghley from the Docks of Calcutta to Sand Heads at the Bay of Bengal, near Kedgeree, from where most ship departures we are reported.

879 The EIC, General Correspondence from Bengal, E/4/138–142 (BL, IRO).

880 There are a few exceptions, when the examiner of the EIC has made a note that the first copy had arrived by another ship, usually earlier. The date when received was always marked on the letter, as well as the name of the ship by which it had arrived. There are no postal markings in the correspondence. Most of the thick letters have just been folded in half lengthwise and sent in bundles.

881 The EIC General Correspondence, E74/143 (BL, IRO); *Lloyd's Register for Underwriters 1833; Lloyd's List* 8.11.1833.

There is an astonishing difference in the total speed of information transmission if we compare the EIC mails with the news sent by Lloyd's agents from Bengal to England during the same period,[882] partly by the same ships on the very same journeys. For example the *Hooghley*, which carried to *Lloyd's List* the news that the ships *Duke of York*, *Lord Amherst*, and *Eamont,* driven on shore near Calcutta, had been condemned in June, arrived in early November after a rather slow trip of 146 days. But the age of the letters which the ship carried simultaneously for the EIC varied between 163 and 274 days. The fastest vessels which brought Lloyd's news in the examples did not seem to carry EIC letters at all, even though some of them did on an earlier or a later voyage.

Despite Lord Ellenborough's efforts to speed up the EIC communications between India and London, letters from Calcutta did not always follow his instructions. Instead of writing a separate letter on each issue – although this did often happen – the reports could just as well include two to four hundred carefully numbered paragraphs, all written by hand, extending up to 200 pages.[883] A long memorial by Sir Charles Metcalfe to the Court of Directors in London, dated on 24 July, 1832, included answers to 38 earlier letters from 11 May to 10 August 1831, plus one from 4 November 1831. His topics covered Bombay, China, Company's Servants, College, Miscellaneous, Marine, Navy, Post Office, Public Instructions, Pension, Profit & Loss, Prince of Wales Island, Singapore & Malacca, Telegraph, Vaccination and Law – in nearly alphabetical order. The letter was received in London by the ship *Juliana* on 23 December, 1833.[884] Thus, the Court received answers to their questions sent two and a half years earlier.

The communications from London to Bengal were no faster than in the other direction. Although the draft books of the Company in the India Record Office do not include information about the ships by which the letters were sent and thus no indication of how long it took to receive them, the contents give some idea of the speed of the EIC communications as a whole.

With reference to the figures above, it is no wonder that the Company had no interest in investing in faster communications between London and Calcutta. Its own system of communications was so outdated that there was really no significant difference whether a letter was received one or two months earlier or later.

In Bombay, the culture was rather different. As can be noticed from Table 74 (in the end of the book, p. 430), most ships stayed in Bombay for a shorter period than in Calcutta, and letters were not kept waiting for so long. Even though the duration of the sailings from Bombay to London was approximately the same as from Calcutta, the letters from Bombay were never older than ten months on arrival. The usual time lag of the Bombay letters was six to eight months, while from Calcutta several letters were

---

882 See Chapter VII.1.

883 For example, letters from Calcutta 31.12.1832 (339 paragraphs, 170 pages); 13.7.1833 (263 paragraphs, 94 pages); 22.8.1833 (402 paragraphs, 200 pages)); and 21.11.1833 (453 paragraphs, more than 200 pages). The EIC, General Correspondence from Bengal, E/4/141–144 (BL, IRO).

884 The EIC, General Correspondence from Bengal, E/4/140 (BL, IRO).

TABLE 75. *Time lag between writing letters and drafting the answers between London and Bengal, the East India Company, 1832.*

Date of writing the draft in London	Answer to a letter from Bengal	Date of the letter(s) now answered	Time lag between writing the original letter and writing the answer
4.7.1832	Territorial Finance Department	20.6.1831	380 days
4.7.1832	Commercial Department	28.9.1830	645 days
4.7.1832	Commercial Department	6.7.1830	729 days
11.7.1832	Public Department	1.11.1831	253 days
25.7.1832	General Department	27.4.1830 22.9.1830 26.10.1830 8.3.1831 31.5.1831	820 days 672 days 638 days 505 days 421 days
1.8.1832	Law Department	8.2.1831	540 days

Source: The EIC, General Correspondence from London to Bengal, E/4/ 735 (BL: IRO).

more than 12 months old when received in London. In the best cases, communications from Bombay worked really well: for example the letters written on 23 January, 1833 arrived in London by the *Lady Raffles* on 24 May, 1833, in 121 days.

Where did the difference derive from? Ever since the emancipation of the East Indian trade in 1813, Bombay had been more open to private merchandise, while Bengal had been more strictly under the old rule. No fewer than 22 of the 31 sailing vessels which brought EIC mails from Bombay, dated between January 1832 and June 1833, were private merchant vessels without any connection to the Company, and none of them sailed under a valid EIC charter.[885]

Of the 436 Bombay letters of that period, no fewer than 90 were carried by Liverpool vessels.[886] These dispatches arrived in England by three vessels at the end of the period, in March–April 1833. The *Cordelia* brought no originals, but ten duplicates and six triplicates; the *John Taylor* carried five originals, two duplicates and 25 triplicates; and the *Royal George* eight originals and 35 duplicates. Most originals had evidently been sent by London vessels, and the Liverpool ships had been relied on as second and third carriers because nothing else was available. However, they arrived before

885 The EIC, General Correspondence from Bombay, E/4/ 517–519 (BL, IRO); *Lloyd's Register for Underwriters* 1833.
886 The EIC, General Correspondence from Bombay, E/4/ 517–519 (BL, IRO).

FIG. 30. *The letter dated on 19.3.1832 in Madras, was carried by one of the three Navy vessels which took mails home to England that year. The letter was handstamped by the Madras G. P. O. on 27.4.1832 and carried by the* HMS Crocodile, *arriving in London on 10.9.1832, in 175 days from the writing and 136 days from Post Office to Post Office.*

the vessels which carried the originals, and therefore these letters have been kept in the Company's records.

Even though there was a steamship connection by the *Hugh Lindsay*, only one letter from Bombay was carried by that vessel and further via the Overland route during January 1832 – June 1833. This small letter, consisting of two thin sheets and a normal sheet for cover, was written on 4 January, 1833, with instructions to be carried by steamer and further via Malta. The letter was from the Management of the Medical Retirement Fund in Bombay, claiming that they had not received any government aid for three and a half years, 'which has nearly proved fatal to the institution'. The letter arrived in London on 9 April, 95 days after being written.[887]

887 The EIC, General Correspondence from Bombay, E/4/ 519 (BL, IRO).

The location of Madras made its communications different from both Calcutta and Bombay. Many ships put in on their way to Bengal or on the way homewards. However, it seems that the ships which took mails from Calcutta did not carry the mails from Madras even if they stopped there, and vice versa. Of 292 letters sent from Madras to London in 1832, less than a third were carried by ships which had a former or current connection with the EIC. A significant portion of the mails (69 out of 292, or 24%) were taken home by three Navy vessels, while no letters were sent by this means from Calcutta or Bombay (see Fig. 30). Liverpool ships were not used for carrying EIC mails from Madras. As the ships usually did not stay long at that port, the letters left sooner from there than from Calcutta. In addition, the durations of the sailings from Madras were clearly shorter than from Calcutta or Bombay due to the shorter sea voyage.[888]

Compared with the manner by which Lloyd's agents used the existing network of private communications to send maritime intelligence to England, the EIC had definitely lost its touch – and obviously also its interest – in improving information transmission. The unbelievable inefficiency of the management, combined with general conservative attitudes must have been one of the main reasons for the Company's final collapse. While it had been possible to ignore the changing times in the shelter of a monopoly, the EIC soon noticed that it could not keep its earlier position in the new environment, in which the competitors were entrepreneurs instead of government officials and accustomed to using all existing means of communication for their benefit.

Building a Monopoly

In search of better communications – The Peninsular Company enters the scene – Via Marseilles – Mixed service – Royal Charter for the P&O – The EIC service to India – Mail sailings to China – The P&O mail monopoly begins – Geographical distance, a relative concept

In search of better communications

At home in England, Select Committees of the House of Commons resolved in 1832 and 1834 that steam communication with India via the Red Sea was practicable, that under proper arrangements the expenses could be greatly reduced, and that a regular service should be opened, the net costs of which should be defrayed equally by the British Government and the EIC.[889]

The Committee also supported an alternative route from Alexandretta, on the Syrian coast, overland to the Euphrates, and then down that river for 1,000 miles to the Persian Gulf, and on to India. This plan was originally

---

888 The EIC General Correspondence from Madras, E/4/ 364–365 (BL, IRO); *Lloyd's List,* January 1832 – June 1834, passim.
889 See Thorner, 26; Sidebottom, 59.

placed before the Committee and warmly endorsed by the EIC, and it was supported by the British Government which wanted to counteract Russian interests in the Middle East. The mercantile houses looked at the Euphrates plan rather coldly, considering that it was yet another attempt by the EIC to defer any effective action. The efforts by the Company and the Government to operate steamers on the Euphrates in 1835–1837 were not successful, and one of the small vessels was in fact lost in a sudden storm with almost all hands.[890]

Additionally, the Select Committee of 1834 determined that the Admiralty's Malta packets should be extended to Egypt and/or Syria as necessary. In addition to the old Falmouth sailing packet route to Vigo, Oporto and Lisbon, the Admiralty had conducted a naval steam packet service on the England – Gibraltar – Malta (– Corfu) route since 1830. The Mediterranean service was needed for British control over Malta and the Ionian Islands, conquered during the Napoleonic wars, as well as Gibraltar, which had belonged to Britain since 1713. In March 1835, this naval steamship mail service was extended to Alexandria.[891]

Now there was a steam-powered European leg for the East India service via Alexandria and Suez. In the Indian Ocean, the EIC finally added two large steamers to the Indian Navy for the Suez–Bombay run, to the delight of Bombay and the discomfiture of Calcutta. The Overland route between Alexandria and Suez was pioneered by Mr. Waghorn, whose efforts to carry mails through the desert proved to be so much more efficient than the official service that he was appointed by the EIC as Deputy Agent and Superintendent for the Indian mails in Egypt from June 1837.[892]

The Indian mails were made up at the General Post Office in London on the first of each month and the naval steam packet sailed from Falmouth on the 3rd or 4th, depending on the weekday. The average duration of the voyage by the Admiralty steam packets via Malta to Alexandria was 22.5 days, varying between 20 and 26 days, while the homebound voyage took a few days more.[893]

The Overland trip was made by donkeys and river boats from Cosseir or Alexandria to Cairo, and from there by camels to Suez. The crossing took several days. In Suez, the mails were taken on board the *Hugh Lindsay* which took them to Aden, from where they were taken to Bombay by one of the EIC's two new steamers, the *Atalanta* or the *Berenice*. By these means, the mails were carried from England to India in 74 days and in the other direction within 64 days on average. These figures are calculated by Sidebottom from the dates of postmarks on some covers carried by the Waghorn service. The duration of the trip varied between 60 and 81 days eastwards and between 56 and 123 days westwards.[894]

890 See Thorner, 26–27.
891 For the Mediterranean mail routes and services, see Moubray & Moubray, 142–143, 155–162; and Tabeart (2002), passim.
892 See Sidebottom, 63–72.
893 For the sailing dates of 1835, see Tabeart (2002), 27–30.
894 Tabeart (2002), 25–28; Sidebottom, 38–39, 61–69. Lively descriptions about the early overland crossings can be found in Cable, 81–84; and Sidebottom 73–75. – The donkey

From Bombay, the mails were sent to Calcutta by runners (dawks), which normally made the trip between the two ports in a fortnight.[895] But the mail service by the EIC steamers did not function satisfactorily. It was more or less mismanaged, highly irregular, and at times quite unsafe. In June 1838, one batch of mail from Calcutta was delayed for so long at Bombay that it took 135 days to reach London; the next batch from Calcutta was again delayed at Bombay and finally dispatched via the Persian Gulf route, where Arabs captured part of it and scattered the letters over the desert. The Calcutta community's frustration and disappointments reached a climax in the summer of 1839 when the EIC steamers left Bombay for Suez on two successive occasions without waiting for mails known to be on the way from Calcutta.[896]

Besides these postal arrangements, the London merchants had in 1836 formed a committee to set up a commercial enterprise, the East India Steam Navigation Company, in order to link Britain via the Suez–Overland route with all the Indian ports, China and Australia. The reaction to this plan in Calcutta was somewhat mixed. Although a better mail service was naturally welcomed, the Calcutta community disliked the idea that Bombay would be the company's initial terminus. With little support from India and strong opposition from the EIC, the new company soon foundered. A revised plan, submitted by a chief London lobbyist for Calcutta interests, was accepted by the leading India houses in London in late 1838. In Calcutta, however, the opinions were again split due to a simultaneous local plan to start a mail service by at least one direct steamer on the Calcutta–Suez run.[897]

The Peninsular Company enters the scene

The steps which the British Government and the EIC now took separately, but not unconnectedly, to improve the steamship service between Britain and Egypt and between Suez and India, undermined all the plans and campaigning of the Anglo-India merchant houses during 1825–1840. When the EIC finally gave way, the Directors were not anxious to strengthen their longstanding opponents. Instead, taking advantage of the dissension and controversies which separated Bombay merchants from Calcutta merchants, and Calcutta merchants from London merchants, the EIC bypassed them all and awarded its coveted support and the contract to a complete newcomer to the eastern seas, later known as the P&O.[898]

Obviously there was also a practical reason for this decision. The Peninsula Steam Navigation Company (PSNCo), as the company was called at that time, had already gained a good reputation in conducting a mail service on the Falmouth–Vigo–Oporto–Lisbon–Cadiz–Gibraltar route from 1837,

service ended when the railway was opened between Alexandria and Cairo in 1856 and the camel transport in 1859, when the railway was finally extended from Cairo to Suez. See Sidebottom, 80–81.
895 Thorner, 28.
896 Thorner, 30.
897 Thorner, 29–31.
898 See Thorner, 32, 38–39.

after having won the postal contract advertised by the Government for public competition. The company carried mails from England to the Iberian Peninsula once a week, using five steamers, for an annual payment of £29,600 and with fines for each delay of 12 hours or more.[899]

From September 1837, the Indian mails had been carried by the PSNCo steamers from Falmouth to Gibraltar, from there by the Admiralty packets via Malta to Alexandria, by different means along the Overland route to Suez, and finally by the EIC steamers from Suez to Bombay.[900] The chain of the different services, here in the homeward direction due to lack of eastward dates, can be described by using an example:

The mails from Calcutta were sent by runners across India for Bombay on 11 September, 1837, and taken there on board the EIC steamer *Atalanta,* which sailed for Suez on 27 September. The sources available do not enable us to calculate the duration of the 1,700-mile sea voyage, but the mails – having meanwhile also been taken across the desert via Cairo by camels, riverboats and donkeys organized by Mr. Waghorn and his partners – left from Alexandria by HMS *Volcano* on 7 November. The ship arrived at Malta on 11 November and another naval steamer, HMS *Firefly* proceeded with the mails on 17 November, arriving at Gibraltar on the 23rd to forward the mails to the PSNCo's *Iberia,* which sailed for England on the following day. The ship arrived at Falmouth on 2 December and the mails were forwarded by mail coach to London, where they arrived on 4 December.[901] The trip took 84 days, which was not immensely better than what could be achieved by the fastest sailing vessels directly – and much more cheaply – from India.

In 1838, the Overland trip from Bombay to London took 64 days on average, the duration of the voyage varying between 50 and 100 days. To this, about a fortnight should be added for the dawk service between Calcutta and Bombay, and two days for the mail coach between Falmouth and London. Thus the Calcutta mails arrived in London in 80 days on average. The fastest mail arrived in 65 days while the slowest dispatch took 118 days.[902]

Via Marseilles

Mr. Waghorn's private express service was still able to make faster voyages than the official mail by using alternative means of transport where available. To avoid transit delays, typical for the official mail, he opened agencies at

---

899 Reg Kirk, *The Postal History of P&O Service to the Peninsula* (London, 1987), 1–11. – The PSNCo had started privately on the route already in 1834. Its main partners, Brodie McGhie Willcox and Arthur Anderson, were from Ostend (although originating from English-Scottish parents) and Shetland respectively, and were therefore not highly appreciated by the London merchant houses. The main proprietor and shipowner, Richard Bourne, was from Dublin, and in fact some of the first vessels used Liverpool as a branch terminal. About the early history, owners, etc. see Cable, 6–36.

900 See Kirk (1987), 12–13; Tabeart (2002), 40–46. Tabeart also corrects some dates published by Kirk, referring to the ships' logs.

901 See Kirk (1987), 13; Tabeart (2002), 44. – The sources available for this study lack information about the EIC's eastbound sailing dates of this period, thus making it impossible to calculate information circles.

902 Calculated from the sailing dates published by Kirk (1987), 13.

Alexandria and Malta to forward dispatches by the quickest steamers to Marseilles, to proceed by railway, coach and steamer for England, where they arrived some ten days before the Post Office mails. The arrangement soon received official attention by the Lords of the Admiralty and the Postmaster General, and to stop this uncomfortable competition, new arrangements were soon made for sending mails to India via Marseilles, from where the Admiralty packets would take the dispatches to Malta, to be forwarded to Alexandria.[903]

In May 1839, the new overland route via Marseilles was taken as an official alternative to the Post Office mails. The single postage rate for a letter to India by British packets via Marseilles would be 2s. 8d. and by French packets, in case British were not available, 3s. 1d., while the postage rate 2s. 6d. for the all-sea route from Falmouth by the PSNCo would remain unaltered.[904] Compared to the private ship letter rate via the Cape, which was 4d. plus the inland rate only, the costs of greater speed were still high.

The faster route via Marseilles was soon given preference by the Admiralty steamers. The all-sea mails via Gibraltar had to wait at Malta for several extra days, even ten or 12, for a packet while the mails for Marseilles left soon after the steamer had arrived from Alexandria.[905] The mails from Alexandria arrived now via Malta at Marseilles in 11 or 12 days, while about five more days were calculated for the journey between Marseilles and Calais on the English Channel.[906]

Mixed service

In 1840, there was thus a mail steamship service from England to India, via the Red Sea, and mails could be sent from Bombay or Calcutta even further

---

903 This arrangement was enabled by the Anglo-French postal convention of 1839, which allowed closed mails through France for India. See Sidebottom, 84–90, Tabeart (2002), 187–190. – Tabeart notes that 'a number of failures by the PSNCo ships slowed the average course of the mails from Malta to Falmouth to 19 days, with a correspondingly poor Alexandria–Falmouth time, averaging 29 days. These compare very unfavourably with the last all-RN figures homewards of 16 ½ and 23 days respectively'. In fact, also the transit times at Malta between the two Royal Navy steamers compared very unfavourably in 1838: instead of the normally one or two days' transit time at Malta during the 'all-RN' service in 1837, it now took three to four days, even six, to get the mails from one Admiralty vessel to another. At Gibraltar, the reasons for lengthened transit times were different. Even if normally smoothly conducted, in four cases the mails were delayed in transit between an Admiralty packet and a PSNCo vessel due to a breakdown of the latter. The delay in these occasions was seven to nine days. For the quote, see Tabeart, (2002), 50, and for the transit dates and notes, 38, 49–52.

904 Sidebottom, 89. – The convention was a major improvement compared with the earlier period when the charges for a letter to India via Marseilles were 10d. British, 3s. 9d. French plus 1s. steam postage from Suez to Bombay, the total being 5s. 7d. See Tabeart (2002), 187. – The French Post Office had started several steamship lines on the Mediterranean routes in 1837. They carried mail between Marseilles and Malta, Athens, Constantinople, and Alexandria. The service was three times monthly. Yet the Overland service by the French started only in the 1860s, when the Egyptian railway had already been built. For the early French services in the Mediterranean, see Salles, Tome II, 9–35.

905 See the sailing dates by Tabeart (2002), 54–55, 189–190.

906 Tabeart (2002), 189.

FIG. 31. *The letter dated in Manila, the Philippines, on 10.2.1842 includes a bill of lading, informing the Fredrick Huth banking company in London about sending goods to their customer in England by two ships (one of which was the* Garland Grove, *an English frigate on her way homewards after having carried female convicts to Australia). The letter was written by a clerk but the owner of the company added with his own handwriting on the top right corner that the original letter should be sent via Bombay (the Overland route) while this letter should be sent by the Spanish merchant ship* Dos Amigos *on her way to Cadiz. In Cadiz, the letter was forwarded by the British Consulate ('B. C. Cadiz' handstamp on the cover) to the P&O's Peninsula route steamer* Royal Tar *on her way from Gibraltar homewards. The ship arrived in Falmouth on 13.8. and the letter arrived in London on 15.8.1842, in 186 days.*

to the East, although not yet by steamer. There were several independent players taking part in the long transmission process, and delays here and there could not be avoided. The duration of business information transmission was still far from satisfactory.

As the sailing dates of the Eastern route are well covered by several postal historians, there is no need to go to the archives to find out when the different mail carriers departed or arrived at ports on their way to Australasia. Reg Kirk's monumental studies on the P&O schedules have been published in several volumes, mainly in the late 1980s. Lee C. Scamp has found lots of interesting details especially concerning the China route, published in a large volume in 1997. And finally, Colin Tabeart has collected the Admiralty steam packet sailing dates of the Mediterranean service, published in 2002. Having all this data in hand, we can pick up an example to see how the system worked in practice (see Table 76).

TABLE 76. *Duration of mail transmission between England, India and China, 1840, an example.*

Means of communications	Port 1 – Port 2	Departure – arrival	Days	Delay at port, days
All-sea route: By mail coach	London–Falmouth	18.1.–20.1.	2	
Royal Adelaide (P&O)	Falmouth– Gibraltar	24.1.–1.2.	8	4
HMS Volcano (Adm.)	Gibraltar–Malta	1.2.–6.2.	5	
Express route: By railway	London–Marseilles	4.2.– ~9.2.	5	
HMS Alecto (Adm.)	Marseille–Malta	~10.2.–13.2.	3	1
Both mails: continued by *HMS Megaera (Adm.)*	Malta–Alexandria	14.2.–20.2.	6	8 / 1
Overland Egypt, by camels etc.	Alexandria–Suez	between 20.2. and 27.2.	7 (?)	incl.
Berenice (EIC)	Suez–Bombay	27.2.–13.3.	15 (?)	
Overland India, by runners	Bombay–Calcutta	between 13.3. and 27.3.	14	incl.
HMS Larne (Adm.)	Calcutta– Singapore	27.3.– ~15.4.	~19	~18
Actif (private sailing vessel)	Singapore–Canton	3.5.–30.5.	27	
Total, all-sea	London–Canton	24.1.–30.5.	**127**	incl.
Total, express	London–Canton	4.2.–30.5.	**116**	incl.

Sources: Kirk (1987), 65; Tabeart (2002), 62, 191; and Scamp, 10. – February had 29 days in 1840.

The example enables a few observations. First of all, the bulk of mails from Falmouth were in this case delayed due to the late departure of the *Royal Adelaide*. With the Saturday mails from London, she should have sailed on Monday, 20 January but was reported to have left on the 24th. She arrived at Gibraltar via Lisbon and Cadiz on 1 February. The transfer of dispatches seems to have been conducted smoothly, as the Admiralty packet *Volcano* started her voyage from Gibraltar to Malta on the same day. However, the mails from Falmouth had to wait at Malta no fewer than eight days, until the Admiralty packet *Alecto* arrived from Marseilles with the express mails and all the dispatches could be taken on to Alexandria.[907]

The Overland voyage across Egypt and the time taken by the *Berenice* to steam from Suez to Bombay was 22 days in total. The mails arrived in Bombay on 13 March, the all-sea mail via Falmouth and Gibraltar in 55 days and the express dispatches via Marseilles in 38 days, a very good record compared with earlier information transmission by private sailing vessels in 125 days on average.[908] The China mails were then probably carried to Calcutta by the dawk service, as they were taken from that port to Singapore by HMS *Larne*, reported to have departed on 27 March. As the trip to Singapore took no more than three weeks, she arrived there in mid-April. The following vessel for Canton, being the *Actif*, departed on 5 May and arrived, probably via some other port, at Canton on 30 May with the 4 February mails.[909]

The last part of the trip could not be called effective by any measurement. The 'express' mails arrived in China 78 days later than the Bombay merchants had received their part of the dispatches which had been sent on the same day from London. The 116-day express mail transmission from London by the Overland route to China actually took longer than the fastest direct sailings by the East Indiamen in 1832.[910]

Royal Charter for the P&O

In 1840, the second contract between the Post Office and the PSNCo stretched the company's activities to the Mediterranean as the European link in the Indian service. This was an exclusive Royal Charter for a mail steamship service to the East, comparable with the Cunard Line's in the North Atlantic and the Royal Mail Line's in the West Indies.

The charter included an annual subsidy of £34,200 for the Alexandria service during the next five years, as well as the right of incorporation with limited liability – a lucrative deal as the shareholders of the rival companies

---

907 Also Tabeart notes the poor connectivity at Malta between the Admiralty packets and the all-sea route via Gibraltar. The Malta–Marseilles packets clearly had priority in the mail service, which was 'quite understandable – a principle reason for establishing the entire packet network was for the Government to get the earliest possible intelligence from [or to] the far-flung British Empire'. Tabeart (2002), 66.
908 See Chapter VII.1.
909 For the last leg, see Scamp, 10.
910 The last commercial East Indiamen, which departed from London in April and May, 1832, sailed to Canton via Anjer, Java, in 107 to 111 days. See Chapter VII.1.

would be unlimited. The geographical enlargement of operations caused a need to change the company's name to the Peninsular and Oriental Steam Navigation Company. The capital of the new company was fixed at £1,000,000. In addition to the five steamers of the former PNSCo, two larger ones – the *Great Liverpool* of 1,400 tons, and the *Oriental* of 1,787 tons – were chartered from a company which had lost the transatlantic mail contract given to the Cunard Line.[911]

From September 1840, the all-sea mail service between Falmouth and Alexandria was taken care of by the P&O. The packets departed from Falmouth on the second of each month, called at Gibraltar and Malta only, and proceeded immediately after coaling. The ships were larger than the Admiralty steamers used earlier on that route, and one and the same vessel took the mails all the way from Falmouth to Alexandria, thus avoiding delays in transfer from one ship to another at the different ports. As a result, the duration of the all-sea trip from Southampton via Gibraltar reduced from an average of 28 days in 1839 to 16 in 1841.[912]

The P&O mail contract included a clause that the company would provide a service from Suez to India within two years. Which part of India, was not specified. While the attitudes among the disappointed Anglo-Indian merchant houses towards the P&O remained cool, their financial support for any route was limited.[913]

The EIC offered a rather modest bonus of £20,000 a year for five years if the P&O successfully inaugurated a service between Calcutta, Madras and Egypt – which left to the EIC the monopoly of the shortest and most direct route to Bombay, which they were then covering with their own naval steamers. And indeed, this arrangement by the EIC continued until the P&O took over the Bombay route in 1852.[914]

The British Government finally awarded the P&O a contract for the route Suez–Ceylon–Madras–Calcutta for an annual payment of £115,000.[915] For this service, and to cover the whole route from England to India – and later to China and other places in the East – much preparation was needed.

---

911 Norman L. Middlemiss, *Merchant Fleets. P&O Lines* (Newcastle-upon-Tyne, 2004), 17; Tabeart (2002), 59; Thorner, 35–36. – The Royal Charter of 1840 is reprinted by Kirk (1987), 92–94.

912 Calculated from Tabeart's figures (2002), 52–53; for the P&O sailings, see 69–70. See also Tabeart (2002), 59–66.

913 As late as 1847, three-quarters of P&O's shares were held in Ireland, presumably by Richard Bourne and his business allies. See Cable, 68–71; Thorner, 36–38.

914 Cable, 69; Thorner 36. – In 1849, P&O made a further attempt to dislodge the EIC from the Bombay route by offering a £24,700/year contract for an extended Suez to Bombay to Australia link. The EIC service between Suez and Bombay was costing the British and Indian governments no less than £105,000/year at that time. The offer was declined even though it was at that time often quicker to send the mails to Bombay by the P&O service via Calcutta. The matter was hotly debated in the Parliament and the EIC was left in no doubt what the country thought of it. Three years later the EIC lost a complete ship load of mail in the Red Sea; and during the next few years the Bombay–Suez link was gradually transferred to P&O. See Middlemiss (2004), 18–19; and Reg Kirk, *P&O Bombay & Australian Lines – 1852–1914* (Norfolk, no printing year given), 43.

915 See Cable, 78; Middlemiss (2004), 18.

The P&O organized overland route facilities of its own, including small tugs and barges to convey passengers along the Mahmoudieh Canal between Alexandria and Atfeh, and a larger Nile river steamer. As the goods had to be carried by camel, caravans of 3,000 to 4,000 animals were needed to transport a single shipload. Even the coal for vessels in the Red Sea area went across Egypt by camel-back. This was necessary as, due to the unfavourable monsoons, it could not be sent by sailing vessels as was the normal practice in sending fuel to the eastern stations. The P&O also opened a hotel in Cairo, reserving it almost exclusively for its own passengers.[916]

On 24 September 1842, the 'large and powerful' *Hindostan* of 2,018 tons departed from Southampton and arrived in Calcutta on Christmas Eve, in 91 days, having coaled at Gibraltar, Cape Verde, Ascension, St. Helena, Cape Town, Mauritius, and Galle in Ceylon. Two more purpose-built vessels arrived in 1843 and 1844.[917] Now when there were enough steamers for the service, a new contract was made between the Government and the P&O for the Calcutta line, and another for a new China line from Galle via Singapore and Penang to Hong Kong. The latter was opened in August 1845.[918]

The EIC service to India

Until the P&O started their mail service to Bengal, both the Bombay and Calcutta merchants were served by EIC steamers from Suez to Bombay. This part of the trip, together with the overland crossing in Egypt, took 20 days in 1841, while the total voyage between London and Bombay took 36 days.[919] Even if this was a radical improvement compared with the duration of information transmission only a few years earlier, a brief look at the information circles raises some questions.

As can be seen from Table 77 (in the end of the book, p. 431), the departures from England were punctual. Although there was not always a sailing from Bombay on the first day of each month that year, it happened nine times out of 12, however. Yet long delays – from 17 to 29 days – at both ends of the journey between the arrivals and departures were typical. If there had been a more frequent service, the duration of the voyage itself would have enabled 4.5 consecutive information circles per year, leaving a good four days margin at both ends.[920]

For the mails to and from Calcutta, the service was even poorer. At least one month had to be counted for the return trip between the ports of Bombay and Calcutta, and in real life this was hardly enough. As there was no direct steam ship service to Calcutta, the existing means of information transmission worked as follows:

916 Middlemiss (2004), 17–18. – More about the Overland route arrangements by the P&O, see Cable, 85–93.
917 Kirk, *The P&O Lines...* 11; Middlemiss (2004), 18.
918 Kirk, *The P&O Lines..*, 11; Middlemiss (2004), 18.
919 Calculated from the sailing dates published by Scamp, 10, 31–32, 47.
920 Calculated from the sailing lists of Scamp, 31–32, 37–38, 47.

TABLE 78. *Consecutive information circles enabled by the express services between London and Calcutta, 1841.*

London departure	Via Marseilles, Malta and Alexandria by Admiralty and P&O; EIC ship to Bombay	Bombay arrival	Bombay-Calcutta-Bombay by dawks 2 x 15 days	Bombay departure	By EIC ship from Bombay; P&O and Admiralty services, arriving at Marseilles, ship and date	London arrival	Information circle, days
4.1. (1841)	*Victoria*	12.2.	~30 days	1.4.	*Promethius* 30.4.	5.5.	121 (7+4)
5.6.	*Victoria*	7.7.	~30 days	2.9.	*Alecto* 3.10.	7.10.	124 (8+4)
4.11.	*Berenice*	12.12.	~30 days				

Source: *Sailing lists of Scamp, 31–32, 37–38, 47; Tabeart (2002), 69–73, 191–192.*

Compared to 3.5 information circles per year between London and Bombay, only 2.5 could be managed by the existing means of communication between London and Calcutta. In the example, the mails from Calcutta arrived in London on 5 May, and answers to them just missed the India mail, which left on the day before. This happened again, when the India mails arrived on 7 October, and the express dispatches had been sent three days earlier on the 4th.[921] Letters from Calcutta always missed the next mail ship departure from Bombay due to the long and troublesome voyage between the two ports. In terms of information circles, there was no real use for the Marseilles express service, as answers to letters could not be sent sooner than they were, anyway. But if the message was urgent, the express service naturally saved a few days in the one-way voyage.

The P&O Calcutta Line from Suez to Madras and Calcutta started in early 1843, first with only one steamer, and finally from the beginning of 1845 with three vessels. From January 1845, the service was conducted monthly. The China Line started a monthly service in the summer of 1845.[922] Until then, all business information transmission to the East was taken care of by a combination of the P&O, Admiralty, EIC and various private merchant vessels as described above.

A memorandum of covers received at Bombay by the EIC steamer *Berenice* in March 1845 gives an idea of the number of letters and newspapers carried from England to India and China at that time. The all-sea mail via Southampton included 24,400 letters, 30,000 newspapers and seventy-five

---

921 See the sailing lists of Scamp, 31–32, 37–38, 47.
922 See Kirk, *The P&O Lines...*, 23–24; Scamp, 94 , 101, 123–130.

TABLE 79. *Consecutive information circles enabled by the co-operating services of the P&O Calcutta Line and the EIC Bombay Line between London and Calcutta, 1845.*

P&O ship / or by rail via Marseilles	South-ampton, depar-ture	Ship from Suez	Cal-cutta arrival	Ship from Calcutta	Calcutta departure	Route	Lon-don arri-val	Infor-mation circle, days
Great Liver-pool	20.1. (1845)	Hin-dostan	8.3.	Bentick	10.3.	Via Mar-seilles	22.4.	92
By rail	24.4.	Hin-dostan	6.6.	Akbar / Queen (EIC) from Bombay to Suez 20.6.	9.6. deadline for dawk service 11.6. for Bombay	Via Mar-seilles with Bombay mails	1.8.	99
By rail	7.8.	Queen (EIC) to Bom-bay, arrival 6.9.	15.9. by dawk service	Semira-mis (EIC) from Bombay to Suez 1.10.	By dawk service for Bombay ~20.9.	Via Mar-seilles with Bombay mails	3.11.	88
By rail	7.11.	Details missing						

Sources: Scamp, 93–103, 108–117; Kirk, The P&O Lines..., 11, 23–24. – There are several differences in the sailing data between Kirk and Scamp. The latter has been used here in case of confusion, as it is newer and based on thorough examination of local newspapers as well as Kirk's studies. – From 1843, the P&O mail departures and arrivals were directed via Southampton instead of Falmouth, which was sensible due to the newly opened railway connection. The arriving mails were normally postmarked in London on the same or the next day after the ship's arrival. See Kirk (1987), 20–21.

boxes, while 6,000 letters, 8,000 newspapers and 38 boxes arrived by the express service via Marseilles. Additionally, the mails carried by the *Berenice* included 1,700 letters from foreign countries, as well as 5,000 newspapers and 28 boxes.[923]

The monthly P&O steamship service all the way from Europe via Suez to Calcutta was definitely an improvement, but it could not alone serve the Bengal merchants satisfactorily. It often happened that the steamer from Calcutta had just departed, or she departed on the same day as the mails from Europe arrived. In these cases, the EIC steamer from Bombay to Suez could still be reached by the dawk service across the Indian mainland. According

923 The memorandum was originally published by the *Bombay Times* on 26.3.1843, see Scamp, 98. On arrival, the *Berenice* was about ten days delayed due to engine problems. See Scamp, 93, 98.

to Scamp who refers to the Calcutta newspapers, the service was in general use, this route thus complementing the direct P&O all-sea mail service.[924]

Many of the local problems were classic examples, typical also in the early mail services in the Atlantic and the West Indies, as has been shown in the previous chapters. When the *Hindostan* arrived at Calcutta on 8 March, 1845, the *Bentick* departed on the same day, or two days later, depending on the sailing data used. The *Hindostan* met serious problems on her way to Calcutta in early June and arrived on the day after the mail ship for Suez had departed. But using the dawk service, answers to the letters could be sent via Bombay, from where the EIC mail steamer was leaving for Suez on the 20th. Thus there was, in fact, a bi-monthly mail service from Calcutta, even if it did not enable heavy bulk mail dispatches.[925]

Mail sailings to China

The real difficulty in Eastern communications was between India and China. The mails were carried by an *ad hoc* basis from Bombay or Calcutta, probably via Singapore, to Canton by varying merchant ships, which happened to sail for China. By comparing the sailing data published by Scamp with a 'Chinese Repository' list of port arrivals in Hong Kong between August 1841 and June 1843, we get some interesting background to the mail-carrying sailing vessels between India and China. Having dispatched the mails at Canton, many of the ships arrived within a few days in Hong Kong. Of the 17 mail carriers on the list, eight were loaded with opium, five reported general cargo or sundries, one carried cotton, one coals, and two arrived in ballast.[926] It is clear that the main interest of these ships was not to carry mail as rapidly as possible, but to take care of their own businesses.

There were different mixtures of mail routes also in the Southeast Asian leg of the journey. An example: the EIC steamer *Cleopatra* took the European mails from Aden to Bombay, where she arrived on 5 August, 1841. At the port of Bombay, most of the mails were taken on board a private merchantman, the *Parkfield*, which sailed for China with a general cargo on the 10th. The EIC steamer *Madagascar* left Calcutta on 16 August, but without any of the dispatches that would probably arrive from Bombay on the 19th by the dawk service. Instead, the ship arrived at Canton on 12 September with fresh Singapore newspapers and a few London papers that she had picked up from HMS *Larne* in Singapore. The *Larne* arrived at Canton from Madras on 19 September with some Indian government dispatches and Madras letters, but with no business letters from Bombay. The *Parkfield* arrived at Canton with the London mails from July as late as 4 October, after '56 days out' as the Repository noted.[927]

---

924 See Table 80.
925 For the sailing dates, see Scamp, 93–103, 108–117; and Kirk, *The P&O Lines...*, 11, 23–24. See also Table 79 for the consecutive information circles.
926 For the sailing lists, see Scamp, 31, 47–48, and 62; for the 'Chinese Repository' see Scamp, 398–413.
927 See Scamp, 31, 35, 399. If the '56' is correct, the ship departed from Bombay on 9.8. and not on 10.8. as has been estimated by Scamp. For the information circulation, see Table 80.

As the last irritant in the matter, those few dispatches brought by the *Madagascar* 'though landed at the Hotel, could not be opened in consequence of a recent order of yours to the contrary, but were sent to Hong Kong and returned here four days afterwards'. This was due to an order by the British Superintendent of Trade that all mail arriving at Macau was to be sent to the new Post Office at Hong Kong for processing, even though most of the merchants still resided at Macau. In consequence, the merchants who received dispatches by the *Madagascar* were unable to reply to their letters by the *City of Palaces*, which soon left Macau for Calcutta.[928]

As long as there was no organized mail system in the Southeast Asian part of the route, the dispatches were carried as described above. It often happened that a minor part of the mails arrived before the bulk, but whether these were the mails for which senders had paid an extra fee in London cannot be verified without seeing the rate markings on letters which were carried by these different means. This could probably be discovered by postal historians collecting covers from Asian mail routes.

TABLE 80. *Consecutive information circles enabled by the fastest mail services between London and Canton, 1841, an example.*

London, departure of express mail, by rail via Marseilles	EIC ship from Suez to Bombay, arrival date	Ship for China, departure port, date	Arrival at Canton	Ship from China, departure port, ship, date	All mails carried by EIC ship from Bombay to Suez, departure	Express mail, London arrival date	Information circle, days
4.1.	*Victoria* 12.2.	1) *Sir Herbert Compton* Bombay 13.2.; 2) *Cowas-jee Family* Calcutta 1.3.	1) 17.4. 2) 15.4.	1) *Ardasser* Canton 15.5 . for Bombay 2) *Sir Herbert Compton*, Canton 21.5. for Bombay	*Auckland* 20.7. to Aden; from there *Berenice* 17.8. to Suez	4.9.	243
6.9.	*Victoria* 25.9.	1) *Water-witch* Calcutta 28.10. 2) *Sir Herbert Compton* Bombay 28.10.	1) 10.12. 2) 23.12.				

Source: Sailing lists of Scamp, 31–32, 37–38, 47.

928 The quote is from the merchants' complaint to the British Superintendent of Trade. See Scamp, 35. Hong Kong was established by the British in 1841.

The mails often arrived by nearly identical merchantmen from Bombay to China, but the duration of the journey varied greatly. For example, the major part of the mails was sent from Bombay by the merchant ship *Westmoreland* on 12 September, 1841. She arrived at Canton on 21 December while some the mails already arrived by the *Monarch* on 6 November. The latter had sailed from Bombay on 16 September. The same letters from London could be taken from Bombay to China in 51 or in 100 days, depending on which vessel the authorities in Bombay happened to put them on board at the port.[929]

The duration of the fastest possible information transmission via the Overland route from London to Canton varied between 79 and 126 days in 1840, between 65 and 119 days in 1841, and between 61 and 110 days in 1842.[930] But most of the business letters did not arrive by these fastest communications, as has been shown by Scamp, who has examined a wide range of newspapers for more details.[931]

Canton Press calculated the following averages for the voyage between London and China: 104 days in 1840, 91 days in 1841 and 88 days for 1842. Yet these were not the averages for the normal mail, but the very first news arriving in Canton by different ships, often not the main mail carriers.[932]

It was normal that arriving vessels carried on board some latest newspapers from the port of departure, and therefore general news often reached the East Asian colonies faster than business letters, which formed one major shipment. Table 80 shows the information circulation enabled by the mixed service in 1841.

This mixed service, with the leg from India to China covered by private sailing vessels, enabled only 1.5 consecutive information circles per year between London and Canton, one circle taking some eight months. And yet it was fortuitous that the mails from India arrived in London on 4 September, just two days before the next departure date of the express mail. If the London mails had been sent off just before the Asian dispatches arrived, the next opportunity to reply to letters from Asia would have been several weeks later. In this case, the replies from England would have arrived in China on 23 January, 1842.[933]

The new trade port of Hong Kong was growing rapidly. The 'Chinese Repository' reported 147 arrivals in August–December 1841, and 371 arrivals in the whole calendar year 1842. Most vessels were on different inter-Asian routes, but 20 ships sailed directly from London or Portsmouth, and 14 from Liverpool. On arrival, these vessels had been out for 135 and 130 days, respectively, on average.[934]

The *John O'Gaunt* sailed from Liverpool in 108 days, arriving in China on 9 July, 1842. If she carried private ship letters, they must have been sent on 23 March at the latest. This was a week earlier than the bulk mail from

929 For the example, see Scamp, 10, 15.
930 See the table about arrival dates of the Overland mails from England in China 1840–1843 by *Canton Press* 11.3.1843, republished by Scamp, 16.
931 For the year 1841, see Scamp, 32–35.
932 For the *Canton Press* table of 11.3.1843, see Scamp, 16.
933 For the sailing dates, see Scamp, 31–32, 37–38.
934 For the 'Chinese Repository' 1842–1843, see Scamp 398–406.

England left for the Overland route, and about ten days earlier than the last dispatches of express mails could be sent via Marseilles. And in this month, the Overland mail reached Canton rather quickly, via Bombay by the *Sir Herbert Compton* and via Calcutta by the famous opium clipper, the *Red Rover,* both arriving on 22 June.[935] The fastest mails arrived in 77 days, which was close to a record. The Overland route appeared to be a better choice, at least this time, but private ship letters were naturally more economical.[936]

Private merchant vessels continued to carry the official China mails from India until the first P&O steamer, the *Lady Mary Wood,* made her first voyage from Galle via Penang and Singapore to Hong Kong with the bulk mails of 20 June and express mails of 24 June from England, arriving on 13 August, 1845.[937] This new arrangement took the London mails to Hong Kong in 50 days, thus halving the normal duration of information transmission in one night. This was one of the occasions in the history of world communications, where a mere logistical arrangement was able to revolutionize the duration of information transmission, without radical new inventions, but using what already existed.

When the P&O was allowed to expand its services to China, the government did not even ask for bids from any other company. It was considered that the company had already invested so much in the service that it would have been unjust not to give them the business. Additionally, the cost of the P&O services east of Suez averaged 17s 1d per mile only, while the estimated cost of the Admiralty packets was 42s 6d.[938]

While the P&O Calcutta Line service via Galle actually made no major difference in communications with Bengal compared with the shorter sailing to Bombay and the inland runners, the steamship service from Galle definitely improved the information circulation with China. Instead of sailing via India, the mails were forwarded from Galle directly by a mail steamer to Penang, Singapore and Hong Kong.

As can be noticed from Table 81, the new system enabled 2.5 consecutive information circles each year compared with only 1.5 in 1841 (see Table 80). The new service more than halved the time taken by the sailing vessels around the Cape, the mails now being carried in about two months in each direction.

This happened simultaneously with the beginning of the golden era of the American-built sailing clippers, which took over a great part of the tea trade between China and London in the late 1840s. Since the abolition of

935 See Scamp, 47, 49, 404.
936 There is also evidence of mails arriving by private sailing vessels directly from England faster than the Overland mail. Scamp refers to Chinese newspapers which reported 'news brought by *Folkstone*' which included 'accounts from London to the 3rd October'. The *Folkstone* had sailed from England in three months and three weeks, and the regular October mail was at that time delayed by trouble in Egypt. The newspapers also reported that the *Narranganset*, from Liverpool, brought the latest dates of 20.10.40 'but a very few letters'. Both these ships sailed via the Cape of Good Hope. See Scamp, 32.
937 Scamp, 93, 122.
938 Moubray & Moubray, 187.

the monopoly of the East India Company in China in 1833, the nature of the British tea trade had thoroughly changed. In the days of the EIC monopoly, the term 'new season's tea' did not really exist. Tea, as bought in London from a retailer, was never less than 18 to 24 months old. The East Indiamen always sailed from China during the favourable monsoon between November and March, and when the teas arrived in England some five or six months later, they were stored in bonded warehouses for about a year, since a large reserve was necessary in case the China fleet failed to arrive. When the business was opened for competition, the import of fresh tea became very lucrative. The merchants had no difficulty in selling the new crop as soon as it arrived at the docks, and the glamour attached to tea carried by a well-known ship could procure even higher prices – we still remember, for example, the famous *Cutty Sark*, one of the British tea clippers from the sunset of this period in the 1870s.[939]

TABLE 81. *Consecutive information circles enabled by the new P&O China Line services, London–Hong Kong, 1846.*

London mail departure	P&O arrival from Suez at Galle, ship and date	P&O departure from Galle, ship and date	Hong Kong arrival	Hong Kong departure, ship and date	Ship arrival at Galle	P&O departure from Galle for Suez, ship and date	London mail arrival	Information circle, days
By rail via Marseilles 24.1.	Hindostan 2.3.	Braganza 3.3.	22.3.	Braganza 30.3.	16.4.	Hindostan 18.4.	22.5.*	118
By rail via Marseilles 25.5.	Precursos 26.6.	Braganza 28.6.	13.7.	Braganza 25.7.	14.8.	Precursor ~19.8.	28.9.**	126
By rail via Marseilles 24.10.	Hindostan 7.11.	Lady Mary Wood 7.12.	3.1. 1847					

Source: Kirk, The P&O Lines…, 11, 23–24, Tabeart (2002), 197, Scamp, 131–134.
    * The arrival date is an estimate (Marseilles arrival + four days).
    ** Due to the delay in the Indian Ocean, the express mails seem to have missed the Admiralty packet for Marseilles at Malta and were carried together with the bulk mail to Southampton by the P&O steamer *Oriental*. Thanks to the railway connection, the mails were in London on the same day when the ship arrived in Southampton. As can be noticed, these mails arrived too late to be answered in the September mail.

939 For the British tea trade, see MacGregor (1952), 3–30. – For changes in the construction of private merchant vessels in order to increase the speed, see MacGregor (1952), 33–188, passim.

The fast American clippers, built for the California run in the late 1840s and 1850s, naturally took their share of the profitable tea trade. Instead of returning in ballast to New York after their arrival in San Francisco, they continued across the Pacific to China, loaded rapidly up with tea, and proceeded to London. This was now possible as Britain had abrogated the remaining provisions of the old Navigation Acts in 1848 and opened up commerce to ships of foreign origin on equal terms with British vessels. Up to the time of the American Civil War, at least 139 cargoes of tea were landed in Great Britain by American ships, most of them 'Yankee clippers'.[940]

Even if greatly admired for their speed, the tea clippers were not often an alternative for the steamship mail service via the Overland route. As in the California run, the clippers sailed a much longer seaway than the steamers and could not make a shortcut across an isthmus, as the steamship companies did at Panama and Suez. The fastest journeys in the tea trade took less than 100 days from China to London[941] but compared with the mail transmission of only two months by steamship, the option was not very attractive and was mainly used for consignee's letters. But the new rapid form of tea trade benefited greatly from fast business information transmission, and would be one of the main reasons for further development of communications between Europe and China in the 1860s.

The P&O mail monopoly begins

During the 1850s, the P&O gradually gained a rather complete monopoly on the eastern routes. In addition to the Southampton–Alexandria route already taken care of by the company, the express service between Marseilles and Malta, earlier carried out by the Admiralty, was transferred to the P&O from January 1853 as a part of a new mail contract.

The mails were made up in London on the 8th and 24th of each month to leave at 8 p.m. that day. No more than 60 hours were allowed for the railway transit through France and the shipment in Marseilles. Thus the vessels from Southampton and Marseilles would arrive at Malta simultaneously. The Southampton mails departed on the 4th and 20th of each month respectively. According to the schedule, the trip took 14 days, including a stoppage at Gibraltar and another for coaling at Malta. [942]

Additionally, the P&O voluntarily entered into increasing postal commitments. The Calcutta and China lines were served twice a month instead of monthly. The company also gradually took over the Bombay route, the mails being first carried by the Calcutta steamer and later directly from Suez via Aden to Bombay twice a month. In addition, the P&O started a mail service between Singapore and Australia, via Batavia, although it

---

940 See Cutler (1961), 167–169, 226–239.
941 See sailing lists of the American tea clippers between China and England 1850–1860, published by Cutler (1961), 467–474; and sailing lists of the British tea clippers on the same route 1848–1875, published by MacGregor (1952), 200–232.
942 See Kirk, *The P&O Lines...*, 13; and Kirk (1987), 106.

FIG. 32. *The letter sent on 16.8.1858 from Clifton, England, to Bombay, was carried along the express route via Marseilles and Overland via Suez, arriving in Bombay by the P&O steamer* Cadiz *on 9.9.1858 in 23 days. (See the text.)*

was interrupted three years later due to the need for steamers in the Crimean war.[943] The Australian mails will be discussed later in this chapter.

After the Crimean War in 1854–1856, the British faced further problems in the East – the Second Opium War with China in 1856–1858, and the Indian Mutiny in 1857–1858.[944] In such circumstances, fast information transmission between England and Asia was crucial not only to the interests of the merchant houses, but also to the British crown. To cope with this problem, and apparently also to discourage French plans to dig a canal from Port Said to the Gulf of Suez, the Overland railway across the Egyptian desert was finalized and opened in 1859.[945]

The mail service to Bombay, which had taken over a month in each direction in the early 1840s even via Marseilles and the Overland route in Egypt, could be conducted in just 23 days in 1858. A letter from the writer's collection illustrates a good example of this speed. The cover from Clifton, England, to Bombay on 16 August, 1858, was sent via London on the 17th, being addressed 'via Marseilles'. It was taken by the P&O steamer *Cadiz*

---

943 No fewer than 12 P&O mail steamers served in the Black Sea area during the war. By agreement with the British Government, the line to Australia was abandoned and the China Line was degraded to a monthly one. The new line to Italy – at that time a cargo line – was also dropped. See Kirk, *The P&O Bombay...*, 2–3; Reg Kirk, *Australian Mails via Suez 1852 to 1926* (Kent, 1989), 4.

944 For the Second Opium War, see e.g. James (2000), 238–241. For the Mutiny, see Cain & Hopkins, 284–288; and Lawrence James, *Raj. The Making of British India,* (London, 2003), 233–298.

945 For a French view of Franco-British relations during the building of the Suez Canal, see Zachary Karabell, *Parting the Desert. The Creation of the Suez Canal* (London, 2004), passim.

TABLE 82. *Consecutive information circles between London and Bombay via Southampton, March 1859–March 1860.*

Ship and depar- ture date from South- ampton	Alex- andria arrival	Ship and depar- ture date from Suez	Bom- bay arrival	Ship and depar- ture from Bombay	Suez arri- val	Ship and depar- ture date from Alex- andria	London arrival – via South- ampton	Infor- mation circle, days
Pera 12.3.59	26.3.	Salsette 29.3.	11.4.	Northam 12.4.	26.4.	Ripon 3.5.	18.5.	67
Behar 27.5.	8.6.	Malta* 12.6.	- -	Emeu 6.7.	24.7.	Ceylon 27.7.	8.8.	73
Ripon 12.8.	27.8.	Madras 28.8.	9.9.	Columbian 12.9.	28.9.	Indus 30.9.	14.10.	63
Orissa 27.10.	4.11.	Madras 12.11.	30.11.	Northam 12.12.	24.12	Pera 28.12.	12.1.60	77
N.N. 27.1.	- -	Ottawa 14.2.	1.3.					

Sources: Kirk, The P&O Bombay..., 12, 47.
  * The *Malta* was laid up at Aden due to a breakdown. The mails for Bombay were carried by the *Concordia*, no arrival date in Bombay given.

from Suez on 27 August to Bombay, where it arrived on 9 September and was handstamped in the Bombay Post Office on the same day (see Fig. 32).[946] The one-way voyage from London to Bombay had been considerably shortened, but did the information circulation improve correspondingly?

From March 1859, mail transmission to the East was taken care of by the P&O as a weekly service. The China and Calcutta mails were transmitted from Southampton in the 1st week, the Bombay mails in the 2nd, the China and Calcutta mails in the 3rd, and the Bombay & Australia mails in the 4th week of each month.[947] By examining the consecutive information circles on the India and China routes, we will notice an interesting point.

In 1859–1860, the information circulation between England and Bombay ran as follows: The all-sea mails for Bombay via Southampton, Gibraltar and Malta to Alexandria, overland to Suez and further by another P&O vessel to Bombay were carried in approximately one month on average, i.e. 30 days eastwards and 32.5 days westwards. The number of consecutive information circles was 4.5.

946 SRLC.
947 Kirk, *The P&O Bombay*..., 11–12. The departure dates from Southampton were the 4th, 12th, 20th and 27th of each month. The express mails via Marseilles departed eight or even nine days later for the same steamers from Aden to the different Asian ports. See e.g. Kirk (1989), 57–65; Kirk, *The P&O Lines*..., 45.

The duration of eastward voyages varied between 28 and 34 days, while the westward voyages took 28 to 42 days. An average information circle between London and Bombay via Southampton took 71 days. The shortest time to get an answer to a letter from Bombay by this means was 59 days and the longest time was 82 days.[948]

As the departure dates from Southampton for the Bombay mails were the 12th and the 27th of each month, and one information circle normally took something between two and two and a half months, the system enabled rather fast answers to letters arriving from India. The system served quite well the Southampton bulk mail service. The express route via Marseilles gives us a slightly different view.

TABLE 83. *Consecutive information circles between London and Bombay via Marseilles, March 1859 – March 1860.*

Departure date from London by rail, by ship from Marseilles	Alexandria arrival	Ship and departure date from Suez	Bombay arrival	Ship and departure date from Bombay	Suez arrival	Ship and departure date from Alexandria for Marseilles	London arrival	Information circle, days
18.3.59 *Panther* 20.3.	26.3.	*Salsette* 29.3.	11.4.	*Northam* 12.4.	26.4.	*Nepaul* 2.5.	~12.5.	59
18.5. *Ellora* 20.5.	26.5.	*Ottawa* 27.5.	9.6.	*Ottawa* 23.6.	11.7.	*Ellora* 13.7.	22.7.	57
2.8. *N.N.* 4.8.	~10.8.	*Norna* 12.8.	25.8.	*Columbian* 12.9.	28.9.	*Panther* 30.9.	7.10.	67
18.10. *Vectis* 20.10.	29.10.	*Bombay* 29.10.	13.11.	*Singapore* 26.11.	12.12.	*Vectis* 14.12.	23.12.	66
2.1.60 *N.N.* 4.1.	~10.1.	*Madras* 17.1.	30.1	*Benares* 11.2.	26.2.	*Valetta* 27.2.	6.3.	64

Sources: Kirk, *The P&O Bombay...*, 12, 47; Kirk 1989, 58–64; Proud, 23–51.[949]
– Two P&O vessels from Marseilles to Alexandria ('N.N.') remain unknown. This does not affect the schedules, however.

948 The average duration of the eastward voyages was calculated from 18 trips and of the number of the westward voyages from 19 trips. The average duration of information circles was calculated from 15 consecutive cases during the period. The sailing dates are published by Kirk, *The P&O Bombay...*, 12, 47.

949 Hector Proud (Edward B. Proud, ed.), *The British Sea Post Offices in the East.* British Maritime Postal History Volume 4, (East Sussex, 2003).

As can be noticed, the duration of a single trip varied between about three to four weeks. The shortest information circle took 57 days and the longest 67 days. Even if the one-way express service was usually several days faster than the bulk mail transport and thus shortened the duration of a single voyage notably, the benefit could not be fully transferred to those who paid for rapid communications. The express service enabled five consecutive information circles per year instead of four and a half by bulk mail – but no more.

In information circulation between England and China, the difference between the all-sea mail and the express service was even less significant, as can be noted from Tables 84 and 85.

TABLE 84. *Consecutive information circles London–Hong Kong 1859, via Southampton.*

	Information circle # 1	Information circle # 2	Information circle # 3	Information circle # 4
Ship and departure date from Southampton	Ceylon 6.1.1859	Pera 20.4.	Ceylon 20.8.	Indus 21.12.
Arrival in Alexandria	20.1.	2.5.	2.9.	5.1.1860
Ship and departure date from Suez	Alma 22.1.	Nemesis 6.5.	Simla 5.9.	
Arrival in Galle	6.2.	21.5.	19.9.	
Ship and departure date from Galle	Norna 7.2.	Aden 22.5.	Norna 22.9.	
Arrival in Hong Kong	27.2.	5.6.	8.10.	
Ship and departure date from Hong Kong	Ottawa 27.2.*	Norna 5.6.**	Malabar 13.10.	
Arrival in Galle	15.3.	22.6.	28.10.	
Ship and departure date from Galle	Alma 17.3.	Nemesis 3.7.	Simla 31.10.	
Arrival in Suez	30.3.	20.7.	15.11.	
Ship and departure date from Alexandria	Indus 4.4.	Ripon 22.7.	Indus 21.11.	
Arrival in Southampton	18.4.	6.8.	5.12.	
Duration of the information circle, days	102	108	107	

Sources: Kirk, The P&O Lines..., 45–47, Proud, 18–42.

* The *Ottawa* departed with the European mails on the same day as the *Norna* arrived. The chance that the recipients had an opportunity to answer their letters may be just theoretical. Probably some of the recipients could answer, while the others did not. The following mail steamer departed on 15.3.1859.

** The *Norna* departed with the European mails on the same day as the *Aden* arrived. The following mail steamer departed on 22.6.1859.

TABLE 85. *Consecutive information circles London–Hong Kong 1859, express via Marseilles.*

	Information circle # 1	Information circle # 2	Information circle # 3	Information circle # 4
Departure from London	10.1.1859	26.4.	10.8.	26.11.
Ship and departure date from Marseilles	Panther 12.1.	Ellora 28.4.	Nepaul 12.8.	Panther 28.11.
Arrival in Alexandria	19.1.	4.5.	18.8.	5.12.
Ship and departure date from Suez	Alma 22.1.	Nemesis 6.5.	Nubia 20.8.	Candia 6.12.
Arrival in Galle	6.2.	21.5.	2.9.	23.12.
Ship and departure date from Galle	Norna 7.2.	Aden 22.5.	Singapore 5.9.	Norna 23.12.
Arrival in Hong Kong	27.2.	5.6.	20.9.	13.1.1860
Ship and departure date from Hong Kong	Ottawa 27.2.*	Norna 5.6.**	Singapore 28.9	
Arrival in Galle	15.3.	22.6.	17.10.	
Ship and departure date from Galle	Alma 17.3.	Nemesis 3.7.	Nemesis 18.10.	
Arrival in Suez	30.3.	20.7.	2.11.	
Ship and departure date from Alexandria	Nepaul 4.4.	Panther 22.7.	Valetta 3.11.	
Arrival in Marseilles	11.4.	29.7.	9.11.	
Arrival in London	13.4.	31.7.	11.11.	
Duration of the information circle, days	93	96	93	

Sources: Kirk, The P&O Lines..., 45–47, Proud 18–42.

* The *Ottawa* departed with the European mails on the same day as the *Norna* arrived. The chance that the recipients had an opportunity to answer their letters may be just theoretical. Probably some of the recipients could answer, while the others did not. The following mail steamer departed on 15.3.1859.

** The *Norna* departed with the European mails on the same day as the *Aden* arrived. The following mail steamer departed on 22.6.1859.

The one-way trips between London and Hong Kong were typically six days shorter in each direction via Marseilles than via Southampton, as that was the time lag between the departures from those ports, while the trip east of Suez was made by the same vessels. The system had some apparent benefits, but it also included several elements which could have been improved.

The benefit of shortening the voyage by paying extra for the express service worked only in the European part of the trip. Even there the problem was that the arriving letters could often not be answered immediately, but had to wait for a couple of weeks for the next departure, regardless of whether the

FIG. 33. *The* Ripon, *built in 1846, served the P&O for 26 years, mainly between the UK – and Alexandria. (Cable: A Hundred Year History of the P&O, 1931).*

arrival was by express via Marseilles or by the all-sea mail via Southampton. Even if it was possible to answer quicker by sending the answers by the all-sea mail which departed sooner, they did not arrive at the other end faster, but by the same mail steamer.

There was no express service available in India or China that was similar to using the Marseilles express route in Europe. Instead, there were major disadvantages built into the system, especially at the port of Hong Kong. This can easily be noticed by picking out the arrival and departure dates of the mail steamers, as in Table 86.

In examining mail arrivals in Hong Kong in 1859, we can notice from Table 86 that the P&O mail steamer for Galle, from where the mails were forwarded to Aden, departed in five cases on the same day as the European mails arrived in Hong Kong. Even if the local post office had been efficient enough to dispatch the arriving mails – which naturally depended very much on the time of day the ship arrived – the merchants would not have had many hours to answer their letters. If the mail ship from Galle arrived in the evening, there was no time at all. The next opportunity to send letters to Europe was after some two weeks, varying between 11 and 17 days.

In a few cases the mail ship arrived one to four days after the mails for Europe had departed from Hong Kong, and there was not even a theoretical possibility to reply to the letters earlier than some two weeks later. There were several cases where there were two mail arrivals without any departing mails in between, and two departures without anything arriving in between.

TABLE 86. *Mail arrivals and departures by the P&O steamers in Hong Kong, 1859.*

Mail arrival in Hong Kong, ship and date	The first possibility to send answers to the letters: Departure from Hong Kong, ship and date
Cadiz 15.1.	Singapore 15.1. Cadiz 30.1.
Pekin 27.1.	Cadiz 30.1.
Ottawa 11.2.	Pekin 15.2.
Norna 27.2.	Ottawa 27.2. Norna 15.3.
Malabar 19.3.	Singapore 31.3.
Singapore 26.3.	Singapore 31.3.
Cadiz 10.4.	Aden 13.4.
Pekin 24.4.	Cadiz 24.4. Pekin 5.5.
Ganges 9.5.	Ganges 22.5.
Norna 20.5.	Ganges 22.5.
Aden 5.6.	Norna 5.6. Malabar 22.6.
Singapore 22.6.	Malabar 22.6. Singapore 5.7.
Pekin 9.7.	Pekin 22.7.
Cadiz 23.7.	Cadiz 10.8.
Granada 5.8.	Cadiz 10.8.
Ganges 22.8.	Granada 24.8.
Malabar 7.9.	Ganges 12.9.
Singapore 20.9.	Singapore 28.9.
Norna 8.10.	Malabar 13.10.
Cadiz 23.10.	Norna 29.10. Cadiz 15.11.
Ottawa 16.11.	Ottawa 30.11.
Ganges 29.11.	Ottawa 30.11.
Pekin 14.12.	Ganges 15.12.
Malabar 27.12.	Pekin 30.12.

Sources: Kirk, The P&O Lines..., 42–47, Proud 18–49.

In fact, Table 86 shows a list of lost opportunities, although half of the cases depict a nicely working system. Even if the mails departed punctually from England, there were more than enough opportunities for them to be delayed during a trip consisting of several different steamship journeys, as well as railway trips and reloading at ports between the sea voyages. The arrivals in Hong Kong varied by more than a week and so did the departures. The time that the mail steamers normally spent at port in Hong Kong varied between five days and three weeks, with some longer exceptions.

To speed up mail delivery in the arrival port, the Post Office authorized the shipping companies to arrange sorting of the mails on board during the long sea voyages. The idea was adopted from the French packets in the Mediterranean and first used on the Australian route by the British in 1858, when the European & Australian Royal Mail Company held the Charter for that mail route. There were two authorized clerks on board the ship to sort and handstamp each letter before they were landed upon arrival at the destination port. From 1859, the British packets in the Mediterranean also sorted their mails between Alexandria and Southampton.[950] This arrangement probably saved money for the Post Office as the work could be done during a longer period at sea, instead of the normal rush at the local Post Office at the port of destination, with several clerks trying to sort a large amount of letters and newspapers as quickly as possible. The system was widely used by the railways, too. In addition to increased work efficiency, it naturally speeded up information transmission.

Geographical distance – a relative concept

As discussed in Chapter VII.1., the number of sailings for Australia grew constantly in the 1820s and 1830s. The mails between Europe and Australia were carried by private merchantmen, and especially the mails homeward were often badly delayed. There was no interest among shipowners to commit themselves to regular sailings, as homeward cargoes were difficult to obtain in Sydney.[951] Many ships sailed from Australia to Chinese or Indian waters in hope of more valuable freight[952] and there was no sense in sending European mails in that direction before the Overland route had been introduced.

Finally the British Government made an agreement with the brothers Henry and Calvert Toulmin for a monthly mail service by sailing vessels around the Cape of Good Hope to Australia. The service was in use from 1844 to 1848, but it never worked satisfactorily. The Postmaster General of New South Wales reported in 1846 that the average time taken by the post office packets on their trips to Sydney was 124 days, twelve days more than the average for the private merchantmen. The colonists in Melbourne and Van Diemen's Land were even more dissatisfied with the Toulmin packets, as they sailed to Sydney only. The ships carried Melbourne mails to Sydney

---

950 Proud's study covers the Mediterranean Sea Post Offices as well as the Sea Post Offices on the Bombay–Suez (later Aden), Bombay–Karachi, Rangoon–Calcutta and Penang–Singapore–Hong Kong routes, lists of marine sorters, used cancellations and different timetables, partly up to the 20th century. See Proud, passim. – For the beginning of sorting mail at sea, see Proud 13–17; for the French Sea Post Office markings of the Mediterranean packets, see Salles, Tome II, 51–139.
951 Moubray & Moubray, 198.
952 See Chapter VII.1.

to be returned to Melbourne by boat or by the recently established overland mail. As the complainants put it: 'our letters [are] taken past our doors and sent back to us after a delay of three to six weeks with a six-fold postage'. If the packets had stopped at Melbourne, the Sydney merchants would not have used the service. They definitely did not want to depend on shipments from Melbourne.[953]

This was not the only aspect similar to the long quarrel about the mail service in India. What might be called a 'Battle of the Routes' followed. One alternative for a steamship mail route was a transpacific route via Panama by the Royal Mail Lines. The problem was that the railway across the isthmus did not exist yet. The all-sea route around the Cape of Good Hope was seriously considered as it was used by the merchantmen, emigrant ships and the Toulmin packets. There was also the possibility to diverge from the P&O line at Galle or Singapore, and to come down the western coast of the Australian continent around Cape Leeuwin, or to sail via Torres Strait and straight down the east coast to Sydney. All these alternatives had their pros and cons and the discussion continued.[954]

In 1847, the P&O offered a monthly service from Singapore to Sydney, if they would also get the contract for the Aden–Bombay Line which was still held by the EIC. According to Robinson, the offer was rejected partly due to growing fears of a monopoly being built up by the P&O in the eastern seas and partly because the EIC was unwilling to surrender the Bombay Line.[955] It was clear that the latter was not interested in giving up the service between Bombay and Aden, and it was equally clear that the EIC would not expand its mail service to Australia. So nothing happened.

By 1851, some decision had to be made. Until then, the trade between Britain and the distant Australian colonies had remained modest, but the gold rush changed it all. As Michael K. Stammers puts it: 'As soon as the news of the discovery of the new goldfields was brought back to England, many people were tempted to sail out in the hope of digging up a fortune. Australia had a predominantly agricultural economy at the time of the gold finds. Consequently, the little manufacturing industry that existed could not cope with the needs of the great influx of new settlers and it was also deprived of labour because of the all-powerful attraction of gold. Gold exports enabled the Australians to import vast quantities of all kinds of manufactured goods from England to satisfy the wants of her new people, and also provided capital to invest in projects to extend the economy. The building of railways was one especially important example. All the materials – the rails, the locomotives, the coaches, the bridge components, the signals – were nearly all made in Great Britain and shipped out. Due to the rapidly increasing number of people and large quantity of British exports demanding shipment, the Black Ball Line [of Liverpool, not to be mixed with the

---

953 Robinson (1964), 186–189. When the Toulmin service ended in early 1849, private sailing ships were again the only means of sending letters to Australia.
954 Robinson (1964), 189–190.
955 Robinson (1964), 190–191. For further details, see also Moubray & Moubray, 199.

American namesake in the North Atlantic] and its competitors enjoyed an unprecedented boom.' [956]

The statistics are impressive. The annual number of passengers for Australia rose from about 21,000 in 1851 to almost 88,000 in 1852, and continued on this level for several years. The number of inhabitants in New South Wales expanded from 119,000 in 1841 to 179,000 in 1851 and 249,000 in 1855 and the lately established Victoria (including Melbourne) grew from 12,000 in 1841 to 237,000 in 1851 and 409,000 in 1855.[957]

The passenger fares to Australia rose rapidly, and so did the freight rates. Cargo space was offered by the Black Ball Line, the main shipping line for Australia, in mid-1852 at £7 per ton, while premier express freight, like the new crop of teas from China, never went much above £ 4–5 per ton. It was easy to find a full crew in Liverpool as there were many who wanted to work their way out to Australia, but it was difficult to find crew from Melbourne back home, unless the most highly inflated wages were offered. Nevertheless, the Black Ball Line and several other quickly established – or already existing – shipping lines, including the famous White Star Line, conducted now frequent sailings to the distant colonies.[958]

The Australian sailings were organized as a bi-monthly line service, following the example of the American sailing packets in the Atlantic. Even the competition between the shipping lines followed the Atlantic example: speed was one of the main stepping stones to prestige. Using the latest scientific studies of winds, currents and the technique of 'Great Circle Sailing' by Lieutenant M. F. Maury of the U.S. Navy, and by ordering fast clipper ships from the best American shipyards, the average passages to Australia shortened markedly. It was reported that the average passage of Liverpool ships to Australia was reduced to 110.5 days from the earlier 120 in 1852, and further to 105.5 days in 1853, which compared favourably with the London averages for the same years of 123 and 126 days respectively.[959]

But this was not enough; a mail steamship line was also needed. In 1852, the British Government made a compromise, believing that a trial between two different routes at the same time would show which one was better. The mails would thus be taken by the newly established Australian Royal Mail Steam Navigation Company around the Cape of Good Hope every second month, alternating with the P&O service from Singapore to Sydney, a new leg of the company's Asian services.[960]

The first steamer to reach Australia was the P&O's *Chusan,* a small vessel of only 700 tons and 80 horsepower, which left from Southampton in mid-May 1852 and arrived at Melbourne at the end of July.[961] The trip to Sydney

---

956 Michael K. Stammers, *The Passage Makers* (Sussex, 1978), 109.
957 Stammers, 125; Mitchell, 36.
958 See Stammers, 125–126; and for the early years of the White Star Line on the Australian route, Gardiner, 12–66.
959 Stammers, 78–81.
960 The P&O service went by the west coast of Australia, past Cape Leeuwin to King George's Sound, Melbourne and Sydney. See Robinson (1964), 191–192.
961 To compare, the largest vessels in the North Atlantic service at that time were Collins Line's *Atlantic* and *Baltic,* both 2,860 tons. See e.g. Staff, 131.

took 84 days in all. Her arrival in Australia was celebrated as the beginning of a new era. But it would take several more years before the Australians really had a satisfactorily working mail service.

The Australian Mail Line service was a disappointment from the beginning. The *Australian*, although two times larger than the *Chusan*, and with engines four times as powerful, could not make the journey on the estimated schedule or even near that. On her first trip, she ran out of coal twice and finally arrived at Melbourne in 91 days, and Sydney four days later. Her return trip was even more disappointing, taking 113 days. The *Australian's* second voyage was even worse than the first; she had to return to Plymouth twice with mails that were badly damaged by water. The mails for South Africa were finally sent by the General Screw Steam Shipping Company, which had had a mail contract for that route from 1850, and the Australian bags by the next P&O steamer.[962]

The Australian Mail Line steamers were almost uniformly behind schedule. Machinery breakdowns, insufficient arrangements for fuel and poor management in general were to blame. This was not unique, remembering the typical deficiencies of the time e.g. in the Atlantic, but as the trip was so much longer, the effects multiplied.[963] Within less than a year, the Australian mail line gave up, and in October 1853 the mail service via the Cape was taken over by the General Screw Company. The company turned out to be much more efficient, and its flagship, the *Great Britain* of 3,200 tons, made her first trip to Australia in 65 days.[964]

But the difficulties were not over yet. In the following year, the Crimean War began and the Government needed all available steamers for troop and horse transports. In practice, all mail steamship companies had to reduce their mail sailings due to the war service, including both the P&O and the General Screw Company. In 1855, the mail service for Australia was again carried out by sailing ships, with monthly mail contracts hastily made between the Government and the Liverpool-based sailing ship companies, the Black Ball Line and the White Star Line.[965]

The bold sailing ship companies competed seriously with steam power. One of the Black Ball Line's new American clippers, named the *James Baines* according to the owner, ran from Boston to the Rock Light off the British coast in 12 days, and from Liverpool to Hobson's Bay in Australia in 64 days – 'carrying 700 passengers including 80 first-class, 1400 tons of

962 Robinson (1964), 191–193. – For the General Screw mail contract to South Africa, and for some time even via Mauritius to Calcutta, see Robinson (1964)173–175.
963 For more details on the miserable performance of the Australian Mail Line, see Moubray & Moubray, 200.
964 See Robinson (1964), 193–194.
965 For the Cunard Line ships at the Crimean war, see e.g. Babcock, 117–118; for the P&O see Kirk (1989), 4; for the Royal Mail Line, Bushell, 80–85. For the Australian mail contracts with the Black Ball Line and the White Star Line, see Robinson (1964), 194–195; Stammers, 144–146. – The PR value of a mail contract was so high for any shipping company that it was even used afterwards. The Black Ball Line advertised its Australian service by 'British and Australian ex-Royal Mail Packets' after having lost the contract to the steamships in 1857. The advertisement of James Baines & Co is kept among the Accounts and papers of Henry Eld Symons, LRO, 380 MD, 20.

FIG. 34. *The* Marco Polo *was one of the best known clipper packets on the Australia route in the 1850s. She was owned by the Liverpool-based Black Ball Line, which together with the White Star Line shared the mail contracts to Australia during the Crimean War. On her maiden voyage to Melbourne in 1852, the* Marco Polo *created a world record by sailing out in 68 days and home in 76 days, less than six months out, the first time this had been achieved. (Tabeart 2004, 139) © National Museums Liverpool (Merseyside Maritime Museum).*

cargo and 350 sacks of mail containing over 180,000 letters'. The average outward voyage of the three fastest Black Ball Line clippers took 84 days, and the homeward voyage, run by Cape Horn, 93 days.[966] In fact, there was no great difference whether the Australian mail service was conducted by sail or steam during the early 1850s. Journeys of some 90 days on average – all ships were not at all as speedy as the fastest clippers or steamers – enabled no more than two information circles per year, if even that.[967]

After the war, the British authorities invited tenders for mail contracts via Egypt to Australia. The P&O offered to carry the mails between Suez and Australia for £140,000 per year, while a newcomer, the European & Australian Royal Mail Company, offered a service for £185,000, without including the Malta–Marseilles branch in the tender. It was a heavy blow to the P&O prestige when the contract was awarded to the European & Australian Line. The latter company was quite unprepared to start the

---

966 Stammers, 144; Robinson (1964), 195. Colin Tabeart has collected all the sailing dates of the Australian mail clippers from the contranct period 1855-1856, see Tabeart (2004), 144–160. – There was also a plan to start a mail steamship service via the Pacific in the early 1850s. With the Royal Mail Line heading the project, a new company called the Australasian Pacific Mail Steam Packet Company was formed in order to start a steam traffic service between Europe and Australia via Panama and Tahiti. The project slowed down in early 1854 due to the Crimean War, which postponed the Government's interest in such mail contracts. See Bushell, 90–93.

967 See the sailing data by Tabeart (2004), 144–160.

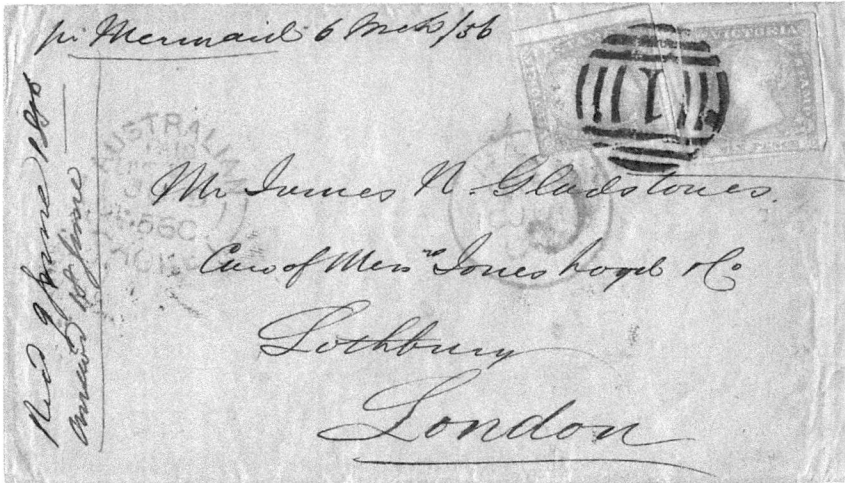

FIG. 35. *The letter dated on 6.3.1856 and sent from Melbourne on 8.3., was carried by the White Star Line clipper packet* Mermaid, *which sailed on 13.3. with 99 passengers, 37,020 ounces of gold, 50,000 sovereigns, wool, etc. and arrived in Liverpool on 9.6.1856. (Tabeart 2004, 153) The letter was on the way for 95 days from the writer to Liverpool and was received latest on the next day in London. The sea journey took 88 days.*

service, having neither ships nor facilities for repair and coaling east of Suez. Beginning with chartered ships, the service started in January 1857.[968]

The European & Australian Line service ended in bankruptcy after 24 round trips. Kirk goes through all the voyages in his study of the Australian mails, depicting the reasons that led to the failure of the company. A few quotes from Kirk tell quite a lot:

'*Oneida* was not available to take the 11.3.57 voyage from Suez – not having arrived at that port. Her next mail voyage was from Galle 31.11.58 when she again broke down, in this case, before reaching Aden. The mails and passengers at Suez on 11.3.57, had to wait for *Simla* on the 28th. The European & Australian Company lost the whole of the subsidy for this mail transit from Sydney to Southampton – it was swallowed up by penalties for late mail.' – 'Despite her [the *Emeu's*] quick passage, she arrived too late to take the August mails from Sydney. What happened to any mails from the French postal service is not known.' – '*European* with engine trouble, lost time between Galle and Sydney. Her arrival time at Sydney [18.10.57]

---

968 Details about the start of this service vary. For example, Robinson states that the P&O lost the contract as they were unwilling to stop at Freemantle and Adelaide, but the timetables published by Kirk show that the European & Australian Line steamers did not stop there either. Kirk also notes that the latter company was not subjected to financial penalties e.g. if the Marseilles steamer was late, although the refusal to submit to the system of penalties was mentioned by Robinson and Cable as the most important reason why the P&O could not accept the details of the contract as desired by the government. See Kirk (1989), 6–8; Robinson (1964), 195–196; Bushell, 93–94.; and Cable 137–140.

was 8 days 19 hours later than specified by contract – for which penalty was £1,800. At first it was advertised that she would leave with the November mails but […] she was unable to leave before 11.12.57. On 19.10.57 the Sydney Post Office advertised that the Aberdeen barque *Oliver Cromwell* would leave with the mails on the 25th, and proceed via the Cape of Good Hope to London…' – 'Naturally she [the *Emeu*] was not available to take the 27.10.57 departure from Suez. As always, the European & Australian Line were handicapped by not having a replacement steamer, or charter steamer, available at the time. Officially: 'No mails from Suez to Sydney, in consequence of the accident to *Emeu*. By an alternation in the terms of the contract, the penalty will be deducted from the next quarterly payment.' By nepotism, most of the penalties were eventually remitted.'[969]

The owners of the European & Australian Line lost over £700,000 within the two years of service,[970] despite the fact that they had a mail contract, showing once again clearly that a government mail subsidy did not make a shipping company prosperous if it could not manage its business. To keep the service going, the Royal Mail Line – the well-known contractor for West Indian mails – took over the management of the European & Australian Line service for half a year until a new contract was made with the P&O for the Australian mail service from Suez via Mauritius to Australia, starting in early 1859.[971]

From the viewpoint of information transmission, the following is how information circulation would have functioned if the sailings had been carried out as planned in the European & Australian Line mail contract, starting from 1857.

TABLE 87. *Consecutive information circles, London–Sydney, as planned in the mail contract, 1857.*

Mails from London	Arr. in Malta	Arr. in Alexandria	Dep. from Suez	Arr. in Sydney	Dep. from Sydney	Arr. in Suez	Dep. from Alexandria	Dep. from Malta	Mails in London
16.1.	21.1.	24.1.	27.1.	9.3.	11.3.	22.4.	25.4.	29.4.	4.5.
16.5.	21.5.	24.5.	27.5.	9.7.	11.7.	22.8.	25.8.	29.8.	4.9.
16.9.	21.9.	24.9.	27.9.	9.11.	11.11.	22.12.	25.12.	29.12.	4.1.

Source: Kirk (1989), 8.

969 Kirk (1989), 13–21. – The barque *Oliver Cromwell* mentioned above sailed to London in 97 days, arriving 30.1.1858. See Kirk (1989), 39.
970 See Robinson (1964), 196; Cable, 140.
971 See Bushell, 94–95; Kirk (1989), 57.

TABLE 88. *Consecutive information circles between London and Sydney enabled by the European & Australian Line service, 1857.*

Mails from London	Ship Marseilles > Malta	Ship Malta > Alexandria	Ship Suez > Sydney	Ship Sydney > Suez	Ship Alexandria > Malta	Ship Malta > Marseilles	Mails in London
14.1.1857 by the *Columbian* via the Cape	–	–	*Columbian* arrived 23.3.1857	*Columbian* *11.4. >* *28.5.*	*Jura 30.5>* *3.6.*	*Cambrian* *3.6. > 6.6.*	~ 8.6.
16.6. from Liverpool by the *Emeu*, chartered from Cunard; sailed via the Cape	–	–	19.8.	*Emeu* 11.9. > 3.11.. (no August mails; and *Emeu* was wrecked off Jeddah 22.10., but refloated)	*Austral-asian 5.11.* *> 9.11.*	By P&O's next steamer *Vectis,* arr. in Marseilles 27.11.	Mails by the *Austral-asian* arrived via South-ampton 18.11. –11days earlier than the express mail via Marseilles
16.12. (Novem-ber mails departed 16.11.)	*Vanguard* *18.12. >* *21.12.*	*Teviot* *21.12. >* *24.12.*	*City of Sydney /* *Victoria* *27.12. >* *25.2.1858*				

Source: Sailing lists published by Kirk (1989), 8–22, 32–36.

The service of the European & Australian Line was nicely planned, enabling three annual information circles between England and Australia. There was enough time between arrivals and departures in Britain, also affording a smooth service for the bulk mails via Southampton, arriving on the 6th and leaving on the 12th. The dispatches would be more hurried in Sydney, but the letters could still have been answered in two days. The colonists in Melbourne would have had more time for their answers, as the ship off-loaded the mails at Melbourne four days before arrival at Sydney, and picked up the homeward mails four days after departure from Sydney.[972]

But the reality was rather different. Table 88 shows the information circles enabled by the European & Australian Line during its first year in service.

Even if the performance of the European & Australian Line was poor compared to the requirements of the mail contract, its service enabled nearly 2.5 consecutive information circles within the first year. This was better than

---

972 Kirk (1989), 8.

could be afforded by the shipping companies which used the route via the Cape exclusively. But also two of the three European & Australian Line ships – which happened to be part of the annual information circulation picked out for the table above – sailed eastwards around Africa to take their positions on the Australia – Suez route. Although they used the Overland route for the mails in 1858, the company's performance was even weaker, and only two consecutive information circles could be achieved.

While this was theory, the practice was even somewhat poorer, probably not only because of problems in the shipping itself, but also due to the business practices or lack of information which would have enabled merchants to use the fastest connections.

The accounts and papers of Henry Eld Symons, already discussed in the context of South America, include a dozen letters from Geelong and Melbourne, both in Victoria, Australia, sent in 1857.[973] They illustrate in an interesting way how communications between a Liverpool merchant house and its distant trade partners worked during this period.

The first letter in chronological order was sent from Melbourne on 14 March, 1857 by the European & Australian Line steamship, *European*. The ship departed from Sydney on 11 March on schedule and the mails arrived at Southampton on 9 May, the letter being handstamped in the Liverpool post office already on the same day. The trip took 56 days. Also the second letter, dated and handstamped in Melbourne on 14 April, was transmitted in a satisfactory way, the *Columbian* departing from Sydney on schedule and the mails arriving in Southampton from Alexandria by the *Jura* on 11 June. The letter arrived in Liverpool on the next day, 58 days after being written.[974]

The next two letters were almost three weeks late on arrival. The first letter was dated on 12 June, but handstamped in the Geelong post office on the 24th. The other was sent from Melbourne on the 22nd. They were carried by the *European* among nearly 15,000 other letters and more than 17,000 newspapers. Her scheduled departure date from Sydney was 11 June, but she left on the 20th, nine days late. This explains why the letter from Geelong was written so early, while the Melbourne letter was written with the knowledge that the ship was late. Further delay was caused to the mails, as there was no European & Australian Line steamer waiting in Alexandria, the *Etna* being elsewhere. The P&O ship *Ripon* finally took the mails after a week's waiting and they arrived at Southampton on 4 September. The mails via Marseilles arrived a week earlier by another P&O vessel, the *Vectis*, but as the letters in question had not been sent by express, they were carried by the all-sea route.[975]

The letter from Geelong was on its way for 85 days, and the letter from Melbourne for 75 days, after being written. It is important once again to notice that the ten days difference between the time of writing and receiving these two letters had nothing to do with the duration of the transport itself but was due to delays on shore.

973 The Accounts and Papers of Henry Eld Symons, LRO, 380 MD, 9–21.
974 For the sailing dates, see Kirk (1989), 14, 32.
975 For the sailing dates, see Kirk (1989), 14, 33.

For some reason, Henry Eld Symons did not answer these letters by the following mail steamer, which left Southampton on 12 September, but by the one after that, in October. This was an unlucky decision for his business communications, as will soon be noticed.

The next two letters from Australia arrived on 25 September, having been sent from Geelong on 21 July and from Melbourne on 22 July, and transferred in 66 and 65 days respectively. This time, too, there were problems in Alexandria. The *Etna* should have been there for the mails arriving on 8 September from Australia, but as there was no European & Australian packet in sight, the British Consul exercised his authority and had them loaded onto the P&O vessels on the 12th.[976]

Henry Eld Symons did not always mark the answering dates on his business letters, but he did mark on the covers from Geelong arriving on 5 and 25 September that he had answered them on 15 October. He sent the letters by the express mail which departed from Marseilles on the 18th. They arrived in Alexandria on the 25th, but there was again no steamer to take the letters from Suez to Australia, as the *Emeu* had grounded a few days earlier on the Guttal el Bunna reef, 120 miles from Jeddah, and was not available. The October mails arrived in Melbourne on 8 January 1858, 85 days after being sent from Liverpool. The answers to the letters sent from Australia in June 1857 were thus dispatched almost seven months later. The delay was partly Mr. Symons' own fault, however. If he had used the opportunity to send the letters of 5th September by the next mail steamer to Australia, they would have arrived in Melbourne on 13 November.[977]

The next letters, sent from Geelong on 11 August and from Melbourne on 12 August arrived in Liverpool on 17 October within 67 and 66 days respectively, but the credit for this was not due to the European and Australian Line, which failed to organize the trip. The August mails from Australia did not arrive until November, together with the September mails. Instead of waiting for that, the letters for Mr. Symons arrived directly in Liverpool by the *Royal Charter*, an auxiliary steamer owned by Gibbs, Bright & Co., a well-known Liverpool merchant house and shipping company.[978]

In December, Mr. Symons received three letters from Australia within three days. Two of them, sent from Geelong on 12 September and from Melbourne on 16 September, arrived on 7 December after a series of adventures. After the *Emeu* had struck a reef off Jeddah on 22 October, the Captain and the Admiralty Agent together with two passengers took the Marseilles portion of the mails and left the ship in an Arab boat. After four days sailing, partly in heavy rain almost filling the boat, they touched Jeddah, where they were hospitably received by the Governor-General. Finally they returned to the Red Sea in the hope of being sighted by a passing ship. They were seen by

---

976 For the sailing dates, see Kirk (1989), 35.

977 For the sailing dates, see Kirk (1989), 33–35, 39.

978 Both letters were directed 'Per *Royal Charter*' and handstamped by 'PAID LIVERPOOL SHIP OC 17 1857' on arrival. For the arrival of the August mails, see Kirk (1989), 35; and for the *Royal Charter,* see Stammers, 164–166, 201, 436, 446. The *Royal Charter* formed together with the famous *Great Britain* the auxiliary steamship service of the Liverpool and Australian Steam Navigation Co. For the *Great Britain*, see Fogg, passim.

the P&O steamer *Madras* on 18 November and the mails arrived at Suez on the 19th. The British Consul at Alexandria reported on 5 November that the *Emeu* had arrived at Suez without the Marseilles portion of the mails. Three weeks later on the 26th the safe arrival of the mails was reported, but at least some of the letters annotated 'via Marseilles' were sent via Southampton. They arrived there on 6 December, including Mr. Symons' dispatches which were delivered in Liverpool on the next day, having been 86 and 82 days on their way. One more letter, sent from Geelong on 12 October arrived on 10 December by the next mail without major difficulties, the trip taking 59 days.[979]

The last letter from Melbourne was dated on 16 November and it arrived via Southampton in Liverpool on 13 January 1858 in 58 days. The reason for the improved service was that the Royal Mail Steam Packet Company, better known for its West Indian mail service, had taken over the management of the European & Australian Line in September 1857. From 1 June 1858 they took over the postal contract as well, until a new contract was made with the P&O from the beginning of 1859.[980]

What happened to the information circles, when the P&O took over the Australian route at the beginning of 1859? The service started in the same way as its predecessors, by sending the first vessels to Australia via the Cape of Good Hope. Table 89 shows how well the first year of the P&O mail service for Australia fulfilled the expectations of faster information transmission.

TABLE 89. *Consecutive information circles between London and Sydney enabled by the P&O service, 1859.*

Mails from London	Ship Marseilles > Alexandria	Ship Suez > Sydney	Ship Sydney > Suez	Ship Alexandria > Marseilles	Mails in London
20.1.1859 by the *Malta* via the Cape	–	*Malta* arrived 8.4.	*Malta* 14.4. > 27.5.	*Ellora* 28.5 > 3.6.	5.6.
18.6.	*Panther* 20.6. > 26.6.	*Bombay* 27.6. > 10.8.	*Northam* 14.7. > 28.8.	*Panther* 5.9. > 12.9.	13.9.
19.9.	*Panther* 21.9. > 27.9.	*Malta* 28.9. > 15.11. (late)	*Malta* 14.12. > 24.1.1860		

Source: Sailing lists published by Kirk (1989), 57–61, 151–156.

979 For the trip to Jeddah, see Kirk (1989), 35–39; Bushell, 94. The stories vary somewhat but it makes no major difference from the postal historical point of view.

980 The cost for the British Government was £6,000 each month in addition to the annual £185,000. The Royal Mail Line also refused to pay any penalties regarding late arrivals under the former contract. See Kirk (1989), 44; Bushell, 94–95.

The P&O would have managed the requirement for three consecutive information circles, if their steamer *Malta* had not been docked at Mauritius for five days in October due to repairs to her air-pump tanks. Now she arrived in Sydney on 15 November, while the *Benares* had departed the day before. This caused a four-week delay in answers to the letters.[981]

In 1860, the P&O service enabled three consecutive information circles between London and Sydney, starting on 18 January, 1860, and ending on 12 January, 1861 – but only just. The steamer *Emeu* arrived at Sydney on 14 March at 4.50 a.m. while the *Northam* sailed on the same day at 15.14 p.m.[982] As the mails had been sorted on board during the voyage, there was some hope of being able to receive the letters and answer them in time. The Melbourne colonists were again luckier, being able to use several more days for their answers. In fact, the P&O ensured three consecutive information circles for Melbourne, but not necessarily for Sydney.

The P&O had received the mail contract to Sydney as a leg for a newly established service from Aden to Mauritius, but they soon realized that there would be several benefits in directing the route via Galle, thus combining several mail routes via one hub. The system had been in use by the Royal Mail Line in the Caribbean since the early 1840s. Although the route via Galle in Ceylon was only 143 miles shorter than the route via Mauritius, 132 hours were saved by proceeding via Galle. And even more important, the stretch of over 3,000 miles between Mauritius and King George's Sound in Australia could be avoided.[983]

The route via Mauritius was abandoned, the last mails being dispatched from London on 18 February and from Sydney on 14 February 1860. The next modification to the routine was the change of departure dates, from the 18th to the 26th in London and from the 14th to the 22nd in Sydney, to find a better match with the other Asian mail routes. From now on, the ship from Suez did not sail to Sydney but via Galle to Calcutta, while the Australian mails were transferred to a ship from Bombay, which took the mails from Galle to Sydney. As a result of these adjustments, the average duration of a normal trip from London via Marseilles and Suez to Sydney decreased from 53 to 49 days. In the other direction, the difference was only one day.[984]

It took about 20 years from the start of the steamship service across the Atlantic to get a working mail service by steamers to Australia. Geography was not on the side of the Australians. While the distance from England to India and China was clearly cut by the Overland route, thus making the

---

981 For the sailing dates of these ships, see Kirk (1989), 61, 155. Also the following month's ship was late, probably due to repairs. She arrived in Sydney on 15 December, while the vessel with mails for Europe had again left on the day before. See Kirk (1989), 62, 156.
982 See the sailing lists published by Kirk (1989), 64–69, 158–162.
983 See Robinson (1964), 197; Kirk (1989), 65.
984 Calculated from the sailing schedules published by Kirk (1989), 57–69, 151–162. Only six 'normal' sailings have been included from both years, leaving out trips via the Cape or trips with exceptional delays due to repairs.

FIG. 35. *The P&O Australasian mail service network, 1861.*

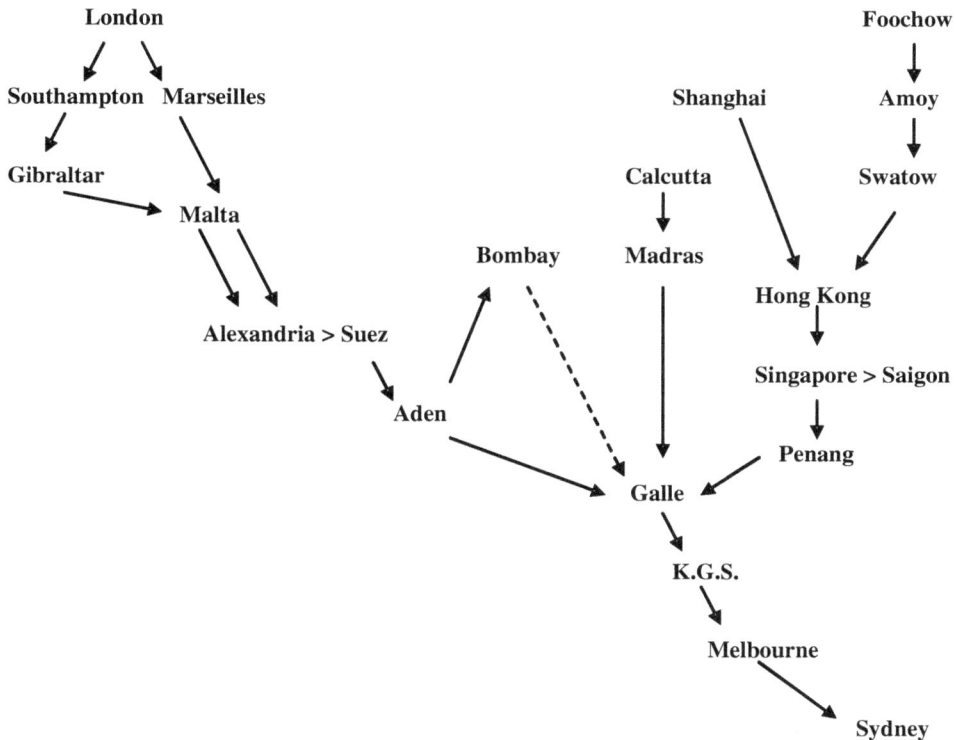

Source: Sailing lists of Kirk (1989), 69, 164; Proud, 76.

use of steamers profitable, the distance to Australia was about the same via Suez as it was via the Cape. Contrary to the India and China routes, or, for example, the route between New York and California in the Western world, there was no 'leverage effect' in using steamers on the Australian route. Only when organized as a leg from Galle, could the special costs of the Australian mails be tolerated. With respect to the voyage to Galle, the mails for Calcutta, Bombay or China could share the costs of the Australian dispatches.

Figure 35 depicts how the P&O mail service was organized in the early 1860s. The example is from January–February 1861. The rather new P&O iron screw steamer, the *Ceylon,* 2,110 tons, sailed from Southampton with the British all-sea mails on 20 January at 2.35 p.m. She made a call at Gibraltar on the 25th and arrived at Malta on the 29th, proceeding for Alexandria on the following day. She arrived there on 2 February at 3.53 p.m.

The express mails left from London by train on the 26th, were taken over the English Channel and across France to Marseilles and there on board the 15-year-old P&O paddle steamer *Euxine,* of 1164 tons. She departed on 28 January at 10 a.m., calling at Malta on the 31st and arriving at Alexandria on 3 February at 3.25 p.m., one day later than the larger shipment of all-sea mails from Southampton had arrived. Even if both vessels called at Malta,

375

no reloading of mails took place there. It was obviously cheaper and faster to let both vessels continue all the way to Alexandria instead of reloading and continuing by one ship only.

The vessels did not stay long at Alexandria. The *Euxine* departed with the Australian, Chinese and Calcutta express mails for Marseilles already on 4 February at 4.05 p.m. and the *Ceylon* with the respective all-sea mails for Southampton five minutes later. They arrived in Marseilles on 10 February at 10.55 p.m. (the mails being in London on the 12th) and Southampton on 16 February at 9 p.m. respectively.

Meanwhile, the mails from Europe were taken from Alexandria by train to Suez on 4 February, the P&O iron screw-steamer *Colombo*, 1,865 tons, departing from there on 5 February at 0.25 a.m. She arrived at Aden on the 10th and at Galle on the 20th. Having unloaded the Australian and China mails at Galle she proceeded to Calcutta on the 21st. She called at Madras on the 24th and arrived in Calcutta on the 27th.

The China mails were taken from Galle by the *Singapore*, which departed on the 22nd, called at Penang on 1 March, Singapore on the 3rd, proceeding the next day and arriving in Hong Kong on 13 March. From there the mails for Shanghai were taken by the *Aden* on 14 March, arriving on the 20th. The mails for Foochow departed on the same day by the *Manilla* which arrived at Swatow on the 16th, proceeding on the following day, staying at Amoy between the 18th and the 20th and arriving finally at Foochow on the 23rd.[985]

The *Singapore* was a ten-year-old vessel of 1,190 tons and the *Aden* and *Manilla* were small coastal steamers (the *Aden* an iron screw) of 812 and 646 tons respectively. They were all owned by the P&O.

The Australian mails were taken from Galle by the 1,330-ton iron screw steamer *Northam*, which had arrived from Bombay on 17 February. The ship now departed for Sydney on the 21st and called at King George's Sound on 11 March and Melbourne on the 18th, before arriving at Sydney on the 21st at 1.50 p.m.[986]

The system was totally in the hands of the P&O and it worked like a clock, mostly. The European mails were sent weekly from Southampton, and six or seven days later from London for the express transmission via Marseilles, in the following order: AC, B, C, B, AC, B, C, B, etc., A being Australia, C being Calcutta and China, and B being Bombay.[987]

The mails arrived by the two routes – via Gibraltar or via Marseilles – in Alexandria, to be forwarded to one and the same vessel in Suez which took them – excluding the Bombay mails – to Galle, where they were transferred to mail steamers for different destinations. There was no unnecessary reloading on the European side, and the ship from Suez also continued with the Calcutta mails from Galle without reloading.

---

985 Swatow, Amoy and Foochow were Chinese ports north of Hong Kong, Foochow being about half-way to Shanghai. The modern names of the ports are Shantou, Xiamen and Fuzhou.

986 Kirk (1989), 69, 164; Proud, 76; Middlemiss, 96–106.

987 The departure dates for the all-sea mails from Southampton were 7th (C), 12th (B), 20th (AC) and 27th (B). See Kirk (1989), 77.

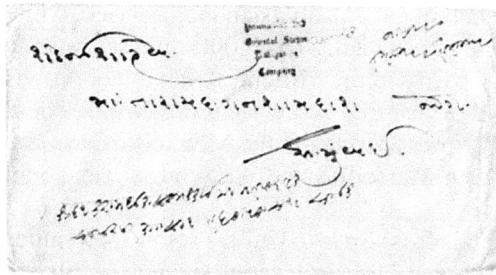

FIG. 36 *The letter, written probably in gujarati, includes a bill of lading as well as a circular, dated on 15.1.1884, showing the changes in the Shanghai stocks of Malwa and Bengal opium. Within a two weeks period, no less than ten steamers had brought new opium to the port. The* Hydaspes, Brindisi *and* Pekin *were P&O mail steamers, and the* Djemnah *was owned by the Messageries Maritimes. The letter has been carried by a P&O steamer, as it bears the ship cancellation 'Peninsular and Oriental Steam Navigation Company' on the front side of the cover.*

Galle in Ceylon was the main hub in the Australasian mail service, while Hong Kong served as the hub for Chinese mails. The 3,000-mile sea voyage from Southampton to Alexandria partly in the difficult Atlantic conditions was carried out by the newest and fastest iron screw steamers, which could make 13 knots. The ships for the express service in the Mediterranean were smaller, while the distance between Marseilles and Alexandria was about 2,000 miles.

The vessel which carried the mails from Suez to Galle – some 3,400 miles in varying monsoons – was also a rather large iron screw steamer, while the long Australian run – about 6,000 miles – was conducted by a medium-size steamer. From this we may conclude that most passengers for Australia generally choose the cheaper sailing vessels and that the P&O route was mainly used for mail and fine freight services. For example the *Northam* could take only 127 passengers.[988]

The Bombay mails were carried separately from the others, alternating with the Calcutta, China and Australia mails. As in the time of the EIC service, the mails were taken from Suez via Aden to Bombay directly without stretching the voyage to the distant Galle. But also the Suez–Aden–Bombay route actually continued to Galle, as the steamer which carried the mails would continue from there to Sydney. For example the *Northam* carried the European mails from Suez on 14.1., arrived in Bombay on 28.1. and left for Galle on 12.2., arrived there on 17.2. and proceeded on 21.2. to Sydney. The route between Bombay and Galle, the main hub of transports for China, was obviously not necessary for the mail service. But the P&O had 'inherited' the opium business from the EIC and was the chief exporter of Malwa opium from Bombay to China, while Bengal opium was mainly carried by local and American companies.[989]

Opium earnings brought relative stability over the whole range of the P&O's lines for about four decades, and finally ceased as late as in 1917, after a ten-year period of reduced trade based on an agreement by the Indian and Chinese governments.[990] This lucrative trade was probably one of the basic reasons for competitors' complaints about the P&O mail contracts. In the late 1860s, when steamship technology had been improved and the Suez Canal had been opened, it was not long before there were several competitors in the Eastern waters, mail contract or not. This will be discussed in the following chapter.

The P&O mail service enabled consecutive information circles between London and the different Australasian ports in 1861 as follows:

---

988 For distances, see e.g. Kirk, *The P&O Bombay...*, 5, for ship details, Middlemiss, 96–106.

989 See Stephen Rabson, 'The Iron Hong. P&O and the Far East from 1845', in Richard Harding, Adrian Jarvis & Alston Kennerley, *British Ships in China Seas: 1700 to the Present Day* (Liverpool, 2004), 120,124.

990 Rabson, 124.

TABLE 90. *Consecutive information circles on the London–Calcutta–London route enabled by the P&O service, 186*

London departure (express via Marseilles)	Calcutta arrival	Calcutta departure	London arrival (express via Marseilles)	Days
26.1.1861	27.2.	9.3.	13.4.	77
26.4.	27.5.	9.6.	17.7.	82
26.7.	2.9.	10.9.	17.10.	83
26.10.	30.11.	10.12.	13.1.1862	79

Source: Sailing lists published by Kirk (1989), 69–75, 162–169

TABLE 91. *Consecutive information circles on the London–Hong Kong–London route enabled by the P&O service, 1861.*

London departure (express via Marseilles	Hong Kong arrival	Hong Kong departure	London arrival (express via Marseilles)	Days
26.1.1861	13.3.	16.3.	26.4.	91
26.4.	6.6.	12.6.	29.7.	94
10.8.	21.9.	15.10*	28.11.	110
10.12.**	24.1.1862			

Source: Sailing lists published by Kirk in The P&O Lines..., 54–55.

* There was no departure for Galle at the end of September due to an attempt to reduce the service to a monthly one. The old system continued in October, however. See Kirk, *The P&O Lines...*, 55.

** The earlier departure date would have been 26.11.

TABLE 92. *Consecutive information circles on the London–Shanghai–London route enabled by the P&O service, 1861.*

London departure (express via Marseilles	Shanghai arrival	Shanghai departure	London arrival (express via Marseilles)	Days
26.1.1861	20.3.	23.3.	13.5.	107
27.5.	11.7.	19.7.	15.9.	111
26.9.	18.11.	23.11.	13.1.1862	109

Source: Sailing lists published by Kirk (1989), 69–75, 162–169.

TABLE 93. *Consecutive information circles on the London–Foochow–London route enabled by the P&O service, 1861.*

London departure (express via Marseilles	Foochow arrival	Foochow departure	London arrival (express via Marseilles)	Days
26.1.1861	21.3.	24.3.	13.5.	107
27.5.	15.7.	19.7.	15.9.	111
26.9.	16.11.	20.11.	13.1.1862	109

Source: Sailing lists published by Kirk (1989), 69–75, 162–169.

TABLE 94. *Consecutive information circles on the London–Sydney–London route enabled by the P&O service, 1861.*

London departure (express via Marseilles	Sydney arrival	Sydney departure	London arrival (express via Marseilles)	Days
26.1.1861	21.3.	22.3.	13.5.	107
27.5.	15.7.	22.7.	15.9.	111
26.9.	21.11.	23.11.	13.1.1862	109

Source: Sailing lists published by Kirk (1989), 69–75, 162–169.

As can be noticed, the system was cleverly built. It combined the different mail routes in an effective way. All ports (except Bombay) were served via Galle, and the schedules matched well. Calcutta's location near Galle – only six days sailing – enabled four consecutive information circles per year, each between 11 and 12 weeks. The mail service from London to Shanghai, Foochow and Sydney enabled three consecutive information circles per year. Each circle took about 3.5 months.[991] As can be seen, the voyage back and forth from Galle to all these places was calculated so that the mails could be carried from Galle to Suez by one and the same steamer.

For the Hong Kong trade, the system was a kind of lucky wheel. Due to its geographical location nearer Galle than Shanghai, for example, its merchants

---

991 From 1866, there was also a contract mail route across the Pacific from Sydney via Wellington, New Zealand, to Panama, across the Isthmus by railway and from Colon by steamer to Southampton. The leg between Australia and Panama was taken care of by the Panama, New Zealand and Australian Royal Mail Company and the leg between Colon and Southampton by existing Royal Mail Line services. This eastbound route enabled 2.5 to three consecutive information circles between Sydney and England per year. The length of the sea voyage sometimes caused the classic situation, where the mails arrived soon after the next ship to Australia had departed. The line existed for only three years. For the sailing data, see Tabeart (2004), 271–281.

could occasionally benefit from the second monthly departure, thus shortening the length of the information circle. But as can see from Table 91, this did not always work, and even if it did, the schedule was tight and for practical reasons probably impossible.

In England, the departures from Southampton enabled the same number of consecutive information circles with each of the Australasian ports (except for the 'extra' Hong Kong mails) as the express route via Marseilles, but a single journey was some six days longer. The time to answer the all-sea letters arriving via Southampton was naturally short, as they arrived later than the express dispatches and departed earlier. But as a whole, the system worked well. It can be stated that the P&O reached the same level of shipping management in the early 1860s as the Royal Mail Line did in the Caribbean and especially in South America during the same period. And in both areas, this was the time when the French entered the scene.

Further Development

Competition with the French – The Suez Canal and the compound engine increase the number of rivals – Mails for South Africa – The introduction of the telegraph

Competition with the French

The French had operated in the Mediterranean mail service since the 1830s, but it was only in the early 1860s that the French Government made a decision to extend the service to the rest of the world. As already discussed in earlier chapters, the Government made a mail contract with Compagnie Générale Transatlantique, or the French Line, for a mail steamship service to and from the United States and the Caribbean and with Compagnie des Messagerie Impériales for a service to and from South America and the Far East.

Messagerie Impériales started its service to the ports east of Egypt only after the railway between Alexandria and Suez had been completed, thus avoiding all the trouble with camel caravans, river boats, and related issues. And as in South America, where the French could just copy a tried and true system already established by the Royal Mail Line, so in the East, Messagerie Impériales could easily follow the guidelines set by the P&O in organizing its routes in a well functioning way.

Messagerie Impériales signed a mail contract in June 1861 and the service started gradually over the next few years. French Post Offices were established at Suez, at Saigon in French Indochina, in Vietnam of today, and at Shanghai; postal agents were appointed at several places and, up to July 1864, no fewer than a dozen mail steamers were placed on the principal line and its branch services.[992]

---

992 See Raymond Salles, *La Poste Maritime Française. Tome V. Les Paquebots de L'Extrême-Orient* (Limassol, 1993), 9–15.

As can be noted in Figure 35 (see p. 375), the P&O had established an extra mail service between Singapore and Saigon already in 1861. This mail route mainly served the French troops in China, until Messagerie Impériales got their own service started in late 1862.[993]

TABLE 95. *Consecutive information circles on the London–Hong Kong–London route, 1865.*

From London	From Marseilles	Arrival in Alexandria	From Suez	Arrival in Hong Kong	From Hong Kong	Arrival in Suez	From Alexandria	Arrival in Marseilles	Arrival in London
10.1. 1865	12.1. British service	19.1.	- -	23.2.	26.2. French service	30.3.	1.4.	7.4.	9.4.
10.4.	12.4. British service	18.4.	19.4.	21.5.	23.5. French service	27.6.	29.6.	5.7.	7.7.
10.7.	12.7. British service	18.7.	19.7.	19.8.	23.8. French service	30.9.	2.10.	8.10.	10.10.
10.10.	12.10. British service	18.10.	21.10.	12.12.*	15.12. British service	15.1. 1866			

Sources: Sailing lists of Salles, Tome II, 189 and Tome V, 28–29; and Kirk, The P&O Lines..., 63–64.

* The P&O steamer *Behar* broke a shaft and was towed to Singapore. The mails for Hong Kong were carried by another P&O vessel, the *Ottawa*, after a notable delay. See Kirk, 63.

The French service included mail transmission from Europe via Marseilles to Alexandria, by train to Suez and from there via Galle and Saigon to Hong Kong. The first mails departed from Suez on 27 October, 1862. A branch line connected Hong Kong with Shanghai from early 1863, and this line was continued from Shanghai to Yokohama in Japan from 1865. Other branch lines served French interests at Calcutta via Galle and Madras from late 1862, and at Bourbon (Réunion) and Mauritius by a direct voyage from Suez from September 1864.[994]

Did the British - French double service to Hong Kong, or later to Shanghai, speed up business information transmission? Not very much, but it was a minor improvement in the development of communications, anyway. Compared to the P&O service between London and Hong Kong in 1861

---

993 The P&O service for Saigon is mentioned for the first time in Kirk's sailing lists at the end of July 1861, but according to Salles the period lasted from February 1861 to June 1862. The French service for Indochina was inaugurated in October 1862. See Kirk (1989), 72, 166; Salles, Tome V, 25–27, 30–31. Kirk reports the last P&O departure from Saigon on 1.12.1862 and the last arrival on 3.1.1863. See the sailing lists by Kirk (1989), 80, 177.
994 See Salles, Tome V, 32–41.

depicted in Table 91, the double service enabled four consecutive information circles per year, at least in theory. In late 1865, the machine breakdown of the P&O steamer *Behar* caused a serious delay in the rest of the chain and made it impossible for merchants to answer the October mails by the November steamer from Hong Kong. Without that incident, the double service would have enabled four full circles that year. On the other hand, the P&O service alone could only accomplish 3.5 consecutive circles. See Table 95.

The French departures from Hong Kong matched nicely with the British arrivals, leaving two to four days' time for answers. This did not always work the other way round, however. During 1865, four departures of the P&O vessels were on the day of a French arrival, three departures were before a French arrival, and only five departures were well-timed at one-to-four days after a French arrival.[995]

In Shanghai, the arrivals and departures of the two mail services did not always match in the optimum way for merchants, or anyone else. It should be remembered that, most probably, as in South America, people used any service that would bring their messages as fast as possible to the destination. Nationalistic feelings did not hinder British merchants from using French services, or vice versa. But even if the departure dates from Marseilles were fixed – the British dates being the 12th and the 18th (closing the mail in London two days earlier) and the French date being the 19th – the arrival and departure dates at Shanghai varied, causing both delays and overlapping.

In 1865, an average passage from Marseilles to Shanghai took 47 days, excluding cases where there were two or three machine breakdowns or other major incidents. The British trips varied between 42 and 54 days, while the French service varied between 45 and 50 days. This naturally caused problems in schedule planning.

As can be noticed in Table 96, there were in fact several periods when the French steamers took home answers to mails carried by their own service, as well as to those carried by the British service, but also vice versa. In between, there were ships leaving Shanghai before any new dispatches had arrived from Europe. Even if the French service was only once a month, they always carried the freshest answers back home, while every second British mail steamer actually left on her homeward trip with a minor portion of important letters, the major part having already been taken home a few days earlier by the French service.

The explanation for this was naturally the hard competition between the two companies, not so much concerning the mails (for which they both got paid through their contracts), but more concerning the passengers and cargo. In the coming years, the P&O could not help but notice that the French steamers were newer, more comfortable, faster and more conveniently scheduled. Such things as a laundry on board could do a lot for the comfort of passengers on a six-week voyage. But already in the 1860s, the P&O had to face the fact that the French were taking over not only its passengers, but also its cargoes. Messagerie Impériales increased its silk transportation from

---

995 Calculated from the sailing lists published by Salles, Tome V, 28–29; and Kirk, *The P&O Lines...*, 63–64.

TABLE 96. *Mail arrivals and departures of the British and French mail steamers in Shanghai, January–June 1865.*

Service	Arrival date	Next departure, service	Departure date
French	~15.1.	French	21.1.
British	19.1.	French British	21.1. 26.1.
British	31.1.	British	9.2.
French	~4.2.	British	9.2.
British	14.2.	French British	21.2. 23.2.
British	28.2.	British	9.3.
French	~6.3.	British	9.3.
British	18.3.	French British	21.3. 26.3.
British	31.3.	British	9.4.
French	~5.4.	British	9.4.
British	15.4.	French British	20.4. 23.4.
British	27.4.	British	6.5.
French	~6.5.	British	6.5.
British	12.5.	French British	18.5. 23.5.
British	27.5.	British	6.6.
French	~3.6.	British	6.6.
British	12.6.	French British	17.6. 22.6.
French	3.7.	British	5.7.
British	25.6.	British	5.7.

Sources: Sailing lists of Salles, Tome V, 37; and Kirk, The P&O Lines..., 62–64. – Most of the French arrival dates are estimates (Hong Kong departure date + four) as Salles does not always give the exact dates for 1865 and 1866.

Shanghai from 11.7% of the total in 1863 to 42.4% in 1866, 'because its ships went direct to Suez, and sailed 2 or 3 days before P&O's'. Silk contributed £119,000 to P&O's income in 1869, but within two years its freight rates dropped by 65%.[996]

---

996 See Rabson, 123. In fact, the Messagerie ships did not sail directly from Shanghai to Suez but there was a change in Hong Kong, and as noted in the text above, P&O changed its departure dates from Shanghai in late 1865 to match the French departures (and the French again changed their departures and the P&O followed). Nevertheless, the P&O cargoes

The Suez Canal and the compound engine increase the number of rivals

The P&O's problems did not end with the strong French competition in Far Eastern waters or with several ship wrecks during these years.[997] Both the company and the British Government had totally misjudged the importance of the Suez Canal, which the French diplomat Ferdinand de Lesseps had promoted with great enthusiasm from the mid-1850s. Instead, the P&O had invested heavily in the Egyptian railway and in the accommodation and related facilities on the Overland route. The British Government and the press were strongly against the Canal, which they thought could be a political risk during a war, if it were in French hands, as it was planned to be. British investors refused to subscribe for Canal Company shares, wishing that the plan would be forgotten because of the economic and technical risks included. Against all presumptions, the Canal project was completed in 1869. The new route shortened the voyage to and from Asia by thousands of miles compared with the traditional seaway around the Cape, which was still in general use, excluding the mail steamers.[998]

Simultaneously with the Canal opening, another great invention facilitated steamship trade with the East. The compound engine, even though it had been in limited use since the mid-1850s, had not earlier been fully appreciated by shipowners. It had mainly been used in the Pacific during its earliest period, as coal was expensive there and fuel economy was thus of great importance. Nearer Britain it was not so highly esteemed, as there was plenty of fuel and it was low-priced.[999]

After 1861, the P&O gradually began to build steamers with compound engines, the *Mooltan* being the first vessel with the new technical construction.[1000] Despite being one of the first to introduce the compound engine, the P&O had an average of 170 sailing ships employed each year to carry coal to the Eastern depots. For example, the company had a coal

and mails were carried by three different ships to Suez with changes in Hong Kong and Galle. The company preferred to serve the Calcutta merchants by direct sailings to Suez with no changes *en route*. See the sailing lists published by Kirk (1989), e.g. 91, 187.

997 At least the following mail-carrying vessels were lost in the P&O service east of Suez between 1843 and 1875: the *Pacha* with 16 lives in 1851, the *Douro* in 1853, the *Erin* in 1857, the *Alma* in 1859, the *Canton* also in 1859, the *Malabar* in 1860, the *Colombo* in 1862, the *Corea* with 103 lives in 1864, the *Niphon* with 13 lives in 1868, the *Benares* also in 1868, the *Carnatic* with 26 lives in 1869, and the *Rangoon* in 1871. See Middlemiss, 92–108. – The French losses between 1862 and 1875 were the *Hydaspe* in 1864, the *Nil* with 142 lives in 1874 and the *Neva* in 1875. See Haws (1999), 20–36.

998 For the Suez Canal project, see Karabell, passim.; for the Canal and the P&O, see Cable, 153–168. – At that time, the eastern seas provided a major source of employment for the sailing fleet, while the Atlantic was already dominated by the steamers. In 1868, over a million tons of sailing ships left British ports for the Far East, a greater tonnage than the sailing fleet that headed for North America that year. See Max E. Fletcher, 'The Suez Canal and World Shipping, 1869–1914' in *The Journal of Economic History, vol. XVIII* (December 1958), No 4, 558.

999 See Fletcher, 557.

1000 After the *Mooltan*, the following steamers in the P&O fleet were also provided with compound engines during the first half of the 1860s: *Poonah, Carnatic, Rangoon* and *Golconda* in 1863, *Delhi* and *Baroda* in 1864, and *Tanjore* in 1865. Many of these and several other P&O steamers were later re-engined with more powerful compound engines. See Middlemiss, 107–110.

shed for 6,000 tons at Shanghai, another for 10,000 tons at Hong Kong, and another for 2,200 tons at Yokohama.[1001]

In the 1860s, coal prices varied greatly in different parts of the world depending on the freight costs. While coal could be shipped to New York for 6 s. per ton and the more expensive Welsh coal for 11 s., a shipment to Gibraltar cost 14 s., to Alexandria 19 s., to Bombay 24 s., to Galle 27 s., to Hong Kong 33 s. and to Shanghai 45 s. Interestingly, the coal freight to Suez was 40 s., more than double the price to Alexandria.[1002] This was because the coal was taken to Suez overland across the desert due to the adverse monsoons in the Indian Ocean.[1003]

The most important innovation of the compound engine was its economical fuel consumption. While the consumption of coal had been reduced from the eight to ten pounds per horsepower per hour used in the 1830s to fewer than four pounds in the mid-1860s, the compound engine further reduced fuel consumption to somewhat over two pounds of good coal per indicated horsepower per hour.[1004] Together with the shortened sea route enabled by the Suez Canal, this notably improved the conditions for profitable shipping. It meant that not only the subsidized mail companies but any shipowner could play a role in the Far Eastern business. Among the most important were the Ocean Steam Ship Co. (the Blue Funnel Line) of Liverpool, the Glen Line owned by MacGregor and Co. of Glasgow, the Castle Line owned by Thomas Skinner and Co., the Shire Line founded by Captain D. J. Jenkins, and other companies operating ships in East Indian and Chinese waters, such as the British India Steam Navigation Co. and Jardine Matheson and Co.[1005]

The hopes of the Mediterranean nations that the opening of the Suez Canal would bring great prosperity to their maritime fleets at the expense of Britain were doomed to disappointment. The advantage of being brought several thousand miles closer to the huge markets and resources of the East by the Canal seemed to have only an illusory cash value for the shipowners of France, Italy, Russia and Austria-Hungary. As far as shipping was concerned, the Canal had been 'cut by French energy and Egyptian money for British advantage'.[1006]

1001 See Cable, 166; Rabson, 121–122.
1002 'Coal from Liverpool, Birkenhead or Garston', in *Boult, English & Brandon's Freight Circular* 6.6.1863. (SRLC).
1003 See Cable, 92. – For further statistics about coal export freight rates from Britain (1818–1913), see Charles K. Harley, 'Coal Exports and British Shipping, 1850–1913' in *Explorations in Economic History,* Vol. 26, Number 3, July 1989, 334–336.
1004 See Fletcher, 557. – For a technical description of the progress of steam shipping, especially the compound engine, see Holt, 1–9. – Alfred Holt, originally a railway engineer, became interested in the Far Eastern trade in the 1860s and started a steamship line by steamers with developed compound engines between Liverpool and the coast of China in 1866. See Francis E. Hyde, *Blue Funnel. A History of Alfred Holt and Company of Liverpool from 1865 to 1914* (Liverpool, 1956), 11–23. See also Cooper, 226–227. – For wider economic aspects of the change from coal to steam during a somewhat later period, see Kaukiainen (2004), 113–128.
1005 See Francis E. Hyde, *Far Eastern Trade 1860–1914* (Liverpool, 1973), 21–23.
1006 Fletcher, 564.

But the growing competition caused a remarkable cut in freight rates. In 1866, the P&O carried specie – partly gold, partly silver – worth nearly £11 million, and earned about £230,000 for it. Six years later, they carried nearly double the amount of specie, but received only £60,000. In another example, having carried 46,000 bales of silk for £110,000 in 1868, the company carried 50,000 bales for only £44,000 three years later – equivalent to only 37 percent of the old rate. The highest classes of cargo moving between England and India or China were quickly transferred to the steamship, including cotton goods, cowhides, ginger, indigo and tea. But the steamers also took a substantial portion of low-value, bulky commodities such as jute cuttings or rice.[1007]

Falling freight rates were a problem not only for the shipping companies trading with the Far East, but everywhere. The decline which started in the 1860s continued right up to the early 1890s, with annual decreases of real freight rates by 2.5 to three percent. According to Harley, the timing of the decline suggests that the introduction of the new technology was the main source of the general decline in rates.[1008]

For the P&O, the increasing competition on the Far Eastern routes was most unwelcome. A great deal of the company's investments in the East lost their significance and they were just written off in the accounting. The P&O lost much of its earlier income, and even the British Post Office used the opportunity to tell the company that if it started transporting the mails through the Canal instead by railway as was stated in the contract, the company's subsidy would be reduced by £30,000 a year. The generously subsidized French, Italian and Austrian shipping companies, which had widened their Mediterranean services east of Suez after the Canal opening, carried all their mails through the cut. Passengers were naturally attracted to these lines and away from the P&O because there was no need for themselves and their baggage to be trans-shipped. The situation led to a farce where the P&O vessels went through the Canal, but the mails were unloaded at Alexandria and taken by train to Suez and there loaded back onto the ship. This continued until a revised contract allowed the mails to be carried through – but only after the company accepted a reduction of the subsidy by £20,000 a year.[1009]

Despite the bitter claims and competing bids for government mail contracts by the British rivals, the P&O continued to conduct the mail service on the Far Eastern routes.[1010] Several branch services were taken care of by

---

1007 Cable, 164; Fletcher, 560–561. For the Far Eastern freight rates, see also Hyde (1973), 24–26.
1008 See Harley (1989), 315.
1009 See Cable, 165–166.
1010 For example, the Ocean Steam Ship Company of Alfred Holt competed seriously for the mail contracts on the China route in 1867 and 1879, but lost. Holt's public arguments about the injurious effects of the subsidies on freight and passage rates may be somewhat exaggerated, in view of the quickly changing business environment and its effects as a whole. And even if he strongly criticised the contract system, Holt continuously repeated attempts to secure one for his own company. See Hyde (1956), 40–42. – This happened simultaneously with William Inman's efforts to capture the mail contract from the Cunard Line in the North Atlantic. Lamport & Holt, the well-known shipping company in which

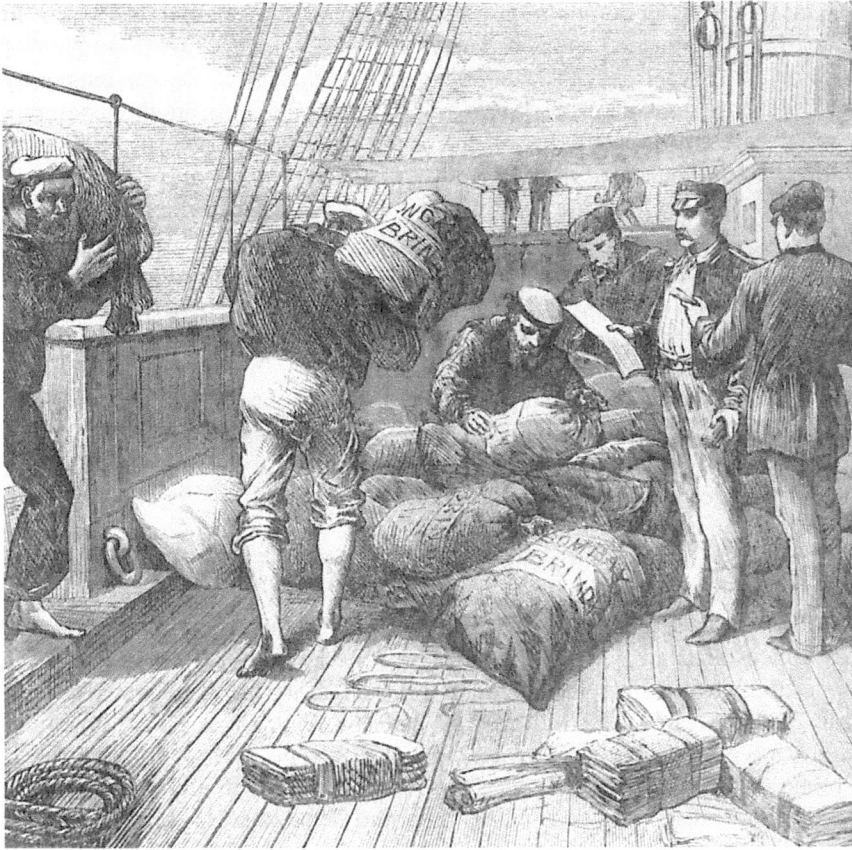

FIG. 38. *Mail bags being brought on board a mail steamship at Brindisi, 1872.*

other companies, e.g. Mackinnon, Mackenzie & Co.'s British India Steam Navigation Co. had served on the Calcutta–Rangoon route from the mid-1850s and on the Calcutta–Karachi, Bombay–Karachi and Bombay–Basra routes from the early 1860s.[1011]

In addition to the already mentioned changes in the business environment concerning the mail service to the Far East, there was an additional challenge to meet in Europe. The Franco-Prussian war of 1870 stopped the railway connection from Calais through France to Marseilles. The bridge over the Oise at Creil was blown up in September that year. For a time, other routes were tried, but they were either overrun by the invading Prussians, or their

Alfred Holt's brother George was a main partner, also held a mail contract between Liverpool and South America in 1868–1876. See Howat, 159–174.

1011 See Duncan Haws, *Merchant Fleets, British India S.N. Co.* (Hereford, 1991), 12–13. Kirk mentions that the company also had a mail contract between Sydney and England via Suez and Naples from 1879. See Kirk (1989), 240–241.

circuitous nature caused unacceptable delays.[1012] In early November, a new route was introduced via Brindisi in Italy. The change did not affect the total duration of information transmission. While the trip by train was longer from the Channel coast to Brindisi than to Marseilles, the trip by steamer from Brindisi to Alexandria was shorter than from Marseilles to Alexandria. Thus, an average trip from Sydney to London in 1870 took 50 to 52 days, independent of the railway route in Europe.[1013]

By the mid-1870s, the speed of the mail services to and from the Far East had reached a level at which it was difficult, and probably unnecessary, to improve it. The systems worked satisfactorily, and the most urgent news could always be transmitted by telegraph. The arrival of the Asian telegraph will be described later in this chapter.

As a final example of the P&O services in the East, Table 97 shows the consecutive information circles enabled by the company's mail sailings to and from Shanghai in 1875.

TABLE 97. *Consecutive information circles enabled by the P&O service between London and Shanghai, 1875.*

From London	From Brindisi	Arrival in Shanghai	From Shanghai	Arrival in Brindisi	Arrival in London
~7.1.1875	11.1.	23.2.	26.2.	7.4.	~11.4.
~15.4.	19.4.	27.5.	30.5.	16.7.	~20.7.
~22.7.	26.7.	1.9.	5.9.	21.10.	~25.10.
~28.10.	1.11.	12.12.	17.12.	27.1.1876	~31.1.

Source: Sailing lists published by Kirk, The P&O Lines..., 86–87. – The London departure and arrival dates are estimates. In the mid-1870s, the railway trip from London to Brindisi probably took three days instead of four, as in 1870. This would leave some more time for answering letters in England.

The P&O service for Shanghai was now working about as well as it could at this time period. The sailings enabled nearly four consecutive information circles a year, and there was no difficulty in answering letters in due time in either Shanghai or England. The one-way trip took about six weeks in each direction. Because the French service was also bi-monthly from mid-1871 and the two companies' departures took place on alternate weeks, there was now a well-working weekly service to and from Shanghai all year round.[1014] This

1012 The reorganizing of mail services, including changing departure dates etc. are explained by Kirk (1989), 127.
1013 Calculated from the sailing dates published by Kirk (1989), 123–130, 211–220.
1014 See the sailing lists published by Kirk, *The P&O Lines...*, 86–87; and Salles, Tome V, 105.

arrangement had been introduced at the same time as Messagerie Impériales doubled their service in July 1871.[1015]

After this, the speed of business information transmission could not easily be improved due to the long voyage.[1016] But using the same model as in the South American mail service, the alternate sailings made it possible for merchants to provide weekly information about their business affairs, even though it took nearly three months to receive a response.

Mails for South Africa

For South Africa or St. Helena, places of such importance during the heyday of canvas, the steamship mail service via the Overland route was of as little significance as it was for Australia. While East India and China had been connected to Europe by regular mail steamers from the early 1840s, South Africa was not considered important enough for subsidised steamship services for a long time. Mails were sent to and from the colony by sailing ships calling at the port, without any certainty of schedule or safe arrival. Prior to 1857, however, there were two attempts to conduct a regular steamship mail service between England and South Africa. From December 1850 to 1854, the General Screw Steam Shipping Company provided a monthly service to the Cape, and from August 1856, there was a contract with the Lindsay Line for less than a year. Despite the £30,000 mail subsidy, both companies ran into trouble and had to abandon the service.[1017]

In 1857, the British Government awarded the South African mail contract to a new company, to be known as the Union Line. It was to provide a bi-monthly service, and would receive an extra bonus of £250 per day from the Cape Colonial Government each time the mail ship arrived from Plymouth in less time than the agreed 35 days. For this reason, the Union Line mail steamers were 'more frequently under contract time than any others, the next being those of the Cunard Line'.[1018]

The progress made in speeding up the voyage over the next few years can be read from the mail contracts. While the Union Line vessels were allowed to use 38 days for a one-way trip in the 1863 contract, the allowed duration of the trip was decreased to 35 days in 1868, 30 days in 1873 and 26 days in 1876.[1019]

This progression was no less remarkable than in any other place where mail steamships took over from traditional sailing vessels. In the early 1830s, the

---

1015 See Salles, Tome V, 104.

1016 For comparison, in 1900 the P&O sailings to Shanghai, via Brindisi or Marseilles, took some 32 to 35 days and enabled approximately five consecutive information circles per year. See the sailing lists published by Kirk, *The P&O Lines...*, 140–141.

1017 See Cattell, 11. – From 1852, the General Screw service was lengthened by a leg via Mauritius to India. This route was never profitable as the P&O already used the Overland route for mails to Calcutta. See Robinson (1964), 172–175.

1018 See Robinson (1964), 175–176. For the early years of the Union Line, see Murray, 1–31. According to Cattell, the first contracts allowed the company to use 38 days for the voyage. Thus, it is possible that Robinson means the contract of 1868. See Cattell, 12.

1019 In the 1893 mail contract, the allowed duration of the trip was only 19 days. See Cattell, 12.

duration of voyages by merchant sailing ships between England and the Cape of Good Hope had been 82 days outward and 72 days homeward on average. The mails departed only if there was a ship available, which meant that the letters were sometimes waiting at Cape Town for several weeks before they were picked up by a homeward bound vessel. The tea clippers of the 1860s and 1870s made the home voyage faster, but even they used about 50 days between passing the Cape and arriving at London. As the sailing ships did not carry public mail at that time, their speed was not of much importance in this regard, however.[1020]

Until 1872, the Union Line kept its mail contract without difficulty, sailing from England on the 10th and 26th of each month.[1021] The factual sailing dates are not published by Cattell or any other postal historian, but a rough calculation shows that the system enabled four consecutive information circles between England and Cape Town. For the colonialists at Durban in Natal on the East Coast of South Africa, the trip was 800 miles longer than to the Cape and needed a further inter-colonial service. To be able to calculate the duration of these voyages, correspondence from that period would be needed for reference.

The situation changed abruptly in 1872, when the Castle Line, established by Donald Currie of Liverpool (who earlier worked for the Cunard Line), started a regular service between England and South Africa. Their ships were newer and faster and made the trip in 25 days, the sensational record of 1873 being 23 days. At that time, the Union Line ships sailed on the 10th and the 26th of each month, so the Castle Line vessels left from Dartmouth three days before the Union Line steamer and as they were faster, arrived at the Cape almost as soon as the competitor ship, which had left Southampton eleven days earlier. Naturally, people started to endorse their letters to be carried by these steamers instead of the official mail service. While the mails carried by the Castle Line steamers were considered private ship letters, they were also notably cheaper, the ½ oz. letter fee being only four pence against the one shilling rate charged for the official mail.[1022]

Before the mail contract with Union Line came to an end in 1876, the Cape Colonial Government negotiated with Donald Currie about a supplement mail contract. The Cape colonialists wanted cheap postage, more frequent mails and no amalgamation between the Union Line and the Castle Line, which would lead to a monopoly. The healthy competition led to a satisfactory situation in which the bi-monthly mail service by the two companies was organized so that there was actually a weekly service in both directions.[1023]

1020 The 1832 averages are calculated from *Lloyd's List* maritime intelligence 1832–1833. The outward trip average covers 45 trips and the homeward average 43 trips made during that period. The tea clippers for London were not often reported passing the Cape, even if those on their way to New York were. The average duration of the trips therefore covers only eight voyages, calculated from the sailing dates published by McGregor, 200–232.
1021 See Cattell, 12–15.
1022 See Cattell, 12–16; Robinson (1964), 178–180.
1023 See Cattell, 16; Robinson (1964), 182–183. The two companies were finally merged in the early 1900s during the South African war, forming the well-

FIG. 39. *Combined use of telegraph and ordinary mail. The telegram, sent Overland by the Alexandria, Cairo & Suez Telegraph Company, was forwarded from Suez (note the B02 handstamp) to Bombay by the P&O steamer* Benares, *which departed from Suez on 12.6.1864 and arrived in Bombay on 24.6.1864. The overland telegraph was most likely built in accordance with the railway, around 1859.*

This must have increased the number of consecutive information circles to five or probably six per year, although it cannot be verified here due to a lack of sailing data.

The introduction of the telegraph

As in other parts of the world, the telegraph came to the East in small portions, shortening the duration of communications by a few days here and there. The principal telegraph lines in Europe were completed in the 1850s and 1860s, and internal networks were linked across national borders to form an international system. From the early 1850s, it was also possible to lay submarine cables on shorter routes, e.g. in the English Channel. Due to economic and political reasons, it was mainly the British companies which were behind the laying of cables between the Mediterranean islands and the mainland in the 1850s. The cable which would run the length of the Mediterranean was started at the eastern end of the sea when Glass, Elliot and Co. prepared a line between Alexandria, Tripoli and Malta. It subsequently became the joint property of the company and the British Government. In 1866, a new and modern cable was laid between Alexandria and Malta by the British-owned Anglo-Mediterranean Telegraph Co.[1024]

known shipping line called the Union-Castle Line. See Marischal Murray, *Union-Castle Chronicle 1853–1953* (Glasgow, 1953), 134–139.

1024 See Jorma Ahvenainen, *The Far Eastern Telegraphs* (Helsinki 1981), 13–14.

With the completion of the cables between Malta and Alexandria, telegraphs from London and other cities in Western Europe reached Alexandria via Sicily and Malta, which had been connected in 1859. In 1870, two important lines were again completed: the line between Marseilles and Malta, which provided a direct link between London and Alexandria via Paris and Marseilles, and the Falmouth, Gibraltar and Malta Company's cable between England and Malta, which provided a British line all the way from London to Alexandria.[1025]

The earliest telegraphic communication with India was established in 1864–1865 using a combination of land and sea lines. The route followed the Turkish Government's line from Constantinople to Fao, via Baghdad. From Fao, the Indo-European Telegraph Department, financed by the Indian Government, laid coastal cables (the Persian Gulf Cables) to Karachi via Bushire and Jask. This line was soon extended by a land line across Persia across Bushire to Teheran. Shortly afterwards a service was inaugurated between Teheran and Moscow via Tiflis. There were now two alternative telegraph communications between Western Europe and India, one via Constantinople and the other via Moscow. However, both these lines proved to be rather week and unreliable, and new options were sought very soon.[1026]

The new telegraph system was built by the Anglo-German Indo-European Telegraph Company, which was established by Werner von Siemens and registered in Britain. The line was built across Continental Europe, through Prussia, then via Kiev, Odessa and the Caucasus to Julfa on the border between Russia and Persia. From there the line continued to Teheran where it was connected with the Indian Government lines. The line was completed in 1869, but for various technical problems, it was brought into general use the following year. Simultaneously a new rival, the British Indian Telegraph Company, entered the scene, building a submarine cable from Alexandria to Bombay via the Red Sea and Aden.[1027]

The cable to Bombay was continued by the Indian Government's land lines to Madras and via Penang to Singapore by the end of 1870. The following year a cable from Singapore to Hong Kong via Saigon was finished and, in addition, Australia and the Dutch East Indies were connected to the British lines. By October 1872, a land telegraph stretched across Australia to the south coast, thus connecting Adelaide and the south-eastern colonies with the mother country.[1028]

For the Far Eastern trade, the new means of communication was naturally very welcome, although the use of it was limited to the most urgent messages. For example, the number of telegrams sent from India grew from 311,000 in 1867 to 577,000 in 1870 and 907,000 in 1876. The respective numbers of mail items sent during these years were also growing fast: from 69 million

---

1025 Ahvenainen (1981), 14.
1026 Ahvenainen (1981), 16.
1027 Ahvenainen (1981), 16–17.
1028 Ahvenainen (1981), 17–19; Robinson (1964), 272.

in 1867 to 86 million in 1870 and 119 million in 1875.[1029] In other words, the number of telegrams sent was 0.45% of the number of items sent by mail in 1867, growing to 0.67% in 1870 and to 0.76% in 1876. It was only in the late 1880s that the number of telegrams sent in India reached 1% of the number of sent mail items. This gives an idea of the nature of telegraph usage. As everywhere else, it was expensive, and often unreliable.

Jorma Ahvenainen describes in an interesting way the political, cultural and economic difficulties met while laying telegraph cables in Chinese waters, as well as building the Siberian line to the East. For further details, his book on the Far Eastern Telegraphs is warmly recommended.[1030]

From the viewpoint of this study, it may be relevant to note that there does not seem to be a specific date when the telegraph 'took over' from traditional business communications. Where the telegraph existed, it was used to shorten the duration of information transmission in critical situations. An early note by Kirk verifies that the new system was immediately adopted by the shipping companies, when such an option was available, and that there also existed an early telegraph line east of Suez: ''Northam' arrived at Suez on 26.4.59 with the Bombay mails and 'Emeu' should have arrived the day after. Both sets of mails should have left Alexandria on 29.4.59 – by 'Nepaul' (Marseilles) or by 'Ripon' (Southampton). But Alexandria had no news of 'Emeu'. The submarine telegraph cable was out of action between Aden and the Red Sea Telegraph Station at Suakin ('the gutta-percha perished' – British Library records). Thus Alexandria would not know about the 'Emeu' until a signal was received from Suakin.'[1031]

An interesting letter by Alfred Holt gives detailed directions to the *Agamemnon's* Captain Middleton for the ship's first voyage to Shanghai in 1866. In addition to orders regarding schedules, ports, coaling, cargo and various agents to be met, as well as arrangements for separate cooking for Chinese passengers, there were also requirements to send information to the owners from different places. From Mauritius, a letter should be sent to an agent in Alexandria to be telegraphed to England with the following short text: 'Agamemnon Mauritius Monday twenty eight May' with the correct date replaced instead of the date given. Holt refers to the foreign telegrams which are sometimes 'almost incomprehensible'.[1032]

Holt also writes that if there is a chance of writing to Ceylon before the mail leaves for Suez, the Captain should write to an agent at Galle and request him to send a similar telegram. 'Of course you will not write to both.' At Galle, the Captain should write by the first mail to the agent and ask him to send a similar telegraph to the one from Mauritius to inform the owners about the ship's safe arrival. On the way homewards, the agent at Galle should telegraph the owners about any deviations from the plan. It would also be a convenience if the Captain could telegraph home when passing

1029 Mitchell, 773.
1030 See Ahvenainen (1981), 17–58.
1031 Kirk (1989), 149.
1032 'Directions to Capt. Middleton when sailing to China with the Agamemnon on her first voyage April 19th 1866', Blue Funnel, Ocean Steamship Co. OA 2583, (MMM).

Lisbon, and if he could not, he should try to telegraph from some place in the English Channel.[1033]

For the mail contract companies, the telegram was a valuable tool as the problems met by one of their vessels often caused a chain of delays in their service. For any shipowner, the telegraph was a management tool which made it possible to keep better control over their businesses far away. To speed up information transmission between Europe and the Far East, it was now possible to ask the agents in e.g. Alexandria to telegraph the most urgent news to London, while the mails were still on their way for a few days.

Thus, from the 1860s, the real duration of information transmission was often shorter than the fastest steam ship connection. As in the case of the North Atlantic mail route (where the telegraphs shortened the duration of information transmission between Ireland and London, or between Newfoundland and New York, long before the Atlantic cable was laid), or as in the case of South America (where merchants could use the telegram between their positions and the northern coast of Brazil, and between Lisbon and London), so the Far Eastern trade benefited from partial solutions for years before the long intercontinental lines were established.

1033 'Directions to Capt. Middleton...', OA 2583, (MMM).

VIII Conclusion

Earlier studies have already shown that the speed of one-way information transmission grew markedly during the 19th century before the introduction of the intercontinental submarine telegraph. The interesting question which has not been systematically examined to date is: Why? What happened? Was the change from sail to steam and from mail coach to railway the only proper answer? And did the shortening of one-way trips automatically improve the information circulation of business enterprises? For a merchant, it was often critical to be able to reply to letters rapidly, not just to receive news from the other side of the ocean.

Due to their own maritime and trade interests, the British became the forerunners in organizing regular overseas mail transmission, first by sailing packets and, as soon as the technology was developed enough, by steamships. Only a few months after the first successful transatlantic crossings entirely by steam power in 1838, the British Government decided to organize regular mail steamship services on the Empire's most important trade routes: to North America, the West Indies and East India.

Instead of building and managing a fleet of steamers itself, the British Post Office 'outsourced' the overseas mail services by giving a Royal Charter to three shipping companies, which would take care of the mail sailings: the Cunard Line, the Royal Mail Line, and the P&O. This happened simultaneously with a few other revolutionary ideas: the change of British inland postage rates from different fees depending on the length of the journey to a uniform one penny rate, and the introduction of the first pre-paid postage stamp in the world, the Penny Black.

From July 1840, the Cunard Line's vessels sailed across the Atlantic on bi-monthly schedule, or monthly in winter. The P&O started their sailings first to the Mediterranean in 1840, and then to India, China and even Australia. The Royal Mail Line started their sailings to the West Indies in early 1842.

Diagram 39 shows the change from sail to steam in the common mail services on the various trade routes. As can be noticed, steamships were taken in use in mail transport within an approximately 15 years' period. Whereas the first mail-carrying steamers crossed the Atlantic in 1838, the first mail steamships started their service to Australia in 1852. The first period of steamship service to Sydney lasted only a couple of years, and started again after the Crimean war in 1857.

As can be noticed in the diagram, there was an 'overnight change' from sail to steam on the West Indian and South American routes, as the British Post Office replaced the Falmouth sailing packets by the Royal Mail Line steamers in January 1842 (the West Indies) and in January 1851 (South America). Even though the other government-sponsored mail steamship companies started their service on specific dates as well, there was generally a shift period of several years when letters were carried by different means of communication. The reasons for the delays varied. On the North Atlantic route, for example, the American sailing packets could compete successfully with the early steamers on the way eastwards due to prevailing winds and currents. At Panama, the construction of the railway across the isthmus took several years. In India and China, the East India Company could fight against changes for several years. And Australia was just too far away to provide a business for the early steamship companies.

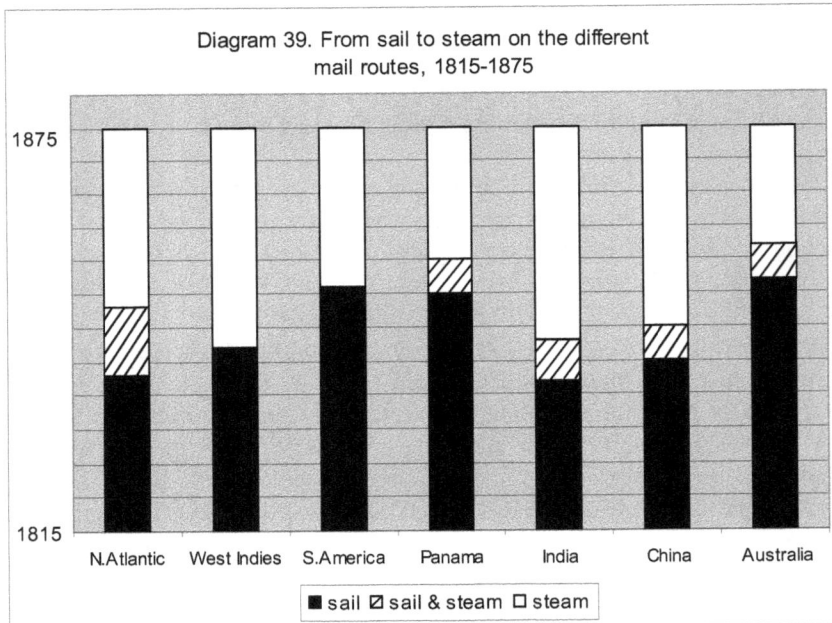

Diagram 39. From sail to steam on the different mail routes, 1815-1875

The development of two-way communications, which was important for business correspondence, has been examined in this study by using the method of calculating the consecutive information circles enabled by various means of communication. The following diagrams will show the development of business information transmission on the different mail routes between 1815 and 1875.

North Atlantic

On the North Atlantic route the number of consecutive information circles enabled by the mail systems of the period grew from three to five per year, when the American sailing packets started their line service between New York and Liverpool. The change from sail to steam in 1838 did not bring a major improvement in the information circulation, even though the duration of westbound voyages in particular decreased remarkably. The reason for this was that the steamship voyages were organized by different independent companies which could not afford a regular line service.

While 15 round voyages by the pioneering steamers enabled only six consecutive information circles per year for merchants in England and New York in 1838 and 1839, the 20 annual round trips of the Cunard Line steamers with regular sailing dates enabled eight consecutive information circles already in the early 1840s.

Although there was a more or less regular steamship service in the North Atlantic from 1838, the shift period during which mail was carried across the ocean by both steamers and sailing packets lasted until the late 1840s. This was due to the fact that the eastbound voyages by steamers were not remarkably faster than by sailing ships and there were weekly sailing packet departures from New York, while the steamship departures took place less often. The captain's fee for carrying a private ship letter was considerably lower than the official postage fee. How relevant the information cost was from the sender's point of view is difficult to estimate, as it was the recipient who mostly paid for the letter.

The general speed and regularity of sailings, as well as the expectations regarding the safety of the mail transmission, were reflected in the business practices of the merchant houses. It was common practice to write duplicates and even triplicates of letters to ensure that at least one would be received, and preferably as soon as possible. During the shift period from sail to steam, the original letter was sent by steamer and the copy by sailing packet, or vice versa. Later on, the original letter and the duplicate were sent by two consecutive steamers, and finally the steamship service was considered so reliable that duplicates were not sent any longer.

The growing trade and improving steamship technology soon attracted competitors to the North Atlantic route. The U.S. Postmaster General awarded subsidized mail contracts to three shipping lines, of which the most important was the Collins Line on the New York – Liverpool route. When the Cunard Line also opened a direct mail route to New York, there were two weekly steamship sailings in both directions between England and the United States from 1850. These changes alone enabled an increase in annual consecutive information circles from eight to twelve without any notable improvement in the speed of one-way voyages during the period when the companies were competing with each other (see Diagram 40).

Diagram 40. Liverpool - New York, development of the number of consecutive information circles per year, 1815-1875

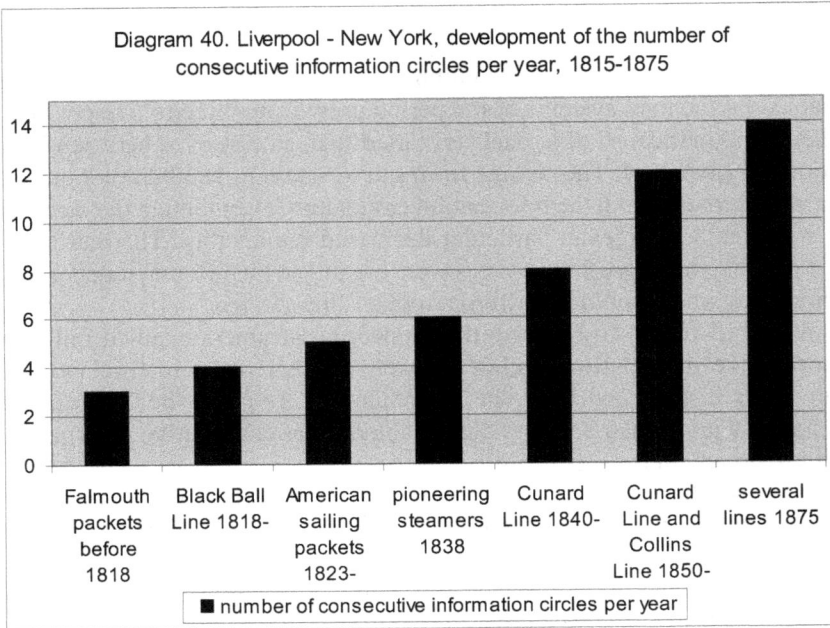

Even though the size and speed of the transatlantic vessels, as well as the frequency of their departures, grew constantly through the period from 1815 to 1875, the number of consecutive information circles enabled by the various services did not improve correspondingly. While there were three times more sailings per year in 1875 than in the early 1850s, the number of options to send letters back and forth consecutively during the year only grew from 12 to 14. Making an allowance for the length of the trip and the number of annual departures, the ideal number of information circles would have been nearly 17. But the transatlantic mail service had reached its maturity and was in fact stagnant at that time. There were several reasons for this.

The steamers had lost their position as 'news bringers' to the submarine telegraph in the same way as the American sailing packets had lost their position to the steamers 30 years earlier. In both cases, this led to growing irregularity and length of sailings. Although the mass of carried bulk mails was still growing decades after the introduction of the telegraph, the excitement of being the first to break the news had gone. The speed at which bulk documents or ordinary business letters were carried was not considered that important.

Secondly, no one was paying for the speed of bulk information transmission. After the lucrative mail contracts had been replaced by monthly agreements about carrying mail as normal freight, the shipping companies started to compete in other business areas, especially the passenger service. Saturday sailings from New York became popular and four companies sailed on the same day. Thus there were several days in the week with no mail departures at all.

The West Indies and South America

The Royal Mail Line started their steamship services to the West Indies one and a half years later than the Cunard Line started their North Atlantic service, and to South America at the beginning of 1851. In both cases, the change occurred overnight, though naturally the last Falmouth packets carried mails from their respective destinations on their home voyages. Diagram 41 shows the change in the number of consecutive information circles during this period with respect to the West Indies. The example is from the Demerara route, but the destination could be some other port in the Caribbean region as well and the result would be the same due to the circular mail route system.

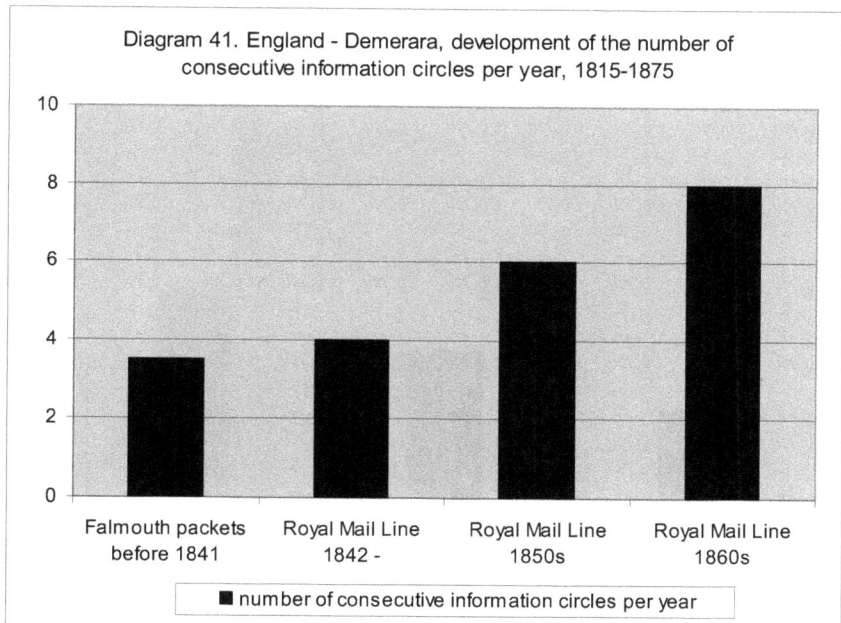

Diagram 41. England - Demerara, development of the number of consecutive information circles per year, 1815-1875

	Falmouth packets before 1841	Royal Mail Line 1842 -	Royal Mail Line 1850s	Royal Mail Line 1860s
number of consecutive information circles per year	3.5	4	6	8

As can be seen by comparing the years 1841 and 1842, the effects of the change from sail to steam were not very impressive on the West Indies route. Even if the duration of one-way sailings from Europe to the Caribbean became shorter, information circulation suffered from the complexity of the inter-island services (see Map 4 on page 238). Improvements took place over the next two decades. By re-routing several inter-island sailings and reducing their number, and by replacing transatlantic vessels with speedier, technologically more advanced ships, it was possible to increase the number of consecutive information circles from four to eight by the early 1860s. The overlapping French service in the Caribbean, starting in 1862, offered an alternative but did not really improve the number of options for faster information circulation.

The course of events on the South American route was different. The British government mail contract was awarded to the Royal Mail Line as late as at the beginning of 1851, while the Falmouth sailing packets had taken care of the mail service until then. By that time, many of the early problems with steamship technology and the streamlining of schedules had been overcome. Thus the overnight change from sail to steam in early 1851 immediately improved the number of consecutive information circles between London and Rio de Janeiro from three to 4.5 and between London and Buenos Aires from two to three. Additionally, the improvements in schedules and the speed of vessels enabled an even better service from 1859. The number of consecutive information circles between London and Rio de Janeiro increased to six and between London and Buenos Aires to four per year.

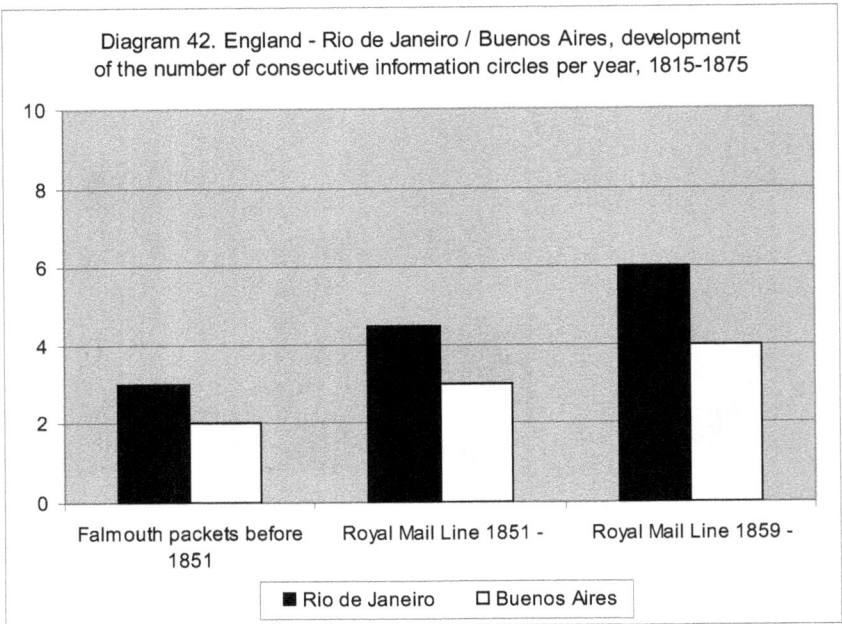

Diagram 42. England - Rio de Janeiro / Buenos Aires, development of the number of consecutive information circles per year, 1815-1875

The French service, which was started in 1860 by Messageries Impériales, could not afford extra consecutive information circles due to the long voyage, but it played an important role in information transmission as the sailings were organized to complement the Royal Mail Line's sailings instead of competing with them by offering simultaneous services.

California

The most striking improvement in the speed of information transmission by traditional means took place between New York and San Francisco. At the time when the Californian gold rush begun in the late 1840s, the only means of communication to the West Coast of the United States was by sailing vessels around Cape Horn. Even by the fastest clippers, it took about four months to sail from New York to San Francisco. When steamship services were established between New York and Colon, as well as between Panama and San Francisco, the one-way travel time was reduced to some six weeks. In 1855, after the opening of the Panama railway, the duration of information transmission between New York and San Francisco was only 3.5 weeks. And finally, in the 1870s, the transcontinental railway took the mails from the East Coast to the West in about one week.

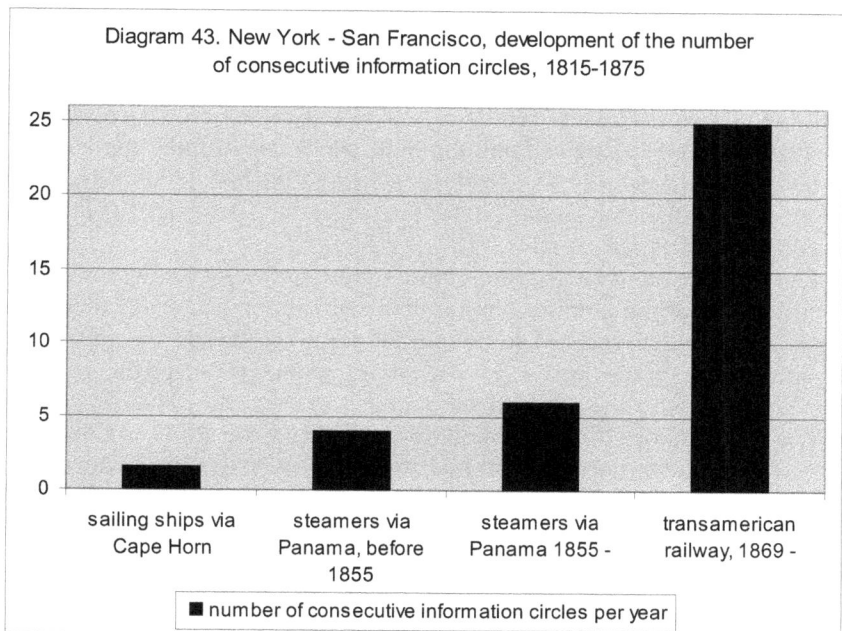

Diagram 43. New York - San Francisco, development of the number of consecutive information circles, 1815-1875

number of consecutive information circles per year

sailing ships via Cape Horn — steamers via Panama, before 1855 — steamers via Panama 1855 - — transamerican railway, 1869 -

The Panama case includes a paradox: by sailing ship, which was the slowest means of communication, the journey in terms of miles was also the longest. The combination of two steamship lines and the overland crossing at Panama caused a double effect: the length of the journey was significantly shortened, while the speed was greatly improved due to the simultaneous change from sail to steam. The railway across the Panama Isthmus made the overland crossing shorter and easier to manage, again speeding up the journey. And finally, by using the shortest possible route and the fastest possible vehicle of the period, the duration of the journey was reduced to less than a week of the original four months or more (see Map 7 on page 284).

In the United States, the telegraph was brought into transcontinental use in the early 1860s, thus making the mail steamers mainly carriers of documents and confirmatory details instead of the first news of great events. This notably demoted the Panama steamship services, which never recovered to their earlier level of performance after the American Civil War. The significance of the transcontinental railway as the 'news bringer' was never recognized, as the telegraph had already taken that place when the railway was completed. From the business information point of view it was nevertheless an important improvement.

East India and other Australasian destinations

On the East India route, the original situation differed from the other routes discussed. There was no government packet service and practically no private merchant ships sailing on the India or China routes due to the monopoly of the East India Company, or the EIC. After the abolition of the EIC monopoly in the India trade in 1813 and the China trade in 1834, great numbers of common merchant ships took over the Eastern routes. They made faster round trips than the East Indiamen and due to their large number, the information circulation between England and the trade ports east of the Cape of Good Hope improved markedly. Due to the long voyage, the number of consecutive information circles increased to only approximately 1.5 per year. The duration of sailings also varied greatly.

The development of the Overland route across Egypt was a major improvement in the communication between Europe and the Asian trade ports. After fifteen years of hesitation between the shorter route with the desert crossing on the one hand and steaming around the Cape on the other, the Overland route was adopted permanently in the early 1840s.

The British Post Office awarded a contract to the P&O for the mail service to India and later to China and other parts of Asia. The European leg,

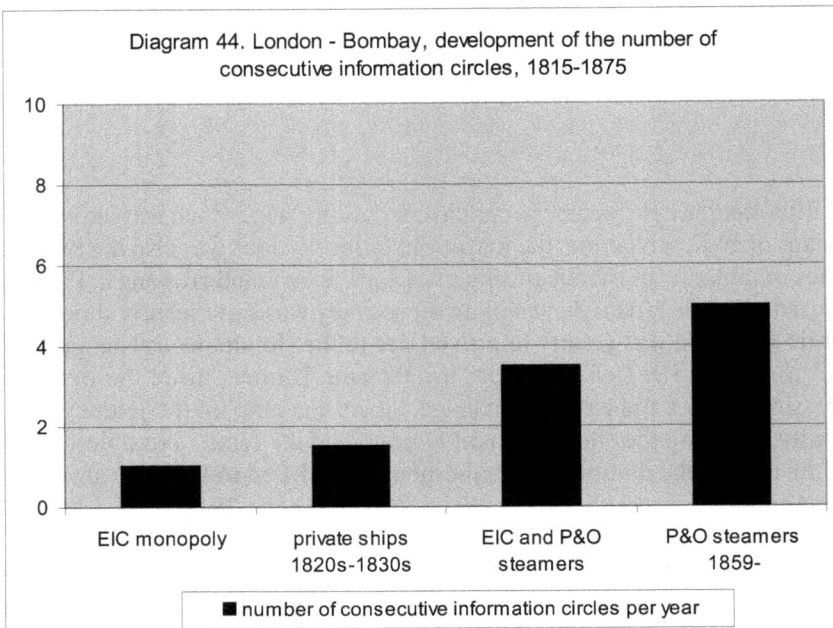

Diagram 44. London - Bombay, development of the number of consecutive information circles, 1815-1875

■ number of consecutive information circles per year

which had been taken care of by the Admiralty, was first transferred to the P&O, while the EIC still took care of the Bombay mails. The P&O started the Calcutta Line in 1843 and the China Line for Hong Kong in 1845.

In the early 1840s, the express mails from London were taken across the Channel, then by railway from Calais to Marseilles, by Admiralty packets to Alexandria, by dromedaries and donkeys across the Egyptian desert, by river boats on the Nile, by steamers from Suez to Bombay and by dawk runners across the Indian mainland. The letters were then carried from Calcutta by private merchant ships to China. This chain of varying services could bring the news from London to Hong Kong in less than four months, of which more than 2.5 months were used for the last leg from Bombay to Canton / Hong Kong. Even a merchant ship sailing directly from England could sometimes bring the latest news faster to China than the expensive and complicated government system, and very much cheaper.

In 1843, the P&O opened its Calcutta route via Galle, Ceylon, and when the leg from Galle to Hong Kong was opened in 1845, the overnight change in the speed of information transmission was remarkable. The new arrangement took the London mails to Hong Kong in fifty days, thus halving the previous duration of the mail transmission. This was one of the occasions in the history of world communications, where just a logistical arrangement could revolutionize the speed of information transmission, without radical new inventions but by applying what already existed. In 1859, the London – Hong Kong service enabled 3.5 consecutive information circles per year, one whole circle taking 93 to 96 days.

By 1861, the P&O had organized its sailings with great expertise. All the Australasian ports except Bombay were served via Galle, from where the

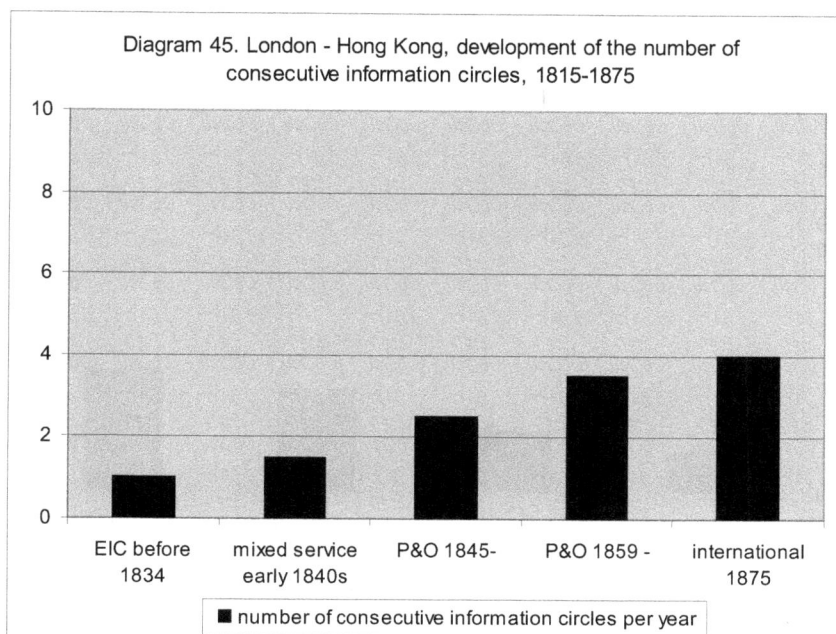

Diagram 45. London - Hong Kong, development of the number of consecutive information circles, 1815-1875

number of consecutive information circles per year

branch steamers continued to Calcutta, to Hong Kong (and from there to Shanghai and Foochow) and to Sydney in Australia. The ships returned to Galle simultaneously to reach the steamer for Suez, from where the mails were forwarded across the Egyptian desert by the newly opened railway and by ship from Alexandria – the express mail via Marseilles and by train directly to London, and the bulk mail via Gibraltar to Southampton.

By avoiding loading and reloading when possible and unnecessary waiting for late arrivals of mail-bringing ships at distant ports, the company had produced a smoothly working system which enabled three consecutive information circles per year with Shanghai, as well as with Foochow and Sydney. It took some 3.5 months to receive an answer to a letter sent to these places, but it was only about a quarter of the duration of the information circle of some thirty years earlier. The French service by Messageries Impériales complemented the system from the 1860s, as it had done on the South America route.

There had been notable geographical 'leverage' in the case of the Panama route combining New York and San Francisco in the 1850s, and the same phenomenon could be seen in the Overland route regarding information transmission to India and the Far Eastern ports. While the steamers were replacing sailing ships, new mail routes could be brought into use, thus considerably shortening the length of the route in miles, as well as the time used for information transmission. By building railways across critical shortcuts, a notable extra benefit could be achieved, e.g. over the Panama and Suez isthmuses, as well as between Calais and Marseilles, or later Brindisi, and across India to replace the dawk runners.

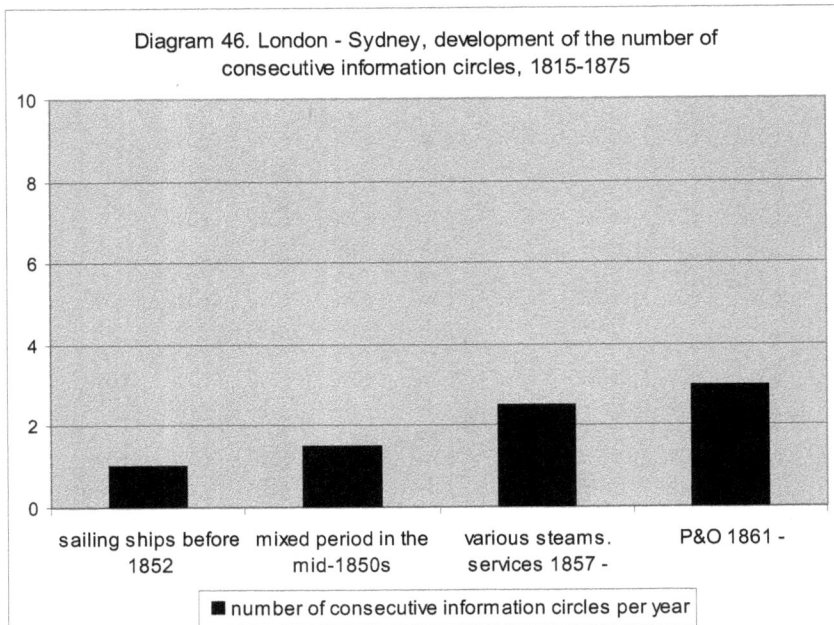

Diagram 46. London - Sydney, development of the number of consecutive information circles, 1815-1875

But not all regions benefited from the shortcuts. For example, the Suez Overland route was a disaster for Australia. When ships travelled from Europe around the Cape of Good Hope, Australia was located almost as near the Cape as the East Indian ports or China – in fact many ships nearly passed Australia on their way to Canton or Manila. But when viewed from Suez, the geography was very different and Australia was thousands of miles away from the main trade routes.

The early steamers were not able to manage these distances and Australia was left alone for many years. The gold rush finally encouraged some companies to try, although with rather weak results. After the Crimean War, 16 years after the company had begun its mail service to Calcutta, the P&O finally started a permanent line service for Australia. By 1872, only a dozen years later, Australia was connected by telegraph with the mother country. When the modern systems finally reached Australia, they entered rapidly.

The submarine telegraph did not cause a sudden revolution in overseas communications, but became an integral part of communications over a longer period. As the telegraph had been partly used for urgent inland connections from the late 1840s, it had benefited communications to some degree for years before direct overseas connections were established. Thus, the duration of information transmission across the Atlantic had been shortened years before the successful Atlantic cable was laid in 1866 by inland telegraph connections both in Britain and Canada / United States. The trip to South America was shortened by a telegraph line between London and Lisbon on the European side, and by a coastal telegraph line in Brazil. There were also several partially working land lines to India before the direct line was opened in 1870.

The laying of submarine telegraph cables between continents caused a shift period in information transmission that was similar to the change from sail to steam. Due to high prices and unreliable services, the telegraph was used only in urgent cases. The use of the telegraph was not usually an alternative to written letters, but these means of communications mainly complemented each other, as letters were needed anyway for sending instructions, explanations and business documents. Thus the information costs were not alternative; the choice was not usually made between sending a letter *or* a telegram but between sending *only* a letter, or a letter *and* a telegram. When the prices of telegrams were reduced, the latter alternative became a part of normal business practice.

Summary

The most notable changes in overseas business information transmission took place in the 1850s or early 1860s, depending on the distance of the region from the mother countries in Europe. This did not occur immediately when sail was transformed to steam but several years later when the shipping network had been organized in a more effective way and there were enough – but not yet too many – companies sharing the market for mail transmission. Additionally, several geographical hurdles were overcome by building railways across critical overland shortcuts like Panama and Suez.

As most of these improvements took place within a decade in the mid-19th century, this period must have been experienced as truly revolutionary by contemporaries. Without the wars and uprisings which consumed a great part of the mail steamship capacity for several years, e.g. the Crimean War, the Indian Mutiny, and the American Civil War, progress could have been even faster.

As long as the ships were considered as important news bringers, they acted accordingly. The departures were punctual and spread more evenly over a time period (offering one weekly departure instead of two simultaneous departures every second week, for example) which was more useful from the business information transmission point of view. The ideal situation was typically based on services by two or several competing companies each having a mail contract. In contrast, mixing a major passenger and freight service with mail transport generally caused declining interest in the speed of information transmission.

The North Atlantic was often the testing field for new information transmission systems, not only due to its economic importance but also because of the shorter run compared to the other routes. The struggle between the Cunard Line and the Collins Line obviously did not speed up specific voyages by more than one or two days, if at all, but their way of organizing sailings on alternative weeks, in the similar way as the American sailing packets had done, led to the same effectiveness of information circulation. Their combined performance was almost equal to what could be achieved 25 years later by much more effective vessels operated by several companies on a nearly daily basis. If there was a revolution in early communications, it was probably in the North Atlantic in around 1850.

The more extensive was the geographical distance, the longer it took before a similar 'revolution' could take place on the other mail routes. The regular and frequent-enough line system conducted by several identical mail carriers was built up all over the world by the early 1860s – only a few years before the laying of the first intercontinental submarine cables. Thus the 'revolutions' followed each other. For contemporaries, it must have been a logical chain of improvements instead of one single event which changed it all.

In our days, the globalization of real-time international communications, first by fax and international phone calls, and then by mobile phones, text messages and the Internet, has changed our way of conducting business or even our personal relationships. Those who saw the development of regular steamship services with strategic overland shortcuts by railways at distant colonies and the speeding up of information circulation coupled with the increasing opportunities to use telegraphs for the most urgent messages, must have felt as we do now. While information and capital were moving faster than ever, people had to adapt their lives to the new communication systems. Hopefully someone will also examine this aspect of the development one day.

IX Epilogue

The introduction of the intercontinental telegraph did not stop the improvement of ocean steamship services but complemented the communication, speeding up world trade and capital movements. For ocean shipping, the development up to 1875 was just the beginning.

The speed of mail steamers, especially on the North Atlantic route, grew steadily through the whole steamship era. While the *Sirius* made her first voyage in 18.5 days, by an average speed of only eight knots, the *Germanic* of the White Star Line doubled that speed to almost 16 knots in the 1870s. By the end of the 19th century, the average speed had risen to 22 knots, and the last record holder, the *United States*, crossed the Atlantic from the Bishop Rock lighthouse at the entrance to the English Channel to the Ambrose lighthouse ship off New York in 3.5 days in 1952, at an average speed of 34.5 knots.[1034]

There clearly was a correlation between the size of the vessel and her speed. From 1838 to 1899 almost all record holders were at the same time the largest ships in the world, excluding the giant *Great Eastern*, built in 1860, which never was a Blue Riband holder, even if she definitely was the largest passenger ship ever built until the 20th century.

The rapid change after 1880 was mainly due to the increasing competition, which started in the 1870s. The ships were built larger and larger, partly to meet the needs of growing masses of emigrants and cargo transport, but also because first class passengers were tempted by more space and comfortable surroundings during their travel.

Luxury indeed became critical in the growing competition, and for instance the new Cunarders of the 1880s provided some 60% of the total net tonnage for cabin class accommodation, compared with only 20% for steerage.[1035] The image of steamship travel in the early 20th century given to the general public by the books and films about the ill-fated *Titanic* of the White Star Line was therefore not incorrect. But in addition to the well known details of the ship's history, it should be remembered that also the *Titanic* bore in her name the abbreviation RMS – Royal Mail Steamer.

1034 Kludas, 146–147.
1035 Hyde (1975), 83.

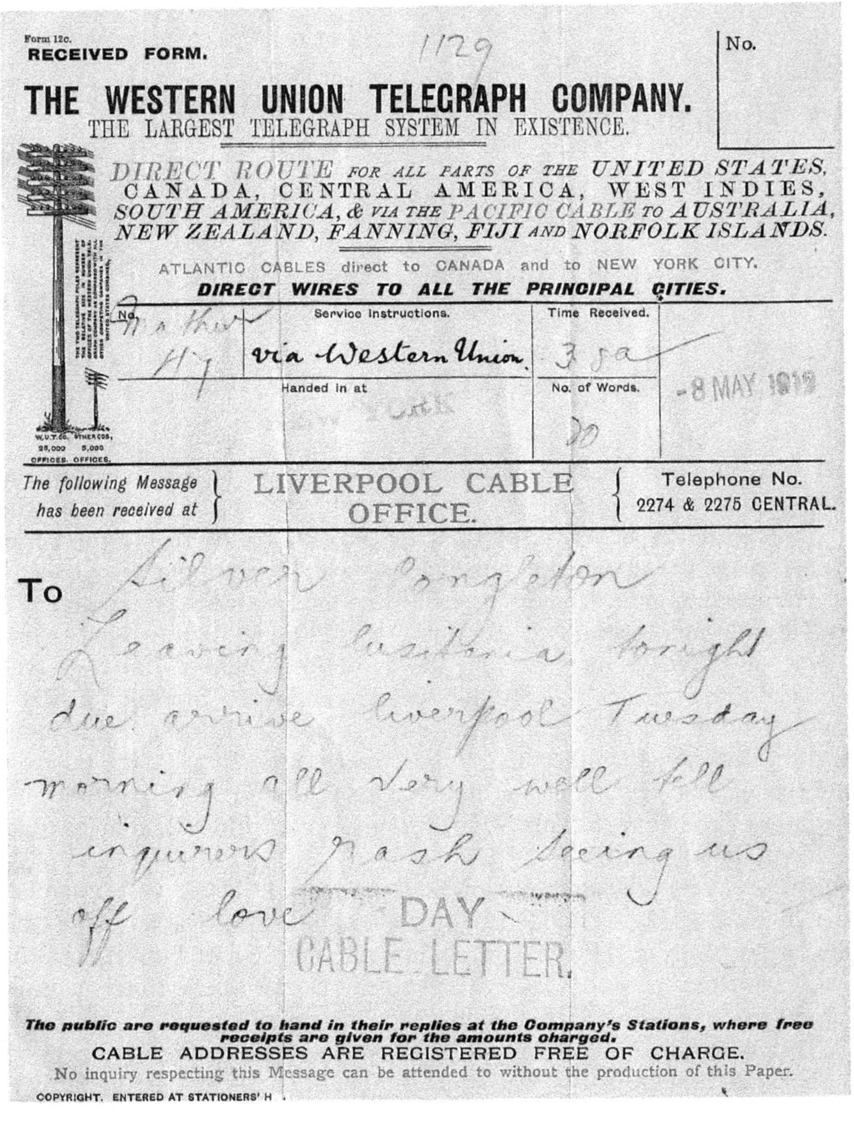

Form 12c.
RECEIVED FORM.

1129

No.

THE WESTERN UNION TELEGRAPH COMPANY.
THE LARGEST TELEGRAPH SYSTEM IN EXISTENCE.

DIRECT ROUTE FOR ALL PARTS OF THE UNITED STATES, CANADA, CENTRAL AMERICA, WEST INDIES, SOUTH AMERICA, & VIA THE PACIFIC CABLE TO AUSTRALIA, NEW ZEALAND, FANNING, FIJI AND NORFOLK ISLANDS.

ATLANTIC CABLES direct to CANADA and to NEW YORK CITY.
DIRECT WIRES TO ALL THE PRINCIPAL CITIES.

W.U.T.Co. 25,000 OFFICES. OTHER COS. 5,000 OFFICES.

No.	Service Instructions.	Time Received.	
47	via Western Union	3 5a	-8 MAY 1912
	Handed in at New York	No. of Words. 30	

The following Message has been received at LIVERPOOL CABLE OFFICE. Telephone No. 2274 & 2275 CENTRAL.

To Silver Congleton

Leaving lusitania tonight due arrive liverpool Tuesday morning all very well tell inquirers rash seeing us off love

DAY CABLE LETTER.

The public are requested to hand in their replies at the Company's Stations, where free receipts are given for the amounts charged.
CABLE ADDRESSES ARE REGISTERED FREE OF CHARGE.
No inquiry respecting this Message can be attended to without the production of this Paper.
COPYRIGHT. ENTERED AT STATIONERS' H

FIG. 40. *The Atlantic cable telegraph from New York to Liverpool on 8.5.1912 informs the family members at home that the senders are going to travel by the* Lusitania: *'Leaving lusitania tonight due arrive liverpool Tuesday morning all very well tell inquirers rash seeing us off love.' The couple who sent the telegraph had arrived in New York three weeks earlier by the* Mauretania *simultaneously with the* Titanic's *sinking on the same route.*

Diagram 47 shows the trend in steamship size and speed from the period of the contest between the Cunard Line and the Collins Line in the 1850s to the end of the 19th century. Later development was even more impressive, as can be seen in Diagram 48.

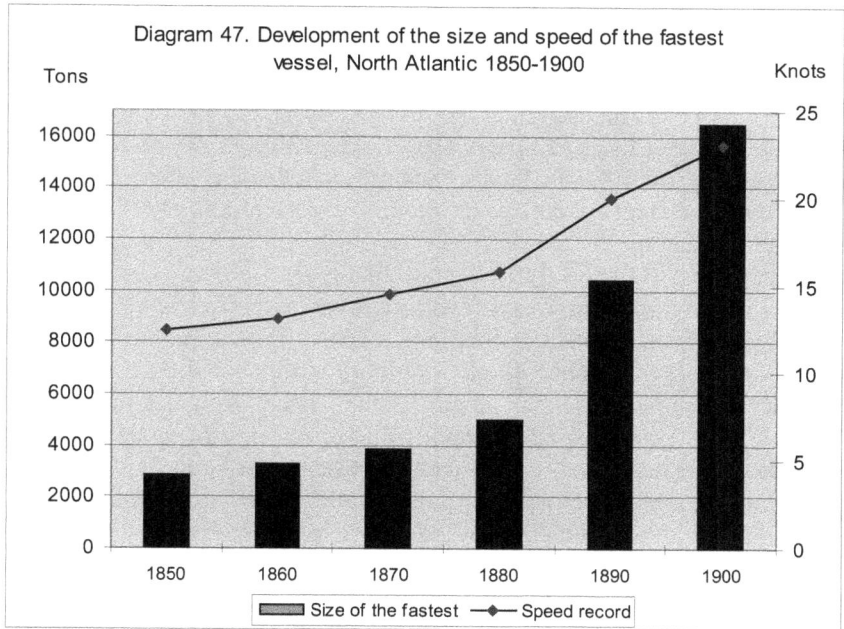

Diagram 47. Development of the size and speed of the fastest vessel, North Atlantic 1850-1900

Source: Kludas, 36, 41, 49, 54, 72, 87 and 146–147.

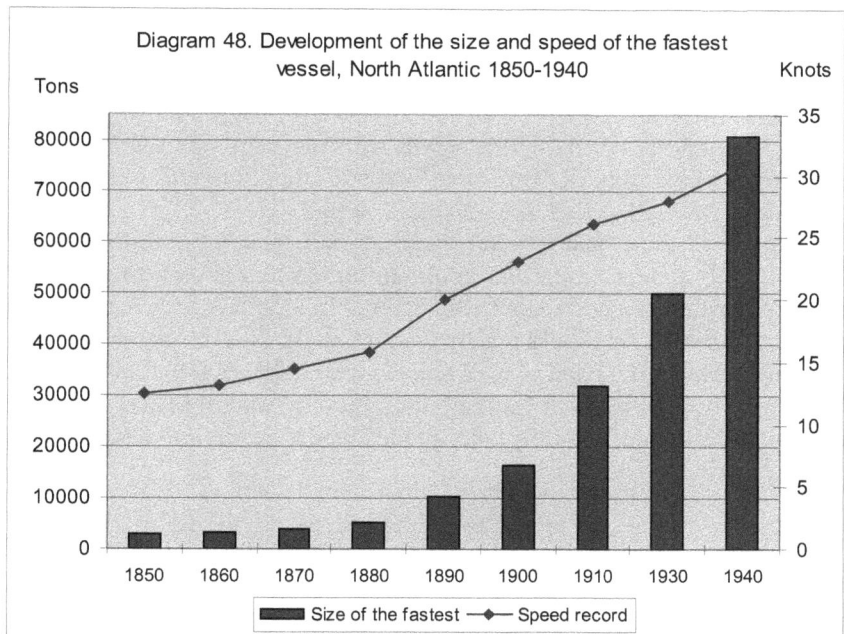

Diagram 48. Development of the size and speed of the fastest vessel, North Atlantic 1850-1940

Source: Kludas, 36, 41, 49, 54, 72, 87, 105, 114, 131, 136 and 146–147. – The *Mauretania* kept the record both in 1910 and 1920.

411

But the progress was not as straightforward as could be assumed by looking at the diagrams. After a period of fast improvement in steamship building around 1910 – including the Cunard Line's *Lusitania* and *Mauretania* in 1907 and *Aquitania* in 1914, the White Star Line's *Olympic* in 1911 and *Titanic* in 1912, the French Line's *France* in 1912, and HAPAG's *Imperator* in 1913 and *Vaterland* in 1914 – WW1 set back progress for years.[1036]

The period of stagnation in the development of speed can easily be noticed from the fact that the *Mauretania* kept the Blue Riband for almost 20 years, from September 1909 to July 1929, until finally the German vessels *Bremen* and *Europa* of Norddeutscher Lloyd took over.[1037] Only a few years later, in 1936, improved maritime technology reached its peak in the form of the *Queen Mary,* 80,774 tons, which was more than a hundred times larger than the first transatlantic mail steamer, the *Sirius* of 703 tons, one century earlier.[1038] The *Queen Mary's* normal Atlantic crossing from New York to Cherbourg took less than 4.5 days at an average speed of almost 30 knots.[1039] During WW2, she once crossed the Atlantic with 15,740 troops and 943 staff – a total of 16,683 people on board, which is still a record.[1040]

The frequency of sailings depended very much on the emigrant flows. One of the peak years was 1913 with almost 1,200 passenger steamship arrivals in New York, over 170 arrivals in Boston, over 90 in Philadelphia, and over 50 in Baltimore – in total more than 1,500 passenger steamship arrivals from Europe at these ports during one year. The Cunard Line's *Mauretania* made 15 round trips that year, arriving in New York every third week. Alone, she could have run more consecutive information circles than all the steamers together that plied the same route in 1875. There was a regular service to New York from Glasgow, Liverpool, London and Southampton, from Antwerp, Bremen, Hamburg, Havre and Rotterdam, and from several Mediterranean and Scandinavian ports.[1041]

Despite the Atlantic cable, which had existed for more than 60 years, fast mail transmission across the ocean was still important and the number of mails was still increasing. The speed was still important and something to be proud of, as well as handling the mails at port.

Whereas all the Cunard vessels together had carried 2.6 million letters in 1851, their steamer *Aquitania* took 16 million letters on a single trip in 1925. According to a newspaper article, the ship's captain 'wirelessed' from the sea that the vessel would reach Quarantine, off New York, at 2.15 p.m. with more than 6,700 bags of mail (each containing 2,000 to 3,000 letters). Three mail boats were sent for the bags, and they were handled, separated and checked to be immediately taken to the Post Office stations and railroads.

1036 For the vessels, see Bonsor (1975), vol. 1, 157, 415; Bonsor (1978), vol. 2, 661, 765.
1037 Kludas, 146–147.
1038 Kludas, 36, 131.
1039 For example, abstracts of logs from the sailings of the *Queen Mary* from New York to Cherbourg and Southampton, 29.7.1936 and 23.6.1937, conducted in rather different weather conditions. (SRLC)
1040 See James Steele, *Queen Mary* (Hong Kong, 1995), 187.
1041 The figures are calculated from Allan Morton, *Directory of European Passenger Steamship Arrivals for the Years 1890 to 1930* (Baltimore, 1998), 165–174.

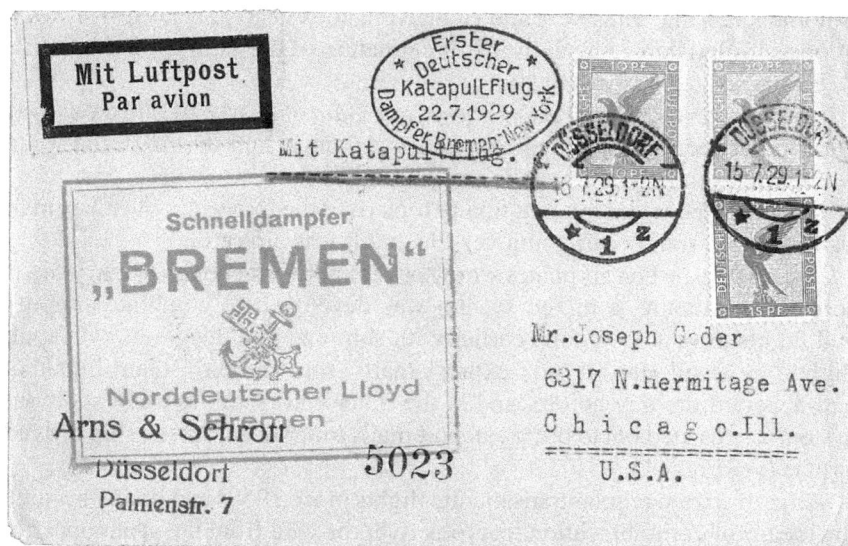

FIG. 41. *Catapult mail was once again a combination of the fastest possible means of carrying mail across the Atlantic. In the late 1920s, despite the fact that the submarine telegraph had already existed for more than 60 years, it was thought to be worth the trouble to organize a system to take the express mails to an ocean steamer by small aircraft when the ship was already at sea, to be sent to the shore by the similar way in the other end. A letter from the first German catapult flight by the NDL steamer* Bremen *in July 1929 arrived from Düsseldorf to New York in seven days, having spent less than five days at sea.*

According to the article, this was done in 84 minutes. The largest single cargo of mails had been carried by the White Star Line's *Olympic* in December 1924, more than 14,000 mailbags. The total number of mailbags handled by the mail boatmen of New York that year was over 960,000.[1042] In 1929, the three Cunard vessels *Aquitania*, *Berengaria* and *Mauretania* carried some 255,000 mailbags from Southampton to New York, with at least 510 million letters in total.[1043]

While the transatlantic mail-carrying steamers continued to increase in size and speed up to WW2, there was no major need for such development on the Asian routes. For example the P&O vessels, which carried mails between London and Shanghai via the Suez Canal in 1913, were about 10,000 tons each, and their service speed varied between 15 and 17 knots. The average journey from London to Shanghai via Gibraltar, Marseilles, Port Said, Aden,

---

1042 *Evening World*, 20.5.1925. PR 3.1/12h (CP). The figures probably included also the coastal mails for New York.

1043 '*Big Three* figures 1929 – From Marine Supt's Records'. PR 3.1/12k (CP). – The *Berengaria* was the former HAPAG ship *Imperator*, which had changed owner after WW1 as part of war indemnities, replacing the Cunard ship *Lusitania* which was sank with great loss of life by German torpedoes in 1915.

Colombo, Penang, Singapore and Hong Kong took nearly 38 days.[1044] The list of ports visited depicts well the different nature of the sailings in the Indian Ocean compared to the Atlantic.

However, in 1929, the P&O's *Viceroy of India* of nearly 20,000 tons made the trip between London and Bombay in 16 days, and the Australia route would see even larger vessels in the long run.[1045]

It was not the telegraph that finally took over the important overseas mail transmission from ocean going vessels, but it was aircraft.

In the 1930s, when air planes were not yet improved enough to carry mails across the Atlantic, a mixed system was developed to combine shipping and flights as had been done earlier with shipping and telegraph. 'Catapult flights' by small aircraft took express mails from shore to steamships that had departed the day before, and at the other end of the journey a similar system was carried out to bring catapult mails to shore before the ship arrived at port (see Fig. 41).

Aircraft started regular transatlantic flights in the 1950s and finally became the means of communication that took over the lead from the steamers after a successful 100-year period of mail transport across the oceans. In taking over the important fine freight, mails and passengers, air planes did not leave much to passenger liners. They died one after another, or merged to stay alive, changing their business to cruising, cargo transport or port systems.

Thus the final 'revolution' in the bulk of business information transmission actually took place several decades after the introduction of electric communications, at a time when telephone, radio and automobiles were already in common use everywhere, and even the TV was taking its first steps in world wide news transmission.

1044 For the Shanghai sailings, see Kirk, *The P&O Lines...*, 159. The mails from Colombo further to Shanghai were carried by even smaller vessels of 8,000 tons or less. See Middlemiss, 121–135.

1045 The P&O steamers reached their peak in size and speed in the early 1960s, when the largest vessels of over 40,000 tons and a speed of 27.5 knots were launched. The Australian service continued up to 1974. See Middlemiss, 147–160.

Bibliography

Records in public archives

British Library, India Record Office, London (BL, IRO)

In General Correspondence of the East India Company:
Correspondence from Bengal to London, 1832–1833, E/4/138–144
Correspondence from Madras to London 1832, E/4/364–365
Correspondence from Bombay to London 1832–1833, E/4/516–519
Correspondence from London to Bengal 1832, E/4/735

Liverpool Record Office (LRO)

Newspapers and registers:

Liverpool Mercury, 1845; 1854 (in microfilm)
Liverpool Street Directories 1818; or Gore's Directory of Liverpool and Its Environs,
Containing an alphabetical list of the Merchants, Traders and Principal Inhabitants,
also lists of the Mayor and Council, officers of the Customs and Excise, Dock duties
and Commissions, Post Office and Pilots' rates and regulations, Bankers, Trading
vessels, Stage and Hackney coaches, carriers, Annal of Liverpool, etc. Liverpool,
printed by J. Gore, Castle Street, 1818. (in microfilm)

Business Records:
Accounts and papers of Henry Eld Symons, of Kirkdale. 1857–1858 (South America–
Liverpool); and 1857 (Australia & New Zealand–Liverpool). 380 MD.

Other primary sources:
The American Chamber of Commerce in Liverpool. Minute Books and Memorials.
1801–1842: 380 AME / 1; 1842–1866: 380 AME/2.

Merseyside Maritime Museum Archives, Liverpool (MMM)

Guides to the records:
Littler, Dawn. *Guide to the Records of Merseyside Maritime Museum, Volume II*. St.
John's, 1999.

Newspapers and registers:

Liverpool Customs Bills of Entry, 1824; 1834–1835 (in microfilm)
Lloyd's List, 1766–1826 (in reprint); 1827–1875 (in microfilm)
Lloyd's Register (for Shipowners / for Underwriters), 1766–1875

Business records:

Bryson Collection:
Correspondence of Daniel Williams, 1854–1872 (South America–Liverpool),
DB/175.

Correspondence of Sandbach, Tinne & Co., 1825–1870 (West Indies–Liverpool), DB/176.

Earle Family and Business Archive:
Correspondence of Thomas and William Earle & Co., 1836–1870 (West Indies–Liverpool), D/Earle 5/1–11.

Business Records of Fraser, Trenholm & Co.:
Correspondence of C.K. Prioleau & Co., 1870–1875 (telegrams), B/FT.

Records of the Ocean Steamship Co.:
'Directions to Capt. Middleton when sailing to China with the *Agamemnon* on her first voyage April 19th 1866'. Blue Funnel, Ocean Steamship Co. OA 2583.

Holt, Alfred. *Review of the Progress of Steam Shipping during the last Quarter of a Century,* and the following discussion. Institute of Civil Engineers. Minutes of Proceedings, vol. 51, Liverpool 1877. OA/2086.

University of Liverpool, Sydney Jones Library Archives (SJ)

Printed records:

British Parliamentary Papers (BPP). Printed in the Irish University Series, Shannon, 1968–1971:

BPP, Transport and Communications. Post and Telegraphs, 1, First and Third Reports from the Select Committee on Postage together with Minutes of Evidence, Appendix and Index, Part I, 1838.

BPP, Transport and Communications. Post and Telegraphs, 2, Second Report from the Select Committee on Postage together with Minutes of Evidence, Appendix and Index, 1838.

BPP, Shipping Safety, 3. First and Second Reports from the Select Committee on Shipwrecks with Minutes of Evidence, Appendix and Index, 1843.

BPP, Colonies. East India 2, Third and Fourth Reports from the Select Committee on the Affairs of the East India Company with Appendices, 1810–12.

BPP, Colonies, East India 3, The Fifth Report from the Select Committee on the Affairs of the East India Company, 1812.

BPP, Colonies. East India 8. Appendix to the Report from Select Committee on the Affairs of the East India Company with an Index (II Finance and Accounts), Part II Commercial, 1831–32.

BPP, Colonies. West Indies 1, Report from the Select Committee on West India Colonies, together with Minutes of Evidence, Appendix and Index, 1842.

BPP, Colonies. West Indies 2, Select Committee Reports and Correspondence on the Trade and Commerce of the West Indies with Minutes of Evidence Appendixes and Index, 1806–49.

BPP, Crime and Punishment Transportation, 2. Report from the Select Committee on Transportation together with the Minutes of Evidence, Appendix and Index, 1837.

Business records:
Correspondence of Rathbone Bros & Co., 1841–1870 (North Atlantic); and 1854–1872 (South America), RP XXIV.2.

Cunard Papers (CP), 1838 –
Miscellaneous papers; *Cunard Passage Books 1848–1881.*

Other printed documents

Pamphlets, speeches:
Ross, Sir John. *On Communication to India, in Large Steam-Ships, by the Cape of Good Hope.* Printed by Order of the India Steam Ship Company, 1838.
Speech of Mr. Edson B. Olds, of Ohio [Chairman of Committee on Post Office and Post Roads]. *On the Collins Line of Steamers.* Delivered in the House of Representatives, February 15, 1855. Washington 1855.

Circulars:
'Coal from Liverpool, Birkenhead or Garston', in *Boult, English & Brandon's Freight Circular,* Liverpool 6.6.1863. (SRLC)

Directories, maps, statistics:
Allan, Morton. *Directory of European Steamship Arrivals* for the Years 1890 to 1930 at the Port of New York and for the Years 1904 to 1926 at the Ports of New York, Philadelphia, Boston and Baltimore. Baltimore 1998.
Lloyd's Maritime Atlas, London, 1964.
Maddison, Angus. *Monitoring the World Economy 1820–1992.* OECD Development Centre Studies, Paris, 1995.
Mitchell, B.R. *International Historical Statistics. Africa, Asia & Oceania 1750–1988.* Second Revised Edition. New York, 1995.

Private philatelic collections

Merchant correspondence:
Frederick Huth & Co., London, 1836–1850. In JAC, SRLC, JSC, STC, RWC (see below)

Miscellaneous merchant correspondence in the following collections:

Arnell, J.C. *Transatlantic Stampless Mail to and from the United States of America* (1986), (JAC)
Hongisto, Heikki. *Sugar in the Life of Mankind* (2005), (HHC)
Laakso, Seija-Riitta. *Development of Transatlantic Mail Services from Sail to Steam,* (2005), (SRLC)
Snellman, Johan. *North Atlantic Mail* (2005), (JSC)
Talvio, Seppo. *North Atlantic Mail* (2006), (STC)
Winter, Richard. *Transatlantic Mails (Steamship)* (1988), (RWC)

Philatelic auction catalogues:
Charles G. Firby Auctions, *British North America Stamps and Postal History.* Dr. Kennethy M. Rosenfeld Collection, June 18, 2005. Waterford, MI, 2005.

Printed sources with important postal historical sailing data

Arnell, J.C. *Atlantic Mails.* A history of the mail service between Great Britain and Canada to 1889. The National Postal Museum, Canada. Ottawa, 1980.
Arnell, J.C. & Ludington, M.H. *The Bermuda Packet Mails and the Halifax–Bermuda Mail Service 1806 to 1886.* The Postal History Society. Great Britain, 1989.
Howat, Rev. J.N.T. *South American Packets.* The British packet service to Brazil, the River Plate, the west coast (via the Straits of Magellan) and the Falkland Islands, 1808–80. The Postal History Society. York, England, 1984.

Hubbard, Walter & Winter, Richard F. *North Atlantic Mail Sailings 1840–75*. U.S. Philatelic Classics Society, Inc., Ohio, 1988.

Kenton, Phil J. & Parsons, Harry G. *Early Routing of the Royal Mail Steam Packet Company 1842–1879*. The Postal History Society. Surrey, England, 1999.

Kirk, Reg. *Australian Mails via Suez 1852 to 1926*. The Postal History Society, Kent, 1989.

Kirk, Reg. *The P&O Bombay & Australian Lines 1852–1914*. British Maritime Postal History, Vol 1.

Kirk, Reg. *The P&O Lines to the Far East*. British Maritime Postal History, Vol 2.

Kirk, Reg. *The Postal History of the P&O service to the Peninsula*. Royal Philatelic Society London, 1987.

Lee Scamp C. *Far East Mail Ship Itineraries. British, Indian, French, American, and Japanese Mail Ship Schedules 1840–1880. Volume I*, Texas, 1997.

Proud, Hector. *The British Sea Post Offices in the East*. British Maritime Postal History. Volume 4. East Sussex, 2003.

Salles, Raymond. *La poste maritime française*. Historique et catalogue. Tome I. Les entrées maritimes depuis 1760 et les bateaux à vapeur depuis 1833. Nicosia, Cyprus, 1992.

Salles, Raymond. *La poste maritime française*. Historique et catalogue. Tome II. Les paquebots de la Méditerranée de 1837 à 1935. Nicosia, Cyprus, 1992.

Salles, Raymond. *La poste maritime française*. Historique et catalogue. Tome III. Les paquebots de l'Atlantique Sud. Brésil–Plata de 1860 à 1939. Cote occidentale d'Afrique de 1889 à 1939. Nicosia, Cyprus, 1992.

Salles, Raymond. *La poste maritime française*. Historique et catalogue. Tome IV. Les paquebots de l'Atlantique Nord. Antilles–Amérique Centrale et Pacifique Sud, États-Unis. Nicosia, Cyprus, 1992.

Salles, Raymond. *La poste maritime française*. Historique et catalogue. Tome V. Les paquebots de l'Extrème-Orient. Saigon–Hong Kong–Shanghai–Yokohama–Kobe. Nicosia, Cyprus, 1993.

Salles, Raymond. *La Poste Maritime Francaise*, Historique et catalogue. Tome VII, Index Alphabétique des Cachets Postaux et Marques Maritimes, Nicosia, Cyprus, 1993.

Tabeart, Colin. *Admiralty Mediterranean Steam Packets 1830 to 1857*. Limassol, Cyprus, 2002.

Tabeart, Colin. *Australia New Zealand UK Mails to 1880. Rates Routes and Ships Out and Home*. Fareham, 2004.

Tabeart, Colin. *Robertson Revisited*. A study of the maritime postal markings of the British Isles based on the work of Alan W. Robertson. Nicosia, Cyprus, 1997.

Wierenga, Theron J. (Winter, Richard F. ed.). *United States Incoming Steamship Mail, 1847–75*. US Philatelic Classics Society, 2000.

Literature

Ahonen, Kalevi. *From Sugar Triangle to Cotton Triangle. Trade and Shipping between America and Baltic Russia, 1783–1860*. Jyväskylä, 2005.

Ahvenainen, Jorma. *The European Cable Companies in South America before the First World War*. Jyväskylä, 2004.

Ahvenainen, Jorma. *The Far Eastern Telegraphs*. Helsinki, 1981.

Ahvenainen, Jorma. *The History of the Caribbean Telegraphs before the First World War*. Helsinki, 1996.

Albion, Robert Greenhalgh. *Square-Riggers on Schedule. The New York Sailing Packets to England, France, and the Cotton Ports*. Princeton, 1938.

Albion, Robert Greenhalgh. *The Rise of New York Port (1815–1860)*. New York and London,1939.

Allington, Peter & Greenhill, Basil. *The First Atlantic liners. Seamanship in the age of paddle wheel, sail and screw*. London, 1997.

Andréadès, A. *History of the Bank of England 1640–1903*. London, 1909.

Armstrong, Warren. *The Collins Story*. London, 1957.

Arnell, Jack C. *Steam and the North Atlantic Mails: The impact of the Cunard Line and subsequent steamship companies on the carriage of transatlantic mails*. Toronto, 1986.

Barbance, Marthe. *Histoire de la Compagnie Générale Transatlantic. Un siècle d'exploitation maritime*. Paris, 1955.

Babcock, F. Lawrence. *Spanning the Atlantic. A history of the Cunard Line*. New York, 1931.

Bolland, O. Nigel. 'Systems of Domination After Slavery: The Control of Land and Labour in the British West Indies After 1838' in Hilary Beckles & Verene Shepherd (eds): *Caribbean Freedom. Economy and Society from Emancipation to the Present*. Princeton, 1996.

Bonsor, N.R.P. *North Atlantic Seaway*. An Illustrated History of the Passenger Services Linking the Old World with the New. Volumes 1–3, 5. New York, 1975–1980.

Bonsor, N.R.P. *South Atlantic Seaway*. Jersey, 1983.

Bowen, H.V. Lincoln, Margarette & Rigby, Nigel (eds.). *The Worlds of the East India Company*, Suffolk, 2004.

Boyce, Gordon. *Information, mediation and institutional development. The rise of large-scale enterprise in British shipping, 1870–1919*, Manchester, 1995.

Britnor, L.E. *The History of the Sailing Packets to the West Indies*. British West Indies Study Circle, 1973.

Brown, John Seely & Duguid, Paul. *The Social Life of Information*. Boston, 2000.

Bulley, Anne. 'The Country Ships from India' in Harding, Richard, Jarvis, Adrian & Kennerley Alston (eds.): *British Ships in China Seas: 1700 to the Present Day*, Liverpool, 2004.

Bushell, T.A. *Royal Mail. A Centenary History of the Royal Mail Line 1839–1939*, London, 1939.

Butler, John A. *Atlantic Kingdom: America's contest with Cunard in the age of sail and steam*. Dulles, Virginia, 2001.

Cable, Boyd. *A Hundred Years of the P&O, 1837–1937*. London, 1937.

Cain, P. J. & Hopkins, A. G. *British Imperialism 1688–2000*. Great Britain, 2002.

Cameron, Gail & Crooke, Stan. *Liverpool – Capital of the Slave Trade*. Liverpool, 1992.

Cattell, Philip. *The Union Castle Ocean Post Office*. British Maritime Postal History, Vol 3. Heathfield.

Charlton, K. 'Liverpool and the East India Trade', Reprinted from *Northern History. A Review od the History of the North of England. Volume VII*. Leeds, 1972.

Checkland, S.G. 'John Gladstone as Trader and Planter', in *Economic History Review*, new series, v. 7, 1954/55.

Clapham, John H. *An Economic History of Modern Britain*. Vol. 1: Britain on the Eve of the Railway Age. Vol. 2: The Early Railway Age 1820–1850. Cambridge, 1930.

Clapham, John H. *An Economic History of Modern Britain*. Vol. 3: Free Trade and Steel 1850–1886. Cambridge, 1932.

Collins, Timothy. *Transatlantic Triumph & Heroic Failure – The Galway Line*. Cork, Ireland, 2002.

Cook, Andrew S. 'Establishing the Sea Routes to India and China: Stages in the Development of Hydrographical Knowledge ', in Bowen, H.V., Lincoln, Margarette & Rigby, Nigel (eds.): *The Worlds of the East India Company*. Suffolk, 2004.

Cookson, Gillian. *The Cable. The Wire that Changed the World*, Gloucestershire, 2003.

Cooper, Malcolm. 'From *Agamemnon* to *Priam*: British liner shipping in the China Seas, 1865–1965' in Richard Harding, Adrian Jarvis & Alston Kennerley, *British Ships in China Seas: 1700 to the Present Day*. Liverpool, 2004.

Cotton, Sir Evan. *East Indiamen. The East-India Company's Maritime Service*. London, 1949.

Cutler, Carl C. *Queens of the Western Ocean*. The Story of America's Mail and Passenger Sailing Lines. Annapolis, Maryland, 1967.

Cutler, Carl C. *Greyhounds of the Sea*. The story of the American clipper ship. Maryland, 1961.

Daniels, Rudolph. *Trains Across the Continent*. North American Railroad History. Indiana, 2000.

Deerr Noel. *The History of Sugar, Volume I*. London, 1949.

Doublet, A.R. *The Pacific Steam Navigation Company*. Its maritime postal history 1840–1853 with particular reference to Chile. Royal Philatelic Society London, 1983.

Drechsel, Edwin. *Norddeutscher Lloyd Bremen 1857–1970*. Vol 1, Vancouver, 1994.

DuBois John L. *Danish West Indies Mails 1754–1917*. Volume I – Postal History. Snow Camp, NC, USA, 2000.

Edwards, Bernard. *The Grey Widow Maker*. The True Stories of Twenty-four Disasters at Sea. London, 1995.

Eibl-Kaye, Geoffrey. 'The Indian Mails 1814 to 1819. Negotiations between the Post Office and the East India Company' in *The London Philatelist*, Volume 113, April 2004. Royal Philatelic Society London, 2004.

Eibl-Kaye, Geoffrey. 'The Indian Mails 1814 to 1819. Administration of the Packet Service and its Demise' in *The London Philatelist*, Volume 113, May 2004. Royal Philatelic Society London, 2004.

Flayhart III, William Henry. *Perils of the Atlantic. Steamship Disasters 1850 to the Present*. New York, 2003.

Flayhart III, William Henry. *The American Line (1871–1902)*. New York, 2000.

Fletcher, Max. E. 'The Suez Canal and World Shipping, 1869–1914' in *Journal of Economic History,* vol. XVIII, December 1958, No 4.

Fogg, Nicholas. *The Voyages of the* Great Britain. Life at sea in the world's first liner. Trowbridge, Wilts, Great Britain, 2002.

Foreman-Peck, James. *A History of the World Economy. International Economic Relations since 1850*. Harvester Press, 1983.

Fox, Stephen. *The Ocean Railway*. London, 2003.

Frajola, Richard C.; Kramer, George J. & Walske, Steven C. *The Pony Express. A Postal History*. New York, 2005.

Fryer, Gavin & Akerman, Clive (ed.). *Reform of the Post Office in the Victorian Era, Vol. 1*. London, 2000.

Furber, Holder. 'The Overland Route to India in the Seventeenth and Eighteenth Centuries'. In Rosane Rocher (ed.): *Private Fortune and Company Profits in the India Trade in the 18th Century*. Variorum, 1997. First published in *Journal of Indian History 29*. Trivandrum, 1951.

Gaastra, Femme S. 'War, Competition and Collaboration: Relations between the English and Dutch East India Company in the Seventeenth and Eighteenth Centuries', in Bowen, H.V., Lincoln, Margarette & Rigby, Nigel (eds.): *The Worlds of the East India Company*. Suffolk, 2004.

Gardiner, Robin. *The History of the White Star Line*. Surrey, England, 2001.

Garratt, G.R.M. *One Hundred Years of Submarine Cables*. London, 1950.

Gibbs, C.R. Vernon. *British Passenger Liners of the Five Oceans*. Great Britain, 1963.

Gibson, John Frederic. *Brocklebanks 1770–1950, Volume I*. Liverpool, 1953.

Gisburn, Harold G. D. *The Postage Stamps and Postal History of the Bahamas*. London, 1950.

Gordon, John Steele. *A Thread Across the Ocean*. The heroic story of the transatlantic cable. Bath, Great Britain, 2002.

Graham, Gerald S. *Empire of the North Atlantic*. The Maritime Struggle for North America. Toronto; London, 1958.

Haggerty, Sheryllynne. 'A Link in the Chain: Trade and the Transhipment of Knowledge in the Late Eighteenth Century', *Forum: Information and Marine History, International Journal of Maritime History,* Vol. XIV No.1, 2002.

Hall, Douglas. 'The Flight from the Estates Reconsidered: The British West Indies, 1838–1842' in Hilary Beckles & Verene Shepherd (eds): *Caribbean Freedom. Economy and Society from Emancipation to the Present*. Princeton, 1996.

Hall, Nigel. 'The Liverpool Cotton Market', *Transactions of the Historic Society of Lancashire and Cheshire*, Vol 149, 1999.

Harding, Richard; Jarvis, Adrian & Kennerley Alston (eds.). *British Ships in China Seas: 1700 to the Present Day*. Liverpool, 2004.

Hargest, George E. *History of Letter Post Communication between the United States and Europe, 1845–75*. Washington, 1971.

Harley, Charles K. 'Coal Exports and British Shipping, 1850–1913' in *Explorations in Economic History*, Vol. 26, Number 3, July 1989.

Harley, Charles K. 'The shift from sailing ships to steamships, 1850–1890: a study in technological change and its diffusion' in Donald N. McCloskey (ed.). *Essays on a Mature Economy: Britain after 1840*. London, 1971.

Haws, Duncan. *Merchant Fleets, British India S.N. Co*. Hereford, 1991.

Haws, Duncan. *Merchant Fleets. French Line. Compagnie Générale Transatlantic*. Pembrokeshire, 1996.

Haws, Duncan. *Merchant Fleets. Messageries Maritimes*. Pembroke, 1998.

Haws, Duncan. *Merchant Fleets. Royal Mail Line & Nelson Line*. Sussex 1982.

Headrick, Daniel R. *When Information Came of Age. Technologies of Knowledge in the Age of Reason and Revolution, 1700–1850*. Oxford, 2000.

Himer, Kurt. *75 Jahre Hamburg-Amerika Linie. Geschichte der Hamburg-Amerika Linie. 1*. Teil: Adolph Godefroy und seine Nachfolger bis 1886. Hamburg, 1922.

Hughes, Paul & Wall, Alan D. 'The Dessiou Hydrographic Work: Its Authorship and Place' in *International Journal of Maritime History, Vol. XVII*, No. 2. St. John's, 2005.

Hyde, Francis E. *Blue Funnel. A History of Alfred Holt and Company of Liverpool from 1865 to 1914*. Liverpool, 1956.

Hyde, Francis E. *Cunard and the North Atlantic, 1840–1973*. A history of shipping and financial management. London, 1975.

Hyde, Francis E. *Far Eastern Trade, 1860–1914*. Edinburgh, 1973.

Hyde, Francis E. *Liverpool & the Mersey. The Development of a Port (An Economic History of a Port) 1700–1970*. Devon, 1971.

James, Lawrence. *Raj. The Making of British India*. London, 2003.

James, Lawrence. *The Rise and Fall of the British Empire*. London, 2000.

Jarvis, Adrian. *Liverpool Central Docks 1799–1905. An Illustrated History*. Bath, Avon, 1991.

Jones, Maldwyn A. *Destination America*. Great Britain, 1976.

Kallioinen, Mika. *Verkostoitu tieto*. Informaatio ja ulkomaiset markkinat Dahlströmin kauppahuoneen liiketoiminnassa 1800-luvulla. Helsinki, 2003.

Karabell, Zachary. *Parting the Desert. The Creation of the Suez Canal*. London, 2004.

Kaukiainen, Yrjö. 'Coal and Canvas: Aspects of the Competition between Steam and Sail, c. 1870–1914' in *Sail and Steam. Selected Maritime Writings of Yrjö Kaukiainen. Research in Maritime History, No. 27*. St. John's, 2004.

Kaukiainen, Yrjö. 'Finnish sailors, 1750–1870' in Lars U. Scholl and Merja-Liisa Hinkkanen (eds), *Sail and Steam. Selected Maritime Writings of Yrjö Kaukiainen. Research in Maritime History No. 27*. St. John's, 2004.

Kaukiainen, Yrjö. *Sailing into Twilight. Finnish Shipping in an Age of Transport Revolution, 1860–1914*. Helsinki, 1991.

Kaukiainen, Yrjö. 'Shrinking the world: Improvements in the speed of information transmission, c. 1820–1870'. *European Review of Economic History, 5*. Cambridge, 2001.

Kemble, John Haskell. *The Panama Route 1848–1869*. South Carolina, 1990.

Kenwood, A.G. & Lougheed, A.L.: *The Growth of the International Economy 1820–1980*, London, 1985.

Kielbowicz, Richard B. 'News Gathering by Mail in the Age of the Telegraph: Adapting to a New Technology' in *Technology and Culture*, Vol. 28, No. 1, Jan. 1987.

Kieve, J. V. *Electric Telegraph. A Social and Economic History*. Devon, 1973.

Kludas, Arnold. *Record Breakers of the North Atlantic. Blue Riband liners 1838–1952*. London, 2000.

Kurchan, Mario D. *Argentine Maritime Postal History*. Buenos Aires, 2002.

Laakso, Seija-Riitta. 'Managing the Distance: Business Information Transmission between Britain and Guiana, 1840' in *International Journal of Maritime History, XVI*, No.2, December 2004.

Lamb, D.P. Lamb. 'Volume and tonnage of the Liverpool slave trade 1772–1807' in Roger Anstey & P.E.H. Hair (ed.): *Liverpool, the African Slave Trade, and Abolition. Essays to illustrate current knowledge and research. Historic Society of Lancashire and Cheshire*. Chippenham, 1989.

Large, Frank. *Faster than the Wind. The Liverpool to Holyhead Telegraph,* Great Britain, 1998.

Littler, Dawn. 'The Earle Collection: Records of a Liverpool Family of Merchants and Shipowners', *Transactions of the Historic Society of Lancashire & Cheshire*, Vol. 146, Liverpool, 1996.

Lubbock, Basil. *The Western Ocean Packets*. Glasgow, 1925.

Ludington, M.H. & Osborne, G. *The Royal Mail Steam Packets to Bermuda & the Bahamas 1842–1859*. London, 1971.

MacGregor, David, R. *The Tea Clippers*. London, 1952.

MacGregor, David. 'The Tea Clippers, 1849–1869' in Harding, Richard, Jarvis, Adrian & Kennerley Alston (eds.): *British Ships in China Seas: 1700 to the Present Day*. Liverpool, 2004.

Marriner, Sheila. *Rathbones of Liverpool 1845–73*. Liverpool, 1961.

McCullough, David. *The Path between the Seas. The creation of the Panama Canal 1870–1914*. New York.

McCusker, John J. 'New York City and the Bristol Packet. A chapter in eighteenth-century postal history', in McCusker, John J. *Essays in the Economic History of the Atlantic World*. London, 1997.

McCusker, John J. 'The Business Press in England before 1775', in McCusker, John J. *Essays in the Economic History of the Atlantic World*. London, 1997.

McCusker, John J. 'The Demise of Distance: The Business Press and the Origins of the Information Revolution in the Early Modern Atlantic World. *The American Historical Review*, Vol. 110, Number 2, April 2005.

McCusker, John J. 'The Italian Business Press in Early Modern Europe', in McCusker, John J. *Essays in the Economic History of the Atlantic World*. London, 1997.

McKay, Richard. *Some Famous Sailing Ships and Their Builder Donald McKay*. New York, 1928.

Middlemiss, Norman L. *Merchant Fleets. P&O Lines*. Great Britain, 2004.

Milne, Graeme J. 'Port Politics: Interest, Faction and Port Management in Mid-Victorian Liverpool', in Lewis R. Fischer & Adrian Jarvis, *Harbours and Havens: Essays in Port History in Honour of Gordon Jackson. Research in Maritime History No. 16*. St. John's, 1999.

Milne, Graeme J. 'Knowledge, Communications and the Information Order in Nineteenth-Century Liverpool', *Forum: Information and Marine History. International Journal of Maritime History,* Vol. XIV No.1, 2002.

Milne, Graeme J. *Trade and Traders in Mid-Victorian Liverpool. Mercantile business and the making of a world port*. Liverpool, 2000.

Moubray, Jane & Moubray, Michael. *British Letter Mail to Overseas Destinations 1840–1875*. Royal Philatelic Society London, 1992.

Murray, Marischal. *Union-Castle Chronicle 1853–1953*. Glasgow, 1953.

Nicol, Stuart. *A history of the Royal Mail Line*. Vol. one & two. Great Britain, 2001.

Ojala, Jari. 'The Principal Agent Problem Revisited: Entrepreneurial networks between Finland and 'world markets' during the eighteenth and nineteenth centuries' in Margrit Schulte Beerbühl and Jörg Vögele (eds.) *Spinning the Commercial Web. International Trade, Merchants, and Commercial Cities, c. 1640–1939*. Frankfurt-am-Main, 2004.

Ojala, Jari. *Tehokasta toimintaa Pohjanmaan pikkukaupungeissa. Purjemerenkulun kannattavuus ja tuottavuus 1700–1800 -luvulla.* Helsinki, 1999.

O'Rourke, Kevin H. & Williamson, Jeffrey G. *Globalization and History. The Evolution of a Nineteenth-Century Atlantic Economy.* Massachusetts, 2000.

Palmer, Sarah. 'Port Economics in an Historical Context: The Nineteenth-Century Port of London', *International Journal of Maritime History.* Vol. XV No. 1, June 2003.

Pawlyn, Tony. *The Falmouth Packets 1689–1851.* Truran, Cornwall, 2003.

Pearson, Michael. *The Indian Ocean.* London & New York, 2003.

Philips, C.H. *The East India Company 1784–1834.* Manchester, 1968.

Pond, E. Le Roy. *Junius Smith: A biography of the father of the Atlantic liner.* New York 1927.

Pred, Allan R. *Urban Growth and the Circulation of Information: The United States System of Cities, 1790–1840.* Harvard University Press, Cambridge, Massachusetts, 1973.

Rabson, Stephen. 'P&O and the Far East since 1845' in Harding, Richard, Jarvis, Adrian & Kennerley Alston (eds.): *British Ships in China Seas: 1700 to the Present Day.* Liverpool, 2004.

Reid, James D. *The Telegraph in America.* New York, 1886.

Ringström Sigurd & Tester, H.E. *The Private Ship Letter Stamps of the World. Part 1. The Caribbean.* Trelleborg.

Risberg, Einar. *Suomen lennätinlaitoksen historia 1855–1955.* Helsinki, 1959.

Robertson, Alan W. *A History of the Ship Letters of the British Isles.* An Encyclopaedia of Maritime Postal History. Bournemouth, 1955.

Robinson, Howard *Carrying British Mails Overseas.* London, 1964.

Robinson, Howard *The British Post Office.* Princeton, 1948.

Rowe, Kenneth. *The Postal History of the Forwarding Agents.* United States, 1984.

Safford, Jeffrey J. 'The decline of the American merchant marine, 1850–1914'. An historiographical appraisal. In Fischer, Lewis R. & Panting, Gerald E. (ed.) *Change and Adaption in Maritime History. The North Atlantic Fleets in the Nineteenth Century.* Maritime History Group. Memorial University of New Foundland, 1985.

Samhaber, Ernst. *Merchants Make History.* How trade has influenced the course of history throughout the world. New York, 1964.

Scholl, Lars U. 'New York's German Suburb: The Creation of the Port of Bremerhaven, 1827–1918' in Fischer, Lewis R. & Jarvis, Adrian, (ed.), *Harbours and Havens: Essays in Port History in Honour of Gordon Jackson. Research of Maritime History No 16,* 1999.

Sidebottom, John K. *The Overland Mail.* A Postal Historical Study of the Mail Route to India. Perth, Scotland, 1948.

Sloan, Edward W. 'The First (and Very Secret) International Steamship Cartel, 1850–1856', in Starkey, David J. & Harlaftis, Gelina (ed.). *Global Markets: the Internalization of the Sea Transport Industries since 1850. Research in Maritime History, No. 14.* St. John's, 1998.

Staff, Frank. *The Transatlantic Mail.* Massachusetts, 1980.

Stammers, Michael K. *The Passage Makers.* Brighton, 1978.

Starkey, David & Harlaftis, Gelina (ed.). *Global Markets: the Internalization of the Sea Transport Industries since 1850. Research in Maritime History, No. 14.* St. John's, 1998.

Steele, Ian K. *The English Atlantic 1675–1740.* An Exploration of Communication and Community. London, 1986.

Steele, James. *Queen Mary.* Hong Kong, 1995.

Thorner, Daniel. *Investment in Empire: British railway and steam shipping enterprise in India, 1825–1849.* Philadelphia, 1950.

Tommila, Päiviö. 'Havaintoja uutisten leviämisnopeudesta ulkomailta Suomeen 1800-luvun alkupuolella', *Historiallinen Aikakauskirja vol. 81, No. 1,* 1960.

Tyler, David Budlong. *Steam Conquers the Atlantic.* New York, 1939.

Valtonen, Pekka. *Latinalaisen Amerikan historia.* Helsinki, 2001.

Vaughan, Adrian. *Railwaymen, Politics and Money. The Great Age of Railways in Britain.* London, 1997.

Williams, David M. 'Abolition and the Re-Deployment of the Slave Fleet, 1807–1811'. *In Merchants and Mariners: Selected Maritime Writings of David M. Williams. Research in Maritime History No. 18*. St. John's, 2000.

Williams, David M. 'Liverpool Merchants and the Cotton Trade 1820–1850'. In *Merchants and Mariners: Selected Maritime Writings of David M. Williams. Research in Maritime History No. 18*. St. John's, 2000.

Winter, Richard F. *Understanding Transatlantic Mail, Vol. 1*. American Philatelic Society, Bellefonte, PA, 2006.

Woods, Oliver & Bishop, James. *The Story of The Times*. London, 1983.

Wright, Charles & Fayle, C. Ernest. *A History of Lloyd's, from the Founding of Lloyd's Coffee House to the Present Day*. London, 1928.

Yates, JoAnne. 'Investing in Information: Supply and Demand Forces in the Use of Information in American Firms, 1850–1920' in Peter Temin (ed.) *Inside the Business Enterprise. Historical Perspective on the Use of Information*. Chicago, 1991.

Internet

http://www.pbbooks.com/webfa.htm

Appendix – Tables

TABLE 15. **The reliability of the American sailing packet service: regularity of sailings from Liverpool and reported disasters, 1844–1845**

Ship (* = new)	Shipping line	Trip 1	Trip 2	Trip 3	Trip 4	Trip 5	Trip 6	Trip 7
Virginian	RS	2.1.44 was fast in the ice, lost sails	27.4.44 arr. in NY with lost bowsprit, etc.	27.8.44	28.12.44 arr. in NY with loss of spars, sails split, etc.	29.4.45	29.7.45	6.12.45
Hottinguer	NL	8.1.44 went on shore off New York	7.5.44	6.9.44	8.1.45	6.5.45	6.9.45	20.12.45
Montezuma	BB	8.1.44 lost masts & sails in hurricane	1.5.44	1.9.44	3.1.45	5.5.45	16.8.45	17.12.45
Roscius	DL	14.1.44	12.5.44	11.9.44	12.1.45	14.5.45	12.9.45	20.12.45
Europe	BB	16.1.44	17.5.44	17.9.44	17.1.45	18.5.45	20.9.45	25.12.45
Independence	BSw	22.1.44	21.5.44	22.9.44	28.12.44 put back leaky; sailed 28.1.45	22.5.45	22.8.45	24.12.45
Samuel Hicks (transient)	RS	1.2.44	26.5.44	26.9.44	29.1.45			
New York	BB	3.2.44	1.6.44	4.10.44	4.2.45	1.6.45	2.10.45	(1846)
Liverpool	NL	6.2.44 grounded but without damage	9.6.44	10.10.44	7.2.45	7.6.45	7.10.45	(1846)
Siddons	DL	11.2.44	11.6.44	12.10.44	11.2.45	12.6.45	13.10.45	(1846)
Columbus	BB	18.2.44	17.6.44	19.10.44	18.2.45	18.6.45	13.12.45	(1846)
Ashburton	BSw	22.2.44	23.6.44	22.10.44	25.2.45	1.6.45	22.9.45	(1846)
Stephen Whitney	RS	5.3.44	26.6.44	26.10.44	28.2.45	27.6.45	29.10.45	(1846)
Yorkshire	BB	5.3.44	2.7.44	1.11.44	4.3.45	2.7.45	2.11.45	(1846)
Queen of the West	NL	6.3.44 arr. in NY with loss of bowsprit, fore top-mast, etc.	- -	8.11.44	7.3.45	7.7.45	7.11.45	(1846)

Ship	Line							
Sheridan	DL	14.3.44	12.7.44	14.11.44	13.3.45	13.7.45	12.11.45	(1846)
Cambridge	BB	17.3.44	17.7.44	17.11.44	19.3.45	18.7.45	21.11.45	(1846)
George Washington	BSw	23.3.44	**21.7.44**	damaged in gale	22.4.45 sold	-	-	-
United States	RS	27.3.44	27.7.44	**26.11.44** went missing, lost with all hands	(26.3. departure by the transient *Empire*)			-
England	BB	2.4.44	3.8.44	**1.12.44** went missing, lost with all hands	-	-	-	-
Rochester	NL	7.4.44	10.8.44	**6.12.44** saved the crew of the sinking Boston packet *Dorchester*	9.4.45	11.8.45	8.12.45	(1846)
Garrick	DL	12.4.44	12.8.44	12.12.44	12.4.45	12.8.45 in contact with a merchant ship, but proceeded	13.12.45	(1846)
Oxford	BB	17.4.44	22.8.44	18.12.44	3.4.45	2.8.45	6.12.45	(1846)
Patrick Henry	BSw	22.4.44	22.8.44	22.11.44	23.3.45	22.7.45	23.11.45	(1846)
*John R. Skiddy**	RS				22.1.45	22.5.45	2.10.45	(1846)
*Waterloo**	RS					27.5.45	29.8.45	29.12.45
*Henry Clay**	BSw					23.6.45	23.10.45	(1846)
*Fidelia**	BB						2.9.45	(1846)

Source: Lloyd's List 1844–1845. – Sailings that took place on the scheduled date are marked in **bold**. The comments are from *Lloyd's List*. BB = Black Ball Line, scheduled sailing dates 1st and 16th of each month; BSw = Blue Swallowtail Line, sailing date probably 21st; DL = Dramatic Line, sailing date 11th, sometimes could have been the 12th, in which case some of the dates above were the correct sailing dates; NL = New Line, sailing date 6th; RS = Red Star Line, sailing date 26th. The sailing schedules are from newspaper advertisements (*Liverpool Mercury*, January–March 1845) and from Cutler (1967), 376–380. – The Blue Swallowtail Line took over the New Line in 1849. It only operated for six years. See Staff, 123–124; Cutler (1967), 380.

TABLE 39. **Falmouth packet round trips and consecutive information circles enabled by them on the Liverpool–Rio de Janeiro–Buenos Aires route, 1840**

Packet	Departure date from Falmouth	Arrival date in Rio de Janeiro (six trips via Pernambuco and Bahia)	Departure date of branch packet from Rio de Janeiro to Buenos Aires	Arrival date in Buenos Aires	Departure date from Buenos Aires	Arrival date in Rio de Janeiro	Packet	Departure date of Falmouth packet from Rio de Janeiro	Arrival date at Falmouth (six trips via Bahia and Pernambuco)	Information circle, days
Alert	**10.1.40**	**28.2.**	**2.3.**	**14.3.**	**21.3.**	**2.4.**	**Pandora**	**15.4.**	**1.6.**	**146**
Pandora	7.2.	31.3.	4.4.	14.4.	23.4.	16.5.	Pigeon	31.5.	11.8.	189
Pigeon	6.3.	23.4.	27.4.	8.5.	22.5.	12.6.	Spey	21.6.	21.8.	172
Spey	10.4.	22.5.	26.5.	9.6.	21.6.	12.7.	Sheldrake	31.7.	26.9.	173
Sheldrake	8.5.	26.6.	1.7.	14.7.	21.7.	7.8.	Delight	13.8.	17.10.	166
Delight	**5.6.**	**29.7.**	**1.8.**	**16.8.**	**26.8.**	**14.9.**	**Alert**	**27.9.**	**20.11.**	**172**
Alert	10.7.	27.8.	30.8.	15.9.	25.9.	13.10.	Magnet	18.10.	30.12.	177
Magnet	7.8.	24.9.	28.9.	8.10.	30.10.	24.11.	Lapwing	26.11.	22.1.41	172
Lapwing	4.9.	25.10.	28.10.	8.11.	16.11.	10.12.	Express	15.12.	11.2.41	164
Express	9.10.	22.11.	26.11.	8.12.	17.12.	3.1.41	Seagull	13.1.41	4.3.41	150
Seagull	7.11.	28.12.	31.12.	9.1.41	19.1.41	13.2.41	Penguin	2.3.41	13.4.41	161
Penguin	**8.12.**	23.1.41	27.1.41	9.2.41	17.2.41	8.3.41	Alert	14.3.41	5.5.41	152

Source: Sailing lists of Howat, 81, 94–95. – The bold figures show the consecutive information circles, starting from early January 1840. In the last column, four days have been added for the inland trip Liverpool–Falmouth–Liverpool. As can be seen, the schedule for answers to the letters arriving at Falmouth on 1 June was very tight as the next packet departed already on 5 June. In practice, letters from Liverpool would probably not have been ready to leave in time. From London it would probably have been possible.

TABLE 73. **Letters received from Calcutta by the East India Company, London, 1833**

Ship	Sailed	Letters received	Ap	My	Ju	Jy	Au	Se	Oc	No	De	Ja	Fe	Ma	Ap	My	Ju	Total
Ferguson	6.9.32	31.1.33	3	1	3	21	3											31
Catherine	17.9.32	5.2.33	1			5	10	7										23
Heroine		8.2.33	1	1		2	1											5
Palmyra		7.4.33			1		2	14	5									22
Isabella		9.4.33	1	2	2	4	4	2	11	5								31
Genl Palmer		1.5.33			1	4	1	2										8
Caesar	7.1.33	11.5.33				1	1		1	6	12							21
Bolton		14.5.33					3	2	2	1	3							11
D. of N-land	20.1.33	18.5.33							1		1							2
Barretto		29.5.33									3							3
Layton		30.5.33			1	1					3							5
Recovery		3.6.33			2					1								3
Bencoolen	5.2.33	14.6.33							1	2	3	17						23
Malcolm	8.2.33	22.6.33										10						10
James Pattison	18.2.33	24.8.33									2	1						3
Exmouth	14.4.33	1.9.33				1			1		2	1	3	18	4			30
Robert		5.9.33									1							1
Georgiana		6.9.33				2	1	3	1	1	3	4	11	3				29
Susan	25.4.33	4.10.33										1	2	1	2			4
Ann & Amelia*		4.11.33						1	1		5	1	2	2				12
Hooghley	13.6.33	11.11.33											1	2	5	19		27
Hindoo	8.7.33	18.11.33															1	1
Lord Amherst* (Juliana)	20.5.33	23.12.33									1				2	3		6
Juliana	16.7.33	23.12.33										3	2	2	3	9	6	27
Total			5	4	12	42	26	31	24	16	39	37	19	28	16	31	7	338
Total 2			29	31	23	45	26	31	24	16	39	38	19	29	16	33	23	422

Source: The EIC General Correspondence from Bengal, E/4/139–143 (BL, IRO). The sailing dates originate from Lloyd's List maritime intelligence, 1833 passim. – The monthly figures indicate the time period when the letters were written, starting from April 1832 and ending in June 1833. Total = total number of letters arrived in 1833. Total 2 = total number of letters sent during those months (including the letters received in 1832 or 1834). The actual number of letters carried was larger than the totals due to copies sent by alternative vessels.
* Wrecked during the homeward voyage. The letters were carried to London by other ships.

TABLE 74. **Letters received from Bombay by the East India Company in London, 1833.**

Ship	Arrived	Sailed	Letters received	Ju	Jy	Au	Se	Oc	No	De	Ja	Fe	Ma	Ap	My	Ju	Total
Cordelia	20.8.32		7.3.33				4	12									16
John Taylor	18.8.32		31.3.33			19	12	1									32
Boyne	16.7.32	30.9.32	2.4.33	2	2	11	10										25
Earl of Eldon	21.8.32		6.4.33			3	5										8
s/s Hugh Lindsay			9.4.33								1						1
Marquis of Hastings	20.10.32	2.12.32	22.4.33				1	3									4
Royal George		20.12.32	22.4.33				1	22	14	6							43
Hero of Malone		12.1.33	23.5.33							2	2						4
Lady Raffles		27.1.33	24.5.33							1	10						11
Lady Nugent	14.1.33	10.2.33	24.6.33							5	1	7					13
Upton Castle	17.1.33	17.2.33	8.7.33								2	3					5
Prince George	17.1.33	3.4.33	6.9.33									4					4
Parsee			12.9.33										1				1
Triumph		28.4.33	21.9.33									4	10	14			28
Palambang			13.10.33											4	18	2	24
Duke of Roxburgh			19.10.33												4		4
Hero			27.12.33											1	15	16	32
Diamond			27.12.33												1	2	3
Total				2	2	33	33	38	14	14	16	18	11	19	38	20	258
Total 2				31	19	46	33	38	14	14	16	18	12	23	39	21	324

Source: The EIC, General Correspondence from Bombay, E/4/517–519 (BL, IRO). The arrival and sailing dates originate from *Lloyd's List* maritime intelligence, 1833 passim. – The monthly figures indicate the time period when the letters were written, starting from June 1832 and ending in June 1833. Total = total number of letters arrived in 1833. Total 2 = total number of letters sent during those months (including the letters which were received in 1832 or 1834).

TABLE 77. **Consecutive information circles enabled by the express mail services between London and Bombay, 1841**

London, departure of express mail, by rail via Marseilles	Admiralty ship, Marseilles to Malta, departure /arrival	The P&O ship, Malta to Alexandria with bulk mails from Southampton 1st/2nd of each month	The EIC ship from Suez to Bombay, departure /arrival	The EIC ship from Bombay to Suez, departure /arrival	The P&O ship, Alexandria to Malta with bulk mails to Falmouth	Admiralty ship, Malta to Marseilles, departure /arrival	Express mail, London arrival date	Information circle, days (via Falmouth)
4.1. (1841)	Acheron 10.1./13.1.	Oriental 14.1./18.1.	Victoria 25.1./12.2.	Victoria 1.3./22.3.	Oriental 26.3./30.3.	Alecto 30.3./4.4.	9.4.	95 (98+4)
4.5.	Prometheus 9.5./12.5.	Oriental 14.5./18.5.	Auckland 22.5./6.6.	Cleopatra + Berenice 19.6./15.7.	Oriental 20.7./23.7.	Alecto 24.7./28.7.	2.8.	90 (93+4)
5.8.*	Alecto 9.8./12.8.	Great Liverpool 13.8./18.8.	Berenice 21.8./6.9.	Cleopatra 1.10./18.10.	Great Liverpool 22.10./26.10.	Prometheus 26.10/31.10.	5.11.	92 (98+4)
4.12.	Polyphemus 10.12./13.12.	Great Liverpool+ Montrose 17.12./22.12.	Victoria 27.12./15.1. (1842)					

Source: Sailing lists of Scamp, 31–32, 37–38, 47; Tabeart (2002), 69–73, 191–192. In the example, the express route via Marseilles has been used instead of the all-sea service via Gibraltar. From Marseilles, the letters were carried by the Admiralty's mail steam packets to Malta, where they joined the P&O all-sea mails. The length of the information circles using the all-sea mail is in brackets. The marking "+4" is added to indicate that the trip to Falmouth by mail coach added a two-day extra delay in both directions.

* This connection worked only for the express service. The all-sea mails arrived at Falmouth on 3.8. by the *Oriental*, on the same day that the P&O steamer *Great Liverpool* departed. However, answers to the letters arriving by express on 2.8. could catch the train for Marseilles on 5.8.1841. – As there was plague in Alexandria, the *Oriental* was ordered to Motherbank (off Portsmouth) for quarantine until 13.8. when the passengers could finally take the train to London. Most ships arriving from Alexandria that year had to spend an extra week or ten days in quarantine off the coast before the passengers were released. It seems that the mails were not subject to quarantine or even disinfection on arrival in England at this time. See Tabeart (2002), 73–75. – For the quarantine system, see Robertson, A33–A44.

List of Diagrams, Maps and Tables

Diagrams

Maps

Tables

General Index

Ship Index

(s) = steamer

452

Studia Fennica Ethnologica

Making and Breaking of Borders
Ethnological Interpretations, Presentations, Representations
Edited by Teppo Korhonen, Helena Ruotsala & Eeva Uusitalo
Studia Fennica Ethnologica 7
2003

Memories of My Town
The Identities of Town Dwellers and Their Places in Three Finnish Towns
Edited by Anna-Maria Åström, Pirjo Korkiakangas & Pia Olsson
Studia Fennica Ethnologica 8
2004

Passages Westward
Edited by Maria Lähteenmäki & Hanna Snellman
Studia Fennica Ethnologica 9
2006

Studia Fennica Folkloristica

Creating Diversities
Folklore, Religion and the Politics of Heritage
Edited by Anna-Leena Siikala, Barbro Klein & Stein R. Mathisen
Studia Fennica Folkloristica 14
2004

Pertti J. Anttonen
Tradition through Modernity
Postmodernism and the Nation-State in Folklore Scholarship
Studia Fennica Folkloristica 15
2005

Narrating, Doing, Experiencing
Nordic Folkloristic Perspectives
Edited by Annikki Kaivola-Bregenhøj, Barbro Klein & Ulf Palmenfelt
Studia Fennica Folkloristica 16
2006

Studia Fennica Historica

Medieval History Writing and Crusading Ideology
Edited by Tuomas M. S. Lehtonen & Kurt Villads Jensen with Janne Malkki
and Katja Ritari
Studia Fennica Historica 9
2005

Moving in the USSR
Western anomalies and Northern wilderness
Edited by Pekka Hakamies
Studia Fennica Historica 10
2005

Derek Fewster
Visions of Past Glory
Nationalism and the Construction of Early Finnish History
Studia Fennica Historica 11
2006

Modernisation in Russia since 1900
Edited by Markku Kangaspuro & Jeremy Smith
Studia Fennica Historica 12
2006

Seija-Riitta Laakso
Across the Oceans
Development of Overseas Business Information Transmission 1815–1875
Studia Fennica Historica 13
2007

Industry and Modernism
Companies, Architecture and Identity in the Nordic and Baltic Countries during
the High-Industrial Period
Edited by Anja Kervanto Nevanlinna
Studia Fennica Historica 14
2007

Studia Fennica Linguistica

Minna Saarelma-Maunumaa
Edhina Ekogidho – Names as Links
The Encounter between African and European Anthroponymic Systems among
the Ambo People in Namibia
Studia Fennica Linguistica 11
2003

Minimal reference
The use of pronouns in Finnish and Estonian discourse
Edited by Ritva Laury
Studia Fennica Linguistica 12
2005

Antti Leino
On Toponymic Constructions
as an Alternative to Naming Patterns in Describing Finnish Lake Names

Studia Fennica Linguistica 13
2007

Studia Fennica Litteraria

Changing Scenes
Encounters between European and Finnish Fin de Siècle
Edited by Pirjo Lyytikäinen
Studia Fennica Litteraria 1
2003

Women's Voices
Female Authors and Feminist Criticism in the Finnish Literary Tradition
Edited by Lea Rojola & Päivi Lappalainen
Studia Fennica Litteraria 2
2007

Studia Fennica Anthropologica

On Foreign Ground
Moving between Countries and Categories
Edited by Minna Ruckenstein & Marie-Louise Karttunen
Studia Fennica Anthropologica 1
2007